COLLINS

CONCISE DICTIONARY OF
QUOTATIONS

HarperCollins*Publishers*

HarperCollins Publishers
P.O. Box, Glasgow G4 0NB

With thanks to Elaine Henderson and Hazel Mills for their
efforts in compiling this book

ISBN 0 00 472004 0
Reprint 10 9 8 7 6 5 4 3 2 1 0

Printed and bound in Great Britain by
Caledonian International Book Manufacturing Ltd, Glasgow

CONTENTS

CONTENTS

INTRODUCTION
by Reginald Hill

Do we need another dictionary of quotations?

Hell, yes!

Like underpants in the Urals, you can never have enough of them.

Quotation is the cosmetic of speech, the cruet of literature.

It seasons sentiment, spices wit, adds grace to compliment and gravitas to wisdom.

For the dedicated quoter, a new dictionary should perform two functions.

The first is to establish its authority by being packed with old favourites. More than the simple pleasure of reunion is involved here. Familiarity breeds inaccuracy, and we need to make sure we are getting it right; or, if you follow Hesketh Pearson's advice under QUOTATIONS, getting it wrong.

The second is the introduction of the new, not too much (books of solely modern quotations often trawl up a deal of dross) but just enough to advance the gentle art.

Collins new *Concise Dictionary of Quotations* gives satisfaction in both areas and its thematic structure is particularly helpful to the speech-maker in need of a quick fix.

Being concise, there must of course be omissions.

But what of that?

The absence of a personal favourite or two from a dictionary is no cause for carping, but rather for self-congratulation that you, dear reader, are one of that happy breed who can enrich their words of wit and wisdom from the storehouse of their own reading without the need to draw upon the common currency of a dictionary of quotations!

ACTING

BAYLIS, Lilian (1874–1937)
[On a less than adequate performance in *King Lear*]
Quite a sweet little Goneril, don't you think?

[*The Guardian*, 1976]

FIELDING, Henry (1707–1754)
He the best player! ... Why, I could act as well as he myself. I am sure, if I had seen a ghost, I should have looked in the very same manner, and done just as he did ... The king for my money! He speaks all his words distinctly, half as loud again as the other. Anybody may see he is an actor.

[*Tom Jones* (1749)]

HULL, Josephine (1886–1957)
Playing Shakespeare is very tiring. You never get to sit down, unless you're a King.

[In Cooper and Hartman, *Violets and Vinegar* (1980)]

LUNT, Alfred (1892–1977)
[On acting]
Speak in a loud clear voice and try not to bump into the furniture.

[In Halliwell, *Filmgoer's Book of Quotes* (1973)]

MOORE, George (1852–1933)
Acting is therefore the lowest of the arts, if it is an art at all.

[*Impressions and Opinions* (1891)]

RICHARDSON, Sir Ralph (1902–1983)
The most precious things in speech are pauses.

[Attr.]

SHAKESPEARE, William (1564–1616)
[On the power of acting]
He would drown the stage with tears,
And cleave the general ear with horrid speech;
Make mad the guilty, and appal the free,
Confound the ignorant, and amaze indeed
The very faculties of eyes and ears.

[*Hamlet*, II.ii]

SHERIDAN, Richard Brinsley (1751–1816)
Burleigh comes forward, shakes his head, and exit.
Sneer: He is very perfect indeed. Now pray, what did he mean by that?
Puff: Why, by that shake of the head, he gave you to understand that even though they had more justice in their cause and wisdom in their measures, yet, if there was not a greater spirit shown on the part of the people, the country would at last fall a sacrifice to the hostile ambition of the Spanish monarchy.
Sneer: The devil! – did he mean all that by shaking his head?
Puff: Every word of it. If he shook his head as I taught him.

[*The Critic* (1779)]

I wish, sir, you would practise this without me. I can't stay dying here all night.

[*The Critic* (1779)]

TERRY, Dame Ellen (1847–1928)
Imagination! imagination! I put it first years ago, when I was asked what qualities I thought necessary for success upon the stage.

[*The Story of My Life* (1933)]

ZE AMI (1363–1443)
In the act of imitation there is the level of no-imitation. When the act of imitation is perfectly accomplished and the actor becomes the thing itself, the actor will no longer have the desire to imitate.

[*Fûshi kaden* (1400–1418)]

See ACTORS; THEATRE

ACTION

AMIEL, Henri-Frédéric (1821–1881)
Action is but coarsened thought – thought become concrete, obscure, and unconscious.

[*Journal*, 1850]

ACTORS

2

BEERBOHM, Sir Max (1872–1956)
Anything that is worth doing has been
done frequently. Things hitherto undone should be given, I suspect, a
wide berth.

[*Mainly on the Air* (1946)]

CANETTI, Elias (1905–1994)
*Was immer ihre Tätigkeit ist, die Tätigen
halten sich für besser.*
Whatever their activity is, the active
think they are better.

[*The Human Province* (1969)]

CARLYLE, Thomas (1795–1881)
*The end of man is an Action and not a
Thought*, though it were the noblest.

[*Sartor Resartus* (1834)]

CORNFORD, F.M. (1874–1943)
Every public action which is not
customary, either is wrong or, if it is
right, is a dangerous precedent. It
follows that nothing should ever be
done for the first time.

[*Microcosmographia Academica* (1908)]

DE GAULLE, Charles (1890–1970)
Deliberation is the work of many men.
Action, of one alone.

[*War Memoirs*]

ELIOT, George (1819–1880)
Our deeds determine us, as much as
we determine our deeds.

[*Adam Bede* (1859)]

EMERSON, Ralph Waldo (1803–1882)
We are taught by great actions that the
universe is the property of every
individual in it.

[*Nature* (1836)]

The reward of a thing well done, is to
have done it.

['New England Reformers' (1844)]

JOWETT, Benjamin (1817–1893)
The way to get things done is not to
mind who gets the credit for doing
them.

[Attr.]

KANT, Immanuel (1724–1804)
*Ich soll niemals anders verfahren als so,
dass ich auch wollen könne, meine
Maxime solle ein allgemeines Gesetz
werden.*
I should always act in such a way that
I may want my maxim to become a
general law.

[*Outline of the Metaphysics of Morals* (1785)]

KEMPIS, Thomas à (c. 1380–1471)
*Certe adveniente die iudicii non
quaeretur a nobis quid legimus sed quid
fecimus.*
Truly, when the day of judgement
comes, it will not be a question of
what we have read, but what we have
done.

[*De Imitatione Christi* (1892 ed.)]

**LA ROCHEFOUCAULD, Duc de
(1613–1680)**
*Nous aurions souvent honte de nos plus
belles actions, si le monde voyait les
motifs qui les produisent.*
We would often be ashamed of our
finest actions if the world could see
the motives behind them.

[*Maximes* (1678)]

SZASZ, Thomas (1920–)
Men are rewarded and punished not
for what they do, but rather for how
their acts are defined. This is why men
are more interested in better justifying
themselves than in better behaving
themselves.

[*The Second Sin* (1973)]

TAWNEY, R.H. (1880–1962)
It is a commonplace that the
characteristic virtue of Englishmen is
their power of sustained practical
activity, and their characteristic vice a
reluctance to test the quality of that
activity by reference to principles.

[*The Acquisitive Society* (1921)]

ACTORS

ANONYMOUS
[On a performance of Cleopatra by
Sarah Bernhardt]
How different, how very different from

the home life of our own dear Queen!

[Remark]

Totus mundus agit histrionem.
The whole world plays the actor.

[Motto of Globe playhouse]

BENCHLEY, Robert (1889–1945)
[Suggesting an epitaph for an actress]
She sleeps alone at last.

[Attr.]

BETTERTON, Thomas (1635–1710)
[Reply to the Archbishop of Canterbury]
Actors speak of things imaginary as if they were real, while you preachers too often speak of things real as if they were imaginary.

[Attr.]

BRANDO, Marlon (1924–)
An actor's a guy who, if you ain't talking about him, ain't listening.

[*The Observer*, 1956]

COLERIDGE, Samuel Taylor (1772–1834)
[Of Edmund Kean]
To see him act is like reading Shakespeare by flashes of lightning.

[*Table Talk* (1835)]

COWARD, Sir Noël (1899–1973)
[Comment on a child star, in a long-winded play]
Two things should be cut: the second act and the child's throat.

[In Richards, *The Wit of Noël Coward*]

DUNDY, Elaine (1927–)
The question actors most often get asked is how they can bear saying the same things over and over again night after night, but God knows the answer to that is, don't we all anyway; might as well get paid for it.

[*The Dud Avocado* (1958)]

FIELD, Eugene (1850–1895)
[Of Creston Clarke as King Lear]
He played the King as though under momentary apprehension that

someone else was about to play the ace.

[Attr.]

FORD, John (1895–1973)
It is easier to get an actor to be a cowboy than to get a cowboy to be an actor.

[Attr.]

HITCHCOCK, Alfred (1899–1980)
Nobody can really *like* an actor.

[*The New Yorker*, 1992]

I deny that I ever said that actors are cattle. What I said was, 'Actors should be treated like cattle'.

[Attr.]

HOPPER, Hedda (1890–1966)
At one time I thought he wanted to be an actor. He had certain qualifications, including no money and a total lack of responsibility.

[*From Under My Hat* (1953)]

JOHNSON, Samuel (1709–1784)
[To Garrick]
I'll come no more behind your scenes, David: for the silk stockings and white bosoms of your actresses excite my amorous propensities.

[In Boswell, *The Life of Samuel Johnson* (1791)]

KAUFMAN, George S. (1889–1961)
[On Raymond Massey's interpretation of Abraham Lincoln]
Massey won't be satisfied until somebody assassinates him.

[In Meredith, *George S. Kaufman and the Algonquin Round Table* (1974)]

LEVANT, Oscar (1906–1972)
Romance on the High Seas was Doris Day's first picture; that was before she became a virgin.

[*Memoirs of an Amnesiac* (1965)]

MALOUF, David (1934–)
Actors don't pretend to be other people; they become themselves by finding other people inside them.

[*Harland's Half Acre* (1984)]

PARKER, Dorothy (1893–1967)
[Remark on a performance by
Katherine Hepburn]
She ran the whole gamut of the
emotions from A to B.

[In Carey, *Katherine Hepburn* (1985)]

Scratch an actor and you'll find an
actress.

[Attr.]

SHAKESPEARE, William (1564–1616)
Like a dull actor now,
I have forgot my part and I am out,
Even to a full disgrace.

[*Coriolanus*, V.iii]

TYNAN, Kenneth (1927–1980)
What, when drunk, one sees in other
women, one sees in Garbo sober.

[*The Sunday Times*, 1963]

WARHOL, Andy (c. 1926–1987)
[Of James Dean]
He is not our hero because he was
perfect. He is our hero because he
perfectly represented the damaged and
beautiful soul of our time.

[In Brandreth, *Great Theatrical Disasters*]

WILLIAMSON, Nicol
[Of Sean Connery]
Guys like him and Caine talk about
acting as if they knew what it was.

[Interview, *Daily Mail*, 1996]

WINCHELL, Walter (1897–1972)
I saw [the show] at a disadvantage –
the curtain was up.

[In Whiteman, *Come to Judgement*]

See ACTING; THEATRE

ADULTERY

AUSTEN, Jane (1775–1817)
I am proud to say that I have a very
good eye at an Adultress, for tho'
repeatedly assured that another in the
same party was the *She*, I fixed upon
the right one from the first.

[Letter to Cassandra Austen, 1801]

BENCHLEY, Robert (1889–1945)
[Comment on an office shared with
Dorothy Parker]
One cubic foot less of space and it
would have constituted adultery.

[Attr.]

BYRON, Lord (1788–1824)
What men call gallantry, and gods
 adultery,
Is much more common where the
 climate's sultry.

[*Don Juan* (1824)]

Merely innocent flirtation.
Not quite adultery, but adulteration.

[*Don Juan* (1824)]

CARTER, Jimmy (1924–)
I've looked on a lot of women with
lust. I've committed adultery in my
heart many times. God recognizes I
will do this and forgives me.

[Interview with *Playboy*, 1976]

DRING, Philip
[Dring is a preacher of the Assembly of
God Mission]
I may commit adultery again if God
moves me to it.

[*The Observer*, 1980]

HUXLEY, Aldous (1894–1963)
There are few who would not rather
be taken in adultery than in
provincialism.

[*Antic Hay* (1923)]

JOHN PAUL II (1920–)
Adultery in your heart is committed
not only when you look with excessive
sexual desire at a woman who is not
your wife, but also if you look in the
same manner at your wife.

[*The Observer*, 1990]

**MAUGHAM, William Somerset
(1874–1965)**
You know, of course, that the
Tasmanians, who never committed
adultery, are now extinct.

[*The Bread-Winner*]

RICHELIEU, Duc de (1766–1822)
[On discovering his wife with her lover]
Madame, you must really be more careful. Suppose it had been someone else who found you like this.

[In Wallechinsky, *The Book of Lists* (1977)]

SHAKESPEARE, William (1564–1616)
Adultery?
Thou shalt not die. Die for adultery?
No.
The wren goes to't, and the small gilded fly
Does lecher in my sight.
Let copulation thrive.

[*King Lear*, IV.vi]

See MARRIAGE; SEX

ADULTS

BEAUVOIR, Simone de (1908–1986)
Qu'est-ce qu'un adulte? Un enfant gonflé d'âge.
What is an adult? A child blown up by age.

[*The Woman Destroyed* (1969)]

HARRIS, Sydney J. (1917–)
We have not passed that subtle line between childhood and adulthood until we move from the passive voice to the active voice – that is, until we have stopped saying 'It got lost', and say, 'I lost it'.

[Attr.]

MILLAY, Edna St Vincent (1892–1950)
Was it for this I uttered prayers,
And sobbed and cursed and kicked the stairs,
That now, domestic as a plate,
I should retire at half-past eight?

['Grown-up' (1920)]

ROSTAND, Jean (1894–1977)
Etre adulte, c'est être seul.
To be an adult is to be alone.

[*Thoughts of a Biologist* (1939)]

SHAKESPEARE, William (1564–1616)
Your lordship, though not clean past your youth, hath yet some smack of age in you, some relish of the saltness of time.

[*Henry IV, Part 2*, I.ii]

SZASZ, Thomas (1920–)
A child becomes an adult when he realizes that he has a right not only to be right but also to be wrong.

[*The Second Sin* (1973)]

ADVERTISING

DOUGLAS, Norman (1868–1952)
You can tell the ideals of a nation by its advertisements.

[*South Wind* (1917)]

HUXLEY, Aldous (1894–1963)
It is far easier to write ten passably effective Sonnets, good enough to take in the not too inquiring critic, than one effective advertisement that will take in a few thousand of the uncritical buying public.

[*On the Margin* (1923), 'Advertisement']

JEFFERSON, Thomas (1743–1826)
Advertisements contain the only truths to be relied on in a newspaper.

[Letter, 1819]

LEACOCK, Stephen (1869–1944)
Advertising may be described as the science of arresting the human intelligence long enough to get money from it.

[In Prochow, *The Public Speaker's Treasure Chest*]

MCDERMOTT, John W.
Ninety-Mile Beach was obviously named by one of New Zealand's first advertising copywriters ... It is fifty-six miles long.

[*How to Get Lost and Found in New Zealand* (1976)]

MCLUHAN, Marshall (1911–1980)
Ads are the cave art of the twentieth century.

[*Culture Is Our Business* (1970)]

ADVICE

ADVICE

NASH, Ogden (1902–1971)
Beneath this slab
John Brown is stowed.
He watched the ads,
And not the road.

['Lather as You Go' (1942)]

ADVICE

BIERCE, Ambrose (1842–c. 1914)
Advice: The smallest current coin.

[*The Cynic's Word Book* (1906)]

BISMARCK, Prince Otto von (1815–1898)
To youth I have but three words of counsel – work, work, work.

[Attr.]

BURTON, Robert (1577–1640)
Who cannot give good counsel? 'tis cheap, it costs them nothing.

[*Anatomy of Melancholy* (1621)]

EDWARD VIII (Later Duke of Windsor) (1894–1972)
Perhaps one of the only positive pieces of advice that I was ever given was that supplied by an old courtier who observed: 'Only two rules really count. Never miss an opportunity to relieve yourself; never miss a chance to sit down and rest your feet.'

[*A King's Story* (1951)]

EMERSON, Ralph Waldo (1803–1882)
It was a high counsel that I once heard given to a young person, – 'Always do what you are afraid to do.'

[*Essays, First Series* (1841)]

HARRIS, George (1844–1922)
[In his address to students at the beginning of a new academic year]
I intended to give you some advice but now I remember how much is left over from last year unused.

[In Braude, *Braude's Second Encyclopedia*]

LA ROCHEFOUCAULD, Duc de (1613–1680)
One gives nothing so generously as advice.

[*Maximes* (1678)]

SULLIVAN, Annie (1866–1936)
It's queer how ready people always are with advice in any real or imaginary emergency, and no matter how many times experience has shown them to be wrong, they continue to set forth their opinions, as if they had received them from the Almighty!

[Letter, 1887]

THOREAU, Henry (1817–1862)
I have lived some thirty years on this planet, and I have yet to hear the first syllable of valuable or even earnest advice from my seniors.

[*Walden* (1854)]

AGE

ADAMS, John Quincy (1767–1848)
I inhabit a weak, frail, decayed tenement; battered by the winds and broken in on by the storms, and, from all I can learn, the landlord does not intend to repair.

[Attr.]

ADENAUER, Konrad (1876–1967)
[To his doctor]
I haven't asked you to make me young again. All I want is to go on getting older.

[Attr.]

ALLEN, Dave (1936–)
I still think of myself as I was 25 years ago. Then I look in a mirror and see an old bastard and I realise it's me.

[*The Independent*, 1993]

ALLEN, Woody (1935–)
I recently turned sixty. Practically a third of my life is over.

[*The Observer Review*, 1996]

ARNOLD, Matthew (1822–1888)
I am past thirty, and three parts iced over.

[Letter to A.H. Clough, 1853]

BARUCH, Bernard M. (1870–1965)
I will never be an old man. To me, old

age is always fifteen years older than I am.

[*The Observer*, 1955]

BINYON, Laurence (1869–1943)
They shall grow not old, as we that are
  left grow old:
Age shall not weary them, nor the
  years condemn.
At the going down of the sun and in
  the morning
We will remember them.

['For the Fallen' (1914)]

BLAKE, Eubie (1883–1983)
[He died five days after his hundredth birthday]
If I'd known I was gonna live this long,
I'd have taken better care of myself.

[*The Observer*, 1983]

BRENAN, Gerald (1894–1987)
Old age takes away from us what we
have inherited and gives us what we
have earned.

[*Thoughts in a Dry Season* (1978)]

BROWNING, Robert (1812–1889)
Grow old along with me!
The best is yet to be,
The last of life for which the first was
  made:
Our times are in His hand
Who saith, 'A whole I planned,
Youth shows but half; trust God: see
  all, nor be afraid!'

['Rabbi Ben Ezra' (1864)]

BURKE, Edmund (1729–1797)
The arrogance of age must submit to
be taught by youth.

[Letter to Fanny Burney, 1782]

BYRON, Lord (1788–1824)
What is the worst of woes that wait on
  age?
What stamps the wrinkle deeper on
  the brow?
To view each loved one blotted from
  life's page,
And be alone on earth, as I am now.

[*Childe Harold's Pilgrimage* (1818)]

Years steal
Fire from the mind as vigour from the
  limb;
And life's enchanted cup but sparkles
  near the brim.

[*Childe Harold's Pilgrimage* (1818)]

I am ashes where once I was fire.

['To the Countess of Blessington' (1823)]

CALMENT, Jeanne (1875–)
[Reply to someone who asked what
she would like for her 121st birthday]
Respect.

[*The Mail on Sunday*, 1996]

CAMPBELL, Joseph (1879–1944)
As a white candle
In a holy place,
So is the beauty
Of an aged face.

['The Old Woman' (1913)]

COLLINS, Mortimer (1827–1876)
A man is as old as he's feeling,
A woman as old as she looks.

['The Unknown Quantity']

DEWEY, John (1859–1952)
It is strange that the one thing that
every person looks forward to, namely
old age, is the one thing for which no
preparation is made.

[Attr.]

DISRAELI, Benjamin (1804–1881)
When a man fell into his anecdotage it
was a sign for him to retire from the
world.

[*Lothair* (1870)]

DRYDEN, John (1631–1700)
None would live past years again,
Yet all hope pleasure in what yet
  remain;
And, from the dregs of life, think to
  receive,
What the first sprightly running could
  not give.

[*Aureng-Zebe* (1675)]

EDMOND, James (1859–1933)
[Caption to a drawing of three women

by Norman Lindsay]
We walk along the gas-lit street in a
    dreadful row, we three,
The woman I was, the woman I am,
    and the woman I'll one day be.
[In Moore, *The Story of Australian Art*]

EMERSON, Ralph Waldo (1803–1882)
Spring still makes spring in the mind,
When sixty years are told.
[*Poems* (1847)]

ESTIENNE, Henri (1531–1598)
Si jeunesse savoit; si vieillesse pouvoit.
If only youth knew; if only age could.
[*Les Prémices* (1594)]

FRANKLIN, Benjamin (1706–1790)
At twenty years of age, the will reigns;
at thirty, the wit; and at forty, the
judgement.
[*Poor Richard's Almanac* (1741)]

GONNE, Maud (1865–1953)
Oh how you hate old age – well so do I
... but I, who am more a rebel against
man than you, rebel less against
nature, and accept the inevitable and
go with it gently into the unknown.
[Letter to W.B. Yeats]

HILTON, James (1900–1954)
Anno domini ... that's the most fatal
complaint of all, in the end.
[*Goodbye, Mr Chips* (1934)]

**HOLMES, Oliver Wendell, Jr.
(1841–1935)**
[Aged 86, on seeing a pretty girl]
Oh, to be seventy again!
[In Fadiman, *The American Treasury*]

IRVING, Washington (1783–1859)
Whenever a man's friends begin to
compliment him about looking young,
he may be sure that they think he is
growing old.
[*Bracebridge Hall* (1822)]

JOHNSON, Samuel (1709–1784)
There is a wicked inclination in most
people to suppose an old man decayed
in his intellects. If a young or middle-
aged man, when leaving a company,

does not recollect where he laid his
hat, it is nothing; but if the same
inattention is discovered in an old
man, people will shrug up their
shoulders, and say, 'His memory is
going.'
[In Boswell, *The Life of Samuel Johnson*
(1791)]

LANG, Andrew (1844–1912)
Our hearts are young 'neath wrinkled
    rind:
Life's more amusing than we thought.
['Ballade of Middle Age']

LARKIN, Philip (1922–1985)
Perhaps being old is having lighted
    rooms
Inside your head, and people in them,
    acting.
People you know, yet can't quite
    name.
['The Old Fools' (1974)]

**MAUGHAM, William Somerset
(1874–1965)**
From the earliest times the old have
rubbed it into the young that they are
wiser than they, and before the young
had discovered what nonsense this
was they were old too, and it profited
them to carry on the imposture.
[*Cakes and Ale* (1930)]

NASH, Ogden (1902–1971)
Do you think my mind is maturing
    late,
Or simply rotted early?
['Lines on Facing Forty' (1942)]

NAYLOR, James Ball (1860–1945)
King David and King Solomon
Led merry, merry lives,
With many, many lady friends
And many, many wives;
But when old age crept over them,
With many, many qualms,
King Solomon wrote the Proverbs
And King David wrote the Psalms.
['King David and King Solomon' (1935)]

ORWELL, George (1903–1950)
At 50, everyone has the face he
deserves.
[Notebook, 1949]

PICASSO, Pablo (1881–1973)
Age only matters when one is ageing.
Now that I have arrived at a great age,
I might just as well be twenty.

[*In Richardson, Picasso in Private*]

POWELL, Anthony (1905–)
Growing old is like being increasingly
penalized for a crime you haven't
committed.

[*A Dance to the Music of Time* (1973)]

POWER, Marguerite, Countess of Blessington (1789–1849)
Tears fell from my eyes – yes, weak
and foolish as it now appears to me, I
wept for my departed youth; and for
that beauty of which the faithful mirror
too plainly assured me, no remnant
existed.

[*The Confessions of an Elderly Lady* (1838)]

REAGAN, Ronald (1911–)
I am delighted to be with you. In fact,
at my age, I am delighted to be anywhere.

[Speech at the Oxford Union, 1992]

RUBINSTEIN, Helena (c. 1872–1965)
I have always felt that a woman has a
right to treat the subject of her age
with ambiguity until, perhaps, she
passes into the realm of over ninety.
Then it is better she be candid with
herself and with the world.

[*My Life for Beauty* (1965)]

SAKI (1870–1916)
The young have aspirations that never
come to pass, the old have reminiscences of what never happened. It's
only the middle-aged who are really
conscious of their limitations.

[*Reginald* (1904)]

SANTAYANA, George (1863–1952)
The young man who has not wept is a
savage, and the old man who will not
laugh is a fool.

[*Dialogues in Limbo* (1925)]

SARTON, May (1912–)
Old age is not an illness, it is a
timeless ascent. As power diminishes,
we grow toward the light.

[*Ms* magazine, 1982]

SEXTON, Anne (1928–1974)
In a dream you are never eighty.

['Old' (1962)]

SHAKESPEARE, William (1564–1616)
Unregarded age in corners thrown.

[*As You Like It*, II.iii]

O, sir, you are old;
Nature in you stands on the very verge
Of her confine.

[*King Lear*, II.iv]

A good old man, sir, he will be talking;
as they say 'When the age is in the wit
is out.'

[*Much Ado About Nothing*, III.v]

Crabbed age and youth cannot live
    together:
Youth is full of pleasance, age is full of
    care ...

Age, I do abhor thee; youth, I do adore
thee.

[*The Passionate Pilgrim*, xii]

That time of year thou mayst in me
    behold
When yellow leaves, or none, or few,
    do hang
Upon those boughs which shake
    against the cold,
Bare ruin'd choirs where late the
    sweet birds sang.
In me thou seest the twilight of such
    day
As after sunset fadeth in the west,
Which by and by black night doth take
    away,
Death's second self, that seals up all in
    rest.

[Sonnet 73]

SHAW, George Bernard (1856–1950)
Old men are dangerous: it doesn't
matter to them what is going to
happen to the world.

[*Heartbreak House* (1919)]

SMITH, Logan Pearsall (1865–1946)
There is more felicity on the far side of

baldness than young men can possibly imagine.

['Last Words' (1933)]

SOLON (c. 638–c. 559 BC)
I grow old ever learning many things.

[In Bergk (ed.), *Poetae Lyrici Graeci*]

SPARK, Muriel (1918–)
Being over seventy is like being engaged in a war. All our friends are going or gone and we survive amongst the dead and the dying as on a battlefield.

[*Memento Mori*]

STONE, I.F. (1907–1989)
If you live long enough, the venerability factor creeps in; you get accused of things you never did and praised for virtues you never had.

[In Laurence J. Peter, *Peter's Quotations*]

SWIFT, Jonathan (1667–1745)
Old men and comets have been reverenced for the same reason; their long beards, and pretences to foretell events.

[*Thoughts on Various Subjects* (1711)]

TALLEYRAND, Charles-Maurice de (1754–1838)
[Remark to young man who boasted that he did not play whist]
Quelle triste vieillesse vous vous préparez.
What a sad old age you are preparing for yourself.

[In J. Amédée Pichot, *Souvenirs intimes sur M. de Talleyrand* (1870)]

THOMAS, Dylan (1914–1953)
Do not go gentle into that good night,
Old age should burn and rave at close of day;
Rage, rage against the dying of the light.

['Do Not Go Gentle into that Good Night' (1952)]

TROTSKY, Leon (1879–1940)
Old age is the most unexpected of all the things that happen to a man.

[*Diary in Exile*, 8 May 1935]

WALPOLE, Horace (1717–1797)
What has one to do, when one grows tired of the world, as we both do, but to draw nearer and nearer, and gently waste the remains of life with friends with whom one began it?

[Letter to George Montagu, 1765]

WEBB, Sidney (1859–1947)
Old people are always absorbed in something, usually themselves; we prefer to be absorbed in the Soviet Union.

[Attr.]

WHITMAN, Walt (1819–1892)
Women sit or move to and fro, some old, some young.
The young are beautiful – but the old are more beautiful than the young.

['Beautiful Women' (1871)]

WILDE, Oscar (1854–1900)
One should never trust a woman who tells one her real age. A woman who would tell one that would tell one anything.

[*A Woman of No Importance* (1893)]

I delight in men over seventy. They always offer one the devotion of a lifetime.

[*A Woman of No Importance* (1893)]

The old believe everything: the middle-aged suspect everything: the young know everything.

[*The Chameleon*, 1894]

WILLIAMS, William Carlos (1883–1963)
In old age
the mind
casts off
rebelliously
an eagle
from its crag.

[*Paterson* (1946–1958)]

WODEHOUSE, P.G. (1881–1975)
He was either a man of about a hundred and fifty who was rather young for his years or a man of about

a hundred and ten who had been aged by trouble.

[In Usborne, *Wodehouse at Work to the End* (1976)]

WORDSWORTH, William (1770–1850)
The wiser mind
Mourns less for what age takes away
Than what it leaves behind.

['The Fountain' (1800)]

YEATS, W.B. (1865–1939)
I thought no more was needed
Youth to prolong
Than dumb-bell and foil
To keep the body young.
O who could have foretold
That the heart grows old?

['A Song' 1918]

An aged man is but a paltry thing,
A tattered coat upon a stick, unless
Soul clap its hands and sing, and
    louder sing
For every tatter in its mortal dress.

['Sailing to Byzantium' (1927)]

See YOUTH

AMBITION

BROWNING, Robert (1812–1889)
'Tis not what man does which exalts
him, but what a man would do!

['Saul' (1855)]

BURKE, Edmund (1729–1797)
Well is it known that ambition can
creep as well as soar.

[*Third Letter ... on the Proposals for Peace with the Regicide Directory of France* (1797)]

CAESAR, Gaius Julius (c. 102–44 BC)
I would rather be the first man here (in Gaul) than second in Rome.

[Attr. in Plutarch, *Lives*]

CONRAD, Joseph (1857–1924)
All ambitions are lawful except those which climb upward on the miseries or credulities of mankind.

[*A Personal Record* (1912)]

GILBERT, W.S. (1836–1911)
If you wish in this world to advance
Your merits you're bound to enhance,
You must stir it and stump it,
And blow your own trumpet,
Or, trust me, you haven't a chance!

[*Ruddigore* (1887)]

KEATS, John (1795–1821)
I am ambitious of doing the world some good: if I should be spared, that may be the work of maturer years – in the interval I will assay to reach to as high a summit in Poetry as the nerve bestowed upon me will suffer.

[Letter to Richard Woodhouse, 1818]

KENEALLY, Thomas (1935–)
It's only when you abandon your ambitions that they become possible.

[*Australian*, 1983]

SHAKESPEARE, William (1564–1616)
I charge thee, fling away ambition:
By that sin fell the angels. How can
    man then,
The image of his Maker, hope to win
    by it?

[*Henry VIII*, III.ii]

'Tis a common proof
That lowliness is young ambition's
    ladder,
Whereto the climber-upward turns his
    face;
But when he once attains the upmost
    round,
He then unto the ladder turns his back,
Looks in the clouds, scorning the base
    degrees
By which he did ascend.

[*Julius Caesar*, II.i]

Thou wouldst be great;
Art not without ambition, but without
The illness should attend it. What thou
    wouldst highly,
That wouldst thou holily; wouldst not
    play false,
And yet wouldst wrongly win.

[*Macbeth*, I.v]

I have no spur
To prick the sides of my intent, but
  only
Vaulting ambition, which o'er-leaps
  itself,
And falls on th' other.

[*Macbeth*, I.vii]

SHAW, George Bernard (1856–1950)
The Gospel of Getting On.

[*Mrs Warren's Profession* (1898), IV]

SMITH, Adam (1723–1790)
And thus, place, that great object
which divides the wives of aldermen,
is the end of half the labours of human
life; and is the cause of all the tumult
and bustle, all the rapine and injustice,
which avarice and ambition have introduced into this world.

[*The Theory of Moral Sentiments* (1759)]

WEBSTER, Daniel (1782–1852)
[On being advised not to join the
overcrowded legal profession]
There is always room at the top.

[Attr.]

AMERICA

ANONYMOUS
Overpaid, overfed, oversexed, and
over here.

[Of GIs in Britain during World War II]

ARNOLD, Matthew (1822–1888)
Our society distributes itself into
Barbarians, Philistines, and Populace;
and America is just ourselves, with the
Barbarians quite left out, and the
Populace nearly.

[*Culture and Anarchy* (1869)]

AUDEN, W.H. (1907–1973)
God bless the U.S.A., so large,
So friendly, and so rich.

['On the Circuit']

AYKROYD, Dan (1952–)
What the American public doesn't
know is what makes it the American
public.

[*Tommy Boy*, film, 1995]

BUTLER, Nicholas Murray (1862–1947)
... a society like ours [USA] of which it
is truly said to be often but three
generations 'from shirt-sleeves to
shirt-sleeves'.

[*True and False Democracy*]

CLEMENCEAU, Georges (1841–1929)
America is the only nation in history
which miraculously has gone directly
from barbarism to degeneration
without the usual interval of civilization.

[Attr.]

COOLIDGE, Calvin (1872–1933)
The business of America is business.

[Speech, 1925]

DÍAZ, Porfirio (1830–1915)
Poor Mexico, so far from God and so
near to the United States!

[Attr.]

**EDWARD VIII (Later Duke of Windsor)
(1894–1972)**
The thing that impresses me most
about America is the way parents obey
their children.

[In *Look*, 1957]

EISENHOWER, Dwight D. (1890–1969)
Whatever America hopes to bring to
pass in this world must first come to
pass in the heart of America.

[Inaugural address, 1953]

EMERSON, Ralph Waldo (1803–1882)
The Americans have little faith. They
rely on the power of a dollar.

[Lecture, 1841, 'Man the Reformer']

FITZGERALD, F. Scott (1896–1940)
Americans, while willing, even eager,
to be serfs, have always been obstinate about being peasantry.

[*The Great Gatsby* (1926)]

FORD, Gerald R. (1913–)
[On becoming President]
I guess it proves that in America
anyone can be President.

[In Reeves, *A Ford Not a Lincoln*]

GREY, Edward (1862–1933)
The United States is like a gigantic boiler. Once the fire is lighted under it there is no limit to the power it can generate.

[In Winston S. Churchill, *Their Finest Hour*]

HOBSON, Sir Harold (1904–1992)
The United States, I believe, are under the impression that they are twenty years in advance of this country; whilst, as a matter of actual verifiable fact, of course, they are just about six hours behind it.

[*The Devil in Woodford Wells*]

JOHNSON, Samuel (1709–1784)
I am willing to love all mankind, *except an American.*

[In Boswell, *The Life of Samuel Johnson* (1791)]

KENNEDY, John F. (1917–1963)
And so, my fellow Americans: ask not what your country can do for you, ask what you can do for your country. My fellow citizens of the world: ask not what America will do for you, but what together we can do for the freedom of man.

[Inaugural address, 1961]

MCCARTHY, Senator Joseph (1908–1957)
McCarthyism is Americanism with its sleeves rolled.

[Speech, 1952]

MADARIAGA, Salvador de (1886–1978)
First, the sweetheart of the nation, then her aunt woman governs America because America is a land where boys refuse to grow up.

['Americans are Boys']

MENCKEN, H.L. (1880–1956)
No one ever went broke underestimating the intelligence of the American people.

[Attr.]

MINIFIE, James M. (1900–1974)
The United States is the glory, jest, and terror of mankind.

[In Purdy (ed.), *The New Romans* (1988)]

ROOSEVELT, Theodore (1858–1919)
There is no room in this country for hyphenated Americanism.

[Speech, 1915]

RUSSELL, Bertrand (1872–1970)
In America everybody is of the opinion that he has no social superiors, since all men are equal, but he does not admit that he has no social inferiors.

['Ideas that have harmed mankind' (1950)]

STAPLEDON, Olaf (1886–1950)
That strange blend of the commercial traveller, the missionary, and the barbarian conqueror, which was the American abroad.

[*Last and First Men* (1930)]

STEIN, Gertrude (1874–1946)
In the United States there is more space where nobody is than where anybody is. That is what makes America what it is.

[*The Geographical History of America* (1936)]

TALLEYRAND, Charles Maurice de (1754–1838)
[Of America]
I found there a country with thirty-two religions and only one sauce.

[In Pedrazzini, *Autant en apportent les mots*]

TOYNBEE, Arnold (1889–1975)
America is a large, friendly dog in a very small room. Every time it wags its tail it knocks over a chair.

[Broadcast news summary, 1954]

WELLS, H.G. (1866–1946)
Every time Europe looks across the Atlantic to see the American eagle, it observes only the rear end of an ostrich.

[*America*]

WILDE, Oscar (1854–1900)
Of course, America had often been discovered before, but it had always been hushed up.

[*Personal Impressions of America* (1883)]

The youth of America is their oldest tradition. It has been going on now for three hundred years.

[*A Woman of No Importance* (1893)]

WILSON, Woodrow (1856–1924)
America ... is the prize amateur nation of the world. Germany is the prize professional nation.

[Speech, 1917]

America is the only idealistic nation in the world.

[Speech, 1919]

ZANGWILL, Israel (1864–1926)
America is God's Crucible, the great Melting-Pot where all the races of Europe are melting and re-forming!

[*The Melting Pot* (1908)]

ANCESTORS

FORRO, (Rev. Fr) Francis Stephen (1914–1974)
[Response to a journalist's comment on the scruffiness of Hungarian refugees arriving at Mascot aerodrome, Australia, in 1956]
Ah, yes, but they will make fine ancestors.

[Attr.]

GILBERT, W.S. (1836–1911)
I can trace my ancestry back to a protoplasmal primordial atomic globule. Consequently, my family pride is something inconceivable.

[*The Mikado* (1885), I]

PLUTARCH (c. 46–c. 120)
It is indeed desirable to be well descended, but the glory belongs to our ancestors.

[*On the Training of Children*]

SHERIDAN, Richard Brinsley (1751–1816)
Our ancestors are very good kind of folks; but they are the last people I should choose to have a visiting acquaintance with.

[*The Rivals* (1775)]

ANGER

ARISTOTLE (384–322 BC)
The man who is angry on the right grounds and with the right people, and in the right manner and at the right moment and for the right length of time, is to be praised.

[*Nicomachean Ethics*]

BACON, Francis (1561–1626)
Anger makes dull men witty, but it keeps them poor.

['Apophthegms' (1679)]

THE BIBLE (King James Version)
A soft answer turneth away wrath.

[*Proverbs*, 15:1]

Be ye angry, and sin not; let not the sun go down upon your wrath.

[*Ephesians*, 4:26]

BLAKE, William (1757–1827)
I was angry with my friend:
I told my wrath, my wrath did end.
I was angry with my foe:
I told it not, my wrath did grow.

[*Songs of Experience* (1794)]

BURNS, Robert (1759–1796)
We think na on the lang Scots miles,
The mosses, waters, slaps, and styles,
That lie between us and our hame,
Whare sits our sulky, sullen dame,
Gathering her brows like gathering storm,
Nursing her wrath to keep it warm.

['Tam o' Shanter' (1790)]

CONGREVE, William (1670–1729)
Heav'n has no rage, like love to hatred turned,
Nor Hell a fury, like a woman scorn'd.

[*The Mourning Bride* (1697)]

CONNOLLY, Cyril (1903–1974)
There is no fury like an ex-wife searching for a new lover.

[*The Unquiet Grave* (1944)]

DILLER, Phyllis (1917–1974)
Never go to bed mad. Stay up and
fight.
[*Phyllis Diller's Housekeeping Hints*]

DRYDEN, John (1631–1700)
Beware the fury of a patient man.
[*Absalom and Achitophel* (1681)]

FULLER, Thomas (1608–1661)
Anger is one of the sinews of the soul;
he that wants it hath a maimed mind.
[*The Holy State and the Profane State* (1642)]

HALIFAX, Lord (1633–1695)
Anger is never without an Argument,
but seldom with a good one.
[*Thoughts and Reflections* (1750)]

HAZLITT, William (1778–1830)
Spleen can subsist on any kind of
food.
['On Wit and Humour' (1819)]

IRVING, Washington (1783–1859)
A tart temper never mellows with age,
and a sharp tongue is the only edged
tool that grows keener with constant
use.
['Rip Van Winkle' (1820)]

SHAW, George Bernard (1856–1950)
Beware of the man who does not
return your blow: he neither forgives
you nor allows you to forgive yourself.
[*Man and Superman* (1903)]

ANIMALS

BLAKE, William (1757–1827)
Tyger Tyger, burning bright
In the forests of the night:
What immortal hand or eye
Could frame thy fearful symmetry?
['The Tyger' (1794)]

CANETTI, Elias (1905–1994)
*Immer wenn man ein Tier genau
betracht, hat man das Gefühl, ein
Mensch, der drin sitzt, macht sich über
einen lustig.*
Whenever you observe an animal
closely, you have the feeling that a
person sitting inside is making fun of
you.
[*The Human Province*]

ELIOT, George (1819–1880)
Animals are such agreeable friends –
they ask no questions, they pass no
criticisms.
[*Scenes of Clerical Life* (1858)]

FOYLE, Christina (1911–)
Animals are always loyal and love you,
whereas with children you never know
where you are.
[*The Times*, 1993]

FROUDE, James Anthony (1818–1894)
Wild animals never kill for sport. Man
is the only one to whom the torture
and death of his fellow creatures is
amusing in itself.
[*Oceana, or England and her Colonies* (1886)]

GOLDSMITH, Oliver (c. 1728–1774)
Brutes never meet in bloody fray,
Nor cut each other's throats, for pay.
['Logicians Refuted' (1759)]

PEACOCK, Thomas Love (1785–1866)
Nothing can be more obvious than
that all animals were created solely
and exclusively for the use of man.
[*Headlong Hall* (1816)]

SHAKESPEARE, William (1564–1616)
No beast so fierce but knows some
touch of pity.
[*Richard III*, I.ii]

SOLZHENITSYN, Alexander (1918–)
Nowadays we don't think much of a
man's love for an animal; we mock
people who are attached to cats. But if
we stop loving animals, aren't we
bound to stop loving humans too?
[*Cancer Ward* (1968)]

SPENCER, Herbert (1820–1903)
People are beginning to see that the
first requisite to success in life, is to be
a good animal.
[*Education* (1861)]

Quarrels would not last long if the fault were on one side only.

[*Maximes* (1678)]

LOWELL, James Russell (1819–1891)
There is no good in arguing with the inevitable. The only argument available with an east wind is to put on your overcoat.

[*Democracy and Other Addresses* (1887)]

ROSTAND, Jean (1894–1977)
A married couple are well suited when both partners usually feel the need for a quarrel at the same time.

[*Le Mariage*]

SHERIDAN, Richard Brinsley (1751–1816)
The quarrel is a very pretty quarrel as it stands – we should only spoil it by trying to explain it.

[*The Rivals* (1775)]

YEATS, W.B. (1865–1939)
We make out of the quarrel with others, rhetoric; but of the quarrel with ourselves, poetry.

['Anima Hominis' (1917)]

ARISTOCRACY

AILESBURY, Maria, Marchioness of (d. 1893)
My dear, my dear, you never know when any beautiful young lady may not blossom into a Duchess!

[In Portland, *Men, Women, and Things* (1937)]

AUSTEN, Jane (1775–1817)
Sir Walter Elliot, of Kellynch Hall, in Somersetshire, was a man who, for his own amusement, never took up any book but the Baronetage; there he found occupation for an idle hour and consolation in a distressed one ... this was the page at which the favourite volume always opened: – ELLIOT OF KELLYNCH-HALL.

[*Persuasion* (1818)]

BURKE, Edmund (1729–1797)
Nobility is a graceful ornament to the civil order. It is the Corinthian capital of polished society.

[*Reflections on the Revolution in France ...* (1790)]

CHARLES, Prince of Wales (1948–)
The one advantage about marrying a princess – or someone from a royal family – is that they do know what happens.

[Attr.]

HOPE, Anthony (1863–1933)
'Bourgeois,' I observed, 'is an epithet which the riff-raff apply to what is respectable, and the aristocracy to what is decent.'

[*The Dolly Dialogues* (1894)]

LEVIS, Duc de (1764–1830)
Noblesse oblige.
Nobility has its obligations.

[*Maximes et réflexions* (1812)]

LLOYD GEORGE, David (1863–1945)
A fully equipped duke costs as much to keep up as two Dreadnoughts; and dukes are just as great a terror and they last longer.

[Speech, 1909]

MACHIAVELLI (1469–1527)
For titles do not reflect honour on men, but rather men on their titles.

[*Dei Discorsi*]

MANNERS, Lord John (1818–1906)
Let wealth and commerce, laws and learning die,
But leave us still our old nobility!

[*England's Trust* (1841)]

MILL, John Stuart (1806–1873)
Persons require to possess a title, or some other badge of rank, or of the consideration of people of rank, to be able to indulge somewhat in the luxury of doing as they like without detriment to their estimation.

[*On Liberty* (1859)]

MITFORD, Nancy (1904–1973)
An aristocracy in a republic is like a

chicken whose head had been cut off: it may run about in a lively way, but in fact it is dead.

[*Noblesse Oblige* (1956)]

NORTHCLIFFE, Lord (1865–1922)
When I want a peerage, I shall buy one like an honest man.

[Attr.]

PEARSON, Hesketh (1887–1964)
There is no stronger craving in the world than that of the rich for titles, except that of the titled for riches.

[Attr.]

SHAW, George Bernard (1856–1950)
Titles distinguish the mediocre, embarrass the superior, and are disgraced by the inferior.

[*Man and Superman* (1903)]

I've been offered titles, but I think they get one into disreputable company.

[In Barrow, *Gossip*]

TENNYSON, Alfred, Lord (1809–1892)
From yon blue heavens above us bent
The gardener Adam and his wife
Smile at the claims of long descent.
Howe'er it be, it seems to me,
'Tis only noble to be good.
Kind hearts are more than coronets,
And simple faith than Norman blood.

['Lady Clara Vere de Vere' (c. 1835)]

THACKERAY, William Makepeace (1811–1863)
Nothing like blood, sir, in hosses, dawgs, and men.

[*Vanity Fair* (1848)]

WELLINGTON, Duke of (1769–1852)
I believe I forgot to tell you I was made a Duke.

[Postscript to a letter to his nephew, 1814]

WOOLF, Virginia (1882–1941)
Those comfortably padded lunatic asylums which are known, euphemistically, as the stately homes of England.

[*The Common Reader* (1925)]

See CLASS

THE ARMY

ANONYMOUS
Any officer who shall behave in a scandalous manner, unbecoming the character of an officer and a gentleman shall ... be CASHIERED.

[*Articles of War*]

[The words of a soldier in the Peninsular War]
I looked along the line; it was enough to assure me. The steady determined scowl of my companions assured my heart and gave me determination.

[In Richardson, *Fighting Spirit: Psychological Factors in War* (1978)]

BAXTER, James K. (1926–1972)
The boy who volunteered at seventeen
At twenty-three is heavy on the booze.

['Returned Soldier' (1946)]

BRODSKY, Joseph (1940–1996)
It is the army that finally makes a citizen of you; without it, you still have a chance, however slim, to remain a human being.

['Less Than One' (1986)]

CHURCHILL, Sir Winston (1874–1965)
[On the Chiefs of Staffs system, 1943]
You may take the most gallant sailor, the most intrepid airman, or the most audacious soldier, put them at a table together – what do you get? *The sum of their fears.*

[In Macmillan, *The Blast of War*]

FREDERICK THE GREAT (1712–1786)
An army, like a serpent, goes on its belly.

[Attr.]

GERRISH, Theodore
The ties that bound us together were of the most sacred nature: they had been gotten in hardship and baptised in blood.

[*Army Life: A Private's Reminiscence of the Civil War* (1882)]

GREEN, Michael (1927–)
Fortunately, the army has had much

practice in ignoring impossible instructions

[*The Boy Who Shot Down an Airship* (1988)]

HELLER, Joseph (1923–)
I had examined myself pretty thoroughly and discovered that I was unfit for military service.

[*Catch-22* (1961)]

HOFFMANN, Max (1869–1927)
[Referring to the performance of the British army in World War I]
Ludendorff: The English soldiers fight like lions.
Hoffman: True. But don't we know that they are lions led by donkeys.

[In Falkenhayn, *Memoirs*]

HULL, General Sir Richard (1907–)
National Service did the country a lot of good but it darned near killed the army.

[Attr.]

KIPLING, Rudyard (1865–1936)
O, it's Tommy this, an' Tommy that,
   an' 'Tommy, go away';
But it's 'Thank you, Mister Atkins,'
   when the band begins to play ...

Then it's Tommy this, an' Tommy that,
   an' 'Tommy 'ow's yer soul?'
But it's 'Thin red line of 'eroes' when
   the drums begin to roll ...

For it's Tommy this, an' Tommy that,
   an' 'Chuck him out, the brute!'
But it's 'Saviour of 'is country' when
   the guns begin to shoot.

['Tommy' (1892)]

KISSINGER, Henry (1923–)
The conventional army loses if it does not win. The guerilla wins if he does not lose.

[*Foreign Affairs*, XIII (1969)]

MANNING, Frederic (1882–1935)
[Of the men in his battalion]
These apparently rude and brutal natures comforted, encouraged, and reconciled each other to fate, with a

tenderness and tact which was more moving than anything in life.

[*Her Privates We* (1929)]

MILLIGAN, Spike (1918–)
The Army works like this: if a man dies when you hang him, keep hanging him until he gets used to it.

[Attr.]

MONASH, Sir John (1865–1931)
Leadership counts for something, of course, but it cannot succeed without the spirit, élan and morale of those led. Therefore I count myself the most fortunate of men in having been placed at the head of the finest fighting machine the world has ever known.

[*Argus*, 1927]

MORAN, Lord (1924–)
A man of character in peace is a man of courage in war.

[*The Anatomy of Courage* (1945)

NAPIER, Sir William (1785–1860)
Then was seen with what a strength and majesty the British soldier fights.

[*History of the War in the Peninsula*]

NAPOLEON I (1769–1821)
[Of his generals]
I made most of mine *de la boue* [out of mud]. Wherever I found talent and courage, I rewarded it. My principle was *la carrière ouverte aux talens* [*sic*] [career open to talent], without asking whether there were any quarters of nobility to show.

[In O'Meara, *Napoleon in Exile* (1822)]

NAPOLEON III (1808–1873)
The army is the true nobility of our country.

[Speech, March 1855]

PATTON, General George S. (1885–1945)
Untutored courage is useless in the face of educated bullets.

[*Cavalry Journal*, 1922]

QUARLES, Francis (1592–1644)
Our God and soldiers we alike adore
Ev'n at the brink of danger; not before:
After deliverance, both alike requited,
Our God's forgotten, and our soldiers
　slighted.
['Of Common Devotion' (1632)]

SASSOON, Siegfried (1886–1967)
Soldiers are citizens of death's gray
land.
['Dreamers' (1917)]

**SELLAR, Walter (1898–1951) and
YEATMAN, Robert (1897–1968)**
Napoleon's armies always used to
march on their stomachs, shouting:
'Vive l'Intérieur!' and so moved about
very slowly.
[1066 And All That (1930)]

SHAKESPEARE, William (1564–1616)
That in the captain's but a choleric
　word
Which in the soldier is flat blasphemy.
[Measure For Measure, II.ii]

SHAW, George Bernard (1856–1950)
You can always tell an old soldier by
the inside of his holsters and cartridge
boxes. The young ones carry pistols
and cartridges: the old ones, grub.
[Arms and the Man (1898)]

SMITHERS, Alan Jack (1919–)
[Of Sir John Monash, Australian
military commander]
He was, above all, the first twentieth-
century general, a man with petrol in
his veins and a computer in his head.
[Sir John Monash]

TRUMAN, Harry S. (1884–1972)
[Of General MacArthur]
I didn't fire him because he was a
dumb son of a bitch, although he was,
but that's not against the law for
generals. If it was, half to three-
quarters of them would be in gaol.
[In Miller, Plain Speaking (1974)]

TUCHMAN, Barbara W. (1912–1989)
Dead battles, like dead generals, hold
the military mind in their dead grip.
[August 1914 (1962)]

TUCHOLSKY, Kurt (1890–1935)
Der französische Soldat ist ein
verkleideter Zivilist, der deutsche Zivilist
ist ein verkleideter Soldat.
The French soldier is a civilian in
disguise, the German civilian is a
soldier in disguise.
['Ocean of Pain' (1973)]

USTINOV, Sir Peter (1921–)
As for being a General, well, at the age
of four with paper hats and wooden
swords we're all Generals. Only some
of us never grow out of it.
[Romanoff and Juliet (1956)]

WASHINGTON, George (1732–1799)
Discipline is the soul of an army. It
makes small numbers formidable;
procures success to the weak, and
esteem to all.
[Letter of Instructions to the Captains of the
Virginia Regiments, 1759]

WELLINGTON, Duke of (1769–1852)
I don't know what effect these men
will have upon the enemy, but, by God,
they frighten me.
[Attr.]

[Of his troops]
The mere scum of the earth.
[In Stanhope, Conversations with the Duke of
Wellington (1888)]

WILDE, Lady Jane (1826–1896)
There's a proud array of soldiers –
what do they round your door?
They guard our master's granaries
from the thin hands of the poor.
['The Famine Years']

See NAVY; WAR

ART

ANOUILH, Jean (1910–1987)
C'est très jolie la vie, mais elle n'a pas
de forme. L'art a pour objet de lui en

ART

donner une précisément.
Life is very nice, but it has no shape. It is the purpose of art to give it shape.

[*The Rehearsal* (1950)]

BELLOW, Saul (1915–)
I feel that art has something to do with the achievement of stillness in the midst of chaos. A stillness which characterizes prayer, too, and the eye of the storm. I think that art has something to do with an arrest of attention in the midst of distraction.

[In Plimpton (ed.), *Writers at Work* (1967)]

BRACK, (Cecil) John (1920–)
I know all about art, but I don't know what I like.

[*The Dictionary of Australian Quotations*]

BRAQUE, Georges (1882–1963)
L'Art est fait pour troubler, la Science rassure.
Art is meant to disturb, science reassures.

[*Day and Night, Notebooks* (1952)]

BRODSKY, Joseph (1940–1996)
Art is not a better, but an alternative existence; it is not an attempt to escape reality but the opposite, an attempt to animate it. It is a spirit seeking flesh but finding words.

[*Less Than One* (1986)]

BUTLER, Samuel (1835–1902)
An art can only be learned in the workshop of those who are winning their bread by it.

[*Erewhon* (1872)]

CHEKHOV, Anton (1860–1904)
The artist may not be a judge of his characters, only a dispassionate witness.

[Attr.]

CHESTERTON, G.K. (1874–1936)
The artistic temperament is a disease that afflicts amateurs.

[*Heretics* (1905)]

CONNOLLY, Cyril (1903–1974)
There is no more sombre enemy of good art than the pram in the hall.

[*Enemies of Promise* (1938)]

CONSTABLE, John (1776–1837)
The sound of water escaping from mill-dams, etc, willows, old rotten planks, slimy posts, and brickwork, I love such things ... those scenes made me a painter and I am grateful.

[Letter to John Fisher, 1821]

CONSTANT, Benjamin (1767–1834)
L'art pour l'art et sans but; tout but dénature l'art. Mais l'art atteint au but qu'il n'a pas.
Art for art's sake, without a purpose; every purpose distorts the true nature of art. But art achieves a purpose which it does not have.

[*Journal intime*, 1804]

CROMWELL, Oliver (1599–1658)
Mr Lely, I desire you would use all your skill to paint my picture freely like me, and not flatter me at all; but remark all these roughnesses, pimples, warts, and everything as you see me, otherwise I will never pay a farthing for it.

[In Horace Walpole, *Anecdotes of Painting in England* (1763)]

DAVY, Sir Humphry (1778–1829)
[His opinion of the art galleries in Paris]
The finest collection of frames I ever saw.

[Attr.]

DEBUSSY, Claude (1862–1918)
L'art est le plus beau des mensonges.
Art is the most beautiful of all lies.

[*Monsieur Croche, antidilettante*]

DEGAS, Edgar (1834–1917)
Art is vice. You don't marry it legitimately, you rape it.

[In Paul Lafond, *Degas* (1918)]

ELIOT, T.S. (1888–1965)
No poet, no artist of any sort, has his complete meaning alone. His significance, his appreciation is the appreciation of his relation to the dead poets and artists.

['Tradition and the Individual Talent' (1919)]

No artist produces great art by a deliberate attempt to express his own personality.

['Four Elizabethan Dramatists' (1924)]

EMERSON, Ralph Waldo (1803–1882)
Art is a jealous mistress, and, if a man
have a genius for painting, poetry,
music, architecture, or philosophy, he
makes a bad husband and an ill
provider.
[*Conduct of Life* (1860)]

Artists must be sacrificed to their art.
Like bees, they must put their lives
into the sting they give.
[*Letters and Social Aims* (1875)]

FLAUBERT, Gustave (1821–1880)
*L'artiste doit être dans son oeuvre
comme Dieu dans la création, invisible
et tout-puissant; qu'on le sente partout,
mais qu'on ne le voie pas.*
The artist must be in his work as God
is in creation, invisible and all-
powerful; his presence should be felt
everywhere, but he should never be
seen.
[Letter to Mlle Leroyer de Chantepie, 1857]

FORSTER, E.M. (1879–1970)
Works of art, in my opinion, are the
only objects in the material universe to
possess internal order, and that is why,
though I don't believe that only art
matters, I do believe in Art for Art's
sake.
[*Two Cheers for Democracy* (1951)]

FRIEL, Brian (1929–)
The hell of it seems to be, when an
artist starts saving the world, he starts
losing himself.
[*Extracts from a Sporadic Diary*]

FRY, Roger (1866–1934)
Art is significant deformity.
[In Virginia Woolf, *Roger Fry* (1940)]

GOETHE (1749–1832)
*Das Klassische nenne ich das Gesunde,
and das Romantische das Kranke.*
Classicism I call health, and roman-
ticism disease.
[*Gespräche mit Eckermann*, 1829]

**HEPWORTH, Dame Barbara
(1903–1975)**
I rarely draw what I see. I draw what I
feel in my body.
[Attr.]

HERBERT, Sir A.P. (1890–1971)
As my poor father used to say
In 1863,
Once people start on all this Art
Good-bye, moralitee!
And what my father used to say
Is good enough for me.
['Lines for a Worthy Person' (1930)]

HIRST, Damien (1965–)
[On winning the Turner Prize]
It's amazing what you can do with an
E in A-level art, twisted imagination
and a chainsaw.
[*The Observer Review*, 1995]

I sometimes feel that I have nothing to
say and I want to communicate this.
[Attr.]

HUXLEY, Aldous (1894–1963)
In the upper and the lower churches of
St Francis, Giotto and Cimabue
showed that art had once worshipped
something other than itself.
[*Those Barren Leaves* (1925)]

INGRES, J.A.D. (1780–1867)
Le dessin est la probité de l'art.
Drawing is the true test of art.
[*Pensées d'Ingres* (1922)]

JOYCE, James (1882–1941)
The artist, like the God of creation,
remains within or behind or beyond or
above his handiwork, invisible, refined
out of existence, indifferent, paring his
fingernails.
[*A Portrait of the Artist as a Young Man* (1916)]

KEATS, John (1795–1821)
The excellence of every art is its
intensity, capable of making all dis-
agreeables evaporate, from their being
in close relationship with Beauty and
Truth.
[Letter to George and Tom Keats,
21 December 1817]

KLEE, Paul (1879–1940)
*Kunst gibt nicht das Sichtbare wieder,
sondern macht sichtbar.*

Art does not reproduce what is visible; it makes things visible.

['Creative Credo' (1920)]

KRAUS, Karl (1874–1936)
Künstler ist nur einer, der aus der Lösung ein Rätsel machen kann.
The only person who is an artist is the one that can make a puzzle out of the solution.

[*By Night* (1919)]

LANDSEER, Sir Edwin Henry (1802–1873)
If people only knew as much about painting as I do, they would never buy my pictures.

[In Campbell Lennie, *Landseer the Victorian Paragon*]

LOW, Sir David (1891–1963)
I do not know whether he draws a line himself. But I assume that his is the direction ... It makes Disney the most significant figure in graphic art since Leonardo.

[In R. Schickel, *Walt Disney*]

MARON, Monika (1941–)
Der Künstler als Bürger kann Demokrat sein, so gut und so schlecht wie alle anderen. Der Künstler als Künstler darf kein Demokrat sein.
The artist as a citizen can be a democrat, just as well and as badly as everybody else. The artist as an artist may not be a democrat.

[Interview in *Der Spiegel*, 1994]

MAYAKOVSKY, Vladimir (1893–1930)
Art is not a mirror to reflect the world, but a hammer with which to shape it.

[*The Guardian*, 1974]

MOORE, George (1852–1933)
Art must be parochial in the beginning to be cosmopolitan in the end.

[*Hail and Farewell: Ave* (1911)]

MOSES, Grandma (1860–1961)
[Of painting]
I don't advise any one to take it up as a business proposition, unless they really have talent, and are crippled so

as to deprive them of physical labor.

[Attr.]

MURDOCH, Iris (1919–)
All art deals with the absurd and aims at the simple. Good art speaks truth, indeed *is* truth, perhaps the only truth.

[*The Black Prince* (1989), 'Bradley Pearson's Foreword']

NOLAN, Sir Sidney Robert (1917–)
A successful artist would have no trouble being a successful member of the Mafia.

[*Good Weekend*, 1985]

PATER, Walter (1839–1894)
All art constantly aspires towards the condition of music.

[*Studies in the History of the Renaissance* (1873)]

PICASSO, Pablo (1881–1973)
[Remark made at an exhibition of children's drawings]
When I was their age, I could draw like Raphael, but it took me a lifetime to learn to draw like them.

[In Penrose, *Picasso: His Life and Work* (1958)]

RENOIR, Pierre-Auguste (1841–1919)
[On why he still painted although he had arthritis of his hands]
The pain passes, but the beauty remains.

[Attr.]

ROSS, Harold W. (1892–1951)
I've never been in there [the Louvre] ... but there are only three things to see, and I've seen colour reproductions of all of them.

[In Hemingway, *A Farewell to Arms* (1929)]

RÜCKRIEM, Ulrich (1938–)
People don't want art, they want football.

[*Scala*, 1992]

RUSKIN, John (1819–1900)
Fine art is that in which the hand, the head, and the heart of man go together.

[*The Two Paths* (1859)]

[Of one of Whistler's works]
I have seen, and heard, much of
Cockney impudence before now; but
never expected to hear a coxcomb ask
two hundred guineas for flinging a pot
of paint in the public's face.

[*Fors Clavigera*, Letter 79, 1877]

SAND, George (1804–1876)
*L'art n'est pas une étude de la réalité
positive; c'est une recherche de la vérité
idéale.*
Art is not a study of positive reality; it
is a search for ideal truth.

[*The Devil's Pond* (1846)]

SANTAYANA, George (1863–1952)
Nothing is really so poor and melancholy as art that is interested in itself
and not in its subject.

[*The Life of Reason* (1906)]

SARGENT, John Singer (1856–1925)
Every time I paint a portrait I lose a
friend.

[In Bentley and Esar, *Treasury of Humorous
Quotations* (1951)]

SHAHN, Ben (1898–1969)
[Outlining the difference between
professional and amateur painters]
An amateur is an artist who supports
himself with outside jobs which enable
him to paint. A professional is someone whose wife works to enable him
to paint.

[Attr.]

SHAW, George Bernard (1856–1950)
The true artist will let his wife starve,
his children go barefoot, his mother
drudge for his living at seventy, sooner
than work at anything but his art.

[*Man and Superman* (1903)]

SONTAG, Susan (1933–)
A photograph is not only an image (as
a painting is an image), an interpretation of the real; it is also a trace,
something directly stencilled off the
real, like a footprint or a death mask.

[*New York Review of Books*, 1977]

SPALDING, Julian (1948–)
The professional art world is becoming
a conspiracy against the public.

[*The Daily Mail*, 1996]

STOPPARD, Tom (1937–)
Skill without imagination is crafts-
manship and gives us many useful
objects such as wickerwork picnic
baskets. Imagination without skill
gives us modern art.

[*Artist Descending a Staircase* (1973)]

What is an artist? For every thousand
people there's nine hundred doing the
work, ninety doing well, nine doing
good, and one lucky bastard who's the
artist.

[*Travesties* (1975)]

TERTZ, Abram (1925–)
Fairy-tales interest me as a mani-
festation of pure art, perhaps the very
first instance of art detaching itself
from real life, and also because – like
pure art – they enhance reality,
remaking it in their own likeness,
separating good from evil, and
bringing all fears and terrors to a
happy conclusion.

[*A Voice From the Chorus* (1973)]

TOLSTOY, Leo (1828–1910)
Art is a human activity which has as
its purpose the transmission to others
of the highest and best feelings to
which men have risen.

[*What is Art?* (1898)]

USTINOV, Sir Peter (1921–)
If Botticelli were alive today he'd be
working for *Vogue*.

[*The Observer*, 1962]

VIDAL, Gore (1925–)
He will lie even when it is inconvenient, the sign of the true artist.

[*Two Sisters* (1970)]

WHARTON, Edith (1862–1937)
Another unsettling element in modern
art is that common symptom of immaturity, the dread of doing what has

been done before.

[*The Writing of Fiction* (1925)]

WHISTLER, James McNeill (1834–1903)
[To a lady who said the two greatest painters were himself and Velasquez]
'Why,' answered Whistler in dulcet tones, 'why drag in Velasquez?'

[In Seitz, *Whistler Stories* (1913)]

[Replying to the question 'For two days' labour, you ask two hundred guineas?']
No, I ask it for the knowledge of a lifetime.

[In Seitz, *Whistler Stories* (1913)]

WHITEHEAD, A.N. (1861–1947)
Art is the imposing of a pattern on experience, and our aesthetic enjoyment is recognition of the pattern.

[*Dialogues* (1954)]

WILDE, Oscar (1854–1900)
All art is quite useless.

[*The Picture of Dorian Gray* (1891)]

WYLLIE, George (1921–)
[On modern art]
Art is like soup. There will be some vegetables you don't like but as long as you get some soup down you it doesn't matter.

[*The Daily Mail*, 1996]

Public art is art that the public can't avoid.

[Attr.]

ATHEISM

BACON, Francis (1561–1626)
I had rather believe all the fables in the legend, and the Talmud, and the Alcoran, than that this universal frame is without a mind.

['Of Atheism' (1625)]

God never wrought miracle to convince atheism, because his ordinary works convince it.

['Of Atheism' (1625)]

It is true, that a little philosophy inclineth man's mind to atheism; but depth in philosophy bringeth men's minds about to religion.

['Of Atheism' (1625)]

BUCHAN, John (1875–1940)
An atheist is a man who has no invisible means of support.

[Attr.]

BUÑUEL, Luis (1900–1983)
I am still an atheist, thank God.

[Attr.]

BURKE, Edmund (1729–1797)
Man is by his constitution a religious animal; ... atheism is against, not only our reason, but our instincts.

[*Reflections on the Revolution in France ...*
(1790)]

DIDEROT, Denis (1713–1784)
Voyez-vous cet oeuf. C'est avec cela qu'on renverse toutes les écoles de théologie, et tous les temples de la terre.
See this egg. It is with this that one overturns all the schools of theology and all the temples on earth.

[*Le Rêve de d'Alembert* (1769)]

ORWELL, George (1903–1950)
He was an embittered atheist (the sort of atheist who does not so much disbelieve in God as personally dislike Him).

[*Down and Out in Paris and London* (1933)]

OTWAY, Thomas (1652–1685)
These are rogues that pretend to be of a religion now!
Well, all I say is, honest atheism for my money.

[*The Atheist* (1683)]

ROSSETTI, Dante Gabriel (1828–1882)
The worst moment for the atheist is when he is really thankful and has nobody to thank.

[Attr.]

RUSSELL, Bertrand (1872–1970)
I was told that the Chinese say they would bury me by the Western Lake and build a shrine to my memory. I have some slight regret that this did not happen, as I might have become a god, which would have been very chic for an atheist.
[*The Autobiography of Bertrand Russell* (1969)]

SARTRE, Jean-Paul (1905–1980)
Elle ne croyait à rien; seul, son scepticisme l'empêchait d'être athée.

She didn't believe in anything; only her scepticism kept her from being an atheist.
[*Words* (1964)]

TURGENEV, Ivan (1818–1883)
The courage to believe in nothing.
[*Fathers and Sons* (1862)]

YOUNG, Edward (1683–1765)
By Night an Atheist half believes a God.
[*Night-Thoughts on Life, Death and Immortality*]

BACON, Francis (1561–1626)
There is no excellent beauty, that hath not some strangeness in the proportion.
['Of Beauty' (1625)]

BLAKE, William (1757–1827)
Exuberance is Beauty.
['Proverbs of Hell' (1793)]

BUCK, Pearl S. (1892–1973)
It is better to be first with an ugly woman than the hundredth with a beauty.
[*The Good Earth* (1931)]

BURKE, Edmund (1729–1797)
Beauty in distress is much the most affecting beauty.
[*A Philosophical Enquiry into the Origin of our Ideas of the Sublime and Beautiful* (1757)]

BYRON, Lord (1788–1824)
She walks in beauty, like the night
Of cloudless climes and starry skies;
And all that's best of dark and bright
Meet in her aspect and her eyes.
['She Walks in Beauty' (1815)]

CONFUCIUS (c. 550–c. 478 BC)
Everything has its beauty but not everyone sees it.
[*Analects*]

CONSTABLE, John (1776–1837)
There is nothing ugly; *I never saw an ugly thing in my life*: for let the form of an object be what it may, – light, shade, and perspective will always make it beautiful.
[In C.R. Leslie, *Memoirs of the Life of John Constable* (1843)]

DRYDEN, John (1631–1700)
When beauty fires the blood, how love exalts the mind.
[*Cymon and Iphigenia* (1700)]

ELLIS, Havelock (1859–1939)
Beauty is the child of love.
[*The New Spirit* (1890)]

The absence of flaw in beauty is itself a flaw.
[*Impressions and Comments* (1914)]

EMERSON, Ralph Waldo (1803–1882)
Though we travel the world over to find the beautiful we must carry it with us or we find it not.
[*Essays, First Series* (1841)]

GALSWORTHY, John (1867–1933)
He [Jolyon] was afflicted by the thought that where Beauty was, nothing ever ran quite straight, which, no doubt, was why so many people looked on it as immoral.
[*In Chancery* (1920)]

HUGO, Victor (1802–1885)
Le beau est aussi utile que l'utile. Plus peut-être.
Beauty is as useful as usefulness. Maybe more so.
[*Les Misérables* (1862)]

HUME, David (1711–1776)
Beauty is no quality in things themselves: It exists merely in the mind which contemplates them; and each mind perceives a different beauty.
[*Essays, Moral, Political, and Literary* (1742)]

KEATS, John (1795–1821)
A thing of beauty is a joy for ever:
Its loveliness increases; it will never
Pass into nothingness; but still will keep
A bower quiet for us, and a sleep
Full of sweet dreams, and health, and quiet breathing.
['Endymion' (1818)]

I never can feel certain of any truth but from a clear perception of its Beauty.
[Letter to George and Georgiana Keats, 16 December 1818–4 January 1819]

MOLIERE (1622–1673)
*La beauté du visage est un frêle ornement,
Une fleur passagère, un éclat d'un moment,*

*Et qui n'est attaché qu'à la simple
épiderme.*
The beauty of a face is a frail
ornament, a passing flower, a
moment's brightness belonging only
to the skin.

[*Les Femmes savantes* (1672)]

PHILIPS, Ambrose (c. 1675–1749)
The flowers anew, returning seasons
   bring!
But beauty faded has no second
   spring.

[*The First Pastoral* (1710)]

PICASSO, Pablo (1881–1973)
I hate that aesthetic game of the eye
and the mind, played by these con-
noisseurs, these mandarins who
'appreciate' beauty. What *is* beauty,
anyway? There's no such thing. I
never 'appreciate', any more than I
'like'. I love or I hate.

[In Gilot and Lake, *Life with Picasso* (1964)]

RUSKIN, John (1819–1900)
Remember that the most beautiful
things in the world are the most
useless; peacocks and lilies for
instance.

[*The Stones of Venice* (1851)]

SAKI (1870–1916)
I always say beauty is only sin deep.

['Reginald's Choir Treat' (1904)]

SAPPHO (fl. 7th–6th centuries BC)
Beauty endures for only as long as it
can be seen; goodness, beautiful
today, will remain so tomorrow.

[In Naim Attallah, *Women* (1987)]

STEVENS, Wallace (1879–1955)
Beauty is momentary in the mind –
The fitful tracing of a portal;
But in the flesh it is immortal.
The body dies; the body's beauty lives.
So evenings die, in their green going,
Aware, interminably flowing.

['Peter Quince at the Clavier' (1923)]

TOLSTOY, Leo (1828–1910)
It is amazing how complete is the

delusion that beauty is goodness.

[*The Kreutzer Sonata* (1890)]

**WOLLSTONECRAFT, Mary
(1759–1797)**
Taught from their infancy that beauty
is woman's sceptre, the mind shapes
itself to the body, and roaming round
its gilt cage, only seeks to adorn its
prison.

[*A Vindication of the Rights of Woman* (1792)]

See ART

BELIEF

AMIEL, Henri-Frédéric (1821–1881)
A belief is not true because it is
useful.

[*Journal*, 1876]

ARNOLD, Matthew (1822–1888)
The Sea of Faith
Was once, too, at the full, and round
   earth's shore
Lay like the folds of a bright girdle
   furl'd.
But now I only hear
Its melancholy, long, withdrawing
   roar,
Retreating, to the breath
Of the night–wind, down the vast
   edges drear
And naked shingles of the world.

['Dover Beach' (1867)]

BAGEHOT, Walter (1826–1877)
So long as there are earnest believers
in the world, they will always wish to
punish opinions, even if their judgement tells them it is unwise, and their
conscience that it is wrong.

[*Literary Studies* (1879)]

THE BIBLE (King James Version)
Lord, I believe; help thou mine
unbelief.

[*Mark*, 9:24]

Blessed are they that have not seen,
and yet have believed.

[*John*, 20:29]

Faith is the substance of things hoped for, the evidence of things not seen.

[*Hebrews*, 11:1]

Faith without works is dead.

[*James*, 2:20]

BROWNE, Sir Thomas (1605–1682)
To believe only possibilities, is not faith, but mere Philosophy.

[*Religio Medici* (1643)]

BUCK, Pearl S. (1892–1973)
I feel no need for any other faith than my faith in human beings.

[*I Believe* (1939)]

CAESAR, Gaius Julius (c. 102–44 BC)
Fere libenter homines id quod volunt credunt.
Men generally believe what they wish.

[*De Bello Gallico*]

CARROLL, Lewis (1832–1898)
'There's no use trying,' she said: 'one *can't* believe impossible things.'
'I dare say you haven't had much practice,' said the Queen. 'When I was your age, I always did it for half an hour a day. Why, sometimes I've believed as many as six impossible things before breakfast.'

[*Through the Looking-Glass* (1872)]

CHESTERTON, G.K. (1874–1936)
Reason is itself a matter of faith. It is an act of faith to assert that our thoughts have any relation to reality at all.

[*Orthodoxy* (1908)]

FRANK, Anne (1929–1945)
In spite of everything I still believe that people are good at heart.

[*The Diary of Anne Frank* (1947)]

GREENE, Graham (1904– 1991)
My belief certainly seems to get stronger in the presence of people whose goodness seems of almost supernatural origin.

[Attr.]

HASKINS, Minnie Louise (1875–1957)
[Quoted by King George VI in his Christmas broadcast, 1939]
And I said to a man who stood at the gate of the year: 'Give me a light that I may tread safely into the unknown.'
And he replied: 'Go out into the darkness and put your hand into the hand of God. That shall be to you better than a light, and safer than a known way.'

[*The Desert* (1908)]

JENKINS, David (1925–)
As I get older I seem to believe less and less and yet to believe what I do believe more and more.

[*The Observer*, 1988]

JOWETT, Benjamin (1817–1893)
My dear child, you must believe in God in spite of what the clergy tell you.

[In M. Asquith, *Autobiography* (1922)]

KANT, Immanuel (1724–1804)
There is only one (true) religion; but there can be many different kinds of belief.

[*Religion within the Boundaries of Mere Reason* (1793)]

MENCKEN, H.L. (1880–1956)
Faith may be defined briefly as an illogical belief in the occurrence of the improbable.

[*Prejudices* (1927)]

NEWMAN, John Henry, Cardinal (1801–1890)
It is as absurd to argue men, as to torture them, into believing.

[Sermon, 1831]

We can believe what we choose. We are answerable for what we choose to believe.

[Letter to Mrs Froude, 1848]

RUSSELL, Bertrand (1872–1970)
Every man, wherever he goes, is encompassed by a cloud of comforting convictions, which move with him like

flies on a summer day.

[*Sceptical Essays* (1928)]

[On being asked if he would be willing to die for his beliefs]
Of course not. After all, I may be wrong.

[Attr.]

UNAMUNO, Miguel de (1864–1936)
Creer en Dios es anhelar que le haya y es además conducirse como si le hubiera.
To believe in God is to yearn for his existence and, moreover, it is to behave as if he did exist.

[*The Tragic Sense of Life* (1913)]

BENEFACTORS

BAGEHOT, Walter (1826–1877)
The most melancholy of human reflections, perhaps, is that, on the whole, it is a question whether the benevolence of mankind does most good or harm.

[*Physics and Politics* (1872)]

CHAMFORT, Nicolas (1741–1794)
Our gratitude to most benefactors is the same as our feeling for dentists who have pulled our teeth. We acknowledge the good they have done and the evil from which they have delivered us, but we remember the pain they occasioned and do not love them very much.

[*Maximes et pensées* (1796)]

COMPTON-BURNETT, Dame Ivy (1884–1969)
At any time you might act for my good. When people do that, it kills something precious between them.

[*Manservant and Maidservant* (1947)]

CREIGHTON, Mandell (1843–1901)
No people do so much harm as those who go about doing good.

[*The Life and Letters of Mandell Creighton* (1904)]

GILBERT, W.S. (1836–1911)
I love my fellow creatures – I do all the
good I can –
Yet everybody says I'm such a
disagreeable man!

[*Princess Ida* (1884)]

GOLDSMITH, Oliver (c. 1728–1774)
And learn the luxury of doing good.

['The Traveller' (1764)]

JOHNSON, Samuel (1709–1784)
Is not a Patron, my Lord, one who looks with unconcern on a man struggling for life in the water, and, when he has reached ground, encumbers him with help?
The notice which you have been pleased to take of my labours, had it been early, had been kind; but it has been delayed till I am indifferent, and cannot enjoy it; till I am solitary, and cannot impart it; till I am known, and do not want it.

[Letter to Lord Chesterfield, 1755]

MACHIAVELLI (1469–1527)
It is the nature of men to be bound by the benefits they confer as much as by those they receive.

[*The Prince* (1532)]

TITUS VESPASIANUS (39–81)
Recordatus quondam super cenam, quod nihil cuiquam toto die praestitisset, memorabilem illam meritoque laudatam vocem edidit: 'Amici, diem perdidi.'
Recalling once after dinner that he had done nothing to help anyone all that day, he gave voice to that memorable and praiseworthy remark: 'Friends, I have lost a day.'

[In Suetonius, *Lives of the Caesars*]

WORDSWORTH, William (1770–1850)
On that best portion of a good man's
life;
His little, nameless, unremembered
acts
Of kindness and of love.

['Lines composed a few miles above Tintern Abbey' (1798)]

See GOODNESS

BIOGRAPHY

AMIS, Martin (1949–)
[Of biography]
To be more interested in the writer
than the writing is just eternal human
vulgarity.

[*The Observer Review*, 1996]

ARBUTHNOT, John (1667–1735)
[Of biography]
One of the new terrors of death.

[In Carruthers, *Life of Pope* (1857)]

**BENTLEY, Edmund Clerihew
(1875–1956)**
The art of Biography
Is different from Geography.
Geography is about Maps,
But Biography is about chaps.

[*Biography for Beginners* (1905)]

CARLYLE, Thomas (1795–1881)
A well-written Life is almost as rare as
a well-spent one.

[*Critical and Miscellaneous Essays* (1839)]

DAVIES, Robertson (1913–)
Biography at its best is a form of
fiction.

[*The Lyre of Orpheus* (1988)]

DISRAELI, Benjamin (1804–1881)
Read no history: nothing but
biography, for that is life without
theory. ·

[*Contarini Fleming* (1832)]

FRYE, Northrop (1912–1991)
There's only one story, the story of
your life.

[In Ayre, *Northrop Frye: A Biography* (1989)]

GRANT, Cary (1904–1986)
Nobody is ever truthful about his own
life. There are always ambiguities.

[*The Observer*, 1981]

GUEDALLA, Philip (1889–1944)
Biography, like big-game hunting, is
one of the recognized forms of sport,
and it is as unfair as only sport can be.

[*Supers and Supermen* (1920)]

LEE, Robert E. (1807–1870)
[Refusing to write his memoirs]
I should be trading on the blood of my
men.

[In M. Ringo, *Nobody Said It Better*]

MACAULAY, Lord (1800–1859)
Biographers, translators, editors, all, in
short, who employ themselves in
illustrating the lives or writings of
others, are peculiarly exposed to the
Lues Boswelliana, or disease of admiration.

[*Collected Essays* (1843)]

SALINGER, J.D. (1919–)
If you really want to hear about it, the
first thing you'll probably want to
know is where I was born and what
my lousy childhood was like, and how
my parents were occupied and all
before they had me, and all that David
Copperfield kind of crap.

[*The Catcher in the Rye* (1951)]

TROLLOPE, Anthony (1815–1882)
In these days a man is nobody unless
his biography is kept so far posted up
that it may be ready for the national
breakfast-table on the morning after
his demise.

[*Doctor Thorne* (1858)]

WALPOLE, Horace (1717–1797)
The life of any man written under the
direction of his family, did nobody
honour.

[Letter, 1778]

WILDE, Oscar (1854–1900)
Every great man has his disciples, but
it is always Judas who writes the
biography.

[Attr.]

BIRDS

CLARE, John (1793–1864)
The crow will tumble up and down
At the first sight of spring
And in old trees around the town
Brush winter from its wing

['Crows in Spring']

GIBBONS, Orlando (1583–1625)
The silver swan, who, living had no note,
When death approached unlocked her silent throat.

['The Silver Swan' (1612)]

LYLY, John (c. 1554–1606)
[The lark]
How at heaven's gates she claps her wings,
The morn not waking till she sings.

[*Campaspe* (1584)]

MANSFIELD, Katherine (1888–1923)
The ostrich burying its head in the sand does at any rate wish to convey the impression that its head is the most important part of it.

[*Journal of Katherine Mansfield* (1954)]

MEREDITH, George (1828–1909)
Lovely are the curves of the white owl sweeping
Wavy in the dusk lit by one large star.
Lone in the fir-branch, his rattle-note unvaried,
Brooding o'er the gloom, spins the brown eve-jar.

[*Nashville Banner*, 1913]

SHELLEY, Percy Bysshe (1792–1822)
Hail to thee, blithe Spirit!
Bird thou never wert,
That from Heaven, or near it,
Pourest thy full heart
In profuse strains of unpremeditated art.

['To a Skylark' (1820)]

THOREAU, Henry (1817–1862)
I once had a sparrow alight upon my shoulder for a moment while I was hoeing in a village garden, and I felt that I was more distinguished by that circumstance than I should have been by any epaulet I could have worn.

[*Walden* (1854)]

WEBSTER, John (c. 1580–c. 1625)
We think caged birds sing, when indeed they cry.

[*The White Devil* (1612)]

WORDSWORTH, William (1770–1850)
O blithe new-comer! I have heard,
I hear thee and rejoice.
O Cuckoo! Shall I call thee bird,
Or but a wandering voice?

['To the Cuckoo' (1807)]

BOOKS

ADDISON, Joseph (1672–1719)
A reader seldom peruses a book with pleasure until he knows whether the writer of it be a black man or a fair man, of a mild or choleric disposition, married or a bachelor.

[*The Spectator*, 1711]

AUDEN, W.H. (1907–1973)
Some books are undeservedly forgotten; none are undeservedly remembered.

[*The Dyer's Hand* (1963)]

BACON, Francis (1561–1626)
Books will speak plain when counsellors blanch.

['Of Counsel' (1625)]

Some books are to be tasted, others to be swallowed, and some few to be chewed and digested; that is, some books are to be read only in parts; others to be read but not curiously; and some few to be read wholly, and with diligence and attention.

['Of Studies' (1625)]

BELLOC, Hilaire (1870–1953)
When I am dead, I hope it may be said:
'His sins were scarlet, but his books were read.'

[*Sonnets and Verse* (1923)]

BURGESS, Anthony (1917–1993)
The possession of a book becomes a substitute for reading it.

[*The New York Times Book Review*]

BYRON, Lord (1788–1824)
'Tis pleasant, sure, to see one's name in print;
A Book's a Book, altho' there is nothing in't.

[*English Bards and Scotch Reviewers* (1809)]

CHANDLER, Raymond (1888–1959)
If my books had been any worse I should not have been invited to Hollywood, and ... if they had been any better, I should not have come.

[Letter to C.W. Morton, 1945]

COWPER, William (1731–1800)
Books are not seldom talismans and spells.

[*The Task* (1785)]

CRABBE, George (1754–1832)
This, books can do – nor this alone:
they give
New views to life, and teach us how to
live;
They soothe the grieved, the stubborn
they chastise;
Fools they admonish, and confirm the
wise,
Their aid they yield to all: they never
shun
The man of sorrow, nor the wretch
undone;
Unlike the hard, the selfish, and the
proud,
They fly not from the suppliant crowd;
Nor tell to various people various
things,
But show to subjects, what they show
to kings.

[*The Library* (1808)]

DAVIES, Robertson (1913–)
A truly great book should be read in youth, again in maturity, and once more in old age, as a fine building should be seen by morning light, at noon, and by moonlight.

[In Grant, *The Enthusiasms of Robertson Davies*]

DESCARTES, René (1596–1650)
La lecture de tous les bons livres est comme une conversation avec les plus honnêtes gens des siècles passés.
The reading of all good books is like a conversation with the finest men of past centuries.

[*Discours de la Méthode* (1637)]

DIODORUS SICULUS
(c. 1st century BC)
[Inscription over library door in Alexandria]
Medicine for the soul.

[*History*]

FORSTER, E.M. (1879–1970)
I suggest that the only books that influence us are those for which we are ready, and which have gone a little farther down our particular path than we have yet got ourselves.

[*Two Cheers for Democracy* (1951)]

FRYE, Northrop (1912–1991)
The book is the world's most patient medium.

[*The Scholar in Society*, film, 1984]

FULLER, Thomas (1608–1661)
Learning hath gained most by those books by which the printers have lost.

[*The Holy State and the Profane State* (1642)]

GOLDSMITH, Oliver (c. 1728–1774)
A book may be amusing with numerous errors, or it may be very dull without a single absurdity.

[*The Vicar of Wakefield* (1766)]

I...shewed her that books were sweet unreproaching companions to the miserable, and that if they could not bring us to enjoy life, they would at least teach us to endure it.

[*The Vicar of Wakefield* (1766)]

HORACE (65–8 BC)
Delere licebit
Quod non edideris; nescit vox missa reverti.
You can destroy what you haven't published; the word once out cannot be recalled.

[*Ars Poetica*]

HUXLEY, Aldous (1894–1963)
The proper study of mankind is books.

[*Crome Yellow* (1921)]

JAMES, Brian (1892–1972)
The book of my enemy has been remaindered
And I am pleased.
['The Book of My Enemy Has Been Remaindered']

KAFKA, Franz (1883–1924)
Ich glaube, man sollte überhaupt nur solche Bücher lesen, die einen beissen und stechen.
I think you should only read those books which bite and sting you.
[Letter to Oskar Pollak, 1904]

... ein Buch muss die Axt sein für das gefrorene Meer in uns.
... a book must be the axe for the frozen sea within us.
[Letter to Oskar Pollak, 1904]

KORAN
Every age hath its book.
[Chapter 13]

LA BRUYERE, Jean de (1645–1696)
C'est un métier que de faire un livre, comme de faire une pendule: il faut plus que de l'esprit pour être auteur.
The making of a book, like the making of a clock, is a craft; it takes more than wit to be an author.
[*Les caractères ou les moeurs de ce siècle* (1688)]

LAMB, Charles (1775–1834)
I mean your *borrowers of books* – those mutilators of collections, spoilers of the symmetry of shelves, and creators of odd volumes.
[*Essays of Elia* (1823)]

I love to lose myself in other men's minds. When I am not walking, I am reading; I cannot sit and think. Books think for me.
[*Last Essays of Elia* (1833)]

LARKIN, Philip (1922–1985)
Get stewed:
Books are a load of crap.
['A Study of Reading Habits' (1964)]

LICHTENBERG, Georg (1742–1799)
There can hardly be a stranger commodity in the world than books. Printed by people who don't understand them; sold by people who don't understand them; bound, criticized and read by people who don't understand them, and now even written by people who don't understand them.
[*A Doctrine of Scattered Occasions*]

MACAULAY, Dame Rose (1881–1958)
It was a book to kill time for those who like it better dead.
[Attr.]

MAUGHAM, William Somerset (1874–1965)
There is an impression abroad that everyone had it in him to write one book; but if by this is implied a good book the impression is false.
[*The Summing Up* (1938)]

MILTON, John (1608–1674)
As good almost kill a Man as kill a good Book; who kills a Man kills a reasonable creature, God's Image; but hee who destroyes a good Booke, kills reason it selfe, kills the Image of God, as it were in the eye. Many a man lives a burden to the Earth; but a good Booke is the pretious life-blood of a master spirit, imbalm'd and treasur'd up on purpose to a life beyond life.
[*Areopagitica* (1644)]

REED, Henry (1914–1986)
I have known her pass the whole evening without mentioning a single book, or *in fact anything unpleasant*, at all.
[*A Very Great Man Indeed* (1953)]

SAMUEL, Lord (1870–1963)
A library is thought in cold storage.
[*A Book of Quotations* (1947)]

SMITH, Logan Pearsall (1865–1946)
A best-seller is the gilded tomb of a mediocre talent.
[*Afterthoughts* (1931)]

SMITH, Sydney (1771–1845)
No furniture so charming as books,
even if you never open them, or read a
single word.

[In Holland, *A Memoir of the Reverend Sydney Smith* (1855)]

**STEVENSON, Robert Louis
(1850–1894)**
Books are good enough in their own
way, but they are a mighty bloodless
substitute for life.

[*Virginibus Puerisque* (1881)]

TUPPER, Martin (1810–1889)
A good book is the best of friends, the
same today and for ever.

[*Proverbial Philosophy* (1838)]

VALERY, Paul (1871–1945)
*Les livres ont les mêmes ennemis que
l'homme: le feu, l'humide, les bêtes, le
temps; et leur propre contenu.*
Books have the same enemies as man:
fire, damp, animals, time; and their
own contents.

[*Littérature*]

WAUGH, Evelyn (1903–1966)
Particularly against books the Home
Secretary is. If we can't stamp out
literature in the country, we can at
least stop it being brought in from
outside.

[*Vile Bodies* (1930)]

WESLEY, John (1703–1791)
Beware you be not swallowed up in
books! An ounce of love is worth a
pound of knowledge.

[In Southey, *Life of Wesley* (1820)]

WILDE, Oscar (1854–1900)
There is no such thing as a moral or
an immoral book. Books are well
written, or badly written. That is all.

[*The Picture of Dorian Gray* (1891)]

WODEHOUSE, P.G. (1881–1975)
[Dedication]
To my daughter Leonora without
whose never-failing sympathy and
encouragement this book would have
been finished in half the time.

[*The Heart of a Goof* (1926)]

See CENSORSHIP; FICTION; LITERATURE; READING; WRITERS; WRITING

BOREDOM

AUSTIN, Warren Robinson (1877–1962)
[On being asked if he found long
debates at the UN tiring]
It is better for aged diplomats to be
bored than for young men to die.

[Attr.]

BIERCE, Ambrose (1842–c. 1914)
Bore: A person who talks when you
wish him to listen.

[*The Cynic's Word Book* (1906)]

BRIDIE, James (1888–1951)
Boredom is a sign of satisfied ignorance, blunted apprehension, crass
sympathies, dull understanding, feeble
powers of attention and irreclaimable
weakness of character.

[*Mr Bolfry* (1943)]

BYRON, Lord (1788–1824)
Society is now one polish'd horde,
Form'd of two mighty tribes, the *Bores*
and *Bored*.

[*Don Juan* (1824)]

CARTER, Angela (1940–1992)
[Rationalization of the Japanese
veneration of boredom]
He loved to be bored; don't think he
was contemptuously dismissive of the
element of boredom inherent in sexual
activity. He adored and venerated
boredom. He said that dogs, for
example, were never bored, nor birds,
so, obviously, the capacity that
distinguished man from the other
higher mammals, from the scaled and
feathered things, was that of boredom.
The more bored one was, the more
one expressed one's humanity.

['The Quilt Maker']

CHESTERTON, G.K. (1874–1936)
There is no such thing on earth as an uninteresting subject; the only thing that can exist is an uninterested person.
[*Heretics* (1905)]

DE VRIES, Peter (1910–)
I wanted to be bored to death, as good a way to go as any.
[*Comfort me with Apples* (1956)]

EMERSON, Ralph Waldo (1803–1882)
Every hero becomes a bore at last.
[*Representative Men* (1850)]

FREUD, Clement (1924–)
If you resolve to give up smoking, drinking and loving, you don't actually live longer; it just seems longer.
[*The Observer*, 1964]

GAUTIER, Théophile (1811–1872)
Plutôt la barbarie que l'ennui.
Sooner barbarity than boredom.
[Attr.]

HOWELLS, W.D. (1837–1920)
Some people can stay longer in an hour than others can in a week.
[In Esar, *Treasury of Humorous Quotations* (1951)]

HUXLEY, Aldous (1894–1963)
I can sympathize with people's pains, but not with their pleasures. There is something curiously boring about somebody else's happiness.
[*Limbo* (1920)]

INGE, William Ralph (1860–1954)
The effect of boredom on a large scale in history is underestimated. It is a main cause of revolutions, and would soon bring to an end all the static Utopias and the farmyard civilization of the Fabians.
[*End of an Age* (1948)]

SAKI (1870–1916)
'I believe I take precedence,' he said coldly; 'you are merely the club Bore; I am the club Liar.'
[*Beasts and Super-Beasts* (1914)]

SHAKESPEARE, William (1564–1616)
Life is as tedious as a twice-told tale
Vexing the dull ear of a drowsy man.
[*King John*, III.iv]

TAYLOR, Bert Leston (1866–1921)
A bore is a man who, when you ask him how he is, tells you.
[*The So-Called Human Race* (1922)]

THOMAS, Dylan (1914–1953)
Dylan talked copiously, then stopped. 'Somebody's boring me,' he said, 'I think it's me.'
[In Heppenstall, *Four Absentees* (1960)]

TREE, Sir Herbert Beerbohm (1853–1917)
[Of Israel Zangwill]
He is an old bore; even the grave yawns for him.
[In Pearson, *Beerbohm Tree* (1956)]

UPDIKE, John (1932–)
A healthy male adult bore consumes one and a half times his own weight in other people's patience.
[*Assorted Prose* (1965)]

VOLTAIRE (1694–1778)
The secret of being boring is to say everything.
[*Discours en vers sur l'homme* (1737)]

BRITAIN

ARTLEY, Alexandra
[On the reprocessing of foreign nuclear waste in Britain]
This is not 'polite and tidy Britain' ...
It's Widow Twankey's Nuclear Laundry.
[In *Britain in the Eighties* (1989)]

ATTLEE, Clement (1883–1967)
I think the British have the distinction above all other nations of being able to put new wine into old bottles without bursting them.
[*Hansard*, 1950]

BULLOCK, Alan, (1914–)
The people Hitler never understood, and whose actions continued to exasperate him to the end of his life, were the British.

[*Hitler, A Study in Tyranny* (1952)]

CAMP, William (1926–)
What annoys me about Britain is the rugged will to lose.

[Attr.]

CASSON, Sir Hugh (1910–)
The British love permanence more than they love beauty.

[*The Observer*, 1964]

EDMOND, James (1859–1933)
I had been told by Jimmy Edmond in Australia that there were only three things against living in Britain: the place, the climate and the people.

[In Low, *Low Autobiography*]

GAITSKELL, Hugh (1906–1963)
[On Britain's joining the European Community]
It does mean, if this is the idea, the end of Britain as an independent European state ... it means the end of a thousand years of history.

[Speech, 1962]

HAMILTON, William (Willie) (1917–)
Britain is not a country that is easily rocked by revolution ... In Britain our institutions evolve. We are a Fabian Society writ large.

[*My Queen and I* (1975)]

HARLECH, Lord (1918–1985)
In the end it may well be that Britain will be honoured by historians more for the way she disposed of an empire than for the way in which she acquired it.

[*New York Times*, 1962]

LLOYD GEORGE, David (1863–1945)
What is our task? To make Britain a fit country for heroes to live in.

[Speech, 1918]

SHAW, George Bernard (1856–1950)
He [the Briton] is a barbarian, and thinks that the custom of his tribe and island are the laws of nature.

[*Caesar and Cleopatra* (1901)]

THOMSON, James (1700–1748)
When Britain first, at heaven's
    command,
Arose from out the azure main,
This was the charter of the land,
And guardian angels sung this strain:
'Rule, Britannia, rule the waves;
Britons never will be slaves.'

[*Alfred: A Masque* (1740)]

WAUGH, Evelyn (1903–1966)
Other nations use 'force'; we Britons alone use 'Might'.

[*Scoop* (1938)]

See ARCHITECTURE

BUREAUCRACY

ACHESON, Dean (1893–1971)
A memorandum is written not to inform the reader but to protect the writer.

[Attr.]

ADENAUER, Konrad (1876–1967)
Es gibt nichts, was durch Beamte nicht wieder kaputtgemacht werden kann.
There's nothing which cannot be made a mess of again by officials.

[*Der Spiegel*, 1975]

ANONYMOUS
A committee is a cul-de-sac down which ideas are lured and then quietly strangled.

[*New Scientist*, 1973]

A camel is a horse designed by a committee.

FONDA, Jane (1937–)
You can run the office without a boss, but you can't run an office without the secretaries.

[*The Observer*, 1981]

FOOT, Michael (1913–)
A Royal Commission is a broody hen
sitting on a china egg.
[Speech, House of Commons, 1964]

GOWERS, Sir Ernest (1880–1966)
It is not easy nowadays to remember
anything so contrary to all appearances as that officials are the servants
of the public; and the official must try
not to foster the illusion that it is the
other way round.
[*Plain Words*]

HUXLEY, Aldous (1894–1963)
Official dignity tends to increase in
inverse ratio to the importance of the
country in which the office is held.
[*Beyond the Mexique Bay* (1934)]

KELLY, Bert (1912–)
Always remember that if a civil
servant had the ability to ... correctly
foresee the demand situation for any
product he would not be working for
the government for long. He would
shortly be sitting in the south of
France with his feet in a bucket of
champagne!
[*Economics Made Easy*]

MCCARTHY, Mary (1912– 1989)
Bureaucracy, the rule of no one, has
become the modern form of
despotism.
[*The New Yorker*, 1958]

MCLUHAN, Marshall (1911–1980)
An administrator in a bureaucratic
world is a man who can feel big by
merging his non-entity with an
abstraction. A real person in touch
with real things inspires terror in him.
[Letter to Ezra Pound, 1951]

SAMPSON, Anthony (1926–)
[Of the Civil Service]
Members rise from CMG (known
sometimes in Whitehall as 'Call Me God')
to the KCMG ('Kindly Call Me God')
to...the GCMG ('God Calls Me God').
[*The Anatomy of Britain* (1962)]

SAMUEL, Lord (1870–1963)
[Referring to the Civil Service]
A difficulty for every solution.
[Attr.]

SANTAYANA, George (1863–1952)
The working of great institutions is
mainly the result of a vast mass of
routine, petty malice, self interest,
carelessness, and sheer mistake.
Only a residual fraction is thought.
[*The Crime of Galileo*]

THOMAS, Gwyn (1913–1981)
My life's been a meeting, Dad, one
long meeting. Even on the few
committees I don't yet belong to, the
agenda winks at me when I pass.
[*The Keep* (1961)]

**TREE, Sir Herbert Beerbohm
(1853–1917)**
A committee should consist of three
men, two of whom are absent.
[In Pearson, *Beerbohm Tree*]

BUSINESS

ANONYMOUS
A Company for carrying on an undertaking of Great Advantage, but no one
to know what it is.
[The South Sea Company Prospectus]

Our company absorbs the cost.
[Useful Arab phrase in modern Arab-English
phrase book for American oil engineers]

AUSTEN, Jane (1775–1817)
Business, you know, may bring money,
but friendship hardly ever does.
[*Emma* (1816)]

BAGEHOT, Walter (1826–1877)
Business is really more agreeable than
pleasure; it interests the whole mind,
the aggregate nature of man more
continuously, and more deeply. But it
does not *look* as if it did.
[*The English Constitution* (1867)]

BALZAC, Honoré de (1799–1850)
*Les gens généreux font de mauvais
commerçants.*

Generous people make bad shop-keepers.

[*Illusions perdues* (1843)]

BARNUM, Phineas T. (1810–1891)
Every crowd has a silver lining.

[Attr.]

BETJEMAN, Sir John (1906–1984)
You ask me what it is I do. Well
  actually, you know,
I'm partly a liaison man and partly
  P.R.O.
Essentially I integrate the current
  export drive
And basically I'm viable from ten
  o'clock till five.

['Executive' (1974)]

CHARLES, Prince of Wales (1948–)
British management doesn't seem to
understand the importance of the
human factor.

[Speech, 1979]

COHEN, Sir Jack (1898–1979)
Pile it high, sell it cheap.

[Business motto]

DENNIS, C.J. (1876–1938)
It takes one hen to lay an egg,
But seven men to sell it.

['The Regimental Hen']

FRANKLIN, Benjamin (1706–1790)
No nation was ever ruined by trade.

[*Essays*]

GALBRAITH, J.K. (1908–)
The salary of the chief executive of the
large corporation is not a market
award for achievement. It is frequently
in the nature of a warm personal ges-
ture by the individual to himself.

[*Annals of an Abiding Liberal* (1980)]

GOLDWYN, Samuel (1882–1974)
Chaplin is no business man – all he
knows is that he can't take anything
less.

[Attr.]

KHRUSHCHEV, Nikita (1894–1971)
[Remark to British businessmen]
When you are skinning your cus-
tomers, you should leave some skin on
to heal so that you can skin them
again.

[*The Observer*, 1961]

LLOYD GEORGE, David (1863–1945)
Love your neighbour is not merely
sound Christianity; it is good business.

[*The Observer*, 1921]

MACMILLAN, Harold (1894–1986)
[Macmillan and Company Limited]
propose to carry on their business at
St Martin's Street, London W.C.2 until
they are either taxed, insured, ARP'd
or bombed out of existence.

[Announcement, 17 September 1939]

MENCKEN, H.L. (1880–1956)
[Referring to the businessman]
He is the only man who is ever
apologizing for his occupation.

[*Prejudices* (1927)]

NAPOLEON I (1769–1821)
*L'Angleterre est une nation de
boutiquiers.*
England is a nation of shopkeepers.

[In O'Meara, *Napoleon in Exile* (1822)]

ONASSIS, Aristotle (1906–1975)
The secret of business is to know
something that nobody else knows.

[*The Economist*, 1991]

PUZO, Mario (1920–)
He's a businessman. I'll make him an
offer he can't refuse.

[*The Godfather* (1969)]

REVSON, Charles (1906–1975)
In the factory we make cosmetics. In
the store we sell hope.

[In Tobias, *Fire and Ice* (1976)]

ROOSEVELT, Theodore (1858–1919)
We demand that big business give the
people a square deal; in return we
must insist that when any one
engaged in big business honestly

endeavors to do right he shall himself
be given a square deal.

[*Theodore Roosevelt: an Autobiography* (1913)]

SHEEN, J. Fulton (1895–1979)
[Referring to his contract for a
television appearance]
The big print giveth and the fine print
taketh away.

[Attr.]

SMITH, Adam (1723–1790)
People of the same trade seldom meet
together, even for merriment and
diversion, but the conversation ends in
a conspiracy against the public, or in
some contrivance to raise prices.

[*Wealth of Nations* (1776)]

THURLOW, Edward, (1731–1806)
Did you ever expect a corporation to
have a conscience, when it has no
soul to be damned, and no body to be
kicked?

[Attr.]

WILDER, Thornton (1897–1975)
A living is made, Mr Kemper, by
selling something that everybody
needs at least once a year. Yes, sir!
And a million is made by producing
something that everybody needs every
day. You artists produce something
that nobody needs at any time.

[*The Merchant of Yonkers* (1939)]

WILSON, Charles E. (1890–1961)
What is good for the country is good
for General Motors, and vice versa.

[Remark to Congressional Committee, 1953]

WILSON, Woodrow (1856–1924)
Business underlies everything in our
national life, including our spiritual
life. Witness the fact that in the Lord's
Prayer the first petition is for daily
bread. No one can worship God or
love his neighbour on an empty
stomach.

[Speech, 1912]

**See ECONOMICS; MONEY AND
WEALTH**

ANONYMOUS
Capitalism is the exploitation of man by man. Communism is the complete opposite.

[Described by Laurence J. Peter as a 'Polish proverb']

CONNOLLY, James (1868–1916)
Governments in a capitalist society are but committees of the rich to manage the affairs of the capitalist class.

[*Irish Worker*, 1914]

GONNE, Maud (1865–1953)
To me judges seem the well paid watch-dogs of Capitalism, making things safe and easy for the devil Mammon.

[Letter to W.B. Yeats]

HAMPTON, Christopher (1946–)
If I had to give a definition of capitalism I would say: the process whereby American girls turn into American women.

[*Savages* (1973)]

HEATH, Sir Edward (1916–)
[On the Lonrho affair (involving tax avoidance)]
The unpleasant and unacceptable face of capitalism.

[Speech, House of Commons, 1973]

ILLICH, Ivan (1926–)
In a consumer society there are inevitably two kinds of slaves: the prisoners of addiction and the prisoners of envy.

[*Tools for Conviviality* (1973)]

KELLER, Helen (1880–1968)
Militarism ... is one of the chief bulwarks of capitalism, and the day that militarism is undermined, capitalism will fail.

[*The Story of My Life* (1902)]

KEYNES, John Maynard (1883–1946)
I think that Capitalism, wisely managed, can probably be made more efficient for attaining economic ends than any alternative system yet in sight, but that in itself it is in many ways extremely objectionable.

['The End of Laissez-Faire' (1926)]

LENIN, V.I. (1870–1924)
Under capitalism we have a state in the proper sense of the word, that is, a special machine for the suppression of one class by another.

[*The State and Revolution* (1917)]

ORTEGA SPOTTORNO, José
I'm convinced that the present form of capitalism will make way for another one which will be more human and less speculative.

[*El País*, 1994]

SAKI (1870–1916)
When she inveighed eloquently against the evils of capitalism at drawing-room meetings and Fabian conferences she was conscious of a comfortable feeling that the system, with all its inequalities and iniquities, would probably last her time. It is one of the consolations of middle-aged reformers that the good they inculcate must live after them if it is to live at all.

[*Beasts and Super-Beasts* (1914)]

STRETTON, Hugh (1924–)
Is it really good for policy-makers to act as if everything has its price, and as if policies should be judged chiefly by their effects in delivering material benefits to selfish citizens? ... It does not ask those individuals whether they also have other values which are not revealed by their shopping.

[*Capitalism, Socialism and the Environment* (1976)]

WAUGH, Evelyn (1903–1966)
Pappenhacker says that every time you are polite to a proletarian you are helping to bolster up the capitalist system.

[*Scoop* (1938)]

CAREERS

BACON, Francis (1561–1626)
I hold every man a debtor to his profession.
[*The Elements of Common Law* (1596)]

BALFOUR, A.J. (1848–1930)
[On being asked whether he was going to marry Margot Tennant]
I rather think of having a career of my own.
[In Asquith, *Autobiography* (1920)]

BENTLEY, Nicolas (1907–1978)
His was the sort of career that made the Recording Angel think seriously about taking up shorthand.
[Attr.]

COLBY, Frank Moore (1865–1925)
I have found some of the best reasons I ever had for remaining at the bottom simply by looking at the men at the top.
[*Essays*]

DISRAELI, Benjamin (1804–1881)
To do nothing and get something, formed a boy's ideal of a manly career.
[*Sybil* (1845)]

EAMES, Emma (1865–1952)
[On giving up her operatic career at 47]
I would rather be a brilliant memory than a curiosity.
[Attr.]

FRANKLIN, Miles (1879–1954)
This was life – my life – my career, my brilliant career! I was fifteen – fifteen! A few fleeting hours and I would be old as those around me. I looked at them as they stood there, weary, and turning down the other side of the hill of life. When young, no doubt they had hoped for, and dreamed of, better things – had even known them. but here they were. This had been their life; this was their career. It was, and

in all probability would be, mine too. My life – my career – my brilliant career!
[*My Brilliant Career* (1901)]

See WORK

CATS

ARNOLD, Matthew (1822–1888)
Cruel, but composed and bland,
Dumb, inscrutable and grand,
So Tiberius might have sat,
Had Tiberius been a cat.
['Poor Matthias']

CHAUCER, Geoffrey (c. 1340–1400)
Lat take a cat, and fostre hym wel with milk
And tendre flessh, and make his couche of silk,
And lat hym seen a mous go by the wal,
Anon he weyveth milk and flessh and al,
And every deyntee that is in that hous,
Swich appetit hath he to ete a mous.
[*The Canterbury Tales* (1387)]

DE LA MARE, Walter (1873–1956)
In Hans' old Mill his three black cats
Watch the bins for the thieving rats.
Whisker and claw, they crouch in the night,
Their five eyes smouldering green and bright ...

Then up he climbs to his creaking mill
Out come his cats all grey with meal-
Jekkel, and Jessup, and one-eyed Jill.
['Five Eyes' (1913)]

ELIOT, T.S. (1888–1965)
Macavity, Macavity, there's no one like Macavity,
There never was a Cat of such deceitfulness and suavity.
He always has an alibi, and one or two to spare:
At whatever time the deed took place
– MACAVITY WASN'T THERE!
['Macavity: the Mystery Cat' (1939)]

HOUSEHOLD, Geoffrey (1900–1988)
I have noticed that what cats most
appreciate in a human being is not the
ability to produce food – which they
take for granted – but his or her
entertainment value.

[*Rogue Male* (1939)]

MONTAIGNE, Michel de (1533–1592)
*Quand je me joue à ma chatte, qui sait
si elle passe son temps de moi plus que
je ne fais d'elle?*
When I play with my cat, who knows
whether she isn't amusing herself with
me more than I am with her?

[*Essais* (1580)]

ROWBOTHAM, David (1924–)
Let some of the tranquillity of the cat
Curl into me.

['The Creature in the Chair']

SACKVILLE-WEST, Vita (1892–1962)
The greater cats with golden eyes
Stare out between the bars.
Deserts are there, and different skies,
And night with different stars.

[*The King's Daughter* (1929)]

SMART, Christopher (1722–1771)
[On his cat]
For he counteracts the powers of
darkness by his electrical skin and
glaring eyes.
For he counteracts the Devil, who is
death, by brisking about the life.

[*Jubilate Agno*]

SMITH, Stevie (1902–1971)
Oh I am a cat that likes to
Gallop about doing good.

['The Galloping Cat' (1972)]

TESSIMOND, A.S.J. (1902–1962)
Cats, no less liquid than their
shadows,
Offer no angles to the wind.
They slip, diminished, neat, through
loopholes
Less than themselves.

['Cats' (1934)]

ANONYMOUS
*Quidquid agas, prudenter agas, et
respice finem.*
Whatever you do, do it warily, and
take account of the end.

[*Gesta Romanorum*]

ARMSTRONG, Dr John (1709–1779)
Distrust yourself, and sleep before you
fight.
'Tis not too late tomorrow to be brave.

[*The Art of Preserving Health* (1744)]

BACON, Francis (1561–1626)
A man ought warily to begin charges
which once begun will continue.

['Of Expense' (1625)]

BELLOC, Hilaire (1870–1953)
And always keep a-hold of Nurse
For fear of finding something worse.

[*Cautionary Tales* (1907)]

COWPER, William (1731–1800)
To combat may be glorious, and
success
Perhaps may crown us; but to fly is
safe.

[*The Task* (1785)]

DRYDEN, John (1631–1700)
But now the world's o'er stocked with
prudent men.

[*The Medal* (1682)]

LINCOLN, Abraham (1809–1865)
When you have got an elephant by the
hind leg, and he is trying to run away,
it's best to let him run.

[Remark, 1865]

SHAW, George Bernard (1856–1950)
Self-denial is not a virtue: it is only the
effect of prudence on rascality.

[*Man and Superman* (1903)]

CENSORSHIP

BOROVOY, A. Alan
It is usually better to permit a piece of
trash than to suppress a work of art.

[*When Freedoms Collide* (1988)]

EMERSON, Ralph Waldo (1803–1882)
Every burned book enlightens the
world.

[Attr.]

GRIFFITH-JONES, Mervyn (1909–1979)
[At the trial of D.H. Lawrence's novel
Lady Chatterley's Lover]
Is it a book you would even wish your
wife or your servants to read?

[*The Times*, 1960]

HEINE, Heinrich (1797–1856)
Dort, wo man Bücher
Verbrennt, verbrennt man auch am
Ende Menschen.
It is there, where they
Burn books, that eventually they burn
people too.

[*Almansor: A Tragedy* (1821)]

MILTON, John (1608–1674)
As good almost kill a Man as kill a
good Book; who kills a Man kills a
reasonable creature, God's image; but
hee who destroyes a good Booke, kills
reason it selfe, kills the Image of God,
as it were in the eye. Many a man
lives a burden to the Earth; but a good
Booke is the pretious life-blood of a
master spirit, imbalm'd and treasur'd
up on purpose to a life beyond life.

[*Areopagitica* (1644)]

PINTER, Harold (1930–)
[On the execution of Nigerian writer
Ken Saro-Wiwa]
Murder is the most brutal form of
censorship.

[*The Observer*, 1995]

ROUSSELOT, Fabrice
Censorship in the UK reveals a deeply
conservative country still in thrall to
its strict Protestant values.

[*Index on Censorship*, 1996]

RUSHDIE, Salman (1946–)
Means of artistic expression that
require large quantities of finance and
sophisticated technology – films, plays,
records – become, by virtue of that

dependence, easy to censor and to
control. But what one writer can make
in the solitude of one room is something no power can easily destroy.

[*Index on Censorship*, 1996]

STROMME, Sigmund
Strict censorship cannot be maintained without terrorism.

[*Index on Censorship*, 1996]

CERTAINTY

BARNFIELD, Richard (1574–1627)
Nothing more certain than
   incertainties;
Fortune is full of fresh variety:
Constant in nothing but inconstancy.

['The Shepherd's Content' (1594)]

BISSELL, Claude T. (1916–)
I prefer complexity to certainty, cheerful mysteries to sullen facts.

[Address, University of Toronto, 1969]

GUEDALLA, Philip (1889–1944)
People who jump to conclusions rarely
alight on them.

[*The Observer*, 1924]

JOHNSON, Samuel (1709–1784)
He is no wise man who will quit a
certainty for an uncertainty.

[*The Idler* (1758–1760)]

PLINY THE ELDER (23–79)
The only certainty is that nothing is
certain.

[Attr.]

TERTULLIAN (c. 160–c. 225)
Certum est quia impossibile.
It is certain because it is impossible.

[*De Carne Christi*]

YEATS, W.B. (1865–1939)
The best lack all conviction, while the
   worst
Are full of passionate intensity.

['The Second Coming' (1920)]

See DOUBT

CHANGE

ANONYMOUS
Tempora mutantur, et nos mutamur in illis.
Times change, and we change with them.

[*In Harrison, Description of Britain (1577)*]

BACON, Francis (1561–1626)
That all things are changed, and that nothing really perishes, and that the sum of matter remains exactly the same, is sufficiently certain.

[*Thoughts on the Nature of Things* (1604)]

BEAUVOIR, Simone de (1908–1986)
Si l'on vit assez longtemps, on voit que toute victoire se change un jour en défaite.
If you live long enough, you'll find that every victory turns into a defeat.

[*All Men are Mortal* (1955)]

BRITTAIN, Vera (1893–1970)
It is probably true to say that the largest scope for change still lies in men's attitude to women, and in women's attitude to themselves.

[*Lady into Woman* (1953)]

CAMBRIDGE, Duke of (1819–1904)
It is said I am against change. I am not against change. I am in favour of change in the right circumstances. And those circumstances are when it can no longer be resisted.

[Attr. by Paul Johnson in *The Spectator*, 1996]

CHESTERTON, G.K. (1874–1936)
All conservatism is based upon the idea that if you leave things alone you leave them as they are. But you do not. If you leave a thing alone you leave it to a torrent of change.

[*Orthodoxy* (1908)]

CONFUCIUS (c. 550–c. 478 BC)
They must often change who would be constant in happiness or wisdom.

[*Analects*]

FALKLAND, Viscount (c. 1610–1643)
When it is not necessary to change, it is necessary not to change.

[Speech concerning Episcopacy, 1641]

HERACLITUS (c. 540–c. 480 BC)
You cannot step twice into the same river.

[In Plato, *Cratylus*]

HOOKER, Richard (c. 1554–1600)
Change is not made without inconvenience, even from worse to better.

[In Johnson, *Dictionary of the English Language* (1755)]

HORACE (65–8 BC)
Immortalia ne speres, monet annus et almum
Quae rapit hora diem.
The changing year and the passing hour that takes away genial day warns you not to build everlasting hopes.

[*Odes*]

IRVING, Washington (1783–1859)
There is a certain relief in change, even though it be from bad to worse; as I have found in travelling in a stage-coach, that it is often a comfort to shift one's position and be bruised in a new place.

[*Tales of a Traveller* (1824)]

KARR, Alphonse (1808–1890)
Plus ça change, plus c'est la même chose.
The more things change the more they remain the same.

[*Les Guêpes* (1849)]

LLOYD GEORGE, David (1863–1945)
[On being asked how he maintained his cheerfulness when beset by numerous political obstacles]
Well, I find that a change of nuisances is as good as a vacation.

[Attr.]

LUCRETIUS (c. 95–55 BC)
Augescunt aliae gentes, aliae minuuntur,
Inque brevi spatio mutantur saecla

animantum
Et quasi cursores vitai lampada
  tradunt.
Some groups increase, others
diminish, and in a short space the
generations of living creatures are
changed and like runners pass on the
torch of life.

[*De Rerum Natura*]

MCCARTNEY, Paul (1942–)
The issues are the same. We wanted
peace on earth, love, and understanding between everyone around
the world. We have learned that
change comes slowly.

[*The Observer*, 1987]

SPENSER, Edmund (c. 1522–1599)
What man that sees the ever-whirling
  wheele
Of Change, the which all mortall
  things doth sway,
But that therby doth find, and plainly
  feele,
How Mutability in them doth play
Her cruell sports, to many men's
  decay?

[*The Faerie Queene* (1596)]

SWIFT, Jonathan (1667–1745)
There is nothing in this world constant, but inconstancy.
[*A Critical Essay upon the Faculties of the Mind*
(1709)]

TENNYSON, Alfred, Lord (1809–1892)
Forward, forward let us range,
Let the great world spin for ever down
  the ringing grooves of change.
['Locksley Hall' (1838)]

The old order changeth, yielding place
  to new,
And God fulfils himself in many ways,
Lest one good custom should corrupt
  the world.

[*The Idylls of the King*]

THOREAU, Henry (1817–1862)
Things do not change; we change.
[*Walden* (1854)]

See TIME

See TIME

CHARACTER

FRISCH, Max (1911–1991)
Jede Uniform verdirbt den Charakter.
Every uniform corrupts one's
character.

[*Diary*, 1948]

GOETHE (1749–1832)
Es bildet ein Talent sich in der Stille,
Sich ein Charakter in dem Strom der
Welt.
Talent is formed in quiet retreat,
Character in the headlong rush of life.
[*Torquato Tasso* (1790)]

KARR, Alphonse (1808–1890)
Every man has three characters: that
which he exhibits, that which he has,
and that which he thinks he has.

[Attr.]

LINCOLN, Abraham (1809–1865)
Character is like a tree and reputation
like its shadow. The shadow is what
we think of it; the tree is the real
thing.

[In Gross, *Lincoln's Own Stories*]

MURRAY, Les A. (1938–)
In the defiance of fashion is the begin-
ning of character.
[*The Boy who Stole the Funeral* (1979)]

REAGAN, Ronald (1911–)
You can tell a lot about a fellow's
character by the way he eats jelly
beans.

[*Daily Mail*, 1981]

WILSON, Woodrow (1856–1924)
Character is a by-product; it is produced in the great manufacture of daily
duty.

[Speech, 1915]

See REPUTATION

CHARITY

BACON, Francis (1561–1626)
In charity there is no excess.
['Of Goodness, and Goodness of Nature'
(1625)]

BROWNE, Sir Thomas (1605–1682)
Charity begins at home, is the voice of the world.

[*Religio Medici* (1643)]

CARNEGIE, Andrew (1835–1919)
Of every thousand dollars spent in so-called charity today, it is probable that nine hundred and fifty dollars is unwisely spent.

['Wealth' (1889)]

FULLER, Thomas (1608–1661)
He that feeds upon charity has a cold dinner and no supper.

[Attr.]

POPE, Alexander (1688–1744)
In Faith and Hope the world will disagree,
But all Mankind's concern is Charity.

[*Essay on Man* (1733)]

ROUSSEAU, Jean-Jacques (1712–1778)
La feinte charité du riche n'est en lui qu'un luxe de plus; il nourrit les pauvres comme des chiens et des chevaux.
The feigned charity of the rich man is for him no more than another luxury; he feeds the poor as he feeds dogs and horses.

[Letter to M. Moulton]

SHERIDAN, Richard Brinsley (1751–1816)
Rowley: I believe there is no sentiment he has more faith in than that 'charity begins at home'.
Sir Oliver Surface: And his, I presume, is of that domestic sort which never stirs abroad at all.

[*The School for Scandal* (1777)]

SMART, Christopher (1722–1771)
Charity is cold in the multitude of possessions, and the rich are covetous of their crumbs.

[*Jubilate Agno* (c. 1758–63)]

VOLTAIRE (1694–1778)
The man who leaves money to charity in his will is only giving away what no longer belongs to him.

[Letter, 1769]

WEST, Dame Rebecca (1892–1983)
[Of charity]
It is an ugly trick. It is a virtue grown by the rich on the graves of the poor. Unless it is accompanied by sincere revolt against the present social system, it is cheap moral swagger.

[*The Clarion*]

CHARM

BARRIE, Sir J.M. (1860–1937)
[On charm]
It's a sort of bloom on a woman. If you have it, you don't need to have anything else; and if you don't have it, it doesn't much matter what else you have.

[*What Every Woman Knows* (1908)]

BIERCE, Ambrose (1842–c. 1914)
Please: To lay the foundation for a superstructure of imposition.

[*The Enlarged Devil's Dictionary* (1961)]

CONNOLLY, Cyril (1903–1974)
All charming people have something to conceal, usually their total dependence on the appreciation of others.

[*Enemies of Promise* (1938)]

FARQUHAR, George (1678–1707)
Charming women can true converts make,
We love the precepts for the teacher's sake.

[*The Constant Couple* (1699)]

LERNER, Alan Jay (1918–1986)
Oozing charm from every pore,
He oiled his way around the floor.

[*My Fair Lady* (1956)]

MACNALLY, Leonard (1752–1820)
On Richmond Hill there lives a lass,
More sweet than May day morn,
Whose charms all other maids surpass,
A rose without a thorn.

['The Lass of Richmond Hill' (1789)]

WOLLSTONECRAFT, Mary (1759–1797)
The woman who has only been taught to please will soon find that her charms are oblique sunbeams, and that they cannot have much effect on her husband's heart when they are seen every day.

[*A Vindication of the Rights of Woman* (1792)]

CHILDREN

AMIS, Kingsley (1922–1995)
It was no wonder that people were so horrible when they started life as children.

[*One Fat Englishman* (1963)]

AUDEN, W.H. (1907–1973)
Only those in the last stages of disease could believe that children are true judges of character.

[*The Orators* (1932)]

AUSTEN, Jane (1775–1817)
On every formal visit a child ought to be of the party, by way of provision for discourse.

[*Sense and Sensibility* (1811)]

BACON, Francis (1561–1626)
Children sweeten labours, but they make misfortunes more bitter.

[*Essays* (1625)]

BALDWIN, James (1924–1987)
Children have never been very good at listening to their elders, but they have never failed to imitate them. They must, they have no other models.

[*Nobody Knows My Name* (1961)]

BOWEN, Elizabeth (1899–1973)
There is no end to the violations committed by children on children, quietly talking alone.

[*The House in Paris* (1935)]

CARROLL, Lewis (1832–1898)
I am fond of children (except boys).

[Letter to Kathleen Eschwege, 1879]

GANDHI, Indira (1917–1984)
To bear many children is considered not only a religious blessing but also an investment. The greater their number, some Indians reason, the more alms they can beg.

[In Fallaci, *New York Review of Books*]

GEORGE V (1865–1936)
My father was frightened of his mother. I was frightened of my father, and I'm damned well going to make sure that my children are frightened of me.

[In R. Churchill, *Lord Derby,'King of Lancashire'* (1959)]

GIBBON, Edward (1737–1794)
Few, perhaps, are the children who, after the expiration of some months or years, would sincerely rejoice in the resurrection of their parents.

[*Memoirs of My Life and Writings* (1796)]

GIBRAN, Kahlil (1883–1931)
Your children are not your children.
They are the sons and daughters of Life's longing for itself...

You may give them your love but not your thoughts.
For they have their own thoughts.
You may house their bodies but not their souls,
For their souls dwell in the house of tomorrow, which you cannot visit, not even in your dreams.
You may strive to be like them, but seek not to make them like you.
For life goes not backward nor tarries with yesterday.
You are the bows from which your children as living arrows are sent forth.

[*The Prophet* (1923)]

HARWOOD, Gwen (1920–)
'It's so sweet
to hear their chatter, watch them grow and thrive'
she says to his departing smile. Then, nursing
the youngest child, sits staring at her feet.
To the wind she says, 'They have eaten me alive.'

[*Poems* (1968)]

INGE, William Ralph (1860–1954)
The proper time to influence the character of a child is about a hundred years berfore he is born.

[The Observer, 1929]

JONSON, Ben (1572–1637)
Rest in soft peace, and, ask'd say here
   doth lye
Ben Jonson his best piece of poetrie.

['On My First Son' (1616)]

KEY, Ellen (1849–1926)
At every step the child should be allowed to meet the real experiences of life; the thorns should never be plucked from his roses.

[The Century of the Child (1909)]

KIPLING, Rudyard (1865–1936)
These were our children who died for
   our lands ...
But who shall return us the children?

['The Children' (1917)]

KNOX, Ronald (1888–1957)
[Definition of a baby]
A loud noise at one end and no sense of responsibility at the other.

[Attr.]

LAMB, Charles (1775–1834)
Riddle of destiny, who can show
What thy short visit meant, or know
What thy errand here below?

['On an Infant Dying as soon as Born']

MILLER, Alice
Society chooses to disregard the mistreatment of children, judging it to be altogether normal because it is so commonplace.

[Pictures of a Childhood (1986)]

MITFORD, Nancy (1904–1973)
I love children – especially when they cry, for then someone takes them away.

[Attr.]

MONTAIGNE, Michel de (1533–1592)
Il faut noter, que les jeux d'enfants ne sont pas jeux: et les faut juger en eux, comme leurs plus sérieuses actions.
It should be noted that children at play are not merely playing; their games should be seen as their most serious actions.

[Essais (1580)]

NASH, Ogden (1902–1971)
Children aren't happy with nothing to
   ignore,
And that's what parents were created
   for.

['The Parent' (1933)]

PAVESE, Cesare (1908–1950)
One stops being a child when one realizes that telling one's trouble does not make it better.

[The Business of Living: Diaries 1935–50]

PLATH, Sylvia (1932–1963)
[On seeing her newborn baby]
What did my fingers do before they
   held him?
What did my heart do, with its love?
I have never seen a thing so clear.
His lids are like the lilac flower
And soft as a moth, his breath.
I shall not let go.
There is no guile or warp in him. May
   he keep so.

['Three Women: A Poem for Three Voices'
(1962)]

SMITH, Sir Sydney (1883–1969)
No child is born a criminal: no child is born an angel: he's just born.

[Remark]

**STEVENSON, Robert Louis
(1850–1894)**
The child that is not clean and neat,
With lots of toys and things to eat,
He is a naughty child, I'm sure –
Or else his dear papa is poor.

[A Child's Garden of Verses (1885)]

A child should always say what's true,
And speak when he is spoken to,
And behave mannerly at table:
At least as far as he is able.

[A Child's Garden of Verses (1885)]

VIDAL, Gore (1925–)
Never have children, only grand-
children.

[*Two Sisters* (1970)]

WILDE, Oscar (1854–1900)
Children begin by loving their parents.
After a time they judge them. Rarely, if
ever, do they forgive them.

[*A Woman of No Importance* (1893)]

YANKWICH, Léon R. (1888–1975)
[Decision, State District Court,
Southern District of California, June
1928, quoting columnist O.O.
McIntyre]
There are no illegitimate children –
only illegitimate parents.

[Attr.]

See PARENTS

CHRISTIANITY

BARTON, Bruce (1886–1967)
[Jesus] picked up twelve men from the
bottom ranks of business and forged
them into an organization that conquered the world.

[*The Man Nobody Knows: A Discovery of the
Real Jesus* (1924)]

BRECHT, Bertolt (1898–1956)
*Da konnt [unser Herr] auch verlangen,
dass man seinen Nächsten liebt, denn
man war satt. Heutzutage ist das
anders.*
In those days [our Lord] could demand
that men love their neighbour, because they'd had enough to eat.
Nowadays it's different.

[*Mother Courage and her Children* (1941)]

BUTLER, Samuel (1835–1902)
They would have been equally
horrified at hearing the Christian
religion doubted, and at seeing it
practised.

[*The Way of All Flesh* (1903)]

CARLYLE, Thomas (1795–1881)
If Jesus Christ were to come to-day,
people would not even crucify him.
They would ask him to dinner, and

hear what he had to say, and make
fun of it.

[In Wilson, *Carlyle at his Zenith* (1927)]

CHESTERTON, G.K. (1874–1936)
Carlyle said that men were mostly
fools. Christianity, with a surer and
more reverend realism, says that they
are all fools.

[*Heretics* (1905)]

The Christian ideal has not been tried
and found wanting. It has been found
difficult; and left untried.

[*What's Wrong with the World* (1910)]

DE BLANK, Joost (1908–1968)
[Of South Africa]
Christ in this country would quite
likely have been arrested under the
Suppression of Communism Act.

[*The Observer*, 1963]

DISRAELI, Benjamin (1804–1881)
A Protestant, if he wants aid or advice
on any matter, can only go to his
solicitor.

[*Lothair* (1870)]

ELLIS, Bob (1942–)
Show me a Wednesday wencher and a
Sunday saint, and I'll show you a
Roman Catholic.

[*The Legend of King O'Malley* (1974)]

FRANCE, Anatole (1844–1924)
*Le Christianisme a beaucoup fait pour
l'amour en en faisant un péché.*
Christianity has done a great deal for
love by making a sin of it.

[*Le Jardin d'Epicure* (1894)]

HALE, Sir Matthew (1609–1676)
Christianity is part of the laws of
England.

[In Blackstone, *Commentaries on the Laws of
England* (1769)]

HOOD, Thomas (1799–1845)
[Of Quakers]
The sedate, sober, silent, serious, sad-
coloured sect.

[*The Comic Annual* (1839)]

HUXLEY, Aldous (1894–1963)
Christianity accepted as given a
metaphysical system derived from
several already existing and mutually
incompatible systems.

[*Grey Eminence (1941)*]

KINGSLEY, Charles (1819–1875)
We have used the Bible as if it was a
constable's handbook – an opium-
dose for keeping beasts of burden
patient while they are being
overloaded.

['Letters to Chartists' (1848)]

LENNON, John (1940–1980)
We're more popular than Jesus Christ
now. I don't know which will go first.
Rock and roll or Christianity.

[*The Beatles Illustrated Lyrics*]

LUTHER, Martin (1483–1546)
*Esto peccator et pecca fortiter, sed
fortius fide et gaude in Christo.*
Be a sinner and sin strongly, but
believe and rejoice in Christ even
more strongly.

[Letter to Melanchton]

MENCKEN, H.L. (1880–1956)
Puritanism – The haunting fear that
someone, somewhere, may be happy.

[*A Mencken Chrestomathy* (1949)]

The chief contribution of Prot-
estantism to human thought is its
massive proof that God is a bore.

[*Notebooks* (1956), 'Minority Report']

MONTESQUIEU, Charles (1689–1755)
*Il n'y a jamais eu de royaume où il y ait
eu tant de guerres civiles que dans celui
du Christ.*
No kingdom has ever had as many
civil wars as the kingdom of Christ.

[*Lettres persanes* (1721)]

NIETZSCHE, Friedrich (1844–1900)
*Der christliche Entschluss, die Welt
hässlich und schlecht zu finden, hat die
Welt hässlich und schlecht gemacht.*
The Christian decision to find the
world ugly and bad has made the
world ugly and bad.

[*The Gay Science*]

PENN, William (1644–1718)
No pain, no palm; no thorns, no
throne; no gall, no glory; no cross, no
crown.

[*No Cross, No Crown* (1669)]

RUSSELL, Bertrand (1872–1970)
There's a Bible on that shelf there. But
I keep it next to Voltaire – poison and
antidote.

[In Harris, *Kenneth Harris Talking To:* (1971)]

SANTAYANA, George (1863–1952)
The Bible is literature, not dogma.

[Introduction to Spinoza's *Ethics*]

TEMPLE, William (1881–1944)
Christianity is the most materialistic of
all great religions.

[*Readings in St John's Gospel* (1939)]

TUTU, Archbishop Desmond (1931–)
For the Church in any country to
retreat from politics is nothing short of
heresy. Christianity is political or it is
not Christianity.

[*The Observer*, 1994]

TWAIN, Mark (1835–1910)
Most people are bothered by those
passages in Scripture which they
cannot understand; but as for me, I
always noticed that the passages in
Scripture which trouble me most are
those that I do understand.

[In Simcox, *Treasury of Quotations on
Christian Themes*]

VAN DER POST, Sir Laurens (1906–)
Organized religion is making
Christianity political rather than
making politics Christian.

[*The Observer, 1986*]

YBARRA, Thomas Russell (1880–)
A Christian is a man who feels
Repentance on a Sunday
For what he did on Saturday
And is going to do on Monday.

['The Christian' (1909)]

THE CHURCH

ANDREWES, Bishop Lancelot (1555–1626)
The nearer the Church the further from God.

[*Sermon 15, Of the Nativity* (1629)]

AUGUSTINE, Saint (354–430)
Salus extra ecclesiam non est.
Outside the church there is no salvation.

[*De Baptismo*]

BANCROFT, Richard (1544–1610)
Where Christ erecteth his Church, the devil in the same churchyard will have his chapel.

[*Sermon,* 1588]

BELLOC, Hilaire (1870–1953)
I always like to associate with a lot of priests because it makes me understand anti-clerical things so well.

[Attr.]

THE BIBLE (King James Version)
Thou art Peter, and upon this rock I will build my church; and the gates of hell shall not prevail against it.

[*Matthew,* 16:18]

BLAKE, William (1757–1827)
But if at the Church they would give us some Ale,
And a pleasant fire our souls to regale:
We'd sing and we'd pray all the live-long day;
Nor ever once wish from the Church to stray.

['The Little Vagabond' (1794)]

BLYTHE, Ronald (1922–)
As for the British churchman, he goes to church as he goes to the bathroom, with the minimum of fuss and no explanation if he can help it.

[*The Age of Illusion* (1963)]

BURKE, Edmund (1729–1797)
Politics and the pulpit are terms that have little agreement. No sound ought to be heard in the church but the healing voice of Christian charity.

[*Reflections on the Revolution in France ...* (1790)]

CYPRIAN, Saint (c. 200–258)
Habere non potest Deum patrem qui ecclesiam non habet matrem.
Who has not the Church as his mother cannot have God as his father.

[*De Unitate Ecclesiae*]

D'ALPUGET, Blanche (1944–)
Convent girls never leave the church, they just become feminists. I learned that in Australia.

[*Turtle Beach* (1981)]

DEVLIN, Bernadette (1947–)
Among the best traitors Ireland has ever had, Mother Church ranks at the very top, a massive obstacle in the path to equality and freedom.

[*The Price of My Soul*]

MELBOURNE, Lord (1779–1848)
While I cannot be regarded as a pillar, I must be regarded as a buttress of the church, because I support it from the outside.

[Attr.]

MUGGERIDGE, Malcolm (1903–1990)
[On *Punch*, which he once edited]
Very much like the Church of England. It is doctrinally inexplicable but it goes on.

[Attr.]

SABIA, Laura
I'm a Roman Catholic and I take a dim view of 2,500 celibates shuffling back and forth to Rome to discuss birth control and not one woman to raise a voice.

[*The Toronto Star,* 1975]

SWIFT, Jonathan (1667–1745)
I never saw, heard, nor read, that the clergy were beloved in any nation where Christianity was the religion of the country. Nothing can render them popular, but some degree of persecution.

[*Thoughts on Religion* (1765)]

TEMPLE, William (1881–1944)
I believe in the Church, One Holy,
Catholic and Apostolic, and I regret
that it nowhere exists.

[Attr.]

TUCHOLSKY, Kurt (1890–1935)
*Was die Kirche nicht verhindern kann,
das segnet sie.*
What the church can't prevent, it
blesses.

[*Scraps* (1973)]

WAUGH, Evelyn (1903–1966)
I have noticed again and again since I
have been in the Church that lay
interest in ecclesiastical matters is
often a prelude to insanity.

[*Decline and Fall* (1928)]

There is a species of person called a
'Modern Churchman' who draws the
full salary of a beneficed clergyman
and need not commit himself to any
religious belief.

[*Decline and Fall* (1928)]

CINEMA

ALTMAN, Robert (1922–)
What's a cult? It just means not
enough people to make a minority.

[*The Observer*, 1981]

BROWN, Geoff (1949–)
Dictators needed a talking cinema to
twist nations round their fingers:
remove the sound from Mussolini and
you are left with a puffing bullfrog.

[*The Times*, 1992]

COLTRANE, Robbie (1950–)
[On film acting]
If anyone asked me what I was doing,
I'd say 'I've come 1500 miles to a
foreign country to pretend to be
someone else in front of a machine'.

[*Arena*, 1991]

DISNEY, Walt (1901–1966)
Girls bored me – they still do. I love
Mickey Mouse more than any woman
I've ever known.

[In Wagner, *You Must Remember This*]

GODARD, Jean-Luc (1930–)
*La photographie, c'est la vérité. Le
cinéma: la vérité vingt-quatre fois par
seconde.*
Photography is truth. Cinema is truth
twenty-four times a second.

[*Le Petit Soldat*, film, 1960]

Of course a film should have a
beginning, a middle and an end. But
not necessarily in that order.

[Attr.]

GOLDWYN, Samuel (1882–1974)
[Before the opening of his film *The
Best Years of Our Lives* in 1946]
I don't care if it doesn't make a nickel,
I just want every man, woman, and
child in America to see it.

[In Zierold, *Moguls* (1969)]

Why should people go out and pay
money to see bad films when they can
stay at home and see bad television
for nothing?

[*The Observer*, 1956]

The trouble with this business is the
dearth of bad pictures.

[Attr.]

GRADE, Lew (1906–1994)
[To Franco Zeffirelli who had ex-
plained that the high cost of the film
Jesus of Nazareth was partly because
there had to be twelve apostles]
Twelve! So who needs twelve!
Couldn't we make do with six?

[*Radio Times*, 1983]

GRIFFITH, D.W. (1874–1948)
[Said when directing an epic film]
Move those ten thousand horses a
trifle to the right. And that mob out
there, three feet forward.

[Attr.]

JUNG, Carl Gustav (1875–1961)
The cinema, like the detective story,
makes it possible to experience
without danger all the excitement,
passion and desire which must be
repressed in a humanitarian ordering
of life.

[Attr.]

KAEL, Pauline (1919–)
Movies are so rarely great art that if we cannot appreciate the great *trash* we have very little reason to be interested in them.
[*Kiss Kiss Bang Bang* (1968)]

KAUFMAN, George S. (1889–1961)
[At a rehearsal of *Animal Crackers* (1930), for which he wrote the script]
Excuse me for interrupting but I actually thought I heard a line I wrote.
[In Meredith, *George S. Kaufman and the Algonquin Round Table* (1974)]

MARX, Groucho (1895–1977)
We in this industry know that behind every successful screenwriter stands a woman. And behind her stands his wife.
[Attr.]

ROGERS, Will (1879–1935)
The movies are the only business where you can go out front and applaud yourself.
[In Halliwell, *Filmgoer's Book of Quotes* (1973)]

TRACY, Spencer (1900–1967)
[Defending his demand for equal billing with Katherine Hepburn]
This is a movie, not a lifeboat.
[Attr.]

WALLACH, Eli (1915–)
[Remarking upon the long line of people at the box office before one of his performances].
There's something about a crowd like that that brings a lump to my wallet.
[Attr.]

See SHOWBUSINESS

CITIES

BURGON, John William (1813–1888)
Match me such marvel save in Eastern clime,
A rose–red city 'half as old as Time'!
['Petra' (1845)]

COLTON, Charles Caleb (c. 1780–1832)
If you would be known, and not know, vegetate in a village; if you would know, and not be known, live in a city.
[*Lacon* (1820)]

COWPER, William (1731–1800)
God made the country, and man made the town.
[*The Task* (1785)]

KEATS, John (1795–1821)
To one who has been long in city pent,
'Tis very sweet to look into the fair
And open face of heaven.
['To one who has been long in city pent' (1816)]

KIPLING, Rudyard (1865–1936)
Cities and Thrones and Powers,
Stand in Time's eye,
Almost as long as flowers,
Which daily die:
But, as new buds put forth,
To glad new men,
Out of the spent and unconsidered Earth,
The Cities rise again.
['Cities and Thrones and Powers' (1906)]

MILTON, John (1608–1674)
Towred Cities please us then,
And the busie humm of men.
['L'Allegro' (1645)]

MORRIS, Charles (1745–1838)
A house is much more to my taste than a tree,
And for groves, oh! a good grove of chimneys for me.
['Country and Town', 1840]

MORRIS, Desmond (1928–)
Clearly, then, the city is not a concrete jungle, it is a human zoo.
[*The Human Zoo* (1969)]

MURDOCH, Sir Walter (1874–1970)
A second-hand bookshop is the sign and symbol of a civilized community ... and the number and quality of these shops give you the exact measure of a city's right to be counted among the great cities of the world ... Show me a

city's second-hand bookshops, and I will tell you what manner of citizens dwell there, and of what ancestry sprung.

[*Collected Essays* (1940)]

BELFAST

CRAIG, Maurice James (1919–)
Red bricks in the suburbs, white horse on the wall,
Eyetalian marbles in the City Hall:
O stranger from England, why stand so aghast?
May the Lord in his mercy be kind to Belfast.

['Ballad to a traditional Refrain']

BIRMINGHAM

AUSTEN, Jane (1775–1817)
One has not great hopes from Birmingham. I always say there is something direful in the sound.

[*Emma* (1816)]

BOSTON

APPLETON, Thomas Gold (1812–1884)
A Boston man is the east wind made flesh.

[Attr.]

BOSSIDY, John Collins (1860–1928)
And this is good old Boston,
The home of the bean and the cod,
Where the Lowells talk only to Cabots,
And the Cabots talk only to God.

[Toast at Harvard dinner, 1910]

EMERSON, Ralph Waldo (1803–1882)
We say the cows laid out Boston. Well, there are worse surveyors.

[*Conduct of Life* (1860)]

GLASGOW

CERNUDA, Luis (1902–1963)
[On leaving Glasgow, where he had lived from 1939 to 1943]
Rara vez me he ido tan a gusto de sitio alguno.
Rarely have I been so pleased to leave a place.

[*Chronicle of a book* (1958)]

MCGONAGALL, William (c. 1830–1902)
Beautiful city of Glasgow, I now conclude my muse,
And to write in praise of thee my pen does not refuse;
And, without fear of contradiction, I will venture to say
You are the second grandest city in Scotland at the present day.

['Glasgow' (1890)]

SMITH, Alexander (1830–1867)
City! I am true son of thine ...

Instead of shores where ocean beats,
I hear the ebb and flow of streets.
Thou hast my kith and kin:
My childhood, youth, and manhood brave;
Thou hast that unforgotten grave
Within thy central din.
A sacredness of love and death
Dwells in thy noise and smoky breath.

['Glasgow' (1857)]

LONDON

AUSTEN, Jane (1775–1817)
Nobody is healthy in London. Nobody can be.

[*Emma* (1816)]

BLAKE, William (1757–1827)
I wander thro' each charter'd street,
Near where the charter'd Thames does flow
And mark in every face I meet
Marks of weakness, marks of woe.

['London' (1794)]

BLÜCHER, Prince (1742–1819)
[Remark made on seeing London in June, 1814]
Was für Plunder!
What junk!

[Attr.]

BRIDIE, James (1888–1951)
London! Pompous Ignorance sits enthroned there and welcomes Pretentious Mediocrity with flattery

and gifts. Oh, dull and witless city!
Very hell for the restless, inquiring,
sensitive soul. Paradise for the snob,
the parasite and the prig; the pimp,
the placeman and the cheapjack.
[*The Anatomist* (1931)]

COBBETT, William (1762–1835)
But what is to be the fate of the great
wen of all? The monster, called...'the
metropolis of the empire'?
['Rural Rides' (1822)]

COLMAN, the Younger, George
(1762–1836)
Oh, London is a fine town,
A very famous city,
Where all the streets are paved with
gold,
And all the maidens pretty.
[*The Heir at Law* (1797)]

DISRAELI, Benjamin (1804–1881)
London; a nation, not a city.
[*Lothair* (1870)]

DOYLE, Sir Arthur Conan (1859–1930)
London, that great cesspool into
which all the loungers of the Empire
are irresistibly drained.
[*A Study in Scarlet* (1887)]

DUNBAR, William (c. 1460–c. 1525)
London, thou art the flower of cities
all!
Gemme of all joy, jasper of jocunditie.
['London' (1834)]

JOHNSON, Samuel (1709–1784)
When a man is tired of London, he is
tired of life; for there is in London all
that life can afford.
[In Boswell, *The Life of Samuel Johnson*
(1791)]

MEYNELL, Hugo (1727–1780)
The chief advantage of London is, that
a man is always so near his burrow.
[In Boswell, *The Life of Samuel Johnson*
(1791)]

MORRIS, William (1834–1896)
Forget six counties overhung with
smoke,

Forget the snorting steam and piston
stroke,
Forget the spreading of the hideous
town;
Think rather of the pack–horse on the
down,
And dream of London, small and
white and clean,
The clear Thames bordered by its
gardens green.
['The Wanderers' (1870)]

WORDSWORTH, William (1770–1850)
Earth has not anything to show more
fair;
Dull would he be of soul who could
pass by
A sight so touching in its majesty:
This city now doth, like a garment,
wear
The beauty of the morning, silent,
bare,
Ships, towers, domes, theatres, and
temples lie
Open unto the fields, and to the sky,
All bright and glittering in the
smokeless air ...

Dear God! the very houses seem
asleep;
And all that mighty heart is lying still!
['Sonnet composed upon Westminster
Bridge' (1807)]

MANCHESTER

BOLITHO, William (1890–1930)
The shortest way out of Manchester is
notoriously a bottle of Gordon's gin.
[*The Treasury of Humorous Quotations*]

MELBOURNE

BEVEN, Rodney Allan (1916–1982)
The people of Melbourne
Are frightfully well-born.
['Observation Sociologique']

BYGRAVES, Max (1922–)
I've always wanted to see a ghost
town. You couldn't even get a para-

chute to open here after 10 p.m.

[Melbourne *Sun*, 1965]

NAPLES

GLADSTONE, William (1809–1898)
This is the negation of God erected
into a system of government.

[*Letter to Lord Aberdeen*, 1851]

NEW YORK

**GILMAN, Charlotte Perkins
(1860–1935)**
New York ... that unnatural city where
every one is an exile, none more so
than the American.

[*The Living of Charlotte Perkins Gilman*
(1935)]

MOORE, Brian (1921–)
This city was full of lunatics, people
who went into muttering fits on the
bus, others who shouted obscenities
in automats, lost souls who walked
the pavements alone, caught up in
imaginary conversations.

[*An Answer From Limbo* (1962)]

SIMON, Neil (1927–)
New York ... is not Mecca. It just
smells like it.

[*California Suite* (1976)]

PARIS

ELMS, Robert
Paris is the paradise of the easily-
impressed – the universal provincial
mind.

[In Burchill, *Sex and Sensibility* (1992)]

HEMINGWAY, Ernest (1898–1961)
If you are lucky enough to have lived
in Paris as a young man, then wherever you go for the rest of your life, it
stays with you, for Paris is a moveable
feast.

[*A Moveable Feast* (1964)]

HENRI IV (1553–1610)
Paris vaut bien une messe.
Paris is well worth a mass.

[Attr.; also attributed to Sully]

KURTZ, Irma (1935–)
Cities are only human. And I had
begun to see Paris for the bitch she is:
a stunning transvestite – vain, narrow-
minded and all false charm.

[*Daily Mail*, 1996]

ROME

BURGESS, Anthony (1917–1993)
Rome's just a city like anywhere else.
A vastly overrated city, I'd say. It
trades on belief just as Stratford trades
on Shakespeare.

[*Inside Mr Enderby* (1968)]

HORACE, (65–8BC)
Fumum et opes strepitumque Romae.
The smoke and wealth and noise of
Rome.

[*Odes*]

See COUNTRY

CIVILISATION

ADDAMS, Jane (1860–1935)
Civilization is a method of living, an
attitude of equal respect for all men.

[Speech, Honolulu, 1933]

ALCOTT, Bronson (1799–1888)
Civilization degrades the many to
exalt the few.

[*Table Talk* (1877)]

BAGEHOT, Walter (1826–1877)
The whole history of civilization is
strewn with creeds and institutions
which were invaluable at first, and
deadly afterwards.

[*Physics and Politics* (1872)]

BATES, Daisy May (1863–1951)
The Australian native can withstand
all the reverses of nature, fiendish
droughts and sweeping floods, horrors
of thirst and enforced starvation – but
he cannot withstand civilisation.

[*The Passing of the Aborigines* ... (1938)]

BUCK, Pearl S. (1892–1973)
Nothing and no one can destroy the

Chinese people. They are relentless survivors. They are the oldest civilized people on earth. Their civilization passes through phases but its basic characteristics remain the same. They yield, they bend to the wind, but they never break.

[*China, Past and Present* (1972)]

DISRAELI, Benjamin (1804–1881)
Increased means and increased leisure are the two civilizers of man.

[Speech, Manchester, 1872]

ELLIS, Havelock (1859–1939)
The more rapidly a civilisation progresses, the sooner it dies for another to rise in its place.

[*The Dance of Life*]

GANDHI (1869–1948)
[When asked what he thought of Western civilization]
I think it would be an excellent idea.

[Attr.]

GARROD, Heathcote William (1878–1960)
[In response to criticism that, during World War I, he was not fighting to defend civilization]
Madam, I am the civilization they are fighting to defend.

[In Balsdon, *Oxford Now and Then* (1970)]

HILLARY, Sir Edmund (1919–)
There is precious little in civilization to appeal to a Yeti.

[*The Observer*, 1960]

HUGO, Victor (1802–1885)
Jésus a pleuré, Voltaire a souri; c'est de cette larme divine et de ce sourire humain qu'est faite la douceur de la civilisation actuelle.
Jesus cried; Voltaire smiled. From that divine tear, from that human smile was born the sweetness of civilisation today.

[Centenary oration on Voltaire, 1878]

KNOX, Ronald (1888–1957)
It is so stupid of modern civilization to have given up believing in the devil

when he is the only explanation of it.

[Attr.]

MILL, John Stuart (1806–1873)
I am not aware that any community has a right to force another to be civilized.

[*On Liberty* (1859)]

PAGLIA, Camille (1947–)
If civilisation had been left in female hands, we would still be living in grass huts.

[*Sex, Art and American Culture: Essays* (1992)]

PARK, Mungo (1771–1806)
[Remark on finding a gibbet in an unexplored part of Africa]
The sight of it gave me infinite pleasure, as it proved that I was in a civilized society.

[Attr.]

POPPER, Sir Karl (1902–1994)
Our civilization ... has not yet fully recovered from the shock of its birth – the transition from the tribal or 'closed society', with its submission to magical forces, to the 'open society' which sets free the critical powers of man.

[*The Open Society and its Enemies* (1945)]

SANTAYANA, George (1863–1952)
Civilisation is perhaps approaching one of those long winters that overtake it from time to time. Romantic Christendom – picturesque, passionate, unhappy episode – may be coming to an end. Such a catastrophe would be no reason for despair.

[*Characters and Opinions in the United States*]

TREVELYAN, G.M. (1876–1962)
Disinterested intellectual curiosity is the life blood of real civilization.

[*English Social History* (1942)]

YEATS, W.B. (1865–1939)
A civilisation is a struggle to keep self-control.

[*A Vision* (1925), 'Dove or Swan']

CLASS

ARNOLD, Matthew (1822–1888)
One has often wondered whether upon the whole earth there is anything so unintelligent, so unapt to perceive how the world is really going, as an ordinary young Englishman of our upper class.

[*Culture and Anarchy* (1869)]

BRENAN, Gerald (1894–1987)
Poets and painters are outside the class system, or rather they constitute a special class of their own, like the circus people and the gipsies.

[*Thoughts in a Dry Season* (1978)]

BROUGH, Robert (1828–1860)
My Lord Tomnoddy is thirty-four;
The Earl can last but a few years
    more.
My Lord in the Peers will take his
    place:
Her Majesty's councils his words will
    grace.
Office he'll hold and patronage sway;
Fortunes and lives he will vote away;
And what are his qualifications? –
    ONE!
He's the Earl of Fitzdotterel's eldest
    son.

['My Lord Tomnoddy' (1855)]

BROUGHAM, Lord Henry (1778–1868)
The great Unwashed.

[Attr.]

BURGESS, Anthony (1917–1993)
Without class differences, England would cease to be the living theatre it is.

[Remark, 1985]

CARTLAND, Barbara (1902–)
[When asked in a radio interview whether she thought that British class barriers had broken down]
Of course they have, or I wouldn't be sitting here talking to someone like you.

[In J. Cooper, *Class* (1979)]

CURZON, Lord (1859–1925)
[On seeing some soldiers bathing]
I never knew the lower classes had such white skins.

[Attr.]

DEFOE, Daniel (c. 1661–1731)
He bid me observe ... that the calamities of life were shared among the upper and lower part of mankind; but that the middle station had the fewest disasters.

[*The Life and Adventures of Robinson Crusoe* (1719)]

EDWARD, Prince (1964–)
We are forever being told we have a rigid class structure. That's a load of codswallop.

[*Daily Mail*, 1996]

ELIZABETH, the Queen Mother (1900–)
My favourite programme is 'Mrs Dale's Diary'. I try never to miss it because it is the only way of knowing what goes on in a middle-class family.

[Attr.]

ENGELS, Friedrich (1820–1895)
The history of all hitherto existing society is the history of class struggles.

[*The Communist Manifesto* (1848)]

FRIEL, Brian (1929–)
The result is that people with a culture of poverty suffer much less repression than we of the middle-class suffer and indeed, if I may make the suggestion with due qualification, they often have a lot more fun than we have.

[*The Freedom of the City* (1973)]

HAILSHAM, Quintin Hogg, Baron (1907–)
I don't see any harm in being middle class, I've been middle class all my life and have benefited from it.

[*The Observer*, 1983]

IPHICRATES (419–353 BC)
[Responding to a descendant of Harmodius (an Athenian hero), who had mocked Iphicrates for being the

son of a shoemaker]
The difference between us is that my family begins with me, whereas yours ends with you.

[Attr.]

LERNER, Alan Jay (1918–1986)
An Englishman's way of speaking absolutely classifies him.

[*My Fair Lady* (1956)]

MARX, Karl (1818–1883)
What I did that was new was prove ... that the class struggle necessarily leads to the dictatorship of the proletariat.

[Letter, 1852]

MIKES, George (1912–1987)
The one class you do *not* belong to and are not proud of at all is the lower-middle class. No one ever describes himself as belonging to the lower-middle class.

[*How to be an Inimitable*]

RATTIGAN, Terence (1911–1977)
You can be in the Horse Guards and still be common, dear.

[*Separate Tables* (1955)]

SCARGILL, Arthur (1941–)
[On John Prescott's description of himself as middle class]
I have little or no time for people who aspire to be members of the middle class.

[Remark at the launch of the Socialist Labour Party, 1996]

STANTON, Elizabeth Cady (1815–1902)
It is impossible for one class to appreciate the wrongs of another.

[In Anthony and Gage, *History of Woman Suffrage* (1881)]

THEROUX, Paul (1941–)
The ship follows Soviet custom: it is riddled with class distinctions so subtle, it takes a trained Marxist to appreciate them.

[*The Great Railway Bazaar* (1975)]

THIERS, Louis Adolphe (1797–1877)
[Defending his social status after someone had remarked that his mother had been a cook]
She was – but I assure you that she was a very bad cook.

[Attr.]

WILDE, Oscar (1854–1900)
Really, if the lower orders don't set us a good example, what on earth is the use of them? They seem, as a class, to have absolutely no sense of moral responsibility.

[*The Importance of Being Earnest* (1895)]

See ARISTOCRACY

COMMON SENSE

DESCARTES, René (1596–1650)
Le bon sens est la chose du monde la mieux partagée, car chacun pense en être bien pourvu.
Common sense is the best distributed thing in the world, for we all think we possess a good share of it.

[*Discours de la Méthode* (1637)]

EINSTEIN, Albert (1879–1955)
Common sense is the collection of prejudices acquired by age eighteen.

[Attr.]

EMERSON, Ralph Waldo (1803–1882)
Nothing astonishes men so much as common-sense and plain dealing.

['Art' (1841)]

SALISBURY, Lord (1830–1903)
No lesson seems to be so deeply inculcated by the experience of life as that you never should trust experts. If you believe the doctors, nothing is wholesome: if you believe the theologians, nothing is innocent: if you believe the soldiers, nothing is safe. They all require to have their strong wine diluted by a very large admixture of insipid common sense.

[Letter to Lord Lytton, 1877]

COMMUNISM

COMMUNISM

ATTLEE, Clement (1883–1967)
Russian Communism is the illegitimate child of Karl Marx and Catherine the Great.

[*The Observer*, 1956]

ELLIOTT, Ebenezer (1781–1849)
What is a communist? One who hath yearnings
For equal division of unequal earnings.

[Epigram, 1850]

GALLACHER, William (1881–1965)
We are for our own people. We want to see them happy, healthy and wise, drawing strength from cooperation with the peoples of other lands, but also contributing their full share to the general well-being. Not a broken-down pauper and mendicant, but a strong, living partner in the progressive advancement of civilization.

[*The Case for Communism* (1949)]

KHRUSHCHEV, Nikita (1894–1971)
[On the possibility that the Soviet Union might one day reject communism]
Those who wait for that must wait until a shrimp learns to whistle.

[Attr.]

LENIN, V.I. (1870–1924)
Communism is Soviet power plus the electrification of the whole country.

[Report at the Congress of Soviets, 1920]

MCCARTHY, Senator Joseph (1908–1957)
[Of someone alleged to have communist sympathies]
It makes me sick, sick, sick way down inside.

[In Lewis, *The Fifties* (1978)]

[On how to spot a communist]
It looks like a duck, walks like a duck, and quacks like a duck.

[Attr.]

MORLEY, Robert (1908–1992)
There's no such thing in Communist countries as a load of old cod's wallop, the cod's wallop is always fresh made.

[*Punch*, 1974]

ROGERS, Will (1879–1935)
Communism is like prohibition, it's a good idea but it won't work.

[Weekly Articles (1981)]

SMITH, F.E. (1872–1930)
[On Bolshevism]
Nature has no cure for this sort of madness, though I have known a legacy from a rich relative work wonders.

[*Law, Life and Letters* (1927)]

SOLZHENITSYN, Alexander (1918–)
For us in Russia, communism is a dead dog, while for many people in the West, it is still a living lion.

[*The Listener*, 1979]

SPARK, Muriel (1918–)
Every communist has a fascist frown, every fascist a communist smile.

[*The Girls of Slender Means*]

See CAPITALISM

COMPASSION

THE BIBLE (King James Version)
Blessed are the merciful: for they shall obtain mercy.

[*Matthew*, 5:7]

BLAKE, William (1757–1827)
Can I see another's woe,
And not be in sorrow too?
Can I see another's grief,
And not seek for kind relief?

['On Another's Sorrow' (1789)]

BRADFORD, John (c. 1510–1555)
[Remark on criminals going to the gallows]
But for the grace of God there goes John Bradford.

[Attr.]

COMPASSION

BURNS, Robert (1759–1796)
Then gently scan your brother man,
Still gentler sister woman;
Tho' they may gang a kennin wrang,
To step aside is human.

['Address to the Unco Guid' (1786)]

DESMOULINS, Camille (1760–1794)
*La clémence aussi est une mesure
révolutionnaire.*
Clemency is also a revolutionary
measure.

[Speech, 1793]

ELIOT, George (1819–1880)
We hand folks over to God's mercy,
and show none ourselves.

[*Adam Bede* (1859)]

GAY, John (1685–1732)
He best can pity who has felt the woe.

[*Dione* (1720)]

GIBBON, Edward (1737–1794)
Our sympathy is cold to the relation of
distant misery.

[*Decline and Fall of the Roman Empire* (1788)]

HOPKINS, Gerard Manley (1844–1889)
My own heart let me more have pity
on; let
Me live to my sad self hereafter
kind,
Charitable; not live this tormented
mind
With this tormented mind tormenting
yet.

['My own Heart let me more have Pity on'
(c. 1885)]

HUXLEY, Aldous (1894–1963)
She was a machine-gun riddling her
hostess with sympathy.

[*Mortal Coils* (1922)]

KINNOCK, Neil (1942–)
Compassion is not a sloppy, sentimental feeling for people who are
underprivileged or sick ... it is an
absolutely practical belief that, regardless of a person's background, ability
or ability to pay, he should be provided
with the best that society has to offer.

[Maiden speech, House of Commons, 1970]

LAZARUS, Emma (1849–1887)
Give me your tired, your poor,
Your huddled masses yearning to
breathe free.

['The New Colossus' (1883); verse inscribed
on the Statue of Liberty]

NIETZSCHE, Friedrich (1844-1900)
*Mitleiden äussern wird als ein Zeichen
der Verachtung empfunden, weil man
ersichtlich aufgehört hat, ein Gegen-
stand der Furcht zu sein, sobald einem
Mitleiden erwiesen wird.*
To show pity is felt to be a sign of
scorn, because one has obviously
stopped being an object of *fear* as
soon as one is pitied.

[*Human, All Too Human* (1886)]

SHAKESPEARE, William (1564–1616)
The quality of mercy is not strain'd;
It droppeth as the gentle rain from
heaven
Upon the place beneath. It is twice
blest:
It blesseth him that gives and him that
takes.

[*The Merchant of Venice*, IV.i]

SMOLLETT, Tobias (1721–1771)
Any man of humane sentiments ...
would have been prompted to offer his
services to the forlorn stranger: but ...
our hero was devoid of all these
infirmities of human nature.

[*The Adventures of Ferdinand Count Fathom*
(1753)]

WHITE, Patrick (1912–1990)
And remember Mother's practical
ethics: *one can drown in compassion if
one answers every call it's another way
of suicide.*

[*The Eye of the Storm* (1973)]

WILDE, Oscar (1854–1900)
Anybody can sympathise with the
sufferings of a friend, but it requires a
very fine nature to sympathise with a
friend's success.

['The Soul of Man under Socialism' (1881)]

CONSCIENCE

DE QUINCEY, Thomas (1785–1859)
Better to stand ten thousand sneers
than one abiding pang, such as time
could not abolish, of bitter self-
reproach.
[*Confessions of an English Opium Eater*
(1822)]

HOBBES, Thomas (1588–1679)
A man's conscience and his judgement is the same thing, and as the
judgement, so also the conscience,
may be erroneous.
[Attr.]

MENCKEN, H.L. (1880–1956)
Conscience is the inner voice that
warns us somebody may be looking.
[*A Mencken Chrestomathy* (1949)]

NASH, Ogden (1902–1971)
He who is ridden by a conscience
Worries about a lot of nonscience;
He without benefit of scruples
His fun and income soon quadruples.
['Reflection on the Fallibility of Nemesis'
(1940)]

SHAKESPEARE, William (1564–1616)
A peace above all earthly dignities,
A still and quiet conscience.
[*Henry VIII*, III.ii]

My conscience hath a thousand
several tongues,
And every tongue brings in a several
tale,
And every tale condemns me for a
villain.
[*Richard III*, V.iii]

Conscience is but a word that cowards
use,
Devis'd at first to keep the strong in
awe.
[*Richard III*, V.iii]

**SHERIDAN, Richard Brinsley
(1751–1816)**
Conscience has no more to do with
gallantry than it has with politics.
[*The Duenna* (1775)]

WASHINGTON, George (1732–1799)
Labour to keep alive in your breast
that little spark of celestial fire, called
conscience.
[*Rules of Civility and Decent Behaviour*]

CONTEMPT

**ALBERTANO OF BRESCIA
(c. 1190–c. 1270)**
Qui omnes despicit, omnibus displicet.
Who despises all, displeases all.
[*Liber Consolationis*]

ASHFORD, Daisy (1881–1972)
Ethel patted her hair and looked very
sneery.
[*The Young Visiters* (1919)]

AUSTEN, Jane (1775–1817)
She was nothing more than a mere
good-tempered, civil and obliging
young woman; as such we could
scarcely dislike her – she was only an
Object of Contempt.
[*Love and Freindship* (1791)]

BIERCE, Ambrose (1842–c. 1914)
Contempt: The feeling of a prudent
man for an enemy who is too
formidable safely to be opposed.
[*The Enlarged Devil's Dictionary* (1961)]

CAREW, Thomas (c. 1595–1640)
I was foretold, your rebell sex,
Nor love, nor pitty knew.
And with what scorne, you use to vex
Poore hearts, that humbly sue.
['A deposition from love']

**CHATEAUBRIAND, François-René
(1768–1848)**
One is not superior merely because
one sees the world in an odious light.
[Attr.]

CONGREVE, William (1670–1729)
A little disdain is not amiss; a little
scorn is alluring.
[*The Way of the World* (1700)]

PALEY, Rev. William (1743–1805)
Who can refute a sneer?
[*Principles of Moral and Political Philosophy* (1785)]

PROVERB
Familiarity breeds contempt.

ROOSEVELT, Theodore (1858–1919)
The poorest way to face life is to face it with a sneer.
[Attr.]

SHAW, George Bernard (1856–1950)
I have never sneered in my life. Sneering doesn't become either the human face or the human soul.
[*Pygmalion* (1916)]

CONVERSATION

ACHEBE, Chinua (1930–)
Among the Ibo the art of conversation is regarded very highly and proverbs are the palm-oil with which words are eaten.
[*Things Fall Apart* (1958)]

BRYAN, William Jennings (1860–1925)
An orator is a man who says what he thinks and feels what he says.
[Attr.]

CARLYLE, Thomas (1795–1881)
Speech is human, silence is divine, yet also brutish and dead: therefore we must learn both arts.
[Attr.]

CHURCHILL, Sir Winston (1874–1965)
[Of Lord Charles Beresford]
He is one of those orators of whom it was well said, 'Before they get up they do not know what they are going to say; when they are speaking, they do not know what they are saying; and when they sit down, they do not know what they have said.'
[Speech, House of Commons, 1912]

To jaw-jaw is better than to war-war.
[Speech, Washington, 1954]

CONFUCIUS (c. 550–c. 478 BC)
For one word a man is often deemed to be wise, and for one word he is often deemed to be foolish. We should be careful indeed what we say.
[*Analects*]

DISRAELI, Benjamin (1804–1881)
I grew intoxicated with my own eloquence.
[*Contarini Fleming* (1832)]

DRYDEN, John (1631–1700)
But far more numerous was the herd of such
Who think too little and who talk too much.
[*Absalom and Achitophel* (1681)]

ELIOT, George (1819–1880)
Half the sorrows of women would be averted if they could repress the speech they know to be useless; nay, the speech they have resolved not to make.
[*Felix Holt* (1866)]

EMERSON, Ralph Waldo (1803–1882)
Conversation is a game of circles. In conversation we pluck up the *termini* which bound the common of silence on every side.
[*Essays, First Series* (1841)]

HALIFAX, Lord (1633–1695)
Most Men make little other use of their Speech than to give evidence against their own Understanding.
['Of Folly and Fools' (1750)]

HOBBES, Thomas (1588–1679)
True and *false* are attributes of speech, not of things. And where speech is not, there is neither *truth* nor *false-hood*.
[*Leviathan* (1651)]

HOLMES, Oliver Wendell (1809–1894)
And, when you stick on conversation's burrs,
Don't strew your pathway with those dreadful urs.
['A Rhymed Lesson' (1848)]

LA BRUYERE, Jean de (1645–1696)
Il y a des gens qui parlent un moment avant que d'avoir pensé.
There are people who speak one moment before they think.

[*Les caractères ou les moeurs de ce siècle* (1688)]

MACAULAY, Lord (1800–1859)
The object of oratory alone is not truth, but persuasion.

['Essay on Athenian Orators' (1898)]

MEREDITH, George (1828–1909)
Speech is the small change of silence.

[*The Ordeal of Richard Feverel* (1859)]

O'BRIAN, Patrick
Question and answer is not a civilized form of conversation.

[*Clarissa Oakes* (1992)]

POST, Emily (1873–1960)
Ideal conversation must be an exchange of thought, and not, as many of those who worry most about their shortcomings believe, an eloquent exhibition of wit or oratory.

[*Etiquette* (1922)]

SENECA (c. 4 BC–AD 65)
Conversation has a kind of charm about it, an insinuating and insidious something that elicits secrets from us just like love or liquor.

[*Epistles*]

SHAKESPEARE, William (1564–1616)
He draweth out the thread of his verbosity finer than the staple of his argument.

[*Love's Labour Lost*, V.i]

TALLEYRAND, Charles-Maurice de (1754–1838)
La parole a été donnée à l'homme pour déguiser sa pensée.
Speech was given to man to disguise his thoughts.

[Attr.]

TANNEN, Deborah (1945–)
Each person's life is lived as a series

of conversations.

[*The Observer*, 1992]

WEST, Dame Rebecca (1892–1983)
There is no such thing as conversation. It is an illusion. There are intersecting monologues, that is all.

[*There is No Conversation* (1935)]

COOKERY

DAVID, Elizabeth (1913–1992)
Delicious meals can, as everybody knows, be cooked with the sole aid of a blackened frying-pan over a primus stove, a camp fire, a gas-ring, or even a methylated spirit lamp.

[*French Country Cooking* (1951)]

FERN, Fanny (1811–1872)
The way to a man's heart is through his stomach.

[*Willis Parton*]

HARNEY, Bill (1895–1962)
[Advice on bush cooking]
You always want to garnish it when it's orf.

['Talkabout', c.1960]

LEITH, Prue (1940–)
Cuisine is when things taste like what they are.

[Lecture, 'The Fine Art of Food', 1987]

MEREDITH, George (1828–1909)
Kissing don't last: cookery do!

[*The Ordeal of Richard Feverel* (1859)]

MEREDITH, Owen (1831–1891)
We may live without poetry, music and art;
We may live without conscience, and live without heart;
We may live without friends; we may live without books;
But civilized man cannot live without cooks.

['Lucile' (1860)]

POST, Emily (1873–1960)
To the old saying that man built the

house but woman made of it a 'home' might be added the modern supplement that woman accepted cooking as a chore but man has made of it a recreation.

[*Etiquette* (1922)]

SAKI (1870–1916)
The cook was a good cook, as cooks go; and as cooks go she went.

[*Reginald* (1904)]

SLATER, Nigel
Cooking is about not cheating yourself of pleasure.

[*Slice of Life*, BBC TV programme]

SMITH, Delia
I truly have tried and we had a microwave to heat things in the filming – but, actually, we mainly use it to keep the ashtrays in. I think it takes the soul out of food. Cooking is about ingredients being put together, and having time to amalgamate.

[Interview, *The Times*, 1990]

See FOOD

THE COUNTRY

BRODERICK, John (1927–)
The city dweller who passes through a country town, and imagines it sleepy and apathetic is very far from the truth: it is watchful as the jungle.

[*The Pilgrimage* (1961)]

CONGREVE, William (1670–1729)
I nauseate walking; 'tis a country diversion, I loathe the country.

[*The Way of the World* (1700)]

COWPER, William (1731–1800)
God made the country, and man made the town.

[*The Task* (1785)]

DOYLE, Sir Arthur Conan (1859–1930)
It is my belief, Watson, founded upon my experience, that the lowest and vilest alleys of London do not present

a more dreadful record of sin than does the smiling and beautiful countryside.

['Copper Beeches' (1892)]

HAZLITT, William (1778–1830)
There is nothing good to be had in the country, or, if there is, they will not let you have it.

[*The Round Table* (1817)]

KILVERT, Francis (1840–1879)
It is a fine thing to be out on the hills alone. A man could hardly be a beast or a fool alone on a great mountain.

[*Diary*, 1871]

SACKVILLE-WEST, Vita (1892–1962)
The country habit has me by the heart,
For he's bewitched for ever who has seen,
Not with his eyes but with his vision, Spring
Flow down the woods and stipple leaves with sun.

['Winter' (1926)]

SMITH, Sydney (1771–1845)
I have no relish for the country; it is a kind of healthy grave.

[Letter to Miss G. Harcourt, 1838]

WILDE, Oscar (1854–1900)
Anybody can be good in the country.

[*The Picture of Dorian Gray* (1891)]

See CITIES

COURAGE

ARISTOTLE (384–322 BC)
I count him braver who overcomes his desires than him who overcomes his enemies.

[In Stobaeus, *Florilegium*]

BARRIE, Sir J.M. (1860–1937)
Courage is the thing. All goes if courage goes.

[Address, St Andrews University, 1922]

COWARDICE

EARHART, Amelia (1898–1937)
Courage is the price that Life exacts
for granting peace.

['Courage' (1927)]

HEMINGWAY, Ernest (1898–1961)
[Definition of 'guts']
Grace under pressure.

[Attr.]

HOWARD, Michael (1922–)
The important thing when you are
going to do something brave is to
have someone on hand to witness it.

[The Observer, 1980]

**IBÁRRURI, Dolores ('La Pasionaria')
(1895–1989)**
Il vaut mieux mourir debout que vivre à
genoux!
It is better to die on your feet than to
live on your knees.

[Speech, Paris, 1936]

LEACOCK, Stephen (1869–1944)
It takes a good deal of physical courage to ride a horse. This, however, I
have. I get it at about forty cents a
flask, and take it as required.

[Literary Lapses (1910)]

NAPOLEON I (1769–1821)
Quant au courage moral, il avait trouvé
fort rare, disait-il, celui de deux heures
après minuit; c'est-à-dire le courage de
l'improviste.
As for moral courage, he said he had
very rarely encountered two o'clock in
the morning courage; that is, the courage of the unprepared.

[Mémorial de Sainte Hélène]

SHAKESPEARE, William (1564–1616)
Courage mounteth with occasion.

[King John, II.i]

**SHERIDAN, Richard Brinsley
(1751–1816)**
My valour is certainly going! – it is
sneaking off! – I feel it oozing out as it
were at the palms of my hands!

[The Rivals (1775)]

USTINOV, Sir Peter (1921–)
Courage is often lack of insight,
whereas cowardice in many cases is
based on good information.

[Attr.]

WALPOLE, Sir Hugh (1884–1941)
'Tisn't life that matters! 'Tis the
courage you bring to it.

[Fortitude (1913)]

COWARDICE

BRONTË, Emily (1818–1848)
No coward soul is mine,
No trembler in the world's storm-
troubled sphere:
I see Heaven's glories shine,
And faith shines equal, arming me
from fear.

['Last Lines' (1846)]

CARROLL, Lewis (1832–1898)
'I'm very brave generally,' he went on
in a low voice: 'only to-day I happen
to have a headache.'

[Through the Looking-Glass (1872)]

ELIZABETH I (1533–1603)
If thy heart fails thee, climb not at all.

[In Fuller, The History of the Worthies of
England (1662)]

GRANVILLE, George (1666–1735)
Cowards in scarlet pass for men of
war.

[The She Gallants (1696)]

HOUSMAN, A.E. (1859–1936)
The man that runs away
Lives to die another day.

[A Shropshire Lad (1896)]

JOHNSON, Samuel (1709–1784)
It is thus that mutual cowardice keeps
us in peace. Were one half of mankind
brave and one half cowards, the brave
would be always beating the cowards.
Were all brave, they would lead a very
uneasy life; all would be continually
fighting; but being all cowards, we go
on very well.

[In Boswell, The Life of Samuel Johnson
(1791)]

JOHNSTON, Brian (1912–1994)
[When asked by his commanding officer what steps he would take if he came across a German battalion]
Long ones, backwards.

[Quoted in his obituary, *Sunday Times*]

ROCHESTER, Earl of (1647–1680)
All men would be cowards if they durst.

['A Satire Against Reason and Mankind' (1679)]

SHAKESPEARE, William (1564–1616)
Instinct is a great matter: I was now a coward on instinct.

[*Henry IV, Part 1*, II.iv]

SHAW, George Bernard (1856–1950)
As an old soldier I admit the cowardice: it's as universal as sea sickness, and matters just as little.

[*Man and Superman* (1903)]

VOLTAIRE (1694–1778)
Marriage is the only adventure open to the cowardly.

[Attr.]

CRIME

ADLER, Freda (1934–)
[On rape]
Perhaps it is the only crime in which the victim becomes the accused and, in reality, it is she who must prove her good reputation, her mental soundness, and her impeccable propriety.

[*Sisters in Crime* (1975)]

ALLEN, Fred (1894–1956)
He's a good boy; everything he steals he brings right home to his mother.

[Attr.]

ANONYMOUS
The fault is great in man or woman
Who steals a goose from off a
   common;
But what can plead that man's excuse
Who steals a common from a goose?

[*The Tickler Magazine*, 1821]

BACON, Francis (1561–16?
Opportunity makes a thief.

[Letter t

THE BIBLE (King James Version)
Whoso sheddeth man's blood, by man shall his blood be shed.

[*Genesis*, 9:6]

BOCCA, Giorgio (1920–)
La mafia è razionale, vuole ridurre al minimo gli omicidi.
The mafia is rational, it wants to reduce homicides to the minimum.

[*Hell* (1992)]

BRECHT, Bertolt (1898–1956)
Was ist ein Einbruch in eine Bank gegen die Gründung einer Bank?
What is robbing a bank compared with founding a bank?

[*The Threepenny Opera* (1928)]

BULWER-LYTTON, Edward (1803–1873)
In other countries poverty is a misfortune – with us it is a crime.

[*England and the English* (1833)]

CAPONE, Al (1899–1947)
I've been accused of every death except the casualty list of the World War.

[In Allsop, *The Bootleggers* (1961)]

CHAUCER, Geoffrey (c. 1340–1400)
Mordre wol out, that se we day by day.

[*The Canterbury Tales* (1387)]

CHESTERTON, G.K. (1874–1936)
Thieves respect property; they merely wish the property to become their property that they may more perfectly respect it.

[Attr.]

CONGREVE, William (1670–1729)
He that first cries out stop thief, is often he that has stolen the treasure.

[*Love for Love* (1695)]

DE QUINCEY, Thomas (1785–1859)
If a man once indulges himself in

murder, very soon he comes to think little of robbing; and from robbing he comes next to drinking and sabbath-breaking, and from that to incivility and procrastination.

['Murder Considered as One of the Fine Arts' (1839)]

DOYLE, Sir Arthur Conan (1859–1930)
Singularity is almost invariably a clue. The more featureless and common-place a crime is, the more difficult it is to bring it home.

['The Boscombe Valley Mystery' (1892)]

FARBER, Barry
Crime expands according to our willingness to put up with it.

[Attr.]

FRY, Elizabeth (1780–1845)
Punishment is not for revenge, but to lessen crime and reform the criminal.

[Journal entry]

GOLDMAN, Emma (1869–1940)
Crime is naught but misdirected energy.

[Anarchism, 1910)]

GREENE, Graham (1904– 1991)
Catholics and Communists have committed great crimes, but at least they have not stood aside, like an established society, and been indif-ferent. I would rather have blood on my hands than water like Pilate.

[The Comedians (1966)]

HANCOCK, Sir William (1898–1988)
Were it possible to compel the prison warders of this past age to produce for our inspection a 'typical' transported convict, they would show us, not the countryman who snared rabbits, but the Londoner who stole spoons.

[Australia (1930)]

HAWTHORNE, Nathaniel (1804–1864)
By the sympathy of your human hearts for sin ye shall scent out all the places – whether in church, bedchamber,

street, field or forest – where crime has been committed, and shall exult to behold the whole earth one stain of guilt, one mighty blood spot.

[Young Goodman Brown (1835)]

HENRY, O. (1862–1910)
A burglar who respects his art always takes his time before taking anything else.

[Makes the Whole World Kin]

LA BRUYERE, Jean de (1645–1696)
Si la pauvreté est la mère des crimes, le défaut d'esprit en est le père.
If poverty is the mother of crime, lack of intelligence is its father.

[Les caractères ou les moeurs de ce siècle (1688)]

LEWES, G.H. (1817–1878)
Murder, like talent, seems occasionally to run in families.

[The Physiology of Common Life (1859)]

LIGHTNER, Candy (1946–)
Death by drunken driving is a socially acceptable form of homicide.

[San José Mercury, 1981]

MEIR, Golda (1898–1978)
[Replying to a member of her Cabinet who proposed a curfew on women after dark in response to a recent outbreak of assaults on women]
But it's the men who are attacking the women. If there's to be a curfew, let the men stay at home, not the women.

[Attr.]

RACINE, Jean (1639–1699)
Ainsi que la vertu, le crime a ses degrés.
Crime has its degrees, as virtue does.

[Phèdre (1677)]

RAINS, Claude (1889–1967)
Major Strasser has been shot. Round up the usual suspects.

[Casablanca, film, 1942; scriptwriters Epstein, Epstein and Koch]

ROOSEVELT, Theodore (1858–1919)
[Dismissing a cowboy who had put

Roosevelt's brand on a steer belonging to a neighbouring ranch]
A man who will steal for me will steal from me.

[In Hagedorn, *Roosevelt in the Bad Lands* (1921)]

ROSS, Nick (1947–)
We're barking mad about crime in this country. We have an obsession with believing the worst, conning ourselves that there was a golden age – typically forty years before the one we're living in.

[*Radio Times*, 1993]

ROSTAND, Jean (1894–1977)
Tue un homme, on est un assassin. On tue des millions d'hommes, on est conquérant. On les tue tous, on est un dieu.
Kill one man, and you are a murderer. Kill millions of men, and you are a conqueror. Kill them all, and you are a god.

[*Thoughts of a Biologist* (1939)]

SHAKESPEARE, William (1564–1616)
[Of stealing]
Why, Hal, 'tis my vocation, Hal; 'tis no sin for a man to labour in his vocation.

[*Henry IV, Part 1*, I.ii]

The robb'd that smiles steals something from the thief.

[*Othello*, I.iii]

SPENCER, Herbert (1820–1903)
A clever theft was praiseworthy amongst the Spartans; and it is equally so amongst Christians, provided it be on a sufficiently large scale.

[*Social Statics* (1850)]

See PUNISHMENT

CRITICISM

ARNOLD, Matthew (1822–1888)
I am bound by my own definition of criticism: a disinterested endeavour to learn and propagate the best that is known and thought in the world.

[*Essays in Criticism* (1865)]

ATWOOD, Margaret (1939–)
Once upon a time I thought there was an old man with a grey beard somewhere who knew the truth, and if I was good enough, naturally he would tell me that this was it. That person doesn't exist, but that's who I write for. The great critic in the sky.

[In Ingersoll, *Margaret Atwood: Conversations* (1990)]

AUDEN, W.H. (1907–1973)
One cannot review a bad book without showing off.

[*The Dyer's Hand and Other Essays* (1963)]

BROWNE, Sir Thomas (1605–1682)
He who discommendeth others obliquely commendeth himself.

[*Christian Morals* (1716)]

BULLET, Gerald (1893–1958)
So, when a new book comes his way,
By someone still alive to-day,
Our Honest John, with right good will,
Sharpens his pencil for the kill.

['A Reviewer']

BURGESS, Anthony (1917–1993)
I know how foolish critics can be, being one myself.

[*The Observer*, 1980]

BUTLER, Samuel (1835–1902)
Talking it over, we agreed that Blake was no good because he learnt Italian at over 60 to study Dante, and we knew Dante was no good because he was so fond of Virgil, and Virgil was no good because Tennyson ran him, and as for Tennyson – well, Tennyson goes without saying.

[*The Note-Books of Samuel Butler* (1912)]

BYRON, Lord (1788–1824)
A man must serve his time to every trade
Save censure – critics all are ready

made.
Take hackney'd jokes from Miller, got
by rote,
With just enough of learning to
misquote.
[*English Bards and Scotch Reviewers* (1809)]

CHURCHILL, Charles (1731–1764)
Though by whim, envy, or resentment
led,
They damn those authors whom they
never read.
[*The Candidate* (1764)]

CHURCHILL, Sir Winston (1874–1965)
I do not resent criticism, even when,
for the sake of emphasis, it parts for
the time with reality.
[Speech, 1941]

**COLERIDGE, Samuel Taylor
(1772–1834)**
Reviewers are usually people who
would have been poets, historians,
biographers, etc., if they could; they
have tried their talents at one or at the
other, and have failed; therefore they
turn critics.
[*Seven Lectures on Shakespeare and Milton*
(1856)]

CONRAN, Shirley (1932–)
[On Julie Burchill]
I cannot take seriously the criticism of
someone who doesn't know how to
use a semicolon.
[Attr.]

DISRAELI, Benjamin (1804–1881)
This shows how much easier it is to
be critical than to be correct.
[Speech, 1860]

Cosmopolitan critics, men who are the
friends of every country save their
own.
[Speech, 1877]

DONATUS, Aelius (fl. 4th century AD)
[Donatus was a commentator on
texts]
*Pereant, inquit, qui ante nos nostra
dixerunt.*
Confound those who have made our

comments before us.
[In St Jerome, *Commentaries on Ecclesiastes*]

ELIOT, T.S. (1888–1965)
The critic, one would suppose, if he is
to justify his existence, should endeavour to discipline his personal
prejudices and cranks – tares to which
we are all subject – and compose his
differences with as many of his fellows
as possible, in the common pursuit of
true judgement.
['The Function of Criticism' (1923)]

FRANCE, Anatole (1844–1924)
*Le bon critique est celui qui raconte les
aventures de son âme au milieu des
chefs-d'oeuvre.*
A good critic is one who tells of his
own soul's adventures among masterpieces.
[*La Vie Littéraire* (1888)]

FRY, Christopher (1907–)
I sometimes think
His critical judgement is so exquisite
It leaves us nothing to admire except
his opinion.
[*The Dark is Light Enough* (1954)]

HAMPTON, Christopher (1946–)
Asking a working writer what he
thinks about critics is like asking a
lamp-post how it feels about dogs.
[*The Sunday Times Magazine*, 1977]

HUXLEY, Aldous (1894–1963)
Parodies and caricatures are the most
penetrating of criticisms.
[*Point Counter Point* (1928)]

JOHNSON, Samuel (1709–1784)
There are two things which I am
confident I can do very well: one is an
introduction to any literary work,
stating what it is to contain, and how
it should be executed in the most
perfect manner; the other is a
conclusion, shewing from various
causes why the execution has not
been equal to what the author
promised himself and to the public.
[In Boswell, *The Life of Samuel Johnson*
(1791)]

CRITICISM

[Of literary criticism]
You *may* abuse a tragedy, though you cannot write one, You may scold a carpenter who has made you a bad table, though you cannot make a table. It is not your trade to make tables.

[In Boswell, *The Life of Samuel Johnson* (1791)]

The man who is asked by an author what he thinks of his work, is put to the torture, and is not obliged to speak the truth.

[In Boswell, *The Life of Samuel Johnson* (1791)]

LA BRUYERE, Jean de (1645–1696)
Le plaisir de la critique nous ôte celui d'être vivement touchés de très belles choses.
The pleasure of criticizing takes away from us the pleasure of being moved by some very fine things.

[*Les caractères ou les moeurs de ce siècle* (1688)]

LEAVIS, F.R. (1895–1978)
Literary criticism provides the test for life and concreteness; where it degenerates, the instruments of thought degenerate too, and thinking, released from the testing and energizing contact with the full living consciousness, is debilitated, and betrayed to the academic, the abstract and the verbal.

[*Towards Standards in Criticism* (1930)]

MARX, Groucho (1895–1977)
I was so long writing my review that I never got around to reading the book.

[Attr.]

MAUGHAM, William Somerset (1874–1965)
People ask you for criticism, but they only want praise.

[*Of Human Bondage* (1915)]

MOORE, George (1852–1933)
The lot of critics is to be remembered by what they failed to understand.

[*Impressions and Opinions* (1891)]

ORWELL, George (1903–1950)
Prolonged, indiscriminate reviewing of books ... not only involves praising trash ... but constantly *inventing* reactions towards books about which one has no spontaneous feelings whatever.

[*Shooting an Elephant* (1950)]

PARKER, Dorothy (1893–1967)
This is not a novel to be tossed aside lightly. It should be thrown with great force.

[In Gaines, *Wit's End*]

POPE, Alexander (1688–1744)
Nor in the Critic let the Man be lost.
Good-nature and good-sense must
   ever join;
To err is human, to forgive, divine.

[*An Essay on Criticism* (1711)]

PORSON, Richard (1759–1808)
[Giving his opinion of Southey's poems]
Your works will be read after Shakespeare and Milton are forgotten – and not till then.

[In Meissen, *Quotable Anecdotes*]

QUILLER-COUCH, Sir Arthur ('Q') (1863–1944)
The best is the best, though a hundred judges have declared it so.

[*Oxford Book of English Verse* (1900)]

REGER, Max (1873–1916)
[Letter written to Rudolf Louis in response to his criticism of Reger's Sinfonietta, 1906]
Ich sitze in dem kleinsten Zimmer in meinem Hause. Ich habe Ihre Kritik vor mir. Im nächsten Augenblick wird sie hinter mir sein.
I am sitting in the smallest room in my house. I have your review in front of me. In a moment it will be behind me.

[In Slonimsky, *The Lexicon of Musical Invective*]

SHAW, George Bernard (1856–1950)
You don't expect me to know what to say about a play when I don't know who the author is, do you? ... If it's by

a good author, it's a good play,
naturally. That stands to reason.

[Fanny's First Play (1911)]

SIBELIUS, Jean (1865–1957)
Pay no attention to what the critics
say. No statue has ever been put up to
a critic.

[Attr.]

SMITH, Sydney (1771–1845)
I never read a book before reviewing
it; it prejudices a man so.

[In Pearson, *The Smith of Smiths* (1934)]

SONTAG, Susan (1933–)
Interpretation is the revenge of the
intellect upon art.

[Evergreen Review, 1964]

STEINBECK, John (1902–1968)
[On critics]
Unless the bastards have the courage
to give you unqualified praise, I say
ignore them.

[In J.K. Galbraith, *A Life in Our Times* (1981)]

SWIFT, Jonathan (1667–1745)
So, naturalists observe, a flea
Hath smaller fleas that on him prey;
And these have smaller fleas to bite
'em,
And so proceed ad infinitum.
Thus every poet, in his kind,
Is bit by him that comes behind.

['On Poetry' (1733)]

TYNAN, Kenneth (1927–1980)
A good drama critic is one who
perceives what is happening in the
theatre of his time. A great drama
critic also perceives what is not
happening.

[Tynan Right and Left (1967)]

A critic is a man who knows the way
but can't drive the car.

[The New York Times Magazine, 1966]

VOLTAIRE (1694–1778)
[Reviewing Rousseau's poem 'Ode to
Posterity']

I do not think this poem will reach its
destination.

[Attr.]

VORSTER, John (1915–1983)
As far as criticism is concerned, we
don't resent that unless it is absolutely
biased, as it is in most cases.

[The Observer, 1969]

WILDE, Oscar (1854–1900)
The man who sees both sides of a
question is a man who sees absolutely
nothing at all.

['The Critic as Artist' (1891)]

[On a notice at a dancing saloon]
I saw the only rational method of art
criticism I have ever come across ...
'Please do not shoot the pianist. He is
doing his best.'

['Impressions of America' (1906)]

CRUELTY

BLAKE, William (1757–1827)
Cruelty has a Human Heart
And Jealousy a Human Face,
Terror the Human Form Divine,
And Secrecy the Human Dress.

['A Divine Image' (c. 1832)]

CALIGULA (12–41)
Ita feri ut se mori sentiat.
Strike him so that he may feel that he
is dying.

[In Suetonius, *Lives of the Caesars*]

COWPER, William (1731–1800)
I would not enter on my list of friends
(Tho' grac'd with polish'd manners
and fine sense,
Yet wanting sensibility) the man
Who needlessly sets foot upon a
worm.

[The Task (1785)]

FROUDE, James Anthony (1818–1894)
Fear is the parent of cruelty.

[Short Studies on Great Subjects (1877)]

GIDE, André (1869–1951)
La cruauté, c'est le premier des attributs

de Dieu.
Cruelty is the first of God's attributes.
[*The Counterfeiters*]

SHELLEY, Percy Bysshe (1792–1822)
Cruel he looks, but calm and strong,
Like one who does, not suffers wrong.
[*Prometheus Unbound* (1820)]

TROTSKY, Leon (1879–1940)
In a serious struggle there is no worse
cruelty than to be magnanimous at an
inappropriate time.
[*The History of the Russian Revolution* (1933)]

CRYING

BYRON, Lord (1788–1824)
Oh! too convincing – dangerously
    dear –
In woman's eye the unanswerable
    tear!
[*The Corsair* (1814)]

CRASHAW, Richard (c. 1612–1649)
Two walking baths; two weeping
    motions;
Portable, and compendious oceans.
['Saint Mary Magdalene, or The Weeper'
(1652)]

CRISP, Quentin (1908–)
Tears were to me what glass beads
are to African traders.
[*The Naked Civil Servant* (1968)]

CROMPTON, Richmal (1890–1969)
Violet Elizabeth dried her tears. She
saw that they were useless and she
did not believe in wasting her effects.
'All right,' she said calmly, 'I'll thcream
then. I'll thcream, an' thcream, an'
thcream till I'm thick.'
[*Still William* (1925)]

DICKENS, Charles (1812–1870)
We need never be ashamed of our
tears.
[*Great Expectations* (1861)]

'It opens the lungs, washes the
countenance, exercises the eyes, and
softens down the temper', said Mr

Bumble. 'So cry away.'
[*Oliver Twist* (1838)]

FLETCHER, Phineas (1582–1650)
Drop, drop, slow tears,
And bathe those beauteous feet,
Which brought from Heav'n
The news and Prince of Peace.
[*Poetical Miscellanies* (1633)]

LIBERACE (1919–1987)
[Remark made after hostile criticism]
I cried all the way to the bank.
[*Autobiography* (1973)]

RHYS, Jean (1894–1979)
I often want to cry. That is the only
advantage women have over men – at
least they can cry.
[*Good Morning, Midnight* (1939)]

**SAINT-EXUPERY, Antoine de
(1900–1944)**
*C'est tellement mystérieux, le pays des
larmes.*
It is such a mysterious place, the land
of tears.
[*The Little Prince* (1943)]

SHAKESPEARE, William (1564–1616)
You think I'll weep.
No, I'll not weep.
I have full cause of weeping; but this
    heart
Shall break into a hundred thousand
    flaws
Or ere I'll weep.
[*King Lear*, II.iv]

WEST, Dame Rebecca (1892–1983)
But there are other things than
dissipation that thicken the features.
Tears, for example.
[*Black Lamb and Grey Falcon* (1942)]

CULTURE

ARNOLD, Matthew (1822–1888)
Culture being a pursuit of our total
perfection by means of getting to
know, on all the matters which most
concern us, the best which has been
thought and said in the world.
[*Culture and Anarchy* (1869)]

Culture, the acquainting ourselves with the best that has been known and said in the world, and thus the history of the human spirit.

[*Literature and Dogma*]

BANDA, Dr Hastings (1905–)
I wish I could bring Stonehenge to Nyasaland to show there was a time when Britain had a savage culture.

[*The Observer*, 1963]

BELLOW, Saul (1915–)
If culture means anything, it means knowing what value to set upon human life; it's not somebody with a mortarboard reading Greek. I know a lot of facts, history. That's not culture. Culture is the openness of the individual psyche ... to the news of being.

[*The Glasgow Herald*, 1985]

We are in the position of savage men who have been educated into believing there are no mysteries.

[*The Independent*, 1990]

CARLYLE, Thomas (1795–1881)
The great law of culture is: let each become all that he was created capable of being.

['Jean Paul Friedrich Richter' (1839)]

DARWIN, Charles (1809–1882)
The highest possible stage in moral culture is when we recognize that we ought to control our thoughts.

[*The Descent of Man* (1871)]

FRYE, Northrop (1912–1991)
Creative culture is infinitely porous – it absorbs influences from all over the world.

[*Maclean's*, 1991]

GOERING, Hermann (1893–1946)
When I hear anyone talk of Culture, I reach for my revolver.

[Attr.]

HELPMAN, Sir Robert Murray (1909–1986)
I don't despair about the cultural scene in Australia because there isn't

one here to despair about.

[In Dunstan, *Knockers* (1972)]

KENNY, Mary (1944–)
Decadent cultures usually fall in the end, and robust cultures rise to replace them. Our own cultural supermarket may eventually be subject to a takeover bid: the most likely challenger being, surely, Islam.

[*Sunday Telegraph*, 1993]

KOESTLER, Arthur (1905–1983)
Two half-truths do not make a truth, and two half-cultures do not make a culture.

[*The Ghost in the Machine* (1961)]

MCLUHAN, Marshall (1911–1980)
In a culture like ours, long accustomed to splitting and dividing all things as a means of control, it is sometimes a bit of a shock to be reminded that, in operational and practical fact, the medium is the message.

[*Understanding Media* (1964)]

MANTEL, Hilary (1953–)
[On travel]
I saw the world as some sort of exchange scheme for my ideals, but the world deserves better than this. When you come across an alien culture you must not automatically respect it. You must sometimes pay it the compliment of hating it.

['Last Months in Al Hamra' (1987)]

MENAND, Louis
Culture isn't something that comes with one's race or sex. It comes only through experience; there isn't any other way to acquire it. And in the end everyone's culture is different, because everyone's experience is different.

[*The New Yorker*, 1992]

MUSSOLINI, Benito (1883–1945)
In un uomo di stato, la cosidetta 'cultura' è in fin dei conti un lusso inutile.
In a statesman so-called 'culture' is,

after all, a useless luxury.

[*Il Populo d'Italia*, 1919]

WALLACE, Edgar (1875–1932)
What is a highbrow? He is a man who has found something more interesting than women.

[*New York Times*, 1932]

WEIL, Simone (1909–1943)
La culture est un instrument manié par des professeurs pour fabriquer des professeurs qui à leur tour fabriqueront des professeurs.
Culture is an instrument wielded by teachers to manufacture teachers, who, in their turn, will manufacture teachers.

[*The Need for Roots* (1949)]

WHARTON, Edith (1862–1937)
Mrs Ballinger is one of the ladies who pursue Culture in bands, as though it were dangerous to meet it alone.

[*Xingu and Other Stories* (1916)]

CURIOSITY

BACON, Francis (1561–1626)
They are ill discoverers that think there is no land, when they can see nothing but sea.

[*The Advancement of Learning* (1605)]

BAX, Sir Arnold (1883–1953)
One should try everything once, except incest and folk-dancing.

[Farewell my Youth (1943)]

THE BIBLE (King James Version)
Be not curious in unnecessary matters: for more things are shewed unto thee than men understand.

[Apocrypha, *Ecclesiasticus*, 3:23]

CARROLL, Lewis (1832–1898)
'If everybody minded their own business,' said the Duchess in a hoarse growl, 'the world would go round a deal faster than it does.'

[*Alice's Adventures in Wonderland* (1865)]

JOHNSON, Samuel (1709–1784)
A generous and elevated mind is distinguished by nothing more certainly than an eminent degree of curiosity.

[In Boswell, *The Life of Samuel Johnson* (1791)]

LAMB, Charles (1775–1834)
Not many sounds in life, and I include all urban and all rural sounds, exceed in interest a knock at the door.

['Valentine's Day' (1823)]

MORITA, Akio
Curiosity is the key to creativity.

[*Made in Japan* (1986)]

PERELMAN, S.J. (1904–1979)
[Giving his reasons for refusing to see a priest as he lay dying]
I am curious to see what happens in the next world to one who dies unshriven.

[Attr.]

CUSTOM

BAILLIE, Joanna (1762–1851)
What custom hath endear'd
We part with sadly, though we prize it not.

[*Basil* (1798)]

BECKETT, Samuel (1906–1989)
The air is full of our cries. But habit is a great deadener.

[*Waiting for Godot* (1955)]

BURKE, Edmund (1729–1797)
Custom reconciles us to everything.

[*A Philosophical Enquiry into the Origin of our Ideas of the Sublime and Beautiful* (1757)]

CRABBE, George (1754–1832)
Habit with him was all the test of truth,
'It must be right: I've done it from my youth.'

[*The Borough* (1810)]

HUME, David (1711–1776)
Custom, then, is the great guide of human life.

[*Philosophical Essays Concerning Human Understanding* (1748)]

CYNICISM

JAMES, William (1842–1910)
Habit is the enormous fly-wheel of
society, its most precious conservative
agent.

[*Principles of Psychology* (1890)]

MORE, Hannah (1745–1833)
Small habits, well pursued betimes,
May reach the dignity of crimes.

[*Florio* (1786)]

PEGUY, Charles (1873–1914)
*La mémoire et l'habitude sont les
fourriers de la mort.*
Memory and habit are the harbingers
of death.

[*Note conjointe sur M. Descartes*]

SHAKESPEARE, William (1564–1616)
Age cannot wither her, nor custom
    stale
Her infinite variety. Other women cloy
The appetites they feed, but she makes
    hungry
Where most she satisfies.

[*Antony and Cleopatra*, II.ii]

Custom calls me to't.
What custom wills, in all things should
    we do't.

[*Coriolanus*, II.iii]

It is a custom
More honour'd in the breach than the
    observance.

[*Hamlet*, I.iv]

How use doth breed a habit in a man!
[*The Two Gentlemen of Verona*, V.iv]

WORDSWORTH, William (1770–1850)
Not choice
But habit rules the unreflecting herd.

['Grant that by this unsparing hurricane'
(1822)]

CYNICISM

BIERCE, Ambrose (1842–c. 1914)
Cynic: A blackguard whose faulty
vision sees things as they are, not as
they ought to be.

[*The Enlarged Devil's Dictionary* (1961)]

CHEKHOV, Anton (1860–1904)
After all, the cynicism of real life can't
be outdone by any literature: one glass
won't get someone drunk when he's
already had a whole barrel.

[Letter to M.V. Kiseleva, 1887]

COZZENS, James Gould (1903–1978)
A cynic is just a man who found out
when he was about ten that there
wasn't any Santa Claus, and he's still
upset.

[Attr.]

HARRIS, Sydney J. (1917–)
A cynic is not merely one who reads
bitter lessons from the past, he is one
who is prematurely disappointed in
the future.

[*On the Contrary* (1962)]

HELLMAN, Lillian (1905–1984)
Cynicism is an unpleasant way of
saying the truth.

[*The Little Foxes* (1939)]

HURST, Fannie (1889–1968)
It takes a clever man to turn cynic,
and a wise man to be clever enough
not to.

[Attr.]

MEREDITH, George (1828–1909)
Cynicism is intellectual dandyism.

[*The Egoist* (1879)]

WILDE, Oscar (1854–1900)
Cecil Graham: What is a cynic?
Lord Darlington: A man who knows
the price of everything and the value
of nothing.

[*Lady Windermere's Fan* (1892)]

79

3

DANCING

AUSTEN, Jane (1775–1817)
Fine dancing, I believe, like virtue, must be its own reward.

[*Emma* (1816)]

BANKHEAD, Tallulah (1903–1968)
[Said on dropping fifty dollars into a tambourine held out by a Salvation Army collector]
Don't bother to thank me. I know what a perfectly ghastly season it's been for you Spanish dancers.

[Attr.]

BURNEY, Fanny (1752–1840)
Dancing? Oh, dreadful! How it was ever adopted in a civilized country I cannot find out; 'tis certainly a Barbarian exercise, and of savage origin.

[*Cecilia* (1782)]

BURNS, Robert (1759–1796)
But the ae best dance ere cam to the land
Was The Deil's Awa wi' th' Exciseman!

['The Deil's Awa wi' th' Exciseman' (1792)]

CHESTERFIELD, Lord (1694–1773)
Custom has made dancing sometimes necessary for a young man; therefore mind it while you learn it, that you may learn to do it well, and not be ridiculous, though in a ridiculous act.

[Letter to his son, 1746]

CICERO (106–43 BC)
Nemo enim fere saltat sobrius, nisi forte insanit.
No sober man dances, unless he happens to be mad.

[*Pro Murena*]

DUNCAN, Isadora (1878–1927)
I have discovered the dance. I have discovered the art which has been lost for two thousand years.

[*My Life* (1927)]

SALLUST (86–c. 34 BC)
Psallere et saltare elegantius, quam necesse est probae.

To play the lyre and dance more beautifully than a virtuous woman need.

[*Catiline*]

SHAKESPEARE, William (1564–1616)
You and I are past our dancing days.

[*Romeo and Juliet*, I.v]

When you do dance, I wish you
A wave o' th' sea, that you might ever do
Nothing but that; move still, still so,
And own no other function.

[*The Winter's Tale*, IV.iv]

SURTEES, R.S. (1805–1864)
These sort of boobies think that people come to balls to do nothing but dance; whereas everyone knows that the real business of a ball is either to look out for a wife, to look after a wife, or to look after somebody else's wife.

[*Mr Facey Romford's Hounds* (1865)]

YEATS, W.B. (1865–1939)
All men are dancers and their tread
Goes to the barbarous clangour of a gong.

['Nineteen Hundred and Nineteen' (1921)]

O chestnut-tree, great-rooted blossomer,
Are you the leaf, the blossom or the bole?
O body swayed to music, O brightening glance,
How can we know the dancer from the dance?

['Among School Children' (1927)]

DANGER

BURKE, Edmund (1729–1797)
Dangers by being despised grow great.

[Speech on the Petition of the Unitarians, 1792]

CHAPMAN, George (c. 1559–c. 1634)
Danger (the spurre of all great mindes) is ever
The curbe to your tame spirits.

[*Revenge of Bussy D'Ambois* (1613)]

CORNEILLE, Pierre (1606–1684)
A vaincre sans péril, on triomphe sans gloire.
When we conquer without danger our triumph is without glory.

[*Le Cid* (1637)]

CURNOW, Allen (1911–)
Always to islanders danger
Is what comes over the sea.

[*Collected Poems 1933–1973* (1974)]

EARHART, Amelia (1898–1937)
[Of her flight in the 'Friendship']
Of course I realized there was a measure of danger. Obviously I faced the possibility of not returning when first I considered going. Once faced and settled there really wasn't any good reason to refer to it.

[*20 Hours: 40 Minutes – Our Flight in the Friendship* (1928)]

EMERSON, Ralph Waldo (1803–1882)
In skating over thin ice, our safety is in our speed.

['Prudence' (1841)]

As soon as there is life there is danger.

[*Society and Solitude* (1870)]

GAY, John (1685–1732)
How, like a moth, the simple maid,
Still plays about the flame!

[*The Beggar's Opera* (1728)]

MACCARTHY, Cormac
There are dragons in the wings of the world.

[*The Guardian*, 1995]

SALINGER, J.D. (1919–)
What I have to do, I have to catch everybody if they start to go over the cliff – I mean if they're running and they don't look where they're going I have to come out from somewhere and *catch* them ... I'd just be the catcher in the rye and all.

[*The Catcher in the Rye* (1951)]

SHAKESPEARE, William (1564–1616)
Out of this nettle, danger, we pluck this flower, safety.

[*Henry IV, Part 1*, II.iii]

STEVENSON, Robert Louis (1850–1894)
The bright face of danger.

['The Lantern-Bearers' (1892)]

DEATH

AUBER, Daniel (1782–1871)
[Remark made at a funeral]
This is the last time I will take part as an amateur.

[Attr.]

BACON, Francis (1561–1626)
Men fear death as children fear to go in the dark; and as that natural fear in children is increased with tales, so is the other.

['Of Death' (1625)]

I have often thought upon death, and I find it the least of all evils.

[*The Remaines of ... Lord Verulam* (1648)]

BHAGAVADGITA
I am become death, the destroyer of worlds.

[Quoted by J. Robert Oppenheimer on seeing the first nuclear explosion]

BION (fl. 280 BC)
Though boys throw stones at frogs in sport, the frogs do not die in sport, but in earnest.

[Quoted by Plutarch]

BOWRA, Sir Maurice (1898–1971)
Any amusing deaths lately?

[Attr.]

BRIDGES, Robert (1844–1930)
When Death to either shall come, –
I pray it be first to me.

['When Death to Either Shall Come']

BROWNE, Sir Thomas (1605–1682)
I am not so much afraid of death, as ashamed thereof; 'tis the very disgrace

81

and ignominy of our natures, that in a moment can so disfigure us that our nearest friends, wife, and children, stand afraid and start at us.

[*Religio Medici* (1643)]

BUCK, Pearl S. (1892–1973)
Euthanasia is a long, smooth-sounding word, and it conceals its danger as long, smooth words do, but the danger is there, nevertheless.

[*The Child Who Never Grew* (1950)]

BUTLER, Samuel (1835–1902)
When you have told anyone you have left him a legacy the only decent thing to do is to die at once.

[In Festing Jones, *Samuel Butler: A Memoir*]

DIBDIN, Charles (1745–1814)
What argufies pride and ambition?
Soon or late death will take us in tow:
Each bullet has got its commission,
And when our time's come we must go.

['Each Bullet has its Commission']

DICKINSON, Emily (1830–1886)
Because I could not stop for Death –
He kindly stopped for me –
The Carriage held but just Ourselves –
And Immortality.

['Because I could not stop for Death' (c.1863)]

DUNBAR, William (c. 1460–c. 1525)
I that in heill wes and gladnes
Am trublit now with gret seiknes
And feblit with infirmitie:
Timor mortis conturbat me...

Our plesance here is all vain glory,
This fals world is but transitory,
The flesh is bruckle, the Feynd is slee:
Timor mortis conturbat me...

Unto the deid gois all Estatis,
Princis, prelatis, and potestatis,
Baith rich and poor of all degree:
Timor Mortis conturbat me.

['Lament for the Makaris' (1834)]

FONTAINE, Jean de la (1621–1695)
La Mort ne surprend point le sage;

Il est toujours prêt à partir.
Death does not take the wise man by surprise, he is always prepared to leave.

['La Mort et le mourant']

FORSTER, E.M. (1879–1970)
Death destroys a man; the idea of Death saves him.

[*Howard's End* (1910)]

HAWTHORNE, Nathaniel (1804–1864)
We sometimes congratulate ourselves at the moment of waking from a troubled dream; it may be so the moment after death.

[*American Notebooks*]

HENLEY, W.E. (1849–1903)
Madam Life's a piece in bloom
Death goes dogging everywhere:
She's the tenant of the room,
He's the ruffian on the stair.

[*Echoes* (1877)]

HOLLAND, Canon Henry Scott (1847–1918)
Death is nothing at all. It does not count. I have only slipped away into the next room. Nothing has happened. Everything remains exactly as it was. I am I, and you are you, and the old life that we lived so fondly together is untouched, unchanged. ... What is death but a negligible accident? Why should I be out of mind because I am out of sight? I am but waiting for you, for an interval, somewhere very near, just round the corner. All is well.

[*Facts of the Faith* (1919)]

HUXLEY, Aldous (1894–1963)
Death ... It's the only thing we haven't succeeded in completely vulgarizing.

[*Eyeless in Gaza* (1936)]

HUXLEY, Henrietta (1825–1915)
And if there be no meeting past the grave,
If all is darkness, silence, yet 'tis rest.
Be not afraid ye waiting hearts that weep;
For still He giveth His beloved sleep,

And if an endless sleep He wills, so best.

[Lines on the grave of her husband, 1895]

KOESTLER, Arthur (1905–1983)
[Of the atomic bomb]
Hitherto man had to live with the idea of death as an individual; from now onward mankind will have to live with the idea of its death as a species.

[Attr.]

LARKIN, Philip (1922–1985)
[On death]
The anaesthetic from which none come round.

['Aubade' (1988)]

LEWIS, D.B. Wyndham (1891–1969)
I am one of those unfortunates to whom death is less hideous than explanations.

[*Welcome to All This*]

MANKIEWICZ, Herman (1897–1953)
[Of death]
It is the only disease you don't look forward to being cured of.

[*Citizen Kane*, film, 1941]

MILLAY, Edna St Vincent (1892–1950)
Down, down, down into the darkness of the grave
Gently they go, the beautiful, the tender, the kind;
Quietly they go, the intelligent, the witty, the brave.
I know. But I do not approve. And I am not resigned.

['Dirge without Music' (1928)]

OUIDA (1839–1908)
Even of death Christianity has made a terror which was unknown to the gay calmness of the Pagan.

[*Views and Opinions* (1895)]

OWEN, Wilfred (1893–1918)
What passing-bells for these who die as cattle?
Only the monstrous anger of the guns.
Only the stuttering rifles' rapid rattle
Can patter out their hasty orisons.

['Anthem for Doomed Youth' (1917)]

PATTEN, Brian (1946–)
Death is the only grammatically correct full-stop ...

Between himself and the grave his parents stand,
monuments that will crumble.

['Schoolboy' (1990)]

POWER, Marguerite, Countess of Blessington (1789–1849)
It is better to die young than to outlive all one loved, and all that rendered one lovable.

[*The Confessions of an Elderly Gentleman* (1836)]

SAKI (1870–1916)
Waldo is one of those people who would be enormously improved by death.

[*Beasts and Super-Beasts* (1914)]

SEVIGNE, Mme de (1626–1696)
Je trouve la mort si terrible, que je hais plus la vie parce qu'elle m'y mène, que par les épines qui s'y rencontrent.
I find death so terrible that I hate life more for leading me towards it than for the thorns encountered on the way.

[Letter to Mme de Grignan, 1672]

SHAKESPEARE, William (1564–1616)
Fear no more the heat o' th' sun
Nor the furious winter's rages;
Thou thy worldly task hast done,
Home art gone, and ta'en thy wages.
Golden lads and girls all must,
As chimney-sweepers, come to dust.

[*Cymbeline*, IV.ii]

O, that this too too solid flesh would melt,
Thaw, and resolve itself into a dew!
Or that the Everlasting had not fix'd
His canon 'gainst self–slaughter! O God! God!
How weary, stale, flat, and unprofitable,
Seem to me all the uses of this world!
Fie on't! Ah, fie! 'tis an unweeded garden,
That grows to seed; things rank and

gross in nature
Possess it merely.

[*Hamlet*, I.ii]

To be, or not to be – that is the
    question;
Whether 'tis nobler in the mind to
    suffer
The slings and arrows of outrageous
    fortune,
Or to take arms against a sea of
    troubles,
And by opposing end them? To die, to
    sleep –
No more; and by a sleep to say we end
The heart-ache and the thousand
    natural shocks
That flesh is heir to. 'Tis a con-
    summation
Devoutly to be wish'd. To die, to sleep;
To sleep, perchance to dream. Ay,
    there's the rub;
For in that sleep of death what dreams
    may come,
When we have shuffled off this mortal
    coil,
Must give us pause.

[*Hamlet*, III.i]

This fell sergeant Death
Is strict in his arrest.

[*Hamlet*, V.ii]

Cowards die many times before their
    deaths:
The valiant never taste of death but
    once.

[*Julius Caesar*, II.ii]

Men must endure
Their going hence, even as their
    coming hither:
Ripeness is all.

[*King Lear*, V.ii]

The weariest and most loathed worldly
    life
That age, ache, penury, and impris-
    onment,
Can lay on nature is a paradise
To what we fear of death.

[*Measure For Measure*, III.i]

SHAW, George Bernard (1856–1950)
Life levels all men: death reveals the
eminent.

[*Man and Superman* (1903)]

SHELLEY, Percy Bysshe (1792–1822)
Death is the veil which those who live
    call life:
They sleep, and it is lifted.

[*Prometheus Unbound* (1820)]

SHIRLEY, James (1596–1666)
The glories of our blood and state
Are shadows, not substantial things;
There is no armour against fate;
Death lays his icy hand on kings:
Sceptre and crown
Must tumble down,
And in the dust be equal made
With the poor crooked scythe and
    spade.

[*The Contention of Ajax and Ulysses* (1659)]

SMITH, Stevie (1902–1971)
If there wasn't death, I think you
couldn't go on.

[*The Observer*, 1969]

SOUTHEY, Robert (1774–1843)
My name is Death: the last best friend
am I.

[*Carmen Nuptiale* (1816)]

SWIFT, Jonathan (1667–1745)
You think, as I ought to think, that it is
time for me to have done with the
world, and so I would if I could get
into a better before I was called into
the best, and not die here in a rage,
like a poisoned rat in a hole.

[Letter to Bolingbroke, 1729]

THOMAS, Dylan (1914–1953)
Though they go mad they shall be
    sane,
Though they sink through the sea they
    shall rise again;
Though lovers be lost love shall not;
And death shall have no dominion.

['And death shall have no dominion' (1936)]

TWAIN, Mark (1835–1910)
Whoever has lived long enough to find

out what life is, knows how deep a debt of gratitude we owe to Adam, the first great benefactor of our race. He brought death into the world.

[*Pudd'nhead Wilson* (1894)]

The report of my death was an exaggeration.

[Cable, 1897]

WEISS, Peter (1916–1982)
*Jeder Tod auch der grausamste
ertrinkt in der völligen Gleichgültigkeit
der Natur
Nur wir verleihen unserm Leben
irgendeinen Wert.*
Every death, even the cruellest, drowns in Nature's complete indifference. We are the only ones who bestow a value on our lives.

[*The Hunting Down and Murder of Jean Paul Marat* (1964)]

WHITMAN, Walt (1819–1892)
Has anyone supposed it lucky to be born?
I hasten to inform him or her it is just as lucky to die, and I know it.

['Song of Myself' (1855)]

WRIGHT, Judith (1915–)
Death marshals up his armies round us now.
Their footsteps crowd too near.
Lock your warm hand above the chilling heart
and for a time I live without my fear.
Grope in the night to find me and embrace,
for the dark preludes of the drums begin,
and round us, round the company of lovers,
death draws his cordons in.

['The Company of Lovers' (1946)]

YEATS, W.B. (1865–1939)
Nor dread nor hope attend
A dying animal;
A man awaits his end
Dreading and hoping all.

['Death' (1933)]

DEATH: DYING

ALLEN, Woody (1935–)
It's not that I'm afraid to die. I just don't want to be there when it happens.

[*Without Feathers* (1976)]

BACON, Francis (1561–1626)
I do not believe that any man fears to be dead, but only the stroke of death.

[*The Remaines of ... Lord Verulam* (1648)]

BARRIE, Sir J.M. (1860–1937)
To die will be an awfully big adventure.

[*Peter Pan* (1904)]

BETJEMAN, Sir John (1906–1984)
There was sun enough for lazing upon beaches,
There was fun enough for far into the night.
But I'm dying now and done for,
What on earth was all the fun for?
For I'm old and ill and terrified and tight.

['Sun and Fun' (1954)]

BROWNE, Sir Thomas (1605–1682)
The long habit of living indisposeth us for dying.

[*Hydriotaphia: Urn Burial* (1658)]

BUTLER, Samuel (1835–1902)
It costs a lot of money to die comfortably.

[*The Note-Books of Samuel Butler* (1912)]

CHARLES II (1630–1685)
He had been, he said, a most unconscionable time dying; but he hoped that they would excuse it.

[In Macaulay, *The History of England* (1849)]

CHILDERS, Erskine (1870–1922)
[Writing about his imminent execution]
It seems perfectly simple and inevitable, like lying down after a long day's work.

[Prison letter to his wife]

CRASHAW, Richard (c. 1612–1649)
And when life's sweet fable ends,
Soul and body part like friends;
No quarrels, murmurs, no delay;
A kiss, a sigh, and so away.
['Temperance' (1652)]

DICKINSON, Emily (1830–1886)
I heard a Fly buzz – when I died ...
With Blue – uncertain stumbling
    Buzz –
Between the light – and me –
And then the Windows failed – and
    then
I could not see to see.
['I heard a Fly buzz – when I died' (c. 1862)]

FARMER, Edward (c. 1809–1876)
I have no pain, dear mother, now;
But oh! I am so dry:
Just moisten poor Jim's lips once more;
And, mother, do not cry!
['The Collier's Dying Child']

HALL, Rodney (1935–)
They're dying just the same in station
    homesteads
they're dying in Home Beautiful
    apartments
in among their lovely Danish furniture
on and across the furniture they're
    dying
spewing blood or stiffening dry and
    seeming never
to have been alive.
[*Black Bagatelles* (1978)]

JOHNSON, Samuel (1709–1784)
It matters not how a man dies, but
how he lives. The act of dying is not of
importance, it lasts so short a time.
[In Boswell, *The Life of Samuel Johnson*
(1791)]

**MAUGHAM, William Somerset
(1874–1965)**
Dying is a very dull, dreary affair. And
my advice to you is to have nothing
whatever to do with it.
[In R. Maugham, *Escape from the Shadows*]

PLATH, Sylvia (1932–1963)
Dying
Is an art, like everything else.

I do it exceptionally well.
['Lady Lazarus' (1963)]

POPE, Alexander (1688–1744)
I mount! I fly!
O Grave! where is thy victory?
O Death! where is thy sting?
['The Dying Christian to his Soul' (1730)]

SHAKESPEARE, William (1564–1616)
Nothing in his life
Became him like the leaving it: he died
As one that had been studied in his
    death
To throw away the dearest thing he
    ow'd
As 'twere a careless trifle.
[*Macbeth*, I.iv]

Dar'st thou die?
The sense of death is most in
    apprehension;
And the poor beetle that we tread
    upon
In corporal sufferance finds a pang as
    great
As when a giant dies.
[*Measure For Measure*, III.i]

SMITH, Logan Pearsall (1865–1946)
I cannot forgive my friends for dying; I
do not find these vanishing acts of
theirs at all amusing.
[*Afterthoughts* (1931)]

THOMAS, Dylan (1914–1953)
Do not go gentle into that good night,
Old age should burn and rave at close
of day;
Rage, rage against the dying of the
light.
['Do Not Go Gentle into that Good Night'
(1952)]

TWAIN, Mark (1835–1910)
All say, 'How hard it is to die' – a
strange complaint to come from the
mouths of people who have had to
live.
[*Pudd'nhead Wilson's Calendar* (1894)]

DEATH: THE DEAD

ADDISON, Joseph (1672–1719)
When I read the several dates of the tombs, of some that died yesterday, and some six hundred years ago, I consider that great day when we shall all of us be contemporaries, and make our appearance together.

[*Thoughts in Westminster Abbey*]

BURKE, Edmund (1729–1797)
I would rather sleep in the southern corner of a little country church-yard, than in the tomb of the Capulets. I should like, however, that my dust should mingle with kindred dust.

[Letter to Matthew Smith, 1750]

CHESTERFIELD, Lord (1694–1773)
[Said when Tyrawley was old and infirm]
Tyrawley and I have been dead these two years; but we don't choose to have it known.

[In Boswell, *The Life of Samuel Johnson* (1791)]

DICKINSON, Emily (1830–1886)
This quiet Dust was Gentlemen and Ladies
And Lads and Girls –
Was laughter and ability and Sighing
And Frocks and Curls.

['This quiet Dust was Gentlemen and Ladies' (c. 1864)]

GORDON, Adam Lindsay (1833–1870)
Let me slumber in the hollow where the wattle blossoms wave,
With never stone or rail to fence my bed;
Should the sturdy station children pull the bush flowers on my grave,
I may chance to hear them romping overhead.

['The Sick Stockrider']

GRAY, Patrick, Lord (d. 1612)
[Advocating the execution of Mary, Queen of Scots]
A dead woman bites not.

[Oral tradition, 1587]

HENDRIX, Jimi (1942–1970)
Once you're dead, you're made for life.

[Attr.]

LAWRENCE, D.H. (1885–1930)
The dead don't die. They look on and help.

[Letter to J. Middleton Murry, 1923]

MAETERLINCK, Maurice (1862–1949)
The living are just the dead on holiday.

[Attr.]

SCHOPENHAUER, Arthur (1788–1860)
After your death you will be what you were before your birth.

[*Parerga and Paralipomena* (1851)]

TENNYSON, Alfred, Lord (1809–1892)
Do we indeed desire the dead
Should still be near us at our side?
Is there no baseness we would hide?
No inner vileness that we dread?

[*In Memoriam A. H. H.* (1850)]

VOLTAIRE (1694–1778)
On doit des égards aux vivants; on ne doit aux morts que la vérité.
We owe respect to the living; we owe nothing but truth to the dead.

['Première Lettre sur *Oedipe*' (1785)]

YOUNG, Edward (1683–1765)
Life is the desert, life the solitude;
Death joins us to the great majority.

[*The Revenge* (1721)]

See GRIEF

DEBTS

COOLIDGE, Calvin (1872–1933)
[Of Allied war debts]
They hired the money, didn't they?

[Remark, 1925]

FOX, Henry Stephen (1791–1846)
[Remark after an illness]
I am so changed that my oldest creditors would hardly know me.

[Quoted by Byron , 1817]

DECEPTION

IBSEN, Henrik (1828–1906)
Home life ceases to be free and
beautiful as soon as it is founded on
borrowing and debt.

[*A Doll's House* (1879)]

SHAKESPEARE, William (1564–1616)
I can get no remedy against this
consumption of the purse; borrowing
only lingers and lingers it out, but the
disease is incurable.

[*Henry IV Part 2*, I.ii]

**SHERIDAN, Richard Brinsley
(1751–1816)**
[Handing one of his creditors an IOU]
Thank God, that's settled.

[In Shriner, *Wit, Wisdom, and Foibles of the
Great* (1918)]

[After being refused a loan of £25 from
a friend who asked him to repay the
£500 he had already borrowed]
My dear fellow, be reasonable; the
sum you ask me for is a very
considerable one, whereas I only ask
you for twenty-five pounds.

[Attr.]

WARD, Artemus (1834–1867)
Let us all be happy, and live within our
means, even if we have to borrer the
money to do it with.

['Science and Natural History']

WODEHOUSE, P.G. (1881–1975)
I don't owe a penny to a single soul –
not counting tradesmen, of course.

['Jeeves and the Hard-Boiled Egg' (1919)]

DECEPTION

AESOP (6th century BC)
The lamb that belonged to the sheep
whose skin the wolf was wearing
began to follow the wolf in the sheep's
clothing.

['The Wolf in Sheep's Clothing']

**BERKELEY, Bishop George
(1685–1753)**
It is impossible that a man who is false
to his friends and neighbours should

be true to the public.

[*Maxims Concerning Patriotism* (1750)]

CARSWELL, Catherine (1879–1946)
It wasn't a woman who betrayed Jesus
with a kiss.

[*The Savage Pilgrimage* (1932)]

CHAUCER, Geoffrey (c. 1340–1400)
The smylere with the knyf under the
cloke.

[*The Canterbury Tales* (1387)]

CONGREVE, William (1670–1729)
Man was by Nature Woman's cully
   made:
We never are, but by ourselves,
   betrayed.

[*The Old Bachelor* (1693)]

FONTAINE, Jean de la (1621–1695)
*C'est double plaisir de tromper le
trompeur.*
It is a double pleasure to trick the
trickster.

['Le coq et le renard']

GAY, John (1685–1732)
To cheat a man is nothing; but the
woman must have fine parts indeed
who cheats a woman!

[*The Beggar's Opera* (1728)]

HENRY, O. (1862–1910)
It was beautiful and simple as all truly
great swindles are.

['The Octopus Marooned' (1908)]

HILL, Joe (1879–1914)
You will eat (You will eat)
Bye and bye (Bye and bye)
In that glorious land above the sky
   (Way up high)
Work and pray (Work and pray)
Live on hay (Live on hay)
You'll get pie in the sky when you die
   (That's a lie.)

['The Preacher and the Slave', song, 1911]

SCOTT, Sir Walter (1771–1832)
O what a tangled web we weave,
When first we practise to deceive!

[*Marmion* (1808)]

SHAKESPEARE, William (1564–1616)
O villain, villain, smiling, damned
villain!
My tables – meet it is I set it down
That one may smile, and smile, and be
a villain.

[*Hamlet*, I.v]

False face must hide what the false
heart doth know.

[*Macbeth*, I.vii]

So may the outward shows be least
themselves;
The world is still deceiv'd with
ornament.

[*The Merchant of Venice*, III.ii]

TAYLOR, Bishop Jeremy (1613–1667)
In the matter of interest we are wary
as serpents, subtle as foxes, vigilant as
the birds of the night, rapacious as
kites, tenacious as grappling-hooks
and the weightiest anchors, and,
above all, false and hypocritical as a
thin crust of ice spread upon the face
of a deep, smooth, and dissembling
pit.

[*XXV Sermons Preached at Golden Grove*]

THURBER, James (1894–1961)
It is not so easy to fool little girls today
as it used to be.

[*Fables for Our Time* (1940)]

You can fool too many of the people
too much of the time.

[*The New Yorker*, 1939]

VIRGIL (70–19 BC)
Quis fallere possit amantem?
Who may deceive a lover?

[*Aeneid*]

See HYPOCRISY

DEMOCRACY

ATTLEE, Clement (1883–1967)
Democracy means government by
discussion but it is only effective if you
can stop people talking.

[Speech, 1957]

BEVERIDGE, William (1879–1963)
The trouble in modern democracy is
that men do not approach to
leadership until they have lost the
desire to lead anyone.

[*The Observer*, 1934]

CHESTERTON, G.K. (1874–1936)
You can never have a revolution in
order to establish a democracy. You
must have a democracy in order to
have a revolution.

[*Tremendous Trifles*]

Democracy means government by the
uneducated, while aristocracy means
government by the badly educated.

[*New York Times*, 1931]

CHURCHILL, Sir Winston (1874–1965)
Many forms of government have been
tried, and will be tried in this world of
sin and woe. No one pretends that
democracy is perfect or all-wise.
Indeed, it has been said that democracy is the worst form of Government
except all those other forms that have
been tried from time to time.

[Speech, 1947]

DEMOSTHENES (c. 384–322 BC)
There is one safeguard, which is an
advantage and security for all, but
especially to democracies against
despots. What is it? Distrust.

[*Philippics*]

**FLERS, Marquis de (1872–1927) and
CAILLAVET, Arman de (1869–1915)**
*Démocratie est le nom que nous
donnons au peuple toutes les fois que
nous avons besoin de lui.*
Democracy is the name we give the
people whenever we need them.

[*L'habit vert*]

FO, Dario (1926–)
*Giusto! L'ha detto! Lo scandalo è il
concime della democrazia.*
Correct! You said it! Scandal is the
manure of democracy.

[*Accidental Death of an Anarchist* (1974)]

FORSTER, E.M. (1879–1970)
So Two cheers for Democracy: one because it admits variety and two because it permits criticism. Two cheers are quite enough: there is no occasion to give three. Only Love the Beloved Republic deserves that.
[*Two Cheers for Democracy* (1951)]

IBSEN, Henrik (1828–1906)
The most dangerous foe to truth and freedom in our midst is the compact majority. Yes, the damned, compact liberal majority.
[*An Enemy of the People* (1882)]

JUNIUS (1769–1772)
The right of election is the very essence of the constitution.
[*Letters* (1769–1771)]

LINCOLN, Abraham (1809–1865)
No man is good enough to govern another man without that other's consent.
[Speech, 1854]

The ballot is stronger than the bullet.
[Speech, 1856]

NIEBUHR, Reinhold (1892–1971)
Man's capacity for justice makes democracy possible, but man's inclination to injustice makes democracy necessary.
[*The Children of Light and the Children of Darkness* (1944)]

PERICLES (c. 495–429)
We enjoy a constitution that does not follow the customs of our neighbours; we are rather an example to them than they to us. Our government is called a democracy because power is in the hands not of the few but of the many.
[In Thucydides, *Histories*]

SHAW, George Bernard (1856–1950)
Our political experiment of democracy, the last refuge of cheap misgovernment.
[*Man and Superman* (1903)]

Democracy substitutes election by the incompetent many for appointment by the corrupt few.
[*Man and Superman* (1903)]

TOCQUEVILLE, Alexis de (1805–1859)
I sought the image of democracy, in order to learn what we have to fear and to hope from its progress.
[*De la Démocratie en Amérique (1840)*]

WEBSTER, Daniel (1782–1852)
The people's government, made for the people, made by the people, and answerable to the people.
[Speech, 1830]

WILLIAMS, Tennessee (1911–1983)
Knowledge – Zzzzzp! Money – Zzzzzp! – Power! That's the cycle democracy is built on!
[*The Glass Menagerie* (1945)]

WILSON, Woodrow (1856–1924)
The world must be made safe for democracy.
[Speech, 1917]

See GOVERNMENT

DESIRE

BLAKE, William (1757–1827)
Man's desires are limited by his perceptions; none can desire what he has not perceiv'd.
[*There is No Natural Religion* (c. 1788)]

The desire of Man being Infinite the possession is Infinite and himself Infinite.
[*There is No Natural Religion* (c. 1788)]

Those who restrain desire, do so because theirs is weak enough to be restrained.
[*The Marriage of Heaven and Hell* (c. 1793)]

Abstinence sows sand all over
The ruddy limbs & flaming hair
But Desire Gratified
Plants fruits of life & beauty there.
['Abstinence sows sand all over' (c. 1793)]

What is it men in women do require?
The lineaments of Gratified Desire.
What is it women do in men require?
The lineaments of Gratified Desire.

['What is it men in women do require']

BROWNE, Sir Thomas (1605–1682)
My desires only are, and I shall be
happy therein, to be but the last man,
and bring up the rear in heaven.

[*Religio Medici* (1643)]

DRAYTON, Michael (1563–1631)
Thus when we fondly flatter our
desires,
Our best conceits do prove the
greatest liars.

[*The Barrons' Wars* (1603)]

JOYCE, James (1882–1941)
[Commenting on the interruption of a
music recital when a moth flew into
the singer's mouth]
The desire of the moth for the star.

[In Ellmann, *James Joyce* (1958)]

PROUST, Marcel (1871–1922)
*Il n'y a rien comme le désir pour
empêcher les choses qu'on dit d'avoir
aucune ressemblance avec ce qu'on a
dans la pensée.*
There is nothing like desire for preventing the things one says from
bearing any resemblance to what one
has in mind.

[*Le Côté de Guermantes* (1921)]

SHAW, George Bernard (1856–1950)
There are two tragedies in life. One is
to lose your heart's desire. The other is
to gain it.

[*Man and Superman* (1903)]

DESPAIR

ALLEN, Woody (1935–)
More than any other time in history,
mankind faces a crossroads. One path
leads to despair and utter hope-
lessness. The other, to total extinction.
Let us pray we have the wisdom to
choose correctly.

[*Side Effects*]

CAMUS, Albert (1913–1960)
He who despairs over an event is a
coward, but he who holds hopes for
the human condition is a fool.

[*The Rebel* (1951)]

CLARE, John (1793–1864)
My life hath been one chain of
contradictions,
Madhouses, prisons, whore-shops ...

Pale death, the grand physician, cures
all pain;
The dead rest well who lived for joys
in vain ...

Hopeless hope hopes on and meets no
end,
Wastes without springs and homes
without a friend.

['Child Harold' (1841)]

FITZGERALD, F. Scott (1896–1940)
In the real dark night of the soul it is
always three o'clock in the morning.

[*The Crack-Up* (1945)]

GREENE, Graham (1904– 1991)
Despair is the price one pays for
setting oneself an impossible aim.

[*Heart of the Matter* (1948)]

HOPKINS, Gerard Manley (1844–1889)
Not, I'll not, carrion comfort, Despair,
not feast on thee;
Not untwist – slack they may be –
these last strands of man
In me or, most weary, cry *I can no
more*. I can;
Can something, hope, wish day come,
not choose not to be.

['Carrion Comfort' (1885)]

I wake and feel the fell of dark, not
day.
What hours, O what black hours we
have spent This night!

['I wake and Feel the Fell of dark, not day'
(c. 1885)]

ST JOHN OF THE CROSS (1542–1591)
Noche oscura del alma.

The dark night of the soul.
[Title of poem]

KAFKA, Franz (1883–1924)
*Nicht verzweifeln, auch darüber nicht,
dass du nicht verzweifelst.*
Do not despair, not even about the
fact that you do not despair.
[*Diary*, 1913]

SHAKESPEARE, William (1564–1616)
I shall despair. There is no creature
    loves me;
And if I die no soul will pity me:
And wherefore should they, since that
    I myself
Find in myself no pity to myself?
[*Richard III*, V.iii]

SHAW, George Bernard (1856–1950)
He who has never hoped can never
despair.
[*Caesar and Cleopatra* (1901)]

WALSH, William (1663–1708)
I can endure my own despair,
But not another's hope.
['Song: Of All the Torments']

DESTINY

AESCHYLUS (525–456 BC)
Things are where things are, and, as
    fate has willed,
So shall they be fulfilled.
[*Agamemnon,* trans. Browning]

**APPIUS CLAUDIUS CAECUS (4th–3rd
century BC)**
Faber est suae quisque fortunae.
Each man is the architect of his own
destiny.
[In Sallust, *Ad Caesarem*]

ARNOLD, Matthew (1822–1888)
Yet they, believe me, who await
No gifts from chance, have conquered
    fate.
['Resignation' (1849)]

AURELIUS, Marcus (121–180)
Nothing happens to any thing which

that thing is not made by nature to
bear.
[*Meditations*]

BACON, Francis (1561–1626)
If a man look sharply, and attentively,
he shall see Fortune: for though she be
blind, yet she is not invisible.
[*Essays* (1625)]

BOWEN, Elizabeth (1899–1973)
Fate is not an eagle, it creeps like a
rat.
[*The House in Paris* (1935)]

BÜCHNER, Georg (1813–1837)
*Puppen sind wir von unbekannten
Gewalten am Draht gezogen; nichts,
nichts wir selbst!*
We are puppets on strings worked by
unknown forces; we ourselves are
nothing, nothing!
[*Danton's Death* (1835)]

CHURCHILL, Sir Winston (1874–1965)
I felt as if I were walking with destiny,
and that all my past life had been but
a preparation for this hour and this
trial.
[*The Gathering Storm*]

CLIVE, Lord (1725–1774)
[Said when his pistol failed to go off
twice, in his attempt to commit
suicide]
I feel that I am reserved for some end
or other.
[In Gleig, *The Life of Robert, First Lord Clive*
(1848)]

CRISP, Quentin (1908–)
Believe in fate, but lean forward where
fate can see you.
[Attr.]

DELILLE, Abbé Jacques (1738–1813)
*Le sort fait les parents, le choix fait les
amis.*
Relations are made by fate, friends by
choice.
[*Malheur et pitié* (1803)]

DRYDEN, John (1631–1700)
[Of Fortune]
I can enjoy her while she's kind;
But when she dances in the wind,
And shakes the wings, and will not stay,
I puff the prostitute away.

[Sylvae (1685)]

ELIOT, George (1819–1880)
'Character', says Novalis, in one of his questionable aphorisms – 'character is destiny.'

[The Mill on the Floss (1860)]

EMERSON, Ralph Waldo (1803–1882)
The bitterest tragic element in life to be derived from an intellectual source is the belief in a brute Fate or Destiny.

[Natural History of Intellect (1893)]

FITZGERALD, Edward (1809–1883)
'Tis all a Chequer-board of Nights and Days
Where Destiny with Men for Pieces plays:
Hither and thither moves, and mates, and slays,
And one by one back in the Closet lays.

[The Rubáiyát of Omar Khayyám (1859)]

The Moving Finger writes; and, having writ,
Moves on: nor all thy Piety nor Wit
Shall lure it back to cancel half a Line,
Nor all thy Tears wash out a Word of it.

[The Rubáiyát of Omar Khayyám (1859)]

FORD, John (c. 1586–1639)
Tempt not the stars, young man, thou canst not play
With the severity of fate.

[The Broken Heart (1633)]

GAY, John (1685–1732)
'Tis a gross error, held in schools,
That Fortune always favours fools.

[Fables (1738)]

HARE, Maurice Evan (1886–1967)
There once was a man who said,
'Damn!
It is borne in upon me I am
An engine that moves
In predestinate grooves,
I'm not even a bus, I'm a tram.'

['Limerick', 1905]

HITLER, Adolf (1889–1945)
Ich gehe mit traumwandlerischer Sicherheit den Weg, den mich die Vorsehung gehen heisst.
I go the way that Providence bids me go with the certainty of a sleepwalker.

[Speech, Munich, 1936]

HORACE (65–8 BC)
Tu ne quaesieris, scire nefas, quem mihi, quem tibi
Finem di dederint.
Do not ask – it is forbidden to know – what end the gods have in store for me or for you.

[Odes]

JONSON, Ben (1572–1637)
Blind Fortune still
Bestows her gifts on such as cannot use them.

[Every Man out of His Humour (1599)]

LOOS, Anita (1893–1981)
Fate keeps on happening.

[Gentlemen Prefer Blondes (1925)]

MACAULAY, Lord (1800–1859)
[Of Rumbold]
He never would believe that Providence had sent a few men into the world ready booted and spurred to ride, and millions ready saddled and bridled to be ridden.

[History of England (1849)]

MACHIAVELLI (1469–1527)
La fortuna, come donna, è amica de giovani, perché sono meno respettivi, più feroci e con più audacia la comandano.
Fortune, like a woman, is friendly to the young, because they show her less respect, they are more daring and command her with audacity.

[The Prince (1532)]

MALLARME, Stéphane (1842–1898)
Un coup de dés jamais n'abolira le hasard.
A throw of the dice will never eliminate chance.

[Title of work, 1897]

SCHOPENHAUER, Arthur (1788–1860)
Das Schicksal mischt die Karten und wir spielen.
Fate shuffles the cards and we play.

['Aphorisms for Wisdom' (1851)]

SHAKESPEARE, William (1564–1616)
Let us sit and mock the good housewife Fortune from her wheel, that her gifts may henceforth be bestowed equally.

[*As You Like It*, I.ii]

Men at some time are masters of their fates:
The fault, dear Brutus, is not in our stars,
But in ourselves, that we are underlings.

[*Julius Caesar*, I.ii]

Fortune is merry,
And in this mood will give us any thing.

[*Julius Caesar*, III.ii]

There is a tide in the affairs of men
Which, taken at the flood, leads on to fortune;
Omitted, all the voyage of their life
Is bound in shallows and in miseries.

[*Julius Caesar*, IV.iii]

SIMPSON, N.F. (1919–)
Each of us as he receives his private trouncings at the hands of fate is kept in good heart by the moth in his brother's parachute, and the scorpion in his neighbour's underwear.

[*A Resounding Tinkle* (1958)]

TERENCE (c. 190–159 BC)
Fortis fortuna adiuvat.
Fortune favours the brave.

[*Phormio*]

WEBSTER, John (c. 1580–c. 1625)
Fortune's a right whore:
If she give aught, she deals it in small parcels,
That she may take away all at one swoop.

[*The White Devil* (1612)]

We are merely the stars' tennis-balls, struck and bandied,
Which way please them.

[*The Duchess of Malfi* (1623)]

THE DEVIL

BAUDELAIRE, Charles (1821–1867)
My dear brothers, never forget when you hear the progress of the Enlightenment praised, that the Devil's cleverest ploy is to persuade you that he doesn't exist.

(var.)

THE BIBLE (King James Version)
Resist the devil, and he will flee from you.

[*James*, 4:7]

BROWNING, Elizabeth Barrett (1806–1861)
The devil's most devilish when respectable.

[*Aurora Leigh* (1857)]

BUTLER, Samuel (1835–1902)
An apology for the devil: it must be remembered that we have heard only one side of the case; God has written all the books.

[*The Note-Books of Samuel Butler* (1912)]

DOSTOEVSKY, Fyodor (1821–1881)
I think if the devil doesn't exist, and man has created him, he has created him in his own image and likeness.

[*The Brothers Karamazov* (1880)]

HILL, Rowland (1744–1833)
[Referring to his writing of hymns]
He did not see any reason why the devil should have all the good tunes.

[In Broome, *The Rev. Rowland Hill* (1881)]

LAWRENCE, D.H. (1885–1930)
It is no good casting out devils. They
belong to us, we must accept them
and be at peace with them.
['The Reality of Peace' (1936)]

MILTON, John (1608–1674)
Abasht the Devil stood,
And felt how awful goodness is.
[*Paradise Lost* (1667)]

SHAKESPEARE, William (1564–1616)
The devil can cite Scripture for his
purpose.
[*The Merchant of Venice*, I.iii]

SHAW, George Bernard (1856–1950)
Is the devil to have all the passions as
well as all the good tunes?
[*Man and Superman* (1903)]

WILDE, Oscar (1854–1900)
We are each our own devil, and we
make
This world our hell.
[*The Duchess of Padua* (1883)]

DINING

BOWRA, Sir Maurice (1898–1971)
I'm a man
More dined against than dining.
[In Betjeman, *Summoned by Bells* (1960)]

EVARTS, William Maxwell (1818–1901)
[Of a dinner given by US President and
temperance advocate Rutherford B.
Hayes]
It was a brilliant affair; water flowed
like champagne.
[Attr.]

GULBENKIAN, Nubar (1896–1972)
The best number for a dinner party is
two: myself and a damn good head
waiter.
[*The Observer*, 1965]

JOHNSON, Samuel (1709–1784)
This was a good dinner enough, to be
sure; but it was not a dinner to *ask* a
man to.
[In Boswell, *The Life of Samuel Johnson*
(1791)]

A man seldom thinks with more
earnestness of anything than he does
of his dinner.
[In Piozzi, *Anecdotes of the Late Samuel
Johnson* (1786)]

A man is in general better pleased
when he has a good dinner upon his
table, than when his wife talks Greek.
[In Hawkins, *Life of Samuel Johnson* (1787)]

MARTIAL (c. 40–c. 104)
*Caenae fercula nostrae malim convivis
quam placuisse cocis.*
I prefer that the courses at our
banquet should give pleasure to the
guests rather than to the cooks.
[*Epigrammata*]

**MAUGHAM, William Somerset
(1874–1965)**
At a dinner party one should eat
wisely but not too well, and talk well
but not too wisely.
[*A Writer's Notebook* (1949)]

PEPYS, Samuel (1633–1703)
Strange to see how a good dinner and
feasting reconciles everybody.
[*Diary*, 1665]

SWIFT, Jonathan (1667–1745)
He showed me his bill of fare to tempt
me to dine with him; Poh, said I, I
value not your bill of fare; give me
your bill of company.
[*Journal to Stella*, 1711]

WILDE, Oscar (1854–1900)
[Said to Frank Harris who was listing
the houses he had dined at]
Dear Frank, we believe you; you have
dined in every house in London – once.
[Attr.]

DIPLOMACY

CROMWELL, Oliver (1599–1658)
A man-of-war is the best ambassador.
[Attr.]

GRANT, Bruce Alexander (1925–)
I recall at least two Australian am-

bassadors who complained to me in the past about the constraints which the inherited British style placed on Australian diplomacy, but, when their time came to resist the invitation of knighthood, their resolve buckled under the terrible strain.

[*Gods and Politicians* (1982)]

PEARSON, Lester B. (1897–1972)
Diplomacy is letting someone else have your way.

[*The Observer*, 1965]

USTINOV, Sir Peter (1921–)
A diplomat these days is nothing but a head-waiter who's allowed to sit down occasionally.

[*Romanoff and Juliet* (1956)]

WOTTON, Sir Henry (1568–1639)
Legatus est vir bonus peregre missus ad mentiendum rei publicae causa.
An ambassador is an honest man sent to lie abroad for the good of his country.

[Written in an album, 1606]

DOGS

BEERBOHM, Sir Max (1872–1956)
You will find that the woman who is really kind to dogs is always one who has failed to inspire sympathy in men.

[*Zuleika Dobson* (1911)]

BENNETT, Alan (1934–)
[On dogs]
It's the one species I wouldn't mind seeing vanish from the face of the earth. I wish they were like the white rhino – six of them left in the Serengeti National Park, and all males.

[Attr.]

ELIOT, George (1819–1880)
Though, as we know, she was not fond of pets that must be held in the hands or trodden on, she was always attentive to the feelings of dogs, and very polite if she had to decline their advances.

[*Middlemarch* (1872)]

HUXLEY, Aldous (1894–1963)
To his dog, every man is Napoleon; hence the constant popularity of dogs.

[Attr.]

MACAULAY, Lord (1800–1859)
We were regaled by a dogfight ... How odd that people of sense should find any pleasure in being accompanied by a beast who is always spoiling conversation.

[In Trevelyan, *Life and Letters of Macaulay* (1876)]

MUIR, Frank (1920–)
Dogs, like horses, are quadrupeds. That is to say, they have four rupeds, one at each corner, on which they walk.

[*You Can't Have Your Kayak and Heat It*, with Dennis Norden]

NASH, Ogden (1902–1971)
A door is what a dog is perpetually on the wrong side of.

['A Dog's Best Friend Is His Illiteracy' (1952)]

POPE, Alexander (1688–1744)
[On the collar of a dog given to Frederick, Prince of Wales]
I am his Highness' dog at Kew;
Pray, tell me sir, whose dog are you?

['Epigram' (1738)]

SPARROW, John (1906–1992)
That indefatigable and unsavoury engine of pollution, the dog.

[Letter to *The Times*, 1975]

STREATFIELD, Sir Geoffrey (1897–1978)
I loathe people who keep dogs. They are cowards who haven't got the guts to bite people themselves.

[*A Madman's Diary*]

DOUBT

BACON, Francis (1561–1626)
If a man will begin with certainties, he shall end in doubts; but if he will be content to begin with doubts, he shall end in certainties.

[*The Advancement of Learning* (1605)]

THE BIBLE (King James Version)
O thou of little faith, wherefore didst
thou doubt?

[*Matthew*, 14:31]

BLAKE, William (1757-1827)
He who shall teach the Child to Doubt
The rotting Grave shall ne'er get out ...

He who Doubts from what he sees
Will ne'er Believe do what you Please.
If the Sun & Moon should doubt,
They'd immediately Go out.

['Auguries of Innocence' (c. 1803)]

BORGES, Jorge Luis (1899-1986)
*He conocido io que ignoran los griegos:
la incertidumbre.*
I have known what the Greeks knew
not: uncertainty.

[*The Garden of Paths which Diverge* (1941)]

BOYD, William (1952-)
What now? What next? All these
questions. All these doubts. So few
certainties. But then I have taken new
comfort and refuge in the doctrine that
advises one not to seek tranquillity in
certainty, but in permanently suspended judgement.

[*Brazzaville Beach* (1990)]

BROWNING, Robert (1812-1889)
All we have gained then by our
    unbelief
Is a life of doubt diversified by faith,
For one of faith diversified by doubt:
We called the chess-board white, – we
    call it black.

['Bishop Blougram's Apology' (1855)]

BUTLER, Samuel (1835-1902)
My Lord, I do not believe. Help thou
mine unbelief.

[*Samuel Butler's Notebooks* (1951)]

DARROW, Clarence (1857-1938)
[Remark during the trial of John
Scopes, 1925, for teaching evolution in
school]
I do not consider it an insult but rather
a compliment to be called an agnostic.
I do not pretend to know where many

ignorant men are sure – that is all that
agnosticism means.

[Attr.]

DENT, Alan (1905-1978)
This is the tragedy of a man who could
not make up his mind.

[Introduction to film *Hamlet*, 1948]

EMERSON, Ralph Waldo (1803-1882)
I am the doubter and the doubt,
And I the hymn the Brahmin sings.

['Brahma' (1867)]

HARDWICKE, Earl of (1690-1764)
[Referring to Dirleton's *Doubts*]
His doubts are better than most
people's certainties.

[In Boswell, *The Life of Samuel Johnson*
(1791)]

HUXLEY, T.H. (1825-1895)
I am too much of a sceptic to deny the
possibility of anything.

[Letter to Herbert Spencer, 1886]

KORAN
There is no doubt in this book.

[Chapter 1]

LICHTENBERG, Georg (1742-1799)
*Zweifle an allem wenigstens einmal,
und wäre es auch der Satz: zweimal
zwei ist vier.*
Doubt everything at least once – even
the proposition that two and two are
four.

[*Miscellaneous Writings*]

**NEWMAN, John Henry, Cardinal
(1801-1890)**
Ten thousand difficulties do not make
one doubt.

[*Apologia pro Vita Sua* (1864)]

PIRSIG, Robert (1928-)
You are never dedicated to something
you have complete confidence in. No
one is fanatically shouting that the sun
is going to rise tomorrow. They *know*
it's going to rise tomorrow. When
people are fanatically dedicated to
political or religious faiths or any other
kind of dogmas or goals, it's always

because these dogmas or goals are in doubt.

[*Zen and the Art of Motorcycle Maintenance* (1974)]

TENNYSON, Alfred, Lord (1809-1892)
There lives more faith in honest doubt,
Believe me, than in half the creeds.

[*In Memoriam A. H. H.* (1850)]

For nothing worthy proving can be
  proven,
Nor yet disproven: wherefore thou be
  wise,
Cleave ever to the sunnier side of
  doubt.

['The Ancient Sage' (1885)]

See CERTAINTY

DREAMS

BACON, Francis (1561-1626)
Dreams and predictions of astrology ...
ought to serve but for winter talk by
the fireside.

[*Essays* (1625)]

BUNN, Alfred (1796-1860)
I dreamt that I dwelt in marble halls,
With vassals and serfs at my side.

[*The Bohemian Girl* (1843)]

**CALDERÓN DE LA BARCA, Pedro
(1600-1681)**
*Pues veo estando dormido,
que sueñe estando despierto.*
For I see, since I am asleep, that I
dream while I am awake.

[*Life is a Dream* (1636)]

CHUANG TSE (c. 369-286 BC)
I do not know whether I was then a
man dreaming I was a butterfly, or
whether I am now a butterfly
dreaming I am a man.

[*Chuang Tse* (1889), trans. H.A. Giles]

LAWRENCE, T.E. (1888-1935)
All men dream: but not equally. Those
who dream by night in the dusty
recesses of their minds wake in the
day to find that it was vanity; but the
dreamers of the day are dangerous
men, for they may act their dream
with open eyes, to make it possible.

[*The Seven Pillars of Wisdom* (1926)]

MONTAIGNE, Michel de (1533-1592)
*Ceux qui ont apparié notre vie à un
songe, ont eu de la raison, à l'aventure
plus qu'ils ne pensaient ... Nous veillons
dormants, et veillants dormons.*
Those who have compared our life to
a dream were, by chance, more right
than they thought ... We are awake
while sleeping, and sleeping while
awake.

[*Essais* (1580)]

POE, Edgar Allan (1809-1849)
All that we see or seem
Is but a dream within a dream.

['A Dream within a Dream' (1849)]

SHAKESPEARE, William (1564-1616)
O God, I could be bounded in a nut-
shell and count myself a king of
infinite space, were it not that I have
bad dreams.

[*Hamlet*, II.ii]

O, I have pass'd a miserable night,
So full of fearful dreams, of ugly
  sights,
That, as I am a Christian faithful man,
I would not spend another such a
  night
Though 'twere to buy a world of
  happy days –
So full of dismal terror was the time!

[*Richard III*, I.iv]

We are such stuff
As dreams are made on; and our little
  life
Is rounded with a sleep.

[*The Tempest*, IV.i]

Weary with toil, I haste me to my bed,
The dear repose for limbs with travel
  tired;
But then begins a journey in my head
To work my mind when body's work's
  expired.

[Sonnet 27]

TENNYSON, Alfred, Lord (1809–1892)
Dreams are true while they last, and
do we not live in dreams?

['The Higher Pantheism' (1867)]

YEATS, W.B. (1865–1939)
In dreams begins responsibility.

[*Responsibilities* (1914)]

DRESS

AESOP (6th century BC)
It is not only fine feathers that make
fine birds.

['The Jay and the Peacock']

ASHFORD, Daisy (1881–1972)
You look rather rash my dear your
colors dont quite match your face.

[*The Young Visiters* (1919)]

BONGAY, Amy
[Commenting on the fact that the
fashion industry had begun to find
supermodels too demanding]
It's a terrible sign. It will be the death
of this profession if designers start
using real people on the catwalks and
in their advertising.

[*Daily Mail*, 1995]

CHANEL, Coco (1883–1971)
Fashion is architecture: it is a matter
of proportions.

[In Haedrich, *Coco Chanel, Her Life, Her
Secrets* (1971)]

[On Dior's New Look]
These are clothes by a man who
doesn't know women, never had one
and dreams of being one.

[*Scotland on Sunday*, 1995]

CURIE, Marie (1867–1934)
[Referring to a wedding dress]
I have no dress except the one I wear
every day. If you are going to be kind
enough to give me one, please let it be
practical and dark so that I can put it
on afterwards to go to the laboratory.

[Letter to a friend, 1894]

DARROW, Clarence (1857–1938)
I go to a better tailor than any of you

and pay more for my clothes. The only
difference is that you probably don't
sleep in yours.

[In E. Fuller, *2500 Anecdotes*]

EDWARD VII (1841–1910)
I think everyone must know that a
short jacket is always worn with a silk
hat at a private view in the morning.

[In Sir P. Magnus, *Edward VII*]

EMERSON, Ralph Waldo (1803–1882)
[Of the English]
They think him the best dressed man,
whose dress is so fit for his use that
you cannot notice or remember to
describe it.

[*English Traits* (1856)]

The Frenchman invented the ruffle, the
Englishman added the shirt.

[*English Traits* (1856)]

It is only when the mind and character
slumber that the dress can be seen.

[*Letters and Social Aims* (1875)]

FARQUHAR, George (1678–1707)
A lady, if undrest at Church, looks silly,
One cannot be devout in dishabilly.

[*The Stage Coach* (1704)]

FORBES, Miss C.F. (1817–1911)
The sense of being well-dressed gives
a feeling of inward tranquillity which
religion is powerless to bestow.

[In Emerson, *Social Aims* (1876)]

GASKELL, Elizabeth (1810–1865)
[The Cranford ladies'] dress is very
independent of fashion; as they
observe, 'What does it signify how we
dress here at Cranford, where
everybody knows us?' And if they go
from home, their reason is equally
cogent, 'What does it signify how we
dress here, where nobody knows us?'

[*Cranford* (1853)]

HERRICK, Robert (1591–1674)
A sweet disorder in the dresse
Kindles in cloathes a wantonnesse:

A Lawne about the shoulders thrown
Into a fine distraction ...

A winning wave (deserving Note)
In the tempestuous petticote:
A carelesse shooe-string, in whose tye
I see a wilde civility:
Doe more bewitch me, than when Art
Is too precise in every part.

['Delight in Disorder' (1648)]

HEWETT, Dorothy (1923–)
Gentlemen may remove any garment
    consistent with decency.
Ladies may remove any garment
    consistent with charm.

['Beneath the Arches']

JULIA (39 BC–AD 14)
[On being complimented by her father
on the modest dress she was wearing
that day]
Today I dressed to meet my father's
eyes; yesterday it was for my husband's.

[In Macrobius, *Saturnalia*]

NASH, Ogden (1902–1971)
Sure, deck your lower limbs in pants;
Yours are the limbs, my sweeting.
You look divine as you advance –
Have you seen yourself retreating?

['What's the Use?' (1940)]

PARKER, Dorothy (1893–1967)
Where's the man could ease a heart,
Like a satin gown?

['The Satin Dress' (1937)]

Brevity is the soul of lingerie.

[In Woollcott, *While Rome Burns* (1934)]

SWIFT, Jonathan (1667–1745)
She wears her clothes, as if they were
thrown on with a pitchfork.

[*Polite Conversation* (1738)]

WATTS, Isaac (1674–1748)
The tulip and the butterfly
Appear in gayer coats than I:
Let me be dressed fine as I will,
Flies, worms, and flowers, exceed me
    still.

['Against Pride in Clothes' (1715)]

WHITEHORN, Katherine (1926–)
Hats divide generally into three
classes: offensive hats, defensive hats,
and shrapnel.

[*Shouts and Murmurs* (1963)]

WILDE, Oscar (1854–1900)
A well-tied tie is the first serious step
in life.

[*A Woman of No Importance* (1893)]

The only way to atone for being
occasionally a little over-dressed is by
being always absolutely over-
educated.

[*The Chameleon*, 1894]

WODEHOUSE, P.G. (1881–1975)
The Right Hon was a tubby little chap
who looked as if he had been poured
into his clothes and had forgotten to
say 'When!'

['Jeeves and the Impending Doom' (1930)]

DRINKING

AGA KHAN III (1877–1957)
[Justifying his liking for alcohol]
I'm so holy that when I touch wine, it
turns into water.

[Attr. in Compton Miller, *Who's Really Who*
(1983)]

ALDRICH, Henry (1647–1710)
If all be true that I do think,
There are five reasons we should
    drink;
Good wine – a friend – or being dry –
Or lest we should be by and by –
Or any other reason why.

['Five Reasons for Drinking' (1689)]

ANONYMOUS
Hath wine an oblivious power?
Can it pluck out the sting from the
    brain?
The draught might beguile for an hour,
But still leaves behind it the pain.

['Farewell to England'; sometimes attr. to
Byron]

BECON, Thomas (1512–1567)
For when the wine is in, the wit is out.
[*Catechism* (1560)]

BENCHLEY, Robert (1889–1945)
[Reply when asked if he realised that drinking was a slow death]
So who's in a hurry?
[Attr.]

BURNS, Robert (1759–1796)
Freedom and whisky gang thegither,
Tak aff your dram!
['The Author's Earnest Cry and Prayer' (1786)]

BURTON, Robert (1577–1640)
I may not here omit those two main plagues, and common dotages of human kind, wine and women, which have infatuated and besotted myriads of people. They go commonly together.
[*Anatomy of Melancholy* (1621)]

BYRON, Lord (1788–1824)
Man, being reasonable, must get drunk;
The best of life is but intoxication:
Glory, the grape, love, gold, in these are sunk
The hopes of all men, and of every nation.
[*Don Juan* (1824)]

CALVERLEY, C.S. (1831–1884)
The heart which grief hath canker'd
Hath one unfailing remedy – the Tankard.
['Beer' (1861)]

CHANDLER, Raymond (1888–1959)
Alcohol is like love: the first kiss is magic, the second is intimate, the third is routine. After that you just take the girl's clothes off.
[*The Long Good-bye* (1953)]

CHURCHILL, Sir Winston (1874–1965)
[Said during a lunch with the Arab leader Ibn Saud, when he heard that the king's religion forbade smoking and alcohol]
I must point out that my rule of life prescribed as an absolutely sacred rite smoking cigars and also the drinking of alcohol before, after, and if need be during all meals and in the intervals between them.
[*Triumph and Tragedy*]

CLARKE, Marcus (1846–1881)
No man has a right to inflict the torture of bad wine upon his fellow-creatures.
[*The Peripatetic Philosopher* (1870)]

COPE, Wendy (1945–)
All you need is love, love
or, failing that, alcohol.
[Variation on a Lennon and McCartney song]

COREN, Alan (1938–)
Apart from cheese and tulips, the main product of the country [Holland] is advocaat, a drink made from lawyers.
[*The Sanity Inspector* (1974)]

CRABBE, George (1754–1832)
Lo! the poor toper whose untutor'd sense,
Sees bliss in ale, and can with wine dispense;
Whose head proud fancy never taught to steer,
Beyond the muddy ecstasies of beer.
[*Inebriety* (1774)]

DE QUINCEY, Thomas (1785–1859)
It is most absurdly said, in popular language, of any man, that he is *disguised* in liquor; for, on the contrary, most men are disguised by sobriety.
[*Confessions of an English Opium Eater* (1822)]

DIBDIN, Charles (1745–1814)
Then trust me, there's nothing like drinking
So pleasant on this side the grave;
It keeps the unhappy from thinking,
And makes e'en the valiant more brave.
['Nothing like Grog']

DUNNE, Finley Peter (1867–1936)
There is wan thing an' on'y wan thing to be said in favour iv dhrink, an' that is that it has caused manny a lady to be loved that otherwise might've died single.

[*Mr Dooley Says* (1910)]

FARQUHAR, George (1678–1707)
I have fed purely upon ale; I have eat my ale, drank my ale, and I always sleep upon ale.

[*The Beaux' Stratagem* (1707)]

FITZGERALD, Edward (1809–1883)
Drink! for you know not whence you came, nor why:
Drink! for you know not why you go, nor where.

[*The Rubáiyát of Omar Khayyám* (1879)]

FITZGERALD, F. Scott (1896–1940)
First you take a drink, then the drink takes a drink, then the drink takes you.

[In Jules Feiffer, *Ackroyd*]

FLETCHER, John (1579–1625)
And he that will go to bed sober,
Falls with the leaf still in October.

[*The Bloody Brother* (1616)]

FRANKLIN, Benjamin (1706–1790)
There are more old drunkards than old doctors.

[Attr.]

HALIFAX, Lord (1633–1695)
It is a piece of Arrogance to dare to be drunk, because a Man sheweth himself without a Vail.

['Drunkenness' (1750),]

HOWKINS, Alun (1947–)
Real ale is an odd concept, linked more to an imagined real pub with real fire and real bread and cheese, as much as to a scientific definition of a brewing process.

[*New Statesman and Society*, 1989]

JAMES, William (1842–1910)
If merely 'feeling good' could decide, drunkenness would be the supremely valid human experience.

[*Varieties of Religious Experience* (1902)]

JOHNSON, Samuel (1709–1784)
Claret is the liquor for boys; port for men; but he who aspires to be a hero must drink brandy.

[In Boswell, *The Life of Samuel Johnson* (1791)]

A man who exposes himself when he is intoxicated, has not the art of getting drunk.

[In Boswell, *The Life of Samuel Johnson* (1791)]

JUNELL, Thomas
The Finns have a very different alcohol culture from other European countries. Basically, it's nothing to do with socialising – it's about getting drunk.

[*Daily Mail*, 1996]

LARDNER, Ring (1885–1933)
Frenchmen drink wine just like we used to drink water before Prohibition.

[In R.E. Drennan, *Wit's End*]

LAWSON, Henry (1867–1922)
Beer makes you feel as you ought to feel without beer.

[In David Low, *Low's Autobiography*]

LLOYD GEORGE, David (1863–1945)
[To a deputation of ship owners urging a campaign for prohibition during the First World War]
We are fighting Germany, Austria, and drink, and so far as I can see the greatest of these deadly foes is drink.

[Speech, 1915]

MENCKEN, H.L. (1880–1956)
I've made it a rule never to drink by daylight and never to refuse a drink after dark.

[*New York Post*, 1945]

NASH, Ogden (1902–1971)
Candy
Is dandy
But liquor
Is quicker.
['Reflections on Ice-Breaking' (1931)]

OSLER, Sir William
[His description of alcohol]
Milk of the elderly.
[The Globe and Mail, 1988]

O'SULLIVAN, John L. (1813–1895)
[Of whisky]
A torchlight procession marching
down your throat.
[Attr.]

PEACOCK, Thomas Love (1785–1866)
There are two reasons for drinking;
one is, when you are thirsty, to cure it;
the other, when you are not thirsty, to
prevent it ... Prevention is better than
cure.
[Melincourt (1817)]

PLINY THE ELDER (AD 23–79)
In vino veritas.
Wine brings out the truth!
[Historia Naturalis]

POTTER, Stephen (1900–1969)
It is WRONG to do what everyone else
does – namely, to hold the wine list
just out of sight, look for the second
cheapest claret on the list, and say,
'Number 22, please'.
[One-Upmanship (1952)]

RABELAIS, François (c. 1494–c. 1553)
Je boy pour la soif advenir.
I drink for the thirst to come.
[Gargantua (1534)]

RUSSELL, Bertrand (1872–1970)
Drunkenness is temporary suicide: the
happiness that it brings is merely
negative, a momentary cessation of
unhappiness.
[The Conquest of Happiness (1930)]

SAINTSBURY, George (1845–1933)
It is the unbroken testimony of all

history that alcoholic liquors have
been used by the strongest, wisest,
handsomest, and in every way best
races of all times.
[Attr.]

SHAW, George Bernard (1856–1950)
I'm only a beer teetotaller, not a
champagne teetotaller.
[Candida (1898)]

Alcohol is a very necessary article ... It
enables Parliament to do things at
eleven at night that no sane person
would do at eleven in the morning.
[Major Barbara (1907)]

SQUIRE, Sir J.C. (1884–1958)
But I'm not so think as you drunk I
am.
['Ballade of Soporific Absorption' (1931)]

TARKINGTON, Booth (1869–1946)
There are two things that will be
believed of any man whatsoever, and
one of them is that he has taken to
drink.
[Penrod (1914)]

THATCHER, Denis (1915–)
[Reply to someone who asked if he
had a drinking problem]
Yes, there's never enough.
[Daily Mail, 1996]

THURBER, James (1894–1961)
It's a naïve domestic Burgundy, without any breeding, but I think you'll be
amused by its presumption.
[Cartoon caption in The New Yorker, 1937]

WARD, Artemus (1834–1867)
I prefer temperance hotels – although
they sell worse kinds of liquor than
any other kind of hotels.
[Artemus Ward's Lecture]

WODEHOUSE, P.G. (1881–1975)
It was my Uncle George who discovered that alcohol was a food well
in advance of modern medical
thought.
[The Inimitable Jeeves (1923)]

YOUNG, George W. (1846-1919)
Your lips, on my own, when they
   printed 'Farewell',
Had never been soiled by the
   'beverage of hell';
But they come to me now with the
   bacchanal sign,
And the lips that touch liquor must
   never touch mine.
['The lips that touch liquor must never touch
   mine' (c. 1870)]

DUTY

ANONYMOUS
Straight is the line of Duty
Curved is the line of Beauty
Follow the first and thou shallt see
The second ever following thee.

GIBBON, Edward (1737-1794)
Dr Winchester well remembered that
he had a salary to receive, and only
forgot that he had a duty to perform.
[*Memoirs of My Life and Writings* (1796)]

GILBERT, W.S. (1836-1911)
The question is, had he not been a
   thing of beauty,
Would she be swayed by quite as keen
   a sense of duty?
[*The Pirates of Penzance* (1880)]

GOETHE (1749-1832)
Du kannst, denn du sollst!
You can, for you ought to!
['An eighth' (1796); written with Schiller]

GRANT, Ulysses S. (1822-1885)
No personal consideration should
stand in the way of performing a
public duty.
[Note on letter, 1875]

HOOPER, Ellen Sturgis (1816-1841)
I slept, and dreamed that life was
   Beauty;
I woke, and found that life was Duty.
['Beauty and Duty' (1840)]

IBSEN, Henrik (1828-1906)
What's a man's first duty? The
answer's brief: To be himself.
[*Peer Gynt* (1867)]

JOHNSON, Samuel (1709-1784)
It is our first duty to serve society, and,
after we have done that, we may
attend wholly to the salvation of our
own souls. A youthful passion for
abstracted devotion should not be
encouraged.
[In Boswell, *The Life of Samuel Johnson*
(1791)]

LEE, Robert E. (1807-1870)
Duty then is the sublimest word in our
language. Do your duty in all things.
You cannot do more. You should never
wish to do less.
[Inscription in the Hall of Fame]

MILNER, Alfred (1854-1925)
If we believe a thing to be bad, and if
we have a right to prevent it, it is our
duty to try to prevent it and to damn
the consequences.
[Speech, 1909]

NELSON, Lord (1758-1805)
[Nelson's last signal at the Battle of
Trafalgar, 1805]
England expects every man to do his
duty.
[In Southey, *The Life of Nelson* (1860)]

PEACOCK, Thomas Love (1785-1866)
Sir, I have quarrelled with my wife;
and a man who has quarrelled with
his wife is absolved from all duty to his
country.
[*Nightmare Abbey* (1818)]

SHAKESPEARE, William (1564-1616)
Every subject's duty is the King's; but
every subject's soul is his own.
[*Henry V*, IV.i]

SHAW, George Bernard (1856-1950)
When a stupid man is doing
something he is ashamed of, he
always declares that it is his duty.
[*Caesar and Cleopatra* (1901)]

**STEVENSON, Robert Louis
(1850-1894)**
There is no duty we so much
underrate as the duty of being happy.
[*Virginibus Puerisque* (1881)]

TENNYSON, Alfred, Lord (1809–1892)
O hard, when love and duty clash!
[*The Princess* (1847)]

WASHINGTON, George (1732–1799)
To persevere in one's duty and be
silent is the best answer to calumny.
[*Moral Maxims*]

WILSON, Woodrow (1856–1924)
I fancy that it is just as hard to do your
duty when men are sneering at you as
when they are shooting at you.
[Speech, 1914]

WORDSWORTH, William (1770–1850)
Stern Daughter of the Voice of God!
O Duty! if that name thou love
Who art a light to guide, a rod
To check the erring and reprove ...

Thou dost preserve the Stars from
    wrong;
And the most ancient Heavens,
    through Thee, are fresh and strong.
['Ode to Duty' (1807)]

ECONOMICS

BAGEHOT, Walter (1826–1877)
No real English gentleman, in his
secret soul, was ever sorry for the
death of a political economist.
['The First Edinburgh Reviewers' (1858)]

BLAIR, Tony (1953–)
I want Britain to be a stake-holder
economy where everyone has a
chance to get on and succeed, where
there is a clear sense of national
purpose and where we leave behind
some of the battles between Left and
Right which really are not relevant in
the new global economy of today.
[Speech in Singapore, 1996]

CARLYLE, Thomas (1795–1881)
[Of Political Economics]
And the Social Science, – not a 'gay
science', ... no, a dreary, desolate, and
indeed quite abject and distressing
one; what we might call ...the *dismal
science*.
[*Latter-Day Pamphlets* (1850)]

DOUGLAS-HOME, Sir Alec (1903–1995)
When I have to read economic
documents I have to have a box of
matches and start moving them into
position to illustrate and simplify the
points to myself.
[Interview in *The Observer*, 1962]

EISENHOWER, Dwight D. (1890–1969)
Every gun that is made, every warship
launched, every rocket fired signifies,
in the final sense, a theft from those
who hunger and are not fed, those
who are cold and are not clothed. This
world in arms is not spending money
alone. It is spending the sweat of its
labourers, the genius of its scientists,
the hopes of its children.
[Speech, 1953]

FRIEDMAN, Milton (1912–)
There's no such thing as a free lunch.
[Title of book]

GALBRAITH, J.K. (1908–)
Economics is extremely useful as a
form of employment for economists.
[Attr.]

If all else fails, immortality can always
be assured by spectacular error.
[Attr.]

GEORGE, Eddie (1938–)
There are three kinds of economist.
Those who can count and those who
can't.
[*The Observer Review*, 1996]

KEYNES, John Maynard (1883–1946)
But this *long run* is a misleading guide
to current affairs. *In the long run* we
are all dead. Economists set themselves too easy, too useless a task if in
tempestuous seasons they can only
tell us that when the storm is long past
the ocean will be flat again.
[*A Tract on Monetary Reform* (1923)]

It is better that a man should tyrannize
over his bank balance than over his
fellow-citizens.
[*The General Theory of Employment, Interest
and Money* (1936)]

Practical men, who believe themselves
to be quite exempt from any intellectual influences, are usually the slaves
of some defunct economist. Madmen
in authority, who hear voices in the
air, are distilling their frenzy from
some academic scribbler of a few
years back.
[*The General Theory of Employment, Interest
and Money* (1936)]

LEVIN, Bernard (1928–)
Inflation in the Sixties was a nuisance
to be endured, like varicose veins or
French foreign policy.
[*The Pendulum Years* (1970)]

MACLEOD, Iain (1913–1970)
We now have the worst of both worlds
– not just inflation on the one side or
stagnation on the other side, but both
of them together. We have a sort of
'stagflation' situation.
[Speech, 1965]

MALTHUS, Thomas Robert (1766–1834)
Population, when unchecked, increases in a geometrical ratio. Subsistence only increases in an arithmetical ratio.

[*Essay on the Principle of Population* (1798)]

MELLON, Andrew (1855–1937)
A nation is not in danger of financial disaster merely because it owes itself money.

[Attr.]

ROOSEVELT, Franklin Delano (1882–1945)
We have always known that heedless self-interest was bad morals; we know now that it is bad economics.

[First Inaugural Address, 1933]

RUTSKOI, Alexander (1947–)
The dollar is Russia's national currency now, the rouble is just a sweetie paper. We've handed our sword to America.

[*Newsweek*, 1994]

SCHUMACHER, E.F. (1911–1977)
Small is Beautiful. A study of economics as if people mattered.

[Title of book, 1973]

SELLAR, Walter (1898–1951) and YEATMAN, Robert (1897–1968)
The National Debt is a very Good Thing and it would be dangerous to pay it off, for fear of Political Economy.

[*1066 And All That* (1930)]

SHAW, George Bernard (1856–1950)
Whether you think Jesus was God or not, you must admit that he was a first-rate political economist.

[*Androcles and the Lion* (1915)]

If all economists were laid end to end, they would not reach a conclusion.

[Attr.]

TRUMAN, Harry S. (1884–1972)
It's a recession when your neighbour loses his job; it's a depression when you lose your own.

[*The Observer*, 1958]

YELTSIN, Boris (1931–)
I am for the market, not for the bazaar.

[*The Times*, 1992]

EDITING

ALLEN, Fred (1894–1956)
[Remark to writers who had heavily edited one of his scripts]
Where were you fellows when the paper was blank?

[Attr.]

AUBREY, John (1626–1697)
He [Shakespeare] was wont to say that he 'never blotted out a line of his life'; said Ben Jonson, 'I wish he had blotted out a thousand.'

[*Brief Lives* (c. 1693)]

BOILEAU-DESPREAUX, Nicolas (1636–1711)
Si j'écris quatre mots, j'en effacerai trois.
If I write four words, I shall strike out three.

[*Satires* (1666)]

HUBBARD, Elbert (1856–1915)
Editor: a person employed by a newspaper whose business it is to separate the wheat from the chaff and to see that the chaff is printed.

[*A Thousand and One Epigrams* (1911)]

JOHNSON, Samuel (1709–1784)
Read over your compositions, and where ever you meet with a passage which you think is particularly fine, strike it out.

[In Boswell, *The Life of Samuel Johnson* (1791)]

MAYER, Louis B. (1885–1957)
[Comment to writers who had objected to changes in their work]
The number one book of the ages was

written by a committee, and it was called The Bible.

[In Halliwell, *The Filmgoer's Book of Quotes* (1973)]

PASCAL, Blaise (1623–1662)
Je n'ai fait celle-ci plus longue que parce que je n'ai pas eu le loisir de la faire plus courte.
I have made this letter longer only because I have not had time to make it shorter.

[*Lettres Provinciales* (1657)]

TWAIN, Mark (1835–1910)
As to the Adjective: when in doubt, strike it out.

[*Pudd'nhead Wilson's Calendar* (1894)]

EDUCATION

AMIS, Kingsley (1922–1995)
[On 'the delusion' that thousands more young people were capable of benefiting from university education]
I wish I could have a little tape-and-loudspeaker arrangement sewn into the binding of this magazine, to be triggered off by the light reflected from the reader's eyes on to this part of the page, and set to bawl out at several bels: MORE WILL MEAN WORSE.

[*Encounter*, 1960]

ARISTOTLE (384–322 BC)
The roots of education are bitter, but the fruit is sweet.

[In Diogenes Laertius, *Lives of Philosophers*]

BACON, Francis (1561–1626)
Reading maketh a full man; conference a ready man; and writing an exact man.

[*Essays* (1625)]

Histories make men wise; poets, witty; the mathematics, subtile; natural philosophy, deep; moral, grave; logic and rhetoric, able to contend.

[*Essays* (1625)]

BIERCE, Ambrose (1842–c. 1914)
Education: That which discloses to the wise and disguises from the foolish their lack of understanding.

[*The Cynic's Word Book* (1906)]

BROUGHAM, Lord Henry (1778–1868)
Education makes a people easy to lead, but difficult to drive; easy to govern, but impossible to enslave.

[Attr.]

BUCHAN, John (1875–1940)
To live for a time close to great minds is the best kind of education.

[*Memory Hold the Door*]

CHESTERTON, G.K. (1874–1936)
Education is simply the soul of a society as it passes from one generation to another.

[*The Observer*, 1924]

CODY, Henry (1868–1951)
Education is casting false pearls before real swine.

[Attr.]

COOPER, Roger
[On being released after five years in an Iranian prison]
I can say that anyone who, like me, has been educated in English public schools and served in the ranks of the British Army is quite at home in a Third World prison.

[*Newsweek*, 1991]

DICKENS, Charles (1812–1870)
EDUCATION. – At Mr Wackford Squeer's Academy, Dotheboys Hall, at the delightful village of Dotheboys, near Greta Bridge in Yorkshire, Youth are boarded, clothed, booked, furnished with pocket-money, provided with all necessaries, instructed in all languages, living and dead, mathematics, orthography, geometry, astronomy, trigonometry, the use of the globes, algebra, single stick (if required), writing, arithmetic, fortification, and every other branch of classical literature. Terms, twenty guineas per annum. No extras, no vacations, and diet unparalleled.

[*Nicholas Nickleby* (1839)]

Now, what I want is, Facts. Teach these boys and girls nothing but Facts. Facts alone are wanted in life. Plant nothing else, and root out everything else ... Stick to Facts, sir!

[*Hard Times* (1854)]

DIOGENES (THE CYNIC) (c. 400–325 BC)
Education is something that tempers the young and consoles the old, gives wealth to the poor and adorns the rich.

[In Diogenes Laertius, *Lives of Eminent Philosophers*]

EMERSON, Ralph Waldo (1803–1882)
I pay the schoolmaster, but 'tis the schoolboys that educate my son.

[*Journals*]

HUXLEY, Aldous (1894–1963)
The solemn foolery of scholarship for scholarship's sake.

[*The Perennial Philosophy* (1945)]

JOHNSON, Samuel (1709–1784)
Example is always more efficacious than precept.

[*Rasselas* (1759)]

All intellectual improvement arises from leisure.

[In Boswell, *The Life of Samuel Johnson* (1791)]

KANT, Immanuel (1724–1804)
Der Mensch ist das einzige Geschöpf, das erzogen werden muss.
Man is the only creature which must be educated.

[*On Pedagogy* (1803)]

KRAUS, Karl (1874–1936)
Bildung ist das, was die meisten empfangen, viele weitergeben und wenige haben.
Education is what most people receive, many pass on and few actually have.

[*Pro domo et mundo* (1912)]

MCIVER, Charles D. (1860–1906)
When you educate a man you educate an individual; when you educate a woman you educate a whole family.

[Address at women's college]

MILTON, John (1608–1674)
... the right path of a vertuous and noble Education, laborious indeed at the first ascent, but else so smooth, so green, so full of goodly prospect, and melodious sounds on every side, that the harp of Orpheus was not more charming.

[*Of Education: To Master Samuel Hartlib* (1644)]

MORAVIA, Alberto (1907–1990)
The ratio of literacy to illiteracy is constant, but nowadays the illiterates can read and write.

[*The Observer*, 1979]

PARSONS, Tony (1922–1996)
The death of the grammar schools – those public schools without the sodomy – resulted in state education relinquishing its role of nurturing bright young working class kids.

[*Arena*, 1989]

ROUSSEAU, Jean-Jacques (1712–1778)
On n'est curieux qu'à proportion qu'on est instruit.
One is only curious in proportion to one's level of education.

[*Émile ou De l'éducation* (1762)]

SITWELL, Sir Osbert (1892–1969)
Educ: during the holidays from Eton.

[*Who's Who* (1929)]

SPARK, Muriel (1918–)
To me education is a leading out of what is already there in the pupil's soul. To Miss Mackay it is a putting in of something that is not there, and that is not what I call education, I call it intrusion.

[*The Prime of Miss Jean Brodie* (1961)]

STOCKS, Mary, Baroness (1891–1975)
Today we enjoy a social structure which offers equal opportunity in education. It is indeed regrettably true

that there is no equal opportunity to take advantage of the equal opportunity.

[*Still More Commonplace* (1973)]

TREVELYAN, G.M. (1876–1962)
Education ... has produced a vast population able to read but unable to distinguish what is worth reading.

[*English Social History* (1942)]

USTINOV, Sir Peter (1921–)
People at the top of the tree are those without qualifications to detain them at the bottom.

[Attr.]

WILDE, Oscar (1854–1900)
Education is an admirable thing, but it is well to remember from time to time that nothing that is worth knowing can be taught.

['The Critic as Artist' (1891)]

See LEARNING; KNOWLEDGE; SCHOOLS; TEACHERS; UNIVERSITY

EGOISM

ADLER, Alfred (1870–1937)
[On hearing that an egocentric had fallen in love]
Against whom?

[Attr.]

ALI, Muhammad (1942–)
I am the greatest.

[Catchphrase]

BACON, Francis (1561–1626)
It was prettily devised of Aesop, 'The fly sat upon the axletree of the chariot-wheel and said, what a dust do I raise.'

['Of Vain-Glory' (1625)]

BARNES, Peter (1931–)
I know I am God because when I pray to him I find I'm talking to myself.

[*The Ruling Class* (1968)]

BIERCE, Ambrose (1842–c. 1914)
Egotist: A person of low taste, more interested in himself than in me.

[*The Cynic's Word Book* (1906)]

BULMER-THOMAS, Ivor (1905–)
[Of Harold Wilson]
If ever he went to school without any boots it was because he was too big for them.

[Remark, 1949]

BUTLER, Samuel (1835–1902)
The advantage of doing one's praising for oneself is that one can lay it on so thick and exactly in the right places.

[*The Way of All Flesh* (1903)]

CHAMFORT, Nicolas (1741–1794)
Quelqu'un disait d'un homme très personnel; il brûlerait votre maison pour se faire cuire deux oeufs.
Someone said of a great egotist: 'He would burn your house down to cook himself a couple of eggs.'

[*Caractères et anecdotes*]

CHURCHILL, Charles (1731–1764)
[Of Thomas Franklin, Professor of Greek, Cambridge]
He sicken'd at all triumphs but his own.

[*The Rosciad* (1761)]

DISRAELI, Benjamin (1804–1881)
Every day when he looked into the glass, and gave the last touch to his consummate toilette, he offered his grateful thanks to Providence that his family was not unworthy of him

[*Lothair* (1870)]

DULLES, John Foster (1888–1959)
[Reply when asked if he had ever been wrong]
Yes, once – many, many years ago. I thought I had made a wrong decision. Of course, it turned out that I had been right all along. But I was wrong to have *thought* that I was wrong.

[Attr.]

ELIOT, George (1819–1880)
He was like a cock, who thought the
sun had risen to hear him crow.
[*Adam Bede* (1859)]

GORTON, John (1911–)
I am always prepared to recognize
that there can be two points of view –
mine, and one that is probably wrong.
[In Trengove, *John Grey Gorton*]

HARTLEY, L.P. (1895–1972)
'Should I call myself an egoist?' Miss
Johnstone mused. 'Others have called
me so. They merely meant I did not
care for them.'
[*Simonetta Perkins* (1925)]

HAWKE, Bob (1929–)
[On first entering Parliament, 1979]
Well, I don't want to be any more
egotistical than possible. I have total
confidence in my ability.
[*The World According to Hawke*]

JAMES, Brian (1892–1972)
A dominant personality doesn't believe
in its own will. All it needs is the inability to recognise the existence of
anybody else's.
[*Falling Towards England*]

JEROME, Jerome K. (1859–1927)
Conceit is the finest armour a man can
wear.
[*Idle Thoughts of an Idle Fellow* (1886)]

KEITH, Penelope (1940–)
Shyness is just egotism out of its
depth.
[*The Observer*, 1988]

ROUX, Joseph (1834–1886)
The egoist does not tolerate egoism.
[*Meditations of a Parish Priest* (1886)]

SITWELL, Dame Edith (1887–1964)
I have often wished I had time to
cultivate modesty ... But I am too busy
thinking about myself.
[*The Observer*, 1950]

SUZUKI, D.T. (1870–1966)
The individual ego asserts itself
strongly in the West. In the East, there
is no ego. The ego is non-existent and,
therefore, there is no ego to be crucified.
[*Mysticism Christian and Buddhist* (1957)]

TROLLOPE, Anthony (1815–1882)
As for conceit, what man will do any
good who is not conceited? Nobody
holds a good opinion of a man who
has a low opinion of himself.
[*Orley Farm* (1862)]

WEBB, Beatrice (1858–1943)
If I ever felt inclined to be timid as I
was going into a room full of people, I
would say to myself, 'You're the
cleverest member of one of the
cleverest families in the cleverest class
of the cleverest nation in the world,
why should you be frightened?'
[In Russell, *Portraits from Memory* (1956)]

WHISTLER, James McNeill (1834–1903)
[Replying to the pointed observation
that it was as well that we do not see
ourselves as others see us]
Isn't it? I know in my case I would
grow intolerably conceited.
[In Pearson, *The Man Whistler*]

ENEMIES

THE BIBLE (King James Version)
Love your enemies, bless them that
curse you, do good to them that hate
you, and pray for them which de-
spitefully use you, and persecute you.
[*Matthew*, 5:44]

BRETON, Nicholas (c. 1545–c. 1626)
I wish my deadly foe, no worse
Than want of friends, and empty
purse.
['A Farewell to Town' (1577)]

BURKE, Edmund (1729–1797)
He that wrestles with us strengthens
our nerves, and sharpens our skill. Our
antagonist is our helper.
[*Reflections on the Revolution in France* (1790)]

CONRAD, Joseph (1857–1924)
You shall judge of a man by his foes as
well as by his friends.

[*Lord Jim* (1900)]

LESAGE, Alain-René (1668–1747)
*On nous réconcilia: nous nous
embrassâmes, et depuis ce temps-là
nous sommes ennemis mortels.*
They made peace between us; we
embraced, and since that time we
have been mortal enemies.

[*Le Diable boiteux*]

LINKLATER, Eric (1899–1974)
With a heavy step Sir Matthew left the
room and spent the morning designing
mausoleums for his enemies.

[*Juan in America* (1931)]

**MONTAGU, Lady Mary Wortley
(1689–1762)**
People wish their enemies dead – but I
do not; I say give them the gout, give
them the stone!

[Letter from Horace Walpole, 1778]

NARVÁEZ, Ramón María (1800–1868)
[On his deathbed, when asked by a
priest if he forgave his enemies]
I do not have to forgive my enemies, I
have had them all shot.

[Attr.]

**ROOSEVELT, Franklin Delano
(1882–1945)**
I ask you to judge me by the enemies I
have made.

[*The Observer*, 1932]

WHITMAN, Walt (1819–1892)
Beautiful that war and all its deeds of
    carnage must in time be utterly lost,
That the hands of the sisters Death
    and Night incessantly softly wash
    again, and ever again, this soil'd
    world;
For my enemy is dead, a man as
    divine as myself is dead,
I look where he lies white-faced and
    still in the coffin – I draw near,
Bend down and touch lightly with my
    lips the white face in the coffin.

['Reconciliation' (1865)]

WILDE, Oscar (1854–1900)
A man cannot be too careful in the
choice of his enemies.

[*The Picture of Dorian Gray* (1891)]

ENGLAND

AGATE, James (1877–1947)
The English instinctively admire any
man who has no talent and is modest
about it.

[Attr.]

BAGEHOT, Walter (1826–1877)
Of all nations in the world the English
are perhaps the least a nation of pure
philosophers.

[*The English Constitution* (1867)]

BEHAN, Brendan (1923–1964)
He was born an Englishman and remained one for years.

[*The Hostage* (1958)]

BRADBURY, Malcolm (1932–)
I like the English. They have the most
rigid code of immorality in the world.

[*Eating People is Wrong* (1954)]

BRIGHT, John (1811–1889)
England is the mother of Parliaments.

[Speech, 1865]

BROOKE, Rupert (1887–1915)
If I should die, think only this of me:
That there's some corner of a foreign
    field
That is for ever England.

['The Soldier' (1914)]

BROWNE, Sir Thomas (1605–1682)
All places, all airs make unto me one
country; I am in England, everywhere,
and under any meridian.

[*Religio Medici* (1643)]

BROWNING, Robert (1812–1889)
Oh, to be in England
Now that April's there,
And whoever wakes in England
Sees, some morning, unaware,
That the lowest boughs and the
    brushwood sheaf

Round the elm-tree bole are in tiny
leaf,
While the chaffinch sings on the
orchard bough
In England – now!

['Home Thoughts, from Abroad' (1845)]

BUTLER, Samuel (1835–1902)
The wish to spread those opinions that
we hold conducive to our own welfare
is so deeply rooted in the English
character that few of us can escape its
influence.

[*Erewhon* (1872)]

BYRON, Lord (1788–1824)
The English winter – ending in July,
To recommence in August.

[*Don Juan* (1824)]

I am sure my bones would not rest in
an English grave, or my clay mix with
the earth of that country. I believe the
thought would drive me mad on my
deathbed, could I suppose that any of
my friends would be base enough to
convey my carcass back to your soil. I
would not even feed your worms if I
could help it.

[Letter to John Murray, 1819]

CARLYLE, Thomas (1795–1881)
[When asked what the population of
England was]
Thirty millions, mostly fools.

[Attr.]

CHESTERTON, G.K. (1874–1936)
Before the Roman came to Rye or out
to Severn strode,
The rolling English drunkard made the
rolling English road.

['The Rolling English Road' (1914)]

**COMPTON-BURNETT, Dame Ivy
(1884–1969)**
Well, the English have no family
feelings. That is, none of the kind you
mean. They have them, and one of
them is that relations must cause no
expense.

[*Parents and Children* (1941)]

COWPER, William (1731–1800)
England, with all thy faults, I love thee
still.

[*The Task* (1785)]

**CUNNINGHAM, Peter Miller
(1789–1864)**
A young girl, when asked how she
would like to go to England, replied
with great *naïveté*, 'I should be afraid
to go, from the *number of thieves*
there,' doubtless conceiving England
to be a downright hive of such, that
threw off its annual swarms to people
the wilds of this colony.

[*Two Years in New South Wales* (1827)]

DEFOE, Daniel (c. 1661–1731)
Your Roman-Saxon-Danish-Norman
English.

[*The True-Born Englishman* (1701)]

DICKENS, Charles (1812–1870)
'This Island was Blest, Sir, to the
Direct Exclusion of such Other
Countries as – as there may happen to
be. And if we were all Englishmen
present, I would say,' added Mr
Podsnap ... 'that there is in the
Englishman a combination of qualities,
a modesty, an independence, a
responsibility, a repose, combined with
an absence of everything calculated to
call a blush into the cheek of a young
person, which one would seek in vain
among the Nations of the Earth.'

[*Our Mutual Friend* (1865)]

FORSTER, E.M. (1879–1970)
It is not that the Englishman can't feel
– it is that he is afraid to feel. He has
been taught at his public school that
feeling is bad form. He must not
express great joy or sorrow, or even
open his mouth too wide when he
talks – his pipe might fall out if he did.

[*Abinger Harvest* (1936)]

GOLDING, William (1911–1993)
We've got to have rules and obey
them. After all, we're not savages.
We're English; and the English are best

at everything. So we've got to do the right things.

[*Lord of the Flies* (1954)]

HALSEY, Margaret (1910–)
Living in England, provincial England, must be like being married to a stupid but exquisitely beautiful wife.

[*With Malice Toward Some* (1938)]

HERBERT, Sir A.P. (1890–1971)
The Englishman never enjoys himself except for a noble purpose.

[*Uncommon Law* (1935)]

HILL, Reginald (1936–)
Nobody has ever lost money by over-estimating the superstitious credulity of an English jury.

[*Pictures of Perfection* (1994)]

HOWARD, Philip (1933–)
Every time an Englishman opens his mouth, he enables other Englishmen if not to despise him, at any rate to place him in some social and class pigeon-hole.

[*The Times*, 1992]

HUGO, Victor (1802–1885)
England has two books: the Bible and Shakespeare. England made Shakespeare but the Bible made England.

[Attr.]

JOAD, C.E.M. (1891–1953)
It will be said of this generation that it found England a land of beauty and left it a land of beauty spots.

[*The Observer*, 1953]

JOYCE, James (1882–1941)
We feel in England that we have treated you [Irish] rather unfairly. It seems history is to blame.

[*Ulysses* (1922)]

KINGSLEY, Charles (1819–1875)
'Tis the hard grey weather
Breeds hard English men.

['Ode to the North-East Wind' (1854)]

KIPLING, Rudyard (1865–1936)
For Allah created the English mad –
the maddest of all mankind!

[*The Five Nations* (1903)]

[Of the English]
For undemocratic reasons and for
  motives not of State,
They arrive at their conclusions –
  largely inarticulate.
Being void of self-expression they
  confide their views to none;
But sometimes in a smoking-room,
  one learns why things were done.

[*Actions and Reactions* (1909)]

LAWRENCE, D.H. (1885–1930)
It was one of those places where the spirit of aboriginal England still lingers, the old savage England, whose last blood flows still in a few Englishmen, Welshmen, Cornishmen.

[*St Mawr* (1925)]

MACAULAY, Lord (1800–1859)
The history of England is emphatically the history of progress.

['Sir James Mackintosh' (1843)]

MACINNES, Colin (1914–1976)
England is ... a country infested with people who love to tell us what to do, but who very rarely seem to know what's going on.

[*England, Half English*]

MARY, QUEEN OF SCOTS (1542–1587)
England is not all the world.

[Said at her trial, 1586]

MIKES, George (1912–1987)
An Englishman, even if he is alone, forms an orderly queue of one.

[*How to be an Alien* (1946)]

NAPOLEON I (1769–1821)
L'Angleterre est une nation de boutiquiers.
England is a nation of shopkeepers.

[In O'Meara, *Napoleon in Exile* (1822)]

NASH, Ogden (1902–1971)
Let us pause to consider the English

Who when they pause to consider
themselves they get all reticently
thrilled and tinglish.
Englishmen are distinguished by their
traditions and ceremonials,
And also by their affection for their
colonies and their condescension to
their colonials.

['England Expects' (1929)]

O'CONNELL, Daniel (1775–1847)
The Englishman has all the qualities of
a poker except its occasional warmth.

[Attr.]

ORWELL, George (1903–1950)
England is not the jewelled isle of
Shakespeare's much-quoted passage,
nor is it the inferno depicted by Dr
Goebbels. More than either it resembles a family, a rather stuffy
Victorian family, with not many black
sheep in it but with all its cupboards
bursting with skeletons. It has rich
relations who have to be kow-towed
to and poor relations who are horribly
sat upon, and there is a deep conspiracy about the source of the family
income. It is a family in which the
young are generally thwarted and
most of the power is in the hands of
irresponsible uncles and bedridden
aunts. Still, it is a family ... A family
with the wrong members in control.

['England, Your England' (1941)]

PARSONS, Tony (1922–1996)
To be born an Englishman – ah, what
an easy conceit that builds in you,
what a self-righteous nationalism, a
secure xenophobia, what a pride in
your ignorance. No other people speak
so few languages. No other people ...
have an expression that is the equivalent of 'greasy foreign muck'. The
noble, wisecracking savages depicted
everywhere from 'Eastenders' to 'Boys
from the Blackstuff' are exercises in
nostalgia who no longer exist.

[*Arena*, 1989]

PEPYS, Samuel (1633–1703)
But Lord! to see the absurd nature of
Englishmen, that cannot forbear

laughing and jeering at everything that
looks strange.

[*Diary*, 1662]

RHODES, Cecil (1853–1902)
Remember that you are an
Englishman, and have consequently
won first prize in the lottery of life.

[In Ustinov, *Dear Me* (1977)]

SANTAYANA, George (1863–1952)
England is the paradise of individuality, eccentricity, heresy,
anomalies, hobbies, and humours.

[*Soliloquies in England* (1922)]

SEELEY, Sir John (1834–1895)
We [the English] seem as it were to
have conquered and peopled half the
world in a fit of absence of mind.

[*The Expansion of England* (1883)]

SHAKESPEARE, William (1564–1616)
This royal throne of kings, this
    scept'red isle,
This earth of majesty, this seat of
    Mars,
This other Eden, demi-paradise,
This fortress built by Nature for herself
Against infection and the hand of war,
This happy breed of men, this little
    world,
This precious stone set in the silver
    sea,
Which serves it in the office of a wall,
Or as a moat defensive to a house,
Against the envy of less happier lands;
This blessed plot, this earth, this
    realm, this England.

[*Richard II*, II.i]

SHAW, George Bernard (1856–1950)
There is nothing so bad or so good
that you will not find Englishmen
doing it; but you will never find an
Englishman in the wrong. He does
everything on principle. He fights you
on patriotic principles; he robs you on
business principles; he enslaves you
on imperial principles; he bullies you
on manly principles; he supports his
king on loyal principles and cuts off

his king's head on republican principles.

[*The Man of Destiny* (1898)]

SULLY, Duc de (1559–1641)
Les Anglais s'amusent tristement, selon l'usage de leur pays.
The English enjoy themselves sadly, according to the custom of their country.

[*Memoirs* (1638)]

TREE, Sir Herbert Beerbohm (1853–1917)
The national sport of England is obstacle-racing. People fill their rooms with useless and cumbersome furniture, and spend the rest of their lives trying to dodge it.

[In Hesketh Pearson, *Beerbohm Tree* (1956)]

VOLTAIRE (1694–1778)
Le sombre Anglais, même dans ses amours,
Veut raisonner toujours.
On est plus raisonnable en France.
The gloomy Englishman, even in love, always wants to reason. We are more reasonable in France.

[*Les Originaux, Entrée des Diverses Nations*]

WELLS, H.G. (1866–1946)
In England we have come to rely upon a comfortable time-lag of fifty years or a century intervening between the perception that something ought to be done and a serious attempt to do it.

[*The Work, Wealth and Happiness of Mankind* (1931)]

WILDE, Oscar (1854–1900)
The English have a miraculous power of turning wine into water.

[Attr.]

WORDSWORTH, William (1770–1850)
Milton! thou shouldst be living at this hour:
England hath need of thee; she is a fen
Of stagnant waters: altar, sword, and pen,
Fireside, the heroic wealth of hall and bower,

Have forfeited their ancient English dower
Of inward happiness.

['Milton! thou shouldst be living at this hour' (1807)]

YEATS, W.B. (1865–1939)
The Irish mind has still in country rapscallion or in Bernard Shaw an ancient, cold, explosive, detonating impartiality. The English mind, excited by its newspaper proprietors and its schoolmasters, has turned into a bed-hot harlot.

['Ireland after the Revolution' (1939)]

THE ENVIRONMENT

BOTTOMLEY, Gordon (1874–1948)
When you destroy a blade of grass
You poison England at her roots:
Remember no man's foot can pass
Where evermore no green life shoots.

['To Ironfounders and Others' (1912)]

CARSON, Rachel (1907–1964)
As man proceeds towards his announced goal of the conquest of nature, he has written a depressing record of destruction, directed not only against the earth he inhabits but against the life that shares it with him.

[*The Silent Spring* (1962)]

Over increasingly large areas of the United States, spring now comes unheralded by the return of the birds, and the early mornings are strangely silent where once they were filled with the beauty of bird song.

[*The Silent Spring* (1962)]

CHEKHOV, Anton (1860–1904)
Human beings have been endowed with reason and a creative power so that they can add to what they have been given. But until now they have been not creative, but destructive. Forests are disappearing, rivers are drying up, wildlife is becoming extinct, the climate's being ruined and with every passing day the earth is becoming poorer and uglier.

[*Uncle Vanya* (1897)]

MCLEAN, Joyce
There's an old saying which goes:
Once the last tree is cut and the last
river poisoned, you will find you cannot eat your money.

[*The Globe and Mail*, 1989]

MEAD, Margaret (1901–1978)
We are living beyond our means. As a
people we have developed a life-style
that is draining the earth of its price-
less and irreplaceable resources
without regard for the future of our
children and people all around the
world.

[*Redbook*]

ENVY

BEERBOHM, Sir Max (1872–1956)
The dullard's envy of brilliant men is
always assuaged by the suspicion that
they will come to a bad end.

[*Zuleika Dobson* (1911)]

THE BIBLE (King James Version)
Through envy of the devil came death
into the world.

[Apocrypha, *Wisdom of Solomon*, 2:24]

BRONTË, Charlotte (1816–1855)
Had I been in anything inferior to him,
he would not have hated me so
thoroughly, but I knew all that he
knew, and, what was worse, he suspected that I kept the padlock of
silence on mental wealth in which he
was no sharer.

[*The Professor* (1857)]

FIELDING, Henry (1707–1754)
Some folks rail against other folks
because other folks have what some
folks would be glad of.

[*Joseph Andrews* (1742)]

GAY, John (1685–1732)
Fools may our scorn, not envy raise,
For envy is a kind of praise.

[*Fables* (1727)]

MOORE, Brian (1921–)
How many works of the imagination
have been goaded into life by envy of
an untalented contemporary's success.

[*An Answer from Limbo* (1962)]

SHAKESPEARE, William (1564–1616)
[Of Cassius]
Such men as he be never at heart's
ease
Whiles they behold a greater than
themselves,
And therefore are they very
dangerous.

[*Julius Caesar*, I.ii]

The general's disdain'd
By him one step below, he by the next,
That next by him beneath; so every
step,
Exampl'd by the first pace that is sick
Of his superior, grows to an envious
fever
Of pale and bloodless emulation.

[*Troilus and Cressida*, I.iii]

EQUALITY

ANTHONY, Susan B. (1820–1906)
There never will be complete equality
until women themselves help to make
laws and elect lawmakers.

[*The Arena*, 1897]

ARISTOTLE (384–322 BC)
Inferiors agitate in order that they may
be equal and equals that they may be
superior. Such is the state of mind
which creates party strife.

[*Politics*]

BAKUNIN, Mikhail (1814–1876)
[Anarchist declaration, Lyon, 1870]
We wish, in a word, equality – equality
in fact as corollary, or rather, as
primordial condition of liberty. From
each according to his faculties, to each
according to his needs; that is what
we wish sincerely and energetically.

[In J. Morrison Davidson, *The Old Order and
the New* (1890)]

BALZAC, Honoré de (1799–1850)
Equality may perhaps be a right, but
no power on earth can ever turn it into
a fact.

[*La Duchesse de Langeais* (1834)]

BARRIE, Sir J.M. (1860–1937)
His Lordship may compel us to be
equal upstairs, but there will never be
equality in the servants' hall.

[*The Admirable Crichton* (1902)]

BURNS, Robert (1759–1796)
The rank is but the guinea's stamp,
The man's the gowd for a' that ...

For a' that, an' a' that,
It's comin yet for a' that,
That man to man the world o'er
Shall brithers be for a' that.

['A Man's a Man for a' that' (1795)]

EMERSON, Ralph Waldo (1803–1882)
There is a little formula, couched in
pure Saxon, which you may hear in
the corners of the streets and in the
yard of the dame's school, from very
little republicans: 'I'm as good as you
be,' which contains the essence of the
Massachusetts Bill of Rights and of the
American Declaration of Independence.

[*Natural History of Intellect* (1893)]

GILBERT, W.S. (1836–1911)
They all shall equal be!
The Earl, the Marquis, and the Dook,
The Groom, the Butler, and the Cook,
The Aristocrat who banks with Coutts,
The Aristocrat who cleans the boots.

[*The Gondoliers* (1889)]

HUXLEY, Aldous (1894–1963)
That all men are equal is a proposition
to which, at ordinary times, no sane
human being has ever given his
assent.

[*Proper Studies* (1927)]

JOHNSON, Samuel (1709–1784)
Your levellers wish to level *down* as far
as themselves; but they cannot bear

levelling *up* to themselves.

[In Boswell, *The Life of Samuel Johnson*
(1791)]

It is better that some should be
unhappy than that none should be
happy, which would be the case in a
general state of equality.

[In Boswell, *The Life of Samuel Johnson*
(1791)]

KING, Martin Luther (1929–1968)
I have a dream that one day this
nation will rise up and live out the true
meaning of its creed: 'We hold these
truths to be self-evident, that all men
are created equal'.

[Speech, 1963]

MANDELA, Nelson (1918–)
I have fought against white domination, and I have fought against black
domination. I have cherished the ideal
of a democratic and free society in
which all persons will live together in
harmony and with equal opportunities. It is an ideal which I hope to
live for and achieve. But, if needs be, it
is an ideal for which I am prepared to
die.

[Statement in the dock, 1964]

MILL, John Stuart (1806–1873)
The principle which regulates the
existing social relations between the
two sexes – the legal subordination of
one sex to the other – is wrong in
itself, and now one of the chief
hindrances to human improvement;
and ... it ought to be replaced by a
principle of perfect equality, admitting
no power or privilege on the one side,
nor disability on the other.

[*The Subjection of Women* (1869)]

MURDOCH, Iris (1919–)
The cry of equality pulls everyone
down.

[*The Observer*, 1987]

ORWELL, George (1903–1950)
All animals are equal, but some
animals are more equal than others.

[*Animal Farm* (1945)]

RAINBOROWE, Thomas (d. 1648)
The poorest he that is in England hath
a life to live as the greatest he.
[Speech in Army debates, 1647]

WEDGWOOD, Josiah (1730–1795)
Am I not a man and a brother?
[Motto adopted by Anti-Slavery Society]

WILSON, Harold (1916–1995)
Everybody should have an equal
chance – but they shouldn't have a
flying start.
[*The Observer*, 1963]

ERROR

AESCHYLUS (525–456 BC)
Even he who is wiser than the wise
may err.
[*Fragments*]

BANVILLE, Théodore de (1823–1891)
*Et ceux qui ne font rien ne se trompent
jamais.*
Those who do nothing are never
wrong.
[*Odes funambulesques*]

BOLINGBROKE, Henry (1678–1751)
Truth lies within a little and certain
compass, but error is immense.
[*Reflections upon Exile* (1716)]

**BOULAY DE LA MEURTHE, Antoine
(1761–1840)**
[On the execution of the Duc
d'Enghien, 1804]
C'est pire qu'un crime, c'est une faute.
It is worse than a crime; it is a
mistake.
[Attr.]

BROWNE, Sir Thomas (1605–1682)
Many ... have too rashly charged the
troops of error, and remain as trophies
unto the enemies of truth.
[*Religio Medici* (1643)]

**DESTOUCHES, Philippe Néricault
(1680–1754)**
Les absents ont toujours tort.
The absent are always in the wrong.
[*L'Obstacle Imprévu* (1717)]

DRYDEN, John (1631–1700)
Errors, like straws, upon the surface
flow;
He who would search for pearls must
dive below.
[*All for Love* (1678)]

ELIOT, George (1819–1880)
Errors look so very ugly in persons of
small means – one feels they are
taking quite a liberty in going astray;
whereas people of fortune may naturally indulge in a few delinquencies.
[*Scenes of Clerical Life* (1858)]

Among all forms of mistake, prophecy
is the most gratuitous.
[*Middlemarch* (1872)]

JOHNSON, Samuel (1709–1784)
[Asked the reason for a mistake in his
Dictionary]
Ignorance, madam, sheer ignorance.
[In Boswell, *The Life of Samuel Johnson*
(1791)]

LOCKE, John (1632–1704)
It is one thing to show a man that he
is in an error, and another to put him
in possession of truth.
[*Essay concerning Human Understanding*
(1690)]

All men are liable to error; and most
men are, in many points, by passion or
interest, under temptation to it.
[*Essay concerning Human Understanding*
(1690)]

POPE, Alexander (1688–1744)
A man should never be ashamed to
own he has been in the wrong, which
is but saying, in other words, that he is
wiser today than he was yesterday.
[*Miscellanies* (1727)]

REAGAN, Ronald (1911–)
You know, by the time you reach my
age, you've made plenty of mistakes if
you've lived your life properly.
[*The Observer*, 1987]

SCHOPENHAUER, Arthur (1788–1860)
Es gibt nur einen angeborenen Irrtum, und es ist der, dass wir dasind, um glücklich zu sein.
There is only one innate error, and that is that we are here in order to be happy.

[*The World as Will and Idea* (1859)]

See TRUTH

EUROPE

BALDWIN, James (1924–1987)
Europe has what we [Americans] do not have yet, a sense of the mysterious and inexorable limits of life, a sense, in a word, of tragedy. And we have what they sorely need: a sense of life's possibilities.

[Attr.]

CHASE, Ilka (1905–1978)
That is what is so marvellous about Europe; the people long ago learned that space and beauty and quiet refuges in a great city, where children may play and old people sit in the sun, are of far more value to the inhabitants than real estate taxes and contractors' greed.

[*Fresh From the Laundry* (1967)]

DELORS, Jacques (1925–)
Europe is not just about material results, it is about spirit. Europe is a state of mind.

[*The Independent*, 1994]

The hardest thing is to convince European citizens that even the most powerful nation is no longer able to act alone.

[*The Independent*, 1994]

FANON, Frantz (1925–1961)
When I search for man in the technique and style of Europe, I see only a succession of negations of man, and an avalanche of murders.

[*The Wretched of the Earth* (1961)]

FISHER, H.A.L. (1856–1940)
Purity of race does not exist. Europe is a continent of energetic mongrels.

[*History of Europe* (1935)]

GLADSTONE, William (1809–1898)
We are part of the community of Europe, and we must do our duty as such.

[Speech, 1888]

GOLDSMITH, James (1933–)
Brussels is madness. I will fight it from within.

[*The Times*, 1994]

GOLDSMITH, Oliver (c. 1728–1774)
On whatever side we regard the history of Europe, we shall perceive it to be a tissue of crimes, follies, and misfortunes.

[*The Citizen of the World* (1762)]

HAZZARD, Shirley (1931–)
Going to Europe, someone had written, was about as final as going to heaven. A mystical passage to another life, from which no one returned the same.

[*The Transit of Venus* (1980)]

HEALEY, Denis (1917–)
[Of Conservatives]
Their Europeanism is nothing but imperialism with an inferiority complex.

[*The Observer*, 1962]

HUGO, Victor (1802–1885)
I represent a party which does not yet exist: the party of revolution, civilisation. This party will make the twentieth century. There will issue from it first the United States of Europe, then the United States of the World.

[Written on the wall of the room in which Hugo died, Paris, 1885]

LEFEVRE, Théo (1914–1973)
In Western Europe there are now only small countries – those that know it and those that don't know it yet.

[*The Observer*, 1963]

EVIL

MCCARTHY, Mary (1912–1989)
The immense popularity of American movies abroad demonstrates that Europe is the unfinished negative of which America is the proof.

[*On the Contrary* (1961)]

NICHOLSON, Sir Bryan (1932–)
[On the government's non-cooperation with Europe over the ban on exporting British beef]
In this pungent atmosphere of romantic nationalism and churlish xenophobia, I sometimes wonder if there are some among us who have failed to notice that the war with Germany has ended.

[*The Observer*, 1996]

SCANLON, Hugh, Baron (1913–)
[Referring to his union's attitude to the Common Market]
Here we are again with both feet firmly planted in the air.

[*The Observer*, 1973]

SHERMAN, Alfred (1919–)
Britain does not wish to be ruled by a conglomerate in Europe which includes Third World nations such as the Greeks and Irish, nor for that matter the Italians and French, whose standards of political morality are not ours, and never will be.

[*The Independent*, 1990]

SOAMES, Nicholas (1948–)
[Comment during a Commons debate, the topics of which included positive discrimination for women in the armed forces and a European Union directive on equality]
All that EC nonsense is beyond me.

[*The Mail on Sunday*, 1996]

THATCHER, Margaret (1925–)
Historians will one day look back and think it a curious folly that just as the Soviet Union was forced to recognize reality by dispersing power to its separate states and by limiting the powers of its central government, some people in Europe were trying to create a new artificial state by taking powers from national states and concentrating them at the centre.

[Speech, 1994]

EVIL

ANONYMOUS
Honi soit qui mal y pense.
Evil be to him who evil thinks.

[Motto of the Order of the Garter]

ARENDT, Hannah (1906–1975)
[Of Eichmann]
It was as though in those last minutes he was summing up the lessons that this long course in human wickedness had taught us – the lesson of the fearsome, word-and-thought-defying banality of evil.

[*Eichmann in Jerusalem* (1963)]

THE BIBLE (King James Version)
The heart is deceitful above all things, and desperately wicked.

[*Jeremiah*, 17:9]

BOILEAU-DESPREAUX, Nicolas (1636–1711)
Souvent la peur d'un mal nous conduit dans un pire.
The fear of one evil often leads us into a greater one.

[*L'Art Poétique* (1674)]

BRECHT, Bertolt (1898–1956)
Die Gemeinheit der Welt ist gross, und man muss sich die Beine ablaufen, damit sie einem nicht gestohlen werden.
The wickedness of the world is so great that you have to run your legs off so you don't get them stolen from you.

[*The Threepenny Opera* (1928)]

BURKE, Edmund (1729–1797)
The only thing necessary for the triumph of evil is for good men to do nothing.

[Attr.]

CONRAD, Joseph (1857–1924)
The belief in a supernatural source of evil is not necessary; men alone are

quite capable of every wickedness.

[*Under Western Eyes* (1911)]

CRISP, Quentin (1908–)
Vice is its own reward.

[*The Naked Civil Servant* (1968)]

DELBANCO, Andrew
The idea of evil is something on which the health of society depends. We have an obligation to name evil and oppose it in ourselves as well as in others.

[*The Guardian*, 1995]

GOLDSMITH, Oliver (c. 1728–1774)
Don't let us make imaginary evils, when you know we have so many real ones to encounter.

[*The Good Natur'd Man* (1768)]

HATTERSLEY, Roy (1932–)
Familiarity with evil breeds not contempt but acceptance.

[*The Guardian*, 1993]

HAZLITT, William (1778–1830)
Wrong dressed out in pride, pomp, and circumstance, has more attraction than abstract right.

[*Characters of Shakespeare's Plays* (1817)]

To great evils we submit, we resent little provocations.

[*Table-Talk* (1822)]

KEMPIS, Thomas à (c. 1380–1471)
De duobus malis minus est semper eligendum.
Of two evils the lesser is always to be chosen.

[*De Imitatione Christi* (1892)]

LA ROCHEFOUCAULD, Duc de (1613–1680)
Il n'y a guère d'homme assez habile pour connaître tout le mal qu'il fait.
There is scarcely a single man clever enough to know all the evil he does.

[*Maximes* (1678)]

MCCARTHY, Mary (1912–1989)
If someone tells you he is going to make 'a realistic decision', you

immediately understand that he has resolved to do something bad.

[*On the Contrary* (1961)]

NEWMAN, John Henry, Cardinal (1801–1890)
Whatever is the first time persons hear evil, it is quite certain that good has been beforehand with them, and they have a something within them which tells them it is evil.

[*Parochial and Plain Sermons*]

NIETZSCHE, Friedrich (1844–1900)
Wer mit Ungeheurn kämpft, mag zusehn, dass er nicht dabei zum Ungeheuer wird. Und wenn du lange in einen Abgrund blickst, blickt der Abgrund auch in dich hinein.
Whoever struggles with monsters might watch that he does not thereby become a monster. When you stare into an abyss for a long time, the abyss also stares into you.

[*Beyond Good and Evil* (1886)]

POPE, Alexander (1688–1744)
Vice is a monster of so frightful mien,
As, to be hated, needs but to be seen;
Yet soon too oft, familiar with her face,
We first endure, then pity, then embrace.

[*An Essay on Man* (1733)]

SHAKESPEARE, William (1564–1616)
How oft the sight of means to do ill deeds
Make deeds ill done!

[*King John*, IV.ii]

Through tatter'd clothes small vices do appear;
Robed and furr'd gowns hide all.

[*King Lear*, IV.vi]

Oftentimes to win us to our harm,
The instruments of darkness tell us truths,
Win us with honest trifles, to betray's
In deepest consequence.

[*Macbeth*, I.iii]

An evil soul producing holy witness

EVOLUTION

Is like a villain with a smiling cheek,
A goodly apple rotten at the heart.
O, what a goodly outside falsehood
hath!

[*The Merchant of Venice*, I.iii]

WEST, Mae (1892–1980)
Whenever I'm caught between two
evils, I take the one I've never tried.

[*Klondike Annie*, film, 1936]

WILDE, Oscar (1854–1900)
Wickedness is a myth invented by
good people to account for the curious
attractiveness of others.

[*The Chameleon*, 1894]

WOLLSTONECRAFT, Mary (1759–1797)
No man chooses evil because it is evil;
he only mistakes it for happiness, the
good he seeks.

[*A Vindication of the Rights of Men* (1790)]

See GOOD AND EVIL; SIN

EVOLUTION

**BLACKWELL, Antoinette Brown
(1825–1921)**
Mr Darwin ... has failed to hold
definitely before his mind the principle
that the difference of sex, whatever it
may consist in, must itself be subject
to natural selection and to evolution.

[*The Sexes Throughout Nature* (1875)]

CONGREVE, William (1670–1729)
I confess freely to you, I could never
look long upon a monkey, without
very mortifying reflections.

[Letter to Mr Dennis, 1695]

DARWIN, Charles (1809–1882)
I have called this principle, by which
each slight variation, if useful, is
preserved, by the term of Natural
Selection.

[*The Origin of Species* (1859)]

We must, however, acknowledge, as it
seems to me, that man with all his
noble qualities ... still bears in his

bodily frame the indelible stamp of his
lowly origin.

[*The Descent of Man* (1871)]

DARWIN, Charles Galton (1887–1962)
The evolution of the human race will
not be accomplished in the ten
thousand years of tame animals, but in
the million years of wild animals,
because man is and will always be a
wild animal.

[*The Next Ten Million Years*]

DISRAELI, Benjamin (1804–1881)
Is man an ape or an angel? Now I am
on the side of the angels.

[Speech, 1864]

HUXLEY, T.H. (1825–1895)
[Reply to Wilberforce during debate on
Darwin's theory of evolution]
I asserted – and I repeat – that a man
has no reason to be ashamed of
having an ape for his grandfather. If
there were an ancestor whom I should
feel shame in recalling it would rather
be a man – a man of restless and
versatile intellect – who, not content
with an equivocal success in his own
sphere of activity, plunges into scientific questions with which he has no
real acquaintance, only to obscure
them by an aimless rhetoric, and dis-
tract the attention of his hearers from
the real point at issue by eloquent
digressions and skilled appeals to
religious prejudice.

[Speech, Oxford, 1860]

SPENCER, Herbert (1820–1903)
Evolution ... is – a change from an
indefinite, incoherent homogeneity, to
a definite coherent heterogeneity.

[*First Principles* (1862)]

It cannot but happen ... that those will
survive whose functions happen to be
most nearly in equilibrium with the
modified aggregate of external forces
... This survival of the fittest implies
multiplication of the fittest.

[*The Principles of Biology* (1864)]

**WILBERFORCE, Bishop Samuel
(1805–1873)**
[To T.H. Huxley]
And, in conclusion, I would like to ask
the gentleman ... whether the ape from
which he is descended was on his
grandmother's or his grandfather's
side of the family.
[Speech at Oxford, 1860]

EXILE

AYTOUN, W.E. (1813–1865)
They bore within their breasts the grief
That fame can never heal –
The deep, unutterable woe
Which none save exiles feel.
['The Island of the Scots' (1849)]

The earth is all the home I have,
The heavens my wide roof-tree.
['The Wandering Jew' (1867)]

THE BIBLE (King James Version)
I have been a stranger in a strange
land.
[*Exodus*, 2:22]

BROWN, Ford Madox (1821–1893)
The last of England! O'er the sea, my
dear,
Our homes to seek amid Australian
fields.
Us, not our million–acred island yields
The space to dwell in. Thrust out,
forced to hear
Low ribaldry from sots, and share
rough cheer
From rudely nurtured men.
['Sonnet']

GALT, John (1779–1839)
From the lone shieling of the misty
island
Mountains divide us, and the waste of
seas –
Yet still the blood is strong, the heart is
Highland,
And we in dreams behold the
Hebrides!
Fair these broad meads, these hoary
woods are grand;

But we are exiles from our fathers'
land.
[Attr. in *Blackwoods Edinburgh Magazine*,
1829]

GREGORY VII (c. 1020–1085)
[Last words]
*Dilexi justitiam et odivi iniquitatem:
propterea morior in exilio.*
I have loved righteousness and hated
iniquity: therefore I die in exile.
[In Bowden, *The Life and Pontificate of
Gregory VII* (1840)]

SPARK, Muriel (1918–)
It was Edinburgh that bred within me
the conditions of exiledom; and what
have I been doing since then but
moving from exile to exile? It has
ceased to be a fate, it has become a
calling.
['What Images Return']

**STEVENSON, Robert Louis
(1850–1894)**
Be it granted to me to behold you
again in dying,
Hills of home! and to hear again the
call;
Hear about the graves of the martyrs
the peewees crying,
And hear no more at all.
[*Songs of Travel* (1896)]

EXPERIENCE

ANTRIM, Minna (1861–1950)
Experience is a good teacher, but she
sends in terrific bills.
[*Naked Truth and Veiled Allusions* (1902)]

BEERBOHM, Sir Max (1872–1956)
You will think me lamentably crude:
my experience of life has been drawn
from life itself.
[*Zuleika Dobson* (1911)]

BLAKE, William (1757–1827)
What is the price of Experience? do
men buy it for a song?
Or wisdom for a dance in the street?
No, it is bought with the price

Of all that a man hath, his house, his
wife, his children.
Wisdom is sold in the desolate market
where none come to buy,
And in the wither'd field where the
farmer plows for bread in vain.
[*Vala, or the Four Zoas*]

BOWEN, Elizabeth (1899–1973)
Experience isn't interesting till it
begins to repeat itself – in fact, till it
does that, it hardly *is* experience.
[*The Death of the Heart* (1938)]

DISRAELI, Benjamin (1804–1881)
Experience is the child of Thought, and
Thought is the child of Action. We
cannot learn men from books.
[*Vivian Grey* (1826)]

EMERSON, Ralph Waldo (1803–1882)
The years teach much which the days
never know.
['*Experience*' (1844)]

FADIMAN, Clifton (1904–)
Experience teaches you that the man
who looks you straight in the eye,
particularly if he adds a firm hand-
shake, is hiding something.
[*Enter, Conversing*]

HALIFAX, Lord (1633–1695)
The best way to suppose what may
come, is to remember what is past.
[*Political, Moral and Miscellaneous Thoughts
and Reflections* (1750)]

HEGEL, Georg Wilhelm (1770–1831)
*Was die Erfahrung aber und die
Geschichte lehren, ist dieses, dass Völker
und Regierungen niemals etwas aus der
Geschichte gelernt haben.*
What experience and history teach us,
however, is this, that peoples and
governments have never learned
anything from history.
[*Lectures on the Philosophy of History* (1837)]

HOLMES, Oliver Wendell (1809–1894)
A moment's insight is sometimes
worth a life's experience.
[*The Professor at the Breakfast-Table* (1860)]

KEATS, John (1795–1821)
Nothing ever becomes real till it is
experienced – Even a Proverb is no
proverb to you till your Life has
illustrated it.
[Letter to George and Georgiana Keats, 1819]

WILDE, Oscar (1854–1900)
Experience is the name every one
gives to their mistakes.
[*Lady Windermere's Fan* (1892)]

FACTS

BARRIE, Sir J.M. (1860–1937)
Facts were never pleasing to him. He acquired them with reluctance and got rid of them with relief. He was never on terms with them until he had stood them on their heads.
[*The Greenwood Hat* (1937)]

BURNS, Robert (1759–1796)
But facts are chiels that winna ding,
And downa be disputed.
['A Dream' (1786)]

DOYLE, Sir Arthur Conan (1859–1930)
'I should have more faith,' he said; 'I ought to know by this time that when a fact appears opposed to a long train of deductions it invariably proves to be capable of bearing some other interpretation.'
[*A Study in Scarlet* (1887)]

HUXLEY, Aldous (1894–1963)
Facts do not cease to exist because they are ignored.
[*Proper Studies* (1927)]

JAMES, Henry (1843–1916)
The fatal futility of Fact.
[*Prefaces* (1897 edition)]

RYLE, Gilbert (1900–1976)
A myth is, of course, not a fairy story. It is the presentation of facts belonging to one category in the idioms appropriate to another. To explode a myth is accordingly not to deny the facts but to re-allocate them.
[*The Concept of Mind* (1949)]

TINDAL, Matthew (1657–1733)
Matters of fact, which as Mr Budgell somewhere observes, are very stubborn things.
[*The Will of Matthew Tindal* (1733)]

FAILURE

CIANO, Count Galeazzo (1903–1944)
As always, victory finds a hundred fathers, but defeat is an orphan.
[Diary, 1942]

COWARD, Sir Noël (1899–1973)
[On Randolph Churchill]
Dear Randolph, utterly unspoiled by failure.
[Attr.]

HARE, Augustus (1792–1834)
Half the failures in life arise from pulling in one's horse as he is leaping.
[*Guesses at Truth* (1827)]

HEALEY, Denis (1917–)
Examining one's entrails while fighting a battle is a recipe for certain defeat.
[*The Observer*, 1983]

HELLER, Joseph (1923–)
He was a self-made man who owed his lack of success to nobody.
[*Catch-22* (1961)]

HEMINGWAY, Ernest (1898–1961)
But man is not made for defeat ... A man can be destroyed but not defeated.
[*The Old Man and the Sea* (1952)]

KEATS, John (1795–1821)
I would sooner fail than not be among the greatest.
[Letter to James Hessey, 1818]

NEWMAN, Paul (1925–)
Show me a good loser and I'll show you a loser.
[*The Observer*, 1982]

SHAKESPEARE, William (1564–1616)
Macbeth: If we should fail?
Lady Macbeth: We fail!
But screw your courage to the sticking place,
And we'll not fail.
[*Macbeth*, I.vii]

STEVENSON, Robert Louis (1850–1894)
Here lies one who meant well, tried a little, failed much: – surely that may be his epitaph, of which he need not be ashamed.
[*Across the Plains* (1892)]

VICTORIA, Queen (1819–1901)
[Said of the Boer War in 'Black Week', 1899]
We are not interested in the possibilities of defeat; they do not exist.
[In Cecil, *Life of Robert, Marquis of Salisbury*]

VOLTAIRE (1694–1778)
N'ayant jamais pu réussir dans le monde, il se vengeait par en médire.
Never having been able to succeed in the world, he took his revenge by speaking ill of it.
[*Zadig, or Fate* (1747)]

WILDE, Oscar (1854–1900)
We women adore failures. They lean on us.
[*A Woman of No Importance* (1893)]

FAME

ALLEN, Fred (1894–1956)
A celebrity is a person who works hard all his life to become known, then wears dark glasses to avoid being recognized.
[Attr.]

ANONYMOUS
Fame is a mask that eats the face.

BOORSTIN, Daniel J. (1914–)
The celebrity is a person who is known for his well-knownness.
[*The Image* (1962)]

BURKE, Edmund (1729–1797)
Passion for fame; a passion which is the instinct of all great souls.
[*Speech on American Taxation* (1774)]

BYRON, Lord (1788–1824)
[Remark on the instantaneous success of *Childe Harold*]
I awoke one morning and found myself famous.
[In Moore, *Letters and Journals of Lord Byron*]

CALDERÓN DE LA BARCA, Pedro (1600–1681)
Fame, like water, bears up the lighter things, and lets the weighty sink.
[Attr.]

CATO THE ELDER (234–149 BC)
I would much rather have men ask why I have no statue than why I have one.
[In Plutarch, *Lives*]

DOBSON, Henry Austin (1840–1921)
Fame is a food that dead men eat, –
I have no stomach for such meat.
['Fame is a Food' (1906)]

GRAINGER, James (c. 1721–1766)
What is fame? an empty bubble;
Gold? a transient, shining trouble.
['Solitude' (1755)]

HUGO, Victor (1802–1885)
La popularité? c'est la gloire en gros sous.
Fame? It's glory in small change.
[*Ruy Blas* (1838)]

HUXLEY, Aldous (1894–1963)
I'm afraid of losing my obscurity. Genuineness only thrives in the dark. Like celery.
[*Those Barren Leaves* (1925)]

HUXLEY, T.H. (1825–1895)
[Remark to George Howell]
Posthumous fame is not particularly attractive to me, but, if I am to be remembered at all, I would rather it should be as 'a man who did his best to help the people' than by any other title.
[In L. Huxley, *Life and Letters of Thomas Henry Huxley* (1900)]

KEATS, John (1795–1821)
Fame, like a wayward girl, will still be coy
To those who woo her with too slavish knees.
['On Fame (1)' (1819)]

MELBA, Dame Nellie (1861–1931)
[To the editor of the *Argus*]
I don't care what you say, for me or against me, but for heaven's sake say something about me.
[In Thompson, *On Lips of Living Men*]

MONTAIGNE, Michel de (1533–1592)
La gloire et le repos sont choses qui ne peuvent loger en même gîte.
Fame and tranquillity cannot dwell under the same roof.

[*Essais* (1580)]

PECK, Gregory (1916–)
[On the fact that no-one in a crowded restaurant recognized him]
If you have to tell them who you are, you aren't anybody.

[In Harris, *Pieces of Eight*]

POPE, Alexander (1688–1744)
Then teach me, Heav'n! to scorn the guilty bays,
Drive from my breast that wretched lust of praise,
Unblemished let me live, or die unknown;
Oh grant an honest fame, or grant me none!

[*The Temple of Fame* (1715)]

SITWELL, Dame Edith (1887–1964)
A pompous woman of his acquaintance, complaining that the head-waiter of a restaurant had not shown her and her husband immediately to a table, said 'We had to tell him who we were.' Gerald, interested, enquired, 'And who were you?'

[*Taken Care Of* (1965)]

TACITUS (c. 56–c. 120)
Etiam sapientibus cupido gloriae novissima exuitur.
The desire for fame is the last thing to be put aside, even by the wise.

[*Histories*]

WARHOL, Andy (c. 1926–1987)
In the future everyone will be world famous for fifteen minutes.

[Catalogue for an exhibition, 1968]

WILDE, Oscar (1854–1900)
There is only one thing in the world worse than being talked about, and that is not being talked about.

[*The Picture of Dorian Gray* (1891)]

FAMILIES

BEERBOHM, Sir Max (1872–1956)
They were a tense and peculiar family, the Oedipuses, weren't they?

[Attr.]

BUTLER, Samuel (1835–1902)
I believe that more unhappiness comes from this source than from any other – I mean from the attempt to prolong family connection unduly and to make people hang together artificially who would never naturally do so. The mischief among the lower classes is not so great, but among the middle and upper classes it is killing a large number daily. And the old people do not really like it much better than the young.

[*The Note-Books of Samuel Butler* (1912)]

DICKENS, Charles (1812–1870)
Accidents will occur in the best regulated families.

[*David Copperfield* (1850)]

FORSTER, E.M. (1879–1970)
I felt for a moment that the whole Wilcox family was a fraud, just a wall of newspapers and motor-cars and golf-clubs, and that if it fell I should find nothing behind it but panic and emptiness.

[*Howard's End* (1910)]

FREUD, Sigmund (1856–1939)
Philosophers and politicians have agreed that the bonding together in family groups is both instinctive and necessary to human welfare – and therefore essential to the health of a society. The family is the microcosm.

[Attr. in *The Times*, May 1996]

HAZLITT, William (1778–1830)
A person may be indebted for a nose or an eye, for a graceful carriage or a voluble discourse, to a great-aunt or uncle, whose existence he has scarcely heard of.

[*London Magazine*, 1821]

JOHN PAUL II (1920–)
Treasure your families – the future of
humanity passes by way of the family.

[Speech, 1982]

LEACH, Sir Edmund (1910–1989)
Far from being the basis of the good
society, the family, with its narrow
privacy and tawdry secrets, is the
source of all our discontents.

[BBC Reith Lecture, 1967]

LINCOLN, Abraham (1809–1865)
I don't know who my grandfather was;
I am much more concerned to know
what his grandson will be.

[In Gross, *Lincoln's Own Stories*]

MACAULAY, Dame Rose (1881–1958)
A group of closely related persons
living under one roof; it is a convenience, often a necessity, sometimes
a pleasure, sometimes the reverse; but
who first exalted it as admirable, an
almost religious ideal?

[*The World My Wilderness* (1950)]

MONTAIGNE, Michel de (1533–1592)
*Il n'y a guère moins de tourment au
gouvernement d'une famille que d'un
état entier ... et, pour être les
occupations domestiques moins
importantes, elles n'en sont pas moins
importunes.*
There is scarcely any less trouble in
running a family than in governing an
entire state ... and domestic matters
are no less importunate for being less
important.

[*Essais* (1580)]

MOONEY, Bel
[On the need for family life]
I find myself surprised at how its
realism actually unites morality with –
yes – romance. It is that need that
draws us to nest in rows, separated by
thin walls, hoping to be tolerated and
loved forever – and to go on
reproducing ourselves in family
patterns, handing on some misery
(perhaps), but untold happiness too.

[*The Times*, 1996]

NASH, Ogden (1902–1971)
One would be in less danger
From the wiles of a stranger
If one's own kin and kith
Were more fun to be with.

['Family Court' (1931)]

POUND, Ezra (1885–1972)
Oh how hideous it is
To see three generations of one house
    gathered together!
It is like an old tree with shoots,
And with some branches rotted and
    falling.

['Commission' (1916)]

**THACKERAY, William Makepeace
(1811–1863)**
If a man's character is to be abused,
say what you will, there's nobody like
a relation to do the business.

[*Vanity Fair* (1848)]

TOLSTOY, Leo (1828–1910)
All happy families resemble one
another, but every unhappy family is
unhappy in its own way.

[*Anna Karenina* (1877)]

FASCISM

BEVAN, Aneurin (1897–1960)
Fascism is not in itself a new order of
society. It is the future refusing to be
born.

[Attr.]

CASTELLANI, Maria (fl. 1930s)
Fascism recognises women as part of
the life force of the country, laying
down a division of duties between the
two sexes, without putting obstacles in
the way of those women who by their
intellectual gifts reach the highest
positions.

[*Italian Women, Past and Present* (1937)]

**IBÁRRURI, Dolores ('La Pasionaria')
(1895–1989)**
Wherever they pass, they [the fascists]
sow death and desolation.

[*Speeches and Articles* (1938)]

MCKENNEY, Ruth (1911–1972)
If modern civilisation had any meaning it was displayed in the fight against Fascism.

[In Seldes, *The Great Quotations* (1960)]

MOSLEY, Sir Oswald (1896–1980)
Before the organization of the Blackshirt movement free speech did not exist in this country.

[Attr.]

MUSSOLINI, Benito (1883–1945)
[On Hitler's seizing power]
Fascism is a religion; the twentieth century will be known in history as the century of Fascism.

[In Seldes, *Sawdust Caesar*]

PLATH, Sylvia (1932–1963)
Every woman adores a Fascist,
The boot in the face, the brute
Brute heart of a brute like you.

['Daddy' (1963)]

FATHERS

AUBREY, John (1626–1697)
[Of Sir Walter Raleigh]
Sir Walter, being strangely surprised and put out of his countenance at so great a table, gives his son a damned blow over the face. His son, as rude as he was, would not strike his father, but strikes over the face the gentleman that sat next to him and said 'Box about: 'twill come to my father anon.'

[*Brief Lives* (c. 1693)]

THE BIBLE (King James Version)
The fathers have eaten sour grapes, and the children's teeth are set on edge.

[*Ezekiel*, 18:2]

BURTON, Robert (1577–1640)
Diogenes struck the father when the son swore.

[*Anatomy of Melancholy* (1621)]

CHESTERFIELD, Lord (1694–1773)
As fathers commonly go, it is seldom a misfortune to be fatherless; and considering the general run of sons, as seldom a misfortune to be childless.

[Attr.]

CODE NAPOLEON
La recherche de la paternité est interdite.
Investigations into paternity are forbidden.

[Article 340]

MCAULEY, James (1917–1976)
Small things can pit the memory like a cyst:
Having seen other fathers greet their sons,
I put my childish face up to be kissed
After an absence. The rebuff still stuns

My blood. The poor man's embarrassment
At such a delicate proffer of affection
Cut like a saw. But home the lesson went:
My tenderness thenceforth escaped detection.

[*Collected Poems* (1971)]

RUSSELL, Bertrand (1872–1970)
The fundamental defect of fathers is that they want their children to be a credit to them.

[Attr.]

SHAKESPEARE, William (1564–1616)
It is a wise father that knows his own child.

[*The Merchant of Venice*, II.ii]

TENNYSON, Alfred, Lord (1809–1892)
How many a father have I seen,
A sober man, among his boys,
Whose youth was full of foolish noise.

[*In Memoriam A. H. H.* (1850)]

TURNBULL, Margaret (fl. 1920s–1942)
No man is responsible for his father. That is entirely his mother's affair.

[*Alabaster Lamps* (1925)]

TWAIN, Mark (1835–1910)
When I was a boy of 14 my father was so ignorant I could hardly stand to have the old man around. But when I got to be 21, I was astonished at how

much he had learned in seven years.
[In Mackay, *The Harvest of a Quiet Eye* (1977)]

FEAR

BOWEN, Elizabeth (1899–1973)
Proust has pointed out that the pre-
disposition to love creates its own
objects: is this not true of fear?
[*Collected Impressions* (1950)]

BURKE, Edmund (1729–1797)
No passion so effectually robs the
mind of all its powers of acting and
reasoning as fear.
[*A Philosophical Enquiry into the Origin of our
Ideas of the Sublime and Beautiful* (1757)]

The concessions of the weak are the
concessions of fear.
[*Speech on Conciliation with America* (1775)]

BURTON, Robert (1577–1640)
The fear of some divine and supreme
powers, keeps men in obedience.
[*Anatomy of Melancholy* (1621)]

CHURCHILL, Sir Winston (1874–1965)
When I look back on all these worries
I remember the story of the old man
who said on his deathbed that he had
had a lot of trouble in his life, most of
which had never happened.
[*Their Finest Hour*]

COWPER, William (1731–1800)
He has no hope who never had a fear.
['Truth' (1782)]

CURIE, Marie (1867–1934)
Nothing in life is to be feared, it is only
to be understood. Now is the time to
understand more, so that we may fear
less.
[Attr.]

DELANEY, Shelagh (1939–)
I'm not frightened of the darkness
outside. It's the darkness inside houses
I don't like.
[*A Taste of Honey* (1959)]

DRYDEN, John (1631–1700)
I am devilishly afraid, that's certain;
but ... I'll sing, that I may seem valiant.
[*Amphitryon* (1690)]

FOCH, Ferdinand (1851–1929)
None but a coward dares to boast that
he has never known fear.
[Attr.]

MTSHALI, Oswald (1940–)
Man is
a great wall builder ...
but the wall
most impregnable
has a moat
flowing with fright
around his heart.
[*Sounds of a Cowhide Drum* (1971)]

PARRIS, Matthew (1949–)
Terror of discovery and fear of re-
proval slip into our unconscious minds
during infancy and remain there
forever, always potent, usually unacknowledged.
[*The Spectator*, 1996]

PLATO (c. 429–347 BC)
Nothing in the affairs of men is worthy
of great anxiety.
[*Republic*]

**ROOSEVELT, Franklin Delano
(1882–1945)**
The only thing we have to fear is fear
itself.
[First Inaugural Address, 1933]

SHAKESPEARE, William (1564–1616)
I have almost forgot the taste of fears.
The time has been my senses would
  have cool'd
To hear a night–shriek, and my fell of
  hair
Would at a dismal treatise rouse and
  stir
As life were in't. I have supp'd full with
  horrors;
Direness, familiar to my slaughterous
  thoughts,
Cannot once start me.
[*Macbeth*, V.v]

SHAW, George Bernard (1856–1950)
There is only one universal passion:
fear.

[*The Man of Destiny* (1898)]

STEPHENS, James (1882–1950)
Curiosity will conquer fear even more
than bravery will.

[*The Crock of Gold* (1912)]

THOMAS, Lewis (1913–)
Worrying is the most natural and
spontaneous of all human functions. It
is time to acknowledge this, perhaps
even to learn to do it better.

[*More Notes of a Biology Watcher*]

VOLTAIRE (1694–1778)
La crainte suit le crime, et c'est son
châtiment.
Fear follows crime, and is its
punishment.

[*Sémiramis* (1748)]

See DEATH

FEELINGS

ANONYMOUS
What goes on in his chest is firmly
    suppressed
By the weight of his old school tie.

COLERIDGE, Samuel Taylor
(1772–1834)
What comes from the heart, goes to
the heart.

[Attr.]

COLMAN, the Younger, George
(1762–1836)
His heart runs away with his head.

[*Who Wants a Guinea?* (1805)]

LOUIS XIV (1638–1715)
First feelings are always the most
natural.

[Recorded by Mme de Sévigné, 1709]

MUSSOLINI, Benito (1883–1945)
[Maxim to which he attributed his
political success]
Keep your heart a desert.

[Attr.]

PASCAL, Blaise (1623–1662)
Le coeur a ses raisons que la raison ne
connaît point.
The heart has its reasons which the
mind knows nothing of.

[*Pensées* (1670)]

RUSKIN, John (1819–1900)
All violent feelings ... produce in us a
falseness in all our impressions of
external things, which I would generally characterize as the 'Pathetic
Fallacy'.

[*Modern Painters* (1856)]

SAINT-EXUPERY, Antoine de
(1900–1944)
On ne voit bien qu'avec le coeur. Les
choses importantes sont invisibles à
l'oeil nu.
It is only with the heart that one can
see clearly. The important things are
invisible to the naked eye.

[*The Little Prince* (1943)]

WILDE, Oscar (1854–1900)
It is not customary in England ... for a
young lady to speak with such
enthusiasm of any person of the
opposite sex. English women conceal
their feelings till after they are married.

[*A Woman of No Importance* (1893)]

FEMINISM

ANTHONY, Susan B. (1820–1906)
Men their rights and nothing more;
women their rights and nothing less.

[Motto of *The Revolution*, 1868]

ATKINSON, Ti-Grace (c. 1938–)
Feminism is the theory: lesbianism is
the practice.

[Attr. in *Amazons, Bluestockings and Crones: A*
Feminist Dictionary]

FAIRBAIRN, Sir Nicholas (1933–1995)
[On feminism]
It's a cover for lesbian homosexuality.

[*Daily Mail*, 1993]

FAUST, Beatrice 1939–)
If the women's movement can be
summed up in a single phrase, it is
'the right to choose'.

[*Women, Sex and Pornography* (1980)]

FOURIER, François (1772–1837)
*L'extension des privilèges des femmes
est le principe général de tous progrès
sociaux.*
The extension of women's privileges is
the basic principle of all social progress.

[*Théorie des Quatre Mouvements* (1808)]

FRIEDAN, Betty (1921–)
I hope there will come a day when
you, daughter mine, or your daughter,
can truly afford to say 'I'm not a feminist. I'm a person' – and a day, not too
far away, I hope, when I can stop
fighting for women and get onto other
matters that interest me now.

[Letter to her daughter, in *Cosmopolitan*,
1978]

JOHNSTON, Jill (1929–)
Until all women are lesbians there will
be no true political revolution.

[*Lesbian Nation: The Feminist Solution* (1973)]

Feminists who still sleep with men are
delivering their most vital energies to
the oppressor.

[*Lesbian Nation: The Feminist Solution* (1973)]

No one should have to dance backwards all their life.

[In Miles, *The Women's History of the World*
(1988)]

KEY, Ellen (1849–1926)
The emancipation of women is
practically the greatest egoistic
movement of the nineteenth century,
and the most intense affirmation of
the right of the self that history has yet
seen.

[*The Century of the Child* (1909)]

LOOS, Anita (1893–1981)
I'm furious about the Women's
Liberationists. They keep getting up on
soapboxes and proclaiming that

women are brighter than men. That's
true, but it should be kept very quiet or
it ruins the whole racket.

[*The Observer*, 1973]

MARTINEAU, Harriet (1802–1876)
Is it to be understood that the
principles of the Declaration of
Independence bear no relation to half
of the human race?

[*Society in America* (1837)]

O'BRIEN, Edna (1936–)
The vote, I thought, means nothing to
women. We should be armed.

[In Erica Jong, *Fear of Flying* (1973)]

**PANKHURST, Dame Christabel
(1880–1958)**
We are here to claim our right as
women, not only to be free, but to
fight for freedom. It is our privilege, as
well as our pride and our joy, to take
some part in this militant movement,
which, as we believe, means the
regeneration of all humanity.

[Speech, 1911]

SHAW, George Bernard (1856–1950)
Give women the vote, and in five years
there will be a crushing tax on bachelors.

[*Man and Superman* (1903)]

SOLANAS, Valerie (1940–)
[SCUM (Society for Cutting Up Men),
manifesto, 1968]
Every man, deep down, knows he's a
worthless piece of shit.

[In Bassnett, *Feminist Experiences: The
Women's Movement in Four Cultures* (1986)]

STANTON, Elizabeth Cady (1815–1902)
We hold these truths to be self-
evident, that all men and women are
created equal.

['Declaration of Sentiments', 1848]

VICTORIA, Queen (1819–1901)
The Queen is most anxious to enlist
every one who can speak or write to
join in checking this mad, wicked folly
of 'Women's Rights', with all its at-

tendant horrors, on which her poor feeble sex is bent, forgetting every sense of womanly feeling and propriety ... It is a subject which makes the Queen so furious that she cannot contain herself. God created men and women different – then let them remain each in their own position.

[Letter to Sir Theodore Martin, 1870]

WOLLSTONECRAFT, Mary (1759–1797)
[Of women]
I do not wish them to have power over men; but over themselves.

[A Vindication of the Rights of Women (1792)]

See MEN AND WOMEN; WOMEN

FICTION

ALDISS, Brian (1925–)
Science fiction is no more written for scientists than ghost stories are written for ghosts.

[Penguin Science Fiction (1961)]

AUSTEN, Jane (1775–1817)
'And what are you reading, Miss –?' 'Oh! it is only a novel!' replies the young lady; while she lays down her book with affected indifference, or momentary shame. It is only Cecilia, or Camilla, or Belinda; or, in short, only some work in which the greatest powers of the mind are displayed, in which the most thorough knowledge of human nature, the happiest delineation of its varieties, the liveliest effusions of wit and humour, are conveyed to the world in the best chosen language.

[Northanger Abbey (1818)]

BARTH, John (1930–)
If you are a novelist of a certain type of temperament, then what you really want to do is re-invent the world. God wasn't too bad a novelist, except he was a Realist.

[Attr.]

CECIL, Lord David (1902–1986)
It does not matter that Dickens' world is not lifelike: it is alive.

[Early Victorian Novelists (1934)]

CHESTERTON, G.K. (1874–1936)
A good novel tells us the truth about its hero; but a bad novel tells us the truth about its author.

[Heretics (1905)]

[On fiction]
It is the art in which the conquests of woman are quite beyond controversy ... The novel of the nineteenth century was female.

[The Victorian Age in Literature (1913)]

DAVISON, Frank Dalby (1893–1970)
You need a skin as thin as a cigarette paper to write a novel and the hide of an elephant to publish it.

[Meanjin, 1982]

FORSTER, E.M. (1879–1970)
That [the story] is the highest factor common to all novels, and I wish that it was not so, that it could be something different – melody, or perception of the truth, not this low atavistic form.

[Aspects of the Novel (1927)]

FOWLES, John (1926–)
There are many reasons why novelists write, but they all have one thing in common – a need to create an alternative world.

[The Sunday Times Magazine, 1977]

GIBBON, Edward (1737–1794)
The romance of Tom Jones, that exquisite picture of human manners, will outlive the palace of the Escurial and the imperial eagle of the house of Austria.

[Memoirs of My Life and Writings (1796)]

LARKIN, Philip (1922–1985)
[Referring to modern novels]
Far too many relied on the classic formula of a beginning, a muddle, and an end.

[New Fiction, 1978]

LAWRENCE, D.H. (1885–1930)
The novel is the one bright book of life.

['Why the Novel Matters' (1936)]

NABOKOV, Vladimir (1899–1977)
A novelist is, like all mortals, more fully at home on the surface of the present than in the ooze of the past.

[*Strong Opinions* (1973)]

POWELL, Anthony (1905–)
People think that because a novel's invented, it isn't true. Exactly the reverse is the case. Biography and memoirs can never be wholly true, since they cannot include every conceivable circumstance of what happened. The novel can do that.

[*Hearing Secret Harmonies* (1975)]

SHAW, George Bernard (1856–1950)
It is clear that a novel cannot be too bad to be worth publishing ... It certainly is possible for a novel to be too good to be worth publishing.

[*Plays Pleasant and Unpleasant* (1898)]

STENDHAL (1783–1842)
Un roman est un miroir qui se promène sur une grande route.
A novel is a mirror walking along a wide road.

[*Le Rouge et le Noir* (1830)]

TYNAN, Kenneth (1927–1980)
A novel is a static thing that one moves through; a play is a dynamic thing that moves past one.

[*Curtains* (1961)]

WAUGH, Auberon (1939–)
It is a sad feature of modern life that only women for the most part have time to write novels, and they seldom have much to write about.

[*The Observer*, 1981]

WILDE, Oscar (1854–1900)
The good ended happily, and the bad unhappily. That is what Fiction means.

[*The Importance of Being Earnest* (1895)]

WOOLF, Virginia (1882–1941)
A woman must have money and a room of her own if she is to write fiction.

[*A Room of One's Own* (1929)]

See BOOKS; LITERATURE; WRITERS; WRITING

FLATTERY

AUSTEN, Jane (1775–1817)
It is happy for you that you possess the talent of flattering with delicacy. May I ask whether these pleasing attentions proceed from the impulse of the moment, or are the result of previous study?

[*Pride and Prejudice* (1813)]

BIERCE, Ambrose (1842–c. 1914)
Flatter: To impress another with a sense of one's own merit.

[*The Enlarged Devil's Dictionary* (1961)]

COLTON, Charles Caleb (c. 1780–1832)
Imitation is the sincerest form of flattery.

[*Lacon* (1820)]

DUNBAR, William (c. 1460–c. 1525)
Flattery wearis ane furrit gown,
And falsett with the lord does roun,
And truth stands barrit at the dure.

['Into this World May None Assure']

FONTAINE, Jean de la (1621–1695)
Mon bon Monsieur,
Apprenez que tout flatteur
Vit au dépens de celui qui l'écoute.
My dear Monsieur, know that every flatterer lives at the expense of the one who listens to him.

['Le corbeau et le renard']

HALIFAX, Lord (1633–1695)
It is flattering some Men to endure them.

['Of Company' (1750)]

JOHNSON, Samuel (1709–1784)
[Remark to Hannah More]
Madam, before you flatter a man so

grossly to his face, you should consider whether or not your flattery is worth his having.

[*Diary and Letters of Madame d'Arblay* (1842)]

SHAW, George Bernard (1856–1950)
What really flatters a man is that you think him worth flattering.

[*John Bull's Other Island* (1907)]

FOLLY

ANONYMOUS
When I was a little boy, I had but a
  little wit,
'Tis a long time ago, and I have no
  more yet;
Nor ever ever shall, until that I die,
For the longer I live the more fool
  am I.

[In *Wit and Mirth, an Antidote against
Melancholy* (1684)]

ANTRIM, Minna (1861–1950)
A fool bolts pleasure, then complains
of moral indigestion.

[*Naked Truth and Veiled Allusions* (1902)]

BARNUM, Phineas T. (1810–1891)
There's a sucker born every minute.

[Attr.]

BEECHER, Henry Ward (1813–1887)
[On receiving a note containing only
one word: 'Fool']
I have known many an instance of a
man writing a letter and forgetting to
sign his name, but this is the only
instance I have ever known of a man
signing his name and forgetting to
write the letter.

[Attr.]

THE BIBLE (King James Version)
Answer a fool according to his folly.

[*Proverbs*, 26:5]

BLAKE, William (1757–1827)
If the fool would persist in his folly he
would become wise.

['Proverbs of Hell' (1793)]

**BOILEAU-DESPREAUX, Nicolas
(1636–1711)**
*Un sot trouve toujours un plus sot qui
l'admire.*
A fool will always find a greater fool to
admire him.

[*L'Art Poétique* (1674)]

COWPER, William (1731–1800)
A fool must now and then be right, by
chance.

['Conversation' (1782)]

CURTIZ, Michael (1888–1962)
The next time I send a damn fool for
something, I go myself.

[In Zierold, *Moguls* (1969)]

FIELDING, Henry (1707–1754)
One fool at least in every married
couple.

[*Amelia* (1751)]

FRANKLIN, Benjamin (1706–1790)
Experience keeps a dear school, but
fools will learn in no other.

[*Poor Richard's Almanac* (1743)]

GRACIÁN, Baltasar (1601–1658)
*No es necio el que hace la necedad, sino
el que, hecha, no la sabe encubrir.*
It is not the one who commits an act
of foolishness who is foolish, but the
one who, once such an act has been
committed, does not know how to
cover it up.

[*Handbook-Oracle and the Art of Prudence*
(1647)]

HORACE (65–8 BC)
*Misce stultitiam consiliis brevem:
Dulce est desipere in loco.*
Mix a little folly with your plans: it is
sweet to be silly at the right moment.

[*Odes*]

IBSEN, Henrik (1828–1906)
Fools are in a terrible, overwhelming
majority, all the wide world over.

[*An Enemy of the People* (1882)]

MOLIERE (1622–1673)
C'est une folie à nulle autre seconde,

De vouloir se mêler à corriger le monde.
The greatest folly of all is wanting to busy oneself in setting the world to rights.

[*Le Misanthrope* (1666)]

ROWLAND, Helen (1875–1950)
The follies which a man regrets most in his life are those which he didn't commit when he had the opportunity.

[*A Guide to Men* (1922)]

SCHILLER, Johann (1759–1805)
Mit der Dummheit kämpfen Götter selbst vergebens.
Gods themselves struggle in vain with stupidity.

[*The Maid of Orleans* (1801)]

SHAKESPEARE, William (1564–1616)
He uses his folly like a stalking-horse, and under the presentation of that he shoots his wit.

[*As You Like It*, V.iv]

STEVENSON, Robert Louis (1850–1894)
For God's sake give me the young man who has brains enough to make a fool of himself!

[*Virginibus Puerisque* (1881)]

SWIFT, Jonathan (1667–1745)
Hated by fools, and fools to hate,
Be that my motto and my fate.

['To Mr Delany' (1718)]

THOREAU, Henry (1817–1862)
Any fool can make a rule and every fool will mind it.

[Attr.]

TUSSER, Thomas (c. 1524–1580)
A fool and his money be soon at debate.

[*Five Hundred Points of Good Husbandry* (1557)]

WHATELY, Richard (1787–1863)
It is a folly to expect men to do all that they may reasonably be expected to do.

[*Apophthegms* (1854)]

YOUNG, Edward (1683–1765)
Be wise with speed;
A fool at forty is a fool indeed.

[*Love of Fame, the Universal Passion* (1728)]

FOOD

BAREHAM, Lindsey (1948–)
Good mashed potato is one of the great luxuries of life and I don't blame Elvis for eating it every night for the last year of his life.

[*In Praise of the Potato* (1989)]

THE BIBLE (King James Version)
Better is a dinner of herbs where love is, than a stalled ox and hatred therewith.

[*Proverbs*, 15:17]

CAMPBELL, Mrs Patrick (1865–1940)
[To Bernard Shaw, a vegetarian]
Some day you'll eat a pork chop, Joey, and then God help all women.

[In Woollcott, *While Rome Burns* (1934)]

CERVANTES, Miguel de (1547–1616)
La mejon salsa del mundo es la hambre.
Hunger is the best sauce in the world.

[*Don Quixote* (1615)]

DAHL, Roald (1916–1990)
Do you *know* what breakfast cereal is made of? It's made of all those little curly wooden shavings you find in pencil sharpeners!

[*Charlie and the Chocolate Factory* (1964)]

DAVID, Elizabeth (1913–1992)
To eat figs off the tree in the very early morning, when they have been barely touched by the sun, is one of the exquisite pleasures of the Mediterranean.

[*Italian Food* (1954)]

DAVIES, David (1742–1819)
Though the potato is an excellent root, deserving to be brought into general use, yet it seems not likely that the use of it should ever be normal in the country.

[*The Case of the Labourers in Husbandry* (1795)]

137   **FOOD**

DE VRIES, Peter (1910–)
Gluttony is an emotional escape, a
sign something is eating us.
[Comfort me with Apples (1956)]

DURRELL, Lawrence (1912–1990)
The whole Mediterranean, the
sculpture, the palms, the gold beads,
the bearded heroes, the wine, the
ideas, the ships, the moonlight, the
winged gorgons, the bronze men, the
philosophers – all of it seems to rise in
the sour, pungent taste of these black
olives between the teeth. A taste older
than meat, older than wine. A taste as
old as cold water.
[Prospero's Cell (1945)]

FADIMAN, Clifton (1904–)
Cheese – milk's leap toward immor-
tality.
[Any Number Can Play (1957)]

FEUERBACH, Ludwig (1804–1872)
Der Mensch ist, was er isst.
Man is what he eats.
*[In Moleschott, Lehre der Nahrungsmittel: Für
das Volk (1850)]*

FRANKLIN, Benjamin (1706–1790)
To lengthen thy life, lessen thy meals.
[Poor Richard's Almanac (1733)]

FULLER, Thomas (1608–1661)
He was a very valiant man who first
ventured on eating of oysters.
[The History of the Worthies of England (1662)]

HERBERT, George (1593–1633)
A cheerful look makes a dish a feast.
[Jacula Prudentum (1640)]

JOHNSON, Samuel (1709–1784)
I look upon it, that he who does not
mind his belly will hardly mind anything else.
*[In Boswell, The Life of Samuel Johnson
(1791)]*

**LUTYENS, Sir Edwin Landseer
(1869–1944)**
[Comment made in a restaurant]

This piece of cod passes all understanding.
[In R. Lutyens, Sir Edwin Lutyens (1942)]

MOLIERE (1622–1673)
*Il faut manger pour vivre et non pas
vivre pour manger.*
One should eat to live, not live to eat.
[L'Avare (1669)]

PETER, Laurence J. (1919–1990)
The noblest of all dogs is the hot-dog;
it feeds the hand that bites it.
[Quotations for Our Time (1977)]

PIGGY, Miss
Never eat anything at one sitting that
you can't lift.
[Woman's Hour, 1992]

POPE, Alexander (1688–1744)
Fame is at best an unperforming
   cheat;
But 'tis substantial happiness, to *eat*.
['Prologue for Mr D'Urfey's Last Play' (1727)]

PORTLAND, Duke of (1857–1943)
[On being told to reduce his expenses
by dispensing with one of his two
Italian pastry cooks]
What! Can't a fellow even enjoy a
biscuit any more?
[In Winchester, Their Noble Lordships]

ROUSSEAU, Émile
*Les grands mangeurs de viande sont en
général cruels et féroces plus que les
autres hommes ... La barbarie anglaise
est connue.*
Great eaters of meat are in general
more cruel and ferocious than other
men. The English are known for their
cruelty.
[Attr.]

SHAKESPEARE, William (1564–1616)
Methinks sometimes I have no more
wit than a Christian or an ordinary
man has; but I am a great eater of
beef, and I believe that does harm to
my wit.
[Twelfth Night, I.iii]

SHAW, George Bernard (1856–1950)
There is no love sincerer than the love of food.

[Man and Superman (1903)]

SHELLEY, Percy Bysshe (1792–1822)
There are two Italies – the one is the most sublime and lovely contemplation that can be conceived by the imagination of man; the other is the most degraded, disgusting and odious. What do you think? Young women of rank actually eat – you will never guess what – garlick!

[Attr.]

VOLTAIRE (1694–1778)
[On learning that coffee was considered a slow poison]
I think it must be so, for I have been drinking it for sixty-five years and I am not dead yet.

[Attr.]

WEBSTER, John (c. 1580–c. 1625)
I saw him even now going the way of all flesh, that is to say towards the kitchen.

[Westward Hoe (1607)]

WODEHOUSE, P.G. (1881–1975)
The lunches of fifty-seven years had caused his chest to slip down to the mezzanine floor.

[The Heart of a Goof (1926)]

See COOKERY; DINING

FOREIGNERS

DU BELLOY, P.–L.B. (1727–1775)
Plus je vis d'étrangers, plus j'aimai ma patrie.
The more foreigners I saw, the more I loved my native land.

[Le Siège de Calais (1765)]

BRADBURY, Malcolm (1932–)
Sympathy – for all these people, for being foreigners – lay over the gathering like a woolly blanket; and no one was enjoying it at all.

[Eating People is Wrong (1954)]

BROWNE, Sir Thomas (1605–1682)
I feel not in myself those common antipathies that I can discover in others; those national repugnances do not touch me, nor do I behold with prejudice the French, Italian, Spaniard, or Dutch; but where I find their actions in balance with my countrymen's, I honour, love and embrace them in the same degree.

[Religio Medici (1643)]

CRISP, Quentin (1908–)
I don't hold with abroad and think that foreigners speak English when our backs are turned.

[The Naked Civil Servant (1968)]

ERASMUS (c. 1466–1536)
Is not the Turk a man and a brother?

[Querela Pacis]

GOLDSMITH, Oliver (c. 1728–1774)
The Scotch may be compared to a tulip planted in dung, but I never see a Dutchman in his own house, but I think of a magnificent Egyptian Temple dedicated to an ox.

[Letter from Leyden to Rev. Thomas Contarine, 1754]

MEYNELL, Hugo (1727–1780)
For anything I see, foreigners are fools.

[In Boswell, The Life of Samuel Johnson (1791)]

MITFORD, Nancy (1904–1973)
Abroad is unutterably bloody and foreigners are fiends.

[The Pursuit of Love (1945)]

TROLLOPE, Anthony (1815–1882)
We cannot bring ourselves to believe it possible that a foreigner should in any respect be wiser than ourselves. If any such point out to us our follies, we at once claim those follies as the special evidences of our wisdom.

[Orley Farm (1862)]

TWAIN, Mark (1835–1910)
They spell it Vinci and pronounce it

Vinchy; foreigners always spell better than they pronounce.

[*The Innocents Abroad* (1869)]

See TRAVEL

FORGIVENESS

AUSTEN, Jane (1775–1817)
You ought certainly to forgive them as a Christian, but never to admit them in your sight, or allow their names to be mentioned in your hearing.

[*Pride and Prejudice* (1813)]

THE BIBLE (King James Version)
Father, forgive them; for they know not what they do.

[*Luke*, 23:34]

BROWNING, Robert (1812–1889)
Good, to forgive;
Best, to forget!
Living, we fret;
Dying, we live.

[*La Saisiaz* (1878)]

CATHERINE THE GREAT (1729–1796)
Moi, je serai autocrate: c'est mon métier. Et le bon Dieu me pardonnera: c'est son métier.
I shall be an autocrat: that's my job. And the good Lord will forgive me: that's his job.

[Attr.]

DRYDEN, John (1631–1700)
Forgiveness to the injured does belong;
But they ne'er pardon, who have done the wrong.

[*The Conquest of Granada* (1670)]

FROST, Robert (1874–1963)
Forgive, O Lord, my little jokes on Thee
And I'll forgive Thy great big one on me.

['Cluster of Faith' (1962)]

GAY, John (1685–1732)
Well, Polly; as far as one woman can

forgive another, I forgive thee.

[*The Beggar's Opera* (1728)]

PROVERB
To err is human; to forgive divine.

YEATS, W.B. (1865–1939)
Only the dead can be forgiven;
But when I think of that my tongue's a stone.

['A Dialogue of Self and Soul' (1933)]

FRANCE

CARLYLE, Thomas (1795–1881)
France was long a despotism tempered by epigrams.

[*History of the French Revolution* (1837)]

DE GAULLE, Charles (1890–1970)
On ne peut rassembler les Français que sous le coup de la peur. On ne peut pas rassembler à froid un pays qui compte 265 spécialités de fromage.
One can only unite the French under the threat of danger. One cannot simply bring together a nation that produces 265 kinds of cheese.

[Speech, 1951]

DU BELLAY, Joachim (1522–1560)
France, mère des arts, des armes et des lois.
France, mother of arts, of arms, and of laws.

[*Les Regrets* (1558)]

JOHNSON, Samuel (1709–1784)
A Frenchman must be always talking, whether he knows anything of the matter or not; an Englishman is content to say nothing, when he has nothing to say.

[In Boswell, *The Life of Samuel Johnson* (1791)]

NAPOLEON I (1769–1821)
France has more need of me than I have need of France.

[Speech, 1813]

NOVELLO, Ivor (1893–1951)
There's something Vichy about the

French.

[In Marsh, *Ambrosia and Small Beer*]

TOCQUEVILLE, Alexis de (1805–1859)
L'esprit français est de ne pas vouloir de supérieur. L'esprit anglais de vouloir des inférieurs. Le Français lève les yeux sans cesse au-dessus de lui avec inquiétude. L'Anglais les baisse au-dessous de lui avec complaisance. C'est de part et d'autre de l'orgueil, mais entendu de manière différente.
The French want no-one to be their *superior*. The English want *inferiors*. The Frenchman constantly looks above him with anxiety. The Englishman looks beneath him with complacency. On either side it is pride, but understood in a different manner.

[*Voyage en Angleterre et en Irlande de 1835*]

WALPOLE, Horace (1717–1797)
I do not dislike the French from the vulgar antipathy between neighbouring nations, but for their insolent and unfounded airs of superiority.

[Letter, 1787]

WILDER, Billy (1906–)
France is a country where the money falls apart in your hands and you can't tear the toilet paper.

[In Halliwell, *Filmgoer's Book of Quotes* (1973)]

FREEDOM

ANONYMOUS
[Declaration sent to Pope John XXII by the Scottish barons]
For so long as but a hundred of us remain alive, we will in no way yield ourselves to the dominion of the English. For it is not for glory, nor riches, nor honour that we fight, but for Freedom only, which no good man lays down but with his life.

[Declaration of Arbroath, 1320]

ARISTOTLE (384–322 BC)
Where we are free to act, we are also free not to act, and where we are able to say No, we are also able to say Yes.

[*Nicomachean Ethics*]

AURELIUS, Marcus (121–180)
Remember that to change your mind and follow someone who puts you right is to be none the less free than you were before.

[*Meditations*]

BARBOUR, John (c. 1316–1395)
A! fredome is a noble thing!
Fredome mayss man to haiff liking;
Fredome all solace to man giffio:
He levys at ess that frely levys!

[*The Bruce* (1375)]

BELL, Clive (1881–1964)
Only reason can convince us of those three fundamental truths without a recognition of which there can be no effective liberty: that what we believe is not necessarily true; that what we like is not necessarily good; and that all questions are open.

[*Civilisation* (1928)]

BERLIN, Sir Isaiah (1909–)
Liberty is liberty, not equality or fairness or justice or culture, or human happiness or a quiet conscience.

[*Four Essays on Liberty* (1969)]

BURKE, Edmund (1729–1797)
Abstract liberty, like other mere abstractions, is not to be found.

[*Speech on Conciliation with America* (1775)]

Freedom and not servitude is the cure of anarchy; as religion, and not atheism, is the true remedy for superstition.

[*Speech on Conciliation with America* (1775)]

Liberty, too, must be limited in order to be possessed.

[*Letter to the Sheriffs of Bristol on the Affairs of America* (1777)]

The only liberty I mean, is a liberty connected with order; that not only exists along with order and virtue, but which cannot exist at all without them.

[Speech, 1774]

BURNS, Robert (1759–1796)
Scots, wha hae wi' Wallace bled,
Scots, wham Bruce has aften led,
Welcome to your gory bed
Or to victorie! ...

Lay the proud usurpers low!
Tyrants fall in ev'ry foe!
Liberty's in every blow!
Let us do, or die!
[*'Scots, Wha Hae'* (1793)]

BYRON, Lord (1788–1824)
Yet, Freedom! yet thy banner, torn, but flying,
Streams like the thunder-storm *against* the wind.
[*Childe Harold's Pilgrimage* (1818)]

COLERIDGE, Hartley (1796–1849)
But what is Freedom? Rightly understood,
A universal licence to be good.
[*'Liberty'* (1833)]

COLERIDGE, Samuel Taylor (1772–1834)
For what is freedom, but the unfettered use
Of all the powers which God for use had given?
[*'The Destiny of Nations'*]

CONNOLLY, James (1868–1916)
Apostles of Freedom are ever idolised when dead, but crucified when alive.
[*Workers Republic*, 1898]

COWPER, William (1731–1800)
Freedom has a thousand charms to show,
That slaves, howe'er contented, never know.
[*Table Talk* (1782)]

CURRAN, John Philpot (1750–1817)
The condition upon which God hath given liberty to man is eternal vigilance; which condition if he break, servitude is at once the consequence of his crime, and the punishment of his guilt.
[Speech, 1790]

DIDEROT, Denis (1713–1784)
Men will never be free until the last king is strangled with the entrails of the last priest.
[*Dithyrambe sur la Fête des Rois*]

ENGELS, Friedrich (1820–1895)
Freedom is the recognition of necessity.
[In Mackay, *The Harvest of a Quiet Eye* (1977)]

EWER, William (1885–1976)
I gave my life for freedom – This I know:
For those who bade me fight had told me so.
[*'The Souls'* (1917)]

GOLDWATER, Barry (1909–)
[On accepting nomination for the presidency]
Extremism in the defence of liberty is no vice.
[Speech, 1964]

HALIFAX, Lord (1633–1695)
Power is so apt to be insolent and Liberty to be saucy, that they are very seldom upon good Terms.
[*Political, Moral and Miscellaneous Thoughts and Reflections* (1750)]

When the people contend for their Liberty, they seldom get any thing by their Victory but new Masters.
[*Political, Moral and Miscellaneous Thoughts and Reflections* (1750)]

HATTERSLEY, Roy (1932–)
The proposition that Muslims are welcome in Britain if, and only if, they stop behaving like Muslims is incompatible with the principles of a free society.
[*The Independent*, 1995]

HAZLITT, William (1778–1830)
The love of liberty is the love of others; the love of power is the love of ourselves.
[*'The Times Newspaper'* (1819)]

HENRY, Patrick (1736–1799)
Give me liberty, or give me death!
[Speech, 1775]

HOFFER, Eric (1902–1983)
When people are free to do as they please, they usually imitate each other.
[*The Passionate State of Mind* (1955)]

HORACE (65–8 BC)
Quisnam igitur liber? Sapiens qui sibi imperiosus,
Quem neque pauperies neque mors neque vincula terrent,
Responsare cupidinibus, contemnere honores
Fortis, et in se ipso totus, teres, atque rotundus.
Who then is free? The wise man who commands himself, whom neither poverty nor death nor chains can terrify, who is strong enough to defy his passions and to despise distinctions, a man who is complete in himself, polished and well-rounded.
[*Satires*]

JEFFERSON, Thomas (1743–1826)
The tree of liberty must be refreshed from time to time with the blood of patriots and tyrants. It is its natural manure.
[Letter to W.S. Smith, 1787]

KAFKA, Franz (1883–1924)
Es ist oft besser, in Ketten, als frei zu sein.
It's often better to be in chains than to be free.
[*The Trial* (1925)]

KING, Martin Luther (1929–1968)
Free at last, free at last, thank God Almighty, we are free at last!
[Speech, 1963]

LENIN, V.I. (1870–1924)
It is true that liberty is precious – so precious that it must be rationed.
[In Sidney and Beatrice Webb, *Soviet Communism* (1936)]

LINCOLN, Abraham (1809–1865)
Those who deny freedom to others, deserve it not for themselves.
[Speech, 1856]

MACAULAY, Lord (1800–1859)
There is only one cure for the evils which newly acquired freedom produces; and that is freedom.
[*Collected Essays* (1843)]

Many politicians of our time are in the habit of laying it down as a self-evident proposition, that no people ought to be free till they are fit to use their freedom. The maxim is worthy of the fool in the old story, who resolved not to go into the water till he had learnt to swim. If men are to wait for liberty till they become wise and good in slavery, they may indeed wait for ever.
[*Collected Essays* (1843)]

MANDELA, Nelson (1918–)
I cannot and will not give any under-taking at a time when I, and you, the people, are not free. Your freedom and mine cannot be separated.
[Message to a rally in Soweto, 1985]

MANN, W. Edward (1918–)
A sudden access of psychological free-dom often turns from sheer excite-ment to deep panic.
[*The Man Who Dreamed of Tomorrow* (1980)]

MILL, John Stuart (1806–1873)
The sole end for which mankind are warranted, individually or collectively, in interfering with the liberty of action of any of their number, is self-protection.
[*On Liberty* (1859)]

MILTON, John (1608–1674)
Give me the liberty to know, to utter, and to argue freely according to conscience, above all liberties.
[*Areopagitica* (1644)]

None can love freedom heartilie, but good men; the rest love not freedom, but licence.
[*The Tenure of Kings and Magistrates* (1649)]

MONTESQUIEU (1689–1755)
La liberté est le droit de faire tout ce que les lois permettent.
Freedom is the right to do whatever the laws permit.

[*De l'esprit des lois* (1748)]

MUSSOLINI, Benito (1883–1945)
Ci sono le libertà; la libertà non è mai esistita.
There are freedoms; freedom has never existed.

[Speech, 1923]

PANKHURST, Dame Christabel (1880–1958)
What we suffragettes aspire to be when we are enfranchised is ambassadors of freedom to women in other parts of the world, who are not so free as we are.

[Speech, 1915]

PITT, William (1759–1806)
Necessity is the plea for every infringement of human freedom. It is the argument of tyrants; it is the creed of slaves.

[Speech, 1783]

ROLAND, Madame (1754–1793)
[Remark on mounting the scaffold]
O liberté! O liberté! que de crimes on commet en ton nom!
O liberty! O liberty! how many crimes are committed in your name!

[In Lamartine, *Histoire des Girondins* (1847)]

ROOSEVELT, Franklin Delano (1882–1945)
In the future days, which we seek to make secure, we look forward to a world founded upon four essential human freedoms. The first is freedom of speech and expression – everywhere in the world. The second is freedom of every person to worship God in his own way – everywhere in the world. The third is freedom from want ... The fourth is freedom from fear.

[Address, 1941]

SARTRE, Jean-Paul (1905–1980)
Quand une fois la liberté a explosé dans une âme d'homme, les Dieux ne peuvent plus rien contre lui.
Once freedom has exploded in the soul of a man, the gods have no more power over him.

[*The Flies* (1943)]

Man is condemned to be free.
[*Existentialism and Humanism*]

SHAW, George Bernard (1856–1950)
Liberty means responsibility. That is why most men dread it.

[*Man and Superman* (1903)]

SOLZHENITSYN, Alexander (1918–)
You only have power over people as long as you don't take *everything* away from them. But when you've robbed a man of *everything* he's no longer in your power – he's free again.

[*The First Circle* (1968)]

STEVENSON, Adlai (1900–1965)
My definition of a free society is a society where it is safe to be unpopular.

[Speech, Detroit, 1952]

TWAIN, Mark (1835–1910)
It is by the goodness of God that in our country we have those three unspeakably precious things: freedom of speech, freedom of conscience, and the prudence never to practise either of them.

[*Following the Equator* (1897)]

VOLTAIRE (1694–1778)
La Liberté est née en Angleterre des querelles des tyrans.
Liberty was born in England from the quarrels of tyrants.

[*Lettres philosophiques* (1734)]

WASHINGTON, George (1732–1799)
Liberty, when it begins to take root, is a plant of rapid growth.

[Letter, 1788]

WILLKIE, Wendell (1892–1944)
Freedom is an indivisible word. If we
want to enjoy it, and fight for it, we
must be prepared to extend it to
everyone, whether they are rich or
poor, whether they agree with us or
not, no matter what their race or the
colour of their skin.

[*One World* (1943)]

FRIENDSHIP

ADAMS, Henry (1838–1918)
One friend in a lifetime is much; two
are many; three are hardly possible.
Friendship needs a certain parallelism
of life, a community of thought, a
rivalry of aim.

[*The Education of Henry Adams* (1918)]

ARISTOTLE (384–322 BC)
On being asked what is a friend, he
said 'A single soul dwelling in two
bodies.'

[In Diogenes Laertius, *Lives of Philosophers*]

AUBREY, John (1626–1697)
[Of Francis Beaumont]
There was a wonderful consimility of
phansey between him and Mr John
Fletcher, which caused that dearness
of friendship between them ... They
lived together on the Bank side, not far
from the Playhouse, both bachelors;
lay together; had one wench in the
house between them, which they did
so admire; the same clothes and cloak,
&c.; between them.

[*Brief Lives* (c. 1693)]

BACON, Francis (1561–1626)
A false friend is more dangerous than
an open enemy.

[*A Letter of Advice ... to the Duke of
Buckingham* (1616)]

It is the worst solitude, to have no true
friendships.

[*The Advancement of Learning* (1605)]

This communicating of a man's self to
his friend works two contrary effects;
for it redoubleth joys, and cutteth
griefs in halves.

[*Essays* (1625)]

BELLOC, Hilaire (1870–1953)
From quiet homes and first beginning,
Out to the undiscovered ends,
There's nothing worth the wear of
winning,
But laughter and the love of friends.

[*Verses* (1910), 'Dedicatory Ode']

THE BIBLE (King James Version)
A faithful friend is a sturdy shelter: he
that has found one has found a
treasure. There is nothing so precious
as a faithful friend, and no scales can
measure his excellence.

[Apocrypha, *Ecclesiasticus*]

Forsake not an old friend; for the new
is not comparable to him; a new friend
is as new wine; when it is old, thou
shalt drink it with pleasure.

[Apocrypha, *Ecclesiasticus*]

BIERCE, Ambrose (1842–c. 1914)
Antipathy: The sentiment inspired by
one's friend's friend.

[*The Enlarged Devil's Dictionary* (1961)]

BRADBURY, Malcolm (1932–)
I've noticed your hostility towards him
... I ought to have guessed you were
friends.

[*The History Man* (1975)]

BULWER-LYTTON, Edward (1803–1873)
There is no man so friendless but what
he can find a friend sincere enough to
tell him disagreeable truths.

[*What Will He Do With It?* (1857)]

BYRON, Lord (1788–1824)
Friendship is Love without his wings.

['L'amitié est l'amour sans ailes' (1806)]

CANNING, George (1770–1827)
Give me the avowed, erect and manly
foe;
Firm I can meet, perhaps return the
blow;
But of all plagues, good Heaven, thy
wrath can send,
Save me, oh, save me, from the candid
friend.

['New Morality' (1821)]

CHURCHILL, Charles (1731–1764)
Greatly his foes he dreads, but more
  his friends;
He hurts me most who lavishly
  commends.
[*The Apology, addressed to the Critical
Reviewers'* (1761)]

COLETTE (1873–1954)
My true friends have always given me
that supreme proof of devotion, a
spontaneous aversion for the man I
loved.
[*Break of Day* (1928)]

COLTON, Charles Caleb (c. 1780–1832)
Friendship often ends in love; but love
in friendship – never.
[*Lacon* (1820)]

ELIOT, George (1819–1880)
Friendships begin with liking or grati-
tude – roots that can be pulled up.
[*Daniel Deronda* (1876)]

EMERSON, Ralph Waldo (1803–1882)
Let the soul be assured that somewhere in the universe it should rejoin
its friend, and it would be content and
cheerful alone for a thousand years.
['Friendship' (1841)]

A friend is a person with whom I may
be sincere. Before him I may think
aloud.
['Friendship' (1841)]

A friend may well be reckoned the
masterpiece of Nature.
['Friendship' (1841)]

The only reward of virtue is virtue; the
only way to have a friend is to be one.
['Friendship' (1841)]

EPICURUS (341–270 BC)
It is not so much our friends' help that
helps us as the confident knowledge
that they will help us.
[Attr.]

GARCÍA MÁRQUEZ, Gabriel (1928–)
*Un solo minuto de reconciliación tiene
más mérito que toda una vida de
amistad.*

One single minute of reconciliation is
worth more than an entire life of
friendship.
[*One Hundred Years of Solitude* (1968)]

GOLDSMITH, Oliver (c. 1728–1774)
Friendship is a disinterested commerce
between equals; love, an abject intercourse between tyrants and slaves.
[*The Good Natur'd Man* (1768)]

HUMPHRIES, Barry (1934–)
Friendship is tested in the thick years
of success rather than in the thin years
of struggle.
[In Green, *A Dictionary of Contemporary
Quotations* (1982)]

JOHNSON, Samuel (1709–1784)
The endearing elegance of female
friendship.
[*Rasselas* (1759)]

If a man does not make new acquaintance as he advances through life, he
will soon find himself left alone. A
man, Sir, should keep his friendship in
constant repair.
[In Boswell, *The Life of Samuel Johnson*
(1791)]

How few of his friends' houses would
a man choose to be at when he is sick.
[In Boswell, *The Life of Samuel Johnson*
(1791)]

KINGSMILL, Hugh (1889–1949)
Friends are God's apology for re-
lations.
[In Ingrams, *God's Apology* (1977)]

**LA ROCHEFOUCAULD, Duc de
(1613–1680)**
*Dans l'adversité de nos meilleurs amis,
nous trouvons toujours quelque chose
qui ne nous déplait pas.*
In the misfortunes of our closest
friends, we always find something
which is not displeasing to us.
[*Maximes* (1665)]

*Il est plus honteux de se défier de ses
amis que d'en être trompé.*

There is more shame in distrusting one's friends than in being deceived by them.

[*Maximes* (1678)]

LEWIS, C.S. (1898–1963)
Friendship is unnecessary, like philosophy, like art. ... It has no survival value; rather it is one of those things that give value to survival.

[*The Four Loves* (c. 1936)]

MEDICI, Cosimo de' (1389–1464)
We read that we ought to forgive our enemies; but we do not read that we ought to forgive our friends.

[In Bacon, *Apophthegms* (1625)]

POPE, Alexander (1688–1744)
True friendship's laws are by this rule express'd,
Welcome the coming, speed the parting guest.

[*The Odyssey* (1726)]

How often are we to die before we go quite off this stage? In every friend we lose a part of ourselves, and the best part.

[Letter to Swift, 1732]

SHAKESPEARE, William (1564–1616)
Friendship is constant in all other things
Save in the office and affairs of love.

[*Much Ado About Nothing*, II.i]

I count myself in nothing else so happy
As in a soul rememb'ring my good friends.

[*Richard II*, II.iii]

TWAIN, Mark (1835–1910)
The holy passion of Friendship is of so sweet and steady and loyal and enduring a nature that it will last through a whole lifetime, if not asked to lend money.

[*Pudd'nhead Wilson's Calendar* (1894)]

VIDAL, Gore (1925–)
Whenever a friend succeeds, a little something in me dies.

[*The Sunday Times Magazine*, 1973]

WHITMAN, Walt (1819–1892)
I no doubt deserved my enemies, but I don't believe I deserved my friends.

[In Bradford, *Biography and the Human Heart*]

YEATS, W.B. (1865–1939)
Think where man's glory most begins and ends,
And say my glory was I had such friends.

['The Municipal Gallery Revisited' (1937)]

THE FUTURE

ADDISON, Joseph (1672–1719)
'We are always doing,' says he, 'something for Posterity, but I would fain see Posterity do something for us.'

[*The Spectator*, 1714]

BACON, Francis (1561–1626)
Men must pursue things which are just in present, and leave the future to the divine Providence.

[*The Advancement of Learning* (1605)]

BALDWIN, James (1924–1987)
The future is ... black.

[*The Observer*, 1963]

BALFOUR, A.J. (1848–1930)
The energies of our system will decay, the glory of the sun will be dimmed, and the earth, tideless and inert, will no longer tolerate the race which has for a moment disturbed its solitude. Man will go down into the pit, and all his thoughts will perish.

[*The Foundations of Belief* (1895)]

BIERCE, Ambrose (1842–c. 1914)
Future: That period of time in which our affairs prosper, our friends are true and our happiness is assured.

[*The Cynic's Word Book* (1906)]

BURKE, Edmund (1729–1797)
People will not look forward to posterity, who never look backward to their ancestors.

[*Reflections on the Revolution in France* (1790)]

You can never plan the future by the past.

[*Letter to a Member of the National Assembly* (1791)]

CAMUS, Albert (1913–1960)
The future is the only kind of property that the masters willingly concede to slaves.

[*The Rebel* (1951)]

CHURCHILL, Sir Winston (1874–1965)
The empires of the future are empires of the mind.

[Speech,1943]

CLARK, Lord Kenneth (1903–1983)
One may be optimistic, but one can't exactly be joyful at the prospect before us.

[End of TV series, *Civilization*]

COLERIDGE, Samuel Taylor (1772–1834)
Often do the spirits
Of great events stride on before the events,
And in to-day already walks to-morrow.

['Death of Wallenstein' (1800)]

CONFUCIUS (c. 550–c. 478 BC)
Study the past, if you would divine the future.

[*Analects*]

COWARD, Sir Noël (1899–1973)
I don't give a hoot about posterity. Why should I worry about what people think of me when I'm dead as a doornail anyway?

[*Present Laughter* (1943)]

DIX, Dorothy (1870–1951)
I have learned to live each day as it comes, and not to borrow trouble by dreading tomorrow. It is the dark menace of the future that makes cowards of us.

[*Dorothy Dix, Her Book* (1926)]

EINSTEIN, Albert (1879–1955)
I never think of the future. It comes soon enough.

[Interview, 1930]

HILL, Reginald (1936–)
I have seen the future and it sucks.

[*Pictures of Perfection* (1994)]

HUGO, Victor (1802–1885)
In the twentieth century, war will be dead, the scaffold will be dead, hatred will be dead, frontier boundaries will be dead, dogmas will be dead; man will live. He will possess something higher than all these – a great country, the whole earth, and a great hope, the whole heaven.

[*The Future of Man*]

JOHNSON, Samuel (1709–1784)
The future is purchased by the present.

[Attr.]

LEWIS, C.S. (1898–1963)
The Future is something which everyone reaches at the rate of sixty minutes an hour, whatever he does, whoever he is.

[*The Screwtape Letters* (1942)]

MITCHELL, Margaret (1900–1949)
After all, tomorrow is another day.

[*Gone with the Wind* (1936)]

ORTEGA Y GASSET, José (1883–1955)
Con el pasado no se lucha cuerpo a cuerpo. El porvenir lo vence porque se lo traga. Como deje algo de él fuera, está perdido.
You don't fight hand-to-hand with the past. The future conquers it because it swallows it. If it leaves part of it outside, it is lost.

[*The Rebellion of the Masses* (1930)]

ORWELL, George (1903–1950)
If you want a picture of the future, imagine a boot stamping on a human face – for ever.

[*Nineteen Eighty-Four* (1949)]

PROUST, Marcel (1871–1922)
Nous appelons notre avenir l'ombre de lui-même que notre passé projette

THE FUTURE

dcvant nous.
What we call our future is the shadow which our past throws in front of us.

[*A l'ombre des jeunes filles en fleurs* (1918)]

RIFKIN, Jeremy
When the Iroquois made a decision, they said, 'How does it affect seven generations in the future?'

[*The New York Times Magazine*, 1988]

SNOW, C.P. (1905–1980)
[On industrialisation]
Common men can show astonishing fortitude in chasing jam tomorrow. Jam today, and men aren't at their most exciting: jam tomorrow, and one

often sees them at their noblest.

[*The Two Cultures and the Scientific Revolution* (1959)]

STEFFENS, Lincoln (1866–1936)
[Remark after visiting Russia in 1919]
I have seen the future; and it works.

[Letter to Marie Howe, 1919]

WEIL, Simone (1909–1943)
The future is made of the same stuff as the present.

[*On Science, Necessity, and the Love of God*]

WELLS, H.G. (1866–1946)
One thousand years more. That's all *Homo sapiens* has before him.

[In H. Nicolson, *Diary*]

GARDENS

ADDISON, Joseph (1672–1719)
I value my garden more for being full of blackbirds than of cherries, and very frankly give them fruit for their songs.
[*The Spectator*, 1712]

BACON, Francis (1561–1626)
God Almighty first planted a garden. And indeed, it is the purest of human pleasures. It is the greatest refreshment to the spirits of man; without which, buildings and palaces are but gross handiworks.
['Of Gardens' (1625)]

BROWN, Thomas Edward (1830–1897)
A garden is a lovesome thing, God wot!
['My Garden' (1893)]

COWLEY, Abraham (1618–1667)
God the first garden made, and the first city Cain.
['The Garden' (1668)]

EMERSON, Ralph Waldo (1803–1882)
What is a weed? A plant whose virtues have not yet been discovered.
[*Fortune of the Republic* (1878)]

GARDINER, Richard (b. c. 1533)
Sowe Carrets in your Gardens, and humbly praise God for them, as for a singular and great blessing.
[*Profitable Instructions for the Manuring, Sowing and Planting of Kitchen Gardens*]

GURNEY, Dorothy (1858–1932)
The kiss of the sun for pardon,
The song of the birds for mirth,
One is nearer God's Heart in a garden
Than anywhere else on earth.
['God's Garden' (1913)]

KIPLING, Rudyard (1865–1936)
Our England is a garden that is full of stately views,
Of borders, beds and shrubberies and lawns and avenues,
With statues on the terraces and peacocks strutting by;

But the Glory of the Garden lies in more than meets the eye ...

Oh, Adam was a gardener, and God who made him sees
That half a proper gardener's work is done upon his knees,
So when your work is finished, you can wash your hands and pray
For the Glory of the Garden, that it may not pass away!
And the Glory of the Garden it shall never pass away!
['The Glory of the Garden' (1911)]

MARVELL, Andrew (1621–1678)
Here at the fountain's sliding foot,
Or at some fruit-tree's mossy root,
Casting the body's vest aside,
My soul into the boughs does glide.
['The Garden' (1681)]

I have a garden of my own,
But so with roses overgrown,
And lilies, that you would it guess
To be a little wilderness.
['The Nymph Complaining for the Death of her Fawn' (1681)]

MILTON, John (1608–1674)
And add to these retired leisure,
That in trim gardens takes his pleasure.
['Il Penseroso' (1645)]

RUSSELL, Bertrand (1872–1970)
Every time I talk to a savant I feel quite sure that happiness is no longer a possibility. Yet when I talk to my gardener, I'm convinced of the opposite.
[Attr.]

SHAKESPEARE, William (1564–1616)
'Tis in ourselves that we are thus or thus. Our bodies are our gardens to the which our wills are gardeners.
[*Othello*, I.iii]

TENNYSON, Alfred, Lord (1809–1892)
Come into the garden, Maud,
For the black bat, night, has flown,
Come into the garden, Maud,

I am here at the gate alone;
And the woodbine spices are wafted
abroad,
And the musk of the rose is blown.

[*Maud* (1855)]

VOLTAIRE (1694–1778)
*Cela est bien dit, répondit Candide,
mais il faut cultiver notre jardin.*
'That is well said,' replied Candide,
'but we must cultivate our garden.'

[*Candide* (1759)]

GENEROSITY

BARRIE, Sir J.M. (1860–1937)
Never ascribe to an opponent motives
meaner than your own.

[Address, St Andrews University, 1922]

THE BIBLE (King James Version)
It is more blessed to give than to
receive.

[*Acts of the Apostles*, 20:35]

God loveth a cheerful giver.

[*II Corinthians*, 9:7]

BURNS, Robert (1759–1796)
To be overtopped in anything else, I
can bear: but in the tests of generous
love, I defy all mankind!

[Letter to Clarinda, 1788]

CORNEILLE, Pierre (1606–1684)
*Le façon de donner vaut mieux que ce
qu'on donne.*
The manner of giving is worth more
than the gift.

[*Le Menteur* (1643)]

GIBBS, Sir Philip (1877–1962)
It is better to give than to lend, and it
costs about the same.

[Attr.]

LA BRUYERE, Jean de (1645–1696)
*La liberalité consiste moins à donner
beaucoup qu'à donner à propos.*
Liberality consists less in giving a
great deal than in gifts well timed.

[*Les caractères ou les moeurs de ce siècle*
(1688)]

MUIR, Edwin (1887–1959)
I think it possible that all Scots are
illegitimate, Scotsmen being so mean
and Scotswomen so generous.

[*Scottish Journey* (1935)]

**TALLEYRAND, Charles-Maurice de
(1754–1838)**
*Méfiez-vous du premier mouvement; il
est toujours généreux.*
Don't trust first impulses; they are
always generous.

[Attr.]

GENIUS

ALCOTT, Louisa May (1832–1888)
It takes people a long time to learn the
difference between talent and genius,
especially ambitious young men and
women.

[*Little Women* (1869)]

BEERBOHM, Sir Max (1872–1956)
I have known no man of genius who
had not to pay, in some affliction or
defect either physical or spiritual, for
what the gods had given him.

[*And Even Now* (1920)]

**BROWNING, Elizabeth Barrett
(1806–1861)**
Since when was genius found
respectable?

[*Aurora Leigh* (1857)]

BUFFON, Comte de (1707–1788)
*Le génie n'est qu'une plus grande
aptitude à la patience.*
Genius is merely a greater aptitude for
patience.

[In Hérault de Séchelles, *Voyage à Montbar*
(1803)]

BUTLER, Samuel (1835–1902)
Genius ... has been defined as a
supreme capacity for taking trouble ...
It might be more fitly described as a
supreme capacity for getting its
possessors into pains of all kinds, and
keeping them therein so long as the
genius remains.

[*The Note-Books of Samuel Butler* (1912)]

DALI, Salvador (1904–1989)
I'm going to live forever. Geniuses
don't die.

[*The Observer*, 1986]

DOYLE, Sir Arthur Conan (1859–1930)
Mediocrity knows nothing higher than
itself, but talent instantly recognizes
genius.

[*The Valley of Fear* (1914)]

EDISON, Thomas Alva (1847–1931)
Genius is one per cent inspiration and
ninety-nine per cent perspiration.

[*Life*, 1932]

HAZLITT, William (1778–1830)
Rules and models destroy genius and
art.

['Thoughts on Taste' (1818)]

HOPE, Anthony (1863–1933)
Unless one is a genius, it is best to aim
at being intelligible.

[*The Dolly Dialogues* (1894)]

HOPKINS, Jane Ellice (1836–1904)
Gift, like genius, I often think, only
means an infinite capacity for taking
pains.

[*Work amongst Working Men*, 1870]

HUBBARD, Elbert (1856–1915)
One machine can do the work of fifty
ordinary men. No machine can do the
work of one extraordinary man.

[*A Thousand and One Epigrams* (1911)]

JOHNSON, Samuel (1709–1784)
The true genius is a mind of large
general powers, accidentally determined to some particular direction.

['Cowley' (1781)]

KENNEDY, John F. (1917–1963)
[At a dinner held at the White House
for Nobel prizewinners]
... probably the greatest concentration
of talent and genius in this house,
except for perhaps those times when
Thomas Jefferson ate alone.

[*New York Times*, 1962]

MEREDITH, Owen (1831–1891)
Genius does what it must, and Talent
does what it can.

['Last Words of a Sensitive Second-Rate Poet'
(1868)]

**STEPHEN, Sir James Fitzjames
(1829–1894)**
The way in which the man of genius
rules is by persuading an efficient
minority to coerce an indifferent and
self-indulgent majority.

[*Liberty, Equality and Fraternity* (1873)]

SWIFT, Jonathan (1667–1745)
When a true genius appears in the
world, you may know him by this sign,
that the dunces are all in confederacy
against him.

[*Thoughts on Various Subjects* (1711)]

WHISTLER, James McNeill (1834–1903)
[Replying to a lady inquiring whether
he thought genius hereditary]
I cannot tell you that, madam. Heaven
has granted me no offspring.

[In Seitz, *Whistler Stories* (1913)]

WILDE, Oscar (1854–1900)
[Spoken to André Gide]
*Voulez-vous savoir le grand drame de
ma vie? C'est que j'ai mis mon génie
dans ma vie; je n'ai mis que mon talent
dans mes oeuvres.*
Do you want to know the great
tragedy of my life? I have put all of my
genius into my life; all I've put into my
works is my talent.

[In Gide, *Oscar Wilde* (1910)]

[At the New York Customs]
I have nothing to declare except my
genius.

[In Harris, *Oscar Wilde* (1918)]

GENTLEMEN

ALLEN, Fred (1894–1956)
A gentleman is any man who wouldn't
hit a woman with his hat on.

[Attr.]

ANONYMOUS
When Adam delved, and Eve span,
Who was then a gentleman?

[Attr. John Ball, 1381]

BURKE, Edmund (1729–1797)
It is therefore our business carefully to cultivate in our minds, to rear to the most perfect vigour and maturity, every sort of generous and honest feeling that belongs to our nature. To bring the dispositions that are lovely in private life into the service and conduct of the commonwealth; so to be patriots, as not to forget we are gentlemen.

[*Thoughts on the Cause of the Present Discontents* (1770)]

Somebody has said, that a king may make a nobleman but he cannot make a Gentleman.

[Letter to William Smith, 1795]

CHIFLEY, Joseph (1885–1951)
My experience of gentlemen's agreements is that, when it comes to the pinch, there are rarely enough bloody gentlemen about.

[In Crisp, *Ben Chifley* (1960)]

CURZON, Lord (1859–1925)
Gentlemen do not take soup at luncheon.

[In Woodward, *Short Journey* (1942)]

EMERSON, Ralph Waldo (1803–1882)
Living blood and a passion of kindness does at last distinguish God's gentlemen from Fashion's.

['Manners' (1844)]

FURPHY, Joseph (1843–1912)
For there is no such thing as a democratic gentleman; the adjective and the noun are hyphenated by a drawn sword.

[*Such is Life* (1903)]

LINTON, W.J. (1812–1897)
For he is one of Nature's Gentlemen, the best of every time.

[*Nature's Gentleman*]

MATTHEWS, Brander (1852–1929)
A gentleman need not know Latin, but he should at least have forgotten it.

[Attr.]

NELSON, Lord (1758–1805)
[To his midshipmen]
Recollect that you must be a seaman to be an officer; and also, that you cannot be a good officer without being a gentleman.

[In Southey, *The Life of Nelson* (1860)]

NEWMAN, John Henry, Cardinal (1801–1890)
It is almost a definition of a gentleman to say that he is one who never inflicts pain.

['Knowledge and Religious Duty' (1852)]

SHAW, George Bernard (1856–1950)
I am a gentleman: I live by robbing the poor.

[*Man and Superman* (1903)]

STEVENSON, Robert Louis (1850–1894)
Between the possibility of being hanged in all innocence, and the certainty of a public and merited disgrace, no gentleman of spirit could long hesitate.

[*The Wrong Box* (1889)]

SURTEES, R.S. (1805–1864)
The only infallible rule we know is, that the man who is always talking about being a gentleman never is one.

[*Ask Mamma* (1858)]

GLORY

ANONYMOUS
Sic transit gloria mundi.
Thus passes the glory of the world.

[Spoken during the coronation of a new pope]

BACON, Francis (1561–1626)
[Knowledge is] a rich storehouse for the glory of the Creator and the relief of man's estate.

[*The Advancement of Learning* (1605)]

BLAKE, William (1757–1827)
The pride of the peacock is the glory of
God.

['Proverbs of Hell' (c. 1793)]

BYRON, Lord (1788–1824)
Glory, like the phoenix 'midst her fires,
Exhales her odours, blazes, and
expires.

[*English Bards and Scotch Reviewers* (1809)]

Oh, talk not to me of a name great in
story;
The days of our youth are the days of
our glory;
And the myrtle and ivy of sweet
two-and-twenty
Are worth all your laurels, though ever
so plenty.

['Stanzas Written on the Road between
Florence and Pisa, November 1821']

CAMPBELL, Thomas (1777–1844)
The combat deepens. On, ye brave,
Who rush to glory, or the grave!

['Hohenlinden']

DRAKE, Sir Francis (c. 1540–1596)
There must be a beginning of any
great matter, but the continuing unto
the end until it be thoroughly finished
yields the true glory.

[Dispatch to Sir Francis Walsingham, 1587]

FONTAINE, Jean de la (1621–1695)
*Aucun chemin de fleurs ne conduit à la
gloire.*
No flowery path leads to glory.

['Les deux aventuriers et le talisman']

GRAY, Thomas (1716–1771)
The boast of heraldry, the pomp of
pow'r,
And all that beauty, all that wealth e'er
gave,
Awaits alike th' inevitable hour,
The paths of glory lead but to the
grave.

['Elegy Written in a Country Churchyard'
(1751)]

MORDAUNT, Thomas (1730–1809)
Sound, sound the clarion, fill the fife,

Throughout the sensual world
proclaim,
One crowded hour of glorious life
Is worth an age without a name.

['Verses written during the War, 1756–1763'
(1791)]

**PROPERTIUS, Sextus Aurelius
(c. 50–c. 15 BC)**
*Magnum iter ascendo, sed dat mihi
gloria vires.*
Great is the height that I must scale,
but the prospect of glory gives me
strength.

[*Elegies*]

SHAKESPEARE, William (1564–1616)
Like madness is the glory of this life.

[*Timon of Athens*, I.ii]

WEBSTER, John (c. 1580–c. 1625)
Glories, like glow-worms, afar off
shine bright,
But, looked too near, have neither heat
nor light.

[*The Duchess of Malfi* (1623)]

WORDSWORTH, William (1770–1850)
Not in entire forgetfulness,
And not in utter nakedness,
But trailing clouds of glory do we
come
From God, who is our home:
Heaven lies about us in our infancy!

['Ode: Intimations of Immortality' (1807)]

GOALS

BERLIN, Sir Isaiah (1909–)
Injustice, poverty, slavery, ignorance –
these may be cured by reform or
revolution. But men do not live only by
fighting evils. They live by positive
goals, individual and collective, a vast
variety of them, seldom predictable, at
times incompatible.

['Political Ideas in the Twentieth Century'
(1969)]

KAFKA, Franz (1883–1924)
*Es gibt ein Ziel, aber keinen Weg; was
wir Weg nennen, ist Zögern.*
There is a goal but no way of reaching

it; what we call the way is hesitation.
[*Reflections on Sin, Sorrow, Hope and the True Way*]

LONGFELLOW, Henry Wadsworth (1807–1882)
If you would hit the mark, you must
aim a little above it;
Every arrow that flies feels the
attraction of earth.
['Elegiac Verse' (1880)]

SANTAYANA, George (1863–1952)
Fanaticism consists in redoubling your
effort when you have forgotten your
aim.
[*The Life of Reason* (1906)]

SIDNEY, Sir Philip (1554–1586)
Who shoots at the midday sun, though
he be sure he shall never hit the mark,
yet as sure he is he shall shoot higher
than who aims but at a bush.
[*New Arcadia* (1590)]

SMITH, Logan Pearsall (1865–1946)
When people come and talk to you of
their aspirations, before they leave you
had better count your spoons.
[*Afterthoughts* (1931)]

STEVENSON, Robert Louis (1850–1894)
An aspiration is a joy forever.
[*Virginibus Puerisque* (1881)]

WHITE, Patrick (1912–1990)
That is men all over ... They will aim
too low. And achieve what they
expect.
[*Voss* (1957)]

See AMBITION

GOD

AGATHON (c. 445–400 BC)
Even God is deprived of this one thing
only: the power to undo what has
been done.
[In Aristotle, *Nicomachean Ethics*]

ANONYMOUS
The nature of God is a circle of which
the centre is everywhere and the
circumference is nowhere.
[Attr. to Empedocles]

THE BIBLE (King James Version)
In the beginning God created the
heaven and the earth.
And the earth was without form, and
void; and darkness was upon the face
of the deep. And the Spirit of God
moved upon the face of the waters.
And God said, Let there be light: and
there was light.
[*Genesis*, 1:1-3]

For the Lord seeth not as man seeth:
for man looketh on the outward
appearance, but the Lord looketh on
the heart.
[*I Samuel*, 16:7]

God is a Spirit: and they that worship
him must worship him in spirit and in
truth.
[*John*, 4:24]

BONHOEFFER, Dietrich (1906–1945)
*Ein Gott, der sich von uns beweisen
liesse, wäre ein Götze.*
A God who allowed us to prove his
existence would be an idol.
['If you believe it, you have it' (1931)]

*Der Mensch hat gelernt, in allen
wichtigen Fragen mit sich selbst fertig zu
werden ohne Zuhilfenahme der
'Arbeitshypothese: Gott.'*
In all important questions, man has
learned to cope without recourse to
God as a working hypothesis.
[Letter to a friend, 1944]

BROOKE, Rupert (1887–1915)
Because God put His adamantine fate
Between my sullen heart and its
desire,
I swore that I would burst the Iron
Gate,
Rise up, and curse Him on His throne
of fire.
['Failure' (1905–1908)]

GOD

BROWNING, Elizabeth Barrett (1806–1861)
God answers sharp and sudden on
    some prayers,
And thrusts the thing we have prayed
    for in our face,
A gauntlet with a gift in't.

[*Aurora Leigh* (1857)]

CLOUGH, Arthur Hugh (1819–1861)
Youths green and happy in first love,
So thankful for illusion;
And men caught out in what the world
Calls guilt, in first confusion;

And almost every one when age,
Disease, or sorrows strike him,
Inclines to think there is a God,
Or something very like Him.

[*Dipsychus* (1865)]

COWPER, William (1731–1800)
God moves in a mysterious way
His wonders to perform;
He plants his footsteps in the sea,
And rides upon the storm.

[*Olney Hymns* (1779)]

DE VRIES, Peter (1910–)
It is the final proof of God's omnip-
otence that he need not exist in order
to save us.

[*The Mackerel Plaza* (1958)]

DUHAMEL, Georges (1884–1966)
*Je respecte trop l'idée de Dieu pour la
rendre responsable d'un monde aussi
absurde.*
I have too much respect for the idea of
God to make it responsible for such an
absurd world.

[*Chronique des Pasquier* (1948)]

EINSTEIN, Albert (1879–1955)
Before God we are all equally wise –
equally foolish.

[Address, Sorbonne, Paris]

GALILEO GALILEI (1564–1642)
I do not feel obliged to believe that the
same God who has endowed us with
sense, reason, and intellect has intended us to forgo their use.

[Attr.]

HALDANE, J.B.S. (1892–1964)
[Reply when asked what inferences
could be drawn about the nature of
God from a study of his works]
The Creator ... has a special preference
for beetles.

[Lecture, 1951]

HUGHES, Sean (1966–)
I'd like to thank God for fucking up my
life and at the same time not existing,
quite a special skill.

[*The Independent,* 1993]

INGE, William Ralph (1860–1954)
Many people believe that they are
attracted by God, or by Nature, when
they are only repelled by man.

[*More Lay Thoughts of a Dean* (1931)]

KEMPIS, Thomas à (c. 1380–1471)
Nam homo proponit, sed Deus disponit.
For man proposes, but God disposes.

[*De Imitatione Christi* (1892)]

KOESTLER, Arthur (1905–1983)
God seems to have left the receiver off
the hook, and time is running out.

[*The Ghost in the Machine* (1961)]

LOGAU, Friedrich von (1605–1655)
*Gottes Mühlen mahlen langsam, mahlen
    aber trefflich klein;
Ob aus Langmut er sich säumet, bringt
    mit Schärf' er alles ein.*

Though the mills of God grind slowly,
    yet they grind extremely small;
Though his patience makes him tarry,
    with exactness grinds He all.

[*Epigrams* (1653)]

MENCKEN, H.L. (1880–1956)
God is the immemorial refuge of the
incompetent, the helpless, the miserable. They find not only sanctuary in
His arms, but also a kind of superiority, soothing to their macerated
egos; He will set them above their
betters.

[*Notebooks* (1956)]

It takes a long while for a naturally trustful person to reconcile himself to the idea that after all God will not help him.

[*Notebooks* (1956)]

NERVAL, Gérard de (1808–1855)
Dieu est mort! le ciel est vide –
Pleurez! enfants, vous n'avez plus de
père.
God is dead! Heaven is empty – Weep, children, you no longer have a father.

['Le Christ aux Oliviers']

OWEN, John (c. 1560–1622)
God and the doctor we alike adore
But only when in danger, not before;
The danger o'er, both are alike
    requited,
God is forgotten, and the Doctor
    slighted.

[*Epigrams*]

PASCAL, Blaise (1623–1662)
Je ne puis pardonner à Descartes: il
aurait bien voulu, dans toute sa
philosophie, pouvoir se passer de Dieu;
mais il n'a pu s'empêcher de lui faire
donner une chiquenaude, pour mettre le
monde en mouvement; après celà, il n'a
plus eu que faire de Dieu.
I cannot forgive Descartes; in all his philosophy he did his best to dispense with God. But he could not avoid making Him set the world in motion with a flick of His finger; after that he had no more use for God.

[*Pensées* (1670)]

POPE, Alexander (1688–1744)
Nor God alone in the still calm we
    find,
He mounts the storm, and walks upon
    the wind.

[*An Essay on Man* (1733)]

SARTRE, Jean-Paul (1905–1980)
L'absence c'est Dieu. Dieu, c'est la
solitude des hommes.
God is absence. God is the solitude of man.

[*Le Diable et le Bon Dieu* (1951)]

SHAKESPEARE, William (1564–1616)
There's a divinity that shapes our ends,
Rough-hew them how we will.

[*Hamlet*, V.ii]

As flies to wanton boys are we to th'
    gods –
They kill us for their sport.

[*King Lear*, IV.i]

SQUIRE, Sir J.C. (1884–1958)
God heard the embattled nations sing
    and shout
'Gott strafe England!' and 'God save
    the King!'
God this, God that, and God the other
    thing –
'Good God!' said God, 'I've got my
    work cut out.'

[*The Survival of the Fittest* (1916)]

STRACHEY, Lytton (1880–1932)
Yet her conception of God was certainly not orthodox. She felt towards Him as she might have felt towards a glorified sanitary engineer; and in some of her speculations she seems hardly to distinguish between the Deity and the Drains.

['Florence Nightingale' (1918)]

WALKER, Alice (1944–)
I think it pisses God off if you walk by the color purple in a field somewhere and don't notice it.

[*The Color Purple*, film, 1985]

WOLSEY, Thomas (c. 1475–1530)
[Remark to Sir William Kingston]
Had I but served God as diligently as I have served the King, he would not have given me over in my grey hairs.

[In Cavendish, *Negotiations of Thomas Wolsey* (1641)]

See ART; BELIEF

GOOD AND EVIL

THE BIBLE (King James Version)
Ye shall be as gods, knowing good and evil.

[*Genesis*, 3:5]

BRECHT, Bertolt (1898–1956)
Something must be wrong with your world. Why is a price set on wickedness, and why is the good man attended by such harsh punishments?

[*Good Woman of Setzuan* (1943)]

BURNS, Robert (1759–1796)
Whatever mitigates the woes or increases the happiness of others, this is my criterion of goodness; and whatever injures society at large, or any individual in it, this is my measure of iniquity.

[Attr.]

BUTLER, Samuel (1835–1902)
Virtue and vice are like life and death or mind and matter: things which cannot exist without being qualified by their opposite.

[*The Way of All Flesh* (1903)]

GOLDSMITH, Oliver (c. 1728–1774)
We must touch his weaknesses with a delicate hand. There are some faults so nearly allied to excellence, that we can scarce weed out the vice without eradicating the virtue.

[*The Good Natur'd Man* (1768)]

HALIFAX, Lord (1633–1695)
Our *Vices* and *Virtues* couple with one another, and get Children that resemble both their Parents.

['Of the World' (1750)]

LERMONTOV, Mikhail (1814–1841)
What *is* the greatest good and evil? – two ends of an invisible chain which come closer together the further they move apart.

[*Vadim* (1834)]

SHAKESPEARE, William (1564–1616)
Men's evil manners live in brass: their virtues
We write in water.

[*Henry VIII*, IV.ii]

The evil that men do lives after them;
The good is oft interred with their bones.

[*Julius Caesar*, III.ii]

Some rise by sin, and some by virtue fall.

[*Measure for Measure*, II.i]

Virtue that transgresses is but patch'd with sin, and sin that amends is but patch'd with virtue.

[*Twelfth Night*, I.v]

SURTEES, R.S. (1805–1864)
More people are flattered into virtue than bullied out of vice.

[*The Analysis of the Hunting Field* (1846)]

VANBRUGH, Sir John (1664–1726)
Belinda: Ay, but you know we must return good for evil.
Lady Brute: That may be a mistake in the translation.

[*The Provok'd Wife* (1697)]

GOODNESS

ADDISON, Joseph (1672–1719)
Content thyself to be obscurely good.
When vice prevails, and impious men bear sway,
The post of honour is a private station.

[*Cato* (1713)]

ARISTOTLE (384–322 BC)
In all things the middle state is to be praised. But it is sometimes necessary to incline towards overshooting and sometimes to shooting short of the mark, since this is the easiest way of hitting the mean and the right course.

[*Nicomachean Ethics*]

BACON, Francis (1561–1626)
The inclination to goodness is imprinted deeply in the nature of man: insomuch, that if it issue not towards men, it will take unto other living creatures.

['Of Goodness, and Goodness of Nature' (1625)]

BARTH, Karl (1886–1968)
Men have never been good, they are not good, they never will be good.

[*Time*, 1954]

BLAKE, William (1757–1827)
He who would do good to another
must do it in Minute Particulars.
General Good is the plea of the
Scoundrel hypocrite & flatterer.

[*Jerusalem* (1804–1820)]

BUDDHA (c. 563–483 BC)
This Ayrian Eightfold Path, that is to
say: Right view, right aim, right
speech, right action, right living, right
effort, right mindfulness, right contemplation.

[In Woodward, *Some Sayings of the Buddha*]

BURKE, Edmund (1729–1797)
When bad men combine, the good
must associate; else they will fall, one
by one, an unpitied sacrifice in a con-
temptible struggle.

[*Thoughts on the Cause of the Present
Discontents* (1770)]

Good order is the foundation of all
good things.

[*Reflections on the Revolution in France* (1790)]

BUTLER, Samuel (1835–1902)
When the righteous man turneth away
from his righteousness that he hath
committed and doeth that which is
neither quite lawful nor quite right, he
will generally be found to have gained
in amiability what he has lost in
holiness.

[*The Note-Books of Samuel Butler* (1912)]

CONFUCIUS (c. 550–c. 478 BC)
True goodness springs from a man's
own heart. All men are born good.

[*Analects*]

GRACIÁN, Baltasar (1601–1658)
Lo bueno, si breve, dos veces bueno.
Good things, if they are short, are
twice as good.

[Attr.]

GRELLET, Stephen (1773–1855)
I expect to pass through this world but
once; any good thing therefore that I
can do, or any kindness that I can
show to any fellow-creature, let me do
it now; let me not defer or neglect it,
for I shall not pass this way again.

[Attr.]

HUTCHESON, Francis (1694–1746)
That action is best, which procures the
greatest happiness for the greatest
numbers.

[*An Inquiry into the Original of our Ideas of
Beauty and Virtue* (1725)]

LANDOR, Walter Savage (1775–1864)
Goodness does not more certainly
make men happy than happiness
makes them good.

[*Imaginary Conversations* (1853)]

MACHIAVELLI (1469–1527)
*Gli uomini non operano mai nulla nel
bene se non per necessità.*
Men never do anything good except
out of necessity.

[*Discourse*]

MEREDITH, George (1828–1909)
Much benevolence of the passive
order may be traced to a disinclination
to inflict pain upon oneself.

[*Lysis*]

SALLUST (86–c. 34 BC)
[Of Cato]
Esse quam videri bonus malebat.
He preferred to be rather than to seem
good.

[*Catiline*]

SHAKESPEARE, William (1564–1616)
How far that little candle throws his
    beams!
So shines a good deed in a naughty
world.

[*The Merchant of Venice*, V.i]

VOLTAIRE (1694–1778)
Le mieux est l'ennemi du bien.
The best is the enemy of the good.

['Art dramatique' (1770)]

WEST, Mae (1892–1980)
When I'm good I'm very good, but
when I'm bad I'm better.

[*I'm No Angel*, film, 1933]

WILDE, Oscar (1854–1900)
It is better to be beautiful than to be good. But ... it is better to be good than to be ugly.

[*The Picture of Dorian Gray* (1891)]

WORDSWORTH, Dame Elizabeth (1840–1932)
If all the good people were clever,
And all clever people were good,
The world would be nicer than ever
We thought that it possibly could.
But somehow, 'tis seldom or never
The two hit it off as they should;
The good are so harsh to the clever,
The clever so rude to the good.

['The Clever and the Good' (1890)]

See BEAUTY; BENEFACTORS; MORALITY; VIRTUE

GOSSIP

BIERCE, Ambrose (1842–c. 1914)
Backbite: To speak of a man as you find him when he can't find you.

[*The Enlarged Devil's Dictionary* (1961)]

CHESTERFIELD, Lord (1694–1773)
In the case of scandal, as in that of robbery, the receiver is always thought as bad as the thief.

[Letter to his son, 1748]

CONGREVE, William (1670–1729)
Retired to their tea and scandal, according to their ancient custom.

[*The Double Dealer* (1694)]

They come together like the Coroner's Inquest, to sit upon the murdered reputations of the week.

[*The Way of the World* (1700)]

ELIOT, George (1819–1880)
Gossip is a sort of smoke that comes from the dirty tobacco-pipes of those who diffuse it: it proves nothing but the bad taste of the smoker.

[*Daniel Deronda* (1876)]

FARQUHAR, George (1678–1707)
I believe they talked of me, for they laughed consumedly.

[*The Beaux' Stratagem* (1707)]

LONGWORTH, Alice Roosevelt (1884–1980)
[Embroidered on a cushion at her home in Washington]
If you haven't anything nice to say about anyone, come and sit by me.

[*New York Times*, 1980]

OUIDA (1839–1908)
A cruel story runs on wheels, and every hand oils the wheels as they run.

[*Wisdom, Wit and Pathos*, 'Moths']

POPE, Alexander (1688–1744)
At ev'ry word a reputation dies.

[*The Rape of the Lock* (1714)]

RUSSELL, Bertrand (1872–1970)
No one gossips about other people's secret virtues.

[*On Education, especially in early childhood* (1926)]

SHERIDAN, Richard Brinsley (1751–1816)
Tale-bearers are as bad as the tale-makers.

[*The School for Scandal* (1777)]

Here is the whole set! a character dead at every word.

[*The School for Scandal* (1777)]

GOVERNMENT

ACTON, Lord (1834–1902)
The danger is not that a particular class is unfit to govern. Every class is unfit to govern.

[Letter to Mary Gladstone, 1881]

BAGEHOT, Walter (1826–1877)
A severe though not unfriendly critic of our institutions said that 'the cure for admiring the House of Lords was to go and look at it.'

[*The English Constitution* (1867)]

BENTHAM, Jeremy (1748–1832)
It is with government as with medi-

cine, its only business is the choice of evils. Every law is an evil, for every law is an infraction of liberty.

[*An Introduction to the Principles of Morals and Legislation* (1789)]

BEVERIDGE, William Henry (1879–1963)
The object of government in peace and in war is not the glory of rulers or of races, but the happiness of the common man.

[*Report on Social Insurance and Allied Services* (1942)]

BURKE, Edmund (1729–1797)
All government, indeed every human benefit and enjoyment, every virtue, and every prudent act, is founded on compromise and barter.

[*Speech on Conciliation with America* (1775)]

In all forms of Government the people is the true legislator.

[*Tracts on the Popery Laws* (1812)]

CAMPBELL-BANNERMAN, Sir Henry (1836–1908)
Good government could never be a substitute for government by the people themselves.

[Speech, 1905]

GOLDWATER, Barry (1909–)
A government that is big enough to give you all you want is big enough to take it all away.

[*Bachman's Book of Freedom Quotations*]

HERBERT, Sir A.P. (1890–1971)
Well, fancy giving money to the Government!
Might as well have put it down the drain.
Fancy giving money to the Government!
Nobody will see the stuff again.
Well, they've no idea what money's for –
Ten to one they'll start another war.
I've heard a lot of silly things, but, Lor'!

Fancy giving money to the Government!

['Too Much!']

HOBBES, Thomas (1588–1679)
They that are discontented under monarchy, call it tyranny; and they that are displeased with aristocracy, call it oligarchy ... they which find themselves grieved under a democracy, call it anarchy.

[*Leviathan* (1651)]

HUME, David (1711–1776)
Nothing appears more surprising to those, who consider human affairs with a philosophical eye, than the easiness with which the many are governed by the few; and the implicit submission, with which men resign their own sentiments and passions to those of their rulers.

[*Essays, Moral, Political, and Literary* (1742)]

JAMES VI OF SCOTLAND AND I OF ENGLAND (1566–1625)
I will govern according to the common weal, but not according to the common will.

[Remark, 1621]

JOHNSON, Samuel (1709–1784)
I would not give half a guinea to live under one form of government rather than another. It is of no moment to the happiness of an individual.

[In Boswell, *The Life of Samuel Johnson* (1791)]

KEYNES, John Maynard (1883–1946)
The important thing for government is not to do things which individuals are doing already, and to do them a little better or a little worse; but to do those things which at present are not done at all.

['The End of Laissez-Faire' (1926)]

MAISTRE, Joseph de (1753–1821)
Toute nation a le gouvernement qu'elle mérite.
Each country has the government it deserves.

[Letter, 1811]

161   GREATNESS

The worst government is the most moral. One composed of cynics is often very tolerant and human. But when fanatics are on top there is no limit to oppression.

[*Notebooks* (1956)]

O'SULLIVAN, John L. (1813–1895)
The best government is that which governs least.

[*United States Magazine and Democratic Review*, 1837]

PAINE, Thomas (1737–1809)
As to religion, I hold it to be the indispensable duty of government to protect all conscientious professors thereof, and I know of no other business which government hath to do therewith.

[*Common Sense* (1776)]

Man is not the enemy of Man, but through the medium of a false system of government.

[*The Rights of Man* (1791)]

RIPPON, Geoffrey (1924–)
Governments don't retreat, they simply advance in another direction.

[*The Observer*, 1981]

ROGERS, Will (1879–1935)
I don't make jokes – I just watch the government and report the facts.

[Attr.]

RUSKIN, John (1819–1900)
Government and cooperation are in all things the laws of life; anarchy and competition, the laws of death.

[*Unto this Last* (1862)]

SPENCER, Herbert (1820–1903)
The Republican form of government is the highest form of government; but because of this it requires the highest type of human nature – a type nowhere at present existing.

[*Essays* (1891)]

VOLTAIRE (1694–1778)
Il faut, dans le gouvernement, des bergers et des bouchers.
In governments there must be both shepherds and butchers.

['The Piccini Notebooks']

WASHINGTON, George (1732–1799)
Mankind, when left to themselves, are unfit for their own government.

[Letter, 1786]

See CAPITALISM; DEMOCRACY

GREATNESS

AMIEL, Henri-Frédéric (1821–1881)
The age of great men is going; the epoch of the ant-hill, of life in multiplicity, is beginning.

[*Journal*, 1851]

BACON, Francis (1561–1626)
All rising to great place is by a winding stair.

['Of Great Place' (1625)]

BEERBOHM, Sir Max (1872–1956)
Great men are but life-sized. Most of them, indeed, are rather short.

[Attr.]

BURKE, Edmund (1729–1797)
Great men are the guide-posts and landmarks in the state.

[*Speech on American Taxation* (1774)]

CARLYLE, Thomas (1795–1881)
No great man lives in vain. The History of the world is but the Biography of great men.

['The Hero as Divinity' (1841)]

CHAPMAN, George (c. 1559–c. 1634)
They're only truly great who are truly good.

[*Revenge for Honour* (1654)]

EMERSON, Ralph Waldo (1803–1882)
A foolish consistency is the hobgoblin of little minds, adored by little statesmen and philosophers and

divines. With consistency a great soul has simply nothing to do.

['Self-Reliance' (1841)]

Is it so bad, then, to be misunderstood? Pythagoras was misunderstood, and Socrates, and Jesus, and Luther, and Copernicus, and Galileo, and Newton, and every pure and wise spirit that ever took flesh. To be great is to be misunderstood.

['Self-Reliance' (1841)]

FIELDING, Henry (1707–1754)
Greatness consists in bringing all manner of mischief on mankind, and goodness in removing it from them.

[Jonathan Wild (1743)]

FRAZER, Sir James (1854–1941)
The world cannot live at the level of its great men.

[The Golden Bough (1900)]

LA ROCHEFOUCAULD, Duc de (1613–1680)
La gloire des grands hommes se doit toujours mesurer aux moyens dont ils se sont servis pour l'acquérir.
The glory of great men must always be measured by the means they have used to obtain it.

[Maximes (1678)]

LAW, Bonar (1858–1923)
If I am a great man, then a good many of the great men of history are frauds.

[Attr.]

LONGFELLOW, Henry Wadsworth (1807–1882)
The heights by great men reached and kept
Were not attained by sudden flight,
But they, while their companions slept,
Were toiling upward in the night.

['The Ladder of Saint Augustine' (1850)]

SHAKESPEARE, William (1564–1616)
Be not afraid of greatness. Some are born great, some achieve greatness, and some have greatness thrust upon 'em.

[Twelfth Night, II.v]

SPENDER, Sir Stephen (1909–)
I think continually of those who were truly great.

The names of those who in their lives fought for life
Who wore at their hearts the fire's centre.
Born of the sun they travelled a short while towards the sun,
And left the vivid air signed with their honour.

['I think continually of those who were truly great' (1933)]

BRENAN, Gerald (1894–1987)
When we attend the funerals of our friends we grieve for them, but when we go to those of other people it is chiefly our own deaths that we mourn for.

[Thoughts in a Dry Season (1978)]

BYRON, Lord (1788–1824)
[A cypress]
Dark tree, still sad when others' grief is fled,
The only constant mourner o'er the dead!

['The Giaour' (1813)]

COWPER, William (1731–1800)
Grief is itself a med'cine.

['Charity' (1782)]

DICKINSON, Emily (1830–1886)
The Bustle in a House
The Morning after Death
Is solemnest of industries
Enacted upon Earth –

The Sweeping up the Heart
And putting Love away
We shall not want to use again
Until Eternity.

['The Bustle in a House' (c. 1866)]

ELLIOT, Jean (1727–1805)
I've heard them lilting, at our yowe-milking,
Lasses a' lilting before the dawn o' day;

163

GRIEF

But now they are moaning on ilka
  green loaning –
The Flowers of the Forest are a' wede
  away.

['The Flowers of the Forest' (1756)]

FORD, John (c. 1586–1639)
They are the silent griefs which cut the
heart-strings.

[*The Broken Heart* (1633)]

GRAVES, Robert (1895–1985)
His eyes are quickened so with grief,
He can watch a grass or leaf
Every instant grow ...

Across two counties he can hear
And catch your words before you
  speak.
The woodlouse or the maggot's weak
Clamour rings in his sad ear,
And noise so slight it would surpass
Credence.

['Lost Love' (1921)]

JOHNSON, Samuel (1709–1784)
Grief is a species of idleness.

[Letter to Mrs Thrale, 1773]

MACDIARMID, Hugh (1892–1978)
I met ayont the cairney
A lass wi' tousie hair
Singin' till a bairnie
That was nae langer there.

Wund wi' warlds to swing
Dinna sing sae sweet,
The licht that bends owre a' thing
Is less ta'en up wi't.

['Empty Vessel' (1926)]

MILTON, John (1608–1674)
Methought I saw my late espoused
  Saint
Brought to me like Alcestis from the
  grave ...

But O as to embrace me she enclin'd,
I wak'd, she fled, and day brought
  back my night.

['Methought I saw my late espoused Saint'
(1658)]

PROUST, Marcel (1871–1922)
*Le bonheur seul est salutaire pour le
corps, mais c'est le chagrin qui
développe les forces de l'esprit.*
Happiness alone is beneficial for the
body, but it is grief that develops the
powers of the mind.

[*Le Temps retrouvé* (1926)]

SHAKESPEARE, William (1564–1616)
Grief fills the room up of my absent
  child,
Lies in his bed, walks up and down
  with me,
Puts on his pretty looks, repeats his
  words,
Remembers me of all his gracious
  parts,
Stuffs out his vacant garments with his
  form;
Then have I reason to be fond of grief.

[*King John*, III.iv]

Howl, howl, howl, howl! O, you are
  men of stones!
Had I your tongues and eyes, I'd use
  them so
That heaven's vault should crack. She's
  gone for ever.

[*King Lear*, V.iii]

What, man! Ne'er pull your hat upon
  your brows;
Give sorrow words. The grief that does
  not speak
Whispers the o'erfraught heart and
  bids it break.

[*Macbeth*, IV.iii]

Every one can master a grief but he
that has it.

[*Much Ado About Nothing*, III.ii]

What's gone and what's past help
Should be past grief.

[*The Winter's Tale*, III.ii]

SHELLEY, Percy Bysshe (1792–1822)
Ah, woe is me! Winter is come and
  gone,
But grief returns with the revolving
  year.

[*Adonais* (1821)]

STOWE, Harriet Beecher (1811–1896)
The bitterest tears shed over graves
are for words left unsaid and deeds
left undone.

[*Little Foxes* (1866)]

TENNYSON, Alfred, Lord (1809–1892)
I sometimes hold it half a sin
To put in words the grief I feel;
For words, like Nature, half reveal
And half conceal the Soul within.

But, for the unquiet heart and brain,
A use in measured language lies;
The sad mechanic exercise,
Like dull narcotics, numbing pain.

[*In Memoriam A. H. H.* (1850)]

Death has made
His darkness beautiful with thee.

[*In Memoriam A. H. H.* (1850)]

WHITMAN, Walt (1819–1892)
When lilacs last in the dooryard
bloom'd,
And the great stars early droop'd in
the western sky in the night,
I mourn'd, and yet shall mourn with
ever-returning spring.

['When lilacs last in the dooryard bloom'd'
(1865)]

WORDSWORTH, William (1770–1850)
Surprised by joy – impatient as the
Wind
I turned to share the transport – Oh!
with whom
But thee, deep buried in the silent
tomb.

['Surprised by joy' (1815)]

GUILT

ARENDT, Hannah (1906–1975)
It is quite gratifying to feel guilty if you
haven't done anything wrong: how
noble! Whereas it is rather hard and
certainly depressing to admit guilt and
to repent.

[*Eichmann in Jerusalem: A Report on the
Banality of Evil* (1963)]

GOETHE (1749–1832)
Denn alle Schuld rächt sich auf Erden.
For all guilt is avenged on earth.

[*Wilhelm Meister's Apprentice Years* (1796)]

GOLDSMITH, Oliver (c. 1728–1774)
When lovely woman stoops to folly
And finds too late that men betray,
What charm can soothe her
melancholy,
What art can wash her guilt away?

The only art her guilt to cover,
To hide her shame from every eye,
To give repentance to her lover
And wring his bosom – is to die.

[*The Vicar of Wakefield* (1766)]

HORACE (65–8 BC)
Hic murus aeneus esto,
Nil conscire sibi, nulla pallescere culpa.
This be your wall of brass, to have
nothing on your conscience, no reason
to grow pale with guilt.

[*Epistles*]

KAFKA, Franz (1883–1924)
'Ich bin aber nicht schuldig', sagte K.,
'es ist ein Irrtum. Wie kann denn ein
Mensch überhaupt schuldig sein.'
'But I'm not guilty,' said K., 'there's
been a mistake. How can a man be
guilty anyway.'

[*The Trial* (1925)]

MCGOUGH, Roger (1937–)
You will put on a dress of guilt
and shoes with broken high ideals.

['Comeclose and Sleepnow' (1967)]

RUSKIN, John (1819–1900)
Life without industry is guilt.

['The Relation of Art to Morals' (1870)]

SHAKESPEARE, William (1564–1616)
And then it started like a guilty thing
Upon a fearful summons.

[*Macbeth*, I.i]

Will all great Neptune's ocean wash
this blood
Clean from my hand? No; this my hand
will rather

The multitudinous seas incarnadine,
Making the green one red.

[*Macbeth*, II.ii]

Out, damned spot! out, I say! One,
two; why then 'tis time to do't. Hell is
murky. Fie, my lord, fie! a soldier, and
afeard? What need we fear who knows
it, when none can call our pow'r to
account? Yet who would have thought
the old man to have had so much

blood in him?

[*Macbeth*, V.i]

Here's the smell of the blood still. All
the perfumes of Arabia will not
sweeten this little hand.

[*Macbeth*, V.i]

**STEVENSON, Robert Louis
(1850–1894)**
What hangs people ... is the
unfortunate circumstance of guilt.

[*The Wrong Box* (1889)]

HAPPINESS

ARISTOTLE (384–322 BC)
One swallow does not make a
summer, neither does one fine day;
similarly one day or brief time of
happiness does not make a person
entirely happy.

[*Nicomachean Ethics*]

BENTHAM, Jeremy (1748–1832)
[Quoting Francis Hutcheson]
... this sacred truth – that the greatest
happiness of the greatest number is
the foundation of morals and
legislation.

[*Works*]

THE BIBLE (Vulgate)
*Beatus vir, qui timet Dominum, in
mandatis eius cupit nimis!*
Happy is the man who fears the Lord,
who is only too willing to follow his
orders.

[*Psalms*, 111:1]

BOETHIUS, (c. 475–524)
*Nihil est miserum nisi cum putes;
contraque beata sors omnis est
aequanimitate tolerantis.*
Nothing is miserable unless you think
it so; conversely, every lot is happy to
one who is content with it.

[*De Consolatione Philosophiae*]

CAMPBELL, Thomas (1777–1844)
One moment may with bliss repay
Unnumber'd hours of pain.

['The Ritter Bann']

**COLERIDGE, Samuel Taylor
(1772–1834)**
We ne'er can be
Made happy by compulsion.

['The Three Graves' (1809)]

DRYDEN, John (1631–1700)
Happy the man, and happy he alone,
He, who can call to-day his own:
He who, secure within, can say,
Tomorrow do thy worst, for I have
lived to-day.

[*Sylvae* (1685)]

ELIOT, George (1819–1880)
The happiest women, like the happiest
nations, have no history.

[*The Mill on the Floss* (1860)]

FRANKLIN, Benjamin (1706–1790)
Be in general virtuous, and you will be
happy.

['On Early Marriages']

HORACE (65–8 BC)
*Non possidentem multa vocaveris
Recte beatum: rectius occupat
Nomen beati, qui deorum
Muneribus sapienter uti
Duramque callet pauperiem pati
Peiusque leto flagitium timet.*
You would not rightly call the man
who has many possessions happy; he
more rightly deserves to be called
happy who knows how to use the gifts
of the gods wisely, and can endure the
hardship of poverty, and who fears
dishonour more than death.

[*Odes*]

JOHNSON, Samuel (1709–1784)
That all who are happy, are equally
happy, is not true. A peasant and a
philosopher may be equally *satisfied*,
but not equally *happy*. Happiness
consists in the multiplicity of agreeable
consciousness.

[In Boswell, *The Life of Samuel Johnson*
(1791)]

There is nothing which has yet been
contrived by man, by which so much
happiness is produced as by a good
tavern or inn.

[In Boswell, *The Life of Samuel Johnson*
(1791)]

KANT, Immanuel (1724–1804)
*... weil Glückseligkeit nicht ein Ideal der
Vernunft, sondern der Einbildungskraft
ist.*
... because bliss is not an ideal of
reason, but of the powers of imagination.

[Outline of the Metaphysics of Morals (1785)]

Tue das, wodurch du würdig wirst,

glücklich zu sein.
Act in such a way that you will be
worthy of being happy.

[*Critique of Pure Reason* (1787)]

MARMION, Shackerley (1603–1639)
Great joys, like griefs, are silent.

[*Holland's Leaguer* (1632)]

ROUSSEAU, Jean-Jacques (1712–1778)
Happiness: a good bank account, a
good cook, and a good digestion.

[*Treasury of Humorous Quotations*]

SAGAN, Françoise (1935–)
*Quel mur s'impose donc toujours entre
les êtres humains et leur désir le plus
intime, leur effroyable volonté de
bonheur?*
What is that wall that always rises up
between human beings and their most
intimate desire, their frightening will to
be happy?

[*Le Garde du coeur* (1968)]

**SAINT-EXUPERY, Antoine de
(1900–1944)**
*Si tu veux comprendre le mot de
bonheur, il faut l'entendre comme
récompense et non comme but.*
If you want to understand the meaning
of happiness, you must see it as a
reward and not as a goal.

[*Carnets*]

SHAKESPEARE, William (1564–1616)
O, how bitter a thing it is to look into
happiness through another man's eyes!

[*As You Like It*, V.ii]

I swear 'tis better to be lowly born
And range with humble livers in
    content
Than to be perk'd up in a glist'ring
    grief
And wear a golden sorrow.

[*Henry VIII*, II.iii]

SHAW, George Bernard (1856–1950)
We have no more right to consume
happiness without producing it than to
consume wealth without producing it.

[*Candida* (1898)]

A lifetime of happiness! No man alive
could bear it: it would be hell on
earth.

[*Man and Superman* (1903)]

SMITH, Sydney 1771–1845)
Mankind are always happy for having
been happy, so that if you make them
happy now, you make them happy
twenty years hence by the memory of
it.

[*Sketches of Moral Philosophy* (1849)]

SOLON (c. 638–c. 559 BC)
Until [a man] dies, be careful to call
him not happy but lucky.

[In Herodotus, *Histories*]

WAUGH, Evelyn (1903–1966)
I can't quite explain it, but I don't
believe one can ever be unhappy for
long provided one does just exactly
what one wants to and when one
wants to.

[*Decline and Fall* (1928)]

WELDON, Fay (1931–)
I don't believe in happiness: why
should we expect to be happy? In such
a world as this, depression is rational,
rage reasonable.

[*The Observer*, 1995]

YEATS, W.B. (1865–1939)
I think that all happiness depends
upon the energy to assume the mask
of some other self; that all joyous or
creative life is a rebirth as something
not oneself, something which has no
memory and is created in a moment
and perpetually renewed.

[*The Death of Synge and other Passages from
an Old Diary* (1928)]

HATRED

ACCIUS, Lucius (170–86 BC)
Oderint dum metuant.
Let them hate provided that they fear.

[*Atreus*]

BACON, Francis (1561–1626)
Severity breedeth fear, but roughness

breedeth hate. Even reproofs from authority ought to be grave, and not taunting.

['Of Great Place' (1625)]

BYRON, Lord (1788–1824)
Now hatred is by far the longest pleasure;
Men love in haste, but they detest at leisure.

[*Don Juan* (1824)]

DE VRIES, Peter (1910–)
Everybody hates me because I'm so universally liked.

[*The Vale of Laughter* (1967)]

FIELDS, W.C. (1880–1946)
I am free of all prejudice. I hate everyone equally.

[Attr.]

GABOR, Zsa-Zsa (1919–)
I never hated a man enough to give him his diamonds back.

[*The Observer*, 1957]

HAZLITT, William (1778–1830)
Violent antipathies are always suspicious, and betray a secret affinity.

[*Table-Talk* (1822)]

We can scarcely hate any one that we know.

[*Table-Talk* (1825)]

HOFFER, Eric (1902–1983)
Passionate hatred can give meaning and purpose to an empty life.

[Attr.]

JUNG CHANG (1952–)
He [Mao Zedong] was, it seemed to me, really a restless fight promoter by nature and good at it. He understood ugly human instincts such as envy and resentment, and knew how to mobilize them for his ends. He ruled by getting people to hate each other.

[*Wild Swans* (1991)]

NASH, Ogden (1902–1971)
Any kiddie in school can love like a

fool,
But hating, my boy, is an art.

['Plea for Less Malice Toward None' (1933)]

NIXON, Richard (1913–1994)
Always give your best, never get discouraged, never be petty. Always remember, others may hate you, but those who hate you don't win unless you hate them, and then you destroy yourself.

[Farewell speech to his staff, 1974]

ROSTEN, Leo (1908–)
[Of W.C. Fields; often attributed to him]
Any man who hates dogs and babies can't be all bad.

[Speech, 1939]

RUSSELL, Bertrand (1872–1970)
Few people can be happy unless they hate some other person, nation or creed.

[Attr.]

TACITUS (c. 56–c. 120)
Proprium humani ingenii est odisse quem laeseris.
It is part of human nature to hate those whom you have injured.

[*Agricola*]

HEALTH

BUTLER, Samuel (1835–1902)
The healthy stomach is nothing if not conservative. Few radicals have good digestions.

[*The Note-Books of Samuel Butler* (1912)]

DRYDEN, John (1631–1700)
Better to hunt in fields, for health unbought,
Than fee the doctor for a nauseous draught.
The wise, for cure, on exercise depend;
God never made his work, for man to mend.

['To John Driden of Chesterton' (1700)]

JAY, Douglas (1907–)
For in the case of nutrition and health,

just as in the case of education, the gentleman in Whitehall really does know better what is good for people than the people know themselves.

[*The Socialist Case* (1947)]

JUVENAL (c. 60–130)
Orandum est ut sit mens sana in corpore sano.
Your prayers should be for a healthy mind in a healthy body.

[*Satires*]

MARTIAL (c. 40–c. 104)
Non est vivere, sed valere vita est.
It is not to live but to be healthy that makes a life.

[*Epigrammata*]

SMITH, Sydney (1771–1845)
I am convinced digestion is the great secret of life

[Letter to Arthur Kinglake, 1837]

SWIFT, Jonathan (1667–1745)
I row after health like a waterman, and ride after it like a postboy, and find little success.

[Attr.]

TOLSTOY, Leo (1828–1910)
Our body is a machine for living. It is geared towards it, it is its nature. Let life go on in it unhindered and let it defend itself, it will be more effective than if you paralyse it by encumbering it with remedies.

[*War and Peace* (1869)]

TUSSER, Thomas (c. 1524–1580)
Make hunger thy sauce, as a medicine for health.

[*Five Hundred Points of Good Husbandry*]

WALTON, Izaak (1593–1683)
Look to your health; and if you have it, praise God, and value it next to a good conscience; for health is the second blessing that we mortals are capable of; a blessing money cannot buy.

[*The Compleat Angler* (1653)]

See ILLNESS; MEDICINE

HEAVEN

BORGES, Jorge Luis (1899–1986)
Que el cielo exista, aunque mi lugar sea el infierno.
Let heaven exist, even if my place be hell.

['The Library of Babel' (1941)]

BROWN, Helen Gurley (1922–)
[Promotional line for *Cosmopolitan* magazine]
Good girls go to heaven, bad girls go everywhere.

[Attr.]

BROWNING, Robert (1812–1889)
On the earth the broken arcs; in the heaven, a perfect round.

['Abt Vogler' (1864)]

DE QUINCEY, Thomas (1785–1859)
Thou hast the keys of Paradise, oh just, subtle, and mighty opium!

[*Confessions of an English Opium Eater* (1822)]

ELLIS, Havelock (1859–1939)
The Promised Land always lies on the other side of a wilderness.

[*The Dance of Life*]

FITZGERALD, Edward (1809–1883)
Here with a Loaf of Bread beneath the Bough,
A Flask of Wine, a Book of Verse – and Thou
Beside me singing in the Wilderness –
And Wilderness is Paradise enow.

[*The Rubáiyát of Omar Khayyám* (1859)]

LICHTENBERG, Georg Christoph (1742–1799)
Probably no invention came more easily to man than Heaven.

[*Aphorisms*]

MILTON, John (1608–1674)
Heav'n is for thee too high
To know what passes there; be lowlie wise:
Think onely what concerns thee and thy being.

[*Paradise Lost* (1667)]

PROUST, Marcel (1871–1922)
Les vrais paradis sont les paradis qu'on a perdus.
The true paradises are the paradises we have lost.

[*Le Temps retrouvé* (1926)]

SEDGWICK, Catharine Maria (1789–1867)
[Comparing heaven with her home town of Stockbridge, Massachussetts]
I expect no very violent transition.

[Attr.]

SHAKESPEARE, William (1564–1616)
Heaven is above all yet: there sits a Judge
That no king can corrupt.

[*Henry VIII*, III.i]

SHAW, George Bernard (1856–1950)
In heaven an angel is nobody in particular.

[*Man and Superman* (1903)]

Heaven, as conventionally conceived, is a place so inane, so dull, so useless, so miserable, that nobody has ever ventured to describe a whole day in heaven, though plenty of people have described a day at the seaside.

[*Misalliance* (1914)]

SMITH, Sydney (1771–1845)
My idea of heaven is eating *pâté de foie gras* to the sound of trumpets.

[In Pearson, *The Smith of Smiths* (1934)]

WADDELL, Helen (1889–1965)
Would you think Heaven could be so small a thing
As a lit window on the hills at night.

['I Shall Not Go To Heaven']

HELL

BETJEMAN, Sir John (1906–1984)
Maud was my hateful nurse who smelt of soap ...
She rubbed my face in messes I had made
And was the first to tell me about Hell,
Admitting she was going there herself.

[*Summoned by Bells* (1960)]

BUNYAN, John (1628–1688)
Then I saw there was a way to Hell, even from the gates of heaven.

[*The Pilgrim's Progress* (1678)]

BURTON, Robert (1577–1640)
If there is a hell upon earth, it is to be found in a melancholy man's heart.

[*Anatomy of Melancholy* (1621)]

CLARE, Dr Anthony (1942–)
Hell is when you get what you think you want.

[*The Observer*, 1983]

ELIOT, T.S. (1888–1965)
Hell is oneself;
Hell is alone, the other figures in it
Merely projections. There is nothing to escape from
And nothing to escape to. One is always alone.

[*The Cocktail Party* (1950)]

LEWIS, C.S. (1898–1963)
There is wishful thinking in Hell as well as on earth.

[*The Screwtape Letters* (1942)]

MARLOWE, Christopher (1564–1593)
Hell hath no limits nor is circumscrib'd
In one self place, where we are is Hell,
And where Hell is, there must we ever be.
And to be short, when all the world dissolves,
And every creature shall be purified,
All places shall be hell that are not heaven.

[*Doctor Faustus* (1604)]

MILTON, John (1608–1674)
Here we may reign secure, and in my choice
To reign is worth ambition though in Hell:
Better to reign in Hell, then serve in Heav'n.

[*Paradise Lost* (1667)]

Long is the way
And hard, that out of Hell leads up to Light.

[*Paradise Lost* (1667)]

SADE, Marquis de (1740–1814)
Il n'y a d'autre enfer pour l'homme que la bêtise ou la méchanceté de ses semblables.
There is no other hell for man than the stupidity and wickedness of his own kind.

[*Histoire de Juliette* (1797)]

SARTRE, Jean-Paul (1905–1980)
Alors, c'est ça l'enfer. Je n'aurais jamais cru ... Vous vous rappelez: le soufre, le bûcher, le gril ... Ah! quelle plaisanterie. Pas besoin de gril, l'enfer, c'est les Autres.
So that's what Hell is. I'd never have believed it ... Do you remember, brimstone, the stake, the gridiron? ... What a joke! No need of a gridiron, Hell is other people.

[*In Camera* (1944)]

SHAW, George Bernard (1856–1950)
A perpetual holiday is a good working definition of hell.

[Attr.]

TEILHARD DE CHARDIN, Pierre (1881–1955)
Vous m'avez dit, mon Dieu, de croire à l'enfer. Mais vous m'avez interdit de penser, avec absolue certitude, d'un seul homme, qu'il était damné.
You have told me, O God, to believe in hell. But you have forbidden me to think, with absolute certainty, of any man as damned.

[*Le Milieu divin*]

VIRGIL (70–19 BC)
Facilis descensus Averno:
Noctes atque dies patet atri ianua Ditis;
Sed revocare gradum superasque
*   evadere ad auras,*
Hoc opus, hic labor est.
The gates of Hell are open night and day;
Smooth the descent, and easy is the way:
But to return, and view the cheerful skies,
In this the task and mighty labour lies.

[*Aeneid*, trans. Dryden]

WATTS, Isaac (1674–1748)
There is a dreadful Hell,
And everlasting pains;
There sinners must with devils dwell
In darkness, fire and chains.

[*Divine Songs for Children* (1715)]

HEROES

BRECHT, Bertolt (1898–1956)
Andrea: *Unglücklich das Land, das keine Helden hat!* ...
Galileo: *Nein. Unglücklich das Land, das Helden nötig hat.*
Andrea: Unhappy the country that has no heroes!
Galileo: No. Unhappy the country that needs heroes.

[*Life of Galileo* (1939)]

CARLYLE, Thomas (1795–1881)
The Hero can be Poet, Prophet, King, Priest or what you will, according to the kind of world he finds himself born into.

['The Hero as Poet' (1841)]

CORNUEL, Madame de (1605–1694)
Il n'y a point de grand homme pour son valet de chambre.
No man is a hero to his valet.

[In *Lettres de Mlle Aïssé à Madame C* (1787)]

GAMBETTA, Léon (1838–1882)
Les temps héroïques sont passés.
Heroic times have passed away.

[Saying]

HARRIS, Max (1921–1995)
The Australian world is peopled with good blokes and bastards, but not heroes.

[In Coleman (ed.), *Australian Civilization*]

HENDERSON, Hamish (1919–)
There were our own, there were the others.
Their deaths were like their lives, human and animal.
There were no gods and precious few heroes.

['First Elegy, End of a Campaign' (1948)]

LANDOR, Walter Savage (1775–1864)
Hail, ye indomitable heroes, hail!
Despite of all your generals ye prevail.
['The Crimean Heroes']

MACKENZIE, Sir Compton (1883–1972)
Ever since the first World War there
has been an inclination to denigrate
the heroic aspect of man.
[*On Moral Courage* (1962)]

MORELL, Thomas (1703–1784)
See, the conquering hero comes!
Sound the trumpets, beat the drums!
[*Joshua* (1748)]

ORWELL, George (1903–1950)
The high sentiments always win in the
end, leaders who offer blood, toil,
tears and sweat always get more out
of their followers than those who offer
safety and a good time. When it comes
to the pinch, human beings are heroic.
[*Horizon*, 1941]

RILKE, Rainer Maria (1875–1926)
*Wunderlich nah ist der Held doch den
jugendlichen Toten.*
Wondrous close is the hero to those
who die young.
[*Duino Elegies* (1923)]

ROGERS, Will (1879–1935)
Heroing is one of the shortest-lived
professions there is.
[In Grove, *The Will Rogers Book* (1961)]

HISTORY

ANGELOU, Maya (1928–)
History, faced with courage, need not
be lived again.
[Speech at the Inauguration of President
Clinton, 1993]

AUSTEN, Jane (1775–1817)
Real solemn history, I cannot be
interested in ... The quarrels of popes
and kings, with wars or pestilences, in
every page; the men all so good for
nothing, and hardly any women at all,
it is very tiresome.
[*Northanger Abbey* (1818)]

BALFOUR, A.J. (1848–1930)
History does not repeat itself. His-
torians repeat each other.
[Attr.]

BEECHAM, Sir Thomas (1879–1961)
When the history of the first half of
this century comes to be written –
properly written – it will be ac-
knowledged the most stupid and
brutal in the history of civilisation.
[Attr.]

BUTLER, Samuel (1835–1902)
It has been said that though God
cannot alter the past, historians can; it
is perhaps because they can be useful
to Him in this respect that He tolerates
their existence.
[*Erewhon Revisited* (1901)]

CARLYLE, Thomas (1795–1881)
History is the essence of innumerable
biographies.
['On History' (1839)]

Happy the people whose annals are
blank in history-books!
[*History of Frederick the Great* (1865)]

CATHER, Willa (1873–1947)
The history of every country begins in
the heart of a man or a woman.
[*O Pioneers!* (1913)]

**COLERIDGE, Samuel Taylor
(1772–1834)**
If men could learn from history, what
lessons it might teach us! But passion
and party blind our eyes, and the light
which experience gives is a lantern on
the stern, which shines only on the
waves behind us!
[*Table Talk* (1835)]

**DIONYSIUS OF HALICARNASSUS
(fl. 30–7 BC)**
History is philosophy teaching from
examples.
[*Ars Rhetorica*]

EBAN, Abba (1915–)
History teaches us that men and

nations behave wisely once they have exhausted all other alternatives.

[Speech, 1970]

FISHER, H.A.L. (1856–1940)
There can be ... only one safe rule for the historian: that he should recognize in the development of human destinies the play of the contingent and the unforeseen.

[*History of Europe* (1935)]

FORD, Henry (1863–1947)
[Popularly remembered as 'History is bunk']
History is more or less bunk. It's tradition. We don't want tradition. We want to live in the present and the only history that is worth a tinker's damn is the history we make today.

[*Chicago Tribune*, 1916]

GIBBON, Edward (1737–1794)
History ... is, indeed, little more than the register of the crimes, follies, and misfortunes of mankind.

[*Decline and Fall of the Roman Empire* (1776–88)]

JOHNSON, Samuel (1709–1784)
Great abilities are not requisite for an Historian ... Imagination is not required in any high degree.

[In Boswell, *The Life of Samuel Johnson* (1791)]

JOYCE, James (1882–1941)
History is a nightmare from which I am trying to awake.

[*Ulysses* (1922)]

KHRUSHCHEV, Nikita (1894–1971)
Whether you like it or not, history is on our side.

[Speech to Western ambassadors, 1956]

KOESTLER, Arthur (1905–1983)
The most persistent sound which reverberates through men's history is the beating of war drums.

[*Janus: A Summing Up* (1978)]

LANG, Ian (1940–)
History is littered with dead opinion polls.

[*The Independent*, 1994]

MCLUHAN, Marshall (1911–1980)
The hydrogen bomb is history's exclamation point. It ends an age-long sentence of manifest violence.

[Attr.]

MARX, Karl (1818–1883)
Hegel says somewhere that all great events and personalities in world history reappear in one way or another. He forgot to add: the first time as tragedy, the second as farce.

[*The Eighteenth Brumaire of Louis Napoleon*]

ORWELL, George (1903–1950)
To a surprising extent the war-lords in shining armour, the apostles of the martial virtues, tend not to die fighting when the time comes. History is full of ignominious getaways by the great and famous.

['Who are the War Criminals?' (1941)]

POPPER, Sir Karl (1902–1994)
There is no history of mankind, there are only many histories of all kinds of aspects of human life. And one of these is the history of political power. This is elevated into the history of the world.

[*The Open Society and its Enemies* (1945)]

SAKI (1870–1916)
The people of Crete unfortunately make more history than they can consume locally.

[*The Chronicles of Clovis* (1911)]

SAMUEL, Lord (1870–1963)
Hansard is history's ear, already listening.

[*The Observer*, 1949]

SCHILLER, Johann (1759–1805)
Die Weltgeschichte ist das Weltgericht.
The history of the world is its judgement.

['Resignation' (1786)]

SCHLEGEL, Friedrich von (1772-1829)
*Anfang und Ende der Geschichte ist
prophetisch, kein Objekt mehr der
reinen Historie.*
The beginning and end of history are
prophetic, they are no longer the object
of pure history.
[*Fragments on Literature and Poetry*]

*Der Historiker ist ein rückwärts
gekehrter Prophet.*
A historian is a prophet in reverse.
[*Athenäum - Fragmente*]

**SELLAR, Walter (1898-1951) and
YEATMAN, Robert (1897-1968)**
A Bad Thing: America was thus clearly
top nation, and History came to a .
[*1066 And All That* (1930)]

STALIN, Joseph (1879-1953)
History shows that there are no invin-
cible armies.
[Speech on the declaration of war on
Germany, 1941]

TAYLOR, A.J.P. (1906-1990)
[Of Napoleon III]
He was what I often think is a dangerous thing for a statesman to be – a
student of history; and like most of
those who study history, he learned
from the mistakes of the past how to
make new ones.
[*The Listener*, 1963]

TOLSTOY, Leo (1828-1910)
Historians are like deaf people who go
on answering questions that no one
has asked them.
[Attr.]

WEDGEWOOD, Cicely (1910-)
Truth can neither be apprehended nor
communicated ... history is an art like
all other sciences.
[*Truth and Opinion* (1960)]

WELLS, H.G. (1866-1946)
Human history becomes more and
more a race between education and
catastrophe.
[*The Outline of History* (1920)]

YELTSIN, Boris (1931-)
[Said after the failure of the
communist coup]
History will record that the twentieth
century essentially ended on 19-21
August 1991.
[Article in *Newsweek*, 1994]

HOME

ACE, Jane (1905-1974)
Home wasn't built in a day.
[In G. Ace, *The Fine Art of Hypochondria*)]

ANONYMOUS
Be it ever so humble there's no place
like home for sending one slowly
crackers.

There's no place like home after the
other places close.

BEAUVOIR, Simone de (1908-1986)
The ideal of happiness has always
taken material form in the house,
whether cottage or castle; it stands for
permanence and separation from the
world.
[*The Second Sex* (1949)]

CICERO (106-43 BC)
What is more agreeable than one's
home?
[*Ad Familiares*]

CLARKE, John (fl. 1639)
Home is home, though it be never so
homely.
[*Paraemiologia Anglo-Latina* (1639)]

COKE, Sir Edward (1552-1634)
The house of everyone is to him as his
castle and fortress, as well for his
defence against injury and violence, as
for his repose.
[*Semayne's Case*]

DE WOLFE, Elsie (1865-1950)
It is the personality of the mistress that
the home expresses. Men are forever
guests in our homes, no matter how
much happiness they may find there.
[*The House in Good Taste* (1920)]

DOUGLAS, Norman (1868–1952)
Many a man who thinks to found a
home discovers that he has merely
opened a tavern for his friends.
[*South Wind* (1917)]

FLETCHER, John (1579–1625)
Charity and beating begins at home.
[*Wit Without Money* (c. 1614)]

FROST, Robert (1874–1963)
Home is the place where, when you
have to go there,
They have to take you in.
['The Death of the Hired Man' (1914)]

FULLER, Margaret
A house is no home unless it contain
food and fire for the mind as well as
for the body.
[*Woman in the Nineteenth Century* (1845)]

HIGLEY, Brewster (19th century)
Oh give me a home where the buffalo
roam,
Where the deer and the antelope play,
Where seldom is heard a discouraging
word
And the skies are not cloudy all day.
['Home on the Range', song, c. 1873]

KAUFMAN, Sue (1926–)
In violent and chaotic times such as
these, our only chance for survival lies
in creating our own little islands of
sanity and order, in making little
havens of our homes.
[*Falling Bodies* (1974)]

LUCE, Clare Boothe (1903–)
A man's home may seem to be his
castle on the outside; inside, it is more
often his nursery.
[Attr.]

MEYER, Agnes (1887–c. 1970)
What the nation must realise is that
the home, when both parents work, is
non-existent. Once we have honestly
faced the fact, we must act accordingly.
[*Washington Post*, 1943]

MORE, Hannah (1745–1833)
The sober comfort, all the peace which
springs
From the large aggregate of little
things;
On these small cares of daughter, wife,
or friend,
The almost sacred joys of home
depend.
['Sensibility' (1782)]

MORRIS, William (1834–1896)
If you want a golden rule that will fit
everybody, this is it: Have nothing in
your houses that you do not know to
be useful, or believe to be beautiful.
[*Hopes and Fears for Art* (1882)]

PAYNE, J.H. (1791–1852)
Mid pleasures and palaces though we
may roam,
Be it ever so humble, there's no place
like home;
A charm from the skies seems to
hallow us there,
Which, seek through the world, is
ne'er met with elsewhere.
['Home, Sweet Home', song, 1823]

ROWLAND, Helen (1875–1950)
'Home' is any four walls that enclose
the right person.
[*Reflections of a Bachelor Girl* (1909)]

SHAW, George Bernard (1856–1950)
The great advantage of a hotel is that
it's a refuge from home life.
[*You Never Can Tell* (1898)]

SITWELL, Dame Edith (1887–1964)
One's own surroundings mean so
much to one, when one is feeling
miserable.
[*Selected Letters* (1970)]

STOWE, Harriet Beecher (1811–1896)
Home is a place not only of strong
affections, but of entire unreserve; it is
life's undress rehearsal, its backroom,
its dressing room, from which we go
forth to more careful and guarded
intercourse, leaving behind us much
debris of cast-off and everyday
clothing.
[*Little Foxes* (1866)]

THOREAU, Henry (1817–1862)
I had three chairs in my house; one for solitude, two for friendship, three for society.

[*Walden* (1854)]

HONESTY

AUDEN, W.H. (1907–1973)
Only God can tell the saintly from the suburban,
Counterfeit values always resemble the true;
Neither in Life nor Art is honesty bohemian,
The free behave much as the respectable do.

['New Year Letter' (1941)]

BLAKE, William (1757–1827)
Always be ready to speak your mind, and a base man will avoid you.

[Attr.]

BROWNE, Sir Thomas (1605–1682)
I have tried if I could reach that great resolution ... to be honest without a thought of Heaven or Hell.

[*Religio Medici* (1643)]

CARLYLE, Thomas (1795–1881)
Make yourself an honest man and then you may be sure there is one rascal less in the world.

[Attr.]

CROMWELL, Oliver (1599–1658)
A few honest men are better than numbers.

[Letter to Sir William Spring, 1643]

DEFOE, Daniel (c. 1661–1731)
Necessity makes an honest man a knave.
[*Serious Reflections of Robinson Crusoe* (1720)]

FITZGERALD, F. Scott (1896–1940)
I am one of the few honest people that I have ever known.

[*The Great Gatsby* (1926)]

JUVENAL (c. 60–130)
Probitas laudatur et alget.
Honesty is praised and is left out in the cold.

[*Satires*]

MARQUIS, Don (1878–1937)
honesty is a good
thing but
it is not profitable to
its possessor
unless it is
kept under control.

['archygrams' (1933)]

RICHELIEU, Cardinal (1585–1642)
If you give me six lines written by the most honest man, I will find something in them to hang him.

[Attr.]

RUSKIN, John (1819–1900)
Your honesty is not to be based either on religion or policy. Both your religion and policy must be based on *it*. Your honesty must be based, as the sun is, in vacant heaven; poised, as the lights in the firmament, which have rule over the day and over the night.

[*Time and Tide by Weare and Tyne* (1867)]

SHAKESPEARE, William (1564–1616)
O wretched fool,
That liv'st to make thine honesty a vice!
O monstrous world! Take note, take note, O world,
To be direct and honest is not safe.

[*Othello*, III.iii]

Though I am not naturally honest, I am so sometimes by chance.

[*The Winter's Tale*, IV.iv]

WHATELY, Richard (1787–1863)
Honesty is the best policy, but he who is governed by that maxim is not an honest man.

[*Apophthegms* (1854)]

HOPE

BACON, Francis (1561–1626)
Hope is a good breakfast, but it is a bad supper.

['Apophthegms']

177

HUMANITY

CHESTERTON, G.K. (1874–1936)
Hope is the power of being cheerful in
circumstances which we know to be
desperate.

[*Heretics* (1905)]

FRANKLIN, Benjamin (1706–1790)
He that lives upon hope will die
fasting.

[*Poor Richard's Almanac* (1758)]

HERBERT, George (1593–1633)
He that lives in hope danceth without
music.

[*Jacula Prudentum* (1640)]

ILLICH, Ivan (1926–)
We must rediscover the distinction
between hope and expectation.

[*Deschooling Society* (1971)]

KERR, Jean (1923–)
You don't seem to realize that a poor
person who is unhappy is in a better
position than a rich person who is
unhappy. Because the poor person has
hope. He thinks money would help.

[*Poor Richard* (1963)]

Hope is the feeling you have that the
feeling you have isn't permanent.

[*Finishing Touches* (1973)]

OSBORNE, John (1929–1994)
[A notice in his bathroom]
Since I gave up hope I feel so much
better.

[*The Independent*, 1994]

POPE, Alexander (1688–1744)
Hope springs eternal in the human
breast;

[*An Essay on Man* (1733)]

SHAKESPEARE, William (1564–1616)
True hope is swift and flies with
    swallow's wings;
Kings it makes gods, and meaner
    creatures kings.

[*Richard III*, V.ii]

TERENCE (c. 190–159 BC)
Modo liceat vivere, est spes.

Where there's life, there's hope.

[*Heauton Timoroumenos*]

See DESPAIR

HUMANITY

AUDEN, W.H. (1907–1973)
Man is a history-making creature who
can neither repeat his past nor leave it
behind.

[*The Dyer's Hand* (1963)]

BEAUMARCHAIS (1732–1799)
*Boire sans soif et faire l'amour en tout
temps, madame, il n'y a que ça qui
nous distingue des autres bêtes.*
Drinking when we're not thirsty and
making love all the time, madam, that
is all there is to distinguish us from
other animals.

[*Le Barbier de Seville* (1775)]

BEERBOHM, Sir Max (1872–1956)
Mankind is divisible into two great
classes: hosts and guests.

[Attr.]

THE BIBLE (King James Version)
Man is born unto trouble, as the
sparks fly upward.

[*Job*, 5:7]

When I consider thy heavens, the work
of thy fingers, the moon and the stars,
which thou hast ordained;
What is man, that thou art mindful of
him? and the son of man, that thou
visitest him?

[*Psalms*, 8:3–4]

As for man, his days are as grass: as a
flower of the field, so he flourisheth.

[*Psalms*, 103:15]

BRONOWSKI, Jacob (1908–1974)
Every animal leaves traces of what it
was; man alone leaves traces of what
he created.

[*The Ascent of Man* (1973)]

BRONTË, Anne (1820–1849)
The human heart is like Indian rubber:

HUMANITY

a little swells it, but a great deal will
not burst it.

[*Agnes Grey* (1847)]

BÜCHNER, Georg (1813–1837)
*Puppen sind wir von unbekannten
Gewalten am Draht gezogen; nichts,
nichts wir selbst!*
We are puppets on strings worked by
unknown forces; we ourselves are
nothing, nothing!

[*Danton's Death* (1835)]

BURNS, Robert (1759–1796)
Man's inhumanity to man
Makes countless thousands mourn!

['Man was made to Mourn, a Dirge' (1784)]

BUTLER, Samuel (1835–1902)
'Man wants but little here below' but
likes that little good – and not too long
in coming.

[*Further Extracts from the Note-Books of
Samuel Butler* (1934)]

Man is the only animal that can
remain on friendly terms with the
victims he intends to eat until he eats
them.

[*Samuel Butler's Notebooks* (1951)]

CAMUS, Albert (1913–1960)
A single sentence will suffice for
modern man: he fornicated and read
the papers.

[*The Fall* (1956)]

CANNING, George (1770–1827)
Man, only – rash, refined,
  presumptuous man,
Starts from his rank, and mars
  creation's plan.

['Progress of Man' (1799)]

CHESTERTON, G.K. (1874–1936)
Individually, men may present a more
or less rational appearance, eating,
sleeping and scheming. But humanity
as a whole is changeful, mystical,
fickle and delightful. Men are men, but
Man is a woman.

[*The Napoleon of Notting Hill* (1904)]

The human race, to which so many of
my readers belong, has been playing
at children's games from the beginning, and will probably do it till the
end, which is a nuisance for the few
people who grow up.

[*The Napoleon of Notting Hill* (1904)]

**COLERIDGE, Samuel Taylor
(1772–1834)**
A Fall of some sort or other – the
creation as it were, of the non-
absolute – is the fundamental postu-
late of the moral history of man.
Without this hypothesis, man is unin-
telligible; with it, every phenomenon is
explicable.

[*Table-Talk* (1835)]

COLTON, Charles Caleb (c. 1780–1832)
Man is an embodied paradox, a bundle
of contradictions.

[*Lacon* (1820)]

DISRAELI, Benjamin (1804–1881)
Man is only truly great when he acts
from the passions.

[*Coningsby* (1844)]

DONNE, John (1572–1631)
No man is an Island, entire of it self;
every man is a piece of Continent, a
part of the main; if a clod be washed
away by the sea, Europe is the less, as
well as if a promontory were, as well
as if a manor of thy friends or of thine
own were; any man's death diminishes
me, because I am involved in
Mankind;
And therefore never send to know for
whom the bell tolls; it tolls for thee.

[*Devotions upon Emergent Occasions* (1624)]

ELIOT, George (1819–1880)
There is a great deal of unmapped
country within us which would have to
be taken into account in an explanation of our gusts and storms.

[*Daniel Deronda* (1876)]

FROUDE, James Anthony (1818–1894)
Wild animals never kill for sport. Man

is the only one to whom the torture
and death of his fellow creatures is
amusing in itself.

[*Oceana, or England and her Colonies* (1886)]

GOLDSMITH, Oliver (c. 1728–1774)
Man wants but little here below,
Nor wants that little long.

[*The Vicar of Wakefield* (1766)]

GORKY, Maxim (1868–1936)
Man and man alone is, I believe, the
creator of all things and all ideas.

[Attr.]

GREVILLE, Fulke (1554–1628)
Oh wearisome Condition of Humanity!
Borne under one Law, to another,
    bound:
Vainely begot, and yet forbidden
    vanity,
Created sicke, commanded to be
    sound.

[*Mustapha* (1609)]

HAZLITT, William (1778–1830)
Man is an intellectual animal, and
therefore an everlasting contradiction
to himself. His senses centre in himself, his ideas reach to the ends of the
universe; so that he is torn in pieces
between the two, without a possibility
of its ever being otherwise.

[*Characteristics* (1823)]

LAWRENCE, D.H. (1885–1930)
Ideal mankind would abolish death,
multiply itself million upon million,
rear up city upon city, save every
parasite alive, until the accumulation
of mere existence is swollen to a
horror.

[*St Mawr* (1925)]

MONASH, Sir John (1865–1931)
Nothing man does to the animal
creation is equal to the cruelties he
commits on his own kind.

[*The Seals*]

MONTAIGNE, Michel de (1533–1592)
L'homme est bien insensé. Il ne saurait

*forger un ciron, et forge des Dieux à
douzaines.*
Man is quite insane. He wouldn't
know how to create a maggot, yet he
creates Gods by the dozen.

[*Essais* (1580)]

NIETZSCHE, Friedrich (1844–1900)
*Wie? ist der Mensch nur ein Fehlgriff
Gottes? Oder Gott nur ein Fehlgriff des
Meschen?*
What? is man only a mistake made by
God, or God only a mistake made by
man?

[*Twilight of the Idols* (1889)]

PASCAL, Blaise (1623–1662)
*L'homme n'est qu'un roseau, le plus
faible de la nature; mais c'est un roseau
pensant.*
Man is only a reed, the feeblest thing
in nature; but he is a thinking reed.

[*Pensées* (1670)]

POPE, Alexander (1688–1744)
Know then thyself, presume not God
    to scan;
The proper study of Mankind is Man.

[*An Essay on Man* (1733)]

Created half to rise, and half to fall;
Great lord of all things, yet a prey to
    all;
Sole judge of truth, in endless error
    hurl'd:
The glory, jest, and riddle of the world!

[*An Essay on Man* (1733)]

ROUSSEAU, Jean-Jacques (1712–1778)
*La nature a fait l'homme heureux et
bon, mais ... la société le déprave et le
rend misérable.*
Nature made man happy and good,
but ... society corrupts him and makes
him miserable.

[*Rousseau juge de Jean-Jacques*]

RUSKIN, John (1819–1900)
No human being, however great, or
powerful, was ever so free as a fish.

[*The Two Paths* (1859)]

SCHILLER, Johann (1759–1805)
Das Herz und nicht die Meinung ehrt den Mann.
Man is honoured by his heart and not by his opinions.

[*Wallensteins Tod* (1801)]

SHAKESPEARE, William (1564–1616)
What a piece of work is a man! How noble in reason! how infinite in faculties! in form and moving, how express and admirable! in action, how like an angel! in apprehension, how like a god! the beauty of the world! the paragon of animals!

[*Hamlet*, II.ii]

Roses have thorns, and silver
    fountains mud;
Clouds and eclipses stain both moon
    and sun,
And loathsome canker lives in
    sweetest bud.
All men make faults.

[Sonnet 35]

SHAW, George Bernard (1856–1950)
Man can climb to the highest summits; but he cannot dwell there long.

[*Candida* (1898)]

TEMPLE, William (1881–1944)
It is not the ape, nor the tiger in man that I fear, it is the donkey.

[Attr.]

TERENCE (c. 190–159 BC)
Homo sum; humani nil a me alienum puto.
I am a man, I count nothing human indifferent to me.

[*Heauton Timoroumenos*]

TERTZ, Abram (1925–)
Man is always both much worse and much better than is expected of him. The fields of good are just as limitless as the wastelands of evil.

[*A Voice From the Chorus* (1973)]

TWAIN, Mark (1835–1910)
Man is the only animal that blushes.
Or needs to.

[*Following the Equator* (1897)]

UNAMUNO, Miguel de (1864–1936)
El hombre, por ser hombre, por tener conciencia, es ya, respecto al burro o a un cangrejo, un animal enfermo. La conciencia es una enfermedad.
Man, because he is man, because he is conscious, is, in relation to the ass or to a crab, already a diseased animal. Consciousness is a disease.

[*The Tragic Sense of Life* (1913)]

VALERY, Paul (1871–1945)
A man is infinitely more complicated than his thoughts.

[In Auden, *A Certain World*]

VOLTAIRE (1694–1778)
Si Dieu nous a fait à son image, nous le lui avons bien rendu.
If God has created us in his image, we have repaid him well.

[*Le Sottisier* (c. 1778)]

WILDE, Oscar (1854–1900)
It is absurd to divide people into good and bad. People are either charming or tedious.

[*Lady Windermere's Fan* (1892)]

YEVTUSHENKO, Yevgeny (1933–)
In the final analysis, humanity has only two ways out – either universal destruction or universal brotherhood.

['The Spirit of Elbe' (1966)]

HUMAN NATURE

AUSTEN, Jane (1775–1817)
Human nature is so well disposed towards those who are in interesting situations, that a young person, who either marries or dies, is sure of being kindly spoken of.

[*Emma* (1816)]

BACON, Francis (1561–1626)
There is in human nature generally more of the fool than of the wise.

['Of Boldness' (1625)]

Nature is often hidden; sometimes
overcome; seldom extinguished.

['Of Nature in Men' (1625)]

BRADLEY, F.H. (1846–1924)
It is good to know what a man is, and
also what the world takes him for. But
you do not understand him until you
have learnt how he understands
himself.

[*Aphorisms* (1930)]

BROWNE, Sir Thomas (1605–1682)
There is surely a piece of divinity in us,
something that was before the elements, and owes no homage unto
the sun.

[*Religio Medici* (1643)]

CONFUCIUS (c. 550–c. 478 BC)
Men's natures are alike; it is their
habits that carry them far apart

[*Analects*]

DONLEAVY, J.P. (1926–)
I got disappointed in human nature as
well and gave it up because I found it
too much like my own.

[*Fairy Tales of New York* (1961)]

JOHNSON, Samuel (1709–1784)
Almost every man wastes part of his
life in attempts to display qualities
which he does not possess, and to
gain applause which he cannot keep.

[*The Rambler* (1750–1752)]

Sir, are you so grossly ignorant of
human nature, as not to know that a
man may be very sincere in good
principles without having good
practice?

[In Boswell, *Journal of a Tour to the Hebrides*
(1785)]

JUNG, Carl Gustav (1875–1961)
We need more understanding of
human nature, because the only real
danger that exists is man himself ...
We know nothing of man, far too little.
His psyche should be studied because
we are the origin of all coming evil.

[BBC television interview, 1959]

KEATS, John (1795–1821)
Scenery is fine – but human nature is
finer.

[Letter to Benjamin Bailey, 1818]

LA BRUYERE, Jean de (1645–1696)
*La plupart des hommes emploient la
meilleure partie de leur vie à rendre
l'autre misérable.*
Most men spend the best part of their
lives in making their remaining years
unhappy.

[*Les caractères ou les moeurs de ce siècle*
(1688)]

MACHIAVELLI (1469–1527)
*Gli uomini sdimenticano più presto la
morte del padre che la perdita del
patrimonio.*
Men sooner forget the death of their
father than the loss of their possessions.

[*The Prince* (1532)]

SARTRE, Jean-Paul (1905–1980)
*Ainsi, il n'y a pas de nature humaine,
puisqu'il n'y a pas de Dieu pour la
concevoir.*
So there is no human nature, since
there is no God to conceive it.

[*Existentialism and Humanism* (1946)]

HUMOUR

ADDISON, Joseph (1672–1719)
If we may believe our logicians, man is
distinguished from all other creatures
by the faculty of laughter.

[*The Spectator*, 1712]

AYCKBOURN, Alan (1939–)
Few women care to be laughed at and
men not at all, except for large sums
of money.

[*The Norman Conquests* (1975)]

BARKER, Ronnie (1929–)
The marvellous thing about a joke
with a double meaning is that it can
only mean one thing.

[Attr.]

BEAUMARCHAIS (1732–1799)
Je me presse de rire de tout, de peur d'être obligé d'en pleurer.
I make myself laugh at everything, for fear of having to cry.
[*Le Barbier de Seville* (1775)]

BROWN, Thomas Edward (1830–1897)
A rich man's joke is always funny.
['The Doctor' (1887)]

BUTLER, Samuel (1835–1902)
The most perfect humour and irony is generally quite unconscious.
[*Life and Habit* (1877)]

CARLYLE, Thomas (1795–1881)
No man who has once heartily and wholly laughed can be altogether irreclaimably bad.
[*Sartor Resartus* (1834)]

CHESTERFIELD, Lord (1694–1773)
In my mind, there is nothing so illiberal and so ill-bred, as audible laughter ... I am neither of a melancholy, nor a cynical disposition; and am as willing, and as apt, to be pleased as anybody; but I am sure that, since I have had the full use of my reason, nobody has ever heard me laugh.
[Letter to his son, 1748]

COLBY, Frank Moore (1865–1925)
Men will confess to treason, murder, arson, false teeth, or a wig. How many of them will own up to a lack of humour?
[*Essays*]

COLETTE (1873–1954)
Une totale absence d'humour rend la vie impossible.
A total absence of humour makes life impossible.
[*Chance Acquaintances*]

CONGREVE, William (1670–1729)
It is the business of a comic poet to paint the vices and follies of human kind.
[*The Double Dealer* (1694)]

DODD, Ken (1931–)
[Commenting on Freud's theory that a good joke will lead to great relief and elation]
The trouble with Freud is that he never played the Glasgow Empire Saturday night after Rangers and Celtic had both lost.
[TV interview, 1965]

ELIOT, George (1819–1880)
A difference of taste in jokes is a great strain on the affections.
[*Daniel Deronda* (1876)]

GRIFFITHS, Trevor (1935–)
Comedy is medicine.
[*The Comedians* (1979)]

HUMPHRIES, Barry (1934–)
The only people really keeping the spirit of irony alive in Australia are taxi-drivers and homosexuals.
[*Australian Women's Weekly*, 1983]

LA BRUYERE, Jean de (1645–1696)
Il faut rire avant que d'être heureux, de peur de mourir sans avoir ri.
One must laugh before one is happy, for fear of dying without ever having laughed at all.
[*Les caractères ou les moeurs de ce siècle* (1688)]

ORWELL, George (1903–1950)
A dirty joke is not ... a serious attack upon morality, but it is a sort of mental rebellion, a momentary wish that things were otherwise.
['The Art of Donald McGill' (1941)]

PRIESTLEY, J.B. (1894–1984)
Comedy, we may say, is society protecting itself – with a smile.
[*George Meredith* (1926)]

RENARD, Jules (1864–1910)
L'ironie est la pudeur de l'humanité.
Irony is humanity's sense of propriety.
[*Journal*, 1892]

ROGERS, Will (1879–1935)
Everything is funny as long as it is

happening to someone else.
[*The Illiterate Digest* (1924)]

SHAW, George Bernard (1856–1950)
My way of joking is to tell the truth.
It's the funniest joke in the world.
[*John Bull's Other Island* (1907)]

STERNE, Laurence (1713–1768)
I live in a constant endeavour to fence
against the infirmities of ill health, and
other evils of life, by mirth; being
firmly persuaded that every time a
man smiles, – but much more so,
when he laughs, it adds something to
this Fragment of Life.
[*Tristram Shandy*]

'Tis no extravagant arithmetic to say,
that for every ten jokes, – thou hast
got a hundred enemies.
[*Tristram Shandy*]

TUCHOLSKY, Kurt (1890–1935)
*Humor ist ein Element, das dem
deutschen Menschen abhanden
gekommen ist.*
Humour is an element which the
German man has lost.
['What may Satire do –?' (1973)]

WALTON, Izaak (1593–1683)
I love such mirth as does not make
friends ashamed to look upon one
another next morning.
[*The Compleat Angler* (1653)]

WILCOX, Ella Wheeler (1850–1919)
Laugh and the world laughs with you;
Weep, and you weep alone;
For the sad old earth must borrow its
mirth,
But has trouble enough of its own.
['Solitude' (1917)]

WODEHOUSE, P.G. (1881–1975)
She had a penetrating sort of laugh.
Rather like a train going into a tunnel.
[*The Inimitable Jeeves* (1923)]

BACON, Francis (1561–1626)
It is the wisdom of the crocodiles, that
shed tears when they would devour.
['Of Wisdom for a Man's Self' (1625)]

BYRON, Lord (1788–1824)
Even innocence itself has many a wile,
And will not dare to trust itself with
truth,
And love is taught hypocrisy from
youth.
[*Don Juan* (1824)]

CHURCHILL, Charles (1731–1764)
Keep up appearances; there lies the
test;
The world will give thee credit for the
rest.
Outward be fair, however foul within;
Sin if thou wilt, but then in secret sin.
['Night' (1761)]

DICKENS, Charles (1812–1870)
With affection beaming in one eye,
and calculation shining out of the
other.
[*Martin Chuzzlewit* (1844)]

EMERSON, Ralph Waldo (1803–1882)
The book written against fame and
learning has the author's name on the
title-page.
[*Journals*]

GAY, John (1685–1732)
An open foe may prove a curse,
But a pretended friend is worse.
[*Fables* (1727)]

**LA ROCHEFOUCAULD, Duc de
(1613–1680)**
*L'hypocrisie est un hommage que le vice
rend à la vertu.*
Hypocrisy is a homage that vice pays
to virtue.
[*Maximes* (1678)]

**MAUGHAM, William Somerset
(1874–1965)**
Hypocrisy is the most difficult and

nerve-racking vice that any man can pursue; it needs an unceasing vigilance and a rare detachment of spirit. It cannot, like adultery or gluttony, be practised at spare moments; it is a whole-time job.

[*Cakes and Ale* (1930)]

MILTON, John (1608–1674)
For neither Man nor Angel can discern Hypocrisie, the onely evil that walks Invisible, except to God alone.

[*Paradise Lost* (1667)]

TOLSTOY, Leo (1828–1910)
Hypocrisy in anything whatever may

deceive the cleverest and most penetrating man, but the least wide-awake of children recognizes it, and is revolted by it, however ingeniously it may be disguised.

[Attr.]

WILDE, Oscar (1854–1900)
I hope that you have not been leading a double life, pretending to be wicked and being really good all the time. That would be hypocrisy.

[*The Importance of Being Earnest* (1895)]

See DECEPTION

IDEAS

ALAIN (Emile-Auguste Chartier)
(1868–1951)
Rien n'est plus dangereux qu'une idée,
quand on n'a qu'une idée.
Nothing is more dangerous than an
idea, when you only have one idea.
[Remarks on Religion (1938)]

BAGEHOT, Walter (1826–1877)
One of the greatest pains to human
nature is the pain of a new idea.
[Physics and Politics (1872)]

BOWEN, Elizabeth (1899–1973)
One can live in the shadow of an idea
without grasping it.
[The Heat of the Day (1949)]

HOLMES, Oliver Wendell, Jr.
(1841–1935)
Many ideas grow better when trans-
planted into another mind than in the
one where they sprang up.
[In Bowen, Yankee from Olympus (1945)]

HUGO, Victor (1802–1885)
On résiste à l'invasion des armées; on
ne résiste pas à l'invasion des idées.
One can resist the invasion of an
army; but one cannot resist the
invasion of ideas.
[Histoire d'un Crime (1852)]

LEWIS, Wyndham (1882–1957)
'Dying for an idea,' again, sounds well
enough, but why not let the idea die
instead of you?
[The Art of Being Ruled (1926)]

MACDONALD, Ramsay (1866–1937)
Society goes on and on and on. It is
the same with ideas.
[Speech, 1935]

MARQUIS, Don (1878–1937)
An idea isn't responsible for the people
who believe in it.
[New York Sun]

MEDAWAR, Sir Peter (1915–1987)
The human mind treats a new idea the

way the body treats a strange protein –
it rejects it.
[Attr.]

SHAW, George Bernard (1856–1950)
This creature Man, who in his own
selfish affairs is a coward to the
backbone, will fight for an idea like a
hero.
[Man and Superman (1903)]

UNAMUNO, Miguel de (1864–1936)
No suelen ser nuestras ideas las que nos
hacen optimistas o pesimistas, sino que
es nuestro optimismo o nuestro
pesimismo, de origen fisiológico o
patológico quizás ... el que hace
nuestras ideas.
It is not normally our ideas which
make us optimists or pessimists, but it
is our optimism or our pessimism,
which is perhaps of a physiological or
pathological origin ... which makes our
ideas.
[The Tragic Sense of Life (1913)]

See MIND; THOUGHT

IDLENESS AND UNEMPLOYMENT

BOILEAU-DESPREAUX, Nicolas
(1636–1711)
Le pénible fardeau de n'avoir rien à
faire!
What a terrible burden it is to have
nothing to do!
[Epitres (c. 1690)]

BRASCH, Charles Orwell (1909–1973)
[On walking on a week-day in
Dunedin, 1938, when he was unem-
ployed]
It is not only an offence against society
to be seen in the streets flaunting the
fact that one does not work like everyone else; it challenges the settled
order of things, a threat that no right
thinking New Zealander could tolerate.
It makes one an object of suspicion,
and more, an enemy.
[Indirections: A Memoir 1909-1947 (1980)]

BRUMMEL, Beau (1778–1840)
I always like to have the morning
well-aired before I get up.

[In Macfarlane, *Reminiscences of a Literary
Life* (1917)]

CHESTERFIELD, Lord (1694–1773)
Idleness is only the refuge of weak
minds, and the holiday of fools.

[Letter to his son, 1749]

CICERO (106–43 BC)
*Numquam se minus otiosum esse quam
cum otiosus, nec minus solum quam
cum solus esset.*
Never less idle than when free from
work, nor less lonely than when
completely alone.

[*De Officiis*]

CONRAN, Shirley (1932–)
I make no secret of the fact that I
would rather lie on a sofa than sweep
beneath it. But you have to be efficient
if you're going to be lazy.

[*Superwoman* (1975)]

COWPER, William (1731–1800)
How various his employments,
    whom the world
Calls idle.

[*The Task* (1785)]

ELIOT, George (1819–1880)
There's many a one would be idle if
hunger didn't pinch him; but the
stomach sets us to work.

[*Felix Holt* (1866)]

EWART, Gavin (1916–1995)
After Cambridge – unemployment. No
    one wanted much to know.
Good degrees are good for nothing in
    the business world below.

['The Sentimental Education']

FITZGERALD, F. Scott (1896–1940)
'What'll we do with ourselves this
afternoon?' cried Daisy, 'and the day
after that, and the next thirty years?'

[*The Great Gatsby* (1925)]

FURPHY, Joseph (1843–1912)
Unemployed at last!

[*Such is Life* (1903)]

HEWETT, Dorothy (1923–)
For dole bread is bitter bread
Bitter bread and sour
There's grief in the taste of it
There's weevils in the flour.

['Weevils in the Flour']

HOOVER, Herbert (1874–1964)
When a great many people are unable
to find work, unemployment results.

[In Boller, *Presidential Anecdotes* (1981)]

JEROME, Jerome K. (1859–1927)
It is impossible to enjoy idling
thoroughly unless one has plenty of
work to do.

[*Idle Thoughts of an Idle Fellow* (1886)]

George goes to sleep at a bank from
ten to four each day, except Saturdays,
when they wake him up and put him
outside at two.

[*Three Men in a Boat* (1889)]

JOHNSON, Samuel (1709–1784)
If you are idle, be not solitary; if you
are solitary, be not idle.

[Letter to Boswell, 1779]

JOWETT, Benjamin (1817–1893)
Research! A mere excuse for idleness;
it has never achieved, and will never
achieve any results of the slightest
value.

[In Logan Pearsall Smith, *Unforgotten Years*]

KEMPIS, Thomas à (c. 1380–1471)
*Numquam sis ex toto otiosus; sed aut
legens, aut scribens, aut orans, aut
meditans, aut aliquid utilitatis pro
communi laborans.*
Never be completely idle, but be either
reading, or writing, or praying, or
meditating, or working at something
useful for the community.

[*De Imitatione Christi* (1892 ed.)]

MADAN, Geoffrey (1895–1947)
The devil finds mischief still for hands that have not learnt how to be idle.

[*Livre sans nom: Twelve Reflections* (1934)]

MARX, Karl (1818–1883)
Without doubt machinery has greatly increased the number of well-to-do idlers.

[*Das Kapital* (1867)]

MAUGHAM, William Somerset (1874–1965)
It was such a lovely day I thought it was a pity to get up.

[*Our Betters* (1923)]

NASH, Ogden (1902–1971)
I would live my life in nonchalance and insouciance
Were it not for making a living, which is rather a nouciance.

['Introspective Reflection' (1940)]

SAMUEL, Lord (1870–1963)
To help the unemployed is not the same thing as dealing with unemployment.

[*The Observer*, 1933]

SHERIDAN, Richard Brinsley (1751–1816)
[On a notice fixed to his door when he was a Secretary to the Treasury]
No applications can be received here on Sundays, nor any business done during the remainder of the week.

[Attr. in Morwood, *The Life and Works of Sheridan* (1985)]

STEVENSON, Robert Louis (1850–1894)
Extreme *busyness*, whether at school or college, kirk or market, is a symptom of deficient vitality; and a faculty for idleness implies a catholic appetite and a strong sense of personal identity.

[*Virginibus Puerisque* (1881)]

THURBER, James (1894–1961)
It is better to have loafed and lost than never to have loafed at all.

[*Fables for Our Time* (1940)]

WARD, Artemus (1834–1867)
I am happiest when I am idle. I could live for months without performing any kind of labour, and at the expiration of that time I should feel fresh and vigorous enough to go right on in the same way for numerous more months.

[*Artemus Ward in London* (1867)]

ILLNESS

AUBREY, John (1626–1697)
Sciatica: he cured it, by boiling his buttock.

[*Brief Lives* (c. 1693), 'Sir Jonas Moore']

AUSTIN, Alfred (1835–1913)
[On the illness of the Prince of Wales]
Across the wires the electric message came:
'He is no better, he is much the same.'

[Attr.]

BACON, Francis (1561–1626)
The remedy is worse than the disease.

['Of Seditions and Troubles' (1625)]

BROWNE, Sir Thomas (1605–1682)
We all labour against our own cure, for death is the cure of all diseases.

[*Religio Medici* (1643)]

CHEKHOV, Anton (1860–1904)
If many remedies are suggested for a disease, that means the disease is incurable.

[*The Cherry Orchard* (1904)]

DAVIES, Robertson (1913–)
Not to be healthy ... is one of the few sins that modern society is willing to recognise and condemn.

[*The Cunning Man* (1994)]

EMERSON, Ralph Waldo (1803–1882)
A person seldom falls sick, but the bystanders are animated with a faint hope that he will die.

[*Conduct of Life* (1860)]

GALBRAITH, J.K. (1908–)
Much of the world's work, it has been

said, is done by men who do not feel quite well. Marx is a case in point.

[*The Age of Uncertainty*]

HELLER, Joseph (1923–)
Hungry Joe collected lists of fatal diseases and arranged them in alphabetical order so that he could put his finger without delay on any one he wanted to worry about.

[*Catch-22* (1961)]

HIPPOCRATES (c. 460–357 BC)
For extreme illnesses extreme remedies are most fitting.

[*Aphorisms*]

MCAULEY, James (1917–1976)
[After his first cancer operation; to a friend]
Well, better a semi-colon than a full stop!

[In Coleman, *The Heart of James McAuley* (1980)]

PERELMAN, S.J. (1904–1979)
I've got Bright's disease and he's got mine.

[Attr.]

SONTAG, Susan (1933–)
Illness is the night-side of life, a more onerous citizenship. Everyone who is born holds dual citizenship, in the kingdom of the well and in the kingdom of the sick. Although we all prefer to use only the good passport, sooner or later each of us is obliged, at least for a spell, to identify ourselves as citizens of that other place.

[*Illness as Metaphor* (1978)]

STACPOOLE, H. de Vere (1863–1951)
In home-sickness you must keep moving – it is the only disease that does not require rest.

[*The Bourgeois* (1901)]

STEVENSON, Robert Louis (1850–1894)
Even if the doctor does not give you a year, even if he hesitates about a month, make one brave push and see

what can be accomplished in a week.

[*Virginibus Puerisque* (1881)]

SWIFT, Jonathan (1667–1745)
We are so fond of one another, because our ailments are the same.

[*Journal to Stella*, 1711]

See HEALTH; MEDICINE

IMAGINATION

BLAKE, William (1757–1827)
What is now proved was once only imagin'd.

['Proverbs of Hell', (c. 1793)]

EINSTEIN, Albert (1879–1955)
Imagination is more important than knowledge.

[*On Science*]

ELIOT, George (1819–1880)
He said he should prefer not to know the sources of the Nile, and that there should be some unknown regions preserved as hunting-grounds for the poetic imagination.

[*Middlemarch* (1872)]

JOUBERT, Joseph (1754–1824)
Imagination is the eye of the soul.

[Attr.]

KEATS, John (1795–1821)
I am certain of nothing but of the holiness of the Heart's affections and the truth of Imagination – What the imagination seizes as Beauty must be truth – whether it existed before or not.

[Letter to Benjamin Bailey, 1817]

MACAULAY, Lord (1800–1859)
His imagination resembled the wings of an ostrich. It enabled him to run, though not to soar.

['John Dryden' (1843)]

ROBINSON, Roland (1912–1992)
Where does imagination start but from primeval images in man's barbaric heart?

['Mopoke']

STEAD, Christina (1902–1983)
I don't know what imagination is, if not an unpruned, tangled kind of memory.

[*Letty Fox: Her Luck* (1946)]

IMMORTALITY

ALLEN, Woody (1935–)
I don't want to achieve immortality through my work ... I want to achieve it by not dying.

[Attr.]

BECKETT, Samuel (1906–1989)
Clov: Do you believe in the life to come?
Hamm: Mine was always that.

[*Endgame* (1958)]

BUTLER, Bishop Joseph (1692–1752)
That which is the foundation of all our hopes and of all our fears; all our hopes and fears which are of any consideration: I mean a Future Life.

[*The Analogy of Religion* (1736)]

DOSTOEVSKY, Fyodor (1821–1881)
If you were to destroy in mankind the belief in immortality, not only love but every living force maintaining the life of the world would at once dry up. Moreover, nothing then would be immoral, everything would be lawful, even cannibalism.

[*The Brothers Karamazov* (1879–1880)]

EMERSON, Ralph Waldo (1803–1882)
Other world! There is no other world! Here or nowhere is the whole fact.

['Natural Religion']

ERTZ, Susan (1894–1985)
Someone has somewhere commented on the fact that millions long for immortality who don't know what to do with themselves on a rainy Sunday afternoon.

[*Anger in the Sky* (1943)]

HAZLITT, William (1778–1830)
No young man believes he shall ever die.

['On the Feeling of Immortality in Youth' (1827)]

HELLER, Joseph (1923–)
He had decided to live forever or die in the attempt.

[*Catch-22* (1961)]

PINDAR (518–438 BC)
Strive not, my soul, for an immortal life, but make the most of what is possible.

[*Pythian Odes*]

PLATO (c. 429–347 BC)
Let us be persuaded ... to consider that the soul is immortal and capable of enduring all evil and all good, and so we shall always hold to the upward way and pursue justice with wisdom.

[*Republic*]

SPINOZA, Baruch (1632–1677)
Sentimus experimurque, nos aeternos esse.
We feel and know by experience that we are eternal.

[*Ethics* (1677)]

STASSINOPOULOS, Arianna (1950–)
Our current obsession with creativity is the result of our continued striving for immortality in an era when most people no longer believe in an afterlife.

[*The Female Woman* (1973)]

THOREAU, Henry (1817–1862)
[On being asked his opinion of the hereafter]
One world at a time.

[Attr.]

UPANISHADS (c. 800–300 BC)
When all desires that dwell within the human heart are cast away, then a mortal becomes immortal and here he attaineth to Brahman.

[*Katha Upanishad*]

VAUGHAN, Henry (1622–1695)
My Soul, there is a countrie
Far beyond the stars,
Where stands a winged Sentry
All skilfull in the wars;
There above noise and danger,

Sweet peace sits crown'd with smiles,
And one born in a Manger
Commands the Beauteous files.

[*Silex Scintillans* (1655)]

INCOME

AUSTEN, Jane (1775–1817)
An annuity is a very serious business;
it comes over and over every year, and
there is no getting rid of it.

[*Sense and Sensibility* (1811)]

A large income is the best recipe for
happiness I ever heard of. It certainly
may secure all the myrtle and turkey
part of it.

[*Mansfield Park* (1814)]

DICKENS, Charles (1812–1870)
Annual income twenty pounds, annual
expenditure nineteen nineteen six,
result happiness. Annual income
twenty pounds, annual expenditure
twenty pounds ought and six, result
misery.

[*David Copperfield* (1850)]

MORLEY, John
For the average European a job was
an income, for the average Japanese it
was a home.

[*Pictures From the Water Trade – An
Englishman in Japan*]

PARKINSON, C. Northcote (1909–1993)
Expenditure rises to meet income.

[Attr.]

SAKI (1870–1916)
All decent people live beyond their
incomes nowadays, and those who
aren't respectable live beyond other
people's. A few gifted individuals
manage to do both.

[*The Chronicles of Clovis* (1911)]

SAUNDERS, Ernest (1935–)
I was on a basic £100,000 a year. You
don't make many savings on that.

[*The Observer*, 1987]

SHAKESPEARE, William (1564–1616)
Remuneration! O, that's the Latin
word for three farthings.

[*Love's Labour Lost*, III.i]

SMITH, Logan Pearsall (1865–1946)
There are few sorrows, however
poignant, in which a good income is of
no avail.

[*Afterthoughts* (1931)]

See MONEY AND WEALTH

INDECISION

ASQUITH, Margot (1864–1945)
[Of Sir Stafford Cripps]
He has a brilliant mind until he makes
it up.

[In *The Wit of the Asquiths*]

BEVAN, Aneurin (1897–1960)
We know what happens to people who
stay in the middle of the road. They
get run over.

[*The Observer*, 1953]

THE BIBLE (King James Version)
How long halt ye between two
opinions?

[*I Kings*, 18:21]

JAMES, William (1842–1910)
There is no more miserable human
being than one in whom nothing is
habitual but indecision.

[*Principles of Psychology* (1890)]

NASH, Ogden (1902–1971)
If I could but spot a conclusion, I
should race to it.

['All, All Are Gone, The Old Familiar
Quotations' (1952)]

SMITH, Sir Cyril (1928–)
If the fence is strong enough I'll sit on
it.

[*The Observer*, 1974]

INDEPENDENCE

AESOP (6th century BC)
The gods help those who help
themselves.

['Hercules and the Waggoner']

EMERSON, Ralph Waldo (1803–1882)
It is easy in the world to live after the
world's opinion; it is easy in solitude
after our own; but the great man is he
who, in the midst of the crowd, keeps
with perfect sweetness the independence of solitude.
['Self-Reliance' (1841)]

GIBBON, Edward (1737–1794)
The first of earthly blessings, – indepen-
dence.
[Memoirs of My Life and Writings (1796)]

IBSEN, Henrik (1828–1906)
The strongest man in the world is the
man who stands alone.
[An Enemy of the People (1882)]

MARRYAT, Frederick (1792–1848)
I think it much better that ... every
man paddle his own canoe.
[Settlers in Canada (1844)]

SCOTT, Sir Walter (1771–1832)
[Refusing offers of help following his
bankruptcy in 1826]
No! this right hand shall work it all off!
[In Cockburn, Memorials of His Time (1856)]

THOREAU, Henry (1817–1862)
I would rather sit on a pumpkin and
have it all to myself than be crowded
on a velvet cushion.
[Walden (1854)]

INDUSTRIAL RELATIONS

ANONYMOUS
In his chamber, weak and dying,
While the Norman Baron lay,
Loud, without, his men were crying,
'Shorter hours and better pay.'
['A Strike among the Poets']

COOK, A.J. (1885–1931)
Not a penny off the pay, not a minute
on the day.
[Speech, 1926]

FEATHER, Vic, Baron (1906–1976)
Industrial relations are like sexual
relations. It's better between two
consenting parties.
[Guardian Weekly, 1976]

KEYNES, John Maynard (1883–1946)
There are the Trade Unionists, once
the oppressed, now the tyrants, whose
selfish and sectional pretensions need
to be bravely opposed.
['Liberalism and Labour' (1926)]

SHINWELL, Emanuel (1884–1986)
We know that you, the organized
workers of the country, are our friends
... As for the rest, they do not matter a
tinker's curse.
[Speech, 1947]

WILSON, Harold (1916–1995)
We are redefining and we are restating
our socialism in terms of the scientific
revolution ... the Britain that is going
to be forged in the white heat of this
revolution will be no place for
restrictive practices or out-dated
methods on either side of industry.
[Speech, 1963]

One man's wage rise is another man's
price increase.
[The Observer, 1970]

INGRATITUDE

CHILLINGWORTH, William (1602–1644)
I once knew a man out of courtesy
help a lame dog over a stile, and he
for requital bit his fingers.
[The Religion of Protestants (1637)]

GARCÍA MÁRQUEZ, Gabriel (1928–)
La ingratitud humana no tiene limites.
There are no limits to human ingrati-
tude.
[No-one Writes to the Colonel (1961)]

HUXLEY, Aldous (1894–1963)
Most human beings have an almost
infinite capacity for taking things for
granted.
[Themes and Variations (1950)]

**LA ROCHEFOUCAULD, Duc de
(1613–1680)**
Le trop grand empressement qu'on a de
s'acquitter d'une obligation est une
espèce d'ingratitude.

INSULTS

Over-great haste to repay an obligation is a form of ingratitude.

[*Maximes* (1678)]

LOUIS XIV (1638–1715)
Toutes les fois que je donne une place vacante, je fais cent mécontents et un ingrat.
Every time I make an appointment, I make a hundred men discontented and one ungrateful.

[In Voltaire, *Siècle de Louis XIV*]

SHAKESPEARE, William (1564–1616)
Blow, blow, thou winter wind,
Thou art not so unkind
As man's ingratitude ...
Thy tooth is not so keen,

Freeze, freeze, thou bitter sky,
That dost not bite so nigh
As benefits forgot.

[*As You Like It*, II.vii]

INSULTS

BRAHMS, Johannes (1833–1897)
[Said on leaving a gathering of friends]
If there is anyone here whom I have not insulted, I beg his pardon.

[Attr.]

CHESTERFIELD, Lord (1694–1773)
An injury is much sooner forgotten than an insult.

[Letter to his son, 1746]

CORNEILLE, Pierre (1606–1684)
He who allows himself to be insulted, deserves to be.

[*Héraclius* (1646)]

GILBERT, W.S. (1836–1911)
I shouldn't be sufficiently degraded in my own estimation unless I was insulted with a very considerable bribe.

[*The Mikado* (1885)]

GROSSMITH, George and **Weedon**
I am a poor man, but I would gladly give ten shillings to find out who sent me the insulting Christmas card I received this morning.

[*Diary of a Nobody* (1894)]

SHERIDAN, Richard Brinsley (1751–1816)
If it is abuse, – why one is always sure to hear of it from one damned good-natured friend or another!

[*The Critic* (1779)]

THURBER, James (1894–1961)
A man should not insult his wife publicly, at parties. He should insult her in the privacy of the home.

[*Thurber Country* (1953)]

INTELLIGENCE

BALDWIN, Stanley (1867–1947)
The intelligent are to the intelligentsia what a gentleman is to a gent.

[Attr.]

BOGARDE, Dirk (1921–)
I'm not very clever, but I'm quite intelligent.

[Attr.]

BRENAN, Gerald (1894–1987)
Intellectuals are people who believe that ideas are of more importance than values. That is to say, their own ideas and other people's values.

[*Thoughts in a Dry Season* (1978)]

DIDEROT, Denis (1713–1784)
[A retort which comes to mind too late]
L'esprit de l'escalier.
Staircase wit.

[*Paradoxe sur le Comédien* (c. 1778)]

FREUD, Sigmund (1856–1939)
The voice of the intellect is a soft one, but it does not rest till it has gained a hearing.

[*The Future of an Illusion*]

FRISCH, Max (1911–1991)
Wieso haben die Intellektuellen, wenn sie scharenweise zusammenkommen, unweigerlich etwas Komisches?
Why is there invariably something comic about intellectuals when they meet together in crowds?

[*Diary*, 1948]

GOULBURN, Edward (1818–1897)
Let the scintillations of your wit be like
the coruscations of summer lightning,
lambent but innocuous.

[Sermon at Rugby]

KEATS, John (1795–1821)
The only means of strengthening one's
intellect is to make up one's mind
about nothing – to let the mind be a
thoroughfare for all thoughts. Not a
select party.

[Letter to George and Georgiana Keats, 1819]

**LA ROCHEFOUCAULD, Duc de
(1613–1680)**
*C'est une grande habileté que de savoir
cacher son habileté.*
The height of cleverness is to be able
to conceal it.

[Maximes (1678)]

MACAULAY, Lord (1800–1859)
The highest intellects, like the tops of
mountains, are the first to catch and to
reflect the dawn.

['Sir James Mackintosh' (1843)]

MANN, Thomas (1875–1955)
Every intellectual attitude is latently
political.

[The Observer, 1974]

NIETZSCHE, Friedrich (1844–1900)
*Der Witz ist das Epigramm auf dem Tod
eines Gefühls.*
Wit is the epigram for the death of an
emotion.

[Human, All too Human (1886)]

PASCAL, Blaise (1623–1662)
*A mesure qu'on a plus d'esprit, on
trouve qu'il y a plus d'hommes
originaux. Les gens du commun ne
trouvent point de différence entre les
hommes.*
The more intelligence one has the
more people one finds original.
Commonplace people see no
difference between men.

[Pensées (1670)]

SCHOPENHAUER, Arthur (1788–1860)
Intellect is invisible to the man who
has none.

[Aphorismen zur Lebensweisheit]

SHAKESPEARE, William (1564–1616)
Brevity is the soul of wit.

[Hamlet, II.ii]

Look, he's winding up the watch of his
wit; by and by it will strike.

[The Tempest, II.i]

This fellow is wise enough to play the
fool;
And to do that well craves a kind of
wit.

[Twelfth Night, III.i]

SU TUNG-P'O (Su Shih) (1036–1101)
Families, when a child is born
Want it to be intelligent.
I, through intelligence,
Having wrecked my whole life,
Only hope the baby will prove
Ignorant and stupid.
Then he will crown a tranquil life
By becoming a Cabinet Minister.

[In Waley, 170 Chinese Poems]

WHITEHEAD, A.N. (1861–1947)
Intelligence is quickness to apprehend
as distinct from ability, which is capacity to act wisely on the thing
apprehended.

[Dialogues (1954)]

INVENTION

EDISON, Thomas Alva (1847–1931)
To invent, you need a good imagination and a pile of junk.

[Attr.]

EMERSON, Ralph Waldo (1803–1882)
Invention breeds invention.

[Society and Solitude (1870)]

FRANKLIN, Benjamin (1706–1790)
[On being asked the use of a new
invention]
What is the use of a new-born child?

[In Parton, Life and Times of Benjamin
Franklin (1864)]

PROVERB
Necessity is the mother of invention.

VOLTAIRE (1694–1778)
The most amazing and effective inventions are not those which do most honour to the human genius.
[*Lettres philosophiques* (1734)]

IRELAND

ALLINGHAM, William (1824–1889)
Not men and women in an Irish street
But Catholics and Protestants you meet.
[Attr.]

BATES, Daisy May (1863–1951)
There are a few fortunate races that have been endowed with cheerfulness as their main characteristic, the Australian Aborigine and the Irish being among these.
[*The Passing of the Aborigines ...* (1938)]

BEHAN, Brendan (1923–1964)
Pat: He was an Anglo-Irishman.
Meg: In the blessed name of God, what's that?
Pat: A Protestant with a horse.
[*The Hostage* (1958)]

Other people have a nationality. The Irish and the Jews have a psychosis.
[*Richard's Cork Leg* (1972)]

CHILD, Lydia M. (1802–1880)
Not in vain is Ireland pouring itself all over the earth ... The Irish, with their glowing hearts and reverent credulity, are needed in this cold age of intellect and skepticism.
[*Letters from New York* (1842)]

CLINTON, Bill (1946–)
[On the IRA, shortly after they resumed their campaign of violence in 1996]
We must not let the men of the past ruin the future of the children of Northern Ireland.
[*Daily Mail*, 1996]

COLLINS, Michael (1890–1922)
[Said on signing the agreement with Great Britain, 1921, that established the Irish Free State; he was assassinated some months later]
Think – what have I got for Ireland? Something which she has wanted these past seven hundred years. Will anyone be satisfied at the bargain? Will anyone? I tell you this – early this morning I signed my death warrant. I thought at the time how odd, how ridiculous – a bullet may just as well have done the job five years ago.
[Letter to John O'Kane, 1921]

DE VALERA, Eamon (1882–1975)
Whenever I wanted to know what the Irish people wanted, I had only to examine my own heart and it told me straight off what the Irish people wanted.
[Dáil Éireann, 1922]

... a land whose countryside would be bright with cosy homesteads, whose fields and villages would be joyous with the sounds of industry, with the romping of sturdy children, the contests of athletic youths and the laughter of comely maidens, whose firesides would be forums for the wisdom of serene old age.
[Radio broadcast, 1943]

DISRAELI, Benjamin (1804–1881)
A starving population, an absentee aristocracy, and an alien Church, and in addition the weakest executive in the world. That is the Irish question.
[Speech, 1844]

DOYLE, Roddy (1958–)
The Irish are the niggers of Europe ... An' Dubliners are the niggers of Ireland ... An' the northside Dubliners are the niggers o' Dublin – Say it loud. I'm black an' I'm proud.
[*The Commitments* (1987)]

GOGARTY, Oliver St John (1878–1957)
Politics is the chloroform of the Irish people, or rather the hashish.
[*As I Was Going Down Sackville Street* (1937)]

HEWITT, John
The names of a land show the heart of
 the race;
They move on the tongue like the lilt
 of a song.
You say the name and I see the place –
Drumbo, Dungannon, or Annalong.
Barony, townland, we cannot go
 wrong.
['Ulster Names']

THE IRISH CONSTITUTION
The national territory consists of the
whole island of Ireland, its islands and
the territorial seas.

JOHNSON, Samuel (1709-1784)
The Irish are a fair people; – they never
speak well of one another.
[In Boswell, *The Life of Samuel Johnson*
(1791)]

JOYCE, James (1882-1941)
Ireland is the old sow that eats her
farrow.
[*A Portrait of the Artist as a Young Man* (1916)]

My intention was to write a chapter of
the moral history of my country and I
chose Dublin for the scene because
that city seemed to me the centre of
paralysis.
[Letter to Grant Richards, 1905]

LEONARD, Hugh (1926–)
The problem with Ireland is that it's a
country full of genius, but with absolutely no talent.
[Interview in *The Times*, 1977]

MAJOR, John (1943–)
[On the search for peace in Northern
Ireland after the end of the IRA
ceasefire in February 1996]
If we are pushed back, we will start
again. If we are pushed back, we will
start again. If we are pushed back a
third time we will start again.
[*The Observer Review*, 1996]

MORRISON, Danny (1950–)
Who here really believes that we can
win the war through the ballot box?

But will anyone here object if with a
ballot box in this hand and an
Armalite in this hand we take power in
Ireland.
[Provisional Sinn Féin Conference, 1981]

ROBINSON, Mary (1944–)
As the elected choice of the people of
this part of our island I want to extend
the hand of friendship and of love to
both communities in the other part.
[Inaugural speech as President, 1991]

SHAW, George Bernard (1856-1950)
An Irishman's heart is nothing but his
imagination.
[*John Bull's Other Island* (1907)]

If you want to bore an Irishman, play
him an Irish melody, or introduce him
to another Irishman.
[In Holroyd, *Shaw* (1989)]

SMITH, Sydney (1771-1845)
The moment the very name of Ireland
is mentioned, the English seem to bid
adieu to common feeling, common
prudence, and to common sense, and
to act with the barbarity of tyrants,
and the fatuity of idiots.
[*Letters of Peter Plymley* (1807)]

YEATS, W.B. (1865-1939)
Behind Ireland fierce and militant, is
Ireland poetic, passionate, remember-
ing, idyllic, fanciful, and always
patriotic.
['Popular Ballad Poetry of Ireland' (1889)]

[From Yeats's speech on divorce, in
which he stressed the contribution
made by the Protestant minority to the
literary and political life of Ireland]
We against whom you have done this
thing are no petty people. We are one
of the great stocks of Europe. We are
the people of Burke; we are the people
of Grattan; we are the people of Swift,
the people of Emmett, the people of
Parnell. We have created the most of
the modern literature of this country.
We have created the best of its
political intelligence.
[Speech to the Senate, June 1925]

JEALOUSY

MILTON, John (1608–1674)
Nor jealousie
Was understood, the injur'd Lover's
Hell.

[*Paradise Lost* (1667)]

SAGAN, Françoise (1935–)
To jealousy nothing is more frightful
than laughter.

[Attr.]

SHAKESPEARE, William (1564–1616)
O, beware, my lord, of jealousy;
It is the green-ey'd monster which
doth mock
The meat it feeds on.

[*Othello*, III.iii]

Trifles light as air
Are to the jealous confirmations
strong
As proofs of holy writ.

[*Othello*, III.iii]

Jealous souls will not be answer'd so;
They are not ever jealous for the
cause,
But jealous for they are jealous.

[*Othello*, III.iv]

WELLS, H.G. (1866–1946)
Moral indignation is jealousy with a
halo.

[*The Wife of Sir Isaac Harman* (1914)]

THE JEWS

BLUE, Rabbi Lionel (1930–)
There is always a danger in Judaism of
seeing history as a sort of poker game
played between Jews and God, in
which the presence of others is noted
but not given much importance.

[*The Observer*, 1982]

DRYDEN, John (1631–1700)
The Jews, a headstrong, moody,
murmuring race
As ever tried the extent and stretch
of grace,
God's pampered people, whom,
debauched with ease,

No king could govern nor no God
could please.

[*Absalom and Achitophel* (1681)]

HEINE, Heinrich (1797–1856)
It is extremely difficult for a Jew to be
converted, for how can he bring
himself to believe in the divinity of –
another Jew?

[Attr.]

JOHNSON, Paul (1928–)
For me this is a vital litmus test: no
intellectual society can flourish where
a Jew feels even slightly uneasy.

[*The Sunday Times Magazine*, 1977]

LAWRENCE, D.H. (1885–1930)
The very best that is in the Jewish
blood: a faculty for pure disinterestedness, and warm, physically
warm love, that seems to make the
corpuscles of the blood glow.

[*Kangaroo* (1923)]

MARX, Groucho (1895–1977)
[When excluded, on racial grounds,
from a beach club]
Since my daughter is only half-Jewish,
could she go into the water up to her
knees?

[*The Observer*, 1977]

MILLER, Jonathan (1934–)
I'm not really a Jew; just Jew-ish, not
the whole hog.

[*Beyond the Fringe* (1961)]

ROTH, Philip (1933–)
A Jewish man with parents alive is a
fifteen-year-old boy, and will remain a
fifteen-year-old boy until *they die*.

[*Portnoy's Complaint* (1969)]

SHAKESPEARE, William (1564–1616)
Hath not a Jew eyes? Hath not a Jew
hands, organs, dimensions, senses,
affections, passions, fed with the same
food, hurt with the same weapons,
subject to the same diseases, healed
by the same means, warmed and
cooled by the same winter and
summer, as a Christian is? If you prick

us, do we not bleed? If you tickle us, do we not laugh? If you poison us, do we not die? And if you wrong us, shall we not revenge? If we are like you in the rest, we will resemble you in that.

[*The Merchant of Venice*, III.i]

STEIN, Gertrude (1874–1946)
The Jews have produced only three originative geniuses: Christ, Spinoza, and myself.

[In Mellow, *Charmed Circle* (1974)]

USTINOV, Sir Peter (1921–)
I believe that the Jews have made a contribution to the human condition out of all proportion to their numbers: I believe them to be an immense people. Not only have they supplied the world with two leaders of the stature of Jesus Christ and Karl Marx, but they have even indulged in the luxury of following neither one nor the other.

[*Dear Me* (1977)]

ZANGWILL, Israel (1864–1926)
No Jew was ever fool enough to turn Christian unless he was a clever man.

[*Children of the Ghetto* (1892)]

See RACE

JUDGEMENT

AUGUSTINE, Saint (354–430)
Securus iudicat orbis terrarum.
The judgement of the world is sure.

[*Contra Epistolam Parmeniani*]

THE BIBLE (King James Version)
Judge not, that ye be not judged.

[*Matthew*, 7:1]

By their fruits ye shall know them.

[*Matthew*, 7:20]

He that is without sin among you, let him first cast a stone at her.

[*Luke*, 8:7]

CAMUS, Albert (1913–1960)
N'attendez pas le jugement dernier. Il a lieu tous les jours.
Don't wait for the Last Judgement. It is taking place every day.

[*The Fall* (1956)]

COMPTON-BURNETT, Dame Ivy (1884–1969)
Appearances are not held to be a clue to the truth. But we seem to have no other.

[*Manservant and Maidservant* (1947)]

COWPER, William (1731–1800)
Judgment drunk, and brib'd to lose his way,
Winks hard, and talks of darkness at noon-day.

['The Progress of Error' (1782)]

EDGEWORTH, Maria (1767–1849)
We cannot judge either of the feelings or of the characters of men with perfect accuracy, from their actions or their appearance in public; it is from their careless conversations, their half-finished sentences, that we may hope with the greatest probability of success to discover their real character.

[*Castle Rackrent* (1800)]

MONTAIGNE, Michel de (1533–1592)
It is a dangerous and serious presumption, and argues an absurd temerity, to condemn what we do not understand.

[*Essais* (1680)]

SHAKESPEARE, William (1564–1616)
What judgment shall I dread, doing no wrong?

[*The Merchant of Venice*, IV.i]

JUSTICE

BENNETT, Arnold (1867–1931)
The price of justice is eternal publicity.

[*Things That Have Interested Me*]

BINGHAM, Sir Thomas (1933–)
[Discussing the rising costs of going to law]

We cannot for ever be content to acknowledge that in England justice is open to all – like the Ritz Hotel.

[*Independent on Sunday*, 1994]

BLACKSTONE, Sir William (1723–1780)
It is better that ten guilty persons escape than one innocent suffer.

[*Commentaries on the Laws of England* (1765–1769)]

BOWEN, Lord (1835–1894)
The rain it raineth on the just
And also on the unjust fella:
But chiefly on the just, because
The unjust steals the just's umbrella.

[In Sichel, *Sands of Time* (1923)]

CONFUCIUS (c. 550–c. 478 BC)
Recompense injury with justice, and recompense kindness with kindness.

[*Analects*]

DÜRRENMATT, Friedrich (1921–1990)
Die Gerechtigkeit ist etwas Fürchterliches.
Justice is something terrible.

[*Romulus the Great* (1964)]

FERDINAND I, Emperor (1503–1564)
Fiat justitia, et pereat mundus.
Let there be justice though the world perish.

[Attr.]

FIELDING, Henry (1707–1754)
Thwackum was for doing justice, and leaving mercy to Heaven.

[*Tom Jones* (1749)]

FRANCE, Anatole (1844–1924)
Désarmer les forts et armer les faibles ce serait changer l'ordre social que j'ai mission de conserver. La justice est la sanction des injustices établies.
To disarm the strong and arm the weak would be to change a social order which I have been commissioned to preserve. Justice is the means whereby established injustices are sanctioned.

[*Crainquebille* (1904)]

HEWART, Gordon (1870–1943)
It is not merely of some importance but is of fundamental importance that justice should not only be done, but should manifestly and undoubtedly be seen to be done.

[Rex v. Sussex Justices, 1923]

JUNIUS (1769–1772)
The injustice done to an individual is sometimes of service to the public.

[*Letters* (1769–1771)]

JUSTINIAN, Emperor (c. 482–565)
Justitia est constans et perpetua voluntas ius suum cuique tribuens.
Justice is the constant and perpetual wish to give to every one his due.

[*Institutes*]

KELLY, Ned (1855–1880)
There never was such a thing as justice in the English laws but any amount of injustice to be had.

[In *Overland*, 1981]

KIPLING, Rudyard (1865–1936)
The Saxon is not like us Normans. His
    manners are not so polite.
But he never means anything serious
    till he talks about justice and right,
When he stands like an ox in the
    furrow with his sullen set eyes on
    your own,
And grumbles, 'This isn't fair dealing,'
    my son, leave the Saxon alone.

['Norman and Saxon' (1911)]

LA ROCHEFOUCAULD, Duc de (1613–1680)
L'amour de la justice n'est, en la plupart des hommes, que la crainte de souffrir l'injustice.
The love of justice in most men is no more than the fear of suffering injustice.

[*Maximes* (1678)]

LINCOLN, Abraham (1809–1865)
The probability that we may fail in the struggle ought not to deter us from the support of a cause we believe to be just.

[Speech, 1859]

MAGNA CARTA (1215)
Nulli vendemus, nulli negabimus aut
differemus, rectum aut justitiam.
To no one will we sell, to no one will
we deny, or delay, right or justice.
[Clause 40]

MANSFIELD, Earl of (1705–1793)
[Advice given to a new colonial
governor]
Consider what you think justice
requires, and decide accordingly. But
never give your reasons; for your
judgement will probably be right, but
your reasons will certainly be wrong.
[In Campbell, *Lives of the Chief Justices* (1849)]

MILTON, John (1608–1674)
Yet I shall temper so
Justice with Mercie.
[*Paradise Lost* (1667)]

PETERS, Ellis (1913–1995)
'It may well be,' said Cadfael, 'that our
justice sees as in a mirror image, left
where right should be, evil reflected
back as good, good as evil, your angel
as her devil. But God's justice, if it
makes no haste, makes no mistakes.'
[*The Potter's Field* (1989)]

ROUX, Joseph (1834–1886)
We love justice greatly, and just men

but little.
[*Meditations of a Parish Priest* (1886)]

SHAKESPEARE, William (1564–1616)
What stronger breastplate than a heart
untainted?
Thrice is he arm'd that hath his quarrel
just;
And he but naked, though lock'd up in
steel,
Whose conscience with injustice is
corrupted.
[*Henry VI, Part 2*, III.ii]

SHIRLEY, James (1596–1666)
Only the actions of the just
Smell sweet, and blossom in their
dust.
[*The Contention of Ajax and Ulysses* (1659)]

STOPPARD, Tom (1937–)
This is a British murder inquiry and
some degree of justice must be seen to
be more or less done.
[*Jumpers* (1972)]

WILDE, Oscar (1854–1900)
For Man's grim Justice goes its way,
And will not swerve aside:
It slays the weak, it slays the strong,
It has a deadly stride.
[*The Ballad of Reading Gaol* (1898)]

See LAW

KINDNESS

BIRLEY, Mark
You never forget people who were kind to you when you were young.
[*The Observer*, 1989]

CAMUS, Albert (1913–1960)
Ils savaient maintenant que s'il est une chose qu'on puisse désirer toujours et obtenir quelquefois, c'est la tendresse humaine.
They now knew that if there is one thing which can always be desired and sometimes obtained, it is human tenderness.
[*The Plague* (1947)]

CONFUCIUS (c. 550–c. 478 BC)
Recompense injury with justice, and recompense kindness with kindness.
[*Analects*]

DAVIES, William Henry (1871–1940)
I love thee for a heart that's kind –
Not for the knowledge in thy mind.
['Sweet Stay-at-Home' (1913)]

GIDE, André (1869–1951)
True kindness presupposes the faculty of imagining as one's own the suffering and joy of others.
[Attr.]

JACKSON, F.J. Foakes (1855–1941)
[Advice given to a new don at Jesus College, Cambridge]
It's no use trying to be *clever* – we are all clever here; just try to be *kind* – a little kind.
[In Benson's *Commonplace Book*]

JOHNSON, Samuel (1709–1784)
Always, Sir, set a high value on spontaneous kindness. He whose inclination prompts him to cultivate your friendship of his own accord, will love you more than one whom you have been at pains to attach to you.
[In Boswell, *The Life of Samuel Johnson* (1791)]

MARSHALL, Alan (1911–1968)
Beware of people you've been kind to.
[Remark to John Morrison]

SHAKESPEARE, William (1564–1616)
I must be cruel, only to be kind.
[*Hamlet*, III.iv]

WILCOX, Ella Wheeler (1850–1919)
So many gods, so many creeds,
So many paths that wind and wind,
While just the art of being kind
Is all the sad world needs.
['The World's Need' (1917)]

WILLIAMS, Tennessee (1911–1983)
I have always depended on the kindness of strangers.
[*A Streetcar Named Desire* (1947)]

KNOWLEDGE

ADAMS, Henry (1838–1918)
They know enough who know how to learn.
[*The Education of Henry Adams* (1918)]

ALEXANDER THE GREAT (356–323 BC)
I would rather excel in the knowledge of what is excellent, than in the extent of my power.
[In Plutarch, *Lives*, 'Alexander']

BACON, Francis (1561–1626)
Knowledge itself is power.
['Of Heresies' (1597)]

BEECHING, Rev. H.C. (1859–1919)
First come I; my name is Jowett.
There's no knowledge but I know it.
I am Master of this college:
What I don't know isn't knowledge.
['The Masque of Balliol' (late 1870s)]

THE BIBLE (King James Version)
He that increaseth knowledge increaseth sorrow.
[*Ecclesiastes*, 1:18]

CLOUGH, Arthur Hugh (1819–1861)
Grace is given of God, but knowledge is bought in the market.
[*The Bothie of Tober-na-Vuolich* (1848)]

HOLMES, Oliver Wendell (1809–1894)
It is the province of knowledge to speak and it is the privilege of wisdom to listen.

[*The Poet at the Breakfast-Table* (1872)]

HUXLEY, T.H. (1825–1895)
The saying that a little knowledge is a dangerous thing is, to my mind, a very dangerous adage. If knowledge is real and genuine, I do not believe that it is other than a very valuable possession however infinitesimal its quantity may be. Indeed, if a little knowledge is dangerous, where is the man who has so much as to be out of danger?

[*Science and Culture* (1877)]

JOAD, C.E.M. (1891–1953)
There was never an age in which useless knowledge was more important than in ours.

[*The Observer*, 1951]

JOHNSON, Samuel (1709–1784)
Integrity without knowledge is weak and useless, and knowledge without integrity is dangerous and dreadful.

[*Rasselas* (1759)]

If it rained knowledge, I'd hold out my hand; but I would not give myself the trouble to go in quest of it.

[In Boswell, *The Life of Samuel Johnson* (1791)]

LINKLATER, Eric (1899–1974)
For the scientific acquisition of knowledge is almost as tedious as a routine acquisition of wealth.

[*White Man's Saga*]

MACAULAY, Lord (1800–1859)
Knowledge advances by steps, and not by leaps.

['History' (1828)]

MILTON, John (1608–1674)
The first and wisest of them all profess'd
To know this onely, that he nothing knew.

[*Paradise Regained* (1671)]

MUMFORD, Ethel (1878–1940)
Knowledge is power if you know it about the right person.

[In Cowan, *The Wit of Women*]

POPPER, Sir Karl (1902–1994)
Our knowledge can only be finite, while our ignorance must necessarily be infinite.

[*Conjectures and Refutations* (1963)]

SHARPE, Tom (1928–)
His had been an intellectual decision founded on his conviction that if a little knowledge was a dangerous thing, a lot was lethal.

[*Porterhouse Blue* (1974)]

SHERIDAN, Richard Brinsley (1751–1816)
Madam, a circulating library in a town is an ever-green tree of diabolical knowledge! – It blossoms through the year! – And depend on it, Mrs Malaprop, that they who are so fond of handling the leaves, will long for the fruit at last.

[*The Rivals* (1775)]

STERNE, Laurence (1713–1768)
The desire of knowledge, like the thirst of riches, increases ever with the acquisition of it.

[*Tristram Shandy* (1767)]

See **LEARNING; WISDOM**

LANGUAGE

CHURCHILL, Sir Winston (1874–1965)
[Marginal comment on a document]
This is the sort of English up with
which I will not put.

[In Gowers, *Plain Words* (1948)]

Everybody has a right to pronounce
foreign names as he chooses.

[*The Observer*, 1951]

DALY, Mary (1928–)
The liberation of language is rooted in
the liberation of ourselves.

[*Beyond God The Father, Toward a Philosophy
of Women's Liberation* (1973)]

DAY, Clarence Shepard (1874–1935)
Imagine the Lord talking French! Aside
from a few odd words in Hebrew, I
took it completely for granted that God
had never spoken anything but the
most dignified English.

[*Life with Father* (1935)]

DICKENS, Charles (1812–1870)
There was no light nonsense about
Miss Blimber ... She was dry and sandy
with working in the graves of deceased languages. None of your live
languages for Miss Blimber. They must
be dead – stone dead – and then Miss
Blimber dug them up like a Ghoul.

[*Dombey and Son* (1848)]

DOBBS, Kildare (1923–)
My country is the English language.

[In Galt (ed.), *The Saturday Night Traveller*
(1990)]

DUPPA, Richard (1770–1831)
In language, the ignorant have
prescribed laws to the learned.

[*Maxims* (1830)]

ELIOT, George (1819–1880)
Correct English is the slang of prigs
who write history and essays.

[*Middlemarch* (1872)]

EMERSON, Ralph Waldo (1803–1882)
Language is fossil poetry.

['The Poet' (1844)]

FRANKLIN, Benjamin (1706–1790)
Write with the learned, pronounce
with the vulgar.

[*Poor Richard's Almanac* (1738)]

GOETHE (1749–1832)
*Wer fremde Sprachen nicht kennt, weiss
nichts von seiner eigenen.*
Whoever is not acquainted with
foreign languages knows nothing of
his own.

[*On Art and Antiquity* (1827)]

GOLDWYN, Samuel (1882–1974)
Let's have some new clichés.

[*The Observer*, 1948]

JESPERSEN, Otto (1860–1943)
In his whole life man achieves nothing
so great and so wonderful as what he
achieved when he learned to talk.

[*Language* (1904)]

JOHNSON, Samuel (1709–1784)
Language is only the instrument of
science, and words are but the signs of
ideas: I wish, however, that the
instrument might be less apt to decay,
and that signs might be permanent,
like the things which they denote.

[*A Dictionary of the English Language* (1755)]

Language is the dress of thought.

[*The Lives of the Most Eminent English Poets*
(1781)]

I am always sorry when any language
is lost, because languages are the
pedigree of nations.

[In Boswell, *Journal of a Tour to the Hebrides*
(1785)]

LANGLAND, William (c. 1330–c. 1400)
Grammere, that grounde is of alle.

[*The Vision of William Concerning Piers the
Plowman*]

LEVI-STRAUSS, Claude (1908–)
*La langue est une raison humaine qui a
ses raisons, et que l'homme ne connaît
pas.*
Language is a kind of human reason,
which has its own internal logic of

which man knows nothing.

[*The Savage Mind* (1962)]

MACAULAY, Lord (1800–1859)
The English Bible, a book which, if everything else in our language should perish, would alone suffice to show the whole extent of its beauty and power.

['John Dryden' (1843)]

MURROW, Edward R. (1908–1965)
[Of Churchill]
He mobilized the English language and sent it into battle to steady his fellow countrymen and hearten those Europeans upon whom the long dark night of tyranny had descended.

[Broadcast, 1954]

NARAYAN, R. K. (1907–)
English is a very adaptable language. And it's so transparent it can take on the tint of any country.

[Radio conversation, 1968]

SHAW, George Bernard (1856–1950)
The English have no respect for their language, and will not teach their children to speak it ... It is impossible for an Englishman to open his mouth without making some other Englishman hate or despise him.

[*Pygmalion* (1916)]

England and America are two countries separated by the same language.

[*Reader's Digest*, 1942]

SIGISMUND (1368–1437)
[Responding to criticism of his Latin]
I am the Roman Emperor, and am above grammar.

[Attr.]

SPENSER, Edmund (c. 1522–1599)
So now they have made our English tongue, a gallimaufray or hodgepodge of al other speches.

[*The Shepheardes Calender* (1579)]

SULLIVAN, Annie (1866–1936)
Language grows out of life, out of its needs and experiences ... *Language* and *knowledge* are indissolubly connected; they are interdependent.

[Speech, 1894]

TOMLIN, Lily (1939–)
Man invented language in order to satisfy his deep need to complain.

[In Pinker, *The Language Instinct* (1994)]

TUCHOLSKY, Kurt (1890–1935)
Das Englische ist eine einfache, aber schwere Sprache. Es besteht aus lauter Fremdwörtern die falsch ausgesprochen werden.
English is a simple, yet hard language. It consists entirely of foreign words pronounced wrongly.

[*Scraps* (1973)]

TWAIN, Mark (1835–1910)
A verb has a hard time enough of it in this world when it's all together. It's downright inhuman to split it up. But that's just what those Germans do. They take part of a verb and put it down here, like a stake, and they take the other part of it and put it away over yonder like another stake, and between these two limits they just shovel in German.

[Address, 1900]

VOLTAIRE (1694–1778)
Je ne suis pas comme une dame de la cour de Versailles, qui disait: c'est bien dommage que l'aventure de la tour de Babel ait produit la confusion des langues; sans cela tout le monde aurait toujours parlé français.
I am not like a lady at the court of Versailles, who said: 'What a great pity it is that the adventure at the tower of Babel should have produced the confusion of languages; if it weren't for that, everyone would always have spoken French.'

[Letter to Catherine the Great, 1767]

WEINREICH, Professor Max
A language is a dialect that has an army and a navy.

[In Rosten, *The Joys of Yiddish* (1968)]

WHITMAN, Walt (1819–1892)
Language ... is not an abstract
construction of the learned, or of
dictionary-makers, but is something
arising out of the work, needs, ties,
joys, affections, tastes, of long
generations of humanity, and has its
bases broad and low, close to the
ground.

[*November Boughs* (1888)]

WHORF, Benjamin (1897–1941)
We dissect nature along lines laid
down by our native language ...
Language is not simply a reporting
device for experience but a defining
framework for it.

[In Hoyer (ed.), *New Directions in the Study of
Language* (1964)]

See WORDS

LAW

ADAMS, Richard (1846–1908)
You have been acquitted by a Limerick
jury and you may now leave the dock
without any other stain on your
character.

[In Healy, *The Old Munster Circuit*]

BACON, Francis (1561–1626)
One of the Seven was wont to say:
'That laws were like cobwebs; where
the small flies were caught, and the
great brake through.'

[*Apophthegms New and Old* (1624)]

BENTHAM, Jeremy (1748–1832)
Lawyers are the only persons in whom
ignorance of the law is not punished.

[Attr.]

BIERCE, Ambrose (1842–c. 1914)
Lawsuit: A machine which you go into
as a pig and come out as a sausage.

[*The Cynic's Word Book* (1906)]

BRAXFIELD, Lord (1722–1799)
Let them bring me prisoners, and I'll
find them law.

[Attr. by Cockburn]

BURKE, Edmund (1729–1797)
Laws, like houses, lean on one
another.

[*Tracts on the Popery Laws* (1812)]

People crushed by law have no hopes
but from power. If laws are their
enemies, they will be enemies to laws;
and those who have much to hope
and nothing to lose will always be
dangerous more or less.

[Letter to Charles James Fox, 1777]

There is but one law for all, namely,
that law which governs all law – the
law of our Creator, the law of
humanity, justice, equity, the law of
nature, and of nations.

[Speech, 1794]

CARROLL, Lewis (1832–1898)
'I'll be judge, I'll be jury,' said cunning
old Fury:
'I'll try the whole cause, and condemn
you to death.'

[*Alice's Adventures in Wonderland* (1865)]

CHAPMAN, George (c. 1559–c. 1634)
I'me asham'd the law is such an Ass.

[*Revenge for Honour* (1654)]

COETZEE, John Michael (1940–)
All we can do is to uphold the laws, all
of us, without allowing the memory of
justice to fade.

[*Waiting for the Barbarians* (1980)]

DARLING, Charles (1849–1936)
The Law of England is a very strange
one; it cannot compel anyone to tell
the truth. ... But what the Law can do
is to give you seven years for not
telling the truth.

[In Walker-Smith, *Lord Darling*]

DENNING, Lord (1899–)
To every subject of this land, however
powerful, I would use Thomas Fuller's
words over three hundred years ago,
'Be ye never so high, the law is above
you'.

[High Court ruling against the
Attorney-General, 1977]

EMERSON, Ralph Waldo (1803–1882)
Good men must not obey the laws too well.

['Politics' (1844)]

FRANCE, Anatole (1844–1924)
La majestueuse égalité des lois, qui interdit au riche comme au pauvre de coucher sous les ponts, de mendier dans les rues et de voler du pain.
The law, in its majestic equality, forbids the rich as well as the poor to sleep under bridges, to beg in the streets, and to steal bread.

[*Le Lys Rouge* (1894)]

GIRAUDOUX, Jean (1882–1944)
Nous savons tous ici que le droit est la plus puissante des écoles de l'imagination. Jamais poète n'a interprété la nature aussi librement qu'un juriste la réalité.
All of us here know that there is no better way of exercising the imagination than the study of law. No poet has ever interpreted nature as freely as a lawyer interprets reality.

[*La Guerre de Troie n'aura pas lieu (1935)*]

GOETHE (1749–1832)
Wenn man alle Gesetze studieren sollte, so hätte man gar keine Zeit, sie zu übertreten.
If one were to study all the laws, one would have absolutely no time to break them.

['Experience and Life']

GRANT, Ulysses S. (1822–1885)
I know no method to secure the repeal of bad or obnoxious laws so effective as their stringent execution.

[Inaugural Address, 1869]

HOLMES, Hugh (Lord Justice Holmes) (1840–1916)
An elderly pensioner on being sentenced to fifteen years' penal servitude cried 'Ah! my Lord, I'm a very old man, and I'll never do that sentence.' The judge replied 'Well try to do as much of it as you can'.

[In Healy, *The Old Munster Circuit* (1939)]

INGRAMS, Richard (1937–)
I have come to regard the law courts not as a cathedral but rather as a casino.

[*The Guardian*, 1977]

JOHNSON, Samuel (1709–1784)
Johnson observed, that 'he did not care to speak ill of any man behind his back, but he believed the gentleman was an *attorney.*'

[In Boswell, *The Life of Samuel Johnson* (1791)]

KNOX, Philander Chase (1853–1921)
[Reply when Theodore Roosevelt requested legal justification for US acquisition of the Panama Canal Zone]
Oh, Mr President, do not let so great an achievement suffer from any taint of legality.

[Attr.]

LOCKE, John (1632–1704)
Wherever Law ends, Tyranny begins.

[*Second Treatise of Civil Government* (1690)]

MACHIAVELLI (1469–1527)
Li buoni esempi nascano dalla buona educazione; la buona educazione dalle buone leggi: e le buone leggi, da quei tumulti che molti inconsideratamente dannano.
Good examples are borne out of good education, which is the outcome of good legislation; and good legislation is borne out of those uprisings which are unduly damned by so many people.

[*Discourse*]

MAYNARD, Sir John (1602–1690)
[Reply to Judge Jeffreys' suggestion that he was so old he had forgotten the law]
I have forgotten more law than you ever knew, but allow me to say, I have not forgotten much.

[Attr.]

LEADERS

MORTIMER, John (1923–)
No brilliance is needed in the law.
Nothing but common sense, and
relatively clean finger nails.

[*A Voyage Round My Father* (1971)]

POPE, Alexander (1688–1744)
The hungry Judges soon the sentence
sign,
And wretches hang that jury-men may
dine.

[*The Rape of the Lock* (1714)]

PUZO, Mario (1920–)
A lawyer with his briefcase can steal
more than a thousand men with guns.

[*The Godfather* (1969)]

RICHELIEU, Cardinal (1585–1642)
*Faire une loi et ne pas la faire exécuter,
c'est autoriser la chose qu'on veut
défendre.*
To pass a law and not have it enforced
is to authorize the very thing you wish
to prohibit.

[*Mémoires*]

**ROBESPIERRE, Maximilien
(1758–1794)**
*Toute loi qui viole les droits
imprescriptibles de l'homme, est
essentiellement injuste et tyrannique;
elle n'est point une loi.*
Any law which violates the
indefeasible rights of man is in
essence unjust and tyrannical; it is no
law.

[*Déclaration des Droits de l'homme* (1793)]

ROUSSEAU, Jean-Jacques (1712–1778)
*Les lois sont toujours utiles à ceux qui
possèdent et nuisibles à ceux qui n'ont
rien.*
Laws are always useful to those who
have possessions, and harmful to
those who have nothing.

[*Du Contrat Social* (1762)]

SELDEN, John (1584–1654)
Ignorance of the law excuses no man;
not that all men know the law, but
because 'tis an excuse every man will
plead, and no man can tell how to

confute him.

[*Table Talk* (1689)]

SHAKESPEARE, William (1564–1616)
We must not make a scarecrow of the
law,
Setting it up to fear the birds of prey,
And let it keep one shape till custom
make it
Their perch, and not their terror.

[*Measure for Measure*, II.i]

SMITH, F.E. (1872–1930)
Judge Willis: What do you suppose I am
on the Bench for, Mr Smith?
F.E. Smith: It is not for me to attempt
to fathom the inscrutable workings of
Providence.

[In Birkenhead, *Frederick Elwin, Earl of
Birkenhead* (1933)]

[To a judge who complained that he
was no wiser at the end than at the
start of one of Smith's cases]
Possibly not, My Lord, but far better
informed.

[In Birkenhead, *Life of F.E. Smith* (1959)]

See JUSTICE

LEADERS

BYRON, Lord (1788–1824)
And when we think we lead, we are
most led.

[*The Two Foscari* (1821)]

**COMPTON-BURNETT, Dame Ivy
(1884–1969)**
'She still seems to me in her own way a
person born to command,' said Luce ...
'I wonder if anyone is born to obey,'
said Isabel.
'That may be why people command
rather badly, that they have no suitable
material to work on.'

[*Parents and Children* (1941)]

**LEDRU-ROLLIN, Alexandre Auguste
(1807–1874)**
[Trying to force his way through a mob

during the 1848 revolution, of which he was one of the chief instigators]
Eh! je suis leur chef, il fallait bien les suivre.
Ah well! I am their leader, I really should be following them!

[In E. de Mirecourt, *Histoire Contemporaine* (1857)]

MASSINGER, Philip (1583-1640)
He that would govern others, first should be
The master of himself.

[*The Bondman: an Antient Story* (1624)]

MURRAY, Les A. (1938-)
Never trust a lean meritocracy
nor the leader who has been lean;
only the lifelong big have the knack of wedding
greatness with balance.

['Quintets for Robert Morley']

SARTRE, Jean-Paul (1905-1980)
Il est toujours facile d'obéir, si l'on rêve de commander.
It is always easy to obey, if one dreams of being in command.

[*Situations*]

SHAKESPEARE, William (1564-1616)
We were not born to sue, but to command.

[*Richard II*, I.i]

TACITUS (c. 56-c. 120)
[Of the Emperor Galba]
Omnium consensu capax imperii nisi imperasset.
No one would have doubted his ability to rule had he never been emperor.

[*Histories*]

LEARNING

ADDISON, Joseph (1672-1719)
The truth of it is, learning ... makes a silly man ten thousand times more insufferable, by supplying variety of matter to his impertinence, and giving him an opportunity of abounding in absurdities.

[*The Man of the Town*]

ARISTOTLE (384-322 BC)
What we have to learn to do, we learn by doing.

[*Nicomachean Ethics*]

ARMSTRONG, Dr John (1709-1779)
Much had he read,
Much more had seen; he studied from the life,
And in th' original perus'd mankind.

[*The Art of Preserving Health* (1744)]

ASCHAM, Roger (1515-1568)
There is no such whetstone, to sharpen a good wit and encourage a will to learning, as is praise.

[*The Scholemaster* (1570)]

BACON, Francis (1561-1626)
Studies serve for delight, for ornament, and for ability.

['Of Studies' (1625)]

Crafty men contemn studies; simple men admire them; and wise men use them.

['Of Studies' (1625)]

CHESTERFIELD, Lord (1694-1773)
Wear your learning, like your watch, in a private pocket; and do not merely pull it out and strike it merely to show you have one. If you are asked what o'clock it is, tell it; but do not proclaim it hourly and unasked like the watch-man.

[Letter to his son, 1748]

CONFUCIUS (c. 550-c. 478 BC)
Learning without thought is labour lost; thought without learning is perilous.

[*Analects*]

FOOTE, Samuel (1720-1777)
For as the old saying is,
When house and land are gone and spent
Then learning is most excellent.

[*Taste* (1752)]

HUXLEY, T.H. (1825-1895)
Try to learn something about

everything and everything about something.

[Memorial stone]

KNOX, Vicesimus (1752–1821)
That learning belongs not to the female character, and that the female mind is not capable of a degree of improvement equal to that of the other sex, are narrow and unphilosophical prejudices.

[*Essays, Moral and Literary* (1782)]

LESSING, Doris (1919–)
... that is what learning is. You suddenly understand something you've understood all your life, but in a new way.

[*The Four-Gated City* (1969)]

MILL, John Stuart (1806–1873)
As often as a study is cultivated by narrow minds, they will draw from it narrow conclusions.

[*Auguste Comte and Positivism* (1865)]

MILTON, John (1608–1674)
Where there is much desire to learn, there of necessity will be much arguing, much writing, many opinions; for opinion in good men is but knowl-edge in the making.

[*Areopagitica* (1644)]

OVID (43 BC–AD 18)
Adde quod ingenuas didicisse fideliter artes
Emollit mores nec sinit esse feros.
Add the fact that to have diligently studied the liberal arts refines behaviour and does not allow it to be savage.

[*Epistulae Ex Ponto*]

POPE, Alexander (1688–1744)
A little learning is a dangerous thing;
Drink deep, or taste not the Pierian spring:
There shallow draughts intoxicate the brain,
And drinking largely sobers us again.

[*An Essay on Criticism* (1711)]

WHITE, Patrick (1912–1990)
'I dunno,' Arthur said. 'I forget what I was taught. I only remember what I've learnt.'

[*The Solid Mandala* (1966)]

See EDUCATION; KNOWLEDGE; SCHOOL; UNIVERSITY

LIES

ANONYMOUS
An abomination unto the Lord, but a very present help in time of trouble.

[Definition of a lie]

BACON, Francis (1561–1626)
But it is not the lie that passeth through the mind, but the lie that sinketh in, and settleth in it, that doth the hurt.

['Of Truth' (1625)]

BELLOC, Hilaire (1870–1953)
Matilda told such Dreadful Lies,
It made one Gasp and Stretch one's Eyes;
Her Aunt, who, from her Earliest Youth,
Had kept a Strict Regard for Truth,
Attempted to Believe Matilda:
The effort very nearly killed her.

['Matilda' (1907)]

THE BIBLE (King James Version)
God is not a man, that he should lie.

[*Numbers*, 23:19]

BURKE, Edmund (1729–1797)
Falsehood has a perennial spring.

[*Speech on American Taxation* (1774)]

BUTLER, Samuel (1835–1902)
Any fool can tell the truth, but it requires a man of some sense to know how to lie well.

[*The Note-Books of Samuel Butler* (1912)]

BYRON, Lord (1788–1824)
And, after all, what is a lie? 'Tis but
The truth in masquerade.

[*Don Juan* (1824)]

LIES

CALLAGHAN, James (1912–)
A lie can be half-way round the world
before the truth has got its boots on.
[Speech, 1976]

CORNEILLE, Pierre (1606–1684)
*Il faut bonne mémoire après qu'on a
menti.*
One needs a good memory after telling
lies.
[*Le Menteur* (1643)]

DAVIES, Robertson (1913–)
Better a noble lie than a miserable
truth.
[In Twigg, *Conversations with Twenty-four
Canadian Writers* (1981)]

DISRAELI, Benjamin (1804–1881)
There are three kinds of lies: lies,
damned lies and statistics.
[Attr.]

EVANS, Harold (1928–)
The camera cannot lie. But it can be
an accessory to untruth.
[Attr.]

HAMPTON, Christopher (1946–)
You see, I always divide people into
two groups. Those who live by what
they know to be a lie, and those who
live by what they believe, falsely, to be
the truth.
[*The Philanthropist* (1970)]

HERVEY, Lord (1696–1743)
Whoever would lie usefully should lie
seldom.
[In Croker, *Memoirs of the Reign of George II*
(1848)]

HOUSEHOLD, Geoffrey (1900–1988)
It's easy to make a man confess the
lies he tells to himself; it's far harder to
make him confess the truth.
[*Rogue Male* (1939)]

IBSEN, Henrik (1828–1906)
Take the saving lie from the average
man and you take his happiness away,
too.
[*The Wild Duck* (1884)]

**MAUGHAM, William Somerset
(1874–1965)**
She's too crafty a woman to invent a
new lie when an old one will serve.
[*The Constant Wife* (1927)]

MURDOCH, Iris (1919–)
He led a double life. Did that make
him a liar? He did not feel a liar. He
was a man of two truths.
[*The Sacred and Profane Love Machine* (1974)]

NIETZSCHE, Friedrich (1844–1900)
*Wir haben die Lüge nötig ... um zu
leben.*
We need lies ... in order to live.
[*Fragments* (1880–1889)]

PROUST, Marcel (1871–1922)
*Une de ces dépêches dont M. de
Guermantes avait spirituellement fixé le
modèle: 'Impossible venir, mensonge
suit'.*
One of those telegrams of which M. de
Guermantes had wittily fixed the
formula: 'Cannot come, lie follows'.
[*Le Temps retrouvé* (1926)]

SAKI (1870–1916)
A little inaccuracy sometimes saves
tons of explanation.
[*The Square Egg* (1924)]

SHAKESPEARE, William (1564–1616)
For my part, if a lie may do thee grace,
I'll gild it with the happiest terms I
have.
[*1Henry IV, Part 1*, V.iv]

SOLZHENITSYN, Alexander (1918–)
This universal, compulsory, force-
feeding with lies is now the most
agonizing aspect of existence in our
country – worse than all our material
miseries, worse than any lack of civil
liberties.
[*Letter to Soviet Leaders* (1974)]

STEVENSON, Robert Louis (1850–1894)
The cruellest lies are often told in
silence.
[*Virginibus Puerisque* (1881)]

TENNYSON, Alfred, Lord (1809–1892)
A lie which is all a lie may be met and
fought with outright,
But a lie which is part a truth is a
harder matter to fight.

['The Grandmother' (1859)]

VIDAL, Gore (1925–)
He will lie even when it is inconvenient, the sign of the true artist.

[*Two Sisters* (1970)]

WASHINGTON, George (1732–1799)
[On being accused of cutting down a
cherry tree]
Father, I cannot tell a lie; I did it with
my little hatchet.

[Attr., probably apocryphal]

WELLS, H.G. (1866–1946)
The Social Contract is nothing more or
less than a vast conspiracy of human
beings to lie to and humbug themselves and one another for the general
Good. Lies are the mortar that bind the
savage individual man into the social
masonry.

[*Love and Mr Lewisham* (1900)]

WILDE, Oscar (1854–1900)
The final revelation is that Lying, the
telling of beautiful untrue things, is the
proper aim of Art.

['The Decay of Lying' (1889)]

See ART; TRUTH

LIFE

ADAMS, Douglas (1952–)
The Answer to the Great Question Of
... Life, the Universe and Everything ...
Is ... Forty-two.

[*The Hitch Hiker's Guide to the Galaxy* (1979)]

ADAMS, Henry (1838–1918)
Chaos often breeds life, when order
breeds habit.

[*The Education of Henry Adams* (1918)]

AMBROSE, Saint (c. 340–397)
Si fueris Romae, Romano vivito more;
Si fueris alibi, vivito sicut ibi.
If you are in Rome, live in the Roman
fashion; if you are elsewhere, live as
they do there.

[In Taylor, *Ductor Dubitantium* (1660)]

AMIEL, Henri-Frédéric (1821–1881)
Every life is a profession of faith, and
exercises an inevitable and silent
influence.

[*Journal*, 1852]

ANKA, Paul (1941–)
And now the end is near
And so I face the final curtain,
My friends, I'll say it clear,
I'll state my case of which I'm certain.
I've lived a life that's full, I've travelled
each and evr'y high-way
And more, much more than this, I did
it my way.

['My Way', song, 1969]

ANONYMOUS
Be happy while y'er leevin,
For y'er a lang time deid.

[Scottish motto]

ARNOLD, Matthew (1822–1888)
Is it so small a thing
To have enjoy'd the sun,
To have liv'd light in the spring,
To have lov'd, to have thought, to have
done?

['Empedocles on Etna' (1852)]

When we are asked further, what is
conduct? – let us answer: Three
fourths of life.

[*Literature and Dogma* (1873)]

AURELIUS, Marcus (121–180)
Remember that no one loses any other
life than this which he now lives, nor
lives any other than this which he now
loses.

[*Meditations*]

BACON, Francis (1561–1626)
But men must know, that in this
theatre of man's life it is reserved only

for God and angels to be lookers on.

[*The Advancement of Learning* (1605)]

BALFOUR, A.J. (1848-1930)
Nothing matters very much, and very few things matter at all.

[Attr.]

BECKETT, Samuel (1906-1989)
We always find something, eh, Didi, to give us the impression that we exist?

[*Waiting for Godot* (1955)]

BEDE, The Venerable (673-735)
When we compare the present life of man with that time of which we have no knowledge, it seems to me like the swift flight of a lone sparrow through the banqueting-hall where you sit in the winter months ... This sparrow flies swiftly in through one door of the hall, and out through another ... Similarly, man appears on earth for a little while, but we know nothing of what went on before this life, and what follows.

[*Ecclesiastical History*]

BENNETT, Alan (1934–)
You know life ... it's rather like opening a tin of sardines. We are all of us looking for the key.

[*Beyond the Fringe* (1962)]

BENTLEY, Nicolas (1907-1978)
One should not exaggerate the importance of trifles. Life, for instance, is much too short to be taken seriously.

[Attr.]

BLAKE, William (1757-1827)
For every thing that lives is holy, life delights in life.

[*America: a Prophecy* (1793)]

BRENAN, Gerald (1894-1987)
We should live as if we were going to live forever, yet at the back of our minds remember that our time is short.

[*Thoughts in a Dry Season* (1978)]

BRONTË, Charlotte (1816-1855)
Life, believe, is not a dream,
So dark as sages say;
Oft a little morning rain
Foretells a pleasant day!

['Life' (1846)]

BROWNE, Sir Thomas (1605-1682)
Life itself is but the shadow of death, and souls but the shadows of the living. All things fall under this name. The sun itself is but the dark *simulacrum*, and light but the shadow of God.

[*The Garden of Cyrus* (1658)]

The long habit of living indisposeth us for dying.

[*Hydriotaphia: Urn Burial* (1658)]

BUCHAN, John (1875-1940)
It's a great life if you don't weaken.

[*Mr Standfast* (1919)]

BUTLER, Samuel (1835-1902)
Life is one long process of getting tired.

[*The Note-Books of Samuel Butler* (1912)]

To live is like love, all reason is against it, and all healthy instinct for it.

[*The Note-Books of Samuel Butler* (1912)]

CHAMFORT, Nicolas (1741-1794)
Vivre est une maladie dont le sommeil nous soulage toutes les 16 heures. C'est un palliatif. La mort est le remède.
Living is an illness to which sleep provides relief every sixteen hours. It's a palliative. Death is the remedy.

[*Maximes et pensées* (1796)]

CHAPLIN, Charlie (1889-1977)
Life is a tragedy when seen in close-up, but a comedy in long-shot.

[In *The Guardian*, Obituary, 1977]

CLARE, John (1793-1864)
And what is Life? – an hour glass on the run
A mist retreating from the morning sun
A busy bustling still repeated dream

Its length? – A moment's pause, a
moment's thought
And happiness? A Bubble on the
stream
That in the act of seizing shrinks to
nought.

['What is Life?' (1820)]

If life had a second edition, how I
would correct the proofs.

[Letter to a friend]

COCTEAU, Jean (1889–1963)
Vivre est une chute horizontale.
Life is falling sideways.

[*Opium* (1930)]

**COMPTON-BURNETT, Dame Ivy
(1884–1969)**
As regards plots I find real life no help
at all. Real life seems to have no plots.

[In R. Lehmann et al., *Orion I* (1945)]

CONRAN, Shirley (1932–)
Life is too short to stuff a mushroom.

[*Superwoman* (1975)]

CORY, William (1823–1892)
You promise heavens free from strife,
Pure truth, and perfect change of will;
But sweet, sweet is this human life,
So sweet, I fain would breathe it still;
Your chilly stars I can forgo,
This warm kind world is all I know ...

All beauteous things for which we live
By laws of space and time decay.
But Oh, the very reason why
I clasp them, is because they die.

['Mimnermus in Church' (1858)]

COUBERTIN, Pierre de (1863–1937)
*L'important dans la vie ce n'est point le
triomphe mais le combat; l'essentiel ce
n'est pas d'avoir vaincu mais de s'être
bien battu.*
The most important thing in life is not
the winning but the taking part ... The
essential thing is not conquering but
fighting well.

[Speech, 1908]

COWPER, William (1731–1800)
Variety's the very spice of life,
That gives all its flavour.

[*The Task* (1785)]

CROWFOOT (1821–1890)
What is life? It is the flash of a firefly in
the night. It is the breath of a buffalo
in the wintertime. It is the little
shadow which runs across the grass
and loses itself in the sunset.

[Last words]

DAVIES, William Henry (1871–1940)
What is this life if, full of care,
We have no time to stand and stare?

[*Songs of Joy* (1911)]

DICKENS, Charles (1812–1870)
'I am ruminating,' said Mr Pickwick,
'on the strange mutability of human
affairs.'
'Ah, I see – in at the palace door one
day, out at the window the next.
Philosopher, sir?'
'An observer of human nature, sir,'
said Mr Pickwick.

[*The Pickwick Papers* (1837)]

DISRAELI, Benjamin (1804–1881)
Next to knowing when to seize an
opportunity, the most important thing
in life is to know when to forego an
advantage.

[Attr.]

DUNCAN, Isadora (1878–1927)
People do not live nowadays – they get
about ten percent out of life.

[*This Quarter Autumn*, 'Memoirs']

EINSTEIN, Albert (1879–1955)
Only a life lived for others is a life
worthwhile.

['Defining Success']

EMERSON, Ralph Waldo (1803–1882)
Life is good only when it is magical
and musical, a perfect timing and
consent, and when we do not
anatomize it. You must treat the days
respectfully, you must be a day
yourself, and not interrogate it like a
college professor ... You must hear the

bird's song without attempting to render it into nouns and verbs.

[*Society and Solitude* (1870)]

FRANKLIN, Benjamin (1706–1790)
Dost thou love life? Then do not squander time, for that's the stuff life is made of.

[*Poor Richard's Almanac* (1746)]

GAY, John (1685–1732)
Life is a jest; and all things show it.
I thought so once; but now I know it.

['My Own Epitaph' (1720)]

GORDON, Adam Lindsay (1833–1870)
Life is mostly froth and bubble,
Two things stand like stone,
Kindness in another's trouble,
Courage in your own.

[*Ye Wearie Wayfarer* (1866)]

A little season of love and laughter,
Of light and life, and pleasure and pain,
And a horror of outer darkness after,
And dust returneth to dust again.

['The Swimmer' (1903)]

HENSHAW, Bishop Joseph (1603–1679)
One doth but breakfast here, another dines, he that liveth longest doth but sup; we must all go to bed in another world.

[*Horae Succisivae* (1631)]

HERBERT, Sir A.P. (1890–1971)
It may be life, but ain't it slow?

['It May Be Life' (1926)]

HOBBES, Thomas (1588–1679)
No arts; no letters; no society; and which is worst of all, continual fear, and danger of violent death; and the life of man, solitary, poor, nasty, brutish, and short.

[*Leviathan* (1651)]

HODSON, Peregrine
It shows hunger for life, like the Zen parable of a man holding on to a tree root over the edge of a cliff: below him rocks, above him a tiger, and a black

and white mouse nibbling at the root: the man notices a strawberry beside him and picks it.

[*A Circle Round The Sun*]

HUBBARD, Elbert (1856–1915)
Life is just one damned thing after another.

[*Philistine*, 1909]

HUXLEY, Aldous (1894–1963)
Most of one's life ... is one prolonged effort to prevent oneself thinking.

[*Mortal Coils* (1922)]

HUXLEY, T.H. (1825–1895)
The chess-board is the world; the pieces are the phenomena of the universe; the rules of the game are what we call the laws of Nature. The player on the other side is hidden from us. We know that his play is always fair, just, and patient. But we also know, to our cost, that he never overlooks a mistake, or makes the smallest allowance for ignorance.

[*Macmillan's Magazine*, 1868]

JAMES, Henry (1843–1916)
Live all you can; it's a mistake not to. It doesn't so much matter what you do in particular, so long as you have your life. If you haven't had that then what *have* you had?

[*The Ambassadors* (1903)]

JEANS, Sir James Hopwood (1877–1946)
Life exists in the universe only because the carbon atom possesses certain exceptional properties.

[*The Mysterious Universe* (1930)]

JOHNSON, Samuel (1709–1784)
The love of life is necessary to the vigorous prosecution of any undertaking.

[*The Rambler* (1750–1752)]

Human life is everywhere a state in which much is to be endured, and little to be enjoyed.

[*Rasselas* (1759)]

LIFE

JUNG, Carl Gustav (1875–1961)
*Soweit wir zu erkennen vermögen, ist es
der einzige Sinn der menschlichen
Existenz, ein Licht anzuzünden in der
Finsternis des blossen Seins.*
As far as we are able to understand,
the only aim of human existence is to
kindle a light in the darkness of mere
being.
[*Memories, Dreams, Thoughts* (1962)]

KIERKEGAARD, Søren (1813–1855)
Life can only be understood back-
wards; but it must be lived forwards.
[*Life*]

LENNON, John (1940–1980)
Life is what happens to you when
you're busy making other plans.
['Beautiful Boy', song, 1980]

**LESSING, Gotthold Ephraim
(1729–1781)**
*Gestern liebt' ich,
Heute leid' ich,
Morgen sterb' ich.
Dennoch denk' ich
Heut und morgen
Gern an gestern.*
Yesterday I loved, today I suffer,
tomorrow I shall die. Nonetheless I still
think with pleasure, today and
tomorrow, of yesterday.
['Song taken from the Spanish']

LEWIS, C.S. (1898–1963)
Term, holidays, term, holidays, till we
leave school, and then work, work,
work till we die.
[*Surprised by Joy* (1955)]

**LEWIS, Sir George Cornewall
(1806–1863)**
Life would be tolerable but for its
amusements.
[In *Dictionary of National Biography*]

**LONGFELLOW, Henry Wadsworth
(1807–1882)**
Lives of great men all remind us

We can make our lives sublime,
And, departing, leave behind us
Footprints on the sands of time ...
['A Psalm of Life' (1838)]

MANN, Thomas (1875–1955)
*Der Mensch lebt nicht nur sein
persönliches Leben als Einzelwesen,
sondern, bewusst oder unbewusst, auch
das seiner Epoche und Zeitgenossen-
schaft.*
Man does not only live his personal
life as an individual, but also,
consciously or unconsciously, the life
of his era and of his contemporaries.
[*The Magic Mountain* (1924)]

MARTIAL (c. 40–c. 104)
*Non est, crede mihi, sapientis dicere
'Vivam':
Sera nimis vita est crastina: vive
hodie.*
Believe me, 'I shall live' is not the
saying of a wise man. Tomorrow's life
is too late: live today.
[*Epigrammata*]

**MAUGHAM, William Somerset
(1874–1965)**
Life is too short to do anything for
oneself that one can pay others to do
for one.
[*The Summing Up* (1938)]

MONTAIGNE, Michel de (1533–1592)
*L'utilité de vivre n'est pas en l'espace,
elle est en l'usage ... Il gît en votre
volonté, non au nombre des ans, que
vous ayez assez vécu.'*
The value of life does not lie in the
number of years but in the use you
make of them... Whether you have
lived enough depends on your will, not
on the number of your years.
[*Essais* (1580)]

NASH, Ogden (1902–1971)
When I consider how my life is spent,
I hardly ever repent.
['Reminiscent Reflection' (1931)]

NIETZSCHE, Friedrich (1844–1900)
Glaubt es mir! – das Geheimnis, um die

grösste Fruchtbarkeit und den grössten Genuss vom Dasein einzuernten, heisst: gefährlich leben!
Believe me! – the secret of gathering in the greatest fruitfulness and the greatest enjoyment from existence is *living dangerously!*

[*The Gay Science* (1887)]

O'KEEFFE, Georgia (1887–1986)
My feeling about life is a curious kind of triumphant feeling about seeing it bleak, knowing it is so, and walking into it fearlessly because one has no choice.

[Attr.]

O'NEILL, Eugene (1888–1953)
Our lives are merely strange dark interludes in the electric display of God the Father!

[*Strange Interlude* (1928)]

PASCAL, Blaise (1623–1662)
Le dernier acte est sanglant, quelque belle que soit la comédie en tout le reste.
The last act is bloody, however delightful the rest of the play may be.

[*Pensées* (1670)]

RUSSELL, Bertrand (1872–1970)
Brief and powerless is Man's life; on him and all his race the slow, sure doom falls pitiless and dark.

[*Mysticism and Logic* (1918)]

SANTAYANA, George (1863–1952)
There is no cure for birth and death save to enjoy the interval.

[*Soliloquies in England* (1922)]

Life is not a spectacle or a feast; it is a predicament.

[In Sagittarius and George, *The Perpetual Pessimist*]

SHAKESPEARE, William (1564–1616)
All the world's a stage,
And all the men and women merely players;
They have their exits and their entrances;

And one man in his time plays many parts.

[*As You Like It*, II.vii]

O gentlemen, the time of life is short!
To spend that shortness basely were too long.

[*Henry IV Part 1*, V.ii]

To-morrow, and to-morrow, and to-morrow,
Creeps in this petty pace from day to day
To the last syllable of recorded time,
And all our yesterdays have lighted fools
The way to dusty death. Out, out, brief candle!
Life's but a walking shadow, a poor player,
That struts and frets his hour upon the stage,
And then is heard no more; it is a tale
Told by an idiot, full of sound and fury,
Signifying nothing.

[*Macbeth*, V.v]

SHELLEY, Percy Bysshe (1792–1822)
Lift not the painted veil which those who live
Call Life.

['Sonnet' (1818)]

SMITH, Logan Pearsall (1865–1946)
There are two things to aim at in life: first, to get what you want; and, after that, to enjoy it. Only the wisest of mankind achieve the second.

[*Afterthoughts* (1931)]

SOCRATES (469–399 BC)
The unexamined life is not a life worth living for a human being.

[Attr. in Plato, *Apology*]

SOUTHEY, Robert (1774–1843)
Live as long as you may, the first twenty years are the longest half of your life.

[*The Doctor* (1812)]

STOPPARD, Tom (1937–)
Life is a gamble, at terrible odds – if it

was a bet, you wouldn't take it.

[*Rosencrantz and Guildenstern Are Dead* (1967)]

TAYLOR, Bishop Jeremy (1613–1667)
As our life is very short, so it is very miserable, and therefore it is well it is short.

[*The Rule and Exercise of Holy Dying* (1651)]

TERENCE (c. 190–159 BC)
Modo liceat vivere, est spes.
Where there's life, there's hope.

[*Heauton Timoroumenos*]

THALES (c. 624–547 BC)
[His reply when asked why he chose to carry on living after saying there was no difference between life and death]
Because there is no difference.

[In Durant, *The Story of Civilization*]

THOREAU, Henry (1817–1862)
Our life is frittered away by detail ...
Simplify, simplify.

[*Walden* (1854)]

VAUVENARGUES, Marquis de (1715–1747)
Pour exécuter de grandes choses, il faut vivre comme si on ne devait jamais mourir.
In order to achieve great things we must live as though we were never going to die.

[*Réflexions et Maximes* (1746)]

VILLIERS DE L'ISLE-ADAM, Philippe-Auguste (1838–1889)
Vivre? Les serviteurs feront cela pour nous.
Live? The servants will do that for us.

[*Axel* (1890)]

WHITEHEAD, A.N. (1861–1947)
It is the essence of life that it exists for its own sake.

[*Nature and Life* (1934)]

WILDE, Oscar (1854–1900)
One can live for years sometimes without living at all, and then all life comes crowding into one single hour.

[*Vera, or The Nihilist* (1880)]

One's real life is so often the life that one does not lead.

['L'Envoi to Rose-Leaf and Apple-Leaf']

WODEHOUSE, P.G. (1881–1975)
I spent the afternoon musing on Life. If you come to think of it, what a queer thing Life is! So unlike anything else, don't you know, if you see what I mean.

[*My Man Jeeves* (1919)]

XERXES (c. 519–465 BC)
[On surveying his army]
I was thinking, and I was moved to pity that the whole of human life is so short – not one of this great number will be alive a hundred years from now.

[In Herodotus, *Histories*]

YEATS, W.B. (1865–1939)
When I think of all the books I have read, and of the wise words I have heard spoken, and of the anxiety I have given to parents and grand-parents, and of the hopes that I have had, all life weighed in the scales of my own life seems to me preparation for something that never happens.

[*Autobiographies* (1955)]

See ART; DEATH

LITERATURE

BRENAN, Gerald (1894–1987)
The cliché is dead poetry. English, being the language of an imaginative race, abounds in clichés, so that English literature is always in danger of being poisoned by its own secretions.

[*Thoughts in a Dry Season* (1978)]

CONNOLLY, Cyril (1903–1974)
Literature is the art of writing something that will be read twice; journalism what will be grasped at once.

[*Enemies of Promise* (1938)]

GAISFORD, Rev. Thomas (1779–1855)
Nor can I do better, in conclusion, than impress upon you the study of Greek literature, which not only elevates above the vulgar herd, but leads not infrequently to positions of considerable emolument.

[Christmas Day Sermon, Oxford Cathedral]

GOETHE (1749–1832)
Nationalliteratur will jetzt nicht viel sagen, die Epoche der Weltliteratur ist an der Zeit.
National literature does not now have much significance, it is time for the era of world literature.

[*Gespräche mit Eckermann*, 1827]

HELLER, Joseph (1923–)
He knew everything about literature except how to enjoy it.

[*Catch-22* (1961)]

HORACE (65–8 BC)
Inceptis gravibus plerumque et magna professis
Purpureus, late qui splendeat, unus et alter
Adsuitur pannus.
In serious works and ones that promise great things, one or two purple patches are often stitched in, to glitter far and wide.

[*Ars Poetica*]

INGE, William Ralph (1860–1954)
Literature flourishes best when it is half a trade and half an art.

['The Victorian Age' (1922)]

LEWIS, Sinclair (1885–1951)
Our American professors like their literature clear, cold, pure, and very dead.

[Address to Swedish Academy, 1930]

LODGE, David (1935–)
Literature is mostly about having sex and not much about having children; life is the other way round.

[*The British Museum is Falling Down* (1965)]

LOVER, Samuel (1797–1868)
When once the itch of literature comes over a man, nothing can cure it but the scratching of a pen.

[*Handy Andy* (1842)]

NABOKOV, Vladimir (1899–1977)
Literature and butterflies are the two sweetest passions known to man.

[*Radio Times*, 1962]

NAIPAUL, V.S. (1930–1983)
Literature should be read by people privately. English should be abandoned as a silly course, and all the professors should be put out of a job.

[Attr. remark, *The Sunday Times*, May 1996]

POUND, Ezra (1885–1972)
Literature is news that STAYS news.

[*ABC of Reading* (1934)]

SOUTHEY, Robert (1774–1843)
Your true lover of literature is never fastidious.

[*The Doctor* (1812)]

TWAIN, Mark (1835–1910)
[Definition of a classic]
Something that everybody wants to have read and nobody wants to read.

['The Disappearance of Literature']

WILDE, Oscar (1854–1900)
Movement, that problem of the visible arts, can be truly realized by Literature alone. It is Literature that shows us the body in its swiftness and the soul in its unrest.

['The Critic as Artist' (1891)]

WILDER, Thornton (1897–1975)
Literature is the orchestration of platitudes.

[*Time*, 1953]

YEATS, W.B. (1865–1939)
All folk literature, and all literature that keeps the folk tradition, delights in unbounded and immortal things.

['The Celtic Element in Literature' (1902)]

We have no longer in any country a literature as great as the literature of the old world, and that is because the newspapers, all kinds of second-rate books, the preoccupation of men with all kinds of practical changes, have driven the living imagination out of this world.

['First Principles' (1904)]

See FICTION; POETRY; WRITING

LONELINESS

CONRAD, Joseph (1857–1924)
Who knows what true loneliness is – not the conventional word but the naked terror? To the lonely themselves it wears a mask.

[Attr.]

HAMMARSKJÖLD, Dag (1905–1961)
Pray that your loneliness may spur you into finding something to live for, great enough to die for.

[Diaries, 1951]

HUBBARD, Elbert (1856–1915)
Loneliness is to endure the presence of one who does not understand.

[Attr.]

LENNON, John (1940–1980)
Waits at the window, wearing the face that she keeps in a jar by the door
Who is it for? All the lonely people, where do they all come from?
All the lonely people, where do they all belong?

['Eleanor Rigby', 1966, with Paul McCartney]

O'BRIEN, Edna (1936–)
I often get lonely for unrealistic things: for something absolute.

[The Observer, 1992]

SARTON, May (1912–)
Loneliness is the poverty of self; solitude is the richness of self.

[Mrs Stevens Hears the Mermaids Singing (1993)]

See SOLITUDE

LOVE

ANONYMOUS
Western wind, when wilt thou blow,
The small rain down can rain?
Christ, if my love were in my arms
And I in my bed again!

[New Oxford Book of 16th-Century Verse]

ANOUILH, Jean (1910–1987)
Vous savez bien que l'amour, c'est avant tout le don de soi!
Love is, above all else, the gift of oneself.

[Ardèle ou la Marguerite (1949)]

AUDEN, W.H. (1907–1973)
When it comes, will it come without warning
Just as I'm picking my nose?
Will it knock on my door in the morning,
Or tread in the bus on my toes?
Will it come like a change in the weather?
Will its greeting be courteous or rough?
Will it alter my life altogether?
O tell me the truth about love.

['Twelve Songs']

AUSTEN, Jane (1775–1817)
All the privilege I claim for my own sex ... is that of loving longest, when existence or when hope is gone.

[Persuasion (1818)]

BACON, Francis (1561–1626)
They do best who, if they cannot but admit love, yet make it keep quarter; and sever it wholly from their serious affairs and actions of life: for if it check once with business, it troubleth men's fortunes, and maketh men, that they can no ways be true to their own ends.

['Of Love' (1625)]

BALZAC, Honoré de (1799–1850)
It is easier to be a lover than a husband, for the same reason that it is more difficult to show a ready wit all day long than to produce an occasional bon mot.

[Attr.]

BEAUMONT, Francis (1584–1616) and
FLETCHER, John (1579–1625)
Those have most power to hurt us,
that we love.

[*The Maid's Tragedy* (1611)]

THE BIBLE (King James Version)
And Jacob served seven years for
Rachel; and they seemed unto him but
a few days, for the love he had to her.

[*Genesis*, 29:20]

Intreat me not to leave thee, or to
return from following after thee: for
whither thou goest, I will go; and
where thou lodgest, I will lodge: thy
people shall be my people, and thy
God my God.

[*Ruth*, 1:16–17]

Greater love hath no man than this,
that a man lay down his life for his
friends.

[*John*, 15:13]

He that loveth not knoweth not God;
for God is love.

[*I John*, 4:8]

Perfect love casteth out fear.

[*I John*, 4:18]

BICKERSTAFFE, Isaac
(c. 1733–c. 1808)
Perhaps it was right to dissemble your
love,
But – why did you kick me downstairs?

['An Expostulation' (1789)]

BLAKE, William (1757–1827)
Love seeketh not Itself to please,
Nor for itself hath any care;
But for another gives its ease,
And builds a Heaven in Hells despair.

['The Clod & the Pebble' (1794)]

Children of the future Age,
Reading this indignant page:
Know that in a former time,
Love! sweet Love! was thought a
crime.

['A Little Girl Lost' (1794)]

BRENNAN, Christopher (1870–1932)
My heart was wandering in the sands,
a restless thing, a scorn apart;
Love set his fire in my hands,
I clasped the flame into my heart.

[*Poems* (1914)]

BRIDGES, Robert (1844–1930)
When first we met we did not guess
That Love would prove so hard a
master.

['Triolet' (1890)]

BROOKE, Rupert (1887–1915)
I thought when love for you died, I
should die.
It's dead. Alone, mostly strangely, I live on.

['The Life Beyond' (1910)]

BROWNING, Elizabeth Barrett
(1806–1861)
How do I love thee? Let me count the
ways.

[*Sonnets from the Portuguese* (1850)]

BURNS, Robert (1759–1796)
Ae fond kiss, and then we sever!
Ae fareweel, and then forever! ...

But to see her was to love her,
Love but her, and love for ever.

Had we never lov'd sae kindly,
Had we never lov'd sae blindly,
Never met – or never parted –
We had ne'er been broken-hearted.

['Ae Fond Kiss' (1791)]

O, my luve's like a red, red, rose
That's newly sprung in June.
O, my luve's like the melodie,
That's sweetly play'd in tune.

['A Red Red Rose' (1794)]

BURTON, Robert (1577–1640)
No chord, nor cable can so forcibly
draw, or hold so fast, as love can do
with a twined thread.

[*Anatomy of Melancholy* (1621)]

BUTLER, Samuel (1612–1680)
For money has a power above
The stars and fate, to manage love.
[*Hudibras* (1678)]

All love at first, like generous wine,
Ferments and frets until 'tis fine;
But when 'tis settled on the lee,
And from th' impurer matter free,
Becomes the richer still the older,
And proves the pleasanter the colder.
[*Miscellaneous Thoughts*]

BUTLER, Samuel (1835–1902)
'Tis better to have loved and lost than
never to have lost at all.
[*The Way of All Flesh (1903)*]

God is Love, I dare say. But what a
mischievous devil Love is.
[*The Note-Books of Samuel Butler* (1912)]

BYRON, Lord (1788–1824)
In her first passion woman loves her
lover,
In all the others all she loves is love.
[*Don Juan* (1824)]

CHAMFORT, Nicolas (1741–1794)
L'amour, tel qu'il existe dans la société,
n'est que l'échange de deux fantaisies et
le contact de deux épidermes.
Love, as it exists in society, is nothing
more than the exchange of two
fantasies and the contact of two skins.
[*Maximes et pensées* (1796)]

CHEVALIER, Maurice (1888–1972)
Many a man has fallen in love with a
girl in a light so dim he would not
have chosen a suit by it.
[Attr.]

CLARE, John (1793–1864)
Language has not the power to speak
what love indites:
The soul lies buried in the ink that
writes.
[Attr.]

**COLMAN, the Elder, George
(1732–1794)**
Love and a cottage! Eh, Fanny! Ah,
give me indifference and a coach and
six!
[*The Clandestine Marriage* (1766)]

CONGREVE, William (1670–1729)
In my conscience I believe the baggage
loves me, for she never speaks well of
me her self, nor suffers any body else
to rail me.
[*The Old Bachelor* (1693)]

COPE, Wendy (1945–)
2 cures for love
1. Don't see him. Don't phone or write
a letter.
2. The easy way: get to know him
better.
[Attr.]

DIDEROT, Denis (1713–1784)
On a dit que l'amour qui ôtait l'esprit à
ceux qui en avaient en donnait à ceux
qui n'en avaient pas.
They say that love takes wit away from
those who have it, and gives it to those
who have none.
[*Paradoxe sur le Comédien*]

DIETRICH, Marlene (1901–1992)
Latins are tenderly enthusiastic. In
Brazil they throw flowers at you. In
Argentina they throw themselves.
[*Newsweek*, 1959]

DONNE, John (1572–1631)
Love built on beauty, soon as beauty
dies.
[*Elegies* (c. 1595)]

Who ever loves, if he do not propose
The right true end of love, he's one that
goes
To sea for nothing but to make him sick.
[*Elegies* (c. 1600)]

Chang'd loves are but chang'd sorts of
meat,
And when he hath the kernel eat,
Who doth not fling away the shell?
[*Songs and Sonnets* (1611)]

I wonder by my troth, what thou, and I

Did, till we lov'd?
[*Songs and Sonnets* (1611)]

DOUGLAS, Lord Alfred (1870–1945)
I am the Love that dare not speak its name.
['Two Loves' (1896)]

DRYDEN, John (1631–1700)
Pains of love be sweeter far
Than all other pleasures are.
[*Tyrannic Love* (1669)]

For, Heaven be thanked, we live in such an age,
When no man dies for love, but on the stage.
[*Mithridates* (1678)]

ELLIS, Havelock (1859–1939)
Love is friendship plus sex.
[Attr.

ETHEREGE, Sir George (c. 1635–1691)
When love grows diseased, the best thing we can do is put it to a violent death; I cannot endure the torture of a lingering and consumptive passion.
[*The Man of Mode* (1676)]

FARQUHAR, George (1678–1707)
Money is the sinews of love, as of war.
[*Love and a Bottle* (1698)]

FIELDING, Henry (1707–1754)
Love and scandal are the best sweeteners of tea.
[*Love in Several Masques* (1728)]

What is commonly called love, namely the desire of satisfying a voracious appetite with a certain quantity of delicate white human flesh.
[*Tom Jones* (1749)]

FLETCHER, Phineas (1582–1650)
Love is like linen often chang'd, the sweeter.
[*Sicelides* (1614)]

FLORIAN, Jean-Pierre Claris de (1755–1794)
Plaisir d'amour ne dure qu'un moment,
Chagrin d'amour dure toute la vie.

Love's pleasure only lasts a moment; love's sorrow lasts one's whole life long.
['Célestine' (1784)]

FORSTER, E.M. (1879–1970)
Only connect! That was the whole of her sermon. Only connect the prose and the passion, and both will be exalted, and human love will be seen at its highest.
[*Howard's End* (1910)]

FRANKLIN, Benjamin (1706–1790)
The having made a young girl miserable may give you frequent bitter reflection; none of which can attend the making of an old woman happy.
[*On the Choice of a Mistress*]

FRY, Christopher (1907–)
Try thinking of love, or something.
Amor vincit insomnia.
[*A Sleep of Prisoners* (1951)]

GAY, John (1685–1732)
Then nature rul'd, and love, devoid of art,
Spoke the consenting language of the heart.
[*Dione* (1720)]

GOLDSMITH, Oliver (c. 1728–1774)
It seemed to me pretty plain, that they had more of love than matrimony in them.
[*The Vicar of Wakefield* (1766)]

GRAVES, Robert (1895–1985)
In love as in sport, the amateur status must be strictly maintained.
[*Occupation: Writer*]

GREER, Germaine (1939–)
Love, love, love – all the wretched cant of it, masking egotism, lust, masochism, fantasy under a mythology of sentimental postures, a welter of self induced miseries and joys, blinding and masking the essential personalities in the frozen gestures of courtship, in the kissing and the dating and the desire, the compliments and the quarrels which vivify its

barrenness.

[*The Female Eunuch* (1970)]

HARDY, Thomas (1840–1928)
A lover without indiscretion is no lover at all.

[*The Hand of Ethelberta* (1876)]

HARTLEY, L.P. (1895–1972)
Once she had loved her fellow human beings; she did not love them now, she had seen them do too many unpleasant things.

[*Facial Justice* (1960)]

HEWETT, Dorothy (1923–)
My body turns to you as the earth turns.
O for such bitter need you've taken me,
To dub me lover, friend and enemy,
Take neither one can set the other free.
But still there is a loveliness that burns
That burns between us two so tenderly.

['There is a Loveliness that Burns']

HOGG, James (1770–1835)
O, love, love, love!
Love is like a dizziness;
It winna let a poor body
Gang about his biziness!

['Love is Like a Dizziness']

HUDSON, Louise (1958–)
Now I go to films alone
watch a silent telephone
send myself a valentine
whisper softly 'I am mine'.

['Men, Who Needs Them']

JERROLD, Douglas William (1803–1857)
Love's like the measles – all the worse when it comes late in life.

[*Wit and Opinions of Douglas Jerrold* (1859)]

KAFKA, Franz (1883–1924)
Liebe ist, dass Du mir das Messer bist, mit dem ich in mir wühle.
Love is, that you are the knife which I plunge into myself.

[Letter to Milena Jesenká, 1920]

KEY, Ellen (1849–1926)
Love is moral even without legal marriage, but marriage is immoral without love.

['The Morality of Women' (1911)]

KING, Bishop Henry (1592–1669)
Sleep on, my Love, in thy cold bed,
Never to be disquieted!
My last good night! Thou wilt not wake
Till I thy fate shall overtake:
Till age, or grief, or sickness must
Marry my body to that dust
It so much loves; and fill the room
My heart keeps empty in thy tomb.
Stay for me there; I will not fail
To meet thee in that hollow vale ...

But hark! My pulse like a soft drum
Beats my approach, tells thee I come.

['Exequy upon his Wife' (1651)]

LAMARTINE, Alphonse de (1790–1869)
Un seul être vous manque, et tout est dépeuplé.
Only one being is missing, and your whole world is bereft of people.

[*Premières Méditations poétiques* (1820)]

LARKIN, Philip (1922–1985)
What will survive of us is love.

['An Arundel Tomb' (1964)]

LA ROCHEFOUCAULD, Duc de (1613–1680)
Il n'y a guère de gens qui ne soient honteux de s'être aimés quand ils ne s'aiment plus.
There are very few people who are not ashamed of having loved one another once they have fallen out of love.

[*Maximes* (1678)]

LAWRENCE, D.H. (1885–1930)
I'm not sure if a mental relation with a woman doesn't make it impossible to love her. To know the mind of a woman is to end in hating her. Love means the pre-cognitive flow ... it is

the honest state before the apple.

[Letter to Dr Trigant Burrow, 1927]

LINDSAY, Norman (1879–1969)
The best love affairs are those we
never had.

[*Bohemians of the Bulletin* (1965)]

LOWRY, Malcolm (1909–1957)
How alike are the groans of love to
those of the dying.

[*Under the Volcano* (1947)]

MARLOWE, Christopher (1564–1593)
Come live with me, and be my love,
And we will all the pleasures prove.

['The Passionate Shepherd to his Love']

MARVELL, Andrew (1621–1678)
Therefore the love which us doth bind,
But Fate so enviously debars,
Is the conjunction of the mind,
And opposition of the stars.

['The Definition of Love' (1681)]

MOLIERE (1622–1673)
*On est aisément dupé par ce qu'on
aime.*
One is easily taken in by what one
loves.

[*Tartuffe* (1664)]

O'BRIEN, Edna (1936–)
Oh, shadows of love, inebriations of
love, foretastes of love, trickles of love,
but never yet the one true love.

[*Night* (1972)]

OVID (43 BC–AD 18)
*Qui finem quaeris amoris,
Cedet amor rebus; res age, tutus eris.*
You who seek an end to love, love will
yield to business: be busy, and you will
be safe.

[*Remedia Amoris*]

PARKER, Dorothy (1893–1967)
By the time you swear you're his,
Shivering and sighing,
And he vows his passion is
Infinite, undying –
Lady, make a note of this:
One of you is lying.

['Unfortunate Coincidence' (1937)]

PARNELL, Anna (1852–1911)
Two children playing by a stream
Two lovers walking in a dream
A married pair whose dream is o'er,
Two old folks who are quite a bore.

['Love's Four Ages']

PATTERSON, Johnny (1840–1889)
Have you ever been in love, me boys
Oh! have you felt the pain,
I'd rather be in jail, I would,
Than be in love again.

['The Garden where the Praties Grow']

PROUST, Marcel (1871–1922)
*On a tort de parler en amour de
mauvais choix, puisque dès qu'il y a
choix il ne peut être que mauvais.*
It is wrong to speak of making a bad
choice in love, since as soon as there
is choice, it can only be bad.

[*La Fugitive* (1923)]

RACINE, Jean (1639–1699)
*Ah! je l'ai trop aimé pour ne le point
haïr!*
Ah, I have loved him too much not to
hate him!

[*Andromaque* (1667)]

ROCHESTER, Earl of (1647–1680)
[Of love]
That cordial drop heaven in our cup
    has thrown
To make the nauseous draught of life
    go down.

['A letter from Artemisa in the Town to Chloe
in the Country' (1679)]

RUSSELL, Bertrand (1872–1970)
Of all forms of caution, caution in love
is perhaps the most fatal to true
happiness.

[*Marriage and Morals* (1929)]

**SAINT-EXUPERY, Antoine de
(1900–1944)**
*L'expérience nous montre qu'aimer ce
n'est point nous regarder l'un l'autre
mais regarder ensemble dans la même
direction.*

Experience shows us that love is not looking into one another's eyes but looking together in the same direction.

[*Wind, Sand and Stars* (1939)]

SEGAL, Erich (1937–)
Love means never having to say you're sorry.

[*Love Story* (1970)]

SHAKESPEARE, William (1564–1616)
Doubt thou the stars are fire;
Doubt that the sun doth move;
Doubt truth to be a liar;
But never doubt I love.

[*Hamlet*, II.ii]

Ay me! for aught that I could ever read,
Could ever hear by tale or history,
The course of true love never did run smooth.

[*A Midsummer Night's Dream*, I.i]

Love looks not with the eyes, but with the mind;
And therefore is wing'd Cupid painted blind.

[*A Midsummer Night's Dream*, I.i]

I thank God, and my cold blood, I am of your humour for that: I had rather hear my dog bark at a crow than a man swear he loves me.

[*Much Ado About Nothing*, I.i]

My bounty is as boundless as the sea,
My love as deep: the more I give to thee,
The more I have, for both are infinite.

[*Romeo and Juliet*, II.ii]

If music be the food of love, play on,
Give me excess of it, that, surfeiting,
The appetite may sicken and so die.
That strain again! It had a dying fall;
O, it came o'er my ear like the sweet sound
That breathes upon a bank of violets,
Stealing and giving odour! Enough, no more;
'Tis not so sweet now as it was before.

[*Twelfth Night*, I.i]

She never told her love,
But let concealment, like a worm i' th' bud,
Feed on her damask cheek. She pin'd in thought;
And with a green and yellow melancholy
She sat like Patience on a monument,
Smiling at grief. Was not this love indeed?
We men may say more, swear more, but indeed
Our shows are more than will; for still we prove
Much in our vows, but little in our love.

[*Twelfth Night*, II.iv]

Love sought is good, but given unsought is better.

[*Twelfth Night*, III.i]

Fie, fie, how wayward is this foolish love,
That like a testy babe will scratch the nurse,
And presently, all humbled, kiss the rod!

[*Two Gentlemen of Verona*, I.ii]

Let me not to the marriage of true minds
Admit impediments. Love is not love
Which alters when it alteration finds,
Or bends with the remover to remove.

[Sonnet 116]

When my love swears that she is made of truth,
I do believe her, though I know she lies.

[Sonnet 138]

SHAW, George Bernard (1856–1950)
The fickleness of the women I love is only equalled by the infernal constancy of the women who love me.

[*The Philanderer* (1898)]

SHELLEY, Percy Bysshe (1792–1822)
Familiar acts are beautiful through love.

[*Prometheus Unbound* (1820)]

STERNE, Laurence (1713–1768)
Love, an' please your honour, is
exactly like war, in this; that a soldier,
though he has escaped three weeks
complete o' Saturday night, – may
nevertheless be shot through his heart
on Sunday morning.

[*Tristram Shandy*]

TENNYSON, Alfred, Lord (1809–1892)
In the Spring a young man's fancy
lightly turns to thoughts of love.

['Locksley Hall' (1838)]

I hold it true, whate'er befall;
I feel it, when I sorrow most;
'Tis better to have loved and lost
Than never to have loved at all.

[*In Memoriam A. H. H.* (1850)]

To love one maiden only, cleave to her,
And worship her by years of noble
    deeds,
Until they won her; for indeed I knew
Of no more subtle master under
    heaven
Than is the maiden passion for a maid,
Not only to keep down the base in man,
But teach high thought, and amiable
    words
And courtliness, and the desire of
    fame,
And love of truth, and all that makes a
    man.

[*The Idylls of the King*]

TERENCE (c. 190–159 BC)
Amantium irae amoris integratio est.
Lovers' quarrels are the renewal of
love.

[*Andria*]

**THACKERAY, William Makepeace
(1811–1863)**
Werther had a love for Charlotte
Such as words could never utter;
Would you know how first he met her?
She was cutting bread and butter.
Charlotte was a married lady,
And a moral man was Werther,
And for all the wealth of Indies,

Would do nothing for to hurt her.
So he sighed and pined and ogled,
And his passion boiled and bubbled,
Till he blew his silly brains out
And no more was by it troubled.
Charlotte, having seen his body
Borne before her on a shutter,
Like a well-conducted person,
Went on cutting bread and butter.

['Sorrows of Werther' (1855)]

TIBULLUS (c. 54–19 BC)
*Te spectem, suprema mihi cum venerit
    hora,
Et teneam moriens deficiente manu.*
May I be looking at you when my last
hour has come, and as I die may I hold
you with my weakening hand.

[*Elegies*]

TOLSTOY, Leo (1828–1910)
Love is God, and when I die it means
that I, a particle of love, shall return to
the general and eternal source.

[*War and Peace* (1869)]

TROLLOPE, Anthony (1815–1882)
Love is like any other luxury. You have
no right to it unless you can afford it.

[*The Way We Live Now (1875)*]

WEBSTER, John (c. 1580–c. 1625)
Is not old wine wholesomest, old
pippins toothsomest? Does not old
wood burn brightest, old linen wash
whitest? Old soldiers, sweethearts, are
surest, and old lovers are soundest.

[*Westward Hoe* (1607)]

WILCOX, Ella Wheeler (1850–1919)
We flatter those we scarcely know,
We please the fleeting guest,
And deal full many a thoughtless blow
To those who love us best.

['Life's Scars' (1917)]

WILDE, Oscar (1854–1900)
When one is in love one begins by
deceiving oneself. And one ends by
deceiving others.

[*A Woman of No Importance* (1893)]

Yet each man kills the thing he loves,
By each let this be heard,
Some do it with a bitter look,
Some with a flattering word,
The coward does it with a kiss,
The brave man with a sword!

[*The Ballad of Reading Gaol* (1898)]

WYCHERLEY, William (c. 1640–1716)
A mistress should be like a little
country retreat near the town, not to
dwell in constantly, but only for a
night and away.

[*The Country Wife* (1675)]

YEATS, W.B. (1865–1939)
A pity beyond all telling
Is hid in the heart of love.

['The Pity of Love' (1892)]

See FRIENDSHIP; MARRIAGE; SEPARATION

MADNESS

BECKETT, Samuel (1906–1989)
We are all born mad. Some remain so.
[*Waiting for Godot* (1955)]

BEERBOHM, Sir Max (1872–1956)
Only the insane take themselves quite
seriously.
[Attr.]

CHESTERTON, G.K. (1874–1936)
The madman is not the man who has
lost his reason. The madman is the
man who has lost everything except
his reason.
[*Orthodoxy* (1908)]

CLARE, John (1793–1864)
Dear Sir, – I am in a Madhouse and
quite forget your name or who you
are.
[Letter, 1860]

DALI, Salvador (1904–1989)
There is only one difference between a
madman and me. I am not mad.
[*The American*, 1956]

**DAVIES, Scrope Berdmore
(c.1783–1852)**
Babylon in all its desolation is a sight
not so awful as that of the human
mind in ruins.
[Letter to Thomas Raikes, 1835]

DRYDEN, John (1631–1700)
Great wits are sure to madness near
    alli'd,
And thin partitions do their bounds
    divide.
[*Absalom and Achitophel* (1681)]

EURIPIDES (c. 485–406 BC)
Whom God wishes to destroy, he first
makes mad.
[Fragment]

GEORGE II (1683–1760)
[Reply to the Duke of Newcastle who
complained that General Wolfe was a
madman]
Mad, is he? Then I hope he will *bite*

some of my other generals.
[In Wilson, *The Life and Letters of James Wolfe*
(1909)]

GINSBERG, Allen (1926–)
I saw the best minds of my generation
destroyed by madness, starving hys-
terical naked.
[*Howl* (1956)]

GREENE, Graham (1904– 1991)
Innocence is a kind of insanity.
[*The Quiet American* (1955)]

HELLER, Joseph (1923–)
Orr was crazy and could be grounded.
All he had to do was ask; and as soon
as he did, he would no longer be crazy
and would have to fly more missions
... Yossarian was moved very deeply
by the absolute simplicity of this
clause of Catch-22 and let out a
respectful whistle.
[*Catch-22* (1961)]

JOHNSON, Samuel (1709–1784)
I inherited a vile melancholy from my
father, which has made me mad all my
life, at least not sober.
[In Boswell, *Journal of a Tour to the Hebrides*
(1785)]

If a madman were to come into this
room with a stick in his hand, no
doubt we should pity the state of his
mind; but our primary consideration
would be to take care of ourselves. We
should knock him down first, and pity
him afterwards.
[In Boswell, *The Life of Samuel Johnson*
(1791)]

JUNG, Carl Gustav (1875–1961)
Show me a sane man and I will cure
him for you.
[*The Observer*, 1975]

KIPLING, Rudyard (1865–1936)
The mad all are in God's keeping.
[*Kim* (1901)]

KYD, Thomas (1558–1594)
I am never better than when I am

mad. Then methinks I am a brave fellow; then I do wonders. But reason abuseth me, and there's the torment, there's the hell.

[*The Spanish Tragedy* (1592)]

LAING, R.D. (1927–1989)
The statesmen of the world who boast and threaten that they have Doomsday weapons are far more dangerous, and far more estranged from 'reality', than many of the people on whom the label 'psychotic' is affixed.

[*The Divided Self* (1960)]

Schizophrenia cannot be understood without understanding despair.

[*The Divided Self* (1960)]

Madness need not be all breakdown. It may also be break-through. It is potential liberation and renewal as well as enslavement and existential death.

[*The Politics of Experience* (1967)]

LAMB, Charles (1775–1834)
The six weeks that finished last year and begun this, your very humble servant spent very agreeably in a madhouse at Hoxton. I am got somewhat rational now, and don't bite anyone.

[Letter to Coleridge, 1796]

LEE, Nathaniel (c. 1653–1692)
[Objecting to being confined in Bedlam]
They called me mad, and I called them mad, and damn them, they outvoted me.

[In Porter, *A Social History of Madness*]

PROUST, Marcel (1871–1922)
Tout ce que nous connaissons de grand nous vient des nerveux. Ce sont eux et non pas d'autres qui ont fondé les religions et composé les chefs-d'oeuvre.
Everything great in the world is done by neurotics; they alone founded our religions and composed our

masterpieces.

[*Le Côté de Guermantes* (1921)]

Neurosis has an absolute genius for malingering. There is no illness which it cannot counterfeit perfectly ... If it is capable of deceiving the doctor, how should it fail to deceive the patient?

[*Le Côté de Guermantes* (1921)]

SHAKESPEARE, William (1564–1616)
And he repelled, a short tale to make,
Fell into a sadness, then into a fast,
Thence to a watch, thence into a weakness,
Thence to a lightness, and, by this declension,
Into the madness wherein now he raves
And all we mourn for.

[*Hamlet*, II.ii]

O, what a noble mind is here o'erthrown!
The courtier's, soldier's, scholar's, eye, tongue, sword;
Th' expectancy and rose of the fair state,
The glass of fashion and the mould of form,
Th' observ'd of all observers – quite, quite down!

[*Hamlet*, III.i]

O, let me not be mad, not mad, sweet heaven!
Keep me in temper; I would not be mad!

[*King Lear*, I.v]

Canst thou not minister to a mind diseas'd,
Pluck from the memory a rooted sorrow,
Raze out the written troubles of the brain,
And with some sweet oblivious antidote
Cleanse the stuff'd bosom of that perilous stuff
Which weighs upon the heart?

[*Macbeth*, V.iii]

It is the very error of the moon;
She comes more nearer earth than she
    was wont,
And makes men mad.

[*Othello*, V.ii]

SMOLLETT, Tobias (1721–1771)
I think for my part one half of the
nation is mad – and the other not very
sound.

[*The Adventures of Sir Launcelot Greaves*
(1762)]

SZASZ, Thomas (1920–)
Psychiatrists classify a person as
neurotic if he suffers from his problems in living, and a psychotic if he
makes others suffer.

[*The Second Sin* (1973)]

If you talk to God, you are praying; if
God talks to you, you have schizophrenia. If the dead talk to you, you
are a spiritualist; if God talks to you,
you are a schizophrenic.

[*The Second Sin* (1973)]

VOLTAIRE (1694–1778)
Men will always be mad and those
who think they can cure them are the
maddest of all.

[Letter, 1762]

MANNERS

BRADBURY, Malcolm (1932–)
The English are polite by telling lies.
The Americans are polite by telling the
truth.

[*Stepping Westward* (1965)]

COWARD, Sir Noël (1899–1973)
Comedies of manners swiftly become
obsolete when there are no longer any
manners.

[*Relative Values* (1951)]

EASTMAN, Max (1883–1969)
[On chivalry]
It is but the courteous exterior of a
bigot.

[*Woman Suffrage and Sentiment*]

EMERSON, Ralph Waldo (1803–1882)
Good manners are made up of petty
sacrifices.

['Social Aims' (1875)]

JARRELL, Randall (1914–1965)
To Americans English manners are far
more frightening than none at all.

[*Pictures from an Institution* (1954)]

KERR, Jean (1923–)
Man is the only animal that learns by
being hypocritical. He pretends to be
polite and then, eventually, he *becomes* polite.

[*Finishing Touches* (1973)]

LOUIS XVIII (1755–1824)
L'exactitude est la politesse des rois.
Punctuality is the politeness of kings.

[Attr.]

**MAUGHAM, William Somerset
(1874–1965)**
The right people are rude. They can
afford to be.

[*Our Betters* (1923)]

**MONTAGU, Lady Mary Wortley
(1689–1762)**
Civility costs nothing and buys
everything.

[Letter to the Countess of Bute, 1756]

STERNE, Laurence (1713–1768)
Hail ye small sweet courtesies of life.

[*A Sentimental Journey* (1768)]

THEROUX, Paul (1941–)
The Japanese have perfected good
manners and made them indistinguishable from rudeness.

[*The Great Railway Bazaar* (1975)]

TWAIN, Mark (1835–1910)
Good breeding consists in concealing
how much we think of ourselves and
how little we think of other persons.

[*Notebooks* (1935)]

WAUGH, Evelyn (1903–1966)
Manners are especially the need of the
plain. The pretty can get away with

anything.

[*The Observer*, 1962]

WILLIAM OF WYKEHAM (1324–1404)
Manners maketh man.

[Motto of Winchester College and New
College, Oxford]

MARRIAGE

ALBERT, Prince Consort (1819–1861)
Tomorrow our marriage will be 21
years old! How many a storm has
swept over it and still it continues
green and fresh and throws out
vigorous roots.

[Attr.]

ASQUITH, Margot (1864–1945)
To marry a man out of pity is folly;
and, if you think you are going to
influence the kind of fellow who has
'never had a chance, poor devil,' you
are profoundly mistaken. One can only
influence the strong characters in life,
not the weak; and it is the height of
vanity to suppose that you can make
an honest man of anyone.

[*The Autobiography of Margot Asquith* (1920)]

BACON, Francis (1561–1626)
He that hath wife and children, hath
given hostages to fortune; for they are
impediments to great enterprises,
either of virtue or mischief.

['Of Marriage and Single Life' (1625)]

But the most ordinary cause of a
single life, is liberty; especially in
certain self-pleasing and humorous
minds, which are so sensible of every
restraint as they will go near to think
their girdles and garters to be bonds
and shackles.

['Of Marriage and Single Life' (1625)]

Wives are young men's mistresses,
companions for middle age, and old
men's nurses.

['Of Marriage and Single Life' (1625)]

What is it then to have or have no
wife,

But single thraldom, or a double strife?

[*The World* (1629)]

BENNETT, Arnold (1867–1931)
Being a husband is a whole-time job.
That is why so many husbands fail.
They cannot give their entire attention
to it.

[*The Title* (1918)]

THE BIBLE (King James Version)
Therefore shall a man leave his father
and his mother, and shall cleave unto
his wife: and they shall be one flesh.

[*Genesis*, 2:24]

BLACKSTONE, Sir William (1723–1780)
Husband and wife are one, and that
one is the husband.

[In Miles, *The Women's History of the World*
(1988)]

BURTON, Robert (1577–1640)
One was never married, and that's his
hell; another is, and that's his plague.

[*Anatomy of Melancholy* (1621)]

BYRON, Lord (1788–1824)
Though women are angels, yet wed-
lock's the devil.

['To Eliza' (1806)]

Romances paint at full length people's
wooings,
But only give a bust of marriages:
For no one cares for matrimonial
cooings.
There's nothing wrong in a connubial
kiss:
Think you, if Laura had been
Petrarch's wife,
He would have written sonnets all his
life?

[*Don Juan* (1824)]

CHAUCER, Geoffrey (c. 1340–1400)
Experience, though noon auctoritee
Were in this world, is right ynogh for
me
To speke of wo that is in mariage.

[*The Canterbury Tales* (1387)]

MARRIAGE

COLERIDGE, Samuel Taylor (1772–1834)
The most happy marriage I can picture or imagine to myself would be union of a deaf man to a blind woman.
[In Allsop, *Recollections* (1836)]

DISRAELI, Benjamin (1804–1881)
I have always thought that every woman should marry – and no man.
[*Lothair* (1870)]

Marriage is the greatest earthly happiness when founded on complete sympathy.
[Letter to Gladstone]

EASTWOOD, Clint (1930–)
There's only one way to have a happy marriage and as soon as I learn what it is I'll get married again.
[Attr.]

ELIOT, George (1819–1880)
A woman dictates before marriage in order that she may have an appetite for submission afterwards.
[*Middlemarch* (1872)]

FARQUHAR, George (1678–1707)
It is a maxim that man and wife should never have it in their power to hang one another.
[*The Beaux' Stratagem* (1707)]

GABOR, Zsa-Zsa (1919–)
Husbands are like fires. They go out when unattended.
[*Newsweek*, 1960]

GOLDSMITH, Oliver (c. 1728–1774)
I ... chose my wife as she did her wedding gown, not for a fine glossy surface, but such qualities as would wear well.
[*The Vicar of Wakefield* (1766)]

HARDY, Rev. E.J. (1849–1920)
How To Be Happy Though Married.
[Title of book, 1885]

HERBERT, Sir A.P. (1890–1971)
The critical period in matrimony is breakfast-time.
[*Uncommon Law* (1935)]

HUME, David (1711–1776)
I shall tell the women what it is our sex complains of in the married state; and if they be disposed to satisfy us in this particular, all the other difficulties will easily be accommodated. If I be not mistaken, 'tis their love of dominion.
[*Essays, Moral, Political and Literary* (1742)]

JOHNSON, Samuel (1709–1784)
Marriage has many pains, but celibacy has no pleasures.
[*Rasselas* (1759)]

A gentleman who had been very unhappy in marriage married immediately after his wife died. Dr Johnson said, it was the triumph of hope over experience.
[In Boswell, *The Life of Samuel Johnson* (1791)]

It is so far from being natural for a man and woman to live in a state of marriage that we find all the motives which they have for remaining in that connection, and the restraints which civilized society imposes to prevent separation, are hardly sufficient to keep them together.
[In Boswell, *The Life of Samuel Johnson* (1791)]

Marriages would in general be as happy, and often more so, if they were all made by the Lord Chancellor ... without the parties having any choice in the matter.
[In Boswell, *The Life of Samuel Johnson* (1791)]

KEATS, John (1795–1821)
The roaring of the wind is my wife and the Stars through the window pane are my Children ... the opinion I have

of the generality of women – who appear to me as children to whom I would rather give a Sugar Plum than my time, forms a barrier against Matrimony which I rejoice in.

[Letter to George and Georgiana Keats, 1818]

LAMB, Charles (1775–1834)
Nothing to me is more distasteful than that entire complacency and satisfaction which beam in the countenance of a new-married couple.

[*Essays of Elia* (1823)]

MACNEICE, Louis (1907–1963)
So they were married – to be the more together –
And found they were never again so much together,
Divided by the morning tea,
By the evening paper,
By children and tradesmen's bills.

['Les Sylphides' (1941)]

MARTINEAU, Harriet (1802–1876)
Any one must see at a glance that if men and women marry those whom they do not love, they must love those whom they do not marry.

[*Society in America* (1837)]

I am in truth very thankful for not having married at all.

[*Harriet Martineau's Autobiography* (1877)]

MILL, John Stuart (1806–1873)
The moral regeneration of mankind will only really commence, when the most fundamental of the social relations [marriage] is placed under the rule of equal justice, and when human beings learn to cultivate their strongest sympathy with an equal in rights and cultivation.

[*The Subjection of Women* (1869)]

MILTON, John (1608–1674)
Flesh of Flesh,
Bone of my Bone thou art, and from thy State
Mine never shall be parted, weal or woe.

[*Paradise Lost* (1667)]

POPE, Alexander (1688–1744)
She who ne'er answers till a Husband cools,
Or, if she rules him, never shows she rules;
Charms by accepting, by submitting sways,
Yet has her humour most, when she obeys.

['Epistle to a Lady' (1735)]

SAIKAKU, Ihara (1642–1693)
And why do people wilfully exhaust their strength in promiscuous living, when their wives are on hand from bridal night till old age – to be taken when required, like fish from a private pond.

[*The Japanese Family Storehouse* (1688)]

SAKI (1870–1916)
The Western custom of one wife and hardly any mistresses.

[*Reginald in Russia* (1910)]

SHAKESPEARE, William (1564–1616)
Men are April when they woo,
December when they wed: maids are May when they are maids, but the sky changes when they are wives.

[*As You Like It*, IV.i]

Let me give light, but let me not be light,
For a light wife doth make a heavy husband.

[*The Merchant of Venice*, V.i]

Thy husband is thy lord, thy life, thy keeper,
Thy head, thy sovereign; one that cares for thee,
And for thy maintenance commits his body
To painful labour both by sea and land.

[*The Taming of the Shrew*, V.ii]

Let still the woman take
An elder than herself; so wears she to him,
So sways she level in her husband's heart.

For, boy, however we do praise
ourselves,
Our fancies are more giddy and
unfirm,
More longing, wavering, sooner lost
and won,
Than women's are.

[*Twelfth Night*, II.iv]

SHAW, George Bernard (1856–1950)
Those who talk most about the
blessings of marriage and the
constancy of its vows are the very
people who declare that if the chain
were broken and the prisoners left free
to choose, the whole social fabric
would fly asunder. You cannot have
the argument both ways. If the
prisoner is happy, why lock him in? If
he is not, why pretend that he is?

[*Man and Superman* (1903)]

**SHERIDAN, Richard Brinsley
(1751–1816)**
'Tis safest in matrimony to begin with
a little aversion.

[*The Rivals* (1775)]

**STEVENSON, Robert Louis
(1850–1894)**
Even if we take matrimony at its
lowest, even if we regard it as no
more than a sort of friendship
recognized by the police.

[*Virginibus Puerisque* (1881)]

Marriage is a step so grave and
decisive that it attracts light-headed,
variable men by its very awfulness.

[*Virginibus Puerisque* (1881)]

Times are changed with him who
marries; there are no more by-path
meadows, where you may innocently
linger, but the road lies long and
straight and dusty to the grave.

[*Virginibus Puerisque* (1881)]

Trusty, dusky, vivid, true,
With eyes of gold and bramble-dew,
Steel-true and blade-straight,
The great artificer
Made my mate.

['My Wife' (1896)]

TAYLOR, Bishop Jeremy (1613–1667)
He that loves not his wife and children, feeds a lioness at home and
broods a nest of sorrows.

[*XXV Sermons Preached at Golden Grove*
(1653)]

WALES, Princess of (1961–)
[Referring to the Prince of Wales'
relationship with Camilla Parker-
Bowles]
There were three of us in this
marriage, so it was a bit crowded.

[BBC television interview, 1995]

WELDON, Fay (1931–)
... the great wonderful construct
which is marriage – a construct made
up of a hundred little kindnesses, a
thousand little bitings back of spite,
tens of thousands of minor actions of
good intent – this must not, as an
institution, be brought down in ruins.

[*Splitting* (1995)]

WILDE, Oscar (1854–1900)
The real drawback to marriage is that
it makes one unselfish. And unselfish
people are colourless.

[*The Picture of Dorian Gray* (1891)]

Twenty years of romance make a
woman look like a ruin; but twenty
years of marriage make her something
like a public building.

[*A Woman of No Importance* (1893)]

The amount of women in London who
flirt with their own husbands is perfectly scandalous. It looks so bad. It is
simply washing one's clean linen in
public.

[*The Importance of Being Earnest* (1895)]

I am not in favour of long
engagements. They give people the
opportunity of finding out each other's
character before marriage, which I
think is never advisable.

[*The Importance of Being Earnest* (1895)]

WODEHOUSE, P.G. (1881–1975)
All the unhappy marriages come from
the husbands having brains. What

good are brains to a man? They only unsettle him.

[*The Adventures of Sally* (1920)]

Like so many substantial Americans, he had married young and kept on marrying, springing from blonde to blonde like the chamois of the Alps leaping from crag to crag.

[In Usborne, *Wodehouse at Work to the End* (1976)]

See LOVE

MARTYRDOM

BOLEYN, Anne (1507–1536)
[Said on hearing that she was to be executed for adultery]
The king has been very good to me. He promoted me from a simple maid to be a marchioness. Then he raised me to be a queen. Now he will raise me to be a martyr.

[Attr.]

BROWNE, Sir Thomas (1605–1682)
Were the happiness of the next world as closely apprehended as the felicities of this, it were a martyrdom to live.

[*Hydriotaphia: Urn Burial* (1658)]

DRYDEN, John (1631–1700)
For all have not the gift of martyrdom.

[*The Hind and the Panther* (1687)]

IBÁRRURI, Dolores ('La Pasionaria') (1895–1989)
Il vaut mieux mourir debout que vivre à genoux!
It is better to die on your feet than to live on your knees.

[Speech, Paris, 1936]

KIERKEGAARD, Søren (1813–1855)
The tyrant dies and his rule is over; the martyr dies and his rule begins.

[Attr.]

LEWIS, C.S. (1898–1963)
She's the sort of woman who lives for others – you can tell the others by their hunted expression.

[*The Screwtape Letters* (1942)]

VOLTAIRE (1694–1778)
I am very fond of truth, but not at all of martyrdom.

[Letter to d'Alembert, 1776]

WILDE, Oscar (1854–1900)
A thing is not necessarily true because a man dies for it.

[*Sebastian Melmoth* (1904 edition)]

MATHEMATICS

BARRIE, Sir J.M. (1860–1937)
What is algebra exactly; is it those three-cornered things?

[*Quality Street* (1901)]

BROWNE, Sir Thomas (1605–1682)
I have often admired the mystical way of Pythagoras, and the secret magic of numbers.

[*Religio Medici* (1643)]

CARLYLE, Thomas (1795–1881)
It is a mathematical fact that the casting of this pebble from my hand alters the centre of gravity of the Universe.

[*Sartor Resartus* (1834)]

EINSTEIN, Albert (1879–1955)
As far as the laws of mathematics refer to reality, they are not certain, and as far as they are certain, they do not refer to reality.

[In Capra, *The Tao of Physics* (1975)]

EUCLID (fl. c. 300 BC)
A line is length without breadth.

[*Elements*]

[To Ptolemy I]
There is no royal road to geometry.

[In Proclus, *Commentaria in Euclidem*]

FLEMING, Marjory (1803–1811)
The most devilish thing is 8 times 8 and 7 times 7 it is what nature itselfe cant endure.

[In Esdaile, *Journals, Letters and Verses* (1934)]

PLATO (c. 429–347 BC)
[Inscription written over the entrance

to the Academy]
Let no one ignorant of mathematics
enter here.

[Attr.]

RUSSELL, Bertrand (1872–1970)
Mathematics, rightly viewed,
possesses not only truth, but supreme
beauty – a beauty cold and austere,
like that of sculpture.

[*Mysticism and Logic* (1918)]

SMITH, Sydney (1771–1845)
What would life be without arithmetic,
but a scene of horrors.

[*Letters*, To Miss — , 1835]

THE MEDIA

**BJELKE-PETERSEN, Sir Johannes
(1911–)**
The greatest thing that could happen
to the state and the nation is when we
can get rid of all the media. Then we
could live in peace and tranquillity,
and no one would know anything.

[*The Spectator*, 1987]

CHOMSKY, Noam (1928–)
The Internet is an élite organisation;
most of the population of the world
has never even made a phone call.

[*The Observer Review*, 1996]

HOWARD, Philip (1933–)
The proliferation of radio and
television channels has produced a
wilderness of cave-dwellers instead of
the promised global village.

[*The Times*, 1992]

JACKSON, Robert (1946–)
To have open government you need
mature media. It is more difficult for
people to discuss complex issues than
it used to be because of the destructive
power of the tabloids. The TV sound
bite also makes it impossible to
communicate complex arguments. It is
all black and white, cut and dried, yaa-
boo.

[*Independent on Sunday*, 1994]

MCLUHAN, Marshall (1911–1980)
The medium is the message. This is
merely to say that the personal and
social consequences of any medium ...
result from the new scale that is
introduced into our affairs by each
extension of ourselves or by any new
technology.

[*Understanding Media* (1964)]

MURDOCH, Rupert (1931–)
Monopoly is a terrible thing, till you
have it.

[*The New Yorker*, 1979]

REITH, Lord (1889–1971)
It was in fact the combination of
public service motive, sense of moral
obligation, assured finance and the
brute force of monopoly which
enabled the BBC to make of broad-
casting what no other country has
made of it.

[*Into the Wind* (1949)]

WHITLAM, Gough (1916–)
Quite small and ineffectual demon-
strations can be made to look like the
beginnings of a revolution if the
cameraman is in the right place at the
right time.

[*A Dictionary of Contemporary Quotations*
(1982)]

See NEWS; TELEVISION

MEDICINE

ARNOLD, Matthew (1822–1888)
Nor bring, to see me cease to live,
Some doctor full of phrase and fame,
To shake his sapient head and give
The ill he cannot cure a name.

['A Wish' (1867)]

THE BIBLE (King James Version)
Physician, heal thyself.

[*Luke*, 4:23]

CHEKHOV, Anton (1860–1904)
Medicine is my lawful wife but
literature is my mistress. When I'm
bored with one, I spend the night with

the other.

[Letter to Suvorin, 1888]

FLETCHER, John (1579–1625)
I find the medicine worse than the malady.

[*The Lover's Progress* (1623)]

FRANKLIN, Benjamin (1706–1790)
He's the best physician that knows the worthlessness of the most medicines.

[*Poor Richard's Almanac* (1733)]

GOLDSMITH, Oliver (c. 1728–1774)
The doctor found, when she was dead, Her last disorder mortal.

['Elegy on Mrs Mary Blaize' (1759)]

GOLDWYN, Samuel (1882–1974)
Any man who goes to a psychiatrist should have his head examined.

[In Zierold, *Moguls* (1969)]

HAHNEMANN, C.F.S. (1755–1843)
Similia similibus curantur.
Like cures like.

[Motto of homeopathic medicine]

HIPPOCRATES (c. 460–357 BC)
[Of medicine]
Life is short, science is so long to learn, opportunity is elusive, experience is dangerous, judgement is difficult.

[*Aphorisms* (c. 415 BC); often quoted as *Ars longa, vita brevis*]

JOHNSON, Samuel (1709–1784)
It is incident to physicians, I am afraid, beyond all other men, to mistake subsequence for consequence.

[In Boswell, *The Life of Samuel Johnson* (1791)]

LOOS, Anita (1893–1981)
So then Dr Froyd said that all I needed was to cultivate a few inhibitions and get some sleep.

[*Gentlemen Prefer Blondes* (1925)]

MCLUHAN, Marshall (1911–1980)
If the nineteenth century was the age of the editorial chair, ours is the century of the psychiatrist's couch.

[*Understanding Media* (1964)]

QUARLES, Francis (1592–1644)
Physicians of all men are most happy; what good success soever they have, the world proclaimeth, and what faults they commit, the earth covereth.

[*Hieroglyphics of the Life of Man* (1638)]

SHAW, George Bernard (1856–1950)
Taking all the round of professions and occupations, you will find that every man is the worse for being poor; and the doctor is a specially dangerous man when poor.

[*The Socialist Criticism of the Medical Profession* (1909)]

Optimistic lies have such immense therapeutic value that a doctor who cannot tell them convincingly has mistaken his profession.

[*Misalliance* (1914)]

STOCKWOOD, Mervyn (1913–)
A psychiatrist is a man who goes to the Folies-Bergère and looks at the audience.

[*The Observer*, 1961]

SZASZ, Thomas (1920–)
Formerly, when religion was strong and science weak, men mistook magic for medicine, now, when science is strong and religion weak, men mistake medicine for magic.

[*The Second Sin* (1973)]

WILLIAMS, Tennessee (1911–1983)
[Explaining why he had stopped seeing his psychoanalyst]
He was meddling too much in my private life.

[Attr.]

See HEALTH; ILLNESS

MEMORY

APOLLINAIRE, Guillaume (1880–1918)
Les souvenirs sont cors de chasse

Dont meurt le bruit parmi le vent.
Memories are hunting horns whose
sound dies away in the wind.

['Cors de Chasse' (1913)]

ARNOLD, Matthew (1822–1888)
And we forget because we must
And not because we will.

['Absence' (1852)]

AUSTEN, Jane (1775–1817)
There seems something more
speakingly incomprehensible in the
powers, the failures, the inequalities of
memory, than in any other of our
intelligences.

[*Mansfield Park* (1814)]

BRIDGES, Robert (1844–1930)
Rejoice ye dead, where'er your spirits
    dwell,
Rejoice that yet on earth your fame is
    bright,
And that your names, remembered day
    and night,
Live on the lips of those who love you
    well.

['Ode to Music' (1896)]

BRODSKY, Joseph (1940–1996)
What memory has in common with art
is the knack for selection, the taste for
detail ... More than anything, memory
resembles a library in alphabetical
disorder, and with no collected works
by anyone.

['In a Room and a Half' (1986)]

CAMPBELL, Thomas (1777–1844)
To live in hearts we leave behind
Is not to die.

['Hallowed Ground']

DISRAELI, Benjamin (1804–1881)
Nobody is forgotten when it is convenient to remember him.

[Attr.]

**LA ROCHEFOUCAULD, Duc de
(1613–1680)**
*Tout le monde se plaint de sa mémoire,
et personne ne se plaint de son*

jugement.
Everyone complains of his memory;
nobody of his judgment.

[*Maximes* (1678)]

SCHOPENHAUER, Arthur (1788–1860)
To expect a man to retain everything
that he has ever read is like expecting
him to carry about in his body everything that he has ever eaten.

[*Parerga and Paralipomena* (1851)]

SHAKESPEARE, William (1564–1616)
Praising what is lost
Makes the remembrance dear.

[*All's Well That Ends Well*, V.iii]

SHAW, George Bernard (1856–1950)
Reminiscences make one feel so
deliciously aged and sad.

[*The Irrational Knot* (1905)]

MEN

BARRIE, Sir J.M. (1860–1937)
I have always found that the man
whose second thoughts are good is
worth watching.

[*What Every Woman Knows* (1908)]

THE BIBLE (King James Version)
It is not good that the man should be
alone; I will make him an help meet
for him.

[*Genesis*, 2:18]

BOMBECK, Erma (1927–1996)
What's wrong with you men? Would
hair stop growing on your chest if you
asked directions somewhere?

[*When You Look Like Your Passport Photo, It's
Time to Go Home* (1991)]

CONNOLLY, Cyril (1903–1974)
The true index of a man's character is
the health of his wife.

[*The Unquiet Grave* (1944)]

COPE, Wendy (1945–)
There are so many kinds of awful
    men –
One can't avoid them all. She often
    said

She'd never make the same mistake
again:
She always made a new mistake
instead.

['Rondeau Redoublé' (1986)]

DICKINSON, Angie (1931–)
Men should be the ones who succeed.
It makes me feel comfortable if men
are the ones in control.

[*Daily Mail*, 1995]

DRYDEN, John (1631–1700)
Men are but children of a larger
growth;
Our appetites as apt to change as
theirs,
And full as craving too, and full as
vain.

[*All for Love* (1678)]

DWORKIN, Andrea (1946–)
Men love death. In everything they
make, they hollow out a central place
for death ... Men especially love
murder. In art they celebrate it. In life,
they commit it.

[*The Independent*, 1992]

EMERSON, Ralph Waldo (1803–1882)
Men are what their mothers made
them.

[*The Conduct of Life* (1860)]

FORD, Anna (1943–)
It is men who face the biggest problems in the future, adjusting to their
new and complicated role.

[Remark, 1981]

FRANCIS, Clare (1946–)
I think men are intimidated by my
independence and wonder what they
have to offer me when I already have
a house in Kensington and a career.
Men of my generation still need to feel
needed.

[*Daily Mail*, 1995]

FRANKLIN, Miles (1879–1954)
Men are clumsy, stupid creatures
regarding little things, but in their right
place they are wonderful animals.

[*My Brilliant Career* (1901)]

FRENCH, Marilyn (1929–)
Whatever they may be in public life,
whatever their relations with men, in
their relations with women, all men
are rapists, and that's all they are.
They rape us with their eyes, their
laws and their codes.

[*The Women's Room* (1977)]

FRIEDAN, Betty (1921–)
Men weren't really the enemy – they
were fellow victims suffering from an
outmoded masculine mystique that
made them feel unnecessarily inad-
equate when there were no bears to
kill.

[*Christian Science Monitor*, 1974)]

FRYE, Marilyn
Gay men generally are in significant
ways, perhaps in all important ways,
more loyal to masculinity and male-
supremacy than other men. The gay
rights movement may be the funda-
mentalism of the global religion which
is patriarchy.

[In Burchill, *Sex and Sensibility* (1992)]

GABOR, Zsa-Zsa (1919–)
Never despise what it says in the
women's magazines: it may not be
subtle but neither are men.

[*The Observer*, 1976]

GASKELL, Elizabeth (1810–1865)
A man ... is so in the way in the
house!

[*Cranford* (1853)]

GREER, Germaine (1939–)
Probably the only place where a man
can feel really secure is in a maximum
security prison, except for the imminent threat of release.

[*The Female Eunuch* (1970)]

HALL, Jerry (1956–)
My mother said it was simple to keep
a man, you must be a maid in the
living room, a cook in the kitchen and
a whore in the bedroom. I said I'd hire
the other two and take care of the
bedroom bit.

[*The Observer*, 1985]

HILL, Reginald (1936–)
He created a man who was hard of head, blunt of speech, knew which side his bread was buttered on, and above all took no notice of women. Then God sent him forth to multiply in Yorkshire.

[*Pictures of Perfection* (1994)]

KEILLOR, Garrison (1942–)
Years ago, manhood was an opportunity for achievement, and now it is a problem to be overcome.

[*The Book of Guys* (1994)]

KENNEDY, Florynce R. (1916–)
If men could get pregnant, abortion would be a sacrament.

[In Steinem, *The Verbal Karate of Florynce R. Kennedy, Esq.* (1973)]

MARX, Groucho (1895–1977)
A man is only as old as the woman he feels.

[Attr.]

MENCKEN, H.L. (1880–1956)
Every normal man must be tempted, at times, to spit on his hands, hoist the black flag, and begin slitting throats.

[*Prejudices* (1922)]

Men have a much better time of it than women. For one thing, they marry later. For another thing, they die earlier.

[*A Mencken Chrestomathy* (1949)]

NORRIS, Kathleen (1880–1966)
There are men I could spend eternity with. But not this life.

[*The Middle of the World* (1981)]

PALACIO VALDES, Armando (1853–1938)
Cuando un hombre deja de ser un dios para su esposa, puede tener la seguridad de que ya es menos que un hombre.
When a man stops being a god for his wife, he can be sure that he's now less than a man.

[*Doctor Angélico's Papers* (1911)]

SEVIGNE, Mme de (1626–1696)
The more I see of men, the more I admire dogs.

[Attr.]

SHAKESPEARE, William (1564–1616)
O heaven, were man
But constant, he were perfect!

[*The Two Gentlemen of Verona*, V.iv]

TWAIN, Mark (1835–1910)
[Responding to the question 'In a world without women what would men become?']
Scarce, sir. Mighty scarce.

[Attr.]

VAIL, Amanda (1921–1966)
Sometimes I think if there was a third sex men wouldn't get so much as a glance from me.

[*Love Me Little* (1957)]

WEST, Mae (1892–1980)
A man in the house is worth two in the street.

[*Belle of the Nineties*, film, 1934]

WEST, Dame Rebecca (1892–1983)
[Defining an anti-feminist]
The man who is convinced that his mother was a fool.

[*The Clarion*]

WHITEHORN, Katherine (1926–)
No nice men are good at getting taxis.

[*The Observer*, 1977]

MEN AND WOMEN

BURCHILL, Julie (1960–)
Men have charisma; women have vital statistics.

[*Sex and Sensibility* (1992)]

BYRON, Lord (1788–1824)
Man's love is of man's life a thing apart,
'Tis woman's whole existence.

[*Don Juan* (1824)]

The more I see of men, the less I like them. If I could but say so of women too, all would be well.

[Journal, 1814]

CHESTERFIELD, Lord (1694–1773)
Have you found out that every woman is infallibly to be gained by every sort of flattery, and every man by one sort or other?

[Letter to his son, 1752]

COLERIDGE, Samuel Taylor (1772–1834)
The man's desire is for the woman; but the woman's desire is rarely other than for the desire of the man.

[Table Talk (1835)]

DAVIES, Robertson (1913–)
Women tell men things that men are not very likely to find out for themselves.

[In J. Madison Davis, Conversations with Robertson Davies (1989)]

DIETRICH, Marlene (1901–1992)
The average man is more interested in a woman who is interested in him than he is in a woman – any woman – with beautiful legs.

[News item, 1954]

Most women set out to try to change a man, and when they have changed him they do not like him.

[Attr.]

EBNER-ESCHENBACH, Marie von (1830–1916)
Eine gescheite Frau hat Millionen geborener Feinde – alle dummen Männer.
A clever woman has millions of born enemies – all stupid men.

[Aphorisms (1880)]

ELIOT, George (1819–1880)
I'm not denyin' the women are foolish: God Almighty made 'em to match the men.

[Adam Bede (1859)]

A man is seldom ashamed of feeling that he cannot love a woman so well when he sees a certain greatness in her: nature having intended greatness for men.

[Middlemarch (1872)]

EVANS, Dame Edith (1888–1976)
When a woman behaves like a man, why doesn't she behave like a nice man?

[The Observer, 1956]

FAIRBAIRN, Lady Sam
Behind every great man is an exhausted woman.

[The Independent, 1994]

GAY, John (1685–1732)
Man may escape from rope and gun;
Nay, some have out-liv'd the doctor's pill:
Who takes a woman must be undone,
That basilisk is sure to kill.
The fly that sips treacle is lost in the sweets,
So he that tastes woman, woman, woman,
He that tastes woman, ruin meets.

[The Beggar's Opera (1728)]

HENRY, O. (1862–1910)
If men knew how women pass the time when they are alone they'd never marry.

['Memoirs of a Yellow Dog' (1906)]

HOLMES, Oliver Wendell (1809–1894)
Man has his will, – but woman has her way.

[The Autocrat of the Breakfast-Table (1858)]

KIPLING, Rudyard (1865–1936)
Open and obvious devotion from any sort of man is always pleasant to any sort of woman.

[Plain Tales from the Hills (1888)]

LAVER, James (1899–1975)
Man in every age has created woman in the image of his own desire.

[In Neustater, Hyenas in Petticoats: a Look at 20 Years of Feminism (1989)]

LERNER, Alan Jay (1918–1986)
Why can't a woman be more like a man?
Men are so honest, so thoroughly square;
Eternally noble, historically fair.
[*My Fair Lady* (1956)]

MEAD, Margaret (1901–1978)
Women want mediocre men, and men are working to be as mediocre as possible.
[*Quote Magazine*, 1958]

MENCKEN, H.L. (1880–1956)
Women hate revolutions and revolutionists. They like men who are docile, and well-regarded at the bank, and never late at meals.
[*Prejudices* (1922)]

POPE, Alexander (1688–1744)
Men, some to business, some to pleasure take;
But every Woman is at heart a rake:
Men, some to quiet, some to public strife;
But every lady would be queen for life.
['Epistle to a Lady' (1735)]

RAMEY, Estelle (1917–)
More and more it appears that, biologically, men are designed for short, brutal lives and women for long miserable ones.
[*The Observer*, 1985]

RHONDDA, Viscountess (1883–1958)
Women must come off the pedestal. Men put us up there to get us out of the way.
[*The Observer*, 1920]

SCHREINER, Olive (1855–1920)
It is delightful to be a woman; but every man thanks the Lord devoutly that he isn't one.
[*The Story of an African Farm* (1884)]

STEINEM, Gloria (1934–)
A woman needs a man like a fish needs a bicycle.
[Attr.]

TENNYSON, Alfred, Lord (1809–1892)
Man is the hunter; woman is his game:
The sleek and shining creatures of the chase,
We hunt them for the beauty of their skins;
They love us for it, and we ride them down.
[*The Princess* (1847)]

Man for the field and woman for the hearth:
Man for the sword and for the needle she:
Man with the head and woman with the heart:
Man to command and woman to obey;
All else confusion.
[*The Princess* (1847)]

WEST, Mae (1892–1980)
When women go wrong, men go right after them.
[In Weintraub, *The Wit and Wisdom of Mae West* (1967)]

WILDE, Oscar (1854–1900)
Women represent the triumph of matter over mind, just as men represent the triumph of mind over morals.
[*The Picture of Dorian Gray* (1891)]

Men can be analysed, women ... merely adored.
[*An Ideal Husband* (1895)]

All women become like their mothers. That is their tragedy. No man does. That's his.
[*The Importance of Being Earnest* (1895)]

WODDIS, Roger
Men play the game; women know the score.
[*The Observer*, 1982]

WOOLF, Virginia (1882–1941)
It is the masculine values that prevail. Speaking crudely, football and sport are 'important'; the worship of fashion, the buying of clothes 'trivial'... This is an important book, the critic assumes, because it deals with war. This is an insignificant book because it deals

with feelings of women in a drawing-room ... everywhere and much more subtly the difference of values persists.

[A Room of One's Own (1929)]

Women have served all these centuries as looking-glasses possessing the magic and delicious power of reflecting the figure of man at twice its natural size.

[A Room of One's Own (1929)]

Why are women ... so much more interesting to men than men are to women?

[A Room of One's Own (1929)]

See FEMINISM; WOMEN

THE MIND

BERKELEY, Bishop George (1685–1753)
All the choir of heaven and furniture of earth – in a word, all those bodies which compose the mighty frame of the world – have not any subsistence without a mind.

[A Treatise Concerning the Principles of Human Knowledge (1710)]

BRADLEY, F.H. (1846–1924)
His mind is open; yes, it is so open that nothing is retained; ideas simply pass through him.

[Attr.]

BURKE, Edmund (1729–1797)
The march of the human mind is slow.

[Speech on Conciliation with America (1775)]

CHESTERTON, G.K. (1874–1936)
There is a road from the eye to the heart that does not go through the intellect.

[The Defendant (1901)]

DOSTOEVSKY, Fyodor (1821–1881)
The mind is a tool, a machine, moved by spiritual fire.

[Letter to his brother, 1838]

DYER, Sir Edward (c. 1540–1607)
My mind to me a kingdom is,
Such present joys therein I find,
That it excels all other bliss
That earth affords or grows by kind.
Though much I want which most
    would have,
Yet still my mind forbids to crave.

['In praise of a contented mind' (1588). Attr.]

HAMILTON, Sir William (1788–1856)
[Quoting Phavorinus]
On earth there is nothing great but man; in man there is nothing great but mind.

[Lectures on Metaphysics and Logic (1859)]

HUBBARD, Elbert (1856–1915)
Little minds are interested in the extraordinary; great minds in the commonplace.

[A Thousand and One Epigrams (1911)]

LA ROCHEFOUCAULD, Duc de (1613–1680)
L'esprit est toujours la dupe du coeur.
The mind is always fooled by the heart.

[Maximes (1678)]

RYLE, Gilbert (1900–1976)
The dogma of the Ghost in the Machine.

[The Concept of Mind (1949)]

WALPOLE, Horace (1717–1797)
When people will not weed their own minds, they are apt to be overrun with nettles.

[Letter to the Countess of Ailesbury, 1779]

WELCH, Raquel (1940–)
The mind can also be an erogenous zone.

[Attr.]

WILLIAMS, William Carlos (1883–1963)
Minds like beds always made up,
(more stony than a shore)
unwilling or unable.

[Paterson (1958)]

See IDEAS; THOUGHT

MODESTY

BARRIE, Sir J.M. (1860–1937)
I'm a second eleven sort of chap.
[*The Admirable Crichton* (1902)]

**BUCHANAN, Robert Williams
(1841–1901)**
She just wore
Enough for modesty – no more.
['White Rose and Red' (1873)]

CHURCHILL, Sir Winston (1874–1965)
[Of Clement Attlee]
He is a modest man who has a good
deal to be modest about.
[In *Chicago Sunday Tribune Magazine of
Books*, 1954]

CONGREVE, William (1670–1729)
Ah! Madam, ... you know every thing
in the world but your perfections, and
you only know not those, because 'tis
the top of perfection not to know
them.
[*Incognita* (1692)]

GILBERT, W.S. (1836–1911)
Wherever valour true is found,
True modesty will there abound.
[*The Yeoman of the Guard* (1888)]

STEELE, Sir Richard (1672–1729)
These Ladies of irresistible Modesty
are those who make Virtue unamiable.
[*The Tatler*, 1710]

MONARCHY

AMES, Fisher (1758–1808)
A monarchy is a merchantman which
sails well, but will sometimes strike on
a rock, and go to the bottom; a republic is a raft which will never sink,
but then your feet are always in the
water.
[Attr.]

BAGEHOT, Walter (1826–1877)
The mystic reverence, the religious
allegiance, which are essential to a
true monarchy, are imaginative
sentiments that no legislature can

manufacture in any people.
[*The English Constitution* (1867)]

The best reason why Monarchy is a
strong government is, that it is an
intelligible government. The mass of
mankind understand it, and they
hardly anywhere in the world understand any other.
[*The English Constitution* (1867)]

It has been said, not truly, but with a
possible approximation to truth, 'that
in 1802 every hereditary monarch was
insane.'
[*The English Constitution* (1867)]

GILMOUR, Sir Ian (1926–)
The monarch is a person and a
symbol. He makes power and state
both intelligible and mysterious.
[*The Times*, 1992]

HAMILTON, William (Willie) (1917–)
The tourists who come to our island
take in the Monarchy along with
feeding the pigeons in Trafalgar
Square.
[*My Queen and I* (1975)]

SELDEN, John (1584–1654)
A king is a thing men have made for
their own sakes, for quietness' sake.
Just as in a family one man is
appointed to buy the meat.
[*Table Talk* (1689)]

WILSON, Harold (1916–1995)
The monarchy is a labour-intensive
industry.
[*The Observer*, 1977]

ZAMOYSKI, Jan (1541–1605)
The king reigns, but does not govern.
[Speech, Polish Parliament, 1605]

See ROYALTY

MONEY AND WEALTH

ASTOR, John Jacob (1763–1848)
A man who has a million dollars is as

well off as if he were rich.

[Attr.]

BACON, Francis (1561-1626)
Riches are a good handmaid, but the worst mistress.

[*The Advancement of Learning* (1623)]

And money is like muck, not good except it be spread.

['Of Seditions and Troubles' (1625)]

BEHN, Aphra (1640-1689)
Money speaks sense in a language all nations understand.

[*The Rover* (1677)]

BELLOC, Hilaire (1870-1953)
I'm tired of Love: I'm still more tired of Rhyme.
But Money gives me pleasure all the time.

['Fatigue' (1923)]

BENCHLEY, Robert (1889-1945)
[Comment on being told his request for a loan had been granted]
I don't trust a bank that would lend money to such a poor risk.

[Attr.]

THE BIBLE (King James Version)
The love of money is the root of all evil.

[*I Timothy*, 6:10]

THE BIBLE (The New Testament in Scots)
Nae man can sair two maisters: aither he will ill-will the tane an luve the tither, or he will grip til the tane an lichtlifie the tither. Ye canna sair God an Gowd baith.

[*Matthew*, 6:24]

BRENAN, Gerald (1894-1987)
Those who have some means think that the most important thing in the world is love. The poor know that it is money.

[*Thoughts in a Dry Season* (1978)]

BURKE, Edmund (1729-1797)
If we command our wealth, we shall be rich and free: if our wealth commands us, we are poor indeed.

[*Two Letters on the Proposals for Peace with the Regicide Directory of France*]

BUTLER, Samuel (1835-1902)
It has been said that the love of money is the root of all evil. The want of money is so quite as truly.

[*Erewhon* (1872)]

CARNEGIE, Andrew (1835-1919)
Surplus wealth is a sacred trust which its possessor is bound to administer in his lifetime for the good of the community.

[*The Gospel of Wealth*]

DENNIS, Nigel (1912-1989)
But then one is always excited by descriptions of money changing hands. It's much more fundamental than sex.

[*Cards of Identity* (1955)]

FRANCE, Anatole (1844-1924)
Dans tout État policé, la richesse est chose sacrée; dans les démocraties elle est la seule chose sacrée.
In every well-governed state, wealth is a sacred thing; in democracies it is the only sacred thing.

[*Penguin Island* (1908)]

GALBRAITH, J.K. (1908-)
Wealth is not without its advantages, and the case to the contrary, although it has often been made, has never proved widely persuasive.

[*The Affluent Society* (1958)]

Money differs from an automobile, a mistress or cancer in being equally important to those who have it and those who do not.

[Attr.]

GETTY, J. Paul (1892-1976)
If you can actually count your money you are not really a rich man.

[In A. Barrow, *Gossip*]

245

MONEY AND WEALTH

GREGORY, Lady Isabella (1852–1932)
It's a good thing to be able to take up
your money in your hand and to think
no more of it when it slips away from
you than you would of a trout that
would slip back into the stream.

[*Twenty-Five*]

HORACE (65–8 BC)
Rem facias, rem si possis recte, si non,
quocumque modo rem.
Make money: make it honestly if
possible; if not, make it by any means.

[*Epistles*]

HUGHES, Howard (1905–1976)
[Response when called a 'paranoid,
deranged millionaire' by a newspaper]
Goddammit, I'm a *billionaire*.

[Attr.]

HUXLEY, Sir Julian (1887–1975)
We all know how the size of sums of
money appears to vary in a remarkable way according as they are being
paid in or paid out.

[*Essays of a Biologist*]

ILLICH, Ivan (1926–)
Man must choose whether to be rich
in things or in the freedom to use
them.

[*Deschooling Society* (1971)]

JOHNSON, Samuel (1709–1784)
You never find people labouring to
convince you that you may live very
happily upon a plentiful fortune.

[In Boswell, *The Life of Samuel Johnson*
(1791)]

There are few ways in which a man
can be more innocently employed than
in getting money.

[In Boswell, *The Life of Samuel Johnson*
(1791)]

LAWRENCE, D.H. (1885–1930)
Money is our madness, our vast
collective madness.

['Money-Madness' (1929)]

MACNEICE, Louis (1907–1963)
It is particularly vulgar to talk about
one's money – whether one has lots of
it, and boasts about it, or is broke, and
says so. Now I myself cannot see why
a man should not talk about his
money. Everybody is interested in
everybody else's finances, and it seems
hypocrisy to hush the subject up in the
drawing room – as if bank balances
were found under gooseberry bushes.

['In Defence of Vulgarity' (1937)]

MILNE, A.A. (1882–1956)
For one person who dreams of making
fifty thousand pounds, a hundred
people dream of being left fifty thousand pounds.

[*If I May*]

MORAVIA, Alberto (1907–1990)
Ma è morto come potrebbe domani
morire tanta gente come lui: correndo
dietro al denaro e illudendosi che non ci
sia che il denaro; e poi, improvvisamente,
restando agghiacciato dalla paura alla
vista di ciò che sta dietro il denaro.
But he died as many people like him
could die tomorrow, running after
money, and believing that there is
nothing but money; then he was
suddenly frozen by the fear of seeing
what lies behind money.

[*Two Women* (1957)]

REINHARDT, Gottfried (1911–)
Money is good for bribing yourself
through the inconveniences of life.

[In L. Ross, *Picture*]

RUNYON, Damon (1884–1946)
Always try to rub up against money, for
if you rub up against money long
enough, some of it may rub off on you.

[*Furthermore* (1938)]

RUSKIN, John (1819–1900)
Whereas it has long been known and
declared that the poor have no right to
the property of the rich, I wish it also
to be known and declared that the rich
have no right to the property of the

poor.

[*Unto this Last* (1862)]

SCHOPENHAUER, Arthur (1788–1860)
Wealth is like sea-water; the more we drink, the thirstier we become.

[*Parerga and Paralipomena* (1851)]

SHAKESPEARE, William (1564–1616)
Well, whiles I am a beggar, I will rail
And say there is no sin but to be rich;
And being rich, my virtue then shall be
To say there is no vice but beggary.

[*King John*, II.i]

SHAW, George Bernard (1856–1950)
The universal regard for money is the one hopeful fact in our civilization, the one sound spot in our social conscience. Money is the most important thing in the world. It represents health, strength, honour, generosity and beauty as conspicuously and undeniably as the want of it represents illness, weakness, disgrace, meanness and ugliness.

[*Major Barbara* (1907)]

SICKERT, Walter (1860–1942)
Nothing knits man to man ... like the frequent passage from hand to hand of cash.

['The Language of Art']

SMITH, Logan Pearsall (1865–1946)
To suppose, as we all suppose, that we could be rich and not behave as the rich behave, is like supposing that we could drink all day and keep absolutely sober.

[*Afterthoughts* (1931)]

THATCHER, Margaret (1925–)
Pennies do not come from heaven. They have to be earned here on earth.

[*The Sunday Telegraph*, 1982]

TUCKER, Sophie (1884–1966)
From birth to eighteen, a girl needs good parents. From eighteen to thirty-five, she needs good looks. From thirty-five to fifty-five, she needs a good personality. From fifty-five on, she needs good cash.

[In Freedland, *Sophie* (1978)]

I've been poor and I've been rich. Rich is better.

[In Cowan, *The Wit of Women*]

TWAIN, Mark (1835–1910)
[Agreeing with a friend's comment that the money of a particular rich industrialist was 'tainted']
That's right. 'Taint yours, and 'taint mine.

[Attr.]

A banker is a person who lends you his umbrella when the sun is shining and wants it back the minute it rains.

[Attr.]

WILLIAMS, Tennessee (1911–1983)
You can be young without money but you can't be old without it.

[*Cat on a Hot Tin Roof* (1955)]

See INCOME

MORALITY

AYER, A.J. (1910–1989)
No morality can be founded on authority, even if the authority were divine.

[*Essay on Humanism*]

BRECHT, Bertolt (1898–1956)
Erst kommt das Fressen, dann kommt die Moral.
Feeding your face comes first, then morality.

[*The Threepenny Opera* (1928)]

HUXLEY, Aldous (1894–1963)
The quality of moral behaviour varies in inverse ratio to the number of human beings involved.

[*Grey Eminence* (1941)]

JOHNSON, Samuel (1709–1784)
We are perpetually moralists, but we are geometricians only by chance. Our intercourse with intellectual nature is necessary; our speculations upon

247

MORTALITY

matter are voluntary, and at leisure.

['Milton']

LAWRENCE, D.H. (1885–1930)
Morality which is based on ideas, or on an ideal, is an unmitigated evil.

[*Fantasia of the Unconscious* (1922)]

MACAULAY, Lord (1800–1859)
We know of no spectacle so ridiculous as the British public in one of its periodical fits of morality.

['Moore's *Life of Byron*' (1843)]

NIETZSCHE, Friedriech (1844–1900)
Moralität ist Herden-Instinkt im Einzelnen.
Morality is the herd-instinct in the individual.

[*The Gay Science* (1887)]

PROUST, Marcel (1871–1922)
On devient moral dès qu'on est malheureux.
One becomes moral as soon as one is unhappy.

[*A l'ombre des jeunes filles en fleurs* (1918)]

RUSSELL, Bertrand (1872–1970)
We have, in fact, two kinds of morality side by side: one which we preach but do not practise, and another which we practise but seldom preach.

[*Sceptical Essays* (1928)]

SAMUEL, Lord (1870–1963)
Without doubt the greatest injury of all was done by basing morals on myth. For, sooner or later, myth is recognized for what it is, and disappears. Then morality loses the foundation on which it has been built.

[Romanes Lecture, 1947]

SHAW, George Bernard (1856–1950)
An Englishman thinks he is moral when he is only uncomfortable.

[*Man and Superman* (1903)]

SPENCER, Herbert (1820–1903)
Absolute morality is the regulation of conduct in such a way that pain shall not be inflicted.

['Prison Ethics' (1891)]

STEVENSON, Robert Louis (1850–1894)
If your morals make you dreary, depend upon it, they are wrong.

[*Across the Plains* (1892)]

WILDE, Oscar (1854–1900)
Morality is simply the attitude we adopt towards people whom we personally dislike.

[*An Ideal Husband* (1895)]

WITTGENSTEIN, Ludwig (1889–1951)
Ethics does not treat of the world. Ethics must be a condition of the world, like logic.

[In Auden, *A Certain World*]

See GOOD AND EVIL; GOODNESS; VIRTUE

MORTALITY

ANONYMOUS
Gaudeamus igitur,
Juvenes dum sumus
Post jucundam juventutem,
Post molestam senectutem,
Nos habebit humus.
Let us be happy while we are young, for after carefree youth and careworn age, the earth will hold us also.

['Gaudeamus Igitur', 13th century]

BEHN, Aphra (1640–1689)
Faith, Sir, we are here today and gone tomorrow.

[*The Lucky Chance* (1687)]

THE BIBLE (King James Version)
All flesh is grass, and all the goodliness thereof is as the flower of the field.

[*Isaiah*, 40:6]

DOWSON, Ernest (1867–1900)
They are not long, the weeping and the laughter,
Love and desire and hate:
I think they have no portion in us after
We pass the gate.
They are not long, the days of wine and roses;
Out of a misty dream

Our path emerges for a while, then
closes
Within a dream.

['Vitae Summa Brevis Spem Nos Vetat
Incohare Longam' (1896)]

HERRICK, Robert (1591–1674)
Gather ye Rose-buds while ye may,
Old Time is still aflying:
And this same flower that smiles
today,
Tomorrow will be dying.

[*Hesperides* (1648)]

HORACE (65–8 BC)
*Omnem crede diem tibi diluxisse
supremum.*
Believe every day that has dawned is
your last.

[*Epistles*]

LEACOCK, Stephen (1869–1944)
I detest life-insurance agents; they
always argue that I shall someday die,
which is not so.

[*Literary Lapses* (1910)]

MARVELL, Andrew (1621–1678)
But at my back I always hear
Time's wingèd chariot hurrying near.
And yonder all before us lie
Deserts of vast eternity.
Thy beauty shall no more be found;
Nor, in thy marble vault, shall sound
My echoing song: then worms shall try
That long preserved virginity:
And your quaint honour turn to dust;
And into ashes all my lust.
The grave's a fine and private place,
But none I think do there embrace.

['To His Coy Mistress' (1681)]

MILLAY, Edna St Vincent (1892–1950)
Death devours all lovely things:
Lesbia with her sparrow
Shares the darkness, – presently
Every bed is narrow ...

After all, my erstwhile dear,
My no longer cherished,
Need we say it was not love,
Just because it perished?

['Passer Mortuus Est' (1921)]

MONTAIGNE, Michel de (1533–1592)
Il faut être toujours botté et prêt à partir.
One should always have one's boots
on and be ready to leave.

[*Essais* (1580)]

**STEVENSON, Robert Louis
(1850–1894)**
Old and young, we are all on our last
cruise.

[*Virginibus Puerisque* (1881)]

MOTHERS

ACHEBE, Chinua (1930–)
It's true that a child belongs to its
father. But when a father beats his
child, it seeks sympathy in its mother's
hut. A man belongs to his fatherland
when times are good and life is sweet.
But when there is sorrow and bitterness he finds refuge in his motherland.
Your mother is there to protect you.
She is buried there. And that is why
we say that mother is supreme.

[*Things Fall Apart* (1958)]

ALCOTT, Louisa May (1832–1888)
What *do* girls do who haven't any
mothers to help them through their
troubles?

[*Little Women* (1868)]

BALLANTYNE, Sheila (1936–)
I acknowledge the cold truth of her
death for perhaps the first time. She is
truly gone, forever out of reach, and I
have become my own judge.

[*Imaginary Crimes* (1982)]

BARKER, George (1913–1991)
Seismic with laughter,
Gin and chicken helpless in her Irish
hand,
Irresistible as Rabelais, but most
tender for
The lame dogs and hurt birds that
surround her.

['Sonnet: To My Mother' (1944)]

BARZAN, Gerald
Mother always said that honesty was
the best policy, and money isn't

everything. She was wrong about
other things too.

[Attr.]

BEHAN, Brendan (1923–1964)
Never throw stones at your mother,
You'll be sorry for it when she's dead,
Never throw stones at your mother,
Throw bricks at your father instead.

[The Hostage (1958)]

BOMBECK, Erma (1927–1996)
My mother phones daily to ask, 'Did
you just try to reach me?' When I reply,
'No', she adds, 'So, if you're not too
busy, call me while I'm still alive,' and
hangs up.

[The 1992 Erma Bombeck Calendar]

CAMPBELL, David (1915–1979)
The cruel girls we loved
Are over forty,
Their subtle daughters
Have stolen their beauty;
And with a blue stare
Of cool surprise
They mock their anxious mothers
With their mothers' eyes.

['Mothers and Daughters' (c. 1965)]

DAWE, (Donald) Bruce (1930–)
Mum, you would have loved the way
    you went!
one moment, at a barbecue in the
    garden
– the next, falling out of your chair,
hamburger in one hand,
and a grandson yelling.

['Going' (1970)]

EDGEWORTH, Maria (1767–1849)
My mother took too much, a great
deal too much, care of me; she over-
educated, over-instructed, over-dosed
me with premature lessons of
prudence: she was so afraid that I
should ever do a foolish thing, or not
say a wise one, that she prompted my
every word, and guided my eyes,
hearing with her ears, and judging
with her understanding, till, at length,
it was found out that I had no eyes, or

understanding of my own.

[Vivian (1812)]

ELLIS, Alice Thomas (1932–)
Claudia ... remembered that when
she'd had her first baby she had
realised with astonishment that the
perfect couple consisted of a mother
and child and not, as she had always
supposed, a man and woman.

[The Other Side of the Fire]

FISHER, Dorothy Canfield (1879–1958)
A mother is not a person to lean on
but a person to make leaning
unnecessary.

[Her Son's Wife (1926)]

FREUD, Sigmund (1856–1939)
A mother is only brought unlimited
satisfaction by her relation to a son;
this is altogether the most perfect, the
most free from ambivalence of all
human relationships.

[Freud on Women (1990)]

FRIDAY, Nancy (1937–)
Blaming mother is just a negative way
of clinging to her still.

[My Mother/My Self (1977)]

GREER, Germaine (1939–)
Mother is the dead heart of the family,
spending father's earnings on consumer goods to enhance the environment in which he eats, sleeps and
watches the television.

[The Female Eunuch (1970)]

HUBBARD, Kin (1868–1930)
The old-time mother who used to
wonder where her boy was now has a
grandson who wonders where his
mother is.

[Attr.]

JEWISH PROVERB
God could not be everywhere, so
therefore he made mothers.

LAWRENCE, D.H. (1885–1930)
[On his relationship with his mother]
We have loved each other, almost with

a husband and wife love, as well as filial and maternal ... It has been rather terrible and has made me, in some respects, abnormal.

[Attr.]

LAZARRE, Jane (1943–)
At her best, she is ... quietly receptive and intelligent in only a moderate, concrete way; she is of even temperament, almost always in control of her emotions. She loves her children completely and unambivalently. Most of us are not like her.

[*The Mother Knot* (1976)]

LINDBERGH, Anne Morrow (1906–)
By and large, mothers and housewives are the only workers who do not have regular time off. They are the great vacationless class.

[*Gift From the Sea* (1955)]

MAUGHAM, William Somerset (1874–1965)
Few misfortunes can befall a boy which bring worse consequences than to have a really affectionate mother.

[*A Writer's Notebook* (1949)]

OLSEN, Tillie (1913–)
More than in any other human relationship, overwhelmingly more, motherhood means being instantly interruptible, responsive, responsible.

[*Silences: When Writers Don't Write* (1965)]

RILEY, Janet (1915–)
The role of mother is probably the most important career a woman can have.

[*The Times-Picayune*, 1986]

SCOTT-MAXWELL, Florida (1884–1979)
No matter how old a mother is, she watches her middle-aged children for signs of improvement.

[*The Measure of My Days* (1968)]

SHAKESPEARE, William (1564–1616)
Thou art thy mother's glass, and she in thee

Calls back the lovely April of her prime.

[Sonnet 3]

STANTON, Elizabeth Cady (1815–1902)
... mothers of the race, the most important actors in the grand drama of human progress.

[*History of Woman Suffrage* (1881)]

STEAD, Christina (1902–1983)
A mother! What are we really? They all grow up whether you look after them or not.

[*The Man Who Loved Children*]

STEFANO, Joseph (1922–)
A boy's best friend is his mother.

[*Psycho*, screenplay, 1960]

WALLACE, William Ross (c. 1819–1881)
The hand that rocks the cradle
Is the hand that rules the world.

['What Rules the World' (c. 1865)]

WHISTLER, James McNeill (1834–1903)
[Explaining to a snobbish lady why he had been born in such an unfashionable place as Lowell, Massachusetts]
The explanation is quite simple. I wished to be near my mother.

[Attr.]

WILDE, Oscar (1854–1900)
All women become like their mothers. That is their tragedy. No man does. That's his.

[*The Importance of Being Earnest* (1895)]

WOOD, Mrs Henry (1814–1887)
Dead! and ... never called me mother.

[*East Lynne* (stage adaptation, 1874)]

MUSIC

ADDISON, Joseph (1672–1719)
Music, the greatest good that mortals know,
And all of heaven we have below.

['Song for St Cecilia's Day' (1694)]

ADE, George (1866–1944)
The music teacher came twice a week to bridge the awful gap between Dorothy and Chopin.

[Attr.]

ANDERSEN, Hans Christian (1805–1875)
[Of the music to be played at his funeral]
Most of the people who walk after me will be children; make the beat keep time with little steps.

[In Godden, *Hans Christian Andersen* (1955)]

APPLETON, Sir Edward Victor (1892–1965)
I do not mind what language an opera is sung in so long as it is a language I don't understand.

[*The Observer*, 1955]

ARMSTRONG, Louis (1900–1971)
[When asked how he felt about people copying his style]
A lotta cats copy the Mona Lisa, but people still line up to see the original.

[Attr.]

BEECHAM, Sir Thomas (1879–1961)
There are two golden rules for an orchestra: start together and finish together. The public doesn't give a damn what goes on in between.

[In Atkins and Newman, *Beecham Stories* (1978)]

[Of Bach]
Too much counterpoint, what is worse, Protestant counterpoint.

[*The Guardian*, 1971]

The sound of the harpsichord resembles that of a bird-cage played with toasting-forks.

[Attr.]

BEETHOVEN, Ludwig Van (1770–1827)
[Said to a violinist complaining that a passage was unplayable]
When I composed that, I was con-

scious of being inspired by God Almighty. Do you think I can consider your puny little fiddle when He speaks to me?

[Attr.]

BIRTWISTLE, Harrison (1934–)
I get someone to write the programme notes. Then I know what the piece is about.

[*The Observer*, 1996]

BROWNE, Sir Thomas (1605–1682)
For there is a music wherever there is a harmony, order or proportion; and thus far we may maintain the music of the spheres; for those well ordered motions, and regular paces, though they give no sound unto the ear, yet to the understanding they strike a note most full of harmony.

[*Religio Medici* (1643)]

BURNEY, Fanny (1752–1840)
All the delusive seduction of martial music.

[*Diary*, 1802]

BUTLER, Samuel (1835–1902)
How thankful we ought to feel that Wordsworth was only a poet and not a musician. Fancy a symphony by Wordsworth! Fancy having to sit it out! And fancy what it would have been if he had written fugues!

[*The Note-Books of Samuel Butler* (1912)]

CONGREVE, William (1670–1729)
Music has charms to soothe a savage breast.

[*The Mourning Bride* (1697)]

COWARD, Sir Noël (1899–1973)
Extraordinary how potent cheap music is.

[*Private Lives* (1930)]

DRYDEN, John (1631–1700)
What passion cannot Music raise and quell?

['A Song for St. Cecilia's Day' (1687)]

FORSTER, E.M. (1879–1970)
Beethoven's Fifth Symphony is the
most sublime noise that ever
penetrated into the ear of man.

[Howard's End (1910)]

GASKELL, Elizabeth (1810–1865)
We were none of us musical, though
Miss Jenkyns beat time, out of time, by
way of appearing to be so.

[Cranford (1853)]

GELDOF, Bob (1954–)
I'm into pop because I want to get
rich, get famous and get laid.

[Attr.]

HOLST, Gustav (1874–1934)
Never compose anything unless the
not composing of it becomes a
positive nuisance to you.

[Letter to W.G. Whittaker]

HUXLEY, Aldous (1894–1963)
Since Mozart's day composers have
learned the art of making music
throatily and palpitatingly sexual.

[Along the Road (1925)]

JOHNSON, Samuel (1709–1784)
Of music Dr Johnson used to say that
it was the only sensual pleasure
without vice.

[In *European Magazine,* 1795]

MENCKEN, H.L. (1880–1956)
Opera in English is, in the main, just
about as sensible as baseball in
Italian.

[Attr.]

NEWMAN, Ernest (1868–1959)
I sometimes wonder which would be
nicer – an opera without an interval,
or an interval without an opera.

[In Heyworth (ed.), *Berlioz, Romantic and
Classic*]

PARKER, Charlie (1920–1955)
Music is your own experience, your
thoughts, your wisdom. If you don't
live it, it won't come out of your horn.

[In Shapiro and Hentoff, *Hear Me Talkin' to Ya*
(1955)]

PEPYS, Samuel (1633–1703)
Music and women I cannot but give
way to, whatever my business is.

[Diary, 1666]

PREVIN, André (1929–)
The basic difference between classical
music and jazz is that in the former
the music is always greater than its
performance – whereas the way jazz is
performed is always more important
than what is being played.

[In Shapiro, *An Encyclopedia of Quotations
about Music*]

RANDOLPH, David
[On Parsifal]
The kind of opera that starts at six
o'clock and after it has been going
three hours, you look at your watch
and it says 6.20.

[In *The Frank Muir Book* (1976)]

ROSSINI, Gioacchino (1792–1868)
Give me a laundry-list and I will set it
to music.

[Attr.]

**SARASATE (Y NAVASCUES), Pablo
(1844–1908)**
[On being hailed as a genius by a
critic]
A genius! For thirty-seven years I've
practised fourteen hours a day, and
now they call me a genius!

[Attr.]

SARGENT, Sir Malcolm (1895–1967)
[Rehearsing a female chorus in 'For
Unto Us a Child is Born' from Handel's
Messiah]
Just a little more reverence, please,
and not so much astonishment.

[Attr.]

SATIE, Erik (1866–1925)
[Direction on one of his piano pieces]
To be played with both hands in the
pocket.

[Attr.]

SCHNABEL, Artur (1882–1951)
The notes I handle no better than

many pianists. But the pauses between the notes – ah, that is where the art resides.

[*Chicago Daily News*, 1958]

SCHUBERT, Franz (1797–1828)
My compositions spring from my sorrows. Those that give the world the greatest delight were born of my deepest griefs.

[*Diary*, 1824]

SHAKESPEARE, William (1564–1616)
In sweet music is such art,
Killing care and grief of heart
Fall asleep or hearing die.

[*Henry VIII*, III.i]

Music oft hath such a charm
To make bad good and good provoke to harm.

[*Measure For Measure*, IV.i]

The man that hath no music in himself,
Nor is not mov'd with concord of sweet sounds,
Is fit for treasons, stratagems, and spoils;
The motions of his spirit are dull as night,
And his affections dark as Erebus.
Let no such man be trusted.

[*The Merchant of Venice*, V.i]

How sour sweet music is
When time is broke and no proportion kept!
So is it in the music of men's lives.

[*Richard II*, V.v]

SHAW, George Bernard (1856–1950)
At every one of those concerts in England you will find rows of weary people who are there, not because they really like classical music, but

because they think they ought to like it.

[*Man and Superman* (1903)]

STEVENS, Wallace (1879–1955)
Just as my fingers on these keys
Make music, so the self-same sounds
On my spirit make a music, too.
Music is feeling, then, not sound.
And thus it is what I feel,
Here in this room, desiring you.

Thinking of your blue-shadowed silk,
Is music.

['Peter Quince at the Clavier' (1923)]

TENNYSON, Alfred, Lord (1809–1892)
Music that gentlier on the spirit lies,
Than tir'd eyelids upon tir'd eyes.

['The Lotos-Eaters' (1832)]

THOMAS, Irene (1920–)
The cello is not one of my favourite instruments. It has such a lugubrious sound, like someone reading a will.

[Attr.]

WHARTON, Edith (1862–1937)
An unalterable and unquestioned law of the musical world required that the German text of French operas sung by Swedish artists should be translated into Italian for the clearer understanding of English speaking audiences.

[*The Age of Innocence* (1920)]

WILLIAMSON, Malcolm (1931–)
Lloyd Webber's music is everywhere, but so is Aids.

[Attr.]

ZAPPA, Frank (1940–1995)
A composer? What the fuck do they do? All the good music's already been written by people with wigs and stuff.

[Attr.]

NATIONS

BOLINGBROKE, Henry (1678–1751)
Nations, like men, have their infancy.

[*Letters on Study and Use of History* (1752)]

INGE, William Ralph (1860–1954)
A nation is a society united by a delusion about its ancestry and by a common hatred of its neighbours.

[In Sagittarius and George, *The Perpetual Pessimist*]

KUBRICK, Stanley (1928–)
The great nations have always acted like gangsters, and the small nations like prostitutes.

[*The Guardian*, 1963]

MCMILLAN, Joyce (1952–)
Recognition of the suffering inflicted on peoples by their own leaders is undermining the idea of absolute national sovereignty, just as recognition of the unacceptability of domestic violence undermined the idea of absolute patriarchal rights in the family.

[*Scotland on Sunday*, 1992]

PARNELL, Charles Stewart (1846–1891)
No man has a right to fix the boundary of the march of a nation: no man has a right to say to his country – thus far shalt thou go and no further.

[Speech, 1885]

WILSON, Woodrow (1856–1924)
No nation is fit to sit in judgement upon any other nation.

[Speech, 1915]

NATURE

THE BIBLE (King James Version)
While the earth remaineth, seedtime and harvest, and cold and heat, and summer and winter, and day and night shall not cease.

[*Genesis*, 8:22]

BRIDGES, Robert (1844–1930)
Man masters nature not by force but by understanding.

[Attr.]

BROWNE, Sir Thomas (1605–1682)
All things are artificial, for nature is the art of God.

[*Religio Medici* (1643)]

BYRON, Lord (1788–1824)
There is a pleasure in the pathless woods,
There is a rapture on the lonely shore,
There is society, where none intrudes,
By the deep Sea, and music in its roar:
I love not Man the less, but Nature more,
From these our interviews, in which I steal
From all I may be, or have been before,
To mingle with the Universe, and feel
What I can ne'er express, yet cannot all conceal.

[*Childe Harold's Pilgrimage* (1818)]

CHESTERTON, G.K. (1874–1936)
Is ditchwater dull? Naturalists with microscopes have told me that it teems with quiet fun.

[*The Listener*, 1936]

CLARKE, Marcus (1846–1881)
In Australia alone is to be found the Grotesque, the Weird, the strange scribblings of nature learning how to write.

[Preface to A.L. Gordon, *Sea Spray and Smoke Drift* (1867)]

CURIE, Marie (1867–1934)
All my life through, the new sights of Nature made me rejoice like a child.

[*Pierre Curie*]

DARWIN, Charles (1809–1882)
What a book a devil's chaplain might write on the clumsy, wasteful, blundering, low, and horribly cruel works of nature!

[Letter to J.D. Hooker, 1856]

DONNE, John (1572–1631)
There is nothing that God hath
established in a constant course of
nature, and which therefore is done
every day, but would seem a Miracle,
and exercise our admiration, if it were
done but once.

[*LXXX Sermons* (1640)]

GRACIAN, Baltasar (1601–1658)
*No es menester arte donde basta la
Naturaleza.*
Art is not essential where Nature is
sufficient.

[*The Hero* (1637)]

GREY OWL (1888–1938)
Civilisation says, 'Nature belongs to
man.' The Indian says, 'No, man
belongs to nature.'

[Address at Norwich]

HORACE (65–8 BC)
*Naturam expelles furca, tamen usque
recurret.*
You may drive out Nature with a
pitchfork, but she always comes
hurrying back.

[*Epistles*]

HUGO, Victor (1802–1885)
*La nature est impitoyable; elle ne
consent pas à retirer ses fleurs, ses
musiques, ses parfums et ses rayons
devant l'abomination humaine.*
Nature is unforgiving; she will not
agree to withdraw her flowers, her
music, her scents or her rays of light
before the abominations of man.

[*Ninety-three* (1874)]

**INGERSOLL, Robert Greene
(1833–1899)**
In nature there are neither rewards
nor punishments – there are
consequences.

[*Some Reasons Why* (1881)]

LINNAEUS, Carl (1707–1778)
Natura non facit saltus.
Nature does not make progress by
leaps and bounds.

[*Philosophia Botanica*]

**MAUGHAM, William Somerset
(1874–1965)**
Men have an extraordinarily
erroneous opinion of their position in
nature; and the error is ineradicable.

[*A Writer's Notebook* (1949)]

MILTON, John (1608–1674)
In those vernal seasons of the yeer,
when the air is calm and pleasant, it
were an injury and sullennesse
against nature not to go out, and see
her riches, and partake in her
rejoycing with heaven and earth.

[*Of Education: To Master Samuel Hartlib*
(1644)]

NEWTON, Sir Isaac (1642–1727)
Whence is it that nature doth nothing
in vain; and whence arises all that
Order and Beauty which we see in the
World?

[*Opticks* (1730 edition)]

RABELAIS, François (c. 1494–c. 1553)
Natura abhorret vacuum.
Nature abhors a vacuum.

[*Gargantua* (1534)]

SHAKESPEARE, William (1564–1616)
In nature's infinite book of secrecy
A little I can read.

[*Antony and Cleopatra*, I.ii]

SMITH, Alexander (1830–1867)
Nature, who makes the perfect rose
  and bird,
Has never made the full and perfect
  man.

[*City Poems* (1857), 'Horton']

TENNYSON, Alfred, Lord (1809–1892)
So careful of the type she seems,
So careless of the single life ...

Who trusted God was love indeed
And love Creation's final law –
Tho' Nature, red in tooth and claw
With ravine, shrieked against his
  creed.

[*In Memoriam A. H. H.* (1850)]

THOREAU, Henry (1817–1862)
I frequently tramped eight or ten miles through the deepest snow to keep an appointment with a beech-tree, or a yellow birch, or an old acquaintance among the pines.

[*Walden* (1854)]

UVAVNUK
The arch of sky and mightiness of
    storms
Have moved the spirit within me,
Till I am carried away
Trembling with joy.

[In Rasmussen, *Intellectual Culture of the
Igulik Eskimos* (1929)]

VOLTAIRE (1694–1778)
*Sachez que le secret des arts
Est de corriger la nature.*
Know that the secret of the arts is to correct nature.

[*Epîtres*, 'A M. de Verrière']

WHITMAN, Walt (1819–1892)
After you have exhausted what there is in business, politics, conviviality, and so on – have found that none of these finally satisfy, or permanently wear – what remains? Nature remains.

[*Specimen Days and Collect* (1882)]

WORDSWORTH, William (1770–1850)
I have learned
To look on nature, not as in the hour
Of thoughtless youth; but hearing
    often-times
The still, sad music of humanity,
Nor harsh nor grating, though of
    ample power
To chasten and subdue ...

Nature never did betray
The heart that loved her.

['Tintern Abbey' (1798)]

One impulse from a vernal wood
May teach you more of man,
Of moral evil and of good,
Than all the sages can ...

Sweet is the lore which Nature brings;
Our meddling intellect

Misshapes the beauteous forms of
    things:
We murder to dissect.

['The Tables Turned' (1798)]

THE NAVY

CAMPBELL, Thomas (1777–1844)
Britannia needs no bulwarks,
No towers along the steep;
Her march is o'er the mountain waves,
Her home is on the deep.
With thunders from her native oak
She quells the floods below.

['Ye Mariners of England' (1801)]

CHURCHILL, Sir Winston (1874–1965)
Don't talk to me about naval tradition. It's nothing but rum, sodomy and the lash.

[In Gretton, *Former Naval Person* (1968)]

COVENTRY, Thomas (1578–1640)
The dominion of the sea, as it is an ancient and undoubted right of the crown of England, so it is the best security of the land. The wooden walls are the best walls of this kingdom.

[Speech in Star Chamber, 1635]

GLOVER, Denis (1912–1980)
[On overcrowding in Royal Navy ships]
With five or six faces in front of a mirror it sometimes becomes a problem just which one to shave.

[In Lehmann, *I Am My Brother* (1960)]

MACAULAY, Lord (1800–1859)
There were gentlemen and there were seamen in the navy of Charles the Second. But the seamen were not gentlemen; and the gentlemen were not seamen.

[*History of England* (1849), I]

MOUNTBATTEN OF BURMA, Earl (1900–1979)
In my experience, I have always found that you cannot have an efficient ship unless you have a happy ship, and you cannot have a happy ship unless you have an efficient ship. That is the way I intend to start this commission, and

NEWS

that is the way I intend to go on – with a happy and an efficient ship.

[Address to crew of *HMS Kelly*, 1939]

VOLTAIRE (1694–1778)
[Referring to the execution of the English Admiral Byng for refusing to attack a French fleet]
Dans ce pays-ci il est bon de tuer de temps en temps un amiral pour encourager les autres.
In this country it is considered a good idea to kill an admiral from time to time, to encourage the others.

[*Candide* (1759)]

NEIGHBOURS

AUSTEN, Jane (1775–1817)
For what do we live, but to make sport for our neighbours, and laugh at them in our turn?

[*Pride and Prejudice* (1813)]

THE BIBLE (King James Version)
Thou shalt love thy neighbour as thyself.

[*Leviticus*, 19·18]

BRADLEY, F.H. (1846–1924)
The propriety of some persons seems to consist in having improper thoughts about their neighbours.

[*Aphorisms* (1930)]

CARLYLE, Jane Welsh (1801–1866)
Some new neighbours, that came a month or two ago, brought with them an accumulation of all the things to be guarded against in a London neighbourhood, viz, a pianoforte, a lap-dog, and a parrot.

[Letter to Mrs Carlyle, 1839]

CHESTERTON, G.K. (1874–1936)
We make our friends, we make our enemies; but God makes our next-door neighbour.

[*Heretics* (1905)]

CLEESE, John (1939–)
Loving your neighbour as much as yourself is practically bloody impossible... You might as well have a Com-

mandment that states, 'Thou shalt fly'.

[*The Times*, 1993]

HORACE (65–8 BC)
Nam tua res agitur, paries cum proximus ardet.
For your own safety is at stake, when your neighbour's wall catches fire.

[*Epistles*]

PROVERB
Good fences make good neighbours.

NEWS

ARNOLD, Harry
[Commenting on the news that the Queen had started to refer privately to Royal reporters as 'scum']
At least we're la crème de la scum.

[*The Observer*, 1995]

AUSTEN, Jane (1775–1817)
Lady Middleton ... exerted herself to ask Mr Palmer if there was any news in the paper.
'No, none at all,' he replied, and read on.

[*Sense and Sensibility* (1811)]

BENNETT, Arnold (1867–1931)
Journalists say a thing that they know isn't true, in the hope that if they keep on saying it long enough it *will* be true.

[*The Title* (1918)]

BEVAN, Aneurin (1897–1960)
I read the newspapers avidly. It is my one form of continuous fiction.

[*The Observer*, 1960]

BONE, James (1872–1962)
[Referring to C.P. Scott, former editor of *The Manchester Guardian*]
He made righteousness readable.

[Attr.]

BRADBURY, Malcolm (1932–)
Reading someone else's newspaper is like sleeping with someone else's wife. Nothing seems to be precisely in the right place, and when you find what

NEWS

you are looking for, it is not clear then how to respond to it.

[*Stepping Westward* (1965)]

CANTONA, Eric (1966–)
[Commenting on the interest taken by the press in the outcome of his court case]
When the seagulls follow the trawler, it is because they think sardines will be thrown into the sea.

[*The Observer*, 1995]

CARLYLE, Thomas (1795–1881)
Burke said there were Three Estates in Parliament; but, in the Reporters' Gallery yonder, there sat a *Fourth Estate* more important far than they all.

['The Hero as Man of Letters' (1841)]

CHESTERTON, G.K. (1874–1936)
It's not the world that's got so much worse but the news coverage that's got so much better.

[Attr.]

COWPER, William (1731–1800)
Thou god of our idolatry, the press ...
Thou fountain, at which drink the
    good and wise;
Thou ever-bubbling spring of endless
    lies;
Like Eden's dread probationary tree,
Knowledge of good and evil is from
    thee.

['The Progress of Error' (1782)]

CURZON, Lord (1859–1925)
I hesitate to say what the functions of the modern journalist may be; but I imagine that they do not exclude the intelligent anticipation of facts even before they occur.

[Speech, 1898]

DANA, Charles Anderson (1819–1897)
When a dog bites a man that is not news, but when a man bites a dog that is news.

[*New York Sun*, 1882]

DRAYTON, Michael (1563–1631)
Ill news hath wings, and with the wind doth go,
Comfort's a cripple and comes ever slow.

[*The Barrons' Wars* (1603)]

ELDERSHAW, M. Barnard (1897–1987)
Journalists are people who take in one another's washing and then sell it.

[*Plaque with Laurel* (1937)]

FAIRBURN, A.R.D. (1904–1957)
The press: slow dripping of water on
    mud;
thought's daily bagwash, ironing out
    opinion,
scarifying the edges of ideas.

[*Collected Poems* (1966)]

GARCIA MARQUEZ, Gabriel (1928–)
El periodismo es un género literario, muy parecido a la novela, y tiene la gran ventaja de que el reportero puede inventar cosas. Y eso el novelista lo tiene totalmente prohibido.
Journalism is a literary genre very similar to that of the novel, and has the great advantage that the reporter can invent things. And that is completely forbidden to the novelist.

[Speech, 1994]

HANSON, Lord James (1922–)
Destructive journalism fosters the belief that politicians routinely evade the truth and break their promises. It creates a climate in which trust in society as a whole dissolves; in which difficulties are magnified beyond all proportion; in which no one is believed to act except for the most self-centred of motives.

[*The Spectator*, May 1996]

HEARST, William Randolph (1863–1951)
[Instruction to artist Frederic Remington, who wished to return from peaceful Havana in spring 1898]
Please remain. You furnish the pictures and I'll furnish the war.

[Attr. in Winkler, *W.R. Hearst* (1928)]

HEPWORTH, John (1921–)
Most journalists of my generation died early, succumbing to one or other of the two great killers in the craft – cirrhosis or terminal alimony.
[*National Review*, 1974]

IGNATIEFF, Michael (1947–)
News is a genre as much as fiction or drama: it is a regime of visual authority, a coercive organization of images according to a stopwatch.
[*Daedalus*, 1988]

KIPLING, Rudyard (1865–1936)
[Of newspaper barons]
Power without responsibility – the prerogative of the harlot throughout the ages.
[Remark, quoted by Baldwin in 1931]

KRAUS, Karl (1874–1936)
Keinen Gedanken haben und ihn ausdrücken können – das macht den Journalisten.
To have no thoughts and be able to express them – that's what makes a journalist.
[*Pro domo et mundo* (1912)]

LAMB, Charles (1775–1834)
Newspapers always excite curiosity. No one ever lays one down without a feeling of disappointment.
[*Last Essays of Elia* (1833)]

LONGFORD, Lord (1905–)
On the whole I would not say that our Press is obscene. I would say that it trembles on the brink of obscenity.
[*The Observer*, 1963]

MACCARTHY, Sir Desmond (1878–1952)
[Journalists are] more attentive to the minute hand of history than to the hour hand.
[In Tynan, *Curtains* (1961)]

MAILER, Norman (1923–)
Once a newspaper touches a story, the facts are lost forever, even to the protagonists.
[*The Presidential Papers* (1976)]

MARQUIS, Don (1878–1937)
The art of newspaper paragraphing is to stroke a platitude until it purrs like an epigram.
[In Anthony, *O Rare Don Marquis* (1962)]

MILLER, Arthur (1915–)
A good newspaper, I suppose, is a nation talking to itself.
[*The Observer*, 1961]

MURDOCH, Rupert (1931–)
I think the important thing is that there be plenty of newspapers with plenty of people controlling them so there can be choice.
[Film interview, 1967]

MURRAY, David (1888–1962)
A reporter is a man who has renounced everything in life but the world, the flesh, and the devil.
[*The Observer*, 1931]

OCHS, Adolph S. (1858–1935)
All the news that's fit to print.
[Motto of the *New York Times*]

SCOTT, C.P. (1846–1932)
Comment is free, but facts are sacred.
[*Manchester Guardian*, 1921]

SHERIDAN, Richard Brinsley (1751–1816)
The newspapers! Sir, they are the most villainous – licentious – abominable – infernal – Not that I ever read them – No I make it a rule never to look into a newspaper.
[*The Critic* (1779)]

STOPPARD, Tom (1937–)
[Referring to foreign correspondents]
He's someone who flies around from hotel to hotel and thinks the most interesting thing about any story is the fact that he has arrived to cover it.
[*Night and Day* (1978)]

SWAFFER, Hannen (1879–1962)
Freedom of the press in Britain is freedom to print such of the proprietor's prejudices as the

advertisers don't object to.
[In Driberg, *Swaff* (1974)]

TOMALIN, Nicholas (1931–1973)
The only qualities essential for real
success in journalism are rat-like
cunning, a plausible manner, and a
little literary ability.
[*The Sunday Times Magazine*, 1969]

WAUGH, Evelyn (1903–1966)
News is what a chap who doesn't care
much about anything wants to read.
And it's only news until he's read it.
After that it's dead.
[*Scoop* (1938)]

WELLINGTON, Duke of (1769–1852)
Possible? Is anything impossible? Read
the newspapers.
[In Fraser, *Words on Wellington* (1889)]

WILDE, Oscar (1854–1900)
There is much to be said in favour of
modern journalism. By giving us the
opinions of the uneducated, it keeps
us in touch with the ignorance of the
community.
['The Critic as Artist' (1891)]

WOLFE, Humbert (1886–1940)
You cannot hope
To bribe or twist,
thank God! the
British journalist.
But, seeing what
the man will do
unbribed, there's
no occasion to.
['Over the Fire' (1930)]

See MEDIA; TELEVISION

NOSTALGIA

AUGIER, Emile (1820–1889)
La nostalgie de la boue.
Homesickness for the gutter.
[*Le Mariage d'Olympe* (1855)]

BYRON, Lord (1788–1824)
Ah! happy years! once more who
would not be a boy?
[*Childe Harold's Pilgrimage* (1818)]

The 'good old times' – all times when
old are good –
Are gone.
['The Age of Bronze' (1823)]

CARR, J.L. (1912–1994)
We can ask and ask but we can't have
again what once seemed ours forever
– the way things looked, that church
alone in the fields, a bed on a belfry
floor, a loved face ... They'd gone, and
you could only wait for the pain to
pass.
[*A Month in the Country* (1980)]

HOUSMAN, A.E. (1859–1936)
That is the land of lost content,
I see it shining plain,
The happy highways where I went
And cannot come again.
[*A Shropshire Lad* (1896)]

LAMB, Charles (1775–1834)
All, all are gone, the old familiar faces.
['The Old Familiar Faces']

ORWELL, George (1903–1950)
Before the war, and especially before
the Boer War, it was summer all the
year round.
[*Coming Up for Air* (1939)]

STEINBECK, John (1902–1968)
Cannery Row in Monterey in California
is a poem, a stink, a grating noise, a
quality of light, a tone, a habit, a
nostalgia, a dream.
[*Cannery Row* (1939)]

TENNYSON, Alfred, Lord (1809–1892)
Tears, idle tears, I know not what they
mean,
Tears from the depth of some divine
despair
Rise in the heart, and gather to the
eyes,
In looking on the happy Autumn-
fields,
And thinking of the days that are no
more.
[*The Princess* (1847)]

THOMAS, Dylan (1914–1953)
Years and years and years ago, when I
was a boy, when there were wolves in
Wales, and birds the colour of red-
flannel petticoats whisked past the
harp-shaped hills ... when we rode the
daft and happy hills bareback, it
snowed and it snowed.

[*A Child's Christmas in Wales* (1954)]

YEATS, W.B. (1865–1939)
In the Junes that were warmer than
these are, the waves were more gay,
When I was a boy with never a crack
in my heart.

['The Meditation of the Old Fisherman'
(1886)]

OBSTINACY

ARISTOTLE (384–322 BC)
Obstinate people may be subdivided into the opinionated, the ignorant, and the boorish.

[*Nicomachean Ethics*]

MACNEICE, Louis (1907–1963)
One must not dislike people ... because they are intransigent. For that could be only playing their own game.

[*Zoo* (1938)]

MAUGHAM, William Somerset (1874–1965)
Like all weak men he laid an exaggerated stress on not changing one's mind.

[*Of Human Bondage* (1915)]

PROVERB
None so deaf as those who will not hear.

STERNE, Laurence (1713–1768
'Tis known by the name of perseverance in a good cause – and of obstinacy in a bad one.

[*Tristram Shandy* (1767)]

OPINIONS

BAEZ, Joan (1941–)
I've never had a humble opinion. If you've got an opinion, why be humble about it.

[*Scotland on Sunday*, 1992]

BROWNE, Sir Thomas (1605–1682)
I could never divide my self from any man upon the difference of an opinion, or be angry with his judgment for not agreeing with me in that, from which perhaps within a few days I should dissent my self.

[*Religio Medici* (1643)]

CONGREVE, William (1670–1729)
I am always of the opinion with the learned, if they speak first.

[*Incognita* (1692)]

EMERSON, Ralph Waldo (1803–1882)
To-morrow a stranger will say with masterly good sense precisely what we have thought and felt all the time, and we shall be forced to take with shame our own opinion from another.

['Self-Reliance' (1841)]

HALSEY, Margaret (1910–)
The English think of an opinion as something which a decent person, if he has the misfortune to have one, does all he can to hide.

[*With Malice Toward Some* (1938)]

JEFFERSON, Thomas (1743–1826)
Error of opinion may be tolerated where reason is left free to combat it.

[First inaugural address, 1801]

LOCKE, John (1632–1704)
New opinions are always suspected, and usually opposed, without any reason but because they are not already common.

[*Essay concerning Human Understanding* (1690)]

MACKINTOSH, Sir James (1765–1832)
Men are never so good or so bad as their opinions.

['Jeremy Bentham' (1830)]

MAISTRE, Joseph de (1753–1821)
Les fausses opinions ressemblent à la fausse monnaie qui est frappée d'abord par de grands coupables, et dépensée ensuite par d'honnêtes gens qui perpétuent le crime sans savoir ce qu'ils font.
Wrong opinions are like counterfeit coins, which are first minted by great wrongdoers, then spent by decent people who perpetuate the crime without knowing what they are doing.

[*Les soirées de Saint-Pétersbourg*]

MILL, John Stuart (1806–1873)
If all mankind minus one, were of one opinion, and only one person were of the contrary opinion, mankind would be no more justified in silencing that one person, than he, if he had the

power, would be justified in silencing mankind.

[*On Liberty* (1859)]

PALMERSTON, Lord (1784–1865)
What is merit? The opinion one man entertains of another.

[In Carlyle, 'Shooting Niagara and After?' (1837)]

SPENCER, Herbert (1820–1903)
Opinion is ultimately determined by the feelings, and not by the intellect.

[*Social Statics* (1850)]

TERENCE (c. 190–159 BC)
Quot homines tot sententiae: suos quoique mos.
There are as many opinions as there are people: each has his own point of view.

[*Phormio*]

WEBSTER, Daniel (1782–1852)
Inconsistencies of opinion, arising from changes of circumstances, are often justifiable.

[Speech, 1846]

OPTIMISM

CABELL, James Branch (1879–1958)
The optimist proclaims that we live in the best of all possible worlds; and the pessimist fears this is true.

[*The Silver Stallion* (1926)]

ELIOT, George (1819–1880)
I am not an optimist but a meliorist.

[In L. Housman, *A.E.H.* (1937)]

MAILER, Norman (1923–)
Being married six times shows a degree of optimism over wisdom, but I am incorrigibly optimistic.

[*The Observer*, 1988]

SHORTER, Clement King (1857–1926)
The latest definition of an optimist is one who fills up his crossword puzzle in ink.

[*The Observer*, 1925]

USTINOV, Sir Peter (1921–)
I am an optimist, unrepentant and militant. After all, in order not to be a fool an optimist must know how sad a place the world can be. It is only the pessimist who finds this out anew every day.

[*Dear Me* (1977)]

VOLTAIRE (1694–1778)
Tout est pour le mieux dans le meilleur des mondes possibles.
Everything is for the best in the best of all possible worlds.

[*Candide* (1759)]

See PESSIMISM

BACON, Francis (1561–1626)
The joys of parents are secret, and so are their griefs and fears.
['Of Parents and Children' (1625)]

BUTLER, Samuel (1835–1902)
Parents are the last people on earth who ought to have children.
[Attr.]

COMPTON-BURNETT, Dame Ivy (1884–1969)
Don't be too hard on parents. You may find yourself in their place.
[Elders and Betters (1944)]

EMERSON, Ralph Waldo (1803–1882)
Respect the child. Be not too much his parent. Trespass not on his solitude.
[Attr.]

LARKIN, Philip (1922–1985)
They fuck you up, your mum and dad.
They may not mean to, but they do.
They fill you with the faults they had.
And add some extra, just for you.
['This be the Verse' (1974)]

SHAW, George Bernard (1856–1950)
Parentage is a very important profession; but no test of fitness for it is ever imposed in the interest of the children.
[Everybody's Political What's What (1944)]

If you must hold yourself up to your children as an object lesson (which is not necessary), hold yourself up as a warning and not as an example.
[Attr.]

SPARK, Muriel (1918–)
Parents learn a lot from their children about coping with life.
[The Comforters (1957)]

WILDE, Oscar (1854–1900)
To lose one parent may be regarded as a misfortune ... to lose both seems like carelessness.
[The Importance of Being Earnest (1895)]

See CHILDREN

CHAPMAN, George (c. 1559–c. 1634)
For one heate (all know) doth drive out another,
One passion doth expell another still.
[Monsieur D'Olive (1606)]

HUME, David (1711–1776)
We never remark any passion or principle in others, of which, in some degree or other, we may not find a parallel in ourselves.
[A Treatise of Human Nature (1739)]

JUNG, Carl Gustav (1875–1961)
A man who has not gone through the hell of his passions has never overcome them either.
[Memories, Dreams, Thoughts (1962)]

LA ROCHEFOUCAULD, Duc de (1613–1680)
If we resist our passions, it is more because of their weakness than because of our strength.
[Maximes]

L'ESTRANGE, Sir Roger (1616–1704)
It is with our passions as it is with fire and water, they are good servants, but bad masters.
[Translation of Aesop's Fables]

MEREDITH, George (1828–1909)
In tragic life, God wot,
No villain need be! Passions spin the plot:
We are betrayed by what is false within.
[A Sentimental Journey (1768)]

SHAKESPEARE, William (1564–1616)
A man that Fortune's buffets and rewards
Hast ta'en with equal thanks; and blest are those
Whose blood and judgment are so well comeddled
That they are not a pipe for Fortune's finger

To sound what stop she please. Give
  me that man
That is not passion's slave, and I will
  wear him
In my heart's core, ay, in my heart of
  heart,
As I do thee.

[*Hamlet*, III.ii]

**THACKERAY, William Makepeace
(1811–1863)**
Yes, I am a fatal man, Madame
Fribsbi. To inspire hopeless passion is
my destiny.

[*Pendennis* (1850)]

THE PAST

BEERBOHM, Sir Max (1872–1956)
There is always something rather
absurd about the past.

[Attr]

COLETTE (1873–1954)
But the past, the beautiful past striped
with sunshine, grey with mist,
childish, blooming with hidden joy,
bruised with sweet sorrow. ... Ah! if
only I could resurrect one hour of that
time, one alone – but which one?

[*Paysages et portraits* (1958)]

HARTLEY, L.P. (1895–1972)
The past is a foreign country: they do
things differently there.

[*The Go-Between* (1953)]

[Remark just before he died]
I seem to have become part of my
past.

[In Wright, *Foreign Country: The Life of L.P.
Hartley*]

ONDAATJE, Michael (1943–)
The past is still, for us, a place that is
not yet safely settled.

[*The Faber Book of Contemporary Canadian
Short Stories* (1990)]

SANTAYANA, George (1863–1952)
Those who cannot remember the past
are condemned to repeat it.

[*The Life of Reason* (1906)]

TERTZ, Abram (1925–)
In the past, people did not cling to life
quite as much, and it was easier to
breathe.

[*A Voice From the Chorus* (1973)]

WAIN, John (1925–)
Keep off your thoughts from things
  that are past and done;
For thinking of the past wakes regret
  and pain.

[*Resignation*, translated from the Chinese of
Po-Chü-I]

**WHITELAW, William (Viscount
Whitelaw) (1918–)**
I do not intend to prejudge the past.

[*The Times*, 1973]

PATIENCE

BIERCE, Ambrose (1842–c. 1914)
Patience: A minor form of despair,
disguised as a virtue.

[*The Cynic's Word Book* (1906)]

FONTAINE, Jean de la (1621–1695)
Patience et longueur de temps
Font plus que force ni que rage.
Patience and time do more than force
and rage.

['Le lion et le rat']

MASSINGER, Philip (1583–1640)
Patience, the beggar's virtue.

[*A New Way to Pay Old Debts* (1633)]

SHAKESPEARE, William (1564–1616)
How poor are they that have not
  patience!
What wound did ever heal but by
  degrees?

[*Othello*, II.iii]

TAYLOR, Elizabeth (1912–1975)
It is very strange ... that the years
teach us patience; that the shorter our
time, the greater our capacity for
waiting.

[*A Wreath of Roses* (1950)]

PATRIOTISM

BARRINGTON, George (1755–c. 1835)
[Of convicts transported to Botany Bay]
True patriots we; for be it understood,
We left our country for our country's good.
['Prologue' for the opening of the Playhouse, Sydney, 1796]

CAVELL, Edith (1865–1915)
[Said on the eve of her execution]
Standing, as I do, in view of God and eternity I realize that patriotism is not enough. I must have no hatred or bitterness towards anyone.
[*The Times*, 1915]

CHESTERTON, G.K. (1874–1936)
'My country, right or wrong,' is a thing that no patriot would think of saying except in a desperate case. It is like saying, 'My mother, drunk or sober'.
[*The Defendant* (1901)]

DECATUR, Stephen (1779–1820)
[Toast during a banquet, 1815]
Our country! In her intercourse with foreign nations, may she always be in the right; but our country, right or wrong.
[In Mackenzie, *Life of Decatur* (1846)]

DRYDEN, John (1631–1700)
Never was patriot yet, but was a fool.
[*Absalom and Achitophel* (1681)]

FORSTER, E.M. (1879–1970)
I hate the idea of causes, and if I had to choose between betraying my country and betraying my friend, I hope I should have the guts to betray my country.
[*Two Cheers for Democracy* (1951)]

GARIBALDI, Giuseppe (1807–1882)
Soldati, io esco da Roma. Chi vuole continuare la guerra contro lo straniero venga con me. Non posso offrirgli né onori né stipendi; gli offro fame, sete, marcie forzate, battaglie e morte. Chi ama la patria mi segua.

Men, I am leaving Rome. If you want to carry on fighting the invader, come with me. I cannot promise you either honours or wages; I can only offer you hunger, thirst, forced marches, battles and death. If you love your country, follow me.
[In Guerzoni, *Garibaldi* (1929)]

GASKELL, Elizabeth (1810–1865)
That kind of patriotism which consists in hating all other nations.
[*Sylvia's Lovers* (1863)]

GOLDSMITH, Oliver (c. 1728–1774)
Such is the patriot's boast, where'er we roam,
His first best country ever is at home.
['The Traveller' (1764)]

HALE, Nathan (1755–1776)
[Speech before he was executed by the British]
I only regret that I have but one life to lose for my country.
[In Johnston, *Nathan Hale* (1974)]

HORACE (65–8 BC)
Dulce et decorum est pro patria mori.
It is sweet and honourable to die for one's country.
[*Odes*]

HUNT, G.W. (1829–1904)
We don't want to fight, but, by jingo if we do,
We've got the ships, we've got the men, we've got the money too.
[Music hall song, 1878]

JOHNSON, Samuel (1709–1784)
Patriotism is the last refuge of a scoundrel.
[In Boswell, *The Life of Samuel Johnson* (1791)]

KINNOCK, Neil (1942–)
[Of nuclear disarmament]
I would die for my country but I could never let my country die for me.
[Speech, 1987]

OWEN, Wilfred (1893–1918)
If you could hear, at every jolt, the
   blood
Come gargling from the froth-
   corrupted lungs,
Obscene as cancer, bitter as the cud
Of vile, incurable sores on innocent
   tongues, –
My friend, you would not tell with
   such high zest
To children ardent for some desperate
   glory,
The old Lie: *Dulce et decorum est*
Pro patria mori.
                    ['Dulce et decorum est' (1917)]

PAINE, Thomas (1737–1809)
My country is the world, and my
religion is to do good.
                    [*The Rights of Man* (1791)]

PLOMER, William (1903–1973)
Patriotism is the last refuge of the
sculptor.
                                        [Attr.]

RUSSELL, Bertrand (1872–1970)
Patriots always talk of dying for their
country, and never of killing for their
country.
                                        [Attr.]

SCHURZ, Carl (1829–1906)
Our country, right or wrong! When
right, to be kept right; when wrong, to
be put right!
                                [Speech, 1872]

SCOTT, Sir Walter (1771–1832)
Breathes there the man, with soul so
   dead,
Who never to himself hath said,
This is my own, my native land!
                    [*The Lay of the Last Minstrel* (1805)]

SMOLLETT, Tobias (1721–1771)
True Patriotism is of no Party.
         [*The Adventures of Sir Launcelot Greaves*
                                         (1762)]

TROTSKY, Leon (1879–1940)
Patriotism to the Soviet State is a
revolutionary duty, whereas patriotism

to a bourgeois State is treachery.
         [In Fitzroy Maclean, *Disputed Barricade*]

PEACE

ANONYMOUS
Since wars begin in the minds of men,
it is in the minds of men that the
defences of peace must be con-
structed.
                    [Constitution of UNESCO]

BELLOC, Hilaire (1870–1953)
Pale Ebenezer thought it wrong to
   fight,
But Roaring Bill (who killed him)
   thought it right.
                    ['The Pacifist' (1938)]

THE BIBLE (King James Version)
They shall beat their swords into
plowshares, and their spears into
pruninghooks: nation shall not lift up
sword against nation, neither shall
they learn war any more.
                              [*Isaiah*, 2:4]

BIERCE, Ambrose (1842–c. 1914)
Peace: In international affairs, a period
of cheating between two periods of
fighting.
                    [*The Cynic's Word Book* (1906)]

BRECHT, Bertolt (1898–1956)
Sagen sie mir nicht, dass Friede
ausgebrochen ist.
Don't tell me that peace has broken
out.
                    [*Mother Courage* (1939)]

CROMWELL, Oliver (1599–1658)
It's a maxim not to be despised,
'Though peace be made, yet it's
interest that keeps peace.'
                                [Speech, 1654]

EINSTEIN, Albert (1879–1955)
Peace cannot be kept by force. It can
only be achieved by understanding.
                    [*Notes on Pacifism*]

I am an absolute pacifist ... It is an
instinctive feeling. It is a feeling that

possesses me, because the murder of men is disgusting.

[Interview, 1929]

EISENHOWER, Dwight D. (1890–1969)
The peace we seek, founded upon decent trust and co-operative effort among nations, can be fortified, not by weapons of war but by wheat and by cotton, by milk and by wool, by meat and by timber and by rice. These are words that translate into every language on earth. These are needs that challenge this world in arms.

[Speech, 1953]

I think that people want peace so much that one of these days governments had better get out of the way and let them have it.

[Broadcast discussion, 1959]

GANDHI (1869–1948)
I wanted to avoid violence. Non-violence is the first article of my faith. It is also the last article of my creed.

[Speech, 1922]

GEORGE V (1865–1936)
[On the battlefield cemeteries in Flanders, 1922]
I have many times asked myself whether there can be more potent advocates of peace upon earth through the years to come than this massed multitude of silent witnesses to the desolation of war.

[Attr.]

IZETBEGOVIC, Alija (1925–)
[On signing the peace accord in Paris, December 1995]
I feel like a man who is drinking a bitter but useful medicine.

[The Observer Review, 1995]

JERROLD, Douglas William (1803–1857)
We love peace, as we abhor pusillanimity; but not peace at any price.

['Peace' (1859)]

LIE, Trygve (1896–1968)
Now we are in a period which I can characterize as a period of cold peace.

[The Observer, 1949]

MAYHEW, Christopher (1915–)
[On the Munich Agreement]
The peace that passeth all understanding.

[Speech, 1938]

MILTON, John (1608–1674)
Peace hath her victories
No less renowned than war.

['To the Lord General Cromwell' (1652)]

RUSSELL, Lord John (1792–1878)
If peace cannot be maintained with honour, it is no longer peace.

[Speech, 1853]

TACITUS (c. 56–c. 120)
Ubi solitudinem faciunt pacem appellant.
They create a desert, and call it peace.

[Agricola]

WALPOLE, Horace (1717–1797)
When will the world know that peace and propagation are the two most delightful things in it?

[Letter to Sir Horace Mann, 1778]

WILSON, Woodrow (1856–1924)
There is a price which is too great to pay for peace, and that price can be put in one word. One cannot pay the price of self-respect.

[Speech, 1916]

It must be a peace without victory ... only a peace between equals can last.

[Speech, 1917]

See WAR AND PEACE

THE PEOPLE

ALCUIN (735–804)
Nec audiendi qui solent dicere, Vox populi, vox Dei, quum tumultuositas vulgi semper insaniae proxima sit.
Nor should those be heeded who are

wont to say 'The voice of the people is the voice of God', since popular uproar is always akin to madness.

[Letter to Charlemagne]

BROWNE, Sir Thomas (1605–1682)
If there be any among those common objects of hatred I do contemn and laugh at, it is that great enemy of reason, virtue, and religion, the multitude; that numerous piece of monstrosity, which, taken asunder, seem men, and the reasonable creatures of God, but, confused together, make but one great beast, and a monstrosity more prodigious than Hydra.

[Religio Medici (1643)]

BURKE, Edmund (1729–1797)
It is a general popular error to imagine the loudest complainers for the public to be the most anxious for its welfare.

[Observations on 'The Present State of the Nation' (1769)]

The people never give up their liberties but under some delusion.

[Speech, 1784]

BURNS, Robert (1759–1796)
Who will not sing God save the King
Shall hang as high's the steeple;
But while we sing God save the King,
We'll ne'er forget the People!

['Does Haughty Gaul Invasion Threat?' (1795)]

CONFUCIUS (c. 550–c. 478 BC)
The people may be made to follow a course of action, but they may not be made to understand it.

[Analects]

CROMWELL, Oliver (1599–1658)
[Referring to a cheering crowd]
The people would be just as noisy if they were going to see me hanged.

[Attr.]

DICKENS, Charles (1812–1870)
'But suppose there are two mobs?' suggested Mr Snodgrass. 'Shout with the largest,' replied Mr Pickwick.

[The Pickwick Papers (1837)]

DRYDEN, John (1631–1700)
Nor is the people's judgement always true:
The most may err as grossly as the few.

[Absalom and Achitophel (1681)]

HAZLITT, William (1778–1830)
There is not a more mean, stupid, dastardly, pitiful, selfish, spiteful, envious, ungrateful animal than the Public. It is the greatest of cowards, for it is afraid of itself.

[Table-Talk (1822)]

HITLER, Adolf (1889–1945)
Die breite Masse eines Volkes ... [fällt] einer grossen Lüge leichter zum Opfer als einer kleinen.
The broad mass of a people ... falls victim to a big lie more easily than to a small one.

[Mein Kampf (1925)]

JUVENAL (c. 60–130)
Duas tantum res anxius optat,
Panem et circenses.
Two things only the people anxiously desire: bread and circuses.

[Satires]

KENNEDY, Robert F. (1925–1968)
One fifth of the people are against everything all the time.

[The Observer, 1964]

LINCOLN, Abraham (1809–1865)
You can fool some of the people all of the time, and all of the people some of the time, but you cannot fool all of the people all the time.

[Attr.]

POPE, Alexander (1688–1744)
The People's Voice is odd,
It is, and it is not, the voice of God.

[Imitations of Horace (1738)]

SCHULZ, Charles (1922–)
I love mankind – it's people I can't stand.

[Go Fly a Kite, Charlie Brown]

SITWELL, Dame Edith (1887–1964)
During the writing ... of this book, I
realized that the public will believe
anything – so long as it is not founded
on truth.

[*Taken Care Of* (1965)]

VANDERBILT, William H. (1821–1885)
[When asked whether the public
should be consulted about luxury
trains]
The public be damned! I'm working
for my stockholders.

[Remark, 1883]

WELLINGTON, Duke of (1769–1852)
You must build your House of
Parliament upon the river: so ... that
the populace cannot exact their
demands by sitting down round you.

[In Fraser, *Words on Wellington* (1889)]

PESSIMISM

BENNETT, Arnold (1867–1931)
Pessimism, when you get used to it, is
just as agreeable as optimism.

[*Things That Have Interested Me*]

**BEVERIDGE, William Henry
(1879–1963)**
Scratch a pessimist, and you find often
a defender of privilege.

[*The Observer*, 1943]

LOWELL, Robert (1917–1977)
If we see light at the end of the tunnel,
It's the light of the oncoming train.

['Since 1939' (1977)]

MALLET, Robert (1915–)
How many pessimists end up by
desiring the things they fear, in order
to prove that they are right.

[*Apostilles*]

MEIR, Golda (1898–1978)
Pessimism is a luxury that a Jew can
never allow himself.

[*The Observer*, 1974]

PETER, Laurence J. (1919–1990)
A pessimist is a man who looks both
ways before crossing a one-way street.

[Attr.]

See OPTIMISM

PHILOSOPHY

AYER, A.J. (1910–1989)
The principles of logic and metaphysics are true simply because we never
allow them to be anything else.

[*Language, Truth and Logic* (1936)]

BACON, Francis (1561–1626)
All good moral philosophy ... is but an
handmaid to religion.

[*The Advancement of Learning* (1605)]

BOWEN, Lord (1835–1894)
On a metaphysician: A blind man in a
dark room – looking for a black hat –
which isn't there.

[Attr.]

CHAMFORT, Nicolas (1741–1794)
*Je dirais volontiers des métaphysiciens
ce que Scalinger disait des Basques, on
dit qu'ils s'entendent, mais je n'en crois
rien.*
I am tempted to say about
metaphysicians what Scalinger would
say about the Basques: they are said to
understand one another, but I don't
believe a word of it.

[*Maximes et Pensées* (1796)]

CICERO (106–43 BC)
*Sed nescio quo modo nihil tam absurde
dici potest quod non dicatur ab aliquo
philosophorum.*
But somehow there is nothing so
absurd that some philosopher has not
said it.

[*De Divinatione*]

EDWARDS, Oliver (1711–1791)
I have tried too in my time to be a
philosopher; but, I don't know how,
cheerfulness was always breaking in.

[In Boswell, *The Life of Samuel Johnson*
(1791)]

GOLDSMITH, Oliver (c. 1728–1774)
This same philosophy is a good horse in the stable, but an errant jade on a journey.

[*The Good Natur'd Man* (1768)]

HUXLEY, T.H. (1825–1895)
I doubt if the philosopher lives, or has ever lived, who could know himself to be heartily despised by a street boy without some irritation.

[*Evolution and Ethics* (1893)]

JOHNSON, Samuel (1709–1784)
[Kicking a stone in order to disprove Berkeley's theory of the non-existence of matter]
I refute it *thus*.

[In Boswell, *The Life of Samuel Johnson* (1791)]

MACNEICE, Louis (1907–1963)
Good-bye now, Plato and Hegel,
The shop is closing down;
They don't want any philosopher-kings in England,
There ain't no universals in this man's town.

[*Autumn Journal* (1939)]

NIETZSCHE, Friedrich (1844–1900)
Wie ich den Philosophen verstehe, als einen furchtbaren Explosionsstoff, vor dem Alles in Gefahr ist.
What I understand philosophers to be: a terrible explosive, in the presence of which everything is in danger.

[*Ecce Homo* (1888)]

PASCAL, Blaise (1623–1662)
Se moquer de la philosophie, c'est vraiment philosopher.
To ridicule philosophy is truly to philosophize.

[*Pensées* (1670)]

RUSSELL, Bertrand (1872–1970)
Organic life, we are told, has developed gradually from the protozoon to the philosopher, and this development, we are assured, is indubitably an advance. Unfortunately it is the philosopher, not the protozoon, who gives us this assurance.

[*Mysticism and Logic* (1918)]

SHAKESPEARE, William (1564–1616)
There are more things in heaven and earth, Horatio,
Than are dreamt of in your philosophy.

[*Hamlet*, I.v]

VOLTAIRE (1694–1778)
En philosophie, il faut se défier de ce qu'on croit entendre trop trop aisément, aussi bien que des choses qu'on n'entend pas.
In philosophy, we must distrust the things we understand too easily as well as the things we don't understand.

[*Lettres philosophiques* (1734)]

La superstition met le monde entier en flammes; la philosophie les éteint.
Superstition sets the whole world on fire; philosophy quenches the flames.

[*Dictionnaire philosophique* (1764)]

WHITEHEAD, A.N. (1861–1947)
Philosophy is the product of wonder.

[*Nature and Life* (1934)]

WITTGENSTEIN, Ludwig (1889–1951)
Philosophy is a struggle against the bewitching of our minds by means of language.

[*Philosophical Investigations* (1953)]

PLAGIARISM

BIERCE, Ambrose (1842–c. 1914)
Plagiarize: To take the thought or style of another writer whom one has never, never read.

[*The Enlarged Devil's Dictionary* (1961)]

MIZNER, Wilson (1876–1933)
When you steal from one author, it's plagiarism; if you steal from many, it's research.

[Attr.]

MONTAIGNE, Michel de (1533–1592)
Quelqu'un pourrait dire de moi que j'ai

seulement fait ici un amas de fleurs étrangères, n'y ayant fourni du mien que le filet à les lier.
One could say of me that in this book I have only made up a bunch of other men's flowers, providing of my own only the string to tie them together.

[*Essais* (1580)]

MORE, Hannah (1745–1833)
He lik'd those literary cooks
Who skim the cream of others' books;
And ruin half an author's graces
By plucking bon-mots from their
places.

[*Florio* (1786)]

SHERIDAN, Richard Brinsley (1751–1816)
All that can be said is, that two people happened to hit on the same thought – and Shakespeare made use of it first, that's all.

[*The Critic* (1779)]

STRAVINSKY, Igor (1882–1971)
A good composer does not imitate; he steals.

[In Yates, *Twentieth Century Music* (1967)]

SULLIVAN, Sir Arthur (1842–1900)
[Accused of plagiarism]
We all have the same eight notes to work with.

[Attr.]

PLANNING

BIERCE, Ambrose (1842–c. 1914)
Plan: To bother about the best method of accomplishing an accidental result.

[*The Enlarged Devil's Dictionary* (1961)]

BRECHT, Bertolt (1898–1956)
Die schönsten Plän sind schon zuschanden geworden durch die Kleinlichkeit von denen, wo sie ausführen sollten.
The best plans have always been wrecked by the narrow-mindedness of those who should carry them out.

[*Mother Courage and her Children* (1939)]

BURNS, Robert (1759–1796)
The best-laid schemes o' mice an' men
Gang aft agley,
An' lea'e us nought but grief an' pain,
For promis'd joy!

['To a Mouse' (1785)]

DRYDEN, John (1631–1700)
Plots, true or false, are necessary things,
To raise up commonwealths and ruin kings.

[*Absalom and Achitophel* (1681)]

GILMAN, Charlotte Perkins (1860–1935)
Where young boys plan for what they will achieve and attain, young girls plan for whom they will achieve and attain.

[*Women and Economics* (1898)]

OSLER, Sir William (1849–1919)
When schemes are laid in advance, it is surprising how often the circumstances fit in with them.

[Attr.]

YOUNG, Edward (1683–1765)
For her own breakfast she'll project a scheme,
Nor take her tea without a stratagem.

[*Love of Fame, the Universal Passion* (1728)]

PLEASURE

ALCOTT, Bronson (1799–1888)
A sip is the most that mortals are permitted from any goblet of delight.

[*Table Talk* (1877)]

AUSTEN, Jane (1775–1817)
One half of the world cannot understand the pleasures of the other.

[*Emma* (1816)]

BIERCE, Ambrose (1842–c. 1914)
Debauchee: One who has so earnestly pursued pleasure that he has had the misfortune to overtake it.

[*The Cynic's Word Book* (1906)]

BURKE, Edmund (1729–1797)
I am convinced that we have a degree of delight, and that no small one, in the real misfortunes and pains of others.

[*A Philosophical Enquiry into the Origin of our Ideas of the Sublime and Beautiful* (1757)]

BURNS, Robert (1759–1796)
But pleasures are like poppies spread:
You seize the flow'r, its bloom is shed;
Or like the snow falls in the river,
A moment white – then melts for ever.

['Tam o' Shanter' (1790)]

BYRON, Lord (1788–1824)
There's not a joy the world can give like that it takes away.

['Stanzas for Music' (1815)]

Pleasure's a sin, and sometimes sin's a pleasure.

[*Don Juan* (1824)]

Though sages may pour out their wisdom's treasure,
There is no sterner moralist than Pleasure.

[*Don Juan* (1824)]

CABELL, James Branch (1879–1958)
A man possesses nothing certainly save a brief loan of his own body: and yet the body of man is capable of much curious pleasure.

[*Jurgen* (1919)]

COWPER, William (1731–1800)
Remorse, the fatal egg by pleasure laid.

['The Progress of Error' (1782)]

GAY, John (1685–1732)
A miss for pleasure, and a wife for breed.

['The Toilette' (1716)]

HAZLITT, William (1778–1830)
The art of pleasing consists in being pleased.

[*The Round Table* (1817)]

HUNT, Leigh (1784–1859)
A pleasure so exquisite as almost to amount to pain.

[Letter to Alexander Ireland, 1848]

JOHNSON, Samuel (1709–1784)
Pleasure is very seldom found where it is sought; our brightest blazes of gladness are commonly kindled by unexpected sparks.

[*The Idler* (1758–1760)]

If I had no duties, and no reference to futurity, I would spend my life in driving briskly in a post-chaise with a pretty woman.

[In Boswell, *The Life of Samuel Johnson* (1791)]

No man is a hypocrite in his pleasures.

[In Boswell, *The Life of Samuel Johnson* (1791)]

LAMB, Charles (1775–1834)
The greatest pleasure I know, is to do a good action by stealth, and to have it found out by accident.

['Table Talk by the Late Elia']

MOLIERE (1622–1673)
*Le ciel défend, de vrai, certains contentements
Mais on trouve avec lui des accommodements.*
Heaven forbids certain pleasures, it is true, but one can arrive at certain compromises.

[*Tartuffe* (1664)]

O'ROURKE, P.J. (1947–)
After all, what is your hosts' purpose in having a party? Surely not for you to enjoy yourself; if that were their sole purpose, they'd have simply sent champagne and women over to your place by taxi.

[Attr.]

SHAKESPEARE, William (1564–1616)
These violent delights have violent ends.

[*Romeo and Juliet*, II.vi]

SMOLLETT, Tobias (1721–1771)
I consider the world as made for me,
not me for the world: it is my maxim
therefore to enjoy it while I can, and
let futurity shift for itself.

[*The Adventures of Roderick Random* (1748)]

WOOLLCOTT, Alexander (1887–1943)
All the things I really like to do are
either immoral, illegal, or fattening.

[In Drennan, *Wit's End* (1973)]

POETRY

BACON, Francis (1561–1626)
[Poesy] was ever thought to have
some participation of divineness,
because it doth raise and erect the
mind, by submitting the shows of
things to the desires of the mind;
whereas reason doth buckle and bow
the mind unto the nature of things.

[*The Advancement of Learning* (1605)]

BANVILLE, Théodore de (1823–1891)
Licences poétiques. Il n'y en a pas.
Poetic licence. There's no such thing.

[*Petit traité de poésie française*]

BRADSTREET, Anne (c. 1612–1672)
I am obnoxious to each carping
   tongue,
Who sayes my hand a needle better
   fits,
A Poet's Pen, all scorne, I should thus
   wrong;
For such despight they cast on female
   wits:
If what I doe prove well, it won't
   advance,
They'll say it's stolne, or else, it was by
   chance.

['The Prologue' (1650)]

BYRON, Lord (1788–1824)
Nothing so difficult as a beginning
In poesy, unless perhaps the end.

[*Don Juan* (1824)]

What is poetry? – The feeling of a
Former world and Future.

[Journal, 1821]

CAGE, John (1912–1992)
I have nothing to say, I am saying it,
and that is poetry.

[*Silence* (1961)]

**COLERIDGE, Samuel Taylor
(1772–1834)**
Poetry is not the proper antithesis to
prose, but to science. Poetry is
opposed to science, and prose to
metre.

[*Lectures and Notes of 1818*]

I wish our clever young poets would
remember my homely definitions of
prose and poetry; that is prose = words
in their best order; poetry = the best
words in the best order.

[*Table Talk* (1835)]

Poetry is certainly something more
than good sense, but it must be good
sense at all events; just as a palace is
more than a house, but it must be a
house, at least.

[*Table Talk* (1835)]

ELIOT, T.S. (1888–1965)
Poetry is not a turning loose of
emotion, but an escape from emotion;
it is not the expression of personality,
but an escape from personality.

['Tradition and the Individual Talent' (1919)]

EWART, Gavin (1916–1995)
Good light verse is better than bad
heavy verse any day of the week.

[*Penultimate Poems* (1989)]

FARQUHAR, George (1678–1707)
Poetry's a mere drug, Sir.

[*Love and a Bottle* (1698)]

FROST, Robert (1874–1963)
A poem may be worked over once it is
in being, but may not be worried into
being.

[*Collected Poems* (1939)]

Poetry is a way of taking life by the
throat.

[In Sergeant, *Robert Frost: the Trial by
Existence* (1960)]

GRANVILLE-BARKER, Harley (1877–1946)
Rightly thought of there is poetry in peaches ... even when they are canned.

[*The Madras House*]

HARDY, Thomas (1840–1928)
If Galileo had said in verse that the world moved, the Inquisition might have let him alone.

[In F.E. Hardy, *The Later Years of Thomas Hardy* (1930)]

HOPKINS, Gerard Manley (1844–1889)
The poetical language of an age should be the current language heightened.

[Letter to Robert Bridges, 1879]

HOUSMAN, A.E. (1859–1936)
Even when poetry has a meaning, as it usually has, it may be inadvisable to draw it out ... perfect understanding will sometimes almost extinguish pleasure.

['The Name and Nature of Poetry' (1933)]

JAMES VI OF SCOTLAND AND I OF ENGLAND (1566–1625)
Dr Donne's verses are like the peace of God; they pass all understanding.

[Attr.]

JARRELL, Randall (1914–1965)
Some poetry seems to have been written on typewriters by other type-writers.

[Attr.]

KEATS, John (1795–1821)
A long Poem is a test of Invention which I take to be the Polar Star of Poetry, as Fancy is the Sails, and Imagination the Rudder.

[Letter to Benjamin Bailey, 1817]

We hate poetry that has a palpable design upon us – and if we do not agree, seems to put its hand in its breeches pocket. Poetry should be great and unobtrusive, a thing which enters into one's soul, and does not startle it or amaze it with itself, but with its subject.

[Letter to J.H. Reynolds, 1818]

If Poetry comes not as naturally as Leaves to a tree it had better not come at all.

[Letter to John Taylor, 1818]

KENNEDY, John F. (1917–1963)
When power narrows the areas of man's concern, poetry reminds him of the richness and diversity of his existence.

[Speech, 1963]

KLOPSTOCK, Friedrich (1724–1803)
[Of one of his poems]
God and I both knew what it meant once; now God alone knows.
[Attr.]

LARKIN, Philip (1922–1985)
I rather think poetry has given me up, which is a great sorrow to me, but not an enormous, crushing sorrow. It's rather like going bald.

[*The Observer*, 1984]

MACAULAY, Lord (1800–1859)
As civilization advances, poetry almost necessarily declines.

[*Collected Essays* (1843)]

PAZ, Octavio (1914–)
La poesía no es nada sino tiempo, ritmo perpetuamente creador.
Poetry is nothing but time, ceaselessly creative rhythm.

[*The Bow and the Lyre* (1956)]

PRESTON, Keith (1884–1927)
Of all the literary scenes
Saddest this sight to me:
The graves of little magazines
Who died to make verse free.

['The Liberators']

SHELLEY, Percy Bysshe (1792–1822)
[Poetry] lifts the veil from the hidden beauty of the world, and makes familiar objects be as if they were not familiar.

[*A Defence of Poetry* (1821)]

THOMAS, Dylan (1914–1953)
These poems, with all their crudities,
doubts, and confusions, are written for
the love of Man and in praise of God,
and I'd be a damn' fool if they weren't.

[*Collected Poems* (1952), Note]

VALERY, Paul (1871–1945)
Mes vers ont le sens qu'on leur prête.
My poems mean what people take
them to mean.

[*Variety* (1924)]

A poem is never finished, only
abandoned.

[In Auden, *A Certain World*]

WAIN, John (1925–)
Poetry is to prose as dancing is to
walking.

[BBC broadcast, 1976]

WILDE, Oscar (1854–1900)
There seems to be some curious
connection between piety and poor
rhymes.

[In Lucas, *A Critic in Pall Mall* (1919)]

WORDSWORTH, William (1770–1850)
I have said that poetry is the
spontaneous overflow of powerful
feelings: it takes its origin from
emotion recollected in tranquillity.

[*Lyrical Ballads* (1802)]

See LITERATURE; WRITING

POETS

AUDEN, W.H. (1907–1973)
A poet's hope: to be,
like some valley cheese,
local, but prized elsewhere.

['Shorts II']

It is a sad fact about our culture that a
poet can earn much more money
writing or talking about his art than he
can by practising it.

[*The Dyer's Hand* (1963)]

BEER, Thomas (1889–1940)
I agree with one of your reputable

critics that a taste for drawing-rooms
has spoiled more poets than ever did a
taste for gutters.

[*The Mauve Decade* (1926)]

BLAKE, William (1757–1827)
The reason Milton wrote in fetters
when he wrote of Angels & God, and
at liberty when of Devils & Hell, is
because he was a true Poet and of the
Devil's party without knowing it.

['The Voice of the Devil']

BURNS, Robert (1759–1796)
I never had the least thought or
inclination of turning Poet till I once
got heartily in love, and then rhyme
and song were, in a manner, the
spontaneous language of my head.

[Attr.]

**COLERIDGE, Samuel Taylor
(1772–1834)**
No man was ever yet a great poet,
without being at the same time a
profound philosopher.

[*Biographia Literaria* (1817)]

CONGREVE, William (1670–1729)
It is the business of a comic poet to
paint the vices and follies of human
kind.

[*The Double Dealer* (1694)]

ELIOT, T.S. (1888–1965)
The business of the poet is not to find
new emotions, but to use the ordinary
ones and, in working them up into
poetry, to express feelings which are
not in actual emotions at all.

['Tradition and the Individual Talent' (1919)]

GRAVES, Robert (1895–1985)
To be a poet is a condition rather than
a profession.

[Questionnaire in *Horizon*]

HARDY, Thomas (1840–1928)
Of course poets have morals and
manners of their own, and custom is
no argument with them.

[*The Hand of Ethelberta* (1876)]

KEATS, John (1795–1821)
A Poet is the most unpoetical of
anything in existence; because he has
no Identity – he is continually
informing and filling some other Body.
[Letter to Richard Woodhouse, 1818]

PESSOA, Fernando (1888–1935)
*Ser poeta não é una ambição minha.
É a minha maneira de estar sozinho.*
Being a poet is not an ambition of
mine.
It is my way of being alone.
[*The Guardian of Flocks* (1914)]

PLATO (c. 429–347 BC)
Poets utter great and wise things
which they do not themselves understand.
[*Republic*]

POPE, Alexander (1688–1744)
Sir, I admit your gen'ral Rule
That every Poet is a Fool;
But you yourself may serve to show it,
That every Fool is not a Poet.
['Epigram from the French' (1732)]

SHELLEY, Percy Bysshe (1792–1822)
Poets are ... the trumpets which sing
to battle and feel not what they inspire
... Poets are the unacknowledged
legislators of the world.
[*A Defence of Poetry* (1821)]

WALLER, Edmund (1606–1687)
Poets lose half the praise they should
have got,
Could it be known what they discreetly
blot.
['On Roscommon's Translation of Horace']

WOOLF, Virginia (1882–1941)
I would venture to guess that Anon,
who wrote so many poems without
signing them, was often a woman.
[*A Room of One's Own* (1929)]

YEATS, W.B. (1865–1939)
The poet finds and makes his mask in
disappointment, the hero in defeat.
['Anima Hominis']

POLITICIANS

ADAMS, Franklin P. (1881–1960)
The trouble with this country is that
there are too many politicians who
believe, with a conviction based on
experience, that you can fool all of the
people all of the time.
[*Nods and Becks* (1944)]

ALLEN, Dave (1936–)
If John Major was drowning, his whole
life would pass in front of him and he
wouldn't be in it.
[On stage, 1991]

ASQUITH, Margot (1864–1945)
[Of Lloyd George]
He couldn't see a belt without hitting
below it.
[*As I Remember*, 1967]

He [a politician] always has his arm
round your waist and his eye on the
clock.
[*As I Remember*, 1967]

BAGEHOT, Walter (1826–1877)
A constitutional statesman is in
general a man of common opinions
and uncommon abilities.
['The Character of Sir Robert Peel' (1856)]

BALDWIN, Stanley (1867–1947)
[Of the House of Commons, 1918]
A lot of hard-faced men who look as if
they had done very well out of the
war.
[Attr.]

BARNARD, Robert (1936–)
Early on in his stint as a junior
minister a newspaper had called him
'the thinking man's Tory', and the label
had stuck, possibly because there was
so little competition.
[*Political Suicide* (1986)]

BELLOCH, Juan Alberto (1950–)
*Los jueces se rigen por la legalidad; los
politicos por la oportunidad.*
Judges are guided by the law;
politicians by expediency.
[*El país: edición internacional*, 1994]

BEVAN, Aneurin (1897–1960)
[Wishing to address the Prime Minister rather than the Foreign Secretary, in the House of Commons]
If we complain about the tune, there is no reason to attack the monkey when the organ grinder is present.

[Speech, 1957]

[On Churchill]
He is a man suffering from petrified adolescence.

[In Brome, *Aneurin Bevan*]

BRIGHT, John (1811–1889)
[Of Disraeli]
He is a self-made man, and worships his creator.

[Remark, c.1868]

BROWN, Tina (1953–)
[Of Richard Crossman]
[He] has the jovial garrulity and air of witty indiscretion that shows he intends to give nothing away.

[*Loose Talk* (1979)]

BUCHWALD, Art (1925–)
[Of Richard Nixon]
I worship the quicksand he walks in.

[Attr.]

BUTLER, R.A. (1902–1982)
[On Sir Anthony Eden, who had been described as the offspring of a mad baronet and a beautiful woman]
That's Anthony for you – half mad baronet, half beautiful woman.

[Attr.]

CAMERON, Simon (1799–1889)
An honest politician is one who, when he is bought, will stay bought.

[Remark]

CAMPBELL, Menzies (1941–)
[Of John Smith, leader of the Labour Party]
He had all the virtues of a Scottish Presbyterian, but none of the vices.

[*The Guardian*, 1994]

COOK, Peter (1937–1995)
[Giving an impersonation of Harold Macmillan]
We exchanged many frank words in our respective languages.

[*Beyond the Fringe*,1961]

CRITCHLEY, Julian (1930–)
The only safe pleasure for a parliamentarian is a bag of boiled sweets.

[*The Listener*, 1982]

CUMMINGS, e. e. (1894–1962)
a politician is an arse upon which everyone has sat except a man

[*1 x 1* (1944), no. 10]

DE GAULLE, Charles (1890–1970)
Comme un homme politique ne croit jamais ce qu'il dit, il est tout étonné quand il est cru sur parole.
Since a politician never believes what he says, he is quite surprised to be taken at his word.

[Attr.]

In order to become the master, the politician poses as the servant.

[Attr.]

DEVONSHIRE, Duke of (1833–1908)
I dreamt that I was making a speech in the House. I woke up, and by Jove I was!

[In Churchill, *Thought and Adventures*]

DOUGLAS-HOME, Sir Alec (1903–1995)
There are two problems in my life. The political ones are insoluble and the economic ones are incomprehensible.

[Speech, 1964]

FOLEY, Rae (1900–1978)
He had the misleading air of open-hearted simplicity that people have come to demand of their politicians.

[*The Hundredth Door* (1950)]

FORD, Gerald R. (1913–)
[Referring to his own appointment as

President]
I guess it proves that in America anyone can be President.

[In Reeves, *A Ford Not a Lincoln*]

GAREL-JONES, Tristan (1941–)
My profession does not allow me to go swanning around buying pints of milk. I wouldn't be of sufficient service to my constituents if I went into shops.

[*The Independent*, 1994]

GUINAN, Texas (1884–1933)
A politician is a fellow who will lay down your life for his country.

[Attr.]

HEALEY, Denis (1917–)
[On Geoffrey Howe's attack on his Budget proposals]
Like being savaged by a dead sheep.

[Speech, 1978]

[Of Mrs Thatcher]
For the past few months she has been charging about like some bargain basement Boadicea.

[*The Observer*, 1982]

HOGGART, Simon (1946–)
Reagan was probably the first modern president to treat the post as a part-time job, one way of helping to fill the otherwise blank days of retirement.

[*America 1990*]

HORNE, Donald Richmond (1921–)
Politicians cannot help being clowns. Political activity is essentially absurd. The hopes held for it can be high, the results tragic, but the political art itself must lack dignity: it can never match our ideals of how such things should be done.

[*The Legend of King O'Malley*]

HOWAR, Barbara (1934–)
There are no such things as good politicians and bad politicians. There are only politicians, which is to say, they all have personal axes to grind, and all too rarely are they honed for the public good.

[*Laughing All the Way* (1973)]

JARRELL, Randall (1914–1965)
President Robbins was so well adjusted to his environment that sometimes you could not tell which was the environment and which was President Robbins.

[*Pictures from an Institution* (1954)]

KEYNES, John Maynard (1883–1946)
[When asked what happened when Lloyd George was alone in a room]
When he's alone in a room, there's nobody there.

[*As I Remember*, 1967]

KHRUSHCHEV, Nikita (1894–1971)
Politicians are the same everywhere. They promise to build a bridge even when there's no river.

[Remark to journalists in the USA, 1960]

LE GUIN, Ursula (1929–)
He had grown up in a country run by politicians who sent the pilots to man the bombers to kill the babies to make the world safe for children to grow up in.

[*The Lathe of Heaven* (1971)]

LYNNE, Liz (1948–)
[On the behaviour of MPs]
It was like a bunch of 11-year-olds at their first secondary school.

[*The Independent*, 1992]

MACMILLAN, Harold (1894–1986)
When you're abroad you're a states-man: when you're at home you're just a politician.

[Speech, South Africa, 1958]

If people want a sense of purpose they should get it from their archbishop. They should certainly not get it from their politicians.

[In Fairlie, *The Life of Politics* (1968)]

MAJOR, John (1943–)
People with vision usually do more harm than good.

[*The Economist*, 1993]

MENZIES, Sir Robert (1894–1978)
[In answer to a woman shouting, 'I wouldn't vote for you if you were the Archangel Gabriel']
If I were the Archangel Gabriel, madam, I'm afraid you would not be in my constituency.

[In Robinson, *The Wit of Sir Robert Menzies* (1966)]

MOSLEY, Sir Oswald (1896–1980)
I am not, and never have been, a man of the right. My position was on the left and is now in the centre of politics.

[Letter to *The Times*, 1968]

MUGGERIDGE, Malcolm (1903–1990)
[Of Anthony Eden]
He was not only a bore; he bored for England.

[*Tread Softly For You Tread on My Jokes* (1966)]

NIXON, Richard (1913–1994)
There can be no whitewash at the White House.

[*The Observer*, 1973]

PARKER, Dorothy (1893–1967)
[Response to news that President Calvin Coolidge had died]
How could they tell?

[In Keats, *You Might As Well Live* (1970)]

POMPIDOU, Georges (1911–1974)
A statesman is a politician who places himself at the service of a nation. A politician is a statesman who places the nation at his service.

[*The Observer*, 1973]

REAGAN, Ronald (1911–)
[To the surgeons about to operate on him after he was wounded in an assassination attempt]
Please assure me that you are all Republicans!

[In Boller, *Presidential Anecdotes* (1981)]

ROOSEVELT, Franklin Delano (1882–1945)
A radical is a man with both feet firmly planted in the air.

[Radio broadcast, 1939]

ROOSEVELT, Theodore (1858–1919)
The most successful politician is he who says what everybody is thinking most often and in the loudest voice.

[In Andrews, *Treasury of Humorous Quotations*]

SAHL, Mort (1927–)
Washington could not tell a lie; Nixon could not tell the truth; Reagan cannot tell the difference.

[*The Observer*, 1987]

[Of President Nixon]
Would you buy a second-hand car from this man?

[Attr.]

SHERIDAN, Richard Brinsley (1751–1816)
[Reply to Mr Dundas]
The Right Honourable Gentleman is indebted to his memory for his jests, and to his imagination for his facts.

[Speech, House of Commons]

SHORTEN, Caroline
Most Conservatives believe that a creche is something that happens between two Range Rovers in Tunbridge Wells.

[*The Independent*, 1993]

SMITH, F.E. (1872–1930)
Winston [Churchill] has devoted the best years of his life to preparing his impromptu speeches.

[Attr.]

STEVENSON, Adlai (1900–1965)
A politician is a statesman who approaches every question with an open mouth.

[In Harris, *The Fine Art of Political Wit*]

THATCHER, Carol (1953-)
[Of her mother, Margaret Thatcher]
Reality hasn't really intervened in my mother's life since the seventies.

[*Daily Mail*, 1996]

THATCHER, Margaret (1925–)
U-turn if you want to. The lady's not
for turning.

[Speech, 1980]

I don't mind how much my Ministers
talk – as long as they do what I say.

[*The Observer*, 1980]

I think I have become a bit of an
institution – you know, the sort of
thing people expect to see around the
place.

[*The Observer*, 1987]

We have become a grandmother.

[*The Observer*, 1989]

TROLLOPE, Anthony (1815–1882)
It has been the great fault of our
politicians that they have all wanted to
do something.

[*Phineas Finn* (1869)]

TRUMAN, Harry S. (1884–1972)
[Referring to Vice-President Nixon's
nomination for President]
You don't set a fox to watching the
chickens just because he has a lot of
experience in the hen house.

[Speech, 1960]

TWAIN, Mark (1835–1910)
The radical invents the views. When
he has worn them out, the conservative adopts them.

[*Notebooks* (1935)]

USTINOV, Sir Peter (1921–)
When Mrs Thatcher says she has a
nostalgia for Victorian values I don't
think she realises that 90 per cent of
her nostalgia would be satisfied in the
Soviet Union.

[*The Observer*, 1987]

WALPOLE, Robert (1676–1745)
[Of fellow-parliamentarians]
All those men have their price.

[In Coxe, *Memoirs of Sir Robert Walpole*
(1798)]

WEST, Dame Rebecca (1892–1983)
Margaret Thatcher's great strength
seems to be the better people know
her, the better they like her. But, of
course, she has one great disadvantage – she is a daughter of the
people and looks trim, as the
daughters of the people desire to be.
Shirley Williams has such an advantage over her because she's a member
of the upper-middle class and can
achieve that kitchen-sink-revolution-
ary look that one cannot get unless
one has been to a really good school.

[Interview, *The Sunday Times*, 1976]

WHITEHORN, Katherine (1926–)
It is a pity, as my husband says, that
more politicians are not bastards by
birth instead of vocation.

[*The Observer*, 1964]

WILSON, Harold (1916–1995)
Hence the practised performances of
latter-day politicians in the game of
musical daggers: never be left holding
the dagger when the music stops.

[*The Governance of Britain*]

POLITICS

ABBOTT, Diane (1953–)
Being an MP is the sort of job all
working-class parents want for their
children – clean, indoors and no heavy
lifting.

[*The Observer*, 1994]

ADAMS, Henry (1838–1918)
Politics, as a practice, whatever its
professions, has always been the
systematic organization of hatreds.

[*The Education of Henry Adams* (1918)]

ANDERSON, Bruce
[Of Tony Blair's New Labour]
The Labour Party has decided to
renounce its principles, its policies and
its past.

[*The Spectator*, May 1996]

ANONYMOUS
Don't tell my mother I'm in politics –

she thinks I play the piano in a whorehouse.

[American saying from the Depression]

The personal is political.

ARENDT, Hannah (1906-1975)
Truthfulness has never been counted among the political virtues, and lies have always been regarded as justifiable tools in political dealings.

[*Crises of the Republic* (1972)]

ARISTOTLE (384-322 BC)
Man is by nature a political animal.

[*Politics*]

ASHDOWN, Paddy (1941-)
Anybody who thinks that the Liberal Democrats are a racist party are staring the facts in the face.

[ITV news, 1993]

ASTOR, Nancy (1879-1964)
Women are young at politics, but they are old at suffering; soon they will learn that through politics they can prevent some kinds of suffering.

[*My Two Countries* (1923)]

BIERCE, Ambrose (1842-c. 1914)
Nepotism: Appointing your grandfather to office for the good of the party.

[*The Enlarged Devil's Dictionary* (1961)]

BISMARCK, Prince Otto von (1815-1898)
Die Politik ist die Lehre vom Möglichen.
Politics is the art of the possible.

[Remark, 1863]

BRITTAIN, Vera (1893-1970)
Politics is usually the executive expression of human immaturity.

[*The Rebel Passion* (1964)]

BURCHILL, Julie (1960-)
Green politics, in the final analysis, is so popular with the rich because it contains no race or class analysis at all; politics with everything but the glow of involvement taken out.

[*Sex and Sensibility* (1992)]

BURGESS, Anthony (1917-1993)
The US presidency is a Tudor monarchy plus telephones.

[In Plimpton (ed.), *Writers at Work* (1977)]

BURKE, Edmund (1729-1797)
The conduct of a losing party never appears right: at least it never can possess the only infallible criterion of wisdom to vulgar judgments – success.

[*Letter to a Member of the National Assembly* (1791)]

Your representative owes you, not his industry only, but his judgement; and he betrays, instead of serving you, if he sacrifices it to your opinion.

[Speech to the Electors of Bristol, 1774]

CAMUS, Albert (1913-1960)
Politics and the fate of mankind are shaped by men without ideals and without greatness. Men who have greatness within them don't concern themselves with politics.

[*Notebooks, 1935-1942*]

CLARK, Alan (1928-)
There are no true friends in politics. We are all sharks circling and waiting, for traces of blood to appear in the water.

[*Diary*, 1990]

DE GAULLE, Charles (1890-1970)
I have come to the conclusion that politics are too serious a matter to be left to the politicians.

[Attr.]

DERBY, Earl of
The Conservatives are the weakest among the intellectual classes: as is natural.

[Letter to Disraeli]

DISRAELI, Benjamin (1804-1881)
England does not love coalitions.

[Speech, 1852]

Finality is not the language of politics.

[Speech, 1859]

Damn your principles! Stick to your

party.

[Attr.]

EINSTEIN, Albert (1879–1955)
An empty stomach is not a good
political adviser.

[*Cosmic Religion* (1931)]

FIELDS, W.C. (1880–1946)
Hell, I never vote *for* anybody. I always
vote *against*.

[In Taylor, *W. C. Fields: His Follies and
Fortunes* (1950)]

FISHER, H.A.L. (1856–1940)
Politics is the art of human happiness.

[*History of Europe* (1935)]

FOUCAULT, Michel (1926–1984)
Marxism exists in nineteenth-century
thought in the same way as a fish
exists in water; that is, it stops
breathing anywhere else.

[In Erlbon, *Michel Foucault* (1989)]

FROST, Robert (1874–1963)
I never dared be radical when young
For fear it would make me
   conservative when old.

['Precaution' (1936)]

A liberal is a man too broadminded to
take his own side in a quarrel.

[Attr.]

GAITSKELL, Hugh (1906–1963)
All terrorists, at the invitation of the
Government, end up with drinks at the
Dorchester.

[Letter to *The Guardian*, 1977]

GALBRAITH, J.K. (1908–)
Few things are as immutable as the
addiction of political groups to the
ideas by which they have once won
office.

[*The Affluent Society* (1958)]

There are times in politics when you
must be on the right side and lose.

[*The Observer*, 1968]

**HAILSHAM, Quintin Hogg, Baron
(1907–)**
[On the Profumo affair]

A great party is not to be brought
down because of a squalid affair
between a woman of easy virtue and a
proved liar.

[Interview, BBC TV, 1963]

HAVEL, Václav (1936–)
Ideology is a special way of relating to
the world. It offers human beings the
illusion of an identity, of dignity, and of
morality, while making it easier for
them to part with it.

[*Living in Truth* (1987)]

HEALEY, Denis (1917–)
It is a good thing to follow the first law
of holes; if you are in one, stop
digging.

[*The Observer*, 1988]

HELLMAN, Lillian (1905–1984)
I cannot and will not cut my
conscience to fit this year's fashions,
even though I long ago came to the
conclusion that I was not a political
person and could have no comfortable
place in any political group.

[Letter to the US House of Representatives
Committee on Un-American Activities, 1952]

HIGHTOWER, Jim (1933–)
Only things in the middle of the road
are yellow lines and dead armadillos.

[Attr.]

HITLER, Adolf (1889–1945)
*Wesentlich ist die politische Willens-
bildung der gesamten Nation, sie ist der
Ausgangspunkt für politische Aktionen.*
What is essential is the formation of
the political will of the entire nation:
that is the starting point for political
actions.

[Speech, 1932]

HORNE, Donald Richmond (1921–)
Politics is both fraud and vision.

[*The Legend of King O'Malley*]

JENKINS, Roy (1920–)
[Used in connection with the SDP,
established in 1981]
Breaking the mould of British politics.

[Attr.]

JOHNSON, Samuel (1709–1784)
Politics are now nothing more than a means of rising in the world.

[In Boswell, *The Life of Samuel Johnson* (1791)]

JUNIUS (1769–1772)
There is a holy mistaken zeal in politics as well as in religion. By persuading others, we convince ourselves.

[*Letters* (1769–1771)]

LA BRUYERE, Jean de (1645–1696)
L'esprit de parti abaisse les plus grands hommes jusques aux petitesses du peuple.
Party loyalty brings the greatest of men down to the petty level of the masses.

[*Les caractères ou les moeurs de ce siècle* (1688)]

MCCARTHY, Senator Eugene (1916–)
Being in politics is like being a football coach. You have to be smart enough to understand the game and dumb enough to think it's important.

[Interview, 1968]

MACMILLAN, Harold (1894–1986)
[On the life of a Foreign Secretary]
Forever poised between a cliché and an indiscretion.

[*Newsweek*, 1956]

As usual the Liberals offer a mixture of sound and original ideas. Unfortunately none of the sound ideas is original and none of the original ideas is sound.

[*The Observer*, 1961]

I have never found in a long experience of politics that criticism is ever inhibited by ignorance.

[Attr.]

MAJOR, John (1943–)
[Commenting on the Tories' disastrous results in local government elections]
For those people who may suggest that at the moment the Conservative

Party has its back to the wall, I would simply say we will do precisely what the British nation has done all through its history when it had its back to the wall: turn round and fight for the things it believes.

[*The Observer*, May 1996]

MAO TSE-TUNG (1893–1976)
All reactionaries are paper tigers.

[*Quotations from Chairman Mao Tse-Tung*]

MAYHEW, Christopher (1915–)
[On the Munich Agreement]
A policy of *reculer pour mieux reculer.*

[Speech, Oxford Union, 1938]

MENZIES, Sir Robert (1894–1978)
A Prime Minister exercises his greatest public influence by creating a public impression of himself, hoping all the time that the people will be generous rather than just.

[In Mayer and Nelson, *Australian Politics: A Third Reader*]

MILL, John Stuart (1806–1873)
A party of order or stability, and a party of progress or reform, are both necessary elements of a healthy state of political life.

[*On Liberty* (1859)]

MILLIGAN, Spike (1918–)
[Remark made about a pre-election poll]
One day the don't-knows will get in, and then where will we be?

[Attr.]

MORTON, Rogers (1914–1979)
[Refusing to make any last-ditch attempts to rescue President Ford's re-election campaign, 1976]
I'm not going to re-arrange the furniture on the deck of the *Titanic.*

[Attr.]

NAPOLEON I (1769–1821)
[To Josephine in 1809, on divorcing her for reasons of state]
I still love you, but in politics there is no heart, only head.

[Attr.]

ORWELL, George (1903–1950)
No book is genuinely free from political bias. The opinion that art should have nothing to do with politics is itself a political attitude.

['Why I Write' (1946)]

PANKHURST, Emmeline (1858–1928)
The argument of the broken pane of glass is the most valuable argument in modern politics.

[Attr.]

PARKINSON, C. Northcote (1909–1993)
The British, being brought up on team games, enter their House of Commons in the spirit of those who would rather be doing something else. If they cannot be playing golf or tennis, they can at least pretend that politics is a game with very similar rules.

[Parkinson's Law (1958)]

It is now known ... that men enter local politics solely as a result of being unhappily married.

[Parkinson's Law (1958)]

PARRIS, Matthew (1949–)
Being an MP feeds your vanity and starves your self-respect.

[The Times, 1994]

PEACOCK, Thomas Love (1785–1866)
A Sympathizer would seem to imply a certain degree of benevolent feeling. Nothing of the kind. It signifies a ready-made accomplice in any species of political villainy.

[Gryll Grange (1861)]

POWELL, Enoch (1912–)
Above any other position of eminence, that of Prime Minister is filled by fluke.

[The Observer, 1987]

PRESCOTT, John (1938–)
[During a debate between Prescott, Tony Blair and Margaret Beckett at the time of the contest for the Labour leadership]
We're in danger of loving ourselves to death.

[The Observer, 1994]

REAGAN, Ronald (1911–)
Politics is supposed to be the second oldest profession. I have come to understand that it bears a very close resemblance to the first.

[Remark at a conference, 1977]

Politics is not a bad profession. If you succeed there are many rewards, if you disgrace yourself you can always write a book.

[Attr.]

RUSK, Dean (1909–)
[Of the Cuban missile crisis]
We're eye-ball to eye-ball and I think the other fellow just blinked.

[Remark, 1962]

SHAW, George Bernard (1856–1950)
He knows nothing; and he thinks he knows everything. That points clearly to a political career.

[Major Barbara (1907)]

SHERIDAN, Richard Brinsley (1751–1816)
[On being asked to apologize for calling a fellow MP a liar]
Mr Speaker, I said the honourable member was a liar it is true and I am sorry for it. The honourable member may place the punctuation where he pleases.

[Attr.]

SOMOZA, Anastasio (1925–1980)
You won the elections. But I won the count.

[The Guardian, 1977]

SOPER, Donald (1903–)
[On the quality of debate in the House of Lords]
It is, I think, good evidence of life after death.

[The Listener, 1978]

STEVENSON, Adlai (1900–1965)
I will make a bargain with the Republicans. If they will stop telling lies about Democrats, we will stop telling the truth about them.

[Speech, 1952]

STEVENSON, Robert Louis (1850–1894)
Politics is perhaps the only profession for which no preparation is thought necessary.

[*Familiar Studies of Men and Books* (1882)]

These are my politics: to change what we can; to better what we can; but still to bear in mind that man is but a devil weakly fettered by some generous beliefs and impositions; and for no word however sounding, and no cause however just and pious, to relax the stricture of these bonds.

[*The Dynamiter* (1885)]

STOPPARD, Tom (1937–)
The House of Lords, an illusion to which I have never been able to subscribe – reponsibility without power, the prerogative of the eunuch throughout the ages.

[*Lord Malquist and Mr Moon* (1966)]

THATCHER, Margaret (1925–)
Let our children grow tall, and some taller than others if they have it in them to do so.

[Speech, US tour, 1975]

Britain is no longer in the politics of the pendulum, but of the ratchet.

[Speech, 1977]

Victorian values ... were the values when our country became great.

[Television interview, 1982]

No one would have remembered the Good Samaritan if he'd only had good intentions. He had money as well.

[*The Observer*, 1980]

THORPE, Jeremy (1929–)
[Remark on Macmillan's Cabinet purge, 1962]
Greater love hath no man than this, that he lay down his friends for his life.

[Speech, 1962]

TONER, Pauline (1935–1989)
[The credo of the first woman Minister

in the history of the Victorian Parliament]
Why join a women's group to lobby government ministers when you can become a minister yourself?

[*Australian Women's Weekly*, 1982]

TROLLOPE, Anthony (1815–1882)
It is the necessary nature of a political party in this country to avoid, as long as it can be avoided, the consideration of any question which involves a great change ... The best carriage horses are those which can most steadily hold back against the coach as it trundles down the hill.

[*Phineas Redux* (1874)]

VALERY, Paul (1871–1945)
La politique est l'art d'empêcher les gens de se mêler de ce qui les regarde.
Politics is the art of preventing people from becoming involved in affairs which concern them.

[*As Such 2* (1943)]

VIDAL, Gore (1925–)
Any American who is prepared to run for President should automatically, by definition, be disqualified from ever doing so.

[Attr.]

WALDEN, George (1939–)
[On John Major's policy of non-cooperation with Europe over the export ban on British beef]
Patriots are not supposed to make fools of their own people.

[*The Times*, May 1996]

WELLINGTON, Duke of (1769–1852)
[On seeing the first Reformed Parliament]
I never saw so many shocking bad hats in my life.

[In Fraser, *Words on Wellington* (1889)]

WILSON, Harold (1916–1995)
The Labour Party is like a stage-coach. If you rattle along at great speed everybody inside is too exhilarated or too seasick to cause any trouble. But if

you stop everybody gets out and argues about where to go next.

[In L. Smith, *Harold Wilson, The Authentic Portrait*]

ZAPPA, Frank (1940–1993)
Politics is the entertainment branch of industry.

[Attr.]

See COMMUNISM; FASCISM; SOCIALISM

POVERTY

ANOUILH, Jean (1910–1987)
Moi j'adorerais être pauvre! Seulement, je voudrais être vraiment pauvre. Tout ce qui est excessif m'enchante.
I should love to be poor, as long as I was *excessively* poor! Anything in excess is quite delightful.

[*Ring Round the Moon* (1948)]

BAGEHOT, Walter (1826–1877)
Poverty is an anomaly to rich people. It is very difficult to make out why people who want dinner do not ring the bell.

[*Literary Studies* (1879)]

BEHN, Aphra (1640–1689)
Come away; poverty's catching.

[*The Rover* (1677)]

THE BIBLE (King James Version)
The poor always ye have with you.

[*John*, 12:8]

BLAKE, William (1757–1827)
Is this a holy thing to see,
In a rich and fruitful land,
Babes reducd to misery,
Fed with cold and usurous hand?

['Holy Thursday' (1794)]

BOOTH, General William (1829–1912)
This Submerged Tenth – is it, then, beyond the reach of the nine-tenths in the midst of whom they live?

[*In Darkest England* (1890)]

CHAMFORT, Nicolas (1741–1794)
Les pauvres sont les nègres de l'Europe.
The poor are the negroes of Europe.

[*Maximes et Pensées* (1796)]

COBBETT, William (1762–1835)
To be poor and independent is very nearly an impossibility.

[*Advice to Young Men* (1829)]

COWPER, William (1731–1800)
[Of a burglar]
He found it inconvenient to be poor.

['Charity' (1782)]

CRABBE, George (1754–1832)
The murmuring poor, who will not fast in peace.

[*The Newspaper* (1785)]

FARQUHAR, George (1678–1707)
'Tis still my maxim, that there is no scandal like rags, nor any crime so shameful as poverty.

[*The Beaux' Stratagem* (1707)]

GELDOF, Bob (1954–)
I'm not interested in the bloody system! Why has he no food? Why is he starving to death?

[In Care, *Sayings of the Eighties* (1989)]

JEROME, Jerome K. (1859–1927)
It is easy enough to say that poverty is no crime. No; if it were men wouldn't be ashamed of it. It is a blunder, though, and is punished as such. A poor man is despised the whole world over.

[*Idle Thoughts of an Idle Fellow* (1886)]

JOHNSON, Samuel (1709–1784)
A man, doubtful of his dinner, or trembling at a creditor, is not much disposed to abstracted meditation, or remote enquiries.

[*The Lives of the Most Eminent English Poets* (1781)]

Resolve not to be poor: whatever you have, spend less. Poverty is a great enemy to human happiness; it certainly destroys liberty, and it makes some virtues impracticable and others extremely difficult.

[Letter to Boswell, 1782]

JUVENAL (c. 60–130)
Haud facile emergunt quorum virtutibus obstat
Res angusta domi.
Rarely they rise by virtue's aid, who lie
Plung'd in the depths of helpless poverty.

[*Satires*; trans. Dryden]

Cantabit vacuus coram latrone viator.
The poure man when he goth by the weye
Bifore the thieves he may synge and playe.

[*Satires*; trans. Chaucer]

MEUDELL, George Dick (1860–1936)
Until we partially abolish poverty at home we have no right to burden ourselves with millions of paupers from abroad. What we have, we hold.
AUSTRALIA FOR THE AUSTRALIANS.

[*The Pleasant Career of a Spendthrift in London* (1929)]

PEACOCK, Thomas Love (1785–1866)
Respectable means rich, and decent means poor. I should die if I heard my family called decent.

[*Crotchet Castle* (1831)]

SHAW, George Bernard (1856–1950)
The greatest of our evils and the worst of our crimes is poverty.

[*Major Barbara* (1907)]

SHUTER, Edward (1728–1776)
[Explaining why he did not mend the holes in his stocking]
A hole is the accident of a day, but a darn is premeditated poverty.

[*Dictionary of National Biography* (1897)]

TERESA, Mother (1910–)
... the poor are our brothers and sisters ... people in the world who need love, who need care, who have to be wanted.

[*Time*, 1975]

TRACY, Spencer (1900–1967)
[Of leaner times in his life]
There were times my pants were so thin I could sit on a dime and tell if it was heads or tails.

[In Swindell, *Spencer Tracy*]

WILDE, Oscar (1854–1900)
We are often told that the poor are grateful for charity. Some of them are, no doubt, but the best amongst the poor are never grateful. They are ungrateful, discontented, disobedient, and rebellious. They are quite right to be so.

['The Soul of Man under Socialism' (1891)]

POWER

ACTON, Lord (1834–1902)
Power tends to corrupt, and absolute power corrupts absolutely. Great men are almost always bad men ... There is no worse heresy than that the office sanctifies the holder of it.

[Letter to Bishop Mandell Creighton, 1887]

AMIS, Kingsley (1922–1995)
Generally, nobody behaves decently when they have power.

[*Radio Times*, 1992]

ANDREOTTI, Giulio (1919–)
Il potere logora chi non ce l'ha.
Power wears down the man who doesn't have it.

[In Biagi, *The Good and the Bad* (1989]

AUNG SAN SUU KYI
Concepts such as truth, justice, compassion are often the only bulwarks which stand against ruthless power.

[*Index on Censorship*, 1994]

BACON, Francis (1561–1626)
Men in great place are thrice servants: servants of the sovereign or state, servants of fame, and servants of business ... It is a strange desire to seek power and to lose liberty.

['Of Great Place' (1625)]

BEAVERBROOK, Lord (1879–1964)
[Of Lloyd George]
He did not care in which direction the car was travelling, so long as he remained in the driver's seat.

[*New Statesman*, 1963]

BURKE, Edmund (1729–1797)
Those who have been once intoxicated with power, and have derived any kind of emolument from it, even though but for one year, never can willingly abandon it.

[*Letter to a Member of the National Assembly* (1791)]

CLARE, Dr Anthony (1942–)
Apart from the occasional saint, it is difficult for people who have the smallest amount of power to be nice.

[In Care, *Sayings of the Eighties* (1989)]

FAUST, Beatrice (1939)
Women's Liberationists are both right and wrong when they say that rape is not about sex but about power: for men, sex is power, unless culture corrects biology.

[*Women, Sex and Pornography* (1980)]

GOERING, Hermann (1893–1946)
Guns will make us powerful; butter will only make us fat.

[Broadcast, 1936]

HITLER, Adolf (1889–1945)
Deutschland wird entweder Weltmacht oder überhaupt nicht sein.
Germany will either be a world power or will not exist at all.

[*Mein Kampf* (1927)]

JONES, Sir William (1746–1794)
My opinion is, that power should always be distrusted, in whatever hands it is placed.

[In Teignmouth, *Life of Sir W. Jones* (1835)]

KISSINGER, Henry (1923–)
Power is the ultimate aphrodisiac.

[Attr.]

KUNDERA, Milan (1929–)
The struggle of man against power is the struggle of memory against forgetting.

[Attr.]

MAO TSE-TUNG (1893–1976)
Every Communist must grasp the truth. Political power grows out of the barrel of a gun.

[Speech, 1938]

MILL, John Stuart (1806–1873)
The only purpose for which power can be rightfully exercised over any member of a civilized community, against his will, is to prevent harm to others. His own good, either physical or moral, is not sufficient warrant.

[*On Liberty* (1859)]

RENAN, J. Ernest (1823–1892)
'Savoir c'est pouvoir' est le plus beau mot qu'on ait dit.
'Knowledge is power' is the finest idea ever put into words.

[*Dialogues et fragments philosophiques* (1876)]

RUSSELL, Bertrand (1872–1970)
The megalomaniac differs from the narcissist by the fact that he wishes to be powerful rather than charming, and seeks to be feared rather than loved. To this type belong many lunatics and most of the great men of history.

[*The Conquest of Happiness* (1930)]

STEVENSON, Adlai (1900–1965)
Power corrupts, but lack of power corrupts absolutely.

[*The Observer*, 1963]

TURENNE, Henri, Vicomte (1611–1675)
Dieu est toujours pour les gros bataillons.
God is always on the side of the big battalions.

[Attr.]

PRAISE

BACON, Francis (1561–1626)
For as it is said of calumny, 'calumniate boldly, for some of it will stick' so it may be said of ostentation

(except it be in a ridiculous degree of deformity), 'boldly sound your own praises, and some of them will stick.'

[*The Advancement of Learning* (1623)]

BIERCE, Ambrose (1842–c. 1914)
Eulogy: Praise of a person who has either the advantages of wealth and power, or the consideration to be dead.

[*The Enlarged Devil's Dictionary* (1961)]

GAY, John (1685–1732)
Praising all alike, is praising none.

['A Letter to a Lady' (1714)]

LA ROCHEFOUCAULD, Duc de (1613–1680)
Le refus des louanges est un désir d'être loué deux fois.
Refusal of praise reveals a desire to be praised twice over.

[*Maximes* (1678)]

MARTIAL (c. AD 40–c. 104)
Laudant illa sed ista legunt.
They praise those works but they read something else.

[*Epigrammata*]

POPE, Alexander (1688–1744)
Fondly we think we honour merit then,
When we but praise ourselves in other men.

[*An Essay on Criticism* (1711)]

PROVERB
Self-praise is no recommendation.

SMITH, Sidney (1771–1845)
Praise is the best diet for us, after all.

[In Holland, *A Memoir of the Reverend Sydney Smith* (1855)]

THE PRESENT

THE BIBLE (King James Version)
Take therefore no thought for the morrow: for the morrow shall take thought for the things of itself. Sufficient unto the day is the evil thereof.

[*Matthew*, 6:34]

BURKE, Edmund (1729–1797)
To complain of the age we live in, to murmur at the present possessors of power, to lament the past, to conceive extravagant hopes of the future, are the common dispositions of the greatest part of mankind.

[*Thoughts on the Cause of the Present Discontents* (1770)]

CLARE, John (1793–1864)
The present is the funeral of the past,
And man the living sepulchre of life.

['The Past' (1845)]

EMERSON, Ralph Waldo (1803–1882)
Write it on your heart that every day is the best day in the year. No man has learned anything rightly until he knows that every day is Doomsday.

[*Society and Solitude* (1870)]

FRANKLIN, Benjamin (1706–1790)
The golden age never was the present age.

[*Poor Richard's Almanac* (1750)]

HAMMARSKJÖLD, Dag (1905–1961)
Do not look back. And do not dream about the future, either. It will neither give you back the past, nor satisfy your other daydreams. Your duty, your reward – your destiny – are *here* and *now*.

[*Markings* (1965)]

HORACE (65–8 BC)
Carpe diem.
Seize the day.

[*Odes*]

MCLUHAN, Marshall (1911–1980)
The present cannot be revealed to people until it has become yesterday.

[In Marchand, *Marshall McLuhan* (1989)]

MALLARME, Stéphane (1842–1898)
Le vierge, le vivace et le bel aujourd'hui.
That virgin, vital, beautiful day: today.

[*Plusieurs sonnets* (1881)]

SHAKESPEARE, William (1564–1616)
Past and to come seems best; things present, worst.

[*Henry IV, Part 2*, I.iii]

PRIDE

THE BIBLE (King James Version)
Pride goeth before destruction, and an
haughty spirit before a fall.
[*Proverbs*, 16:18]

BRADSHAW, Henry (d. 1513)
Proude as a pecocke.
[*The Life of Saint Werburge* (1521)]

**COLERIDGE, Samuel Taylor
(1772–1834)**
And the Devil did grin, for his darling
sin
Is pride that apes humility.
['The Devil's Thoughts' (1799)]

DAVIES, Sir John (1569–1626)
I know my life's a pain and but a span,
I know my sense is mock'd in every
thing;
And to conclude, I know myself a
man,
Which is a proud and yet a wretched
thing.
[*Nosce Teipsum* (1599)]

DOBREE, Bonamy (1891–1974)
It is difficult to be humble. Even if you
aim at humility, there is no guarantee
that when you have attained the state
you will not be proud of the feat.
[*John Wesley*]

LANDOR, Walter Savage (1775–1864)
I know not whether I am proud,
But this I know, I hate the crowd.
['With an Album']

MACNEICE, Louis (1907–1963)
Pride in your history is pride
In living what your fathers died,
Is pride in taking your own pulse
And counting in you someone else.
['Suite for recorders' (1966)]

POPE, Alexander (1688–1744)
Pride, the never-failing vice of fools.
[*An Essay on Criticism* (1711)]

SHAKESPEARE, William (1564–1616)
O world, how apt the poor are to be
proud!
[*Twelfth Night*, III.i]

SHELLEY, Percy Bysshe (1792–1822)
But human pride
Is skilful to invent most serious names
To hide its ignorance.
[*Queen Mab* (1813)]

PRINCIPLES

ADLER, Alfred (1870–1937)
It is easier to fight for one's principles
than to live up to them.
[Attr.]

BALDWIN, Stanley (1867–1947)
I would rather be an opportunist and
float than go to the bottom with my
principles round my neck.
[Attr.]

**EBNER-ESCHENBACH, Marie von
(1830–1916)**
*Wenn zwei brave Menschen über
Grundsätze streiten, haben immer beide
recht.*
Whenever two good people argue over
principles, both are always right.
[*Aphorisms* (1880)]

MACKENZIE, Sir Compton (1883–1972)
I don't believe in principles. Principles
are only excuses for what we want to
think or what we want to do.
[*The Adventures of Sylvia Scarlett* (1918)]

MELBOURNE, Lord (1779–1848)
Nobody ever did anything very foolish
except from some strong principle.
[Attr.]

**ROOSEVELT, Franklin Delano
(1882–1945)**
To stand upon the ramparts and die
for our principles is heroic, but to sally
forth to battle and win for our
principles is something more than
heroic.
[Speech, 1928]

SADE, Marquis de (1740–1814)
All universal moral principles are idle
fancies.
[*The 120 Days of Sodom* (1784)]

TODD, Ron (1927–)
You don't have power if you surrender all your principles – you have office.

[Attr.]

PRISON

BOTTOMLEY, Horatio William (1860–1933)
[When spotted sewing mailbags during his imprisonment for misappropriation of funds]
Visitor: Ah, Bottomley, sewing?
Bottomley: No, reaping.

[Attr.]

BRONTË, Emily (1818–1848)
Oh dreadful is the check – intense the agony –
When the ear begins to hear and the eye begins to see;
When the pulse begins to throb, the brain to think again;
The soul to feel the flesh and the flesh to feel the chain!

['The Prisoner' (1846)]

DOWLING, Basil Cairns
[On prisons]
Prisoners and warders – we are all of one blood.
They're much alike, except for a different coat
And a different hat;
And they all seem decent, kindly fellows enough
As they work and chat:
How can it be that men like this have been hanged
By men like that?

[In Burton, *In Prison* (1945)]

FRANK, Otto (b. 1889)
When you have survived life in a concentration camp you have ceased to count yourself as a member of the human race. You will forever be outside the experience of the rest of mankind.

[In the *Daily Mail*, 1996]

HAWTHORNE, Nathaniel (1804–1864)
The black flower of civilized society, a prison.

[*The Scarlet Letter* (1850)]

What other dungeon is so dark as one's own heart! What jailer so inexorable as one's self!

[*The House of the Seven Gables* (1851)]

INGRAMS, Richard (1937–)
[On the prospect of going to jail, 1976]
The only thing I really mind about going to prison is the thought of Lord Longford coming to visit me.

[Attr.]

KEENAN, Brian (1950–)
I would be the voyeur of myself. This strategy I employed for the rest of my captivity. I allowed myself to do and be and say and think and feel all the things that were in me, but at the same time could stand outside observing and attempting to understand.

[*An Evil Cradling*]

LEON, Fray Luis de (c. 1527–1591)
[Resuming a lecture after five years' imprisonment]
Dicebamus hesterno die.
As we were saying the other day.

[Attr.]

LEVI, Primo (1919–1987)
[Of the Nazi concentration camps]
The worst survived – that is, the fittest; the best all died.

[*The Drowned and the Saved* (1988)]

LOVELACE, Richard (1618–1658)
Stone walls do not a prison make
Nor iron bars a cage;
Minds innocent and quiet take
That for an hermitage;
If I have freedom in my love,
And in my soul am free;
Angels alone, that soar above,
Enjoy such liberty.

['To Althea, From Prison' (1649)]

RALEIGH, Sir Walter (c. 1552–1618)
But now close kept, as captives wonted are:

That food, that heat, that light I find no
  more;
Despair bolts up my doors, and I alone
Speak to dead walls, but those hear
  not my moan.

[Untitled poem]

[Said after his trial for treason, 1603]
The world itself is but a large prison,
out of which some are daily led to
execution.

[Attr.]

WAUGH, Evelyn (1903–1966)
Anyone who has been to an English
public school will always feel com-
paratively at home in prison.

[*Decline and Fall* (1928)]

WILDE, Oscar (1854–1900)
The vilest deeds like poison-weeds
Bloom well in prison-air;
It is only what is good in Man
That wastes and withers there.

[*The Ballad of Reading Gaol* (1898)]

[Complaining at having to wait in the
rain for transport to take him to
prison]
If this is the way Queen Victoria treats
her prisoners, she doesn't deserve to
have any.

[Attr.]

PROGRESS

ANONYMOUS
We've made great medical progress in
the last generation. What used to be
merely an itch is now an allergy.

BLAKE, William (1757–1827)
Without Contraries is no progression.
Attraction and Repulsion, Reason and
Energy, Love and Hate, are necessary
to Human existence.

[*The Marriage of Heaven and Hell* (c. 1793)]

BORGES, Jorge Luis (1899–1986)
We have stopped believing in
progress. What progress that is!

[*Ibarra, Borges et Borges*]

BUTLER, Samuel (1835–1902)
All progress is based upon a universal
innate desire on the part of every
organism to live beyond its income.

[*The Note-Books of Samuel Butler* (1912)]

**CLIFFORD, William Kingdon
(1845–1879)**
... scientific thought is not an
accompaniment or condition of
human progress, but human progress
itself.

[*Aims and Instruments of Scientific Thought*
(1872)]

COMTE, Auguste (1798–1857)
L'Amour pour principe, l'Ordre pour
base, et le Progrès pour but.
Love our principle, order our foundation, progress our goal.

[*Système de politique positive*]

CUMMINGS, e. e. (1894–1962)
pity this busy monster, manunkind,
not. Progress is a comfortable disease.

[*1 x 1* (1944), no. 14]

DE KLERK, F.W. (1936–)
A man of destiny knows that beyond
this hill lies another and another. The
journey is never complete.

[*The Observer*, 1994]

DOUGLASS, Frederick (c. 1818–1895)
If there is no struggle, there is no
progress.

[Attr.]

DU BOIS, William (1868–1963)
Believe in life! Always human beings
will live and progress to greater,
broader, and fuller life.

[Last message to the world, read at his
funeral]

ELIOT, Charles W. (1834–1926)
In the modern world the intelligence of
public opinion is the one indispensable
condition of social progress.

[Speech, 1869]

ELLIS, Havelock (1859–1939)
What we call 'Progress' is the
exchange of one nuisance for another
nuisance.

[*Impressions and Comments* (1914)]

FREUD, Sigmund (1856–1939)
What progress we are making. In the Middle Ages they would have burned me. Now they are content with burning my books.

[Letter, 1933]

GIBBON, Edward (1737–1794)
All that is human must retrograde if it does not advance.

[*Decline and Fall of the Roman Empire* (1776–88)]

HEGEL, Georg Wilhelm (1770–1831)
The history of the world is none other than the progress of the consciousness of freedom.

[*Philosophy of History*]

HUBBARD, Elbert (1856–1915)
The world is moving so fast these days that the man who says it can't be done is generally interrupted by someone doing it.

[Attr.]

JOHN XXIII (1881–1963)
The social progress, order, security and peace of each country are necessarily connected with the social progress, order, security and peace of all other countries.

[Encyclical letter, April 1963]

LINDBERGH, Anne Morrow (1906–)
Why do progress and beauty have to be so opposed?

[*Hour of Gold, Hour of Lead* (1973)]

SAINT-EXUPERY, Antoine de (1900–1944)
Man's 'progress' is but a gradual discovery that his questions have no meaning.

[*The Wisdom of the Sands*]

SANTAYANA, George (1863–1952)
Progress, far from consisting in change, depends on retentiveness. Those who cannot remember the past are condemned to repeat it.

[*The Life of Reason* (1906)]

The cry was for freedom and indeterminate progress: *Vorwärts! Avanti!* Onwards! Full speed ahead!, without asking whether directly before you was not a bottomless pit.

[*My Host the World* (1953)]

SHAW, George Bernard (1856–1950)
The reasonable man adapts himself to the world: the unreasonable one persists in trying to adapt the world to himself. Therefore all progress depends on the unreasonable man.

[*Man and Superman* (1903)]

THURBER, James (1894–1961)
Progress was all right; only it went on too long.

[Attr.]

VIGNEAUD, Vincent de (1901–1978)
Nothing holds up the progress of science so much as the right idea at the wrong time.

[*Most Secret War* (1978)]

WALKER, Alice (1944–)
People tend to think that life really does progress for everyone eventually, that people progress, but actually only *some* people progress. The rest of the people don't.

[In C. Tate (ed.), *Black Women Writers at Work* (1983)]

PROPERTY

DICKENS, Charles (1812–1870)
Get hold of portable property.

[*Great Expectations* (1861)]

DRUMMOND, Thomas (1797–1840)
Property has its duties as well as its rights.

[Letter to the Earl of Donoughmore, 1838]

EDGEWORTH, Maria (1767–1849)
Well! some people talk of morality, and some of religion, but give me a little snug property.

[*The Absentee* (1812)]

EMERSON, Ralph Waldo (1803–1882)
A man builds a fine house; and now he has a master, and a task for life; he is to furnish, watch, show it, and keep it in repair, the rest of his days.
[*Society and Solitude* (1870)]

INGERSOLL, Robert Greene (1833–1899)
Few rich men own their own property. The property owns them.
[Address, 1896]

JAMES, Henry (1843–1916)
The black and merciless things that are behind the great possessions.
[*The Ivory Tower* (1917 edition)]

LOOS, Anita (1893–1981)
Kissing your hand may make you feel very very good but a diamond and safire bracelet lasts forever.
[*Gentlemen Prefer Blondes* (1925)]

PROUDHON, Pierre-Joseph (1809–1865)
Si j'avais à répondre à la question suivante: qu'est-ce que l'esclavage? et que d'un seul mot je répondisse: c'est l'assassinat, ma pensée serait aussitôt comprise... Pourquoi donc à cette autre demande: qu'est-ce que la propriété? ne puis-je répondre de même: c'est le vol!
If I were asked to answer the following question: 'What is slavery?' and I replied in one word, 'Murder!' my meaning would be understood at once ... Why, then, to this other question: 'What is property?' may I not likewise answer 'Theft'?
[*Qu'est-ce que la propriété?* (1840)]

VANBRUGH, Sir John (1664–1726)
The want of a thing is perplexing enough, but the possession of it is intolerable.
[*The Confederacy* (1705)]

PUNISHMENT

ARENDT, Hannah (1906–1975)
No punishment has ever possessed enough power of deterrence to prevent the commission of crimes.
[*Eichmann in Jerusalem: A Report on the Banality of Evil* (1963)]

BENTHAM, Jeremy (1748–1832)
All punishment is mischief: all punishment in itself is evil.
[*An Introduction to the Principles of Morals and Legislation* (1789)]

DOSTOEVSKY, Fyodor (1821–1881)
Juridical punishment for crime scares a criminal far less than law-makers think, partly because the criminal himself requires it morally.
[Letter to Katkov, 1865]

GILBERT, W.S. (1836–1911)
My object all sublime
I shall achieve in time –
To let the punishment fit the crime –
The punishment fit the crime.
[*The Mikado* (1885)]

HALIFAX, Lord (1633–1695)
Men are not hang'd for stealing Horses, but that Horses may not be stolen.
['Of Punishment' (1750)]

HUBBARD, Elbert (1856–1915)
Men are not punished for their sins, but by them.
[*A Thousand and One Epigrams* (1911)]

JOHNSON, Samuel (1709–1784)
The rod produces an effect which terminates in itself. A child is afraid of being whipped, and gets his task, and there's an end on't; whereas, by exciting emulation and comparisons of superiority, you lay the foundation of lasting mischief; you make brothers and sisters hate each other.
[In Boswell, *The Life of Samuel Johnson* (1791)]

There is now less flogging in our great schools than formerly, but then less is learned there; so that what the boys get at one end they lose at the other.
[In Boswell, *The Life of Samuel Johnson* (1791)]

PUNISHMENT

JUVENAL (c. 60–130)
*Prima est haec ultio, quod se
Iudice nemo nocens absolvitur.*
The chief punishment is this: that no
guilty man is acquitted in his own
judgement.

[*Satires*]

KARR, Alphonse (1808–1890)
*Si l'on veut abolir la peine de mort en ce
cas, que MM les assassins commencent.*
If we want to abolish the death pen-
alty, let our friends the murderers take
the first step.

[*Les Guêpes* (1849)]

KEY, Ellen (1849–1926)
Corporal punishment is as humiliating
for him who gives it as for him who
receives it; it is ineffective besides.
Neither shame nor physical pain have
any other effect than a hardening one.

[*The Century of the Child* (1909)]

MANN, Horace (1796–1859)
The object of punishment is prevention from evil; it never can be
made impulsive to good.

[*Lectures and Reports on Education* (1845)]

PEPYS, Samuel (1633–1703)
I went out to Charing Cross, to see
Major-General Harrison hanged,
drawn and quartered; which was done
there, he looking as cheerful as any
man could do in that condition.

[*Diary*, 1660]

SALMON, George (1819–1904)
[On hearing a colleague claiming to
have been caned only once in his life,
and that, for telling the truth]
Well, it certainly cured you, Mahaffy.

[Attr.]

SHAKESPEARE, William (1564–1616)
Use every man after his desert, and
who shall scape whipping?

[*Hamlet*, II.ii]

Now, as fond fathers,
Having bound up the threat'ning twigs
  of birch,
Only to stick it in their children's sight
For terror, not to use, in time the rod
Becomes more mock'd than fear'd; so
  our decrees,
Dead to infliction, to themselves are
  dead;
And liberty plucks justice by the nose;
The baby beats the nurse, and quite
  athwart
Goes all decorum.

[*Measure For Measure*, I.iii]

STOWE, Harriet Beecher (1811–1896)
Whipping and abuse are like
laudanum; you have to double the
dose as the sensibilities decline.

[*Uncle Tom's Cabin* (1852)]

VIDAL, Gore (1925–)
[When asked for his views about
corporal punishment]
I'm all for bringing back the birch, but
only between consenting adults.

[TV interview with David Frost]

WILDE, Oscar (1854–1900)
A community is infinitely more
brutalised by the habitual employment
of punishment than it is by the
occasional occurrence of crime.

['The Soul of Man under Socialism' (1891)]

See CRIME

CHURCHILL, Sir Winston (1874–1965)
It is a good thing for an uneducated
man to read books of quotations.
[*My Early Life* (1930)]

EMERSON, Ralph Waldo (1803–1882)
Every man is a borrower and a mimic,
life is theatrical and literature a
quotation.
[*Society and Solitude* (1870)]

By necessity, by proclivity, – and by
delight, we all quote.
[*Letters and Social Aims* (1875)]

Next to the originator of a good
sentence is the first quoter of it.
[*Letters and Social Aims* (1875)]

JOHNSON, Samuel (1709–1784)
He that tries to recommend him by
select quotations, will succeed like the
pedant in Hierocles, who, when he
offered his house to sale, carried a
brick in his pocket as a specimen.
[*The Plays of William Shakespeare* (1765)]

MONTAGUE, C.E. (1867–1928)
To be amused at what you read – that
is the great spring of happy quotation.
[*A Writer's Notes on his Trade* (1930)]

PEACOCK, Thomas Love (1785–1866)
A book that furnishes no quotations is,
me judice, no book – it is a plaything.
[*Crotchet Castle* (1831)]

PEARSON, Hesketh (1887–1964)
A widely-read man never quotes
accurately ... Misquotation is the pride

and privilege of the learned.
[*Common Misquotations* (1937)]

Misquotations are the only quotations
that are never misquoted.
[*Common Misquotations* (1937)]

RIBBLESDALE, Lord (1854–1925)
It [is] gentlemanly to get one's
quotations very slightly wrong. In that
way one unprigs oneself and allows
the company to correct one.
[In Cooper, *The Light of Common Day* (1959)]

SHAW, George Bernard (1856–1950)
I often quote myself. It adds spice to
the conversation.
[*Reader's Digest*, 1943]

STOPPARD, Tom (1937–)
It's better to be quotable than to be
honest.
[*The Guardian*]

WAUGH, Evelyn (1903–1966)
In the dying world I come from
quotation is a natural vice. It used to
be classics, now it's lyric verse.
[*The Loved One* (1948)]

WILLIAMS, Kenneth (1926–1988)
The nicest thing about quotes is that
they give us a nodding acquaintance
with the originator which is often
socially impressive.
[*Acid Drops* (1980)]

YOUNG, Edward (1683–1765)
Some, for renown, on scraps of
learning dote,
And think they grow immortal as they
quote.
[*Love of Fame, the Universal Passion* (1728)]

RACE

BIKO, Steve (1946–1977)
We wanted to remove him [the white man] from our table, strip the table of all the trappings put on it by him, decorate it in true African style, settle down and then ask him to join us if he liked.

[Speech, 1971]

BOSMAN, Herman Charles (1905–1951)
Kafirs? (said Oom Schalk Lourens), Yes, I know them. And they're all the same. I fear the Almighty, and I respect His works, but I could never understand why He made the kafir and the rinderpest.

[Mafeking Road (1947)]

CALWELL, Arthur Augustus (1894–1973)
[Defending the deportation of a Chinese refugee who, Calwell claimed, was not eligible to become a permanent resident of Australia]
There are many Wongs in the Chinese community, but I have to say – and I am sure that the honourable member for Balaclava will not mind me doing so – that 'two Wongs do not make a White'.

[Commonwealth Parliamentary Debates, 1947]

DE BLANK, Joost (1908–1968)
I suffer from an incurable disease – colour blindness.

[Attr.]

DISRAELI, Benjamin (1804–1881)
All is race; there is no other truth.

[Tancred (1847)]

EINSTEIN, Albert (1879–1955)
If my theory of relativity is proven successful, Germany will claim me as a German and France will declare that I am a citizen of the world. Should my theory prove untrue, France will say that I am a German and Germany will declare that I am a Jew.

[Address, c. 1929]

FANON, Frantz (1925–1961)
For the black man there is only one destiny. And it is white.

[Black Skin, White Masks]

FORSTER, E.M. (1879–1970)
The so-called white races are really pinko-gray.

[A Passage to India (1924)]

GOEBBELS, Joseph (1897–1945)
... mir in Bälde einen Gesamtentwurf über die organisatorischen, sachlichen und materiellen Vorausmassnanahmen zur Durchführung der angestrebten Endlösung der Judenfrage vorzulegen.
... to place before me soon a complete proposal for the organisational, practical and material preliminary measures which have to be taken in order to bring about the desired Final Solution to the Jewish question.

[Letter to Reinhard Heydrich, 1941]

GORDIMER, Nadine (1923–)
The force of white men's wills, which dispensed and withdrew life, imprisoned and set free, fed or starved, like God himself.

[Six Feet of the Country (1956)]

HITLER, Adolf (1889–1945)
Was nicht gute Rasse ist auf dieser Welt, ist Spreu.
Whoever is not racially pure in this world is chaff.

[Mein Kampf (1925)]

KING, Martin Luther (1929–1968)
I want to be the white man's brother, not his brother-in-law.

[New York Journal – American, 1962]

LESSING, Doris (1919–)
[Referring to South Africa]
When old settlers say 'One has to understand the country', what they mean is, 'You have to get used to our ideas about the native.' They are saying, in effect, 'Learn our ideas, or otherwise get out; we don't want you.'

[The Grass is Singing (1950)]

When a white man in Africa by accident looks into the eyes of a native and sees the human being (which it is his chief preoccupation to avoid), his sense of guilt, which he denies, fumes up in resentment and he brings down the whip.

[*The Grass is Singing* (1950)]

MANDELA, Nelson (1918–)
I have fought against white domination, and I have fought against black domination. I have cherished the ideal of a democratic and free society in which all persons will live together in harmony and with equal opportunities. It is an ideal which I hope to live for and achieve. But, if needs be, it is an ideal for which I am prepared to die.

[Statement in the dock, 1964]

MENAND, Louis
The evil of modern society isn't that it creates racism but that it creates conditions in which people who don't suffer from injustice seem incapable of caring very much about people who do.

[*The New Yorker*, 1992]

MENCKEN, H.L. (1880–1956)
One of the things that makes a Negro unpleasant to white folk is the fact that he suffers from their injustice. He is thus a standing rebuke to them.

[*Notebooks* (1956)]

MILLER, Arthur (1915–)
If there weren't any anti-semitism, I wouldn't think of myself as Jewish.

[*The Observer*, 1995
]

PATON, Alan (1903–1988)
I have one great fear in my heart, that one day when they [whites] are turned to loving, they will find we [blacks] are turned to hating.

[*Cry, the Beloved Country* (1948)]

It was on Wednesday 16 June 1976 that an era came to an end in South Africa. That was the day when black South Africans said to white, 'You can't do this to us any more.' It had taken three hundred years for them to say that.

[*Journey Continued* (1988)]

PLOMER, William (1903–1973)
The warm heart of any human that saw the black man first not as a black but as a man.

[*Turbott Wolfe* (1926)]

POWELL, Enoch (1912–)
[On race relations in Britain]
As I look ahead I am filled with foreboding. Like the Roman I seem to see 'The River Tiber foaming with much blood'.

[Speech, 1968]

PRINGLE, Thomas (1789–1834)
But I brought the handsomest bride of
   them all –
Brown Dinah, the bondmaid who sat
   in our hall ...

Shall the Edict of Mercy be sent forth
   at last,
To break the harsh fetters of Colour
   and Caste?

[*Poetical Works* (1838)]

SHERIDAN, Philip Henry (1831–1888)
The only good Indian is a dead Indian.

[Attr.]

SMITH, Ian (1919–)
I don't believe in black majority rule in Rhodesia ... not in a thousand years.

[Speech, 1976]

SONTAG, Susan (1933–)
The truth is that Mozart, Pascal, Boolean algebra, Shakespeare, parliamentary government, baroque churches, Newton, the emancipation of women, Kant, Marx, and Balanchine ballets don't redeem what this particular civilisation has wrought upon the world. The white race *is* the cancer of human history.

[Attr.]

TECUMSEH (d. 1812)
Where today are the Pequot? Where are the Narragansett, the Mohican, the Pokanoket, and many other once powerful tribes of our people? They have vanished before the avarice and the oppression of the White Man, as snow before a summer sun.

[In Brown, *Bury My Heart at Wounded Knee*]

TOMASCHEK, Rudolphe (b. c. 1895)
Modern Physics is an instrument of Jewry for the destruction of Nordic science ... True physics is the creation of the German spirit.

[In Shirer, *The Rise and Fall of the Third Reich* (1960)]

TUTU, Archbishop Desmond (1931–)
It is very difficult now to find anyone in South Africa who ever supported apartheid.

[*The Observer*, 1994]

X, Malcolm (1925–1965)
I believe in the brotherhood of all men, but I don't believe in wasting brotherhood on anyone who doesn't want to practise it with me.

[Speech, 1964]

We never made one step forward until world pressure put Uncle Sam on the spot ... It has never been out of any internal sense of morality or legality or humanism that we were allowed to advance.

[Speech, 1964]

ZANGWILL, Israel (1864–1926)
The law of dislike for the unlike will always prevail. And whereas the unlike is normally situated at a safe distance, the Jews bring the unlike into the heart of *every milieu*, and must there defend a frontier line as large as the world.

[Speech, 1911]

READING

AUSTEN, Jane (1775–1817)
Oh, Lord! not I; I never read much; I

have something else to do.

[*Northanger Abbey* (1818)]

BACON, Francis (1561–1626)
Read not to contradict and confute, nor to believe and take for granted, nor to find talk and discourse, but to weigh and consider.

['Of Studies' (1625)]

COLTON, Charles Caleb (c. 1780–1832)
Some read to think, – these are rare; some to unite, – these are common; and some to talk, – and these form the great majority.

[*Lacon* (1820)]

DESCARTES, René (1596–1650)
La lecture de tous les bons livres est comme une conversation avec les plus honnêtes gens des siècles passés.
The reading of all good books is like a conversation with the finest men of past centuries.

[*Discours de la Méthode* (1637)]

DISRAELI, Benjamin (1804–1881)
[His customary reply to those who sent him unsolicited manuscripts]
Thank you for the manuscript; I shall lose no time in reading it.

[Attr.]

FLAUBERT, Gustave (1821–1880)
Mais ne lisez pas, comme les enfants lisent, pour vous amuser, ni comme les ambitieux lisent, pour vous instruire. Non, lisez pour vivre.
Do not read, as children do, for the sake of entertainment, or like the ambitious, for the purpose of instruction. No, read in order to live.

[Letter to Mlle Leroyer de Chantepie, 1857]

FRANKLIN, Benjamin (1706–1790)
[On being asked what condition of man he considered the most pitiable]
A lonesome man on a rainy day who does not know how to read.

[In Shriner, *Wit, Wisdom, and Foibles of the Great*]

HAMERTON, P.G. (1834–1894)
The art of reading is to skip judiciously.
[*The Intellectual Life* (1873)]

HANDKE, Peter (1942–)
Der gedankenloseste aller Menschen: der in jedem Buch nur blättert.
The most unthinking person of all: the one who only flicks through every book.
[*The Weight of the World. A Diary* (1977)]

HELPS, Sir Arthur (1813–1875)
Reading is sometimes an ingenious device for avoiding thought.
[*Friends in Council* (1849)]

HOBBES, Thomas (1588–1679)
He was wont to say that if he had read as much as other men, he should have knowne no more than other men.
[In Aubrey, *Brief Lives* (c. 1693)]

JOHNSON, Samuel (1709–1784)
A man ought to read just as inclination leads him; for what he reads as a task will do him little good.
[In Boswell, *The Life of Samuel Johnson* (1791)]

MAO TSE-TUNG (1893–1976)
To read too many books is harmful.
[*The New Yorker*, 1977]

MILTON, John (1608–1674)
Who reads
Incessantly, and to his reading brings not
A spirit and judgment equal or superior
(And what he brings, what needs he elsewhere seek)
Uncertain and unsettl'd still remains,
Deep verst in books and shallow in himself.
[*Paradise Regained* (1671)]

ORTON, Joe (1933–1967)
Reading isn't an occupation we encourage among police officers. We try to keep the paper work down to a minimum.
[*Loot* (1967)]

SMITH, Logan Pearsall (1865–1946)
People say that life is the thing, but I prefer reading.
[*Afterthoughts* (1931)]

STERNE, Laurence (1713–1768)
Digressions, incontestably, are the sunshine; – they are the life, the soul of reading; – take them out of this book for instance, – you might as well take the book along with them.
[*Tristram Shandy*]

WILDE, Oscar (1854–1900)
I never travel without my diary. One should always have something sensational to read in the train.
[*The Importance of Being Earnest* (1895)]

See BOOKS

REALISM

BACON, Francis (1561–1626)
We are much beholden to Machiavel and others, that write what men do, and not what they ought to do.
[*The Advancement of Learning* (1605)]

CERVANTES, Miguel de (1547–1616)
Mire vuestra merced ... que aquellos que allí se parecen no son gigantes, sino molinos de viento.
Look, your worship ... those things which you see over there are not giants, but windmills.
[*Don Quixote*, I (1605)]

DÜRRENMATT, Friedrich (1921–1990)
Wer dem Paradoxen gegenübersteht, setzt sich der Wirklichkeit aus.
Whoever is faced with the paradoxical exposes himself to reality.
[*The Physicists* (1962)]

ELIOT, T.S. (1888–1965)
Human kind
Cannot bear very much reality.
[*Four Quartets* (1944)]

FRY, Christopher (1907–)
There may always be another reality
To make fiction of the truth we think we've arrived at.
[*A Yard of Sun* (1970)]

HEGEL, Georg Wilhelm (1770–1831)
Was vernünftig ist; das ist wirklich: und was wirklich ist, das ist vernünftig.
What is rational is real, and what is real is rational.
[*Basis of Legal Philosophy* (1820)]

KHRUSHCHEV, Nikita (1894–1971)
If you cannot catch a bird of paradise, better take a wet hen.
[Attr.]

TWAIN, Mark (1835–1910)
Don't part with your illusions. When they are gone, you may still exist, but you have ceased to live.
[*Pudd'nhead Wilson's Calendar* (1894)]

WILDE, Oscar (1854–1900)
The nineteenth century dislike of Realism is the rage of Caliban seeing his own face in a glass.
[*The Picture of Dorian Gray* (1891)]

Cecily: When I see a spade I call it a spade.
Gwendolen: I am glad to say that I have never seen a spade. It is obvious that our social spheres have been widely different.
[*The Importance of Being Earnest* (1895)]

See ART

REBELLION

ARENDT, Hannah (1906–1975)
The defiance of established authority, religious and secular, social and political, as a world-wide phenomenon may well one day be accounted the outstanding event of the last decade.
[*Crises of the Republic* (1972)]

ARNOLD, Thomas (1795–1842)
As for rioting, the old Roman way of dealing with that is always the right one; flog the rank and file, and fling the ringleaders from the Tarpeian rock.
[Letter, written before 1828]

BRADSHAW, John (1602–1659)
Rebellion to tyrants is obedience to God.
[In Randall, *Life of Jefferson* (1865)]

BURKE, Edmund (1729–1797)
Make the Revolution a parent of settlement, and not a nursery of future revolutions.
[*Reflections on the Revolution in France* (1790)]

CAMUS, Albert (1913–1960)
Tout révolutionnaire finit en oppresseur ou en hérétique.
Every revolutionary ends as an oppressor or a heretic.
[*The Rebel* (1951)]

Qu'est-ce qu'un homme révolté? Un homme qui dit non.
What is a rebel? A man who says no.
[*The Rebel* (1951)]

Toutes les révolutions modernes ont abouti à un renforcement de l'Etat.
All modern revolutions have led to a reinforcement of the power of the State.
[*The Rebel* (1951)]

CONRAD, Joseph (1857–1924)
The scrupulous and the just, the noble, humane, and devoted natures; the unselfish and the intelligent may begin a movement – but it passes away from them. They are not the leaders of a revolution. They are its victims.
[*Under Western Eyes* (1911)]

DURRELL, Lawrence (1912–1990)
No one can go on being a rebel too long without turning into an autocrat.
[*Balthazar* (1958)]

ENGELS, Friedrich (1820–1895)
The proletariat has nothing to lose but its chains in this revolution. It has a world to win. Workers of the world, unite!
[*The Communist Manifesto* (1848)]

GEORGE V (1865–1936)
[On hearing Mr Wheatley's life story]
Is it possible that my people live in

such awful conditions? ... I tell you, Mr Wheatley, that if I had to live in conditions like that I would be a revolutionary myself.

[In MacNeill Weir, *The Tragedy of Ramsay MacDonald* (1938)]

HILL, Reginald (1936–)
The first thing revolutionaries of the left or right give up is their sense of humour. The second thing is other people's rights.

[In Winks (ed.), *Colloquium on Crime* (1986)]

JEFFERSON, Thomas (1743–1826)
A little rebellion now and then is a good thing.

[Letter to James Madison, 1787]

KHRUSHCHEV, Nikita (1894–1971)
If you feed people with revolutionary slogans alone they will listen today, they will listen tomorrow, they will listen the day after that, but on the fourth day they will say 'To hell with you!'

[Attr.]

LEWIS, Wyndham (1882–1957)
The revolutionary simpleton is everywhere.

[*Time and Western Man* (1927)]

SHAKESPEARE, William (1564–1616)
Rebellion lay in his way, and he found it.

[*Henry IV, Part I*, V.i]

STORR, Dr Anthony (1920–)
It is harder to rebel against love than against authority.

[Attr.]

TROTSKY, Leon (1879–1940)
Insurrection is an art, and like all arts it has its laws.

[*History of the Russian Revolution* (1933)]

VERGNIAUD, Pierre (1753–1793)
[Remark at his trial, 1793]
Il a été permis de craindre que la Révolution, comme Saturne, dévorât successivement tous ses enfants.

There was reason to fear that the Revolution, like Saturn, would eventually devour all her children one by one.

[In Lamartine, *Histoire des Girondins* (1847)]

WEIL, Simone (1909–1943)
On pense aujourd'hui à la révolution, non comme à une solution des problèmes posés par l'actualité, mais comme à un miracle dispensant de résoudre les problèmes.
Nowadays we think of revolution not as the solution to problems posed by current developments but as a miracle which releases us from the obligation to solve these problems.

[*Oppression and Freedom* (1955)]

WELLINGTON, Duke of (1769–1852)
Beginning reform is beginning revolution.

[In Mrs Arbuthnot's Journal, 1830]

RELIGION

ADDISON, Joseph (1672–1719)
We have in England a particular bashfulness in every thing that regards religion.

[*The Spectator*, 1712]

ARNOLD, Matthew (1822–1888)
The true meaning of religion is thus not simply morality, but morality touched by emotion.

[*Literature and Dogma* (1873)]

BARRIE, Sir J.M. (1860–1937)
One's religion is whatever he is most interested in, and yours is Success.

[*The Twelve-Pound Look*]

BEHAN, Brendan (1923–1964)
Pound notes are the best religion in the world.

[*The Wit of Brendan Behan* (1968)]

BLAKE, William (1757–1827)
I went to the Garden of Love,
And saw what I never had seen:
A Chapel was built in the midst,
Where I used to play on the green.

And the gates of this Chapel were
  shut,
And 'Thou shalt not' writ over the
  door ...

And Priests in black gowns were
  walking their rounds,
And binding with briars my joys &
  desires.

['The Garden of Love' (1794)]

BRENAN, Gerald (1894–1987)
Religions are kept alive by heresies,
which are really sudden explosions of
faith. Dead religions do not produce
them.

[*Thoughts in a Dry Season* (1978)]

BROWNE, Sir Thomas (1605–1682)
Persecution is a bad and indirect way
to plant religion.

[*Religio Medici* (1643)]

BURKE, Edmund (1729–1797)
Nothing is so fatal to religion as
indifference, which is, at least, half
infidelity.

[Letter to William Smith, 1795]

BURTON, Robert (1577–1640)
One religion is as true as another.

[*Anatomy of Melancholy* (1621)]

BUTLER, Samuel (1835–1902)
To be at all is to be religious more or
less.

[*The Note-Books of Samuel Butler* (1912)]

CHESTERFIELD, Lord (1694–1773)
Putting moral virtues at the highest,
and religion at the lowest, religion
must still be allowed to be a collateral
security, at least, to virtue; and every
prudent man will sooner trust to two
securities than to one.

[Letter to his son, 1750]

COLTON, Charles Caleb (c. 1780–1832)
Men will wrangle for religion; write for
it; fight for it; anything but – live for it.

[*Lacon* (1820)]

DALY, Mary (1928–)
*Patriarchy is itself the prevailing religion
of the entire planet*, and its essential
message is necrophilia.

[*Gyn/Ecology* (1979)]

DIDEROT, Denis (1713–1784)
Wandering in a vast forest at night, I
have only a faint light to guide me. A
stranger appears and says to me: 'My
friend, you should blow out your
candle in order to find your way more
clearly.' This stranger is a theologian.

[*Addition aux Pensées Philosophiques*]

DIOGENES (THE CYNIC)
(c. 400–325 BC)
I do not know whether there are gods,
but there ought to be.

[In Tertullian, *Ad Nationes*]

DIX, George (1901–1952)
It is no accident that the symbol of a
bishop is a crook, and the sign of an
archbishop is a double-cross.

[Letter to *The Times*, 1977]

ELLIS, Havelock (1859–1939)
The whole religious complexion of the
modern world is due to the absence
from Jerusalem of a lunatic asylum.

[*Impressions and Comments* (1914)]

EMERSON, Ralph Waldo (1803–1882)
The religions we call false were once
true.

['Character' (1866)]

I have heard with admiring submission
the experience of the lady who declared that 'the sense of being well-
dressed gives a feeling of inward
tranquillity which religion is powerless
to bestow.'

['Social Aims' (1875)]

FLEMING, Marjory (1803–1811)
I hope I will be religious again but as
for reganing my charecter I despare for
it.

[In Esdaile (ed.), *Journals, Letters and Verses*
(1934)]

FREUD, Sigmund (1856–1939)
Religion is an illusion and it derives its strength from the fact that it falls in with our instinctual desires.
[*New Introductory Lectures on Psychoanalysis* (1933)]

GIBBON, Edward (1737–1794)
The various modes of worship, which prevailed in the Roman world, were all considered by the people as equally true; by the philosopher, as equally false; and by the magistrate, as equally useful.
[*Decline and Fall of the Roman Empire* (1776–88)]

HOOTON, Harry (1908–1961)
Psychology is the theology of the 20th century.
['Inhuman Race']

INGE, William Ralph (1860–1954)
To become a popular religion, it is only necessary for a superstition to enslave a philosophy.
[*Outspoken Essays*]

JERROLD, Douglas William (1803–1857)
Religion's in the heart, not in the knees.
[*The Devil's Ducat* (1830)]

LUCRETIUS (c. 95–55 BC)
Tantum religio potuit suadere malorum.
So potent a persuasion to evil was religion.
[*De Rerum Natura*]

MARLOWE, Christopher (1564–1593)
I count religion but a childish toy,
And hold there is no sin but ignorance.
[*The Jew of Malta* (c. 1592)]

MARX, Karl (1818–1883)
Religion ... is the opium of the people.
[*A Contribution to the Critique of Hegel's Philosophy of Right* (1844)]

MELBOURNE, Lord (1779–1848)
[On listening to an evangelical sermon]

Things have come to a pretty pass when religion is allowed to invade the sphere of private life.
[In Russell, *Collections and Recollections* (1898)]

MENCKEN, H.L. (1880–1956)
We must respect the other fellow's religion, but only in the sense and to the extent that we respect his theory that his wife is beautiful and his children smart.
[*Notebooks* (1956)]

O'CASEY, Sean (1880–1964)
There's no reason to bring religion into it. I think we ought to have as great a regard for religion as we can, so as to keep it out of as many things as possible.
[*The Plough and the Stars* (1926)]

RUNCIMAN, Sir Steven (1903–)
Unlike Christianity, which preached a peace that it never achieved, Islam unashamedly came with a sword.
[*A History of the Crusades* (1954)]

SHAW, George Bernard (1856–1950)
I can't talk religion to a man with bodily hunger in his eyes.
[*Major Barbara* (1907)]

SHELLEY, Percy Bysshe (1792–1822)
Earth groans beneath religion's iron age,
And priests dare babble of a God of peace,
Even whilst their hands are red with guiltless blood.
[*Queen Mab* (1813)]

STERNE, Laurence (1713–1768)
Whenever a man talks loudly against religion, – always suspect that it is not his reason, but his passions which have got the better of his creed.
[*Tristram Shandy* (1759–67)]

SWIFT, Jonathan (1667–1745)
We have just enough religion to make us hate, but not enough to make us

love one another.

[*Thoughts on Various Subjects* (1711)]

WEBB, Beatrice (1858–1943)
Religion is love; in no case is it logic.

[*My Apprenticeship* (1926)]

ZANGWILL, Israel (1864–1926)
Let us start a new religion with one commandment, 'Enjoy thyself'.

[*Children of the Ghetto* (1892)]

REPUTATION

BURNEY, Fanny (1752–1840)
Nothing is so delicate as the reputation of a woman; it is at once the most beautiful and most brittle of all human things.

[*Evelina* (1778)]

EMERSON, Ralph Waldo (1803–1882)
I trust a good deal to common fame, as we all must. If a man has good corn, or wood, or boards, or pigs, to sell, or can make better chairs or knives, crucibles, or church organs, than anybody else, you will find a broad, hard-beaten road to his house, though it be in the woods.

[*Journals*, 1855]

KEYNES, John Maynard (1883–1946)
Wordly wisdom teaches that it is better for the reputation to fail conventionally than to succeed unconventionally.

[*The General Theory of Employment, Interest and Money* (1936)]

MITCHELL, Margaret (1900–1949)
Until you've lost your reputation, you never realize what a burden it was or what freedom really is.

[*Gone with the Wind* (1936)]

SHAKESPEARE, William (1564–1616)
Good name in man and woman, dear my lord,
Is the immediate jewel of their souls:
Who steals my purse steals trash; 'tis something, nothing;
'Twas mine, 'tis his, and has been slave to thousands;

But he that filches from me my good name
Robs me of that which not enriches him
And makes me poor indeed.

[*Othello*, III.iii]

The purest treasure mortal times afford
Is spotless reputation; that away,
Men are but gilded loam or painted clay.
A jewel in a ten-times barr'd-up chest
Is a bold spirit in a loyal breast.
Mine honour is my life; both grow in one;
Take honour from me, and my life is done.

[*Richard I*, I.i]

WASHINGTON, George (1732–1799)
Associate yourself with men of good quality if you esteem your own reputation; for 'tis better to be alone than in bad company.

[*Rules of Civility and Decent Behaviour*]

See CHARACTER

REVENGE

ATWOOD, Margaret (1939–)
An eye for an eye leads only to more blindness.

[*Cat's Eye* (1988)]

BACON, Francis (1561–1626)
Revenge is a kind of wild justice, which the more man's nature runs to, the more ought law to weed it out.

['Of Revenge' (1625)]

A man that studieth revenge keeps his own wounds green.

['Of Revenge' (1625)]

THE BIBLE (King James Version)
Vengeance is mine; I will repay, saith the Lord.

[*Romans*, 12:19]

CYRANO DE BERGERAC, Savinien de (1619–1655)
Périsse l'Univers, pourvu que je me

venge.
The universe may perish, so long as I
have my revenge.
[*La Mort d'Agrippine* (1654)]

MILTON, John (1608–1674)
Revenge, at first though sweet,
Bitter ere long back on it self recoils.
[*Paradise Lost* (1667)]

SHAKESPEARE, William (1564–1616)
Let's make us med'cines of our great
revenge
To cure this deadly grief.
[*Macbeth*, IV.iii]

Heat not a furnace for your foe so hot
That it do singe yourself.
[*Henry VIII*, I.i]

RIDICULE

ALBEE, Edward (1928–)
I have a fine sense of the ridiculous,
but no sense of humour.
[*Who's Afraid of Virginia Woolf?* (1962)]

NAPOLEON I (1769–1821)
*Du sublime au ridicule il n'y a qu'un
pas.*
It is only one step from the sublime to
the ridiculous.
[In De Pradt, *Histoire de l'Ambassade dans le
grand-duché de Varsovie en 1812* (1815)]

SCOTT, Sir Walter (1771–1832)
Ridicule often checks what is absurd,
and fully as often smothers that which
is noble.
[*Quentin Durward* (1823)]

VOLTAIRE (1694–1778)
I have never made but one prayer to
God, a very short one: 'O Lord, make
my enemies ridiculous.' And God
granted it.
[Letter to Damilaville, 1767]

RIGHTS

**CONDORCET, Antoine-Nicolas de
(1743–1794)**
Either none of mankind possesses

genuine rights, or everyone shares
them equally; whoever votes against
another's rights, whatever his religion,
colour or sex, forswears his own.
[In Vansittart (ed.), *Voices of the Revolution*
(1989)]

JEFFERSON, Thomas (1743–1826)
We hold these truths to be self-
evident: that all men are created
equal; that they are endowed by their
Creator with certain unalienable
rights; that among these are life,
liberty, and the pursuit of happiness.
[Declaration of Independence, 1776]

JOHNSON, Samuel (1709–1784)
I have got no further than this: Every
man has a right to utter what he
thinks truth, and every other man has
a right to knock him down for it.
Martyrdom is the test.
[In Boswell, *The Life of Samuel Johnson*
(1791)]

MAGNA CARTA (1215)
*Nullus liber homo capiatur, vel
imprisonetur, aut disseisiatur, aut
utlagetur, aut exuletur, aut aliquo modo
destruatur, nec super eum ibimus, nec
super eum mittemus, nisi per legale
judicium parium suorum vel per legem
terrae.*
No free man shall be taken or
imprisoned or dispossessed, or
outlawed or exiled, or in any way
destroyed, nor will we go upon him,
nor will we send against him, except
by the lawful judgement of his peers or
by the law of the land.
[Clause 39]

PANKHURST, Emmeline (1858–1928)
Women had always fought for men,
and for their children. Now they were
ready to fight for their own human
rights. Our militant movement was
established.
[*My Own Story* (1914)]

**UNIVERSAL DECLARATION OF HUMAN
RIGHTS**
All human beings are born free and
equal in dignity and rights.
[Article 1]

ROYALTY

ARCHER, Lord Jeffrey (1940–)
An entire family of divorcees, and
they're head of the Church of England.
It's going to make the person out there
wonder if it's all worth it.

[Comment on the Royal Family, 1992]

BURCHILL, Julie (1960–)
[Of Princess Diana]
She is Madonna crossed with Mother
Theresa – a glorious totem of Western
ideals.

[*Sex and Sensibility* (1992)]

CHARLES X (1757–1836)
I would rather hew wood than be a
king under the conditions of the King
of England.

[Attr.]

DISRAELI, Benjamin (1804–1881)
[To Matthew Arnold]
Everyone likes flattery; and when you
come to Royalty you should lay it on
with a trowel.

[Attr.]

**EDWARD VIII (later Duke of Windsor)
(1894–1972)**
I have found it impossible to carry the
heavy burden of responsibility and to
discharge my duties as King as I would
wish to do without the help and
support of the woman I love.

[Abdication speech, 1936]

ELIZABETH I (1533–1603)
I thank God I am endued with such
qualities that if I were turned out of
the Realm in my petticoat I were able
to live in any place in Christome.

[Attr. Speech, 1566]

[Of the approaching Armada]
I know I have the body of a weak and
feeble woman, but I have the heart
and stomach of a king, and of a king
of England too; and think foul scorn
that Parma or Spain, or any prince of
Europe, should dare to invade the
borders of my realm.

[Speech, 1588]

Though God hath raised me high, yet
this I count the glory of my crown: that
I have reigned with your loves.

[The Golden Speech, 1601]

GEORGE VI (1895–1952)
We're not a family; we're a firm.

[Attr. in Lane, *Our Future King*]

LEOPOLD II (1835–1909)
[Instructing Prince Albert, the heir
apparent, to pick up some papers from
the floor]
A constitutional king must learn to
stoop.

[In Kelen, *The Mistress*]

MACHIAVELLI (1469–1527)
*Debbe, pertanto, uno principe non si
curare della infamia di crudele, per
tenere li sudditi suoi uniti e in fede.*
In order to keep his people united and
faithful, a prince must not be
concerned with being reputed as a
cruel man.

[*The Prince* (1532)]

PLATO (c. 429–347 BC)
Every king springs from a race of
slaves, and every slave has had kings
among his ancestors.

[*Theaetetus*]

SELLAR, Walter (1898–1951)
and **YEATMAN, Robert (1897–1968)**
Charles II was always very merry and
was therefore not so much a king as a
Monarch.

[*1066 And All That* (1930)]

SHAKESPEARE, William (1564–1616)
Uneasy lies the head that wears a
crown.

[*Henry IV, Part 2*, III.i]

I think the King is but a man as I am:
the violet smells to him as it doth to
me.

[*Henry V*, IV.i]

WORSTHORNE, Sir Peregrine (1923–)
A little more willingness to bore, and
much less eagerness to entertain,

would do the monarchy no end of
good in 1993.

[*The Sunday Telegraph*, 1993]

See MONARCHY

SCHOOL

BEERBOHM, Sir Max (1872–1956)
Not that I had any special reason for
hating school ... I was a modest, good-
humoured boy. It is Oxford that has
made me insufferable.

[*More* (1899)]

CLARK, Lord Kenneth (1903–1983)
[On boarding schools]
This curious, and, to my mind,
objectionable feature of English
education was maintained solely in
order that parents could get their
children out of the house.

[*Another Part of the Wood* (1974)]

DAVIES, Robertson (1913–)
The most strenuous efforts of the most
committed educationalists in the years
since my boyhood have been quite
unable to make a school into anything
but a school, which is to say a jail with
educational opportunities.

[*The Cunning Man* (1994)]

FIELDING, Henry (1707–1754)
Public schools are the nurseries of all
vice and immorality.

[*Joseph Andrews* (1742)]

FORSTER, E.M. (1879–1970)
[Of public schoolboys]
They go forth into it [the world] with
well-developed bodies, fairly
developed minds, and undeveloped
hearts.

[*Abinger Harvest* (1936)]

GREENE, Graham (1904– 1991)
I had left civilisation behind and
entered a savage country of strange
customs and inexplicable cruelties: a
country in which I was a foreigner and
a suspect, quite literally a hunted
creature, known to have dubious
associates. Was not my father the
headmaster? I was like the son of a
quisling in a country under occupation.

[*A Sort of Life* (1971)]

WELLINGTON, Duke of (1769–1852)
The battle of Waterloo was won on the
playing fields of Eton.

[Attr.]

See EDUCATION; TEACHERS

SCIENCE

AMIS, Martin (1949–)
Not only are all characters and scenes
in this book entirely fictitious; most of
the technical, medical and psychological data are too. My working
maxim here has been as follows: I may
not know much about science but I
know what I like.

[*Dead Babies* (1975)]

AUDEN, W.H. (1907–1973)
The true men of action in our time,
those who transform the world, are
not the politicians and statesmen, but
the scientists. Unfortunately, poetry
cannot celebrate them, because their
deeds are concerned with things, not
persons and are, therefore, speechless.

[*The Dyer's Hand* (1963)]

BAINBRIDGE, Kenneth (1904–)
Now we are all sons of bitches.

[Remark after directing the first atomic test,
1945]

BRIDIE, James (1888–1951)
Eve and the apple was the first great
step in experimental science.

[*Mr Bolfry* (1943)]

BRONOWSKI, Jacob (1908–1974)
That is the essence of science: ask an
impertinent question, and you are on
the way to the pertinent answer.

[*The Ascent of Man* (1973)]

Science has nothing to be ashamed of,
even in the ruins of Nagasaki.

[*Science and Human Values*]

CHOMSKY, Noam (1928–)
As soon as questions of will or
decision or reason or choice of action

arise, human science is at a loss.

[Television interview, 1978]

CLARKE, Arthur C. (1917–)
When a distinguished but elderly scientist states that something is possible, he is almost certainly right. When he states that something is impossible, he is very probably wrong. (Clarke's First Law.)

[*The New Yorker*, 1969]

Technology, sufficiently advanced, is indistinguishable from magic.

[*The Times*, 1996]

CRICK, Francis (1916–)
[On the discovery of the structure of DNA, 1953]
We have discovered the secret of life!

[In Watson, *The Double Helix* (1968)]

CRONENBERG, David (1943–)
A virus is only doing its job.

[*The Sunday Telegraph*, 1992]

DAGG, Fred (1948–)
I can see ... why a man who lives in Colorado is so anxious for all this nuclear activity to go on in Australia, an area famed among nuclear scientists for its lack of immediate proximity to their own residential areas.

[*Dagshead Revisited* (1989)]

DÜRRENMATT, Friedrich (1921–1990)
Unsere Wissenschaft ist schrecklich geworden, unsere Forschung gefährlich, unsere Erkenntnis tödlich.
Our science has become terrible, our research dangerous, our knowledge fatal.

[*The Physicists* (1962)]

EDDINGTON, Sir Arthur (1882–1944)
We used to think that if we knew one, we knew two, because one and one are two. We are finding that we must learn a great deal more about 'and'.

[In Mackay, *The Harvest of a Quiet Eye* (1977)]

EINSTEIN, Albert (1879–1955)
A theory can be proved by experiment; but no path leads from experiment to the birth of a theory.

[In Mackay, *The Harvest of a Quiet Eye* (1977)]

When a man sits with a pretty girl for an hour, it seems like a minute. But let him sit on a hot stove for a minute – and it's longer than any hour. That's relativity.

[Attr.]

FARADAY, Michael (1791–1867)
[On his scientific research]
It may be a weed instead of a fish that, after all my labour, I may at last pull up.

[Letter, 1831]

HEISENBERG, Werner (1901–1976)
Natural science does not simply describe and explain nature, it is part of the interplay between nature and ourselves.

[Attr.]

HUXLEY, T.H. (1825–1895)
The great tragedy of Science – the slaying of a beautiful hypothesis by an ugly fact.

[*British Association Annual Report* (1870)]

JEANS, Sir James Hopwood (1877–1946)
Science should leave off making pronouncements: the river of knowledge has too often turned back on itself.

[*The Mysterious Universe* (1930)]

LEVIN, Bernard (1928–)
Those of our own-day scientists who stir the embers of fires that went out millions of years ago may believe [their theories] but can never know. It would be better for all of us if they said as much.

[*The Times*, 1992]

MEDAWAR, Sir Peter (1915–1987)
Scientific discovery is a private event, and the delight that accompanies it, or

the despair of finding it illusory does not travel.

[*Hypothesis and Imagination*]

MONTAIGNE, Michel de (1533–1592)
Science without conscience is but death of the soul.

[In Simcox, *Treasury of Quotations on Christian Themes*]

NEWTON, Sir Isaac (1642–1727)
If I have seen further it is by standing on the shoulders of giants.

[Letter to Robert Hooke, 1675–76]

OPPENHEIMER, J. Robert (1904–1967)
[On the consequences of the first atomic test]
The physicists have known sin; and this is a knowledge which they cannot lose.

[Lecture, 1947]

PASTEUR, Louis (1822–1895)
Dans les champs de l'observation, l'hasard ne favorise que les esprits préparés.
In the field of observation, chance favours only the prepared mind.

[Lecture, 1854]

PEACOCK, Thomas Love (1785–1866)
I almost think it is the ultimate destiny of science to exterminate the human race.

[*Gryll Grange* (1861)]

PIRSIG, Robert (1928–)
Traditional scientific method had always been at the very *best*, 20–20 hindsight. It's good for seeing where you've been.

[*Zen and the Art of Motorcycle Maintenance* (1974)]

POPPER, Sir Karl (1902–1994)
Science may be described as the art of systematic oversimplification.

[*The Observer*, 1982]

PORTER, Sir George (1920–)
Should we force science down the throats of those that have no taste for

it? Is it our duty to drag them kicking and screaming into the twenty-first century? I am afraid that it is.

[Speech, 1986]

ROUX, Joseph (1834–1886)
Science is for those who learn; poetry, for those who know.

[*Meditations of a Parish Priest* (1886)]

SALK, Jonas E. (1914–)
[On being asked who owned the patent on his antipolio vaccine]
The people – could you patent the sun?

[Attr.]

STENHOUSE, David (1932–)
[On the conservation of biological resources]
I know a man who has a device for converting solar energy into food. Delicious stuff he makes with it, too. Being doing it for years ... It's called a farm.

[*Crisis in Abundance* (1966)]

SZENT-GYÖRGYI, Albert von (1893–1986)
Discovery consists of seeing what everybody has seen and thinking what nobody has thought.

[In Good (ed.), *The Scientist Speculates* (1962)]

VEBLEN, Thorstein (1857–1929)
The outcome of any serious research can only be to make two questions grow where only one grew before.

[*The Place of Science in Modern Civilization* (1919)]

SCOTLAND

BARRIE, Sir J.M. (1860–1937)
There are few more impressive sights in the world than a Scotsman on the make.

[*What Every Woman Knows* (1908)]

BOORDE, Andrew (c. 1490–1549)
Trust your no Skott.

[Letter to Thomas Cromwell, 1536]

The devellysche dysposicion of a
Scottysh man, not to love nor favour
an Englishe man.

[Letter to Thomas Cromwell, 1536]

BURNS, Robert (1759–1796)
My heart's in the Highlands, my heart
   is not here,
My heart's in the Highlands a-chasing
   the deer,
A-chasing the wild deer and following
   the roe –
My heart's in the Highlands, wherever
   I go!

['My Heart's in the Highlands' (1790)]

The story of Wallace poured a Scottish
prejudice in my veins which will boil
along there till the flood-gates of life
shut in eternal rest.

[Letter to Dr Moore, 1787]

CLEVELAND, John (1613–1658)
Had Cain been Scot, God would have
   changed his doom,
Nor forced him wander, but confined
   him home.

['The Rebel Scot' (1647)]

EWART, Gavin (1916–1995)
The Irish are great talkers
Persuasive and disarming,
You can say lots and lots
Against the Scots –
But at least they're never charming!

[The Complete Little Ones (1986)]

HAMILTON, Ian (1925–)
[On the performance of Scottish
National Party MPs in Westminster]
Courage is a quality Scots lack only
when they become MPs. They should
be twisting the lion's tail until it comes
out by the roots.

[Daily Mail, May 1996]

JENKINS, Robin (1912–)
Football has taken the place of religion
in Scotland.

[A Would-Be Saint]

JOHNSON, Samuel (1709–1784)
Oats. A grain, which in England is

generally given to horses, but in
Scotland supports the people.

[A Dictionary of the English Language (1755)]

A Scotchman must be a very sturdy
moralist who does not love Scotland
better than truth.

[A Journey to the Western Islands of Scotland
(1775)]

Norway, too, has noble wild prospects;
and Lapland is remarkable for prodigious noble wild prospects. But, Sir,
let me tell you, the noblest prospect
which a Scotchman ever sees, is the
high road that leads him to England!

[In Boswell, The Life of Samuel Johnson
(1791)]

Much may be made of a Scotchman, if
he be caught young.

[In Boswell, The Life of Samuel Johnson
(1791)]

Seeing Scotland, Madam, is only
seeing a worse England. It is seeing
the flower fade away to the naked
stalk.

[In Boswell, The Life of Samuel Johnson
(1791)]

KEILLOR, Garrison (1942–)
Lutherans are like Scottish people,
only with less frivolity.

[The Independent, 1992]

LAMB, Charles (1775–1834)
I have been trying all my life to like
Scotchmen, and am obliged to desist
from the experiment in despair.

['Imperfect Sympathies' (1823)]

LOCKIER, Francis (1667–1740)
In all my travels I have never met with
any one Scotchman but what was a
man of sense. I believe everybody of
that country that has any, leaves it as
fast as they can.

[In Spence, Anecdotes (1858)]

MACDIARMID, Hugh (1892–1978)
It's easier to lo'e Prince Charlie

THE SEA

Than Scotland – mair's the shame!
['Bonnie Prince Charlie' (1930)]

The rose of all the world is not for me
I want for my part
Only the little white rose of Scotland
That smells sharp and sweet – and
breaks the heart.
['The Little White Rose']

NICHOLSON, Emma (1941–)
England treats Scotland as if it was an
island off the coast of West Africa in
the 1830s.
[*Daily Mail*, 1996]

NORTH, Christopher (1785–1854)
Minds like ours, my dear James, must
always be above national prejudices,
and in all companies it gives me true
pleasure to declare, that, as a people,
the English are very little indeed
inferior to the Scotch.
[*Blackwood's Edinburgh Magazine*, 1826]

OGILVY, James, (1663–1730)
[On signing the Act of Union]
Now there's an end of ane old song.
[Remark, 1707]

SCOTT, Sir Walter (1771–1832)
O Caledonia! stern and wild,
Meet nurse for a poetic child!
Land of brown heath and shaggy
wood,
Land of the mountain and the flood,
Land of my sires! what mortal hand
Can e'er untie the filial band,
That knits me to thy rugged strand!
[*The Lay of the Last Minstrel* (1805)]

Still from the sire the son shall hear
Of the stern strife, and carnage drear,
Of Flodden's fatal field,
Where shiver'd was fair Scotland's
spear,
And broken was her shield!
[*Marmion* (1808)]

SMITH, Sydney (1771–1845)
It requires a surgical operation to get a
joke well into a Scotch understanding.

Their only idea of wit ... is laughing
immoderately at stated intervals.
[In Holland, *A Memoir of the Reverend Sydney
Smith* (1855)]

WODEHOUSE, P.G. (1881–1975)
It is never difficult to distinguish
between a Scotsman with a grievance
and a ray of sunshine.
[*Blandings Castle and Elsewhere* (1935)]

THE SEA

AESCHYLUS (525–456 BC)
The ceaseless twinkling laughter of the
waves of the sea.
[*Prometheus Bound*]

ARNOLD, Matthew (1822–1888)
Sand-strewn caverns, cool and deep,
Where the winds are all asleep;
Where the spent lights quiver and
gleam;
Where the salt weed sways in the
stream;
Where the sea-beasts ranged all round
Feed in the ooze of their pasture-
ground...
Where great whales come sailing by,
Sail and sail, with unshut eye,
Round the world for ever and aye.
['The Forsaken Merman' (1849)]

BYRON, Lord (1788–1824)
Roll on, thou deep and dark blue
Ocean – roll!
Ten thousand fleets sweep over thee
in vain;
Man marks the earth with ruin – his
control
Stops with the shore.
[*Childe Harold's Pilgrimage* (1818)]

Dark-heaving – boundless, endless,
and sublime,
The image of eternity.
[*Childe Harold's Pilgrimage* (1818)]

CARSON, Rachel (1907–1964)
In its mysterious past, it encompasses
all the dim origins of life and receives
in the end ... the dead husks of that
same life. For all at last return to the

sea – to Oceanus, the ocean river, like the ever-flowing stream of time, the beginning and the end.

[*The Sea Around Us* (1951)]

CHOPIN, Kate (1851–1904)
The voice of the sea speaks to the soul. The touch of the sea is sensuous, enfolding the body in its soft, close embrace.

[*The Awakening* (1899)]

CLAYTON, Keith (1928–)
[Of sewage]
You can do far worse than putting it into a deep and well-flushed sea. As far as poisoning the fish is concerned, that's rubbish. The sewage has probably kept the poor fish alive.

[*The Times*, 1992]

COLERIDGE, Samuel Taylor (1772–1834)
As idle as a painted ship
Upon a painted ocean.

Water, water, every where,
And all the boards did shrink;
Water, water, every where
Nor any drop to drink.

['The Rime of the Ancient Mariner' (1798)]

CONRAD, Joseph (1857–1924)
This could have occurred nowhere but in England, where men and sea interpenetrate, so to speak.

[*Youth* (1902)]

The sea has never been friendly to man. At most it has been the accomplice of human restlessness.

[Attr.]

CUNNINGHAM, Allan (1784–1842)
A wet sheet and a flowing sea,
A wind that follows fast
And fills the white and rustling sail
And bends the gallant mast.

['A Wet Sheet and a Flowing Sea' (1825)]

DICKENS, Charles (1812–1870)
I want to know what it says ... The sea, Floy, what it is that it keeps on saying?

[*Dombey and Son* (1848)]

'People can't die, along the coast,' said Mr Peggotty, 'except when the tide's pretty nigh out. They can't be born, unless it's pretty nigh in – not properly born, till flood. He's a going out with the tide.'

[*David Copperfield* (1850)]

DONNE, John (1572–1631)
The sea is as deepe in a calme as in a storme.

[*Sermons*]

FLECKER, James Elroy (1884–1915)
The dragon-green, the luminous, the dark, the serpent-haunted sea.

[*The Golden Journey to Samarkand* (1913)]

JOYCE, James (1882–1941)
The snotgreen sea. The scrotum-tightening sea.

[*Ulysses* (1922)]

KIPLING, Rudyard (1865–1936)
What is a woman that you forsake her,
And the hearth-fire and the home-
acre,
To go with the old grey Widow-maker?

['Harp Song of the Dane Women' (1906)]

LONGFELLOW, Henry Wadsworth (1807–1882)
'Wouldst thou' – so the helmsman
answered –
'Learn the secret of the sea?
Only those who brave its dangers
Comprehend its mystery!'

['The Secret of the Sea' (1904)]

MASEFIELD, John (1878–1967)
I must go down to the seas again, to
the lonely sea and the sky,
And all I ask is a tall ship and a star to
steer her by.

['Sea Fever' (1902)]

RIMBAUD, Arthur (1854–1891)
*Je me suis baigné dans le Poème
De la Mer, infusé d'astres, et lactescent,
Dévorant les azurs verts.*

I have bathed in the Poem
Of the Sea, steeped in stars, milky,
Devouring the green azures.

['Le Bâteau ivre' (1870)]

ROSSETTI, Dante Gabriel (1828–1882)
The sea hath no king but God alone.

['The White Ship']

**SWINBURNE, Algernon Charles
(1837–1909)**
I will go back to the great sweet
    mother,
Mother and lover of men, the sea.
I will go down to her, I and no other,
Close with her, kiss her and mix her
    with me ...

I shall sleep, and move with the
    moving ships,
Change as the winds change, veer in
    the tide;
My lips will feast on the foam of thy
    lips,
I shall rise with thy rising and with
    thee subside.

['The Triumph of Time' (1866)]

SYNGE, J.M. (1871–1909)
'A man who is not afraid of the sea
will soon be drownded,' he said, 'for
he will be going out on a day he
shouldn't. But we do be afraid of the
sea, and we do only be drownded now
and again.'

[The Aran Islands (1907)]

UVAVNUK
The great sea
Has set me adrift
It moves me as the weed in the river,
Earth and the great weather
Move me,
Have carried me away
And move my inward parts with joy.

[In Rasmussen, Intellectual Culture of the
Igulik Eskimos (1929)]

WHITING, William (1825–1878)
Eternal Father, strong to save,
Whose arm hath bound the restless
    wave,
... O hear us when we cry to Thee

For those in peril on the sea.

[Hymn, 1869]

THE SEASONS

ADAMS, Richard (1920–)
Many human beings say that they
enjoy the winter, but what they really
enjoy is feeling proof against it.

[Watership Down (1974)]

**ANDREWES, Bishop Lancelot
(1555–1626)**
It was no summer progress. A cold
coming they had of it, at this time of
the year; just, the worst time of the
year, to take a journey, and specially a
long journey, in. The ways deep, the
weather sharp, the days short, the sun
farthest off in solstitio brumali, the very
dead of Winter.

[Sermon 15, Of the Nativity (1629)]

**COLERIDGE, Samuel Taylor
(1772–1834)**
Summer has set in with its usual
severity.

[Letters of Charles Lamb (1888)]

HOLMES, Oliver Wendell (1809–1894)
For him in vain the envious seasons
    roll
Who bears eternal summer in his soul.

['The Old Player' (1861)]

HOOD, Thomas (1799–1845)
I saw old Autumn in the misty morn
Stand shadowless like Silence,
    listening
To silence.

['Ode: Autumn' (1823)]

KEATS, John (1795–1821)
Where are the songs of Spring? Ay,
    where are they?
Think not of them, thou hast thy music
too.

['To Autumn' (1819)]

SANTAYANA, George (1863–1952)
To be interested in the changing
seasons is, in this middling zone, a
happier state of mind than to be

hopelessly in love with spring.

[*Little Essays* (1920)]

SHAKESPEARE, William (1564–1616)
At Christmas I no more desire a rose
Than wish a snow in May's new-
fangled shows;
But like of each thing that in season
grows.

[*Love's Labour's Lost*, I.i]

WALPOLE, Horace (1717–1797)
The way to ensure summer in England
is to have it framed and glazed in a
comfortable room.

[Letter to William Cole, 1774]

See WEATHER

SECRETS

ACTON, Lord (1834–1902)
Everything secret degenerates ...
nothing is safe that does not show
how it can bear discussion and
publicity.

[Attr.]

CERVANTES, Miguel de (1547–1616)
*Mucho más dañan a las honras de las
mujeres las desenvolturas y libertades
públicas que las maldades secretas.*
Brazenness and public liberties do
much more harm to a woman's
honour than secret wickedness.

[*Don Quixote*, II (1615)]

CONGREVE, William (1670–1729)
I know that's a secret, for it's whis-
pered everywhere.

[*Love for Love* (1695)]

CRABBE, George (1754–1832)
Secrets with girls, like loaded guns
with boys,
Are never valued till they make a
noise.

[*Tales of the Hall* (1819)]

DRYDEN, John (1631–1700)
For secrets are edged tools,
And must be kept from children and
from fools.

[*Sir Martin Mar-All* (1667)]

FRANKLIN, Benjamin (1706–1790)
Three may keep a secret, if two of
them are dead.

[*Poor Richard's Almanac* (1735)]

FRANKS, Oliver, Baron (1905–1992)
It is a secret in the Oxford sense: you
may tell it to only one person at a
time.

[*Sunday Telegraph*, 1977]

FROST, Robert (1874–1963)
We dance round in a ring and
suppose,
But the Secret sits in the middle and
knows.

['The Secret Sits' (1942)]

SHAKESPEARE, William (1564–1616)
But that I am forbid
To tell the secrets of my prison-house,
I could a tale unfold whose lightest
word
Would harrow up thy soul, freeze thy
young blood,
Make thy two eyes, like stars, start
from their spheres,
Thy knotted and combined locks to
part,
And each particular hair to stand on
end,
Like quills upon the fretful porpentine.
But this eternal blazon must not be
To ears of flesh and blood.

[*Hamlet*, I.v]

STEPHENS, James (1882–1950)
A secret is a weapon and a friend.
Man is God's secret, Power is man's
secret, Sex is woman's secret.

[*The Crock of Gold* (1912)]

SELF

ARNOLD, Matthew (1822–1888)
Resolve to be thyself; and know, that he,
Who finds himself, loses his misery!

['Self-Dependence' (1852)]

BACON, Francis (1561–1626)
It is a poor centre of a man's actions,
himself.

['Of Wisdom for a Man's Self' (1625)]

BRONTË, Emily (1818–1848)
He is more myself than I am.

[*Wuthering Heights* (1847)]

BURNS, Robert (1759–1796)
O wad some Power the giftie gie us
To see oursels as ithers see us!
It wad frae monie a blunder free us,
An' foolish notion:
What airs in dress an' gait wad lea'e us,
An' ev'n devotion!

['To a Louse' (1786)]

CARLYLE, Thomas (1795–1881)
A certain inarticulate Self-conscious-
ness dwells dimly in us ... Hence, too,
the folly of that impossible precept,
Know thyself; till it be translated into
this partially possible one, *Know what
thou canst work at.*

[*Sartor Resartus* (1834)]

CONNOLLY, Cyril (1903–1974)
I have always disliked myself at any
given moment; the total of such
moments is my life.

[*Enemies of Promise* (1938)]

EMERSON, Ralph Waldo (1803–1882)
All sensible people are selfish, and
nature is tugging at every contract to
make the terms of it fair.

[*Conduct of Life* (1860)]

HILLEL, `The Elder' (c. 60 BC–c. 10 AD)
If I am not for myself who is for me;
and being for my own self what am I?
If not now when?

[In Taylor (ed.), *Sayings of the Jewish Fathers*
(1877)]

HUXLEY, Aldous (1894–1963)
There's only one corner of the
universe you can be certain of
improving, and that's your own self.

[*Time Must Have a Stop* (1944)]

JOAD, C.E.M. (1891–1953)
Whenever I look inside myself I am
afraid.

[*The Observer*, 1942]

KEMPIS, Thomas à (c. 1380–1471)
*Humilis tui cognitio, certior via est ad
Deum; quam profunda scientiae
inquisitio.*
The humble knowledge of thyself is a
surer way to God than the deepest
search after learning.

[*De Imitatione Christi* (1892)]

**LA ROCHEFOUCAULD, Duc de
(1613–1680)**
*L'amour-propre est le plus grand de tous
les flatteurs.*
Self-love is the greatest flatterer of all.

[*Maximes* (1678)]

*L'intérêt parle toutes sortes de langues,
et joue toutes sortes de personnages,
même celui de désintéressé.*
Self-interest speaks every kind of
language, and plays every role, even
that of disinterestedness.

[*Maximes* (1678)]

MANSFIELD, Katherine (1888–1923)
[On human limitations]
To have the courage of your excess –
to find the limit of yourself.

[*Journal of Katherine Mansfield* (1954)]

**MAUGHAM, William Somerset
(1874–1965)**
I recognize that I am made up of
several persons and that the person
that at the moment has the upper
hand will inevitably give place to
another. But which is the real one? All
of them or none?

[*A Writer's Notebook* (1949)]

MOLIÈRE (1622–1673)
*On doit se regarder soi–même un fort
    long temps,
Avant que de songer à condamner les
    gens.*
We should look long and carefully at
ourselves before we consider judging
others.

[*Le Misanthrope* (1666)]

MONTAIGNE, Michel de (1533–1592)
*La plus grande chose du monde, c'est
de savoir être à soi.*
The greatest thing in the world is to
know how to belong to oneself.

[*Essais* (1580)]

POWELL, Anthony (1905–)
He fell in love with himself at first
sight and it is a passion to which he
has always remained faithful. Self-love
seems so often unrequited.

[*The Acceptance World* (1955)]

RUSSELL, Bertrand (1872–1970)
Man is not a solitary animal, and so
long as social life survives, self-
realization cannot be the supreme
principle of ethics.

[*A History of Western Philosophy* (1946)]

SHAKESPEARE, William (1564–1616)
This above all – to thine own self be
   true,
And it must follow, as the night the
   day,
Thou canst not then be false to any
   man.

[*Hamlet*, I.iii]

SHAW, George Bernard (1856–1950)
It is easy – terribly easy – to shake a
man's faith in himself. To take
advantage of that to break a man's
spirit is devil's work.

[*Candida* (1898)]

Don't fuss, my dear, I'm not unhappy. I
am enjoying the enormous freedom of
having found myself out and got myself off my mind; it is the beginning of
hope and the end of hypocrisy.

[*On the Rocks*]

SITWELL, Dame Edith (1887–1964)
Why not be oneself? That is the whole
secret of a successful appearance. If
one is a greyhound, why try to look
like a Pekingese?

['Why I look the Way I do' (1955)]

TOLSTOY, Leo (1828–1910)
I am always with myself, and it is I
who am my own tormentor.

[*Memoirs of a Madman* (1943)]

TROLLOPE, Anthony (1815–1882)
Never think that you're not good
enough yourself. A man should never
think that. My belief is that in life
people will take you very much at your
own reckoning.

[*The Small House at Allington* (1864)]

TWAIN, Mark (1835–1910)
When people do not respect us we are
sharply offended; yet deep down in his
heart no man much respects himself.

[*Notebooks* (1935)]

WHITMAN, Walt (1819–1892)
Behold, I do not give lectures or a little
   charity,
When I give I give myself.

['Song of Myself' (1855)]

WILDE, Oscar (1854–1900)
Other people are quite dreadful. The
only possible society is oneself.

[*An Ideal Husband* (1895)]

SEPARATION

BAYLY, Thomas Haynes (1797–1839)
Absence makes the heart grow fonder,
Isle of Beauty, Fare thee well!

['Isle of Beauty', song, 1830]

BRENNAN, Christopher (1870–1932)
I am shut out of mine own heart
because my love is far from me.

['I Am Shut Out of Mine Own Heart' (1914)]

**BUSSY-RABUTIN, Comte de
(1618–1693)**
*L'absence est à l'amour ce qu'est au feu
le vent; il éteint le petit, il allume le
grand.*
Absence is to love what the wind is to
fire; it extinguishes the small, it kindles
the great.

[*Histoire Amoureuse des Gaules* (1665)]

COPE, Wendy (1945–)
The day he moved out was terrible –
That evening she went through hell.

His absence wasn't a problem
But the corkscrew had gone as well.

['Loss' (1992)]

COWPER, William (1731–1800)
Absence from whom we love is worse
than death.

['Hope, like the Short-lived Ray' (1791)]

DICKINSON, Emily (1830–1886)
My life closed twice before its close –
It yet remains to see
If Immortality unveil
A third event to me

So huge, so hopeless to conceive
As these that twice befell.
Parting is all we know of heaven,
And all we need of hell.

['My life closed twice before its close' (1896)]

JAGO, Rev. Richard (1715–1781)
With leaden foot time creeps along
While Delia is away.

[*Absence*]

KEATS, John (1795–1821)
I wish you could invent some means
to make me at all happy without you.
Every hour I am more and more con-
centrated in you; every thing else
tastes like chaff in my Mouth.

[Letter to Fanny Brawne, 1820]

KING, Bishop Henry (1592–1669)
We that did nothing study but the way
To love each other, with which
thoughts the day
Rose with delight to us, and with them
set,
Must learn the hateful art, how to
forget.

['The Surrender' (1651)]

POUND, Ezra (1885–1972)
And if you ask how I regret that
parting:
It is like the flowers falling at Spring's
end
Confused, whirled in a tangle.
What is the use of talking, and there is
no end of talking,
There is no end of things in the heart.

['Exile's Letter' (1915)]

SCHOPENHAUER, Arthur (1788–1860)
*Jede Trennung gibt einen Vorschmack
des Todes, – und jedes Wiedersehen
einen Vorschmack der Auferstehung.*
Every separation gives a foretaste of
death, – and every reunion a foretaste
of resurrection.

[*Parerga und Paralipomena* (1851)]

SHAKESPEARE, William (1564–1616)
Parting is such sweet sorrow
That I shall say good night till it be
morrow.

[*Romeo and Juliet*, II.ii]

SEX

ALLEN, Woody (1953–)
Hey, don't knock masturbation! It's sex
with someone I love.

[*Annie Hall*, film, 1977]

On bisexuality: It immediately doubles
your chances for a date on Saturday
night.

[*New York Times*, 1975]

I want to tell you a terrific story about
oral contraception. I asked this girl to
sleep with me and she said 'no'.

[Attr.]

ANONYMOUS
Post coitum omne animal triste.
After coition every animal is sad.

[Post-classical saying]

AUGUSTINE, Saint (354–430)
*Da mihi castitatem et continentiam, sed
noli modo.*
Give me chastity and continence, but
not yet.

[*Confessions* (398)]

BANKHEAD, Tallulah (1903–1968)
[To an admirer]
I'll come and make love to you at five
o'clock. If I'm late start without me.

[In Morgan, *Somerset Maugham* (1980)]

BETJEMAN, Sir John (1906–1984)
[When asked if he had any regrets]
Yes, I haven't had enough sex.

[*Time With Betjeman*, BBC TV, 1983]

'BOY GEORGE' (1961–)
I'd rather have a cup of tea than go to bed with someone – any day.

[Remark, variously expressed, 1983]

BROME, Richard (c. 1590–1652)
Doctor: But there the maids doe woe the Batchelors, and tis most probable, The wives lie uppermost.
Diana: That is a trim, upside-downe Antipodian tricke indeed.

[*The Antipodes* (1638)]

BROWNE, Sir Thomas (1605–1682)
I could be content that we might procreate like trees, without conjunction, or that there were any way to perpetuate the World without this trivial and vulgar way of coition: it is the foolishest act a wise man commits in all his life; nor is there any thing that will more deject his cool'd imagination, when he shall consider what an odd and unworthy piece of folly he hath committed.

[*Religio Medici* (1643)]

BURCHILL, Julie (1960–)
Sex, on the whole, was meant to be short, nasty and brutish. If what you want is cuddling, you should buy a puppy.

[*Sex and Sensibility* (1992)]

CAMPBELL, Mrs Patrick (1865–1940)
I don't mind where people make love, so long as they don't do it in the street and frighten the horses.

[Attr.]

CHESTERFIELD, Lord (1694–1773)
[On sex]
The pleasure is momentary, the position ridiculous, and the expense damnable.

[Attr.]

COMFORT, Alex (1920–)
A woman who has the divine gift of lechery will always make a superlative partner.

[Attr.]

COOGAN, Tim Pat (1935–)
[Describing the rulings of the Catholic Church on matters of sexual morality]
It's rather like teaching swimming from a book without ever having got wet oneself.

[*Disillusioned Decades: Ireland, 1966–87* (1987)]

CRISP, Quentin (1908–)
What is wrong with pornography is that it is a successful attempt to sell sex for more than it is worth.

[In Kettlehack (ed.), *The Wit and Wisdom of Quentin Crisp*]

DAVIES, Robertson (1913–)
Sex that is not an evidence of a strong human tie is just like blowing your nose; it's not a celebration of a splendid relationship.

[Interview, 1974]

DONNE, John (1572–1631)
Licence my roving hands, and let them go,
Before, behind, between, above, below.
O my America! my new-found-land,
My kingdom, safeliest when with one man mann'd.

['To His Mistress Going to Bed' (c. 1595)]

DURRELL, Lawrence (1912–1990)
No more about sex, it's too boring.

[*Tunc* (1968)]

DWORKIN, Andrea (1946–)
Intercourse as an act often expresses the power men have over women.

[*Intercourse* (1987)]

Seduction is often difficult to distinguish from rape. In seduction, the rapist often bothers to buy a bottle of wine.

[*The Independent*, 1992]

FAIRBAIRN, Sir Nicholas (1933–1995)
Sex is a human activity like any other. It's a natural urge, like breathing, thinking, drinking, laughing, talking with friends, golf. They are not crimes

if you plan them with someone other than your wife. Why should sex be?

[*The Independent*, 1992]

Most cases of rape are reported as an act of vengeance because the fellow has got himself another woman. Or guilt.

[*Daily Mail*, 1993]

FIGES, Eva (1932–)
When modern woman discovered the orgasm it was (combined with modern birth control) perhaps the biggest single nail in the coffin of male dominance.

[In Morgan, *The Descent of Woman* (1972)]

FRY, Stephen (1957–)
I gave coitus the red card for utilitarian reasons: the displeasure, discomfort and aggravation it caused outweighed any momentary explosions of pleasure, ease or solace.

[*Paperweight*]

GREER, Germaine (1939–)
No sex is better than bad sex.

[Attr.]

GWYN, Nell (1650–1687)
[On prostitution]
As for me, it is my profession, I do not pretend to anything better.

[In Miles, *The Women's History of the World* (1988)]

HELLER, Joseph (1923–)
Prostitution gives her an opportunity to meet people. It provides fresh air and wholesome exercise, and it keeps her out of trouble.

[*Catch-22* (1961)]

HERRICK, Robert (1591–1674)
Night makes no difference 'twixt the
   Priest and Clark;
Jone as my Lady is as good i' th' dark.

[*Hesperides* (1648)]

HILLINGDON, Lady Alice (1857–1940)
I am happy now that Charles calls on my bedchamber less frequently than of

old. As it is, I now endure but two calls a week and when I hear his steps outside my door I lie down on my bed, close my eyes, open my legs and think of England.

[*Journal* (1912)]

HUXLEY, Aldous (1894–1963)
Mr Mercaptan went on to preach a brilliant sermon on that melancholy sexual perversion known as continence.

[*Antic Hay* (1923)]

'Bed,' as the Italian proverb succinctly puts it, 'is the poor man's opera.'

[*Heaven and Hell* (1956)]

LANDERS, Ann (1918–)
Women complain about sex more often than men. Their gripes fall into two major categories: (1) Not enough (2) Too much.

[*Ann Landers Says Truth Is Stranger Than ...* (1968)]

LAWRENCE, D.H. (1885–1930)
How wonderful sex can be, when men keep it powerful and sacred, and it fills the world! Like sunshine through and through one!

[*The Plumed Serpent* (1926)]

It's all this cold-hearted fucking that is death and idiocy.

[*Lady Chatterley's Lover* (1928)]

LEWIS, Wyndham (1882–1957)
The 'homo' is the legitimate child of the 'suffragette'.

[*The Art of Being Ruled* (1926)]

LONGFORD, Lord (1905–)
No sex without responsibility.

[*The Observer*, 1954]

MACKENZIE, Sir Compton (1883–1972)
From the days of Eve women have always faced sexual facts with more courage and realism than men.

[*Literature in My Time* (1933)]

I told him [D.H. Lawrence] that if he was determined to convert the world to proper reverence for the sexual act ... he would always have to remember one handicap for such an undertaking – that except to the two people who are indulging in it the sexual act is a comic operation.

[*My Life and Times*]

MACLAINE, Shirley (1934–)
The more sex becomes a non-issue in people's lives, the happier they are.

[Attr.]

MIKES, George (1912–1987)
Continental people have sex life; the English have hot-water bottles.

[*How to be an Alien* (1946)]

MILLER, Henry (1891–1980)
Sex is one of the nine reasons for reincarnation ... The other eight are unimportant.

[*Big Sur and the Oranges of Hieronymus Bosch*]

MILTON, John (1608–1674)
Into thir inmost bower
Handed they went; and eas'd the putting off
These troublesom disguises which wee wear,
Strait side by side were laid, nor turned I weene
Adam from his fair Spouse, nor Eve the Rites
Mysterious of connubial Love refus'd:
Whatever Hypocrits austerely talk
Of puritie and place and innocence,
Defaming as impure what God declares
Pure, and commands to som, leaves free to all.

[*Paradise Lost* (1667)]

MONTGOMERY, Viscount (1887–1976)
[Comment on a bill to relax the laws against homosexuals]
This sort of thing may be tolerated by the French, but we are British – thank God.

[Speech, 1965]

MUGGERIDGE, Malcolm (1903–1990)
An orgy looks particularly alluring seen through the mists of righteous indignation.

[*The Most of Malcolm Muggeridge* (1966)]

The orgasm has replaced the Cross as the focus of longing and the image of fulfilment.

[*The Most of Malcolm Muggeridge* (1966)]

NASH, Ogden (1902–1971)
Home is heaven and orgies are vile
But you *need* an orgy, once in a while.

['Home, 99.44/100% Sweet Home' (1935)]

NEWBY, P.H. (1918–)
He felt that he could love this woman with the greatest brutality. The situation between them was electric. When he was in a room with her the only thing he could think of was sex.

[*A Journey to the Interior* (1945)]

ORTON, Joe (1933–1967)
You were born with your legs apart. They'll send you to the grave in a Y-shaped coffin.

[*What the Butler Saw* (1969)]

PHILIP, Prince, Duke of Edinburgh (1921–)
I don't think a prostitute is more moral than a wife, but they are doing the same thing.

[*The Observer*, 1988]

PINTER, Harold (1930–)
I tend to believe that cricket is the greatest thing that God ever created on earth ... certainly greater than sex, although sex isn't too bad either.

[Interview in *The Observer*, 1980]

SALINGER, J.D. (1919–)
Sex is something I really don't understand too hot. You never know *where* the hell you are. I keep making up these sex rules for myself, and then I break them right away.

[*The Catcher in the Rye* (1951)]

SAYERS, Dorothy L. (1893–1957)
As I grow older and older,
And totter towards the tomb,
I find that I care less and less
Who goes to bed with whom.

[In Hitchman, *Such a Strange Lady* (1975)]

SCOTT, Valerie
[Toronto prostitute-by-choice]
We don't sell our bodies. Housewives
do that. What we do is *rent* our bodies
for sexual services.

[*The Toronto Star*, 1989]

SHAKESPEARE, William (1564–1616)
Is it not strange that desire should so
many years outlive performance?

[*Henry IV, Part 2*, II.iv]

STEINEM, Gloria (1934–)
[On transsexualism]
If the shoe doesn't fit, must we change
the foot?

[*Outrageous Acts and Everyday Rebellions* (1984)]

STEWART, Rod (1945–)
[On his sexual partners]
The most memorable is always the
current one; the rest just merge into a
sea of blondes.

[Attr.]

SZASZ, Thomas (1920–)
Traditionally, sex has been a very
private, secretive activity. Herein perhaps lies its powerful force for uniting
people in a strong bond. As we make
sex less secretive, we may rob it of its
power to hold men and women
together.

[*The Second Sin* (1973)]

Masturbation: the primary sexual
activity of mankind. In the nineteenth
century it was a disease; in the twentieth, it's a cure.

[*The Second Sin* (1973)]

THURBER, James (1894–1961)
[On being accosted at a party by a
drunk woman who claimed she would

like to have a baby by him]
Surely you don't mean by unartificial
insemination!

[Attr.]

VIDAL, Gore (1925–)
[On being asked if his first sexual
experience had been heterosexual or
homosexual]
I was too polite to ask.

[*Forum*, 1987]

VOLTAIRE (1694–1778)
*C'est une des superstitions de l'esprit
humain d'avoir imaginé que la virginité
pouvait être une vertu.*
It is one of the superstitions of the
human mind to have imagined that
virginity could be a virtue.

['The Leningrad Notebooks' (c. 1735–1750)]

WAUGH, Evelyn (1903–1966)
All this fuss about sleeping together.
For physical pleasure I'd sooner go to
my dentist any day.

[*Vile Bodies* (1930)]

WAX, Ruby (1953–)
This 'relationship' business is one big
waste of time. It is just Mother Nature
urging you to breed, breed, breed.
Learn from nature. Learn from our
friend the spider. Just mate once and
then kill him.

[*Spectator*, 1994]

YEATS, W.B. (1865–1939)
The tragedy of sexual intercourse is
the perpetual virginity of the soul.

[Attr. in Jeffares, *W.B. Yeats: man and poet* (1949)]

SHAKESPEARE

ARNOLD, Matthew (1822–1888)
Others abide our question. Thou art
free.
We ask and ask – Thou smilest and art
still,
Out-topping knowledge.

['Shakespeare' (1849)]

AUBREY, John (1626-1697)
He was a handsome, well-shaped man: very good company, and of a very ready and pleasant smooth wit.
[*Brief Lives* (c. 1693)]

AUSTEN, Jane (1775-1817)
We all talk Shakespeare, use his similes, and describe with his descriptions.
[*Mansfield Park* (1814)]

CHESTERFIELD, Lord (1694-1773)
If Shakespeare's genius had been cultivated, those beauties, which we so justly admire in him, would have been undisgraced by those extravagancies and that nonsense with which they are frequently accompanied.
[Letter to his son, 1748]

COLERIDGE, Samuel Taylor (1772-1834)
I believe Shakespeare was not a whit more intelligible in his own day than he is now to an educated man, except for a few local allusions of no consequence. He is of no age – nor of any religion, or party or profession. The body and substance of his works came out of the unfathomable depths of his own oceanic mind: his observation and reading, which was considerable, supplied him with the drapery of his figures.
[*Table Talk* (1835)]

DARWIN, Charles (1809-1882)
I have tried lately to read Shakespeare, and found it so intolerably dull that it nauseated me.
[*Autobiography* (1877]

ELIOT, T.S. (1888-1965)
We can say of Shakespeare, that never has a man turned so little knowledge to such great account.
[Lecture, 1942]

EMERSON, Ralph Waldo (1803-1882)
When Shakespeare is charged with debts to his authors, Landor replies: 'Yet he was more original than his

originals. He breathed upon dead bodies and brought them into life.'
[*Letters and Social Aims* (1875)]

GRAVES, Robert (1895-1985)
The remarkable thing about Shakespeare is that he is really very good – in spite of all the people who say he is very good.
[*The Observer*, 1964]

KEATS, John (1795-1821)
Shakespeare led a life of Allegory: his works are the comments on it.
[Letter to George and Georgiana Keats, 1819]

OLIVIER, Laurence (1907-1989)
Shakespeare – the nearest thing in incarnation to the eye of God.
[*Kenneth Harris Talking To:* 'Sir Laurence Olivier']

PHILIP, Prince, Duke of Edinburgh (1921-)
A man can be forgiven a lot if he can quote Shakespeare in an economic crisis.
[Attr.]

POWYS, John Cowper (1872-1963)
He combined scepticism of everything with credulity about everything ... and I am convinced this is the true Shakespearian way wherewith to take life.
[*Autobiography*]

SHAW, George Bernard (1856-1950)
With the single exception of Homer, there is no eminent writer, not even Sir Walter Scott, whom I can despise so entirely as I despise Shakespeare when I measure my mind against his ... it would positively be a relief to me to dig him up and throw stones at him.
['Blaming the Bard' (1906)]

WALPOLE, Horace (1717-1797)
One of the greatest geniuses that ever existed, Shakespeare, undoubtedly wanted taste.
[Letter to Christopher Wren, 1764]

ANONYMOUS

Can't act, can't sing, slightly bald. Can dance a little.

[Comment by a Hollywood executive on Fred Astaire's first screen test]

BROOKS, Mel (1926–)

That's it, baby, if you've got it, flaunt it.

[*The Producers*, film, 1968]

CHASEN, Dave

Bogart's a helluva nice guy until 11.30 p.m. After that he thinks he's Bogart.

[In Halliwell, *The Filmgoer's Book of Quotes* (1973)]

CHER (1946–)

Mother told me a couple of years ago, 'Sweetheart, settle down and marry a rich man.' I said, 'Mom, I am a rich man.'

[*The Observer Review*, 1995]

COCHRAN, Charles B. (1872–1951)

I still prefer a good juggler to a bad Hamlet.

[*The Observer*, 1943]

DAVIS, Bette (1908–1989)

[Of a starlet]
I see – she's the original good time that was had by all.

[In Halliwell, *Filmgoer's Book of Quotes* (1973)]

DAVIS, Sammy, Junior (1925–1990)

Being a star has made it possible for me to get insulted in places where the average Negro could never hope to get insulted.

[*Yes I can* (1965)]

DILLINGHAM, Charles Bancroft (1868–1934)

[Said at the funeral of Harry Houdini, the escapologist, while carrying his coffin]
I bet you a hundred bucks he ain't in here.

[Attr.]

GARBO, Greta (1905–1990)

I never said, 'I want to be alone.' I only said, 'I want to be *let* alone.' There is all the difference.

[In Colombo, *Wit and Wisdom of the Moviemakers*]

GARLAND, Judy (1922–1969)

I was born at the age of twelve on a Metro-Goldwyn-Mayer lot.

[*The Observer*, 1951]

GOLDWYN, Samuel (1882–1974)

Directors [are] always biting the hand that lays the golden egg.

[In Zierold, *Moguls* (1969)]

I'll give you a definite maybe.

[In Colombo, *Wit and Wisdom of the Moviemakers*]

In two words: im possible.

[Attr.; in Zierold, *Moguls* (1969)]

What we want is a story that starts with an earthquake and works its way up to a climax.

[Attr.]

GRABLE, Betty (1916–1973)

There are two reasons why I'm in show business, and I'm standing on both of them.

[Attr.]

GRADE, Lew (1906–1994)

All my shows are great. Some of them are bad. But they are all great.

[*The Observer*, 1975]

GUINAN, Texas (1884–1933)

[When she and her troupe were refused entry to France in 1931]
It goes to show that fifty million Frenchmen *can* be wrong.

[Attr.]

HELPMAN, Sir Robert Murray (1909–1986)

[Commenting on *Oh, Calcutta!*]
The trouble with nude dancing is that not everything stops when the music stops.

[In *The Frank Muir Book* (1976)]

LEVANT, Oscar (1906–1972)
Strip the phony tinsel off Hollywood
and you'll find the real tinsel underneath.
[In Halliwell, *Filmgoer's Book of Quotes*
(1973)]

MIZNER, Wilson (1876–1933)
[On Hollywood]
A trip through a sewer in a glass-
bottomed boat.
[Attr.]

MONROE, Marilyn (1926–1962)
I guess I *am* a fantasy.
[In Steinem, *Outrageous Acts and Everyday
Rebellions* (1984)]

Hollywood is a place where they'll pay
you $50,000 for a kiss and 50 cents for
your soul.
[Attr.]

REED, Rex (1938–)
In Hollywood, if you don't have
happiness you send out for it.
[In Colombo, *Colombo's Hollywood*]

RICHARD, Sir Cliff (1940–)
There's no room in my life for drugs,
fights, divorce, adultery, sadism, unnecessary fuss and sex.
[*Daily Mail*, 1996]

Stars who debauch themselves, get
addicted to drugs then kick them get
all the praise. Wouldn't you think that
people who have never been addicted
should be praised all the more?
[*The Observer Review*, 1996]

ROWLAND, Richard (c. 1881–1947)
[When United Artists was established
in 1919 by Mary Pickford, Douglas
Fairbanks, Charlie Chaplin and D.W.
Griffith]
The lunatics have taken over the
asylum.
[Attr.]

SHAW, George Bernard (1856–1950)
The trouble, Mr Goldwyn, is that you
are only interested in art and I am only
interested in money.
[In Johnson, *The Great Goldwyn* (1937)]

SKELTON, Red (1913–)
[Commenting on the large crowds
attending the funeral of Hollywood
producer Harry Cohn]
It proves what they say, give the public
what they want to see and they'll
come out for it.
[Remark, 1958]

SOUTHERN, Terry (1924–)
She says, 'Listen, who do I have to
fuck to get *off* this picture?'
[*Blue Movie* (1970)]

THOMAS, Irene (1920–)
It was the kind of show where the girls
are not auditioned – just measured.
[Attr.]

TRACY, Spencer (1900–1967)
[Explaining what he looked for in a
script]
Days off.
[Attr.]

WELLES, Orson (1915–1985)
I began at the top and I've been
working my way down ever since.
[In Colombo, *Wit and Wisdom of the
Moviemakers*]

See CINEMA

SILENCE

AUSTEN, Jane (1775–1817)
From politics, it was an easy step to
silence.
[*Northanger Abbey* (1818)]

BACON, Francis (1561–1626)
Silence is the virtue of fools.
[*The Advancement of Learning* (1623)]

CARLYLE, Thomas (1795–1881)
Under all speech that is good for
anything there lies a silence that is
better. Silence is deep as Eternity;
speech is shallow as Time.
['Memoirs of the Life of Scott' (1839)]

FLECKNOE, Richard (d. c. 1678)
Still-born Silence! thou that art
Floodgate of the deeper heart.
['Invocation of Silence' (1653)]

HOLMES, Oliver Wendell (1809–1894)
And silence, like a poultice, comes
To heal the blows of sound.
['The Music-Grinders' (1836)]

HOOD, Thomas (1799–1845)
There is a silence where hath been no
sound,
There is a silence where no sound
may be,
In the cold grave – under the deep,
deep sea,
Or in the wide desert where no life is
found.
['Sonnet: Silence' (1823)]

HUXLEY, Aldous (1894–1963)
Silence is as full of potential wisdom
and wit as the unhewn marble of great
sculpture.
[*Point Counter Point* (1928)]

JONSON, Ben (1572–1637)
Calumnies are answered best with
silence.
[*Volpone* (1607)]

**LA ROCHEFOUCAULD, Duc de
(1613–1680)**
*Le silence est le parti le plus sûr de celui
qui se défie de soi-même.*
Silence is the safest policy for the man
who distrusts himself.
[*Maximes* (1678)]

LINCOLN, Abraham (1809–1865)
Better to remain silent and be thought
a fool than to speak out and remove
all doubt.
[Attr.]

MANDELSTAM, Nadezhda (1899–1980)
If nothing else is left, one must
scream. Silence is the real crime
against humanity.
[*Hope Against Hope* (1970)]

PASCAL, Blaise (1623–1662)
*Le silence éternel de ces espaces infinis
m'effraie.*
The eternal silence of these infinite
spaces terrifies me.
[*Pensées* (1670)]

SAINTE-BEUVE (1804–1869)
Le silence seul est le souverain mépris.
Silence is the supreme contempt.
['Mes Poisons']

SIDNEY, Sir Philip (1554–1586)
Shallow brookes murmur moste,
Depe sylent slyde away.
[*Old Arcadia* (1581)]

TUPPER, Martin (1810–1889)
Well-timed silence hath more elo-
quence than speech.
[*Proverbial Philosophy* (1838)]

VIRGIL (70–19 BC)
Tacitae per amica silentia lunae.
Through the friendly silence of the
soundless moonlight.
[*Aeneid*]

WITTGENSTEIN, Ludwig (1889–1951)
What can be said at all can be said
clearly; and whereof one cannot speak,
thereon one must keep silent.
[*Tractatus Logico-Philosophicus* (1922)]

See CONVERSATION

SIN

AUDEN, W.H. (1907–1973)
All sin tends to be addictive, and the
terminal point of addiction is what is
called damnation.
[*A Certain World* (1970)]

THE BIBLE (King James Version)
Be sure your sin will find you out.
[*Numbers*, 32:23]

He that is without sin among you, let
him first cast a stone.
[*John*, 8:7]

The wages of sin is death.
[*Romans*, 6:23]

BULGAKOV, Mikhail (1891–1940)
Cowardice is, without a doubt, one of
the greatest sins.
[*The Master and Margarita* (1967)]

BUNYAN, John (1628–1688)
One leak will sink a ship, and one sin
will destroy a sinner.

[*The Pilgrim's Progress* (1678)]

COOLIDGE, Calvin (1872–1933)
[On being asked what had been said
by a clergyman who preached on sin]
He said he was against it.

[Attr.]

COWLEY, Abraham (1618–1667)
Lukewarmness I account a sin
As great in love as in religion.

['The Request' (1647)]

DONNE, John (1572–1631)
Wilt thou forgive that sin, where I
begun,
Which is my sin, though it were done
before?
Wilt thou forgive those sins through
which I run
And do them still, though still I do
deplore?
When thou hast done, thou hast not
done,
For I have more.

Wilt thou forgive that sin, by which I
have won
Others to sin, and made my sin their
door?
Wilt thou forgive that sin which I did
shun
A year or two, but wallowed in a
score?
When thou hast done, thou hast not
done,
For I have more.

['Hymn to God the Father' (1623)]

EDDY, Mary Baker (1821–1910)
Sin brought death, and death will
disappear with the disappearance of
sin.

[*Science and Health* (1875)]

JUVENAL (c. 60–130)
*Summum crede nefas animam praeferre
pudori
Et propter vitam vivendi perdere causas.*

Count it the greatest sin to put life
before honour, and for the sake of life
to lose the reasons for living.

[*Satires*]

LAWRENCE, D.H. (1885–1930)
There's nothing so artificial as sinning
nowadays. I suppose it once was real.

[*St Mawr* (1925)]

MOLIERE (1622–1673)
*Le scandale du monde est ce qui fait
l'offense,
Et ce n'est pas pécher que pécher en
silence.*
Public scandal is what constitutes
offence; to sin in secret is no sin at all.

[*Tartuffe* (1664)]

**QUEVEDO Y VILLEGAS, Francisco
Gómez de (1580–1645)**
*Tan ciego estoy a mi mortal enredo
que no te oso llamar, Señor, de miedo
de que querrás sacarme de pecado.*
So blind am I to my mortal
entanglement
that I dare not call upon thee, Lord, for
fear
that thou wouldst take me away from
my sin.

[*Christian Heraclitus* (1613)]

ROOSEVELT, Theodore (1858–1919)
The worst sin towards our fellow
creatures is not to hate them, but to be
indifferent to them: that's the essence
of inhumanity.

[*The Devil's Disciple* (1901)]

SHAKESPEARE, William (1564–1616)
Plate sin with gold,
And the strong lance of justice hurtless
breaks;
Arm it in rags, a pigmy's straw does
pierce it.

[*King Lear*, IV.vi]

Few love to hear the sins they love to
act.

[*Pericles, Prince of Tyre*, I.i]

Nothing emboldens sin so much as
mercy.

[*Timon of Athens*, III.v]

WILDE, Oscar (1854–1900)
It has been said that the great events
of the world take place in the brain. It
is in the brain, and the brain only, that
the great sins of the world take place.
[*The Picture of Dorian Gray* (1891)]

See EVIL

SLAVERY

BURKE, Edmund (1729–1797)
Slavery they can have anywhere. It is a
weed that grows in every soil.
[*Speech on Conciliation with America* (1775)]

GANDHI (1869–1948)
The moment the slave resolves that he
will no longer be a slave, his fetters
fall. He frees himself and shows the
way to others. Freedom and slavery
are mental states.
[*Non-Violence in Peace and War* (1949)]

GILL, Eric (1882–1940)
That state is a state of Slavery in
which a man does what he likes to do
in his spare time and in his working
time that which is required of him.
['Slavery and Freedom' (1929)]

JOHNSON, Samuel (1709–1784)
How is it that we hear the loudest
yelps for liberty among the drivers of
negroes?
[*Taxation No Tyranny* (1775)]

LINCOLN, Abraham (1809–1865)
In giving freedom to the slave, we
assure freedom to the free – honourable alike in what we give and what
we preserve.
[Speech, 1862]

MACKENZIE, Sir Compton (1883–1972)
The slavery of being waited upon that
is more deadening than the slavery of
waiting upon other people.
[*The Adventures of Sylvia Scarlett* (1918)]

STANTON, Elizabeth Cady (1815–1902)
The prolonged slavery of woman is the
darkest page in human history.
[In Anthony and Gage, *History of Woman
Suffrage* (1881)]

WEDGWOOD, Josiah (1730–1795)
Am I not a man and a brother?
[Motto adopted by Anti-Slavery Society]

SLEEP

BROWNE, Sir Thomas (1605–1682)
Sleep is a death, O make me try,
By sleeping what it is to die.
And as gently lay my head
On my grave, as now my bed.
[*Religio Medici* (1643)]

Half our days we pass in the shadow
of the earth; and the brother of death
exacteth a third part of our lives.
[*Pseudodoxia Epidemica* (1646)]

CERVANTES, Miguel de (1547–1616)
*Bien haya el que inventó el sueño, capa
que cubre todos los humanos
pensamientos, manjar que quita la
hambre, agua que ahuyenta la sed,
fuego que calienta el frío, frío que
templa el ardor, y, finalmente, moneda
general con que todas las cosas se
compran, balanza y peso que iguala al
pastor con el rey y al simple con el
discreto.*
God bless whoever invented sleep, the
cloak that covers all human thoughts.
It is the food that satisfies hunger, the
water that quenches thirst, the fire that
warms cold, the cold that reduces
heat, and, lastly, the common currency
which can buy anything, the balance
and compensating weight that makes
the shepherd equal to the king, and
the simpleton equal to the sage.
[*Don Quixote* (1615)]

DANIEL, Samuel (1562–1619)
Care-charmer Sleep, son of the sable
  Night,
Brother to Death, in silent darkness
  born.
[*Delia* (1592)]

DICKENS, Charles (1812–1870)
It would make any one go to sleep,
that bedstead would, whether they
wanted to or not.
[*The Pickwick Papers* (1837)]

HENRI IV (1553–1610)
*Les grands mangeurs et les grands
dormeurs sont incapables de rien faire
de grand.*
Great eaters and great sleepers are not
capable of doing anything great.

[Attr.]

NIETZSCHE, Friedrich (1844–1900)
*Keine geringe Kunst ist schlafen: es tut
schon not, den ganzen Tag darauf hin
zu wachen.*
Sleeping is no mean art: it is necessary
to stay awake for it all day.

[*Thus Spake Zarathustra* (1884)]

SHAKESPEARE, William (1564–1616)
Weariness
Can snore upon the flint, when resty
    sloth
Finds the down pillow hard.

[*Cymbeline*, III.vi]

Methought I heard a voice cry 'Sleep
    no more;
Macbeth does murder sleep' – the
    innocent sleep,
Sleep that knits up the ravell'd sleave
    of care,
The death of each day's life, sore
    labour's bath,
Balm of hurt minds, great nature's
    second course,
Chief nourisher in life's feast.

[*Macbeth*, II.ii]

Not poppy, nor mandragora,
Nor all the drowsy syrups of the world,
Shall ever medicine thee to that sweet
    sleep
Which thou owed'st yesterday.

[*Othello*, III.iii]

SIDNEY, Sir Philip (1554–1586)
Come, Sleepe, O Sleepe, the certaine
    knot of peace,
The bathing place of wits, the balm of
    woe,
The poore man's wealth, the
    prysoner's release,
The indifferent Judge betweene the hie
    and lowe.

[*Astrophel and Stella* (1591)]

SOUTHEY, Robert (1774–1843)
Thou hast been call'd, O Sleep! the
    friend of Woe,
But 'tis the happy who have called
    thee so.

[*The Curse of Kehama* (1810)]

TERTZ, Abram (1925–)
Sleep is the watering place of the soul
to which it hastens at night to drink at
the sources of life.
In sleep we receive confirmation ...
that we must go on living.

[*A Voice From the Chorus* (1973)]

SMOKING

CALVERLEY, C.S. (1831–1884)
How they who use fusees
All grow by slow degrees
Brainless as chimpanzees,
Meagre as lizards:
Go mad, and beat their wives;
Plunge (after shocking lives)
Razors and carving knives
Into their gizzards.

['Ode to Tobacco' (1861)]

DOYLE, Sir Arthur Conan (1859–1930)
A little monograph on the ashes of
one hundred and forty different
varieties of pipe, cigar, and cigarette
tobacco.

['The Boscombe Valley Mystery' (1892)]

ELIZABETH I (1533–1603)
[To Sir Walter Raleigh]
I have known many persons who
turned their gold into smoke, but you
are the first to turn smoke into gold.

[In Chamberlin, *The Sayings of Queen
Elizabeth*]

HELPS, Sir Arthur (1813–1875)
What a blessing this smoking is!
perhaps the greatest that we owe to
the discovery of America.

[*Friends in Council* (1859)]

**JAMES VI OF SCOTLAND AND I OF
ENGLAND (1566–1625)**
A custom loathesome to the eye,
hateful to the nose, harmful to the
brain, dangerous to the lungs, and in

the black, stinking fume thereof, nearest resembling the horrible Stygian smoke of the pit that is bottomless.

[*A Counterblast to Tobacco* (1604)]

JONSON, Ben (1572–1637)
I do hold it, and will affirm it before any prince in Europe, to be the most sovereign and precious weed that ever the earth rendered to the use of man.

[*Every Man in His Humour* (1598)]

Ods me, I marvel what pleasure or felicity they have in taking their roguish tobacco. It is good for nothing but to choke a man, and fill him full of smoke and embers.

[*Every Man in His Humour* (1598)]

KIPLING, Rudyard (1865–1936)
And a woman is only a woman, but a good cigar is a Smoke.

['The Betrothed' (1886)]

LAMB, Charles (1775–1834)
Dr Parr ... asked him, how he had acquired his power of smoking at such a rate? Lamb replied, 'I toiled after it, sir, as some men toil after virtue.'

[In Talfourd, *Memoirs of Charles Lamb* (1892)]

LINDSAY, Norman (1879–1969)
'You ain't got any tobacco,' he said scornfully to Bunyip Bluegum. 'I can see that at a glance. You're one of the non-smoking sort, all fur and feathers.'

[*The Magic Pudding* (1918)]

NAPOLEON III (1808–1873)
[On being asked to ban smoking] This vice brings in one hundred million francs in taxes every year. I will certainly forbid it at once – as soon as you can name a virtue that brings in as much revenue.

[In Hoffmeister, *Anekdotenschatz*]

SATIE, Erik (1866–1925)
Mon médecin m'a toujours dit de fumer. Il ajoute à ses conseils: 'Fumez, mon

ami: sans cela, un autre fumera à votre place.'
My doctor has always told me to smoke. He explains himself thus: 'Smoke, my friend. If you don't, someone else will smoke in your place.'

[*Mémoires d'un amnésique* (1924)]

TWAIN, Mark (1835–1910)
[Saying how easy it is to give up smoking]
I've done it a hundred times!

[Attr.]

WILDE, Oscar (1854–1900)
A cigarette is the perfect type of a perfect pleasure. It is exquisite, and it leaves one unsatisfied. What more can one want?

[*The Picture of Dorian Gray* (1891)]

SOCIALISM

BENNETT, Alan (1934–)
Why is it always the intelligent people who are socialists?

[*Forty Years On* (1969)]

BEVAN, Aneurin (1897–1960)
The language of priorities is the religion of Socialism.

[Attr.]

DURANT, Will (1885–1982)
There is nothing in Socialism that a little age or a little money will not cure.

[Attr.]

EDWARD VIII (later Duke of Windsor) (1894–1972)
[Quoting Sir William Harcourt]
We are all socialists now.

[Attr.]

KEYNES, John Maynard (1883–1946)
Marxian Socialism must always remain a portent to the historians of opinion – how a doctrine so illogical and so dull can have exercised so powerful and enduring an influence over the minds of men, and, through

them, the events of history.

['The End of Laissez-Faire' (1926)]

KINNOCK, Neil (1942–)
The idea that there is a model Labour voter, a blue-collar council house tenant who belongs to a union and has 2.4 children, a five-year-old car and a holiday in Blackpool, is patronizing and politically immature.

[Speech, 1986]

LENIN, V.I. (1870–1924)
Under socialism *all* will govern in turn and will soon become accustomed to no one governing.

[*The State and Revolution* (1917)]

ORWELL, George (1903–1950)
As with the Christian religion, the worst advertisement for Socialism is its adherents.

[*The Road to Wigan Pier* (1937)]

To the ordinary working man, the sort you would meet in any pub on Saturday night, Socialism does not mean much more than better wages and shorter hours and nobody bossing you about.

[*The Road to Wigan Pier* (1937)]

STOPPARD, Tom (1937–)
Socialists treat their servants with respect and then wonder why they vote Conservative.

[*Lord Malquist and Mr Moon* (1966)]

STRETTON, Hugh (1924–)
Most capacities for love develop (or don't) in childhood; the largest quantity of willing human cooperation occurs within and between house-holds; cooperation there is the pattern, and has to be the continuing basis, for cooperation anywhere else. To put it in the most shocking possible language, socialism should cease to be the factory-floor and chicken-battery party, and become the hearth-and-home, do-it-yourself party.

[*Capitalism, Socialism and the Environment* (1976)]

THATCHER, Margaret (1925–)
State socialism is totally alien to the British character.

[*The Times*, 1983]

WARREN, Earl (1891–1974)
Many people consider the things which government does for them to be social progress, but they consider the things government does for others as socialism.

[*Peter's Quotations*]

SOCIETY

ARISTOTLE (384–322 BC)
A person who cannot live in society, or does not need to because he is self-sufficient, is either a beast or a god.

[*Politics*]

AURELIUS, Marcus (121–180)
What is not good for the beehive, cannot be good for the bees.

[*Meditations*]

BACON, Francis (1561–1626)
Man seeketh in society comfort, use, and protection.

[*The Advancement of Learning* (1605)]

CICERO (106–43 BC)
O tempora! O mores!
What times! What manners!

[*In Catilinam*]

CLAUDEL, Paul (1868–1955)
Il n'y a de société vivante que celle qui est animée par l'inégalité et l'injustice.
The only living societies are those which are animated by inequality and injustice.

[*Conversations dans le Loir-et-Cher*]

COUNIHAN, Noel Jack (1913–1986)
In human society the warmth is mainly at the bottom.

[*Age*, 1986]

CURRY, George
[On the young people involved in the 1991 riots in Tyneside]
It's not sex and drug advice these kids need, so much as help in acquiring a

world view, in motivating them to take responsibility and enabling them to build proper relationships. But if you say that sort of thing to the social work agencies, they just turn off and say: 'Oh, those are moral issues – we can't be going into those.' But we have to! Otherwise, we shall simply be raising generations of animals, of Calibans.

[*Daily Mail*, 1996]

EMERSON, Ralph Waldo (1803–1882)
Society everywhere is in conspiracy against the manhood of every one of its members.

['Self-Reliance' (1841)]

GALBRAITH, J.K. (1908–)
In the affluent society, no sharp distinction can be made between luxuries and necessaries.

[*The Affluent Society* (1958)]

HOWKINS, Alun (1947–)
The English pub is, we are told from childhood, a unique institution. Nothing 'quite like it' exists anywhere else. That's true. The pub uniquely represents, even in metropolitan England, the precise inequalities of gender, race and class that construct our society. From the inclusive white, male and proletarian 'public' of many northern pubs to the parasitic blazer and cotton dress 'locals' of the home counties, our unique institution divides our society and our social life.

[*New Statesman and Society*, 1989]

HUME, Basil (1923–)
[On the killing of London headmaster Philip Lawrence]
We have really lost in our society the sense of the sacredness of life.

[*The Observer Review*, 1995]

JENKINS, Roy (1920–)
The permissive society has been allowed to become a dirty phrase. A better phrase is the civilized society.

[Speech, 1969]

MANDELA, Nelson (1918–)
We enter into a covenant that we shall build the society in which all South Africans, both black and white, will be able to walk tall, without any fear in their hearts, assured of their inalienable right to human dignity – a rainbow nation at peace with itself and the world.

[Inaugural Address, 1994]

MENCKEN, H.L. (1880–1956)
A society made up of individuals who were all capable of original thought would probably be unendurable. The pressure of ideas would simply drive it frantic.

['Minority Report' (1956)]

ROOSEVELT, Theodore (1858–1919)
The men with the muck-rakes are often indispensable to the well-being of society; but only if they know when to stop raking the muck.

[Speech, 1906]

SMITH, Adam (1723–1790)
No society can surely be flourishing and happy, of which the far greater part of the members are poor and miserable.

[*Wealth of Nations* (1776)]

SPENCER, Herbert (1820–1903)
No one can be perfectly free till all are free; no one can be perfectly moral till all are moral; no one can be perfectly happy till all are happy.

[*Social Statics* (1850)]

SPINOZA, Baruch (1632–1677)
Homo sit animale sociale.
Man is a social animal.

[*Ethics* (1677)]

THACKERAY, William Makepeace (1811–1863)
It is impossible, in our condition of Society, not to be sometimes a Snob.

[*The Book of Snobs* (1848)]

THATCHER, Margaret (1925–)
There is no such thing as society.

There are individual men and women and there are families.

[Attr.]

THOREAU, Henry (1817–1862)
Wherever a man goes, men will pursue him and paw him with their dirty institutions, and, if they can, constrain him to belong to their desperate oddfellow society.

[*Walden* (1854)]

WILDE, Oscar (1854–1900)
[Of society]
To be in it is merely a bore. But to be out of it simply a tragedy.

[*A Woman of No Importance* (1893)]

WILSON, Harold (1916–1995)
[Referring to Christine Keeler]
There is something utterly nauseating about a system of society which pays a harlot 25 times as much as it pays its Prime Minister, 250 times as much as it pays its Members of Parliament, and 500 times as much as it pays some of its ministers of religion.

[Speech, 1963]

See CAPITALISM

SOLITUDE

BACON, Francis (1561–1626)
It had been hard for him that spake it to have put more truth and untruth together, in a few words, than in that speech: 'Whosoever is delighted in solitude is either a wild beast, or a god.'

['Of Friendship'] (1625)]

COWPER, William (1731–1800)
I praise the Frenchman, his remark was shrewd –
How sweet, how passing sweet, is solitude!
But grant me still a friend in my retreat,
Whom I may whisper – solitude is sweet.

['Retirement' (1782)]

ECO, Umberto (1932–)
Solitude is a kind of freedom.

[*The Observer Review*, 1995]

GIBBON, Edward (1737–1794)
I was never less alone than when by myself.

[*Memoirs of My Life and Writings* (1796)]

MANN, Thomas (1875–1955)
Einsamkeit zeitigt das Originale, das gewagt und befremdend Schöne, das Gedicht. Einsamkeit zeitigt aber auch das Verkehrte, das Unverhältnismässige, das Absurde und Unerlaubte.
Solitude gives rise to what is original, to what is daringly and displeasingly beautiful, to poetry. Solitude however also gives rise to what is wrong, excessive, absurd and forbidden.

[*Death in Venice* (1912)]

MONTAIGNE, Michel de (1533–1592)
Il se faut réserver une arrière boutique toute nôtre, toute franche, en laquelle nous établissons notre vraie liberté et principale retraite et solitude.
We should keep for ourselves a little back shop, all our own, untouched by others, in which we establish our true freedom and chief place of seclusion and solitude.

[*Essais* (1580)]

SASSOON, Siegfried (1886–1967)
Alone ... The word is life endured and known.
It is the stillness where our spirits walk
And all but inmost faith is overthrown.

[*The Heart's Journey* (1928)]

SCHOPENHAUER, Arthur (1788–1860)
Einsamkeit ist das Los aller hervorragenden Geister: sie werden solche bisweilen beseufzen; aber stets sie als das kleinere von zwei Übeln erwählen.
Solitude is the fate of all outstanding minds: it will at times be deplored; but it will always be chosen as the lesser of two evils.

['Aphorisms for Wisdom' (1851)]

THE SOUL

SCHREINER, Olive (1855–1920)
She thought of the narrowness of the limits within which a human soul may speak and be understood by its nearest of mental kin, of how soon it reaches that solitary land of the individual experience in which no fellow footfall is ever heard.

[*The Story of an African Farm* (1884)]

THOREAU, Henry (1817–1862)
I never found the companion that was so companionable as solitude.

[*Walden* (1854)]

See LONELINESS

THE SOUL

THE BIBLE (King James Version)
What is a man profited, if he shall gain the whole world, and lose his own soul?

[*Matthew*, 16:26]

CRABBE, George (1754–1832)
It is the soul that sees; the outward eyes
Present the object, but the mind descries.

[*The Lover's Journey*]

DICKINSON, Emily (1830–1886)
The Soul selects her own Society –
Then – shuts the Door –
To her divine Majority –
Present no more ...
I've known her- from an ample nation -
Choose One –
Then – close the Valves of her attention –
Like Stone.

['The Soul selects her own Society' (c. 1862)]

EMERSON, Ralph Waldo (1803–1882)
When divine souls appear men are compelled by their own self-respect to distinguish them.

[*Journals*]

HADRIAN (AD 76–138)
Ah fleeting Spirit! wand'ring Fire,
That long hast warm'd my tender Breast,
Must thou no more this Frame inspire?
No more a pleasing, cheerful Guest?

['Ad Animam Suam', trans. Pope]

ST JOHN OF THE CROSS (1542–1591)
Keep your heart in peace; let nothing in this world disturb it: all things have an end. In all circumstances, however hard they may be, we should rejoice rather than be cast down, that we may not lose the greatest good, the peace and tranquillity of our soul.

[Attr.]

JUVENAL (c. 60–130)
Mors sola fatetur
Quantula sint hominum corpuscula.
Death only this mysterious truth unfolds,
The mighty soul, how small a body holds.

[*Satires*; trans. Dryden]

KEATS, John (1795–1821)
A man should have the fine point of his soul taken off to become fit for this world.

[Letter to J.H. Reynolds, 1817]

LUCRETIUS (c. 95–55 BC)
Nil igitur mors est ad nos neque pertinet hilum,
Quandoquidem natura animi mortalis habetur.
What has this bugbear death to frighten man
If souls can die as well as bodies can?

[*De Rerum Natura*; trans. Dryden]

MCAULEY, James (1917–1976)
The soul must feed on something for its dreams,
In those brick suburbs, and there wasn't much:
It can make do with little, so it seems.

['Wisteria' (1971)]

MEREDITH, George (1828–1909)
There is nothing the body suffers the soul may not profit by.

[*Modern Love* (1862)]

SHELLEY, Percy Bysshe (1792–1822)
The soul of man, like unextinguished
    fire,
Yet burns towards heaven with fierce
    reproach.
            [*Prometheus Unbound* (1820)]

SMITH, Logan Pearsall (1865–1946)
Most people sell their souls, and live
with a good conscience on the
proceeds.
            [*Afterthoughts* (1931)]

STERNE, Laurence (1713–1768)
I am positive I have a soul; nor can all
the books with which materialists
have pestered the world ever convince
me to the contrary.
            [*A Sentimental Journey* (1768)]

WEBSTER, John (c. 1580–c. 1625)
My soul, like to a ship in a black
    storm,
Is driven, I know not whither.
            [*The White Devil* (1612)]

WORDSWORTH, William (1770–1850)
Our birth is but a sleep and a
    forgetting.
The Soul that rises with us, our life's
    Star,
Hath had elsewhere its setting,
And cometh from afar.
        ['Ode: Intimations of Immortality' (1807)]

See IMMORTALITY

SPACE

ADDISON, Joseph (1672–1719)
The spacious firmament on high,
With all the blue ethereal sky,
And spangled heavens, a shining
    frame,
Their great Original proclaim.
            [*The Spectator*, 1712]

ALFONSO X (1221–1284)
[On the Ptolemaic system of astron-
omy]
If the Lord Almighty had consulted me
before embarking upon Creation, I
should have recommended something
simpler.
            [Attr.]

ARMSTRONG, Neil (1930–)
[On stepping on to the moon]
That's one small step for a man, one
giant leap for mankind.
            [*New York Times*, 1969)]

THE BIBLE (King James Version)
The heavens declare the glory of God;
and the firmament sheweth his
handywork.
            [*Psalms*, 19:1]

BYRON, Lord (1788–1824)
Ye stars! which are the poetry of
heaven!
            [*Childe Harold's Pilgrimage* (1818)]

CHESTERTON, G.K. (1874–1936)
The cosmos is about the smallest hole
that a man can hide his head in.
            [*Orthodoxy* (1908)]

DE VRIES, Peter (1910–)
Anyone informed that the universe is
expanding and contracting in
pulsations of eighty billion years has a
right to ask, 'What's in it for me?'
            [*The Glory of the Hummingbird* (1974)]

FROST, Robert (1874–1963)
They cannot scare me with their
    empty spaces
Between stars – on stars where no
    human race is.
I have it in me so much nearer home
To scare myself with my own desert
    places.
            ['Desert Places' (1936)]

**FULLER, Richard Buckminster
(1895–1983)**
I am a passenger on the spaceship,
Earth.
            [*Operating Manual for Spaceship Earth* (1969)]

GALILEO GALILEI (1564–1642)
[Remark made after he was forced to
withdraw his assertion that the Earth
moved round the Sun]
Eppur si muove.
But it does move.
            [Attr., 1632]

HOLMES, Rev. John H. (1879–1964)
This universe is not hostile, nor yet is
it friendly. It is simply indifferent.
[*A Sensible Man's View of Religion* (1932)]

HOPKINS, Gerard Manley (1844–1889)
Look at the stars! look, look up at the
skies!
Oh look at all the fire-folk sitting in
the air!
The bright boroughs, the circle-citadels
there!
['The Starlight Night' (1877)]

SHAKESPEARE, William (1564–1616)
Look how the floor of heaven
Is thick inlaid with patines of bright
gold;
There's not the smallest orb which
thou behold'st
But in his motion like an angel sings,
Still quiring to the young-ey'd
cherubins.
[*The Merchant of Venice*, V.i]

SIDNEY, Sir Philip (1554–1586)
With how sad steps O Moone thou
clim'st the skyes,
How silently, and with how meane a
face,
What may it be, that even in heavenly
place,
That busie Archer his sharpe Arrowes
tryes?
[*Astrophel and Stella* (1591)]

VIDAL, Gore (1925–)
The astronauts! ... Rotarians in outer
space.
[*Two Sisters* (1970)]

VIRGIL (70–19 BC)
*Nosque ubi primus equis Oriens adflavit
anhelis,*
Illic sera rubens accendit lumina Vesper.
And when the rising sun has first
breathed on us with his panting
horses, over there the glowing
evening-star is lighting his late lamps.
[*Georgics*]

YOUNG, Andrew (1885–1971)
But moon nor star-untidy sky

Could catch my eye as that star's eye;
For still I looked on that same star,
That fitful, fiery Lucifer,
Watching with mind as quiet as moss
Its light nailed to a burning cross.
['The Evening Star' (1922)]

SPORT AND GAMES

ALI, Muhammad (1942–)
Float like a butterfly, sting like a bee.
[Catchphrase]

ALLISON, Malcolm (1927–)
Professional football is no longer a
game. It's a war. And it brings out the
same primitive instincts that go back
thousands of years.
[*The Observer*, 1973]

ANONYMOUS
Say it ain't so, Joe. Please say it ain't
so.
[Plea to 'Shoeless' Joe Jackson, when he and
seven other US baseball players were banned
for life after being found guilty of throwing
the World Series in 1920]

Shooting is a popular sport in the
countryside ... Unlike many other
countries, the outstanding
characteristic of the sport has been
that it is not confined to any one class.
[The Northern Ireland Tourist Board, 1969]

They'll be dancing in the streets of
Raith tonight.
[Falsely attributed to both Kenneth
Wolstenholme and David Coleman, this
reference to Raith Rovers fans dancing in a
non-existent Scottish town – the team plays
in Kirkcaldy – almost certainly originated in a
BBC radio broadcast from London in 1963,
after Raith Rovers defeated Aberdeen in a
Scottish Cup tie]

'Well, what sort of sport has Lord —
had?'
'Oh, the young Sahib shot divinely, but
God was very merciful to the birds.'
[In Russell, *Collections and Recollections*
(1898)]

ARCHER, Mark
In the case of almost every sport one can think of, from tennis to billiards, golf to skittles, it was royalty or the aristocracy who originally developed, codified and popularised the sport, after which it was taken up by the lower classes.

[*The Spectator*, 1996]

BALL, Alan (1943–)
[After making a substitution which enabled his team to win a key relegation battle]
I thought if we were going to lose it, we might as well lose it by trying to win it.

[*Daily Mail*, 1996]

BARBARITO, Luigi (1922–)
[Papal emissary, commenting on a sponsored snooker competition at a convent]
Playing snooker gives you firm hands and helps to build up character. It is the ideal recreation for dedicated nuns.

[*The Daily Telegraph*, 1989]

BARNES, Simon (1951–)
Sport is something that does not matter, but is performed as if it did. In that contradiction lies its beauty.

[*The Spectator*, 1996]

BELASCO, David (1853–1931)
Boxing is showbusiness with blood.

[Attr., 1915]

BENNETT, Alan (1934–)
If you think squash is a competitive activity, try flower arrangement.

[*Talking Heads* (1988)]

BERNHARDT, Sarah (1844–1923)
[Remark while watching a game of football]
I do love cricket – it's so very English.

[Attr.]

BLAINEY, Geoffrey Norman (1930–)
We forget that the nineteenth century often turned work into sport. We, in contrast, often turn sport into work.

[*Victorian Historical Journal*, 1978]

BROWN, Rita Mae (1944–)
Sport strips away personality, letting the white bone of character shine through.

[*Sudden Death* (1983)]

BYRON, H.J. 1834–1884)
Life's too short for chess.

[*Our Boys*]

CANTERBURY, Tom
The trouble with referees is that they just don't care which side wins.

[*The Guardian*, 1980]

COLEMAN, David (1926–)
That's the fastest time ever run – but it's not as fast as the world record.

[In Fantoni, *Private Eye's Colemanballs (3)* (1986)]

CONNORS, Jimmy (1952–)
New Yorkers love it when you spill your guts out there. Spill your guts at Wimbledon and they make you stop and clean it up.

[*The Guardian*, 1984]

COWPER, William (1731–1800)
[Of hunting]
Detested sport,
That owes its pleasures to another's pain.

[*The Task* (1785)]

CROOKS, Garth (1958–)
Football is football; if that weren't the case, it wouldn't be the game it is.

[In Fantoni, *Private Eye's Colemanballs (2)* (1984)]

DAVIS, Steve (1957–)
Sport is cut and dried. You always know when you succeed ... You are not an actor: you don't wonder 'did my performance go down all right?' You've lost.

[Remark]

DEMPSEY, Jack (1895–1983)
Kill the other guy before he kills you.

[Motto]

DISRAELI, Benjamin (1804–1881)
Yesterday at the racket court, sitting in the gallery among strangers, the ball ... fell at my feet. I picked it up, and observing a young rifleman excessively stiff, I humbly requested him to forward its passage into the court, as I really had never thrown a ball in my life.

[Letter to his father]

DUFFY, Jim
[Of goalkeeper Andy Murdoch]
He has an answerphone installed on his six-yard line and the message says: 'Sorry, I'm not in just now, but if you'd like to leave the ball in the back of the net, I'll get back to you as soon as I can.'

[In *Umbro Book of Football Quotations* (1993)]

EUBANK, Chris (1966–)
Any boxer who says he loves boxing is either a liar or a fool. I'm not looking for glory ... I'm looking for money. I'm looking for readies.

[*The Times*, 1993]

FITZSIMMONS, Robert (1862–1917)
[Remark before a boxing match, 1900]
The bigger they come, the harder they fall.

[Attr.]

FORD, Henry (1863–1947)
Exercise is bunk. If you are healthy, you don't need it: if you are sick, you shouldn't take it.

[Attr.]

FOX, Dixon Ryan
I listened to a football coach who spoke straight from the shoulder – at least I could detect no higher origin in anything he said.

[Attr.]

GASCOIGNE, Paul (1967–)
I get on a train and sit in second class and people think, 'tight bastard.

Money he's got and he sits in second class.' So I think, — them' and I go in first class and then they say, 'look at that — ing flash bastard in first class'.

[*The Herald*, 1995]

GRACE, W.G. (1848–1915)
[Refusing to leave the crease after being bowled first ball in front of a large crowd]
They came to see me bat not to see you bowl.

[Attr.]

GREAVES, Jimmy (1940–)
The only thing that Norwich didn't get was the goal that they finally got.

[In Fantoni, *Private Eye's Colemanballs (2)* (1984)]

HEMINGWAY, Ernest (1898–1961)
Bullfighting is the only art in which the artist is in danger of death and in which the degree of brilliance in the performance is left to the fighter's honour.

[*Death in the Afternoon* (1932)]

HUISTRA, Peter (1967–)
Soccer in Japan is interesting, in Glasgow it's a matter of life and death.

[*Daily Mail*, 1996]

INGHAM, Bernard (1932–)
Blood sport is brought to its ultimate refinement in the gossip columns.

[Remark, 1986]

JACOBS, Joe (1896–1940)
[Remark made after Max Schmeling, whom he managed, lost his boxing title to Jack Sharkey in 1932]
We was robbed!

[Attr.]

JOHNSON, Samuel (1709–1784)
I am sorry I have not learned to play at cards. It is very useful in life: it generates kindness and consolidates society.

[In Boswell, *Journal of a Tour to the Hebrides* (1785)]

It is very strange, and very melancholy, that the paucity of human pleasures

SPORT AND GAMES

should persuade us ever to call hunting one of them.

[In Piozzi, *Anecdotes of the Late Samuel Johnson* (1786)]

Fly fishing may be a very pleasant amusement; but angling or float fishing I can only compare to a stick and a string, with a worm at one end and a fool at the other.

[Attr. in Hawker, *Instructions to Young Sportsmen* (1859)]

KING, Billie-Jean (1943–)
It's really impossible for athletes to grow up. As long as you're playing, no one will let you. On the one hand, you're a child, still playing a game ... But on the other hand, you're a superhuman hero that everyone dreams of being. No wonder we have such a hard time understanding who we are.

[*Billie-Jean* (1982)]

KINGLAKE, Edward (1864–1935)
Every Australian worships the Goddess of Sport with profound adoration, and there is no nation in the world which treats itself to so many holidays.

[*The Australian at Home*]

LAMB, Charles (1775–1834)
Man is a gaming animal. He must always be trying to get the better in something or other.

['Mrs Battle's Opinions on Whist' (1823)]

LOUIS, Joe (1914–1981)
[Referring to the speed of an opponent, Billy Conn]
He can run, but he can't hide.

[Attr.]

MCGUIGAN, Barry (1961–)
The gladiators and champions through the ages confirm quite clearly that aggressive competition is part of the human makeup. For the sport of professional boxing to be banned would be the most terrible error.

[*The Observer*, 1994]

MOURIE, Graham (1952–)
Nobody ever beats Wales at rugby, they just score more points.

[In Keating, *Caught by Keating*]

MUIR, Edwin (1887–1959)
[On hunting trophies]
To find these abominations on the walls of Highland hotels, among people of such delicacy in other things, is peculiarly revolting.

[*Scottish Journey*]

O'REILLY, Tony (1936–)
[Commenting on the voice of Winston McCarthy, the noted rugby commentator]
The love call of two pieces of sandpaper.

[*New Zealand Listener*, 1984]

O'ROURKE, P.J. (1947–)
The sport of skiing consists of wearing three thousand dollars' worth of clothes and equipment and driving two hundred miles in the snow in order to stand around at a bar and get drunk.

[*Modern Manners* (1984)]

ORWELL, George (1903–1950)
Serious sport has nothing to do with fair play. It is bound up with hatred, jealousy, boastfulness, disregard for all rules and sadistic pleasure in witnessing violence; in other words it is war minus the shooting.

[*Shooting an Elephant* (1950)]

OVETT, Steve (1955–)
There is no way sport is so important that it can be allowed to damage the rest of your life.

[Remark at the Olympic Games, 1984]

PALMER, Arnold (1929–)
[Replying to an onlooker who observed that he was playing so well he must have plenty of luck on his side]
The more I practise the luckier I get.

[Attr.]

RICE, Grantland (1880–1954)
For when the One Great Scorer comes
  to mark against your name,
He marks – not that you won or lost –
but how you played the Game.
['Alumnus Football' (1941)]

SEAL, Christopher
Hunting people tend to be churchgoers
on a higher level than ordinary folk.
One has a religious experience in the
field.
[The Times, 1993]

SHANKLY, Bill (1914–1981)
Some people think football is a matter
of life and death. I don't like that attitude. I can assure them it is much
more serious than that.
[Remark on BBC TV, 1981]

SHAW, George Bernard (1856–1950)
[An R.S.V.P. to an invitation to attend
an athletic meeting at the Wangamui
Domain]
I take athletic competitive sports very
seriously indeed ... as they seem to
produce more bad feeling, bad
manners and international hatred than
any other popular movement.
[Auckland Star, 1934]

SNAGGE, John (1904–1996)
I don't know who's ahead – it's either
Oxford or Cambridge.
[Radio commentary on the Boat Race, 1949]

**STEVENSON, Robert Louis
(1850–1894)**
The harmless art of knucklebones has
seen the fall of the Roman Empire and
the rise of the United States.
[Across the Plains (1892)]

STUBBES, Philip (c. 1555–1610)
Football ... causeth fighting, brawling,
contention, quarrel picking, murder,
homicide and great effusion of blood,
as daily experience teacheth.
[Anatomy of Abuses (1583)]

VIERA, Ondina
Other nations have history. We have
football.
[The Spectator, 1996]

WALTON, Izaak (1593–1683)
As no man is born an artist, so no
man is born an angler.
[The Compleat Angler (1653)]

Sir Henry Wotton ... was also a most
dear lover, and a frequent practiser of
the art of angling; of which he would
say, 'it was an employment for his idle
time, which was then not idly spent ...
a rest to his mind, a cheerer of his
spirits, a diverter of sadness, a calmer
of unquiet thoughts, a moderator of
passions, a procurer of contentedness;
and that it begat habits of peace and
patience in those that professed and
practised it.'
[The Compleat Angler (1653)]

WILDE, Oscar (1854–1900)
The English country gentleman galloping after a fox – the unspeakable in
full pursuit of the uneatable.
[A Woman of No Importance (1893)]

WODEHOUSE, P.G. (1881–1975)
The least thing upset him on the links.
He missed short putts because of the
uproar of the butterflies in the ad-
joining meadows.
[The Clicking of Cuthbert (1922)]

THE STATE

ARISTOTLE (384–322 BC)
Blessed is the state in which those in
power have moderate and sufficient
means since where some are immoderately wealthy and others have
nothing, the result will be extreme
democracy or absolute oligarchy, or a
tyranny may result from either of these
extremes.
[Politics, IV]

BOUTROS-GHALI, Boutros (1922–)
The time of absolute and exclusive
national sovereignty has passed.
[Scotland on Sunday, 1992]

BURKE, Edmund (1729–1797)
A state without the means of some
change is without the means of its

conservation.

[*Reflections on the Revolution in France* (1790)]

CROMWELL, Oliver (1599–1658)
The State, in choosing men to serve it, takes no notice of their opinions. If they be willing faithfully to serve it, that satisfies.

[Said before the Battle of Marston Moor, 1644]

INGE, William Ralph (1860–1954)
The nations which have put mankind and posterity most in their debt have been small states – Israel, Athens, Florence, Elizabethan England.

[*Outspoken Essays: Second Series* (1922)]

LANDOR, Walter Savage (1775–1864)
States, like men, have their growth, their manhood, their decrepitude, their decay.

[*Imaginary Conversations* (1876)]

LENIN, V.I. (1870–1924)
So long as the state exists there is no freedom. When there is freedom there will be no state.

[*The State and Revolution* (1917)]

LOUIS XIV (1638–1715)
L'État c'est moi.
I am the State.

[Attr.]

MILL, John Stuart (1806–1873)
The worth of a State, in the long run, is the worth of the individuals composing it.

[*On Liberty* (1859)]

A State which dwarfs its men, in order that they may be more docile instruments in its hands even for beneficial purposes – will find that with small men no great thing can really be accomplished.

[*On Liberty* (1859)]

PLATO (c. 429–347 BC)
It is the rulers of the state, if anybody, who may lie in dealing with citizens or enemies, for reasons of state.

[*Republic*]

RUSKIN, John (1819–1900)
I hold it for indisputable, that the first duty of a State is to see that every child born therein shall be well housed, clothed, fed and educated, till it attain years of discretion.

[*Time and Tide by Weare and Tyne* (1867)]

SHELLEY, Percy Bysshe (1792–1822)
The rich have become richer, and the poor have become poorer; and the vessel of the state is driven between the Scylla and Charybdis of anarchy and despotism.

[*A Defence of Poetry* (1821)]

STALIN, Joseph (1879–1953)
The state is a machine in the hands of the ruling class for suppressing the resistance of its class enemies.

[*Foundations of Leninism* (1924)]

STYLE

ARNOLD, Matthew (1822–1888)
People think that I can teach them style. What stuff it all is! Have something to say, and say it as clearly as you can. That is the only secret of style.

[In Russell, *Collections and Recollections* (1898)]

BUFFON, Comte de (1707–1788)
Ces choses sont hors de l'homme, le style est l'homme même.
These things [subject matter] are external to the man; style is the essence of man.

['Discours sur le Style' (1753)]

CAMUS, Albert (1913–1960)
Le style, comme la popeline, dissimule trop souvent de l'eczéma.
Style, like sheer silk, too often hides eczema.

[*The Fall* (1956)]

RENARD, Jules (1864–1910)
Un mauvais style, c'est une pensée imparfaite.
Poor style reflects imperfect thought.

[*Journal*, 1898]

SWIFT, Jonathan (1667–1745)
Proper words in proper places, make the true definition of a style.

[*Letter to a Young Gentleman Lately Entered Into Holy Orders* (1720)]

WESLEY, Samuel (1662–1735)
Style is the dress of thought; a modest dress,
Neat, but not gaudy, will true critics please.

['An Epistle to a Friend concerning Poetry' (1700)]

WILDE, Oscar (1854–1900)
In matters of grave importance, style, not sincerity, is the vital thing.

[*The Importance of Being Earnest* (1895)]

SUCCESS

BROOKNER, Anita (1928–)
[On the myth of the tortoise and the hare]
In real life, of course, it is the hare who wins. Every time. Look around you. And in any case it is my contention that Aesop was writing for the tortoise market ... Hares have no time to read. They are too busy winning the game.

[*Hotel du Lac* (1984)]

BROWNING, Robert (1812–1889)
A minute's success pays the failure of years.

['Apollo and the Fates' (1887)]

BURKE, Edmund (1729–1797)
The only infallible criterion of wisdom to vulgar minds – success.

[*Letter to a Member of the National Assembly* (1791)]

CHURCHILL, Charles (1731–1764)
Where he falls short, 'tis Nature's fault alone;
Where he succeeds, the merit's all his own.

[*The Rosciad* (1761)]

DEWAR, Lord (1864–1930)
The road to success is filled with

women pushing their husbands along.

[Epigram]

DICKINSON, Emily (1830–1886)
Success is counted sweetest
By those who ne'er succeed.
To comprehend a nectar
Requires sorest need.

['Success is counted sweetest' (c. 1859)]

JAMES, William (1842–1910)
The moral flabbiness born of the exclusive worship of the bitch-goddess *success*. That – with the squalid cash interpretation put on the word success – is our national disease.

[Letter to H.G. Wells, 1906]

LA ROCHEFOUCAULD, Duc de (1613–1680)
Pour s'établir dans le monde, on fait tout ce que l'on peut pour y paraître établi.
To succeed in the world we do all we can to appear successful.

[*Maximes* (1678)]

MEIR, Golda (1898–1978)
I can honestly say that I was never affected by the question of the success of an undertaking. If I felt it was the right thing to do, I was for it regardless of the possible outcome.

[In Syrkin, *Golda Meir: Woman with a Cause* (1964)]

RENOIR, Jean (1894–1979)
Est-il possible de réussir sans trahir?
Is it possible to succeed without betrayal?

[*My Life and My Films* (1974)]

VIDAL, Gore (1925–)
It is not enough to succeed. Others must fail.

[In Irvine, *Antipanegyric for Tom Driberg* (1976)]

VIRGIL (70–19 BC)
Hos successus alit: possunt, quia posse videntur.
To these success gives heart: they can because they think they can.

[*Aeneid*]

SUFFERING

ANONYMOUS
Three things one does not recover
  from –
oppression that knows the backing of
  brute force,
poverty that knows the destitution of
  one's home,
and being deprived of children.
[Somali poem]

AUDEN, W.H. (1907–1973)
About suffering they were never
  wrong,
The Old Masters: how well they
  understood
Its human position; how it takes place
While someone else is eating or
  opening a window or just walking
  dully along ...

They never forgot
That even the dreadful martyrdom
  must run its course
Anyhow in a corner, some untidy spot
Where the dogs go on with their doggy
  life and the torturer's horse
Scratches its innocent behind on a
  tree.
['Musée des Beaux Arts']

AUSTEN, Jane (1775–1817)
One does not love a place the less for
having suffered in it, unless it has all
been suffering, nothing but suffering.
[Persuasion (1818)]

BACON, Francis (1561–1626)
It is a miserable state of mind to have
few things to desire and many things
to fear.
['Of Empire' (1625)]

BOETHIUS (c. 475–524)
Nihil est miserum nisi cum putes;
contraque beata sors omnis est
aequanimitate tolerantis.
Nothing is miserable unless you think
it so; conversely, every lot is happy to
one who is content with it.
[De Consolatione Philosophiae (c. 524)]

BONO, Edward de (1933–)
Unhappiness is best defined as the
difference between our talents and our
expectations.
[The Observer, 1977]

**BROWNING, Elizabeth Barrett
(1806–1861)**
For frequent tears have run
The colours from my life.
[Sonnets from the Portuguese (1850)]

CARLYLE, Thomas (1795–1881)
Man's Unhappiness, as I construe,
comes of his Greatness; it is because
there is an Infinite in him, which with
all his cunning he cannot quite bury
under the Finite.
[Sartor Resartus (1834)]

CHAUCER, Geoffrey (c. 1340–1400)
For of fortunes sharpe adversitee
The worste kynde of infortune is this,
A man to han ben in prosperitee,
And it remembren, whan it passed is.
[Troilus and Criseyde]

CORNEILLE, Pierre (1606–1684)
A raconter ses maux, souvent on les
soulage.
Telling one's sorrows often brings
comfort.
[Polyeucte (1643)]

COWPER, William (1731–1800)
But misery still delights to trace
Its semblance in another's case.
['The Castaway' (1799)]

DICKINSON, Emily (1830–1886)
After great pain, a formal feeling
  comes –
The Nerves sit ceremonious, like
  Tombs –
The stiff Heart questions was it He,
  that bore,
And Yesterday, or Centuries before? ...

This is the Hour of Lead –
Remembered, if outlived,
As Freezing persons, recollect the
  Snow –

First – Chill – then Stupor – then the
letting go.

['After great pain, a formal feeling comes'
(c. 1862)]

GAY, John (1685–1732)
A moment of time may make us
unhappy forever.

[*The Beggar's Opera* (1728)]

HAZLITT, William (1778–1830)
The least pain in our little finger gives
us more concern and uneasiness, than
the destruction of millions of our
fellow-beings.

[*Edinburgh Review*, 1829]

HEMINGWAY, Ernest (1898–1961)
The world breaks everyone and
afterward many are strong at the
broken places.

[*A Farewell to Arms* (1929)]

HOGG, James (1770–1835)
How often does the evening cup of joy
lead to sorrow in the morning!

[Attr.]

HOPKINS, Gerard Manley (1844–1889)
No worst, there is none. Pitched past
  pitch of grief,
More pangs will, schooled at
  forepangs, wilder wring.
Comforter, where, where is your
  comforting? ...

O the mind, mind has mountains; cliffs
  of fall
Frightful, sheer, no-man-fathomed ...

Here! creep,
Wretch, under a comfort serves in a
  whirlwind: all
Life death does end and each day dies
  with sleep.

['No Worst, there is None' (1885)]

HUGO, Victor (1802–1885)
Souffrons, mais souffrons sur les cimes.
Let us suffer if we must, but let us
suffer on the heights.

[*Contemplations* (1856)]

JOHNSON, Samuel (1709–1784)
I shall long to see the miseries of the
world, since the sight of them is
necessary to happiness.

[*Rasselas* (1759)]

There is no wisdom in useless and
hopeless sorrow.

[Letter to Mrs Thrale, 1781]

Depend upon it that if a man talks of
his misfortunes there is something in
them that is not disagreeable to him;
for where there is nothing but pure
misery there never is any recourse to
the mention of it.

[In Boswell, *The Life of Samuel Johnson*
(1791)]

KEATS, John (1795–1821)
Is there another Life? Shall I awake
and find all this a dream? There must
be, we cannot be created for this sort
of suffering.

[Letter to Charles Brown, 1820]

KEMPIS, Thomas à (c. 1380–1471)
Si libenter crucem portas portabit te.
If you bear the cross willingly, it will
bear you.

[*De Imitatione Christi* (1892 ed.)]

**LA ROCHEFOUCAULD, Duc de
(1613–1680)**
*On n'est jamais si malheureux qu'on
croit, ni si heureux qu'on espère.*
One is never as unhappy as one
thinks, or as happy as one hopes to
be.

[*Maximes* (1664)]

*Nous avons tous assez de force pour
supporter les maux d'autrui.*
We are all strong enough to bear the
sufferings of others.

[*Maximes* (1678)]

LOWELL, James Russell (1819–1891)
The misfortunes hardest to bear are
those which never come.

['Democracy' (1887)]

MILLER, Arthur (1915–)
Years ago a person, he was unhappy,
didn't know what to do with himself –
he'd go to church, start a revolution –
something. Today you're unhappy?
Can't figure it out? What is the salvation? Go shopping.

[*The Price* (1968)]

MONTAIGNE, Michel de (1533–1592)
*Qui craint de souffrir, il souffre déjà de
ce qu'il craint.*
A man who fears suffering is already
suffering from what he fears.

[*Essais* (1580)]

NEAVES, Lord (1800–1876)
We can't for a certainty tell
What mirth may molest us on Monday;
But, at least, to begin the week well,
Let us all be unhappy on Sunday.

[*Songs and Verses*]

NIETZSCHE, Friedrich (1844–1900)
*Was eigentlich gegen das Leiden empört,
ist nicht das Leiden an sich, sondern das
Sinnlose des Leidens.*
What actually fills you with indignation
as regards suffering is not suffering in
itself but the pointlessness of suffering.

[*On the Genealogy of Morals* (1881)]

PASCAL, Blaise (1623–1662)
*Tout le malheur des hommes vient
d'une seule chose, qui est de ne savoir
pas demeurer en repos dans une
chambre.*
All the troubles of men are caused by
one single thing, which is their
inability to stay quietly in a room.

[*Pensées* (1670)]

SAKI (1870–1916)
He's simply got the instinct for being
unhappy highly developed.

[*The Chronicles of Clovis* (1911)]

SHAKESPEARE, William (1564–1616)
When sorrows come, they come not
    single spies,
But in battalions.

[*Hamlet*, IV.v]

In sooth I know not why I am so sad.
It wearies me; you say it wearies you;
But how I caught it, found it, or came
    by it,
What stuff 'tis made of, whereof it is
    born,
I am to learn;
And such a want-wit sadness makes
    of me
That I have much ado to know myself.

[*The Merchant of Venice*, I.i]

Misery acquaints a man with strange
bedfellows.

[*The Tempest*, II.ii]

SHAW, George Bernard (1856–1950)
The secret of being miserable is to
have leisure to bother about whether
you are happy or not.

[*Misalliance* (1914)]

TOLSTOY, Leo (1828–1910)
Pure and complete sorrow is just as
impossible as pure and complete joy.

[*War and Peace* (1869)]

VERLAINE, Paul (1844–1896)
*Il pleure dans mon coeur
Comme il pleut sur la ville.*
Tears fall in my heart as rain falls on
the city.

[*Romances sans paroles* (1874)]

WHITTIER, John Greenleaf (1807–1892)
For all sad words of tongue or pen,
The saddest are these: 'It might have
been!'

['Maud Muller' (1854)]

WILDE, Oscar (1854–1900)
Where there is sorrow, there is holy
ground.

[*De Profundis* (1897)]

SUICIDE

BUDGELL, Eustace (1686–1737)
[Lines found on his desk after his
suicide]
What Cato did, and Addison approved
Cannot be wrong.

[Attr.]

GREER, Germaine (1939–)
Suicide is an act of narcissistic manipulation and deep hostility.

[*The Observer Review*, 1995]

IBSEN, Henrik (1828–1906)
[Judge Brack, on Hedda Gabler's suicide]
People don't do such things!

[*Hedda Gabler* (1890)]

NIETZSCHE, Friedrich (1844–1900)
Der Gedanke an den Selbstmord ist ein starkes Trostmittel: mit ihm kommt man gut über manche böse Nacht hinweg.
The thought of suicide is a great comfort: it's a good way of getting through many a bad night.

[*Beyond Good and Evil* (1886)]

PARKER, Dorothy (1893–1967)
Razors pain you;
Rivers are damp;
Acids stain you;
And drugs cause cramp.
Guns aren't lawful;
Nooses give;
Gas smells awful;
You might as well live.

['Résumé' (1937)]

PARKES, Sir Henry (1815–1896)
[On William Nicholas Willis]
Ho! the honourable member for Bourke, who is believed to have committed every crime in the calendar, – except the one we could so easily have forgiven him – suicide.

[In Wannan, *With Malice Aforethought*]

RHYS, Jean (1894–1979)
Next week, or next month, or next year I'll kill myself. But I might as well last out my month's rent, which has been paid up, and my credit for breakfast in the morning.

[*Good Morning, Midnight* (1939)]

SANDERS, George (1906–1972)
Dear World, I am leaving you because I am bored. I am leaving you with your worries. Good luck.

[Suicide note]

TENNYSON, Alfred, Lord (1809–1892)
Nor at all can tell
Whether I mean this day to end
    myself,
Or lend an ear to Plato where he says,
That men like soldiers may not quit
    the post
Allotted by the Gods.

['Lucretius' (1868)]

SUPERSTITION

AUBREY, John (1626–1697)
Anno 1670, not far from Cirencester, was an apparition; being demanded whether a good spirit or a bad? returned no answer, but disappeared with a curious perfume and most melodious twang. Mr W. Lilly believes it was a fairy.

[*Miscellanies* (1696)]

BACON, Francis (1561–1626)
There is a superstition in avoiding superstition.

['Of Superstition' (1625)]

BARRIE, Sir J.M. (1860–1937)
Every time a child says 'I don't believe in fairies,' there is a little fairy somewhere that falls down dead.

[*Peter Pan* (1904)]

BOHR, Niels (1885–1962)
[Explaining why he had a horseshoe on his wall]
Of course I don't believe in it. But I understand that it brings you luck whether you believe in it or not.

[Attr.]

BROWNE, Sir Thomas (1605–1682)
For my part, I have ever believed, and do now know, that there are witches.

[*Religio Medici* (1643)]

BURKE, Edmund (1729–1797)
Superstition is the religion of feeble minds.

[*Reflections on the Revolution in France* (1790)]

GOETHE (1749–1832)
Der Aberglaube ist die Poesie des Lebens.

Superstition is the poetry of life.
['Literature and Language' (1823)]

HUME, David (1711–1776)
We soon learn that there is nothing
mysterious or supernatural in the case,
but that all proceeds from the usual
propensity of mankind towards the
marvellous, and that, though this
inclination may at intervals receive a
check from sense and learning, it can
never be thoroughly extirpated from
human nature.
['Of Miracles' (1748)]

Opposing one species of superstition
to another, set them a quarrelling;
while we ourselves, during their fury
and contention, happily make our
escape into the calm, though obscure,
regions of philosophy.
[*The Natural History of Religion* (1757)]

JOHNSON, Samuel (1709–1784)
[Of ghosts]
All argument is against it; but all belief
is for it.
[In Boswell, *The Life of Samuel Johnson*
(1791)]

TASTE

ADAMS, Henry (1838–1918)
Every one carries his own inch-rule of taste, and amuses himself by applying it, triumphantly, wherever he travels.
[*The Education of Henry Adams* (1918)]

BENNETT, Arnold (1867–1931)
Good taste is better than bad taste, but bad taste is better than no taste.
[*The Observer*, 1930]

FITZGERALD, Edward (1809–1883)
Taste is the feminine of genius.
[Letter to J.R. Lowell, 1877]

HUXLEY, Aldous (1894–1963)
The aristocratic pleasure of displeasing is not the only delight that bad taste can yield. One can love a certain kind of vulgarity for its own sake.
[*Vulgarity in Literature* (1930)]

REYNOLDS, Sir Joshua (1723–1792)
Taste does not come by chance: it is a long and laborious task to acquire it.
[In Northcote, *Life of Sir Joshua Reynolds* (1818)]

VALERY, Paul (1871–1945)
Le goût est fait de mille dégoûts.
Taste is created from a thousand distastes.
[*Unsaid Things*]

TAXES

BURKE, Edmund (1729–1797)
To tax and to please, no more than to love and to be wise, is not given to men.
[*Speech on American Taxation* (1774)]

CAPONE, Al (1899–1947)
[Objecting to US Government attempts to force him to pay taxes]
They can't collect legal taxes from illegal money.
[In Kobler, *Capone* (1971)]

DICKENS, Charles (1812–1870)
'It was as true,' said Mr Barkis, '... as taxes is. And nothing's truer than them.'
[*David Copperfield* (1850)]

LOWE, Robert (1811–1892)
The Chancellor of the Exchequer is a man whose duties make him more or less of a taxing machine. He is intrusted with a certain amount of misery which it is his duty to distribute as fairly as he can.
[Speech, 1870]

MITCHELL, Margaret (1900–1949)
Death and taxes and childbirth? There's never any convenient time for any of them!
[*Gone with the Wind* (1936)]

OTIS, James (1725–1783)
Taxation without representation is tyranny.
[Attr.]

SHAW, George Bernard (1856–1950)
A government which robs Peter to pay Paul can always depend on the support of Paul.
[*Everybody's Political What's What* (1944)]

SMITH, Adam (1723–1790)
There is no art which one government sooner learns of another than that of draining money from the pockets of the people.
[*Wealth of Nations* (1776)]

TEA

ADDISON, Joseph (1672–1719)
The infusion of a China plant sweetened with the pith of an Indian cane.
[*The Spectator*, 1711]

COBBETT, William (1762–1835)
Resolve to free yourselves from the slavery of the tea and coffee and other slop-kettle.
[*Advice to Young Men* (1829)]

COWPER, William (1731–1800)
Now stir the fire, and close the
  shutters fast,

Let fall the curtains, wheel the sofa
round,
And, while the bubbling and
loud-hissing urn
Throws up a steamy column, and the
cups,
That cheer but not inebriate, wait on
each,
So let us welcome peaceful ev'ning
in.

[*The Task* (1785)]

GLADSTONE, William (1809–1898)
The domestic use of tea is a powerful
champion able to encounter alcoholic
drink in a fair field and throw it in a
fair fight.

[Budget Speech, 1882]

PRIESTLEY, J.B. (1894–1984)
Our trouble is that we drink too much
tea. I see in this the slow revenge of
the Orient, which has diverted the
Yellow River down our throats.

[*The Observer*, 1949]

SMITH, Sydney (1771–1845)
Thank God for tea! What would the
world do without tea? How did it
exist? I am glad I was not born before
tea.

[Attr.]

TEACHERS

AUDEN, W.H. (1907–1973)
A professor is one who talks in someone else's sleep.

[Attr.]

BERLIOZ, Hector (1803–1869)
Time is a great teacher, but unfortunately it kills all its pupils.

[Attr.]

BROUGHAM, Lord Henry (1778–1868)
The schoolmaster is abroad, and I
trust more to him, armed with his
primer, than I do to the soldier in full
military array, for upholding and
extending the liberties of his country.

[Speech, 1828]

CARLYLE, Thomas (1795–1881)
It were better to perish than to
continue schoolmastering.

[In Wilson, *Carlyle Till Marriage* (1923)]

CHURCHILL, Sir Winston (1874–1965)
Headmasters have powers at their
disposal with which Prime Ministers
have never yet been invested.

[*My Early Life* (1930)]

HUXLEY, T.H. (1825–1895)
Some experience of popular lecturing
had convinced me that the necessity
of making things plain to uninstructed
people was one of the very best
means of clearing up the obscure
corners of one's own mind.

[*Man's Place in Nature* (1894)]

MONTESSORI, Maria (1870–1952)
We teachers can only help the work
going on, as servants wait upon a
master.

[*The Absorbent Mind*]

SHAW, George Bernard (1856–1950)
He who can, does. He who cannot,
teaches.

[*Man and Superman* (1903)]

TROLLOPE, Anthony (1815–1882)
[Of his headmaster]
He must have known me had he seen
me as he was wont to see me, for he
was in the habit of flogging me constantly. Perhaps he did not recognize
me by my face.

[*Autobiography* (1883)]

WAUGH, Evelyn (1903–1966)
We schoolmasters must temper
discretion with deceit.

[*Decline and Fall* (1928)]

Assistant masters came and went ...
Some liked little boys too little and
some too much.

[*A Little Learning* (1964)]

WILDE, Oscar (1854–1900)
Everybody who is incapable of
learning has taken to teaching.

['The Decay of Lying' (1889)]

YEATMAN, Robert (1897–1968)
For every person wishing to teach
there are thirty not wanting to be
taught.

[*And Now All This* (1932)]

See EDUCATION; LEARNING; SCHOOL; UNIVERSITY

TELEVISION

BAKEWELL, Joan (1933–)
The BBC is full of men appointing men
who remind them of themselves when
young, so you get the same back-
grounds, the same education, and the
same programmes.

[*The Observer*, 1993]

BIAGI, Enzo (1920–)
*La televisione ha fatto per la nostra
unità più di Garibaldi e Cavour, ha dato
un linguaggio e un costume comuni.*
Television has done more for the
unification of Italy than Garibaldi and
Cavour did; it has given us a commu-
nal custom and language.

[*The Good and the Bad* (1989)]

BIRT, John (1944–)
There is a bias in television
journalism. It is not against any
particular party or point of view – it is
a bias against *understanding*.

[*The Times*, 1975]

COREN, Alan (1938–)
Television is more interesting than
people. If it were not, we should have
people standing in the corners of our
rooms.

[Attr.]

COWARD, Sir Noël (1899–1973)
Television is for appearing on, not
looking at.

[Attr.]

CRISP, Quentin (1908–)
If any reader of this book is in the grip
of some habit of which he is deeply
ashamed, I advise him not to give way
to it in secret but to do it on television.

No-one will pass him with averted
gaze on the other side of the street.
People will cross the road at the risk of
losing their own lives in order to say
'We saw you on the telly'.

[*How to Become a Virgin*]

DEBRAY, Régis (1942–)
The darkest spot in modern society is
a small luminous screen.

[*Teachers, Writers, Celebrities*]

ECO, Umberto (1932–)
*La TV non offre, come ideale in cui
immedesimarsi, il superman ma
l'everyman. La TV presenta come ideale
l'uomo assolutamente medio.*
Television doesn't present, as an ideal
to aspire to, the superman but the
everyman. Television puts forward, as
an ideal, the absolutely average man.

[*Diario Minimo*]

FROST, Sir David (1939–)
Television is an invention that permits
you to be entertained in your living
room by people you wouldn't have in
your home.

[Remark, 1971]

HANSON, Lord James (1922–)
Television exacerbates the concentration on personality and trivia at the
expense of serious discussion and
analysis, but its tendency to unbalance
and to displace what really matters
goes much further and is potentially
very damaging to our lives and beliefs.
It tends to destroy public trust.

[*The Spectator*, 1996]

HITCHCOCK, Alfred (1899–1980)
Television has brought murder back
into the home – where it belongs.

[*The Observer*, 1965]

MCLUHAN, Marshall (1911–1980)
Television brought the brutality of war
into the comfort of the living room.
Vietnam was lost in the living rooms
of America – not on the battle fields of
Vietnam.

[Montreal *Gazette*, 1975]

PARRIS, Matthew (1949–)
Television lies. All television lies. It lies persistently, instinctively and by habit ... A culture of mendacity surrounds the medium, and those who work there live it, breathe it and prosper by it ... I know of no area of public life – no, not even politics – more saturated by professional cynicism.

[*The Spectator*, 1996]

SCOTT, C.P. (1846–1932)
Television? The word is half Latin and half Greek. No good can come of it.

[Attr.]

See MEDIA; NEWS

TEMPTATION

BECKFORD, William (1760–1844)
I am not over-fond of resisting temptation.

[*Vathek* (1787)]

DRYDEN, John (1631–1700)
Thou strong seducer, opportunity!

[*The Conquest of Granada* (1670)]

GRAHAM, Clementina (1782–1877)
The best way to get the better of temptation is just to yield to it.

[*Mystifications* (1859)]

HOPE, Anthony (1863–1933)
'You oughtn't to yield to temptation.'
'Well, somebody must, or the thing becomes absurd.'

[*The Dolly Dialogues* (1894)]

JERROLD, Douglas William (1803–1857)
Honest bread is very well – it's the butter that makes the temptation.

[*The Catspaw* (1850)]

SHAW, George Bernard (1856–1950)
I never resist temptation, because I have found that things that are bad for me do not tempt me.

[*The Apple Cart* (1930)]

WILDE, Oscar (1854–1900)
I couldn't help it. I can resist everything except temptation.

[*Lady Windermere's Fan* (1892)]

THEATRE

ADAMOV, Arthur (1908–1970)
[Remark at the International Drama Conference, Edinburgh, 1963]
The reason why Absurdist plays take place in No Man's Land with only two characters is primarily financial.

[Attr.]

ADDISON, Joseph (1672–1719)
A perfect tragedy is the noblest production of human nature.

[*The Spectator*, 1711]

AGATE, James (1877–1947)
Long experience has taught me that in England nobody goes to the theatre unless he or she has bronchitis.

[Attr.]

ARISTOTLE (384–322 BC)
Tragedy, then, is the imitation of an action that is serious, has magnitude, and is complete in itself ... through incidents arousing pity and fear it effects a catharsis of these and similar emotions.

[*Poetics*]

The plot is the first principle and, as it were, the soul of tragedy; character comes second.

[*Poetics*]

BANKHEAD, Tallulah (1903–1968)
It's one of the tragic ironies of the theatre that only one man in it can count on steady work – the night watchman.

[*Tallulah* (1952)]

BERNARD, Tristan (1866–1947)
In the theatre the audience want to be surprised – but by things that they expect.

[Attr.]

BROOKS, Mel (1926–)
Tragedy is if I cut my finger. Comedy is if I walk into an open sewer and die.
[*The New Yorker*, 1978]

BUCKINGHAM, Duke of (1628–1687)
What the devil does the plot signify, except to bring in fine things?
[*The Rehearsal* (1663)]

BURNEY, Fanny (1752–1840)
'Do you come to the play without knowing what it is?' 'Oh, yes, sir, yes, very frequently. I have no time to read play-bills. One merely comes to meet one's friends, and show that one's alive.'
[*Evelina* (1778)]

BYRON, Lord (1788–1824)
All tragedies are finish'd by a death,
All comedies are ended by a marriage.
[*Don Juan* (1824)]

COOK, Peter (1937–1995)
You know, I go to the theatre to be entertained ... I don't want to see plays about rape, sodomy and drug addiction ... I can get all that at home.
[*The Observer*, cartoon caption, 1962]

CRAIG, Sir Gordon (1872–1966)
Farce is the essential theatre. Farce refined becomes high comedy: farce brutalized becomes tragedy.
[Attr.]

DENNIS, John (1657–1734)
[Remark at a production of *Macbeth*, which used his new technique for producing stage thunder]
See how the rascals use me! They will not let my play run and yet they steal my thunder!
[Attr.]

DENT, Alan (1905–1978)
This is the tragedy of a man who could not make up his mind.
[Introduction to film *Hamlet*, 1948]

EVELYN, John (1620–1706)
I saw Hamlet Prince of Denmark played: but now the old playe began to disgust this refined age.
[*Diary*, 1661]

GUINNESS, Sir Alec (1914–)
[Vowing never to perform again in the West End when he saw the blank faces of uncomprehending tourists]
I'd rather go to the provinces where they still speak English and not Japanese.
[*Scotsman*, 1992]

GWENN, Edmund (1875–1959)
[Reply on his deathbed, when someone said to him, 'It must be very hard']
It is. But not as hard as farce.
[*Time*, 1984]

HITCHCOCK, Alfred (1899–1980)
What is drama but life with the dull bits cut out?
[*The Observer*,1960]

HOPE, Anthony (1863–1933)
[On the first night of J. M. Barrie's play *Peter Pan*]
Oh, for an hour of Herod!
[In Birkin, *J. M. Barrie and the Lost Boys*]

HUXLEY, Aldous (1894–1963)
We participate in a tragedy; at a comedy we only look.
[*The Devils of Loudun* (1952)]

KEMBLE, John Philip (1757–1823)
[Said during a play which was continually interrupted by a crying child]
Ladies and gentlemen, unless the play is stopped, the child cannot possibly go on.
[Attr.]

PAVLOVA, Anna (1881–1931)
Although one may fail to find happiness in theatrical life, one never wishes to give it up after having once tasted its fruits.
[In Franks (ed.), *Pavlova: A Biography*]

PINTER, Harold (1930–)
I've never regarded myself as the one

authority on my plays just because I wrote the damned things.

RATTIGAN, Terence (1911–1977)
A nice, respectable, middle-class, middle-aged, maiden lady, with time on her hands and the money to help her pass it ... Let us call her Aunt Edna ... Aunt Edna is universal, and to those who might feel that all the problems of the modern theatre might be solved by her liquidation, let me add that ... she is also immortal.

[*Collected Plays* (1953)]

SHAW, George Bernard (1856–1950)
You don't expect me to know what to say about a play when I don't know who the author is, do you? ... If it's by a good author, it's a good play, naturally. That stands to reason.

[*Fanny's First Play* (1911)]

[Responding to a solitary boo amongst the mid-act applause at the first performance of *Arms and the Man* in 1894]
I quite agree with you, sir, but what can two do against so many?

[*Oxford Book of Literary Anecdotes*]

STOPPARD, Tom (1937–)
The bad end unhappily, the good unluckily. That is what tragedy means.

[*Rosencrantz and Guildenstern Are Dead* (1967)]

VICTORIA, Queen (1819–1901)
[Giving her opinion of *King Lear*]
A strange, horrible business, but I suppose good enough for Shakespeare's day.

[Attr.]

VOLTAIRE (1694–1778)
[When asked why no woman had ever written a tolerable tragedy]
The composition of a tragedy requires *testicles*.

[In a letter from Byron to John Murray, 1817]

See ACTING; ACTORS

BIERCE, Ambrose (1842–c. 1914)
Brain: An apparatus with which we think that we think.

[*The Cynic's Word Book* (1906)]

CONFUCIUS (c. 550–c. 478 BC)
Learning without thought is labour lost; thought without learning is perilous.

[*Analects*]

DESCARTES, René (1596–1650)
Cogito, ergo sum.
I think, therefore I am.

[*Discours de la Méthode* (1637)]

EMERSON, Ralph Waldo (1803–1882)
Beware when the great God lets loose a thinker on this planet. Then all things are at risk.

['Circles' (1841)]

GOETHE (1749–1832)
Alles Gescheite ist schon gedacht worden, man muss nur versuchen, es noch einmal zu denken.
Everything worth thinking has already been thought, our concern must only be to try to think it through again.

['Thought and Action' (1829)]

HAZLITT, William (1778–1830)
The most fluent talkers or most plausible reasoners are not always the justest thinkers.

[*Atlas* (1830), 'On Prejudice']

HEATH, Sir Edward (1916–)
The real problem in life is to have sufficient time to think.

[*The Observer*, 1981]

HORVÁTH, Ödön von (1901–1938)
Denken tut weh.
Thinking hurts.

[*A Child of our Time* (1938)]

JAMES, William (1842–1910)
A great many people think they are thinking when they are merely re-arranging their prejudices.

[Attr.]

JOHNSON, Samuel (1709–1784)
Whatever withdraws us from the power of our senses; whatever makes the past, the distant, or the future, predominate over the present, advances us in the dignity of thinking beings.

[*A Journey to the Western Islands of Scotland* (1775)]

LUTHER, Martin (1483–1546)
Gedanken sind zollfrei.
Thoughts are not subject to duty.

[*On Worldly Authority* (1523)]

MILL, John Stuart (1806–1873)
No great improvements in the lot of mankind are possible, until a great change takes place in the fundamental constitution of their modes of thought.

[*Autobiography* (1873)]

NEWTON, Sir Isaac (1642–1727)
If I have done the public any service, it is due to patient thought.

[Letter to Dr Bentley, 1713]

REITH, Lord (1889–1971)
You can't think rationally on an empty stomach, and a whole lot of people can't do it on a full one either.

[Attr.]

RUSKIN, John (1819–1900)
The purest and most thoughtful minds are those which love colour the most.

[*The Stones of Venice*, II (1853)]

RUSSELL, Bertrand (1872–1970)
People don't seem to realize that it takes time and effort and preparation to think. Statesmen are far too busy making speeches to think.

[In Harris, *Kenneth Harris Talking To:* (1971)]

Many people would sooner die than think. In fact they do.

[In Flew, *Thinking about Thinking* (1975)]

SARTRE, Jean-Paul (1905–1980)
Ma pensée, c'est moi: voilà pourquoi je ne peux pas m'arrêter. J'existe par ce que je pense ... et je ne peux pas m'empêcher de penser.
My thought is *me*: that is why I cannot stop. I exist by what I think ... and I can't prevent myself from thinking.

[*Nausea* (1938)]

SHAKESPEARE, William (1564–1616)
There is nothing either good or bad, but thinking makes it so.

[*Hamlet*, II.ii]

SHELLEY, Percy Bysshe (1792–1822)
A single word even may be a spark of inextinguishable thought.

[*A Defence of Poetry* (1821)]

VALERY, Paul (1871–1945)
A gloss on Descartes: Sometimes I think: and sometimes I am.

[*The Faber Book of Aphorisms* (1962)]

VAUVENARGUES, Marquis de (1715–1747)
Les grandes pensées viennent du coeur.
Great thoughts come from the heart.

[*Réflexions et Maximes* (1746)]

VOLTAIRE (1694–1778)
Ils ne servent de la pensée que pour autoriser leurs injustices, et n'emploient les paroles que pour déguiser leurs pensées.
People use thought only to justify their injustices, and they use words only to disguise their thoughts.

[*Dialogues* (1763)]

WEBSTER, John (c. 1580–c. 1625)
There's nothing of so infinite vexation As man's own thoughts.

[*The White Devil* (1612)]

WITTGENSTEIN, Ludwig (1889–1951)
In order to draw a limit to thinking, we should have to be able to think both sides of this limit.

[*Tractatus Logico-Philosophicus* (1922)]

See IDEAS; MIND

TIME

AURELIUS, Marcus (121–180)
Time is like a river made up of the things which happen, and its current is strong; no sooner does anything appear than it is carried away, and another comes in its place, and will be carried away too.

[*Meditations*]

BACON, Francis (1561–1626)
He that will not apply new remedies, must expect new evils; for time is the greatest innovator.

['Of Innovations' (1625)]

BASHÓ, Matsuo (1644–1694)
Days and months are itinerants on an eternal journey; the years that pass by are also travellers.

['Narrow Roads of Oku' (1703)]

THE BIBLE (King James Version)
To every thing there is a season, and a time to every purpose under the heaven:
A time to be born, and a time to die ...
A time to love, and a time to hate; a time of war, and a time of peace.

[*Ecclesiastes*, 3:1–8]

BOUCICAULT, Dion (1822–1890)
Men talk of killing time, while time quietly kills them.

[*London Assurance* (1841)]

BROWNE, Sir Thomas (1605–1682)
The night of time far surpasseth the day, and who knows when was the equinox?

[*Hydriotaphia: Urn Burial* (1658)]

CARLYLE, Thomas (1795–1881)
The illimitable, silent, never-resting thing called Time, rolling, rushing on, swift, silent, like an all-embracing ocean-tide, on which we and all the Universe swim like exhalations, like apparitions which *are*, and then *are not*.

['The Hero as Divinity' (1841)]

COMPTON-BURNETT, Dame Ivy (1884–1969)
Time has too much credit ... I never agree with the compliments paid to it. It is not a great healer. It is an indifferent and perfunctory one. Sometimes it does not heal at all. And sometimes when it seems to, no healing has been necessary.

[*Darkness and Day* (1951)]

COWARD, Sir Noël (1899–1973)
Time is the reef upon which all our frail mystic ships are wrecked.

[*Blithe Spirit* (1941)]

DISRAELI, Benjamin (1804–1881)
Time is the great physician.

[*Henrietta Temple* (1837)]

DOBSON, Henry Austin (1840–1921)
Time goes, you say? Ah no!
Alas, Time stays, *we* go.

['The Paradox of Time' (1877)]

EMERSON, Ralph Waldo (1803–1882)
[To a person complaining that he had not enough time]
'Well,' said Red Jacket, 'I suppose you have all there is.'

['Works and Days' (1870)]

A day is a miniature eternity.

[*Journals*]

FRAME, Janet (1924–)
There is no past present or future. Using tenses to divide time is like making chalk marks on water.

[*Faces in the Water* (1961)]

HODGSON, Ralph (1871–1962)
Time, you old gypsy man,
Will you not stay,
Put up your caravan,
Just for one day?

['Time, You Old Gypsy Man' (1917)]

MCLUHAN, Marshall (1911–1980)
For tribal man space was the uncontrollable mystery. For technological man it is time that occupies the same role.

[*The Mechanical Bridge* (1951)]

TOLERANCE

MAXWELL, Gavin (1914–1969)
Yet while there is time, there is the certainty of return.

[*Ring of Bright Water* (1960)]

PERICLES (c. 495–429)
Wait for that wisest of counsellors, Time.

[In Plutarch, *Life*]

RALEIGH, Sir Walter (c. 1552–1618)
[Written the night before his execution]
Even such is Time, which takes in trust
Our youth, our joys, and all we have,
And pays us but with age and dust;
Who in the dark and silent grave,
When we have wandered all our ways,
Shuts up the story of our days.

[Untitled poem (1618)]

ROGERS, Will (1879–1935)
Half our life is spent trying to find something to do with the time we have rushed through life trying to save.

[*The New York Times*, 1930]

SHAKESPEARE, William (1564–1616)
But thoughts, the slaves of life, and life, time's fool,
And time, that takes survey of all the world,
Must have a stop.

[*Henry IV, Part 1*, V.iv]

Come what come may,
Time and the hour runs through the roughest day.

[*Macbeth*, I.iii]

I wasted time, and now doth time waste me.

[*Richard II*, V.v]

STOPPARD, Tom (1937–)
Eternity's a terrible thought. I mean, where's it all going to end?

[*Rosencrantz and Guildenstern Are Dead* (1967)]

THOMAS, Dylan (1914–1953)
Oh as I was young and easy in the mercy of his means,
Time held me green and dying
Though I sang in my chains like the sea.

['Fern Hill' (1946)]

THOREAU, Henry (1817–1862)
Time is but the stream I go a-fishing in.

[*Walden* (1854)]

VAUGHAN, Henry (1622–1695)
I saw Eternity the other night
Like a great Ring of pure and endless light,
All calm, as it was bright,
And round beneath it, Time in hours, days, years
Driv'n by the spheres
Like a vast shadow mov'd, in which the world
And all her train were hurl'd.

[*Silex Scintillans*]

WATTS, Isaac (1674–1748)
Time, like an ever-rolling stream,
Bears all its sons away;
They fly forgotten, as a dream
Dies at the opening day.

[*The Psalms of David Imitated* (1719)]

YOUNG, Edward (1683–1765)
Procrastination is the Thief of Time.

[*Night-Thoughts on Life, Death and Immortality*]

See CHANGE

TOLERANCE

THE BIBLE (King James Version)
For ye suffer fools gladly, seeing ye yourselves are wise.

[*Paul*, 3:67]

BROWNE, Sir Thomas (1605–1682)
No man can justly censure or condemn another, because indeed no man truly knows another.

[*Religio Medici* (1643)]

BURKE, Edmund (1729–1797)
There is, however, a limit at which
forbearance ceases to be a virtue.
[*Observations on 'The Present State of the
Nation'* (1769 ed.)]

SADE, Marquis de (1740–1814)
La tolérance est la vertu du faible.
Tolerance is the virtue of the weak.
[*La nouvelle Justine* (1797)]

STAËL, Mme de (1766–1817)
Tout comprendre rend très indulgent.
Understanding everything makes one
very tolerant.
[*Corinne* (1807)]

TROLLOPE, Anthony (1815–1882)
It is because we put up with bad
things that hotel-keepers continue to
give them to us.
[*Orley Farm* (1862)]

TRADITION

CHESTERTON, G.K. (1874–1936)
Tradition means giving votes to the
most obscure of all classes, our
ancestors. It is the democracy of the
dead. Tradition refuses to submit to
the small and arrogant oligarchy of
those who merely happen to be
walking about. All democrats object to
men being disqualified by the accident
of birth; tradition objects to their being
disqualified by the accident of death.
[*Orthodoxy* (1908)]

COKE, Sir Edward (1552–1634)
How long soever it hath continued, if it
be against reason, it is of no force in
law.
['Commentary upon Littleton']

We have a maxim in the House of
Commons ... that old ways are the
safest and surest ways.
[Speech, 1628]

DISRAELI, Benjamin (1804–1881)
A precedent embalms a principle.
[Attr.]

HARDY, Thomas (1840–1928)
Five decades hardly modified the cut
of a gaiter, the embroidery of a smock-
frock, by the breadth of a hair. Ten
generations failed to alter the turn of a
single phrase. In these Wessex nooks
the busy outsider's ancient times are
only old; his old times are still new; his
present is futurity.
[*Far From the Madding Crowd* (1874)]

BOOK OF COMMON PRAYER
There was never any thing by the wit
of man so well devised, or so sure
established, which in continuance of
time hath not been corrupted.
[*The Preface*]

TRANSLATION

BORGES, Jorge Luis (1899–1986)
[On Henley's translation of Beckford's
Vathek]
El original es infiel a la traducción.
The original is not faithful to the
translation.
[*Sobre el 'Vathek' de William Beckford* (1943)]

BORROW, George (1803–1881)
Translation is at best an echo.
[*Lavengro* (1851)]

CAMPBELL, Roy (1901–1957)
Translations (like wives) are seldom
strictly faithful if they are in the least
attractive.
[*Poetry Review*, 1949]

DENHAM, Sir John (1615–1669)
Such is our pride, our folly, or our fate,
That few, but such as cannot write,
translate.
['To Richard Fanshaw' (1648)]

FROST, Robert (1874–1963)
Poetry is what is lost in translation.
[In Untermeyer, *Robert Frost: a Backward
Look* (1964)]

JOHNSON, Samuel (1709–1784)
A translator is to be like his author; it
is not his business to excel him.
[Attr.]

ARNOLD, Matthew (1822–1888)
A wanderer is man from his birth.
He was born in a ship
On the breast of the river of Time.

['The Future']

BUCHAN, William
Canadian trains did not rush and rock.
They pounded steadily along, every so
often giving a warning blast on their
sirens. I remember those sirens
blowing in the icy darkness of winter
nights in Ottawa, the most haunting
sound, at once melancholy and
stirring, like the mourning of some
strange, sad beast.

[A Memoir]

**CHERRY-GARRARD, Apsley
(1886–1959)**
Polar exploration is at once the
cleanest and most isolated way of
having a bad time which has been
devised.

[The Worst Journey in the World (1922)]

**COLERIDGE, Samuel Taylor
(1772–1834)**
From whatever place I write you will
expect that part of my 'Travels' will
consist of excursions in my own mind.

[Satyrane's Letters (1809)]

COWPER, William (1731–1800)
How much a dunce that has been sent
    to roam
Excels a dunce that has been kept at
    home.

['The Progress of Error' (1782)]

DIDION, Joan (1934–)
Certain places seem to exist mainly
because someone has written about
them.

[The White Album (1979)]

DREW, Elizabeth (1887–1965)
Too often travel, instead of broadening
the mind, merely lengthens the
conversation.

[The Literature of Gossip (1964)]

ELIOT, T.S. (1888–1965)
The first condition of understanding a
foreign country is to smell it.

[Attr.]

EMERSON, Ralph Waldo (1803–1882)
Travelling is a fool's paradise. Our first
journeys discover to us the indifference
of places.

['Self-Reliance' (1841)]

**FLANDERS, Michael (1922–1975) and
SWANN, Donald (1923–1994)**
If God had intended us to fly, he'd
never have given us the railways.

['By Air', 1963]

GALBRAITH, J.K. (1908–)
The Great Wall, I've been told, is the
only man-made structure on earth that
is visible from the moon. For the life of
me I cannot see why anyone would go
to the moon to look at it, when, with
almost the same difficulty, it can be
viewed in China.

[The Sunday Times Magazine]

GEORGE VI (1895–1952)
Abroad is bloody.

[In Auden, A Certain World (1970)]

HAZLITT, William (1778–1830)
Give me the clear blue sky over my
head, and the green turf beneath my
feet, a winding road before me, and a
three hours' march to dinner – and
then to thinking! It is hard if I cannot
start some game on these lone heaths.

['On Going a Journey' (1822)]

JOHNSON, Amy (1903–1941)
Had I been a man I might have
explored the Poles or climbed Mount
Everest, but as it was my spirit found
an outlet in the air.

[In Margot Asquith (ed.), Myself When Young]

JOHNSON, Samuel (1709–1784)
[Of the Giant's Causeway]
Worth seeing? yes; but not worth
going to see.

[In Boswell, The Life of Samuel Johnson
(1791)]

KERR, Jean (1923–)
I feel about airplanes the way I feel about diets. It seems to me that they are wonderful things for other people to go on.

[*The Snake Has All the Lines* (1958)]

KILVERT, Francis (1840–1879)
Of all noxious animals, too, the most noxious is a tourist. And of all tourists, the most vulgar, ill-bred, offensive and loathsome is the British tourist.

[*Diary*, 1870]

KIPLING, Rudyard (1865–1936)
Down to Gehenna or up to the Throne,
He travels the fastest who travels
    alone.

['The Winners' (1888)]

MACAULAY, Dame Rose (1881–1958)
The great and recurrent question about abroad is, is it worth getting there?

[Attr.]

MCLUHAN, Marshall (1911–1980)
The car has become the carapace, the protective and aggressive shell, of urban and suburban man.

[*Understanding Media* (1964)]

MANSFIELD, Katherine (1888–1923)
Whenever I prepare for a journey I prepare as though for death. Should I never return, all is in order. That is what life has taught me.

[*Journal of Katherine Mansfield* (1954)]

MOORE, George (1852–1933)
A man travels the world over in search of what he needs and returns home to find it.

[*The Brook Kerith* (1916)]

PEARY, Robert Edwin (1856–1920)
The Eskimo had his own explanation. Said he: 'The devil is asleep or having trouble with his wife, or we should never have come back so easily.'

[*The North Pole* (1910)]

SACKVILLE-WEST, Vita (1892–1962)
Travel is the most private of pleasures. There is no greater bore than the travel bore. We do not in the least want to hear what he has seen in Hong Kong.

[*Passenger to Tehran* (1926)]

SANTAYANA, George (1863–1952)
[On being asked why he always travelled third class]
Because there's no fourth class.

[In Thomas, *Living Biographies of the Great Philosophers*]

SCOTT, Captain Robert (1868–1912)
[Of the South Pole]
Great God! this is an awful place.

[*Journal*, 1912]

STARK, Dame Freya (1893–)
The beckoning counts, and not the clicking latch behind you.

[*The Sunday Telegraph*, 1993]

STERNE, Laurence (1713–1768)
A man should know something of his own country too, before he goes abroad.

[*Tristram Shandy* (1767)]

STEVENSON, Robert Louis (1850–1894)
For my part, I travel not to go anywhere, but to go. I travel for travel's sake. The great affair is to move.

[*Travels with a Donkey in the Cévennes* (1879)]

To travel hopefully is a better thing than to arrive, and the true success is to labour.

[*Virginibus Puerisque* (1881)]

But all that I could think of, in the
    darkness and the cold,
Was that I was leaving home and my
    folks were growing old.

['Christmas at Sea' (1890)]

TRUST

There's nothing under Heav'n so blue
That's fairly worth the travelling to.

['A Song of the Road' (1896)]

THOMSON, Joseph (1858–1895)
[His reply when J.M. Barrie asked what
was the most hazardous part of his
expedition to Africa]
Crossing Piccadilly Circus.

[In Dunbar, *J.M. Barrie*]

VIZINCZEY, Stephen (1933–)
I was told I am a true cosmopolitan. I
am unhappy everywhere.

[*The Guardian*, 1968]

WHITE, E.B. (1899–1985)
Commuter – one who spends his life
In riding to and from his wife;
A man who shaves and takes a train,
And then rides back to shave again.

['The Commuter' (1982)]

See FOREIGNERS

TRUST

CAMUS, Albert (1913–1960)
*C'est si vrai que nous nous confions
rarement à ceux qui sont meilleurs que
nous.*
It is very true that we seldom confide
in those who are better than ourselves.

[*The Fall* (1956)]

FIELDING, Henry (1707–1754)
Never trust the man who hath reason
to suspect that you know that he hath
injured you.

[*Jonathan Wild* (1743)]

GREENE, Graham (1904– 1991)
His smile explained everything; he
carried it always with him as a leper
carried his bell; it was a perpetual
warning that he was not to be trusted.

[*England Made Me* (1935)]

JEFFERSON, Thomas (1743–1826)
When a man assumes a public trust,
he should consider himself as public
property.

[Remark, 1807]

PITT, William (1708–1778)
I cannot give them my confidence;
pardon me, gentlemen, confidence is a
plant of slow growth in an aged
bosom: youth is the season of
credulity.

[Speech, 1766]

RUBIN, Jerry (1936–)
Don't trust anyone over thirty.

[In Flexner, *Listening to America*]

**SHERIDAN, Richard Brinsley
(1751–1816)**
There is no trusting appearances.

[*The School for Scandal* (1777)]

WILLIAMS, Tennessee (1911–1983)
We have to distrust each other. It's our
only defence against betrayal.

[*Camino Real* (1953)]

TRUTH

ANONYMOUS
Se non è vero, è molto ben trovato.
If it is not true, it is a happy invention.

[16th century]

BACON, Francis (1561–1626)
What a man had rather were true he
more readily believes.

[*The New Organon* (1620)]

Some in their discourse desire rather
commendation of wit, in being able to
hold all arguments, than of judgement
in discerning what is true.

['Of Discourse' (1625)]

This same truth is a naked and open
daylight, that doth not show the
masques and mummeries and
triumphs of the world half so stately
and daintily as candlelights.

['Of Truth' (1625)]

BALDWIN, Stanley (1867–1947)
A platitude is simply a truth repeated
until people get tired of hearing it.

[Attr.]

BALFOUR, A.J. (1848–1930)
It is unfortunate, considering that enthusiasm moves the world, that so few enthusiasts can be trusted to speak the truth.

[Letter to Mrs Drew, 1891]

BERKELEY, Bishop George (1685–1753)
Truth is the cry of all, but the game of the few.

[*Siris* (1744)]

THE BIBLE (King James Version)
Magna est veritas et praevalet.
Great is Truth, and mighty above all things.

[Apocrypha, *I Esdras*, 4:41]

And ye shall know the truth, and the truth shall make you free.

[*John*, 8:32]

BLAKE, William (1757–1827)
Truth can never be told so as to be understood, and not be believ'd.

['Proverbs of Hell' (c. 1793)]

A truth that's told with bad intent
Beats all the Lies you can invent.

['Auguries of Innocence' (c. 1803)]

BOLINGBROKE, Henry (1678–1751)
Plain truth will influence half a score of men at most in a nation, or an age, while mystery will lead millions by the nose.

[Letter, 1721]

BOWEN, Elizabeth (1899–1973)
Nobody speaks the truth when there's something they must have.

[*The House in Paris* (1935)]

BRAQUE, Georges (1882–1963)
La vérité existe; on n'invente que le mensonge.
Truth exists; only lies are invented.

[*Day and Night, Notebooks* (1952)]

BROWNE, Sir Thomas (1605–1682)
A man may be in as just possession of truth as of a city, and yet be forced to surrender.

[*Religio Medici* (1643)]

CARROLL, Lewis (1832–1898)
What I tell you three times is true.

['The Hunting of the Snark' (1876)]

COWPER, William (1731–1800)
And diff'ring judgments serve but to declare
That truth lies somewhere, if we knew but where.

['Hope' (1782)]

DARLING, Charles (1849–1936)
Much truth is spoken, that more may be concealed.

[*Scintillae Juris* (1877)]

DOYLE, Sir Arthur Conan (1859–1930)
It is an old maxim of mine that when you have excluded the impossible, whatever remains, however improbable, must be the truth.

['The Beryl Coronet' (1892)]

DRYDEN, John (1631–1700)
I never saw any good that came of telling truth.

[*Amphitryon* (1690)]

FRAME, Janet (1924–)
In an age of explanation one can always choose varieties of truth.

[*Living in the Maniototo* (1979)]

HUXLEY, T.H. (1825–1895)
Irrationally held truths may be more harmful than reasoned errors.

[*Science and Culture, and Other Essays* (1881)]

It is the customary fate of new truths to begin as heresies and to end as superstitions.

[*Science and Culture, and Other Essays* (1881)]

IBSEN, Henrik (1828–1906)
A man should never have his best trousers on when he goes out to battle for freedom and truth.

[*An Enemy of the People* (1882)]

JOHNSON, Samuel (1709–1784)
[On sceptics]
Truth, Sir, is a cow which will yield such people no more milk, and so they are gone to milk the bull.

[In Boswell, *The Life of Samuel Johnson* (1791)]

LA BRUYERE, Jean de (1645–1696)
Il y a quelques rencontres dans la vie où la vérité et la simplicité sont le meilleur manège du monde.
There are some circumstances in life where truth and simplicity are the best strategy in the world.

[*Les caractères ou les moeurs de ce siècle* (1688)]

LEACOCK, Stephen (1869–1944)
A half truth in argument, like a half brick, carries better.

[In Flesch, *The Book of Unusual Quotations*]

LE GALLIENNE, Richard (1866–1947)
[Of Oscar Wilde]
Paradox with him was only Truth standing on its head to attract attention.

[*The Romantic 90s*]

MILL, John Stuart (1806–1873)
History teems with instances of truth put down by persecution ... It is a piece of idle sentimentality that truth, merely as truth, has any inherent power denied to error, of prevailing against the dungeon and the stake.

[*On Liberty* (1859)]

MILTON, John (1608–1674)
Beholding the bright countenance of truth in the quiet and still air of delightfull studies.

[*The Reason of Church-government Urg'd against Prelaty* (1642)]

NIXON, Richard (1913–1994)
Let us begin by committing ourselves to the truth, to see it like it is and to tell it like it is, to find the truth, to speak the truth and live with the truth. That's what we'll do.

[Nomination acceptance speech, 1968]

PROUST, Marcel (1871–1922)
Une vérité clairement comprise ne peut plus être écrite avec sincérité.
A truth which is clearly understood can no longer be written with sincerity.

['Senancour c'est moi']

SAMUEL, Lord (1870–1963)
A truism is on that account none the less true.

[*A Book of Quotations* (1947)]

SMITH, Sydney (1771–1845)
It is the calling of great men, not so much to preach new truths, as to rescue from oblivion those old truths which it is our wisdom to remember and our weakness to forget.

[Attr.]

SOLZHENITSYN, Alexander (1918–)
When truth is discovered by someone else, it loses something of its attractiveness.

[*Candle in the Wind*]

TWAIN, Mark (1835–1910)
When in doubt, tell the truth.

[*Pudd'nhead Wilson's New Calendar*]

WHITEHEAD, A.N. (1861–1947)
There are no whole truths; all truths are half-truths. It is trying to treat them as whole truths that plays the devil.

[*Dialogues* (1954), Prologue]

WILDE, Oscar (1854–1900)
If one tells the truth, one is sure, sooner or later, to be found out.

[*The Chameleon*, 1894]

WRIGHT, Frank Lloyd (1869–1959)
The truth is more important than the facts.

[In Simcox, *Treasury of Quotations on Christian Themes*]

YELTSIN, Boris (1931–)
Truth is truth, and the truth will

overcome the left, the right and the centre.

[Interview in *Newsweek*, 1994]

See ART; ERROR; LIES

TYRANNY

ARENDT, Hannah (1906–1975)
Under conditions of tyranny it is far easier to act than to think.

[In Auden, *A Certain World* (1970)]

BELLOW, Saul (1915–)
It is not inconceivable that a man might find freedom and identity by killing his oppressor. But as a Chicagoan, I am rather skeptical about this. Murderers are not improved by murdering.

['A World Too Much With Us' (1975)]

BIKO, Steve (1946–1977)
The most potent weapon in the hands of the oppressor is the mind of the oppressed.

[Address to students, 1971]

BROWNING, Robert (1812–1889)
Oppression makes the wise man mad.

[*Luria* (1846)]

BURKE, Edmund (1729–1797)
Bad laws are the worst sort of tyranny.

[*Speech at Bristol* (1780)]

CHURCHILL, Sir Winston (1874–1965)
Dictators ride to and fro upon tigers which they dare not dismount. And the tigers are getting hungry.

[*While England Slept* (1936)]

DEFOE, Daniel (c. 1661–1731)
And of all plagues with which
    mankind are curst,
Ecclesiastic tyranny's the worst.

[*The True-Born Englishman* (1701)]

Nature has left this tincture in the
    blood,
That all men would be tyrants if they
    could.

['The Kentish Petition' (1713)]

HERRICK, Robert (1591–1674)
'Twixt Kings & Tyrants there's this
    difference known;
Kings seek their Subjects good: Tyrants
    their owne.

[*Hesperides* (1648)]

JUNG CHANG (1952–)
Mao had managed to turn the people into the ultimate weapon of dictatorship. That was why under him there was no real equivalent of the KGB in China. There was no need. In bringing out and nourishing the worst in people, Mao had created a moral wasteland and a land of hatred.

[*Wild Swans* (1991)]

MANDELA, Nelson (1918–)
Never, never and never again shall it be that this beautiful land will again experience the oppression of one by another and suffer the indignity of being the skunk of the world.

[Inauguration speech, 1994]

MILL, John Stuart (1806–1873)
Whatever crushes individuality is despotism, by whatever name it may be called.

[*On Liberty* (1859), 3]

NIEMÖLLER, Martin (1892–1984)
In Germany, the Nazis came for the Communists and I didn't speak up because I was not a Communist. Then they came for the Jews and I didn't speak up because I was not a Jew. Then they came for the trade unionists and I didn't speak up because I was not a trade unionist. Then they came for the Catholics and I was a Protestant so I didn't speak up. Then they came for me ... By that time there was no one to speak up for anyone.

[In Neil, *Concise Dictionary of Religious Quotations*]

PITT, William (1708–1778)
Where law ends, there tyranny begins.

[Speech, 1770]

See CENSORSHIP

UNIVERSITY

BACON, Francis (1561–1626)
Universities incline wits to sophistry and affectation.

[*Valerius Terminus of the Interpretation of Nature* (1603)]

BATESON, Mary (1939–)
Most higher education is devoted to affirming the traditions and origins of an existing elite and transmitting them to new members.

[*Composing a Life* (1989)]

CONGREVE, William (1670–1729)
Aye, 'tis well enough for a servant to be bred at an University. But the education is a little too pedantic for a gentleman.

[*Love for Love* (1695)]

FRY, Stephen (1957–)
The competitive spirit is an ethos which it is the business of universities ... to subdue and neutralise.

[*Paperweight* (1992)]

HODSON, Peregrine
He probably doesn't understand what he's looking at but he's reluctant to ask, because this is Japan and the student doesn't ask questions but waits to be told by the teacher.

[*A Circle Round The Sun – A Foreigner in Japan*]

ILLICH, Ivan (1926–)
Any attempt to reform the university without attending to the system of which it is an integral part is like trying to do urban renewal in New York City from the twelfth storey up.

[*Deschooling Society* (1971)]

JOHNSON, Paul (1928–)
In a growing number of countries everyone has a qualified right to attend a university ... The result is the emergence of huge caravanserais ... where higher education is doled out rather like gruel in a soup kitchen.

[*The Spectator*, 1996]

LODGE, David (1935–)
Rummidge ... had lately suffered the mortifying fate of most English universities of its type (civic redbrick): having competed strenuously for fifty years with two universities chiefly valued for being old, it was, at the moment of drawing level, rudely overtaken in popularity and prestige by a batch of universities chiefly valued for being new.

[*Changing Places* (1975)]

Universities are the cathedrals of the modern age. They shouldn't have to justify their existence by utilitarian criteria.

[*Nice Work*]

MCLUHAN, Marshall (1911–1980)
The reason universities are so full of knowledge is that the students come with so much and they leave with so little.

[*Antigonish Review*, 1988]

MELVILLE, Herman (1819–1891)
A whale ship was my Yale College and my Harvard.

[*Moby Dick* (1851)]

NABOKOV, Vladimir (1899–1977)
Like so many ageing college people, Pnin had long ceased to notice the existence of students on the campus.

[*Pnin* (1957)]

O'CONNOR, Flannery (1925–1964)
Everywhere I go I'm asked if I think the university stifles writers. My opinion is that they don't stifle enough of them. There's many a bestseller that could have been prevented by a good teacher.

[In Fitzgerald, *The Nature and Aim of Fiction*]

OZICK, Cynthia (1928–)
It is the function of a liberal university not to give the right answers, but to ask right questions.

['Women and Creativity' (1969)]

PEACOCK, Thomas Love (1785–1866)
He was sent, as usual, to a public school, where a little learning was painfully beaten into him, and from thence to the university, where it was carefully taken out of him.

[*Nightmare Abbey* (1818)]

TRAPP, Joseph (1679–1747)
The King, observing with judicious eyes,
The state of both his universities,
To Oxford sent a troop of horse, and why?
That learned body wanted loyalty;

To Cambridge books, as very well discerning,
How much that loyal body wanted learning.

[Epigram on George I's donation of Bishop Ely's Library to Cambridge University]

WALKER, Alice (1944–)
Ignorance, arrogance and racism have bloomed as Superior Knowledge in all too many universities.

[*In Search of our Mothers' Gardens* (1983)]

See EDUCATION; LEARNING; SCHOOL; TEACHERS

THE BIBLE (King James Version)
Vanity of vanities, saith the Preacher,
vanity of vanities; all is vanity.

[*Ecclesiastes*, 1:2]

COWLEY, Hannah (1743–1809)
Vanity, like murder, will out.

[*The Belle's Stratagem* (1780)]

**EBNER-ESCHENBACH, Marie von
(1830–1916)**
*Wir sind so eitel, dass uns sogar an der
Meinung der Leute, an denen uns nichts
liegt, etwas gelegen ist.*
We are so vain that we are even
concerned about the opinion of those
people who are of no concern to us.

[*Aphorisms* (1880)]

**STEVENSON, Robert Louis
(1850–1894)**
Vanity dies hard; in some obstinate
cases it outlives the man.

[*Prince Otto*]

SWIFT, Jonathan (1667–1745)
'Tis an old maxim in the schools,
That vanity's the food of fools;
Yet now and then your men of wit
Will condescend to take a bit.

['Cadenus and Vanessa' (c. 1712)]

UNAMUNO, Miguel de (1864–1936)
*Cúrate de la afección de preocuparte
cómo aparezcas a los demás. Cuídate
sólo de cómo aparezcas ante Dios,
cuídate de la idea que de ti Dios tenga.*
Cure yourself of the disease of
worrying about how you appear to
others. Concern yourself only with
how you appear before God, concern
yourself with the idea which God has
of you.

[*Vida de Don Quijote y Sancho* (1914 ed.)]

ASIMOV, Isaac (1920–1992)
Violence is the last refuge of the
incompetent.

[*Foundation* (1951)]

BRIEN, Alan (1925–)
Violence is the repartee of the illiterate.

[*Punch*, 1973]

BRIGHT, John (1811–1889)
Force is not a remedy.

[Speech, 1880]

BRONOWSKI, Jacob (1908–1974)
The wish to hurt, the momentary
intoxication with pain, is the loophole
through which the pervert climbs into
the minds of ordinary men.

[*The Face of Violence* (1954)]

BURKE, Edmund (1729–1797)
The use of force alone is but
temporary. It may subdue for a
moment; but it does not remove the
necessity of subduing again: and a
nation is not governed, which is
perpetually to be conquered.

[*Speech on Conciliation with America* (1775)]

FONTAINE, Jean de la (1621–1695)
*La raison du plus fort est toujours la
meilleure.*
The reason of the strongest is always
the best.

['Le loup et l'agneau']

HORACE (65–8 BC)
Vis consili expers mole ruit sua.
Brute force without judgement col-
lapses under its own weight.

[*Odes*]

INGE, William Ralph (1860–1954)
A man may build himself a throne of
bayonets, but he cannot sit upon it.

[*Philosophy of Plotinus* (1923)]

KING, Martin Luther (1929–1968)
A riot is at bottom the language of the
unheard.

[*Chaos or Community* (1967)]

KORAN
Let there be no violence in religion.

[Chapter 2]

MACKENZIE, Sir Compton (1883–1972)
There is little to choose morally between beating up a man physically and beating him up mentally.
[*On Moral Courage* (1962)]

MILTON, John (1608–1674)
Who overcomes
By force, hath overcome but half his foe.
[*Paradise Lost* (1667)]

ROOSEVELT, Theodore (1858–1919)
There is a homely old adage which runs, 'Speak softly and carry a big stick; you will go far.'
[Speech, 1903]

SAINT-PIERRE, Bernardin de (1737–1814)
Les femmes sont fausses dans les pays où les hommes sont des tyrans. Partout la violence produit la ruse.
Women are false in countries where men are tyrants. Violence everywhere leads to deception.
[*Paul et Virginie* (1788)]

TROTSKY, Leon (1879–1940)
Where force is necessary, one should make use of it boldly, resolutely, and right to the end. But it is as well to know the limitations of force; to know where to combine force with manoeuvre, assault with conciliation.
[*What Next?* (1932)]

UNAMUNO, Miguel de (1864–1936)
[Of Franco's supporters]
Vencer no es convencer.
To conquer is not to convince.
[Speech, 1936]

VIRTUE

ARISTOTLE (384–322 BC)
Moral virtues we acquire through practice like the arts.
[*Nicomachean Ethics*]

BACON, Francis (1561–1626)
Virtue is like a rich stone, best plain set.
['Of Beauty' (1625)]

BAGEHOT, Walter (1826–1877)
Nothing is more unpleasant than a virtuous person with a mean mind.
[*Literary Studies* (1879)]

BROWNE, Sir Thomas (1605–1682)
There is no road or ready way to virtue.
[*Religio Medici* (1643)]

CONFUCIUS (c. 550–c. 478 BC)
Virtue is not left to stand alone. He who practises it will have neighbours.
[*Analects*]

To be able to practise five things everywhere under heaven constitutes perfect virtue ... gravity, generosity of soul, sincerity, earnestness, and kindness.
[*Analects*]

FLETCHER, John (1579–1625)
'Tis virtue, and not birth that makes us noble:
Great actions speak great minds, and such should govern.
[*The Prophetess* (1622)]

GOLDSMITH, Oliver (c. 1728–1774)
The virtue which requires to be ever guarded, is scarce worth the sentinel.
[*The Vicar of Wakefield* (1766)]

LA ROCHEFOUCAULD, Duc de (1613–1680)
Il faut de plus grandes vertus pour soutenir la bonne fortune que la mauvaise.
Greater virtues are needed to sustain good fortune than bad.
[*Maximes* (1678)]

MILTON, John (1608–1674)
Most men admire
Virtue, who follow not her lore.
[*Paradise Regained* (1671)]

MOLIERE (1622–1673)
Il faut, parmi le monde, une vertu traitable.
Virtue, in this world, should be accommodating.
[*Le Misanthrope* (1666)]

MONTAIGNE, Michel de (1533–1592)
*La vertu refuse la facilité pour compagne
... elle demande un chemin âpre et
épineux.*
Virtue shuns ease as a companion. It
needs a rough and thorny path.

[*Essais* (1580)]

POPE, Alexander (1688–1744)
For Virtue's self may too much zeal be
    had;
The worst of Madmen is a Saint run
    mad.

[*Imitations of Horace* (1738)]

SHAKESPEARE, William (1564–1616)
Dost thou think, because thou art
virtuous, there shall be no more cakes
and ale?

[*Twelfth Night*, II.iii]

SHAW, George Bernard (1856–1950)
What is virtue but the Trade Unionism
of the married?

[*Man and Superman* (1903)]

WALPOLE, Horace (1717–1797)
Tell me, ye divines, which is the most

virtuous man, he who begets twenty
bastards, or he who sacrifices an
hundred thousand lives?

[Letter to Sir Horace Mann, 1778]

Virtue knows to a farthing what it has
lost by not having been vice.

[In Kronenberger, *The Extraordinary Mr.
Wilkes* (1974)]

WALTON, Izaak (1593–1683)
Good company and good discourse are
the very sinews of virtue.

[*The Compleat Angler* (1653)]

WASHINGTON, George (1732–1799)
Few men have virtue to withstand the
highest bidder.

[*Moral Maxims*]

WHITE, Patrick (1912–1990)
Virtue is ... frequently in the nature of
an iceberg, the other parts of it
submerged.

[*The Tree of Man* (1955)]

See GOOD AND EVIL;
GOODNESS; MORALITY

WAR

ANONYMOUS
To save the town, it became necessary to destroy it.
[American officer, during the Tet offensive, 1968]

AUSTEN, Jane (1775–1817)
[Of the Battle of Albuera in 1811]
How horrible it is to have so many people killed! – And what a blessing that one cares for none of them!
[Letter to Cassandra Austen, 1811]

BARUCH, Bernard M. (1870–1965)
Let us not be deceived – we are today in the midst of a cold war.
[Speech, 1947]

BENNETT, Alan (1934–)
I have never understood this liking for war. It panders to instincts already catered for within the scope of any respectable domestic establishment.
[*Forty Years On* (1969)]

THE BIBLE (King James Version)
All they that take the sword shall perish with the sword.
[*Matthew*, 26:52]

BISMARCK, Prince Otto von (1815–1898)
[Remark made just before he died]
If there is ever another war in Europe, it will come out of some damned silly thing in the Balkans.
[Attr.]

BORGES, Jorge Luis (1899–1986)
[On the Falklands War of 1982]
The Falklands thing was a fight between two bald men over a comb.
[*Time*, 1983]

BOSQUET, Pierre (1810–1861)
[Remark on witnessing the Charge of the Light Brigade, 1854]
C'est magnifique mais ce n'est pas la guerre.
It is magnificent, but it is not war.
[Attr.]

BRADLEY, Omar Nelson (1893–1981)
[On General MacArthur's proposal to carry the Korean war into China]
The wrong war, at the wrong place, at the wrong time, and with the wrong enemy.
[Senate inquiry, 1951]

BRIGHT, John (1811–1889)
[Referring to the Crimean War]
The angel of death has been abroad throughout the land; you may almost hear the beating of his wings.
[Speech, 1855]

CHAMBERLAIN, Neville (1869–1940)
[On the annexation by Germany of the Sudetenland]
How horrible, fantastic, incredible, it is that we should be digging trenches and trying on gas-masks here because of a quarrel in a far-away country between people of whom we know nothing.
[Speech, 1938]

CHRISTIE, Dame Agatha (1890–1976)
One is left with the horrible feeling now that war settles *nothing*; that to *win* a war is as disastrous as to lose one!
[*An Autobiography* (1977)]

CHURCHILL, Sir Winston (1874–1965)
[On RAF pilots in the Battle of Britain]
Never in the field of human conflict was so much owed by so many to so few.
[Speech, 1940]

CICERO (106–43 BC)
Silent enim leges inter arma.
Laws are silent in war.
[*Pro Milone*]

CLAUSEWITZ, Karl von (1780–1831)
Der Krieg ist nichts als eine Fortsetzung des politischen Verkehrs mit Einmischung anderer Mittel.
War is nothing but a continuation of politics by other means.
[*On War* (1834)]

CLEMENCEAU, Georges (1841–1929)
La guerre! C'est une chose trop grave pour la confier à des militaires.
War is much too serious a thing to be left to the military.

[In Suarez, *Sixty Years of French History: Clemenceau*]

CORNFORD, Frances Crofts (1886–1960)
How long ago Hector took off his plume,
Not wanting that his little son should cry,
Then kissed his sad Andromache goodbye –
And now we three in Euston waiting-room.

['Parting in Wartime' (1948)]

EDEN, Anthony (1897–1977)
We are not at war with Egypt. We are in armed conflict.

[Speech, 1956]

ELLIS, Havelock (1859–1939)
In many a war it has been the vanquished, not the victor, who has carried off the finest spoils.

[*The Soul of Spain* (1908)]

ERASMUS (c. 1466–1536)
Dulce bellum inexpertis.
War is sweet to those who do not fight.

[*Adagia* (1500)]

FONTENELLE, Bernard (1657–1757)
I detest war: it ruins conversation.

[In Auden, *A Certain World* (1970)]

FORGY, Howell (1908–1983)
[Remark at Pearl Harbour, 1941]
Praise the Lord and pass the ammunition.

[Attr.]

GOLDWATER, Barry (1909–)
You've got to forget about this civilian. Whenever you drop bombs, you're going to hit civilians.

[Speech, 1967]

GREY, Edward, Viscount of Fallodon (1862–1933)
[To a caller at the Foreign Office in August 1914]
The lamps are going out all over Europe; we shall not see them lit again in our lifetime.

[In *Twenty-five Years*]

HAIG, Douglas, Earl (1861–1928)
Every position must be held to the last man: there must be no retirement. With our backs to the wall, and believing in the justice of our cause, each one of us must fight on to the end.

[Order to British forces, 1918]

HANRAHAN, Brian (1949–)
[Reporting the British attack on Port Stanley airport, during the Falklands war]
I'm not allowed to say how many planes joined the raid but I counted them all out and I counted them all back.

[BBC report, 1 May 1982]

HIROHITO, Emperor (1901–1989)
The war situation has developed not necessarily to Japan's advantage.

[Announcing Japan's surrender, 15 August 1945]

HITLER, Adolf (1889–1945)
[Said in 1939]
In starting and waging a war it is not right that matters, but victory.

[In Shirer, *The Rise and Fall of the Third Reich* (1960)]

HOBBES, Thomas (1588–11679
Force, and fraud, are in war the two cardinal virtues.

[*Leviathan* (1651)]

HOOVER, Herbert (1874–1964)
Older men declare war. But it is youth that must fight and die.

[Speech, 1944]

HOPE, Alec (1907–)
[An ironic parody of the Greek epitaph

commemorating the Spartans who
died at Thermopylae in 480 BC]
Go tell those old men, safe in bed,
We took their orders and are dead.

['Inscription for Any War']

JARRELL, Randall (1914–1965)
From my mother's sleep I fell into the
State,
And I hunched in its belly till my wet
fur froze.
Six miles from earth, loosed from its
dream of life,
I woke to black flak and the nightmare
fighters.
When I died they washed me out of
the turret with a hose.

['The Death of the Ball Turret Gunner' (1969)]

JOHNSON, Hiram (1866–1945)
The first casualty when war comes is
truth.

[Speech, US Senate, 1917]

KEY, Ellen (1849–1926)
Everything, everything in war is
barbaric ... But the worst barbarity of
war is that it forces men collectively to
commit acts against which individually
they would revolt with their whole
being.

[*War, Peace, and the Future* (1916)]

LEE, Robert E. (1807–1870)
It is well that war is so terrible – we
would grow too fond of it.

[Remark after the Battle of Fredericksburg, 1862]

LLOYD GEORGE, David (1863–1945)
[Referring to the popular opinion that
World War I would be the last major
war]
This war, like the next war, is a war to
end war.

[Attr.]

MACAULAY, Lord (1800–1859)
[Of John Hampden]
He knew that the essence of war is
violence, and that moderation in war
is imbecility.

[*Collected Essays* (1843)]

MACDONALD, Ramsay (1866–1937)
We hear war called murder. It is not: it
is suicide.

[*The Observer*, 1930]

MAO TSE-TUNG (1893–1976)
We are advocates of the abolition of
war, we do not want war; but war can
only be abolished through war, and in
order to get rid of the gun it is necessary to take up the gun.

[*Quotations from Chairman Mao Tse-Tung*]

MARLOWE, Christopher (1564–1593)
Accurs'd be he that first invented war!

[*Tamburlaine the Great* (1590)]

MEIR, Golda (1898–1978)
A leader who doesn't hesitate before
he sends his nation into battle is not fit
to be a leader.

[I. and M. Shenker, *As Good as Golda* (1943)]

MENCKEN, H.L. (1880–1956)
War will never cease until babies
begin to come into the world with
larger cerebrums and smaller adrenal
glands.

[*Notebooks* (1956)]

MICHAELIS, John H. (1912–1985)
[Said to his regiment during the
Korean War]
You're not here to die for your country.
You're here to make those — die for
theirs.

[Attr.]

MILTON, John (1608–1674)
For what can Warr, but endless warr
still breed.

['On the Lord Generall Fairfax at the seige of Colchester' (1648)]

MOLTKE, Helmuth von (1800–1891)
*Der ewige Friede ist ein Traum, und
nicht einmal ein schöner und der Krieg
ein Glied in Gottes Weltordnung ... Ohne
den Krieg würde die Welt in
Materialismus versumpfen.*
Eternal peace is a dream, and not
even a pleasant one; and war is an
integral part of the way God has

WAR

ordered the world ... Without war, the world would sink in the mire of materialism.

[Letter to Dr J.K. Bluntschli, 1880]

MONTAGUE, C.E. (1867–1928)
War hath no fury like a non-combatant.

[*Disenchantment* (1922)]

NELSON, Lord (1758–1805)
[At the Battle of Copenhagen, 1801]
Leave off action? Now, damn me if I do! ... I have only one eye – I have a right to be blind sometimes ... I really do not see the signal! ... Damn the signal!

[In Southey, *The Life of Nelson*]

OWEN, Wilfred (1893–1918)
What passing-bells for these who die as cattle?
Only the monstrous anger of the guns.
Only the stuttering rifles' rapid rattle
Can patter out their hasty orisons.

['Anthem for Doomed Youth' (1917)]

PANKHURST, Sylvia (1882–1960)
I could not give my name to aid the slaughter in this war, fought on both sides for grossly material ends, which did not justify the sacrifice of a single mother's son. Clearly I must continue to oppose it, and expose it, to all whom I could reach with voice or pen.

[*The Home Front*]

PLOMER, William (1903–1973)
Out of that bungled, unwise war
An alp of unforgiveness grew.

['The Boer War' (1932)]

PYRRHUS (319–272 BC)
[After a hard-won battle]
If we are victorious against the Romans in one more battle we shall be utterly ruined.

[In Plutarch, *Lives*]

RABELAIS, François (c. 1494–c. 1553)
Les nerfs des batailles sont les pécunes.
Money is the sinews of battle.

[*Gargantua* (1534)]

RAE, John (1931–)
War is, after all, the universal perversion. We are all tainted: if we cannot experience our perversion at first hand we spend our time reading war stories, the pornography of war; or seeing war films, the blue films of war; or titillating our senses with the imagination of great deeds, the masturbation of war.

[*The Custard Boys* (1960)]

ROOSEVELT, Franklin Delano (1882–1945)
More than an end to war, we want an end to the beginnings of all wars.

[Speech, 1945]

SANDBURG, Carl (1878–1967)
Sometime they'll give a war and nobody will come.

[*The People, Yes* (1936)]

SASSOON, Siegfried (1886–1967)
[From the statement sent to his commanding officer, July 1917]
I am making this statement as an act of wilful defiance of military authority, because I believe that the War is being deliberately prolonged by those who have the power to end it ... I have seen and endured the sufferings of the troops, and I can no longer be a party to prolong these sufferings for ends which I believe to be evil and unjust.

[*Memoirs of an Infantry Officer* (1930)]

SHAKESPEARE, William (1564–1616)
Once more unto the breach, dear friends, once more;
Or close the wall up with our English dead.
In peace there's nothing so becomes a man
As modest stillness and humility;
But when the blast of war blows in our ears,
Then imitate the action of the tiger:
Stiffen the sinews, summon up the blood,
Disguise fair nature with hard-favour'd rage;
Then lend the eye a terrible aspect.

[*Henry V*, III.i]

We few, we happy few, we band of
  brothers;
For he to-day that sheds his blood
  with me
Shall be my brother; be he ne'er so
  vile,
This day shall gentle his condition;
And gentlemen in England now a-bed
Shall think themselves accurs'd they
  were not here,
And hold their manhoods cheap
  whiles any speaks
That fought with us upon Saint
  Crispin's day.

[Henry V, IV.iii]

**SHERMAN, William Tecumseh
(1820–1891)**
There is many a boy here today who
looks on war as all glory, but, boys, it
is all hell.

[Speech, 1880]

STRACHEY, Lytton (1880–1932)
[Reply when asked by a Tribunal what
he, as a conscientious objector, would
do if he saw a German soldier trying to
rape his sister]
I should try and come between them.

[In Holroyd, Lytton Strachey: A Critical
Biography (1968)]

TABER, Robert (20th century)
The guerrilla fights the war of the flea,
and his military enemy suffers the
dog's disadvantages: too much to
defend; too small, ubiquitous, and
agile an enemy to come to grips with.

[The War of the Flea]

UREY, Harold (1893–1981)
The next war will be fought with atom
bombs and the one after that with
spears.

[The Observer, 1946]

VIRGIL (70–19 BC)
Bella, horrida bella,
Et Thybrim multo spumantem sanguine
  cerno.
I see wars, dreadful wars, and the
Tiber foaming with much blood.

[Aeneid]

VULLIAMY, Ed
[A pacifist until the war in the Balkans
forced him to change his convictions]
Ironically, the horrors of war have
taught me that there are things that
are worse than war, and against them
determined and careful war should be
waged, in the name of the innocent
and the weak.

[The Weekend Guardian, 1992]

WAUGH, Evelyn (1903–1966)
When the war broke out she took
down the signed photograph of the
Kaiser and, with some solemnity, hung
it in the menservants' lavatory; it was
her one combative action.

[Vile Bodies (1930)]

[Giving his opinions of warfare after
the battle of Crete, 1941]
Like German opera, too long and too
loud.

[Attr.]

WELLINGTON, Duke of (1769–1852)
I always say that, next to a battle lost,
the greatest misery is a battle gained.

[In Rogers, Recollections (1859)]

[Refusing permission to shoot at
Napoleon during the Battle of
Waterloo]
It is not the business of generals to
shoot one another.

[Attr.]

WILSON, Woodrow (1856–1924)
Once lead this people into war and
they'll forget there ever was such a
thing as tolerance.

[In Dos Passos, Mr Wilson's War (1917)]

YOUNG, Edward (1683–1765)
One to destroy, is murder by the law;
And gibbets keep the lifted hand in
  awe;
To murder thousands, takes a specious
  name,
War's glorious art, and gives immortal
  fame.

[Night-Thoughts on Life, Death and
Immortality]

WAR AND PEACE

CHURCHILL, Sir Winston (1874–1965)
Those who can win a war well can rarely make a good peace and those who could make a good peace would never have won the war.

[*My Early Life* (1930)]

In war, resolution; in defeat, defiance; in victory, magnanimity; in peace, goodwill.

[*The Gathering Storm*]

CLEMENCEAU, Georges (1841–1929)
Il est plus facile de faire la guerre que la paix.
It is easier to make war than to make peace.

[Speech, 1919]

KETTLE, Thomas (1880–1916)
If I live, I mean to spend the rest of my life working for perpetual peace. I have seen war and faced artillery and know what an outrage it is against simple men.

[*Poems and Parodies*]

SHAKESPEARE, William (1564–1616)
Let me have war, say I; it exceeds peace as far as day does night; it's spritely, waking, audible, and full of vent. Peace is a very apoplexy, lethargy; mull'd, deaf, sleepy, insensible; a getter of more bastard children than war's a destroyer of men.

[*Coriolanus*, IV.v]

VEGETIUS RENATUS, Flavius (fl. c. AD 375)
Qui desiderat pacem, praeparet bellum.
Let him who desires peace be prepared for war.

[*Epitoma Rei Militaris*]

WILDER, Thornton (1897–1975)
When you're at war you think about a better life; when you're at peace you think about a more comfortable one.

[*The Skin of Our Teeth* (1942)]

See PEACE

THE WEATHER

AUSTEN, Jane (1775–1817)
What dreadful hot weather we have! It keeps me in a continual state of inelegance.

[Letter, 1796]

CHEKHOV, Anton (1860–1904)
He who doesn't notice whether it is winter or summer is happy. I think that if I were in Moscow, I wouldn't notice what the weather was like.

[*The Three Sisters* (1901)]

CONGREVE, William (1670–1729)
Is there in the world a climate more uncertain than our own? And, which is a natural consequence, is there any where a people more unsteady, more apt to discontent, more *saturnine, dark* and *melancholic* than our selves? Are we not of all people the most unfit to be alone, and most unsafe to be trusted with our selves?

[*Amendments of Mr Collier's False and Imperfect Citations* (1698)]

ELLIS, George (1753–1815)
Snowy, Flowy, Blowy,
Showery, Flowery, Bowery,
Hoppy, Croppy, Droppy,
Breezy, Sneezy, Freezy.

['The Twelve Months']

GOGARTY, Oliver St John (1878–1957)
In my best social accent I addressed him. I said, 'It is most extraordinary weather for this time of year!' He replied, 'Ah, it isn't this time of year at all.'

[*It Isn't This Time of Year at All* (1954)]

JOHNSON, Samuel (1709–1784)
When two Englishmen meet, their first talk is of the weather.

[*The Idler* (1758–1760)]

KEATS, John (1795–1821)
[Of Devon]
It is impossible to live in a country which is continually under hatches ... Rain! Rain! Rain!

[Letter to J.H. Reynolds, 1818]

LODGE, David (1935–)
The British, he thought, must be gluttons for satire: even the weather forecast seemed to be some kind of spoof, predicting every possible combination of weather for the next twenty-four hours without actually committing itself to anything specific.

[*Changing Places* (1975)]

MACAULAY, Dame Rose (1881–1958)
Owing to the weather, English social life must always have largely occurred either indoors, or, when out of doors, in active motion.

['Life Among The English' (1942)]

POUND, Ezra (1885–1972)
Winter is icummen in,
Lhude sing Goddamn,
Raineth drop and staineth slop,
And how the wind doth ramm!
Sing: Goddamn.

['Ancient Music' (1916)]

RUSKIN, John (1819–1900)
There is really no such thing as bad weather, only different kinds of good weather.

[Attr.]

SMITH, Logan Pearsall (1865–1946)
Thank heavens, the sun has gone in, and I don't have to go out and enjoy it.

[*All Trivia* (1933), 'Last Words']

SMITH, Sydney (1771–1845)
[Discussing the recent hot weather]
Heat, Ma'am! It was so dreadful here, that I found there was nothing left for it but to take off my flesh and sit in my bones.

[In Holland, *A Memoir of the Rev. Sydney Smith*]

See SEASONS

WIDOWS

FIELDING, Henry (1707–1754)
When widows exclaim loudly against second marriages, I would always lay a wager, that the man, if not the wedding-day, is absolutely fixed on.

[*Amelia* (1751)]

GAY, John (1685–1732)
The comfortable estate of widowhood, is the only hope that keeps up a wife's spirits.

[*The Beggar's Opera* (1728)]

I think, you must do like other widows – buy your self weeds, and be cheerful.

[*The Beggar's Opera* (1728)]

GUITRY, Sacha (1885–1957)
[Responding to his fifth wife's jealousy of his previous wives]
The others were only my wives. But you, my dear, will be my widow.

[Attr.]

HOFFNUNG, Gerard (1925–1959)
There is a French widow in every bedroom (affording delightful prospects).

[Speech, 1958]

IBÁRRURI, Dolores ('La Pasionaria') (1895–1989)
It is better to be the widow of a hero than the wife of a coward.

[Speech, Valencia, 1936]

WYCHERLEY, William (c. 1640–1716)
Well, a widow, I see, is a kind of sinecure.

[*The Plain Dealer* (1677)]

WISDOM

AESCHYLUS (525–456 BC)
It is a fine thing even for an old man to learn wisdom.

[*Fragments*]

ARISTOPHANES (c. 445–385 BC)
One may learn wisdom even from one's enemies.

[*Birds*]

BACON, Francis (1561–1626)
A wise man will make more opportunities than he finds.

['Of Ceremonies and Respects' (1625)]

THE BIBLE (King James Version)
Wisdom is the principal thing; there-

fore get wisdom: and with all thy
getting get understanding.

[*Proverbs*, 4:7]

BLAKE, William (1757–1827)
I care not whether a Man is Good or
  Evil; all that I care
Is whether he is a Wise Man or a Fool.
Go! put off Holiness
And put on Intellect.

[*Jerusalem* (1820)]

CHESTERFIELD, Lord (1694–1773)
Be wiser than other people if you can;
but do not tell them so.

[Letter to his son, 1745]

CONFUCIUS (c. 550–c. 478 BC)
Gravity is only the bark of wisdom's
tree, but it preserves it.

[*Analects*]

The heart of the wise, like a mirror,
should reflect all objects without being
sullied by any.

[*Analects*]

COWPER, William (1731–1800)
Knowledge dwells
In heads replete with thoughts of other
  men;
Wisdom in minds attentive to their
  own.

[*The Task* (1785)]

Knowledge is proud that he has
  learn'd so much;
Wisdom is humble that he knows no
  more.

[*The Task* (1785)]

EMERSON, Ralph Waldo (1803–1882)
Now that is the wisdom of a man, in
every instance of his labor, to hitch his
wagon to a star, and see his chore
done by the gods themselves.

[*Society and Solitude* (1870)]

HORACE (65–8 BC)
*Dimidium facti qui coepit habet: sapere
aude.*
To have made a beginning is half of
the business; dare to be wise.

[*Epistles*]

HUTCHESON, Francis (1694–1746)
Wisdom denotes the pursuing of the
best ends by the best means.

[*An Inquiry into the Original of our Ideas of
Beauty and Virtue* (1725)]

LEVI-STRAUSS, Claude (1908–)
*Le savant n'est pas l'homme qui fournit
les vraies réponses; c'est celui qui pose
les vraies questions.*
The wise man is not the man who
gives the right answers; he is the one
who asks the right questions.

[*The Raw and the Cooked*]

PLATO (c. 429–347 BC)
That man is wisest who, like Socrates,
has realized that in truth his wisdom is
worth nothing.

[*The Apology of Socrates*]

QUARLES, Francis (1592–1644)
Be wisely worldly, not worldly wise.

[*Emblems*, II (1635)]

ROOSEVELT, Theodore (1858–1919)
Nine-tenths of wisdom is being wise in
time.

[Speech, 1917]

SMOLLETT, Tobias (1721–1771)
Some folks are wise, and some are
otherwise.

[*The Adventures of Roderick Random* (1748)]

SWIFT, Jonathan (1667–1745)
No wise man ever wished to be
younger.

[*Thoughts on Various Subjects* (1711)]

SZASZ, Thomas (1920–)
The stupid neither forgive nor forget;
the naive forgive and forget; the wise
forgive but do not forget.

[*The Second Sin* (1973)]

TROLLOPE, Anthony (1815–1882)
It may almost be a question whether
such wisdom as many of us have in
our mature years has not come from
the dying out of the power of temptation, rather than as the results of
thought and resolution.

[*The Small House at Allington* (1864)]

WORDSWORTH, William (1770–1850)
Wisdom is oftimes nearer when we
    stoop
Than when we soar.
                          [*The Excursion* (1814)]

See KNOWLEDGE

WOMEN

ANONYMOUS
In particular, the State recognises that
by her life within the home, woman
gives to the State a support without
which the common good cannot be
achieved.
                          [*The Irish Constitution*]

AUSTEN, Jane (1775–1817)
Where people wish to attach, they
should always be ignorant. To come
with a well-informed mind, is to come
with an inability of administering to
the vanity of others, which a sensible
person would always wish to avoid. A
woman especially, if she have the
misfortune of knowing any thing,
should conceal it as well as she can.
                          [*Northanger Abbey* (1818)]

In nine cases out of ten, a woman had
better show more affection than she
feels.
                          [Letter]

BEAUVOIR, Simone de (1908–1986)
On ne naît pas femme: on le devient.
One is not born a woman: one
becomes a woman.
                          [*The Second Sex* (1950)]

THE BIBLE (King James Version)
And the rib, which the Lord God had
taken from man, made he a woman.
                          [*Genesis*, 2:22]

Who can find a virtuous woman? for
her price is far above rubies.
                          [*Proverbs*, 31:10]

All wickedness is but little to the
wickedness of a woman.
                          [Apocrypha, *Ecclesiasticus*, 25:19]

**BURNET, Sir Frank Macfarlane
(1899–1985)**
In an affluent society most healthy
women would like to have four
healthy children.
                          [*Dominant Mammal* (1970)]

BURNS, Robert (1759–1796)
Auld nature swears, the lovely dears
Her noblest work she classes, O:
Her prentice han' she try'd on man,
An' then she made the lasses, O.
                          ['Green Grow the Rashes' (1783)]

BUTLER, Samuel (1612–1680)
The souls of women are so small,
That some believe they've none at all.
                          [*Miscellaneous Thoughts*]

BUTLER, Samuel (1835–1902)
Brigands demand your money or your
life; women require both.
                          [Attr.]

BYRON, Lord (1788–1824)
There is something to me very
softening in the presence of a woman,
– some strange influence, even if one
is not in love with them – which I
cannot at all account for, having no
very high opinion of the sex.
                          [Journal, 1814]

CATULLUS (84–c. 54 BC)
Sed mulier cupido quod dicit amanti,
In vento et rapida scribere oportet aqua.
But what a woman says to her eager
lover, she ought to write in the wind
and the running water.
                          [*Carmina*]

CERVANTES, Miguel de (1547–1616)
La mujer honrada, la pierna quebrada, y
en casa; y la doncella honesta, el hacer
algo es su fiesta.
An honest woman and a broken leg
should be at home; and for a decent
maiden, working is her holiday.
                          [*Don Quixote* (1615)]

CHISHOLM, Caroline (1808–1877)
For all the churches you can build, and
all the books you can export, will

never do much good without what a
gentleman in that Colony very
appropriately called 'God's police' –
wives and little children – good and
virtuous women.

[*Emigration and Transportation Relatively
Considered* (1847)]

EKLAND, Britt (1942–)
As a single woman with a child, I
would love to have a wife.

[*The Independent*, 1994]

ELIOT, George (1819–1880)
I should like to know what is the
proper function of women, if it is not
to make reasons for husbands to stay
at home, and still stronger reasons for
bachelors to go out.

[*The Mill on the Floss* (1860)]

A woman can hardly ever choose ...
she is dependent on what happens to
her. She must take meaner things,
because only meaner things are within
her reach.

[*Felix Holt* (1866)]

FARQUHAR, George (1678–1707)
There's some diversion in a talking
blockhead; and since a woman must
wear chains, I would have the
pleasure of hearing 'em rattle a little.

[*The Beaux' Stratagem* (1707)]

FITZGERALD, Edward (1809–1883)
Mrs Browning's death is rather a relief
to me, I must say: no more Aurora
Leighs, thank God! A woman of real
genius, I know; but what is the upshot
of it all? She and her sex had better
mind the kitchen and their children;
and perhaps the poor: except in such
things as little novels, they only devote
themselves to what men do much
better, leaving that which men do
worse or not at all.

[Letter to W.H. Thompson, 1861]

FRAYN, Michael (1933–)
No woman so naked as one you can
see to be naked underneath her
clothes.

[*Constructions*]

FREUD, Sigmund (1856–1939)
The great question ... which I have not
been able to answer, despite my thirty
years of research into the feminine
soul, is 'What does a woman want?'

[In Robb, *Psychiatry in American Life*]

GRANVILLE, George (1666–1735)
Of all the plagues with which the
    world is curst,
Of every ill, a woman is the worst.

[*The British Enchanters*]

HAKIM, Catherine
The unpalatable truth is that a
substantial proportion of women still
accept the sexual division of labour
which sees home-making as women's
principal activitiy and income-earning
as men's principal activity in life.

[*The Observer Review*, 1996]

HARMAN, Sir Jeremiah (1930–)
I've always thought there were only
three kinds of women: wives, whores
and mistresses.

[Attr. in *Daily Mail*, 1996]

IRVING, Washington (1783–1859)
A woman's whole life is a history of
the affections.

[*The Sketch Book* (1820)]

JAMES I OF SCOTLAND (1394–1437)
[On being introduced to a young girl
proficient in Latin, Greek, and Hebrew]
These are rare attainments for a
damsel, but pray tell me, can she spin?

[Attr.]

JOHNSON, Samuel (1709–1784)
Sir, a woman's preaching is like a
dog's walking on his hinder legs. It is
not done well; but you are surprised to
find it done at all.

[In Boswell, *The Life of Samuel Johnson*
(1791)]

**LA ROCHEFOUCAULD, Duc de
(1613–1680)**
*On peut trouver des femmes qui n'ont
jamais eu de galanterie, mais il est rare
d'en trouver qui n'en aient jamais eu
qu'une.*

One can find women who have never
had a love affair, but it is rare to find a
woman who has only had one.

[*Maximes* (1678)]

LERNER, Alan Jay (1918–1986)
I'd be equally as willing
For a dentist to be drilling
Than to ever let a woman in my life.

[*My Fair Lady* (1956)]

LOOS, Anita (1893–1981)
So this gentleman said a girl with
brains ought to do something with
them besides think.

[*Gentlemen Prefer Blondes* (1925)]

MCCARTHY, Abigail (c. 1914–)
For those of us whose lives have been
defined by others – by wifehood and
motherhood – there is no individual
achievement to measure, only the
experience of life itself.

[*Private Faces/Public Places* (1972)]

MASEFIELD, John (1878–1967)
To get the whole world out of bed
And washed, and dressed, and
   warmed, and fed,
To work, and back to bed again,
Believe me, Saul, costs worlds of pain.

['The Everlasting Mercy' (1911)]

**MAUGHAM, William Somerset
(1874–1965)**
A woman will always sacrifice herself
if you give her the opportunity. It is her
favourite form of self-indulgence.

[*The Circle* (1921)]

MENCKEN, H.L. (1880–1956)
When women kiss, it always reminds
me of prize-fighters shaking hands.

[Attr.]

MILTON, John (1608–1674)
Nothing lovelier can be found
In Woman, than to studie household
   good,
And good works in her Husband to
   promote.

[*Paradise Lost* (1667)]

O why did God,
Creator wise, that peopl'd highest
   Heav'n
With Spirits Masculine, create at last
This noveltie on Earth, this fair defect
Of Nature?

[*Paradise Lost* (1667)]

[Reply when asked if he would allow
his daughters to learn foreign
languages]
One tongue is sufficient for a woman.

[Attr.]

NASH, Ogden (1902–1971)
Women would rather be right than
reasonable.

['Frailty, Thy Name is a Misnomer' (1942)]

NIETZSCHE, Friedrich (1844–1900)
*Alles am Weibe ist ein Rätsel, und alles
am Weibe hat eine Lösung: sie heisst
Schwangerschaft.*
Everything to do with women is a
mystery, and everything to do with
women has one solution: it's called
pregnancy.

[*Thus Spake Zarathustra* (1884)]

NIN, Anais (1903–1977)
Women (and I, in this Diary) have
never separated sex from feeling, from
love of the whole man.

[*Delta of Venus* (1977)]

POPE, Alexander (1688–1744)
Most Women have no Characters at
all.

['Epistle to a Lady' (1735)]

Woman's at best a Contradiction still.

['Epistle to a Lady' (1735)]

RACINE, Jean (1639–1699)
*Elle flotte, elle hésite; en un mot, elle est
femme.*
She wavers, she hesitates; in a word,
she is a woman.

[*Athalie* (1691)]

ROWLAND, Helen (1875–1950)
It takes a woman twenty years to

make a man of her son, and another woman twenty minutes to make a fool of him.

[*Reflections of a Bachelor Girl* (1909)]

RUBINSTEIN, Helena (c. 1872–1965)
There are no ugly women, only lazy ones.

[*My Life for Beauty* (1965)]

SCHOPENHAUER, Arthur (1788–1860)
One needs only to see the way she is built to realise that woman is not intended for great mental labour.

[Attr.]

SHAKESPEARE, William (1564–1616)
Do you not know I am a woman? When I think, I must speak.

[*As You Like It*, III.ii]

Frailty, thy name is woman!

[*Hamlet*, I.ii]

She's beautiful, and therefore to be woo'd;
She is a woman, therefore to be won.

[*Henry VI, Part 1*, V.iii]

A woman mov'd is like a fountain troubled –
Muddy, ill-seeming, thick, bereft of beauty.

[*The Taming of the Shrew*, V.ii]

SHARIF, Omar (1932–)
The truth is I worship women ... the kind who can use both intelligence and femininity. The woman must give the impression that she needs a man.

[In Spada, *Streisand: The Intimate Biography* (1995)]

SHAW, George Bernard (1856–1950)
The one point on which all women are in furious secret rebellion against the existing law is the saddling of the right to a child with the obligation to become the servant of a man.

[*Getting Married* (1911)]

SOUTHEY, Robert (1774–1843)
What will not woman, gentle woman, dare,

When strong affection stirs her spirit up?

[*Madoc* (1805)]

STOCKS, Mary, Baroness (1891–1975)
It is clearly absurd that it should be possible for a woman to qualify as a saint with direct access to the Almighty while she may not qualify as a curate.

[Attr.]

TENNYSON, Alfred, Lord (1809–1892)
The woman is so hard
Upon the woman.

[*The Princess* (1847)]

VANBRUGH, Sir John (1664–1726)
Once a woman has given you her heart you can never get rid of the rest of her.

[*The Relapse, or Virtue in Danger* (1696)]

WELLS, H.G. (1866–1946)
There's no social differences – till women come in.

[*Kipps: the Story of a Simple Soul* (1905)]

WOLFF, Charlotte (1904–1986)
Women have always been the guardians of wisdom and humanity which makes them natural, but usually secret, rulers. The time has come for them to rule openly, but together with and not against men.

[*Bisexuality: A Study*]

WYNNE-TYSON, Esme (1898–1972)
Scheherazade is the classical example of a woman saving her head by using it.

[Attr.]

See FEMINISM; MEN AND WOMEN

WORDS

AESCHYLUS (525–456 BC)
Words are physic to the distempered mind.

[*Prometheus Bound*]

BACON, Francis (1561–1626)
The ill and unfit choice of words wonderfully obstructs the understanding.

[*The New Organon* (1620)]

CARROLL, Lewis (1832–1898)
'When I use a word,' Humpty Dumpty said in rather a scornful tone, 'it means just what I choose it to mean – neither more nor less.'

[*Through the Looking-Glass* (1872)]

CONFUCIUS (c. 550–c. 478 BC)
Without knowing the force of words, it is impossible to know men.

[*Analects*]

ELIOT, T.S. (1888–1965)
Words strain,
Crack and sometimes break, under the burden,
Under the tension, slip, slide, perish,
Decay with imprecision, will not stay in place,
Will not stay still.

[*Four Quartets* (1944)]

EMERSON, Ralph Waldo (1803–1882)
Words are also actions, and actions are a kind of words.

['The Poet' (1844)]

HOBBES, Thomas (1588–1679)
Words are wise men's counters, they do but reckon by them; but they are the money of fools.

[*Leviathan* (1651)]

HOLMES, Oliver Wendell (1809–1894)
I am omniverbivorous by nature and training. Passing by such words as are poisonous, I can swallow most others, and chew such as I cannot swallow.

[*The Autocrat of the Breakfast-Table* (1858)]

HUXLEY, Aldous (1894–1963)
Thanks to words, we have been able to rise above the brutes; and thanks to words, we have often sunk to the level of the demons.

[*Adonis and the Alphabet* (1956)]

KIPLING, Rudyard (1865–1936)
Words are, of course, the most powerful drug used by mankind.

[Speech, 1923]

LYDGATE, John (c. 1370–c. 1451)
Woord is but wynd; leff woord and tak the dede.

['Secrets of Old Philosophers']

OGDEN, C.K. (1889–1957) and
RICHARDS, I.A. (1893–1979)
The belief that words have a meaning of their own account is a relic of primitive word magic, and it is still a part of the air we breathe in nearly every discussion.

[*The Meaning of Meaning* (1923)]

POPE, Alexander (1688–1744)
Words are like leaves; and where they most abound,
Much fruit of sense beneath is rarely found.

[*An Essay on Criticism* (1711)]

SHAKESPEARE, William (1564–1616)
But words are words: I never yet did hear
That the bruis'd heart was pierced through the ear.

[*Othello*, I.iii]

SPENCER, Herbert (1820–1903)
How often misused words generate misleading thoughts.

[*Principles of Ethics* (1879)]

SPENDER, Sir Stephen (1909–)
The word bites like a fish.
Shall I throw it back, free
Arrowing to that sea
Where thoughts lash tail and fin?
Or shall I pull it in
To rhyme upon a dish?

['Word']

See CONVERSATION;
LANGUAGE

WORK

ACHESON, Dean (1893–1971)
[Remark made on leaving his post as

Secretary of State, 1952]
I will undoubtedly have to seek what
is happily known as gainful employment, which I am glad to say does not
describe holding public office.

[Attr.]

ALLEY, Rewi (1897–1987)
[The motto of the Chinese Industrial
Co-operatives Association]
Gung Ho!
Work Together!

[In Chapple, *Rewi Alley of China* (1980)]

ANONYMOUS
Laborare est orare.
Work is prayer.

[Unknown origin]

The working class can kiss my arse –
I've got the boss's job at last.

[Australian Labor movement, traditional folk
saying]

BACON, Francis (1909–1993)
How can I take an interest in my work
when I don't like it?

[Attr.]

BALDWIN, James (1924–1987)
The price one pays for pursuing any
profession or calling is an intimate
knowledge of its ugly side.

[*Nobody Knows My Name* (1961)]

THE BIBLE (King James Version)
The labourer is worthy of his hire.

[*Luke*, 10:7]

If any would not work, neither should
he eat.

[*II Thessalonians*, 3:10]

BURNS, Robert (1759–1796)
We labour soon, we labour late,
To feed the titled knave, man,
And a' the comfort we're to get,
Is that ayont the grave, man.

['The Tree of Liberty' (1838)]

BUTLER, Samuel (1835–1902)
Every man's work, whether it be
literature or music or pictures or
architecture or anything else, is always

a portrait of himself.

[*The Way of All Flesh* (1903)]

CARLYLE, Thomas (1795–1881)
Be no longer a Chaos, but a World, or
even Worldkin. Produce! Produce!
Were it but the pitifullest infinitesimal
fraction of a Product, produce it, in
God's name! 'Tis the utmost thou hast
in thee: out with it, then. Up, up!
Whatsoever thy hand findeth to do, do
it with thy whole might.

[*Sartor Resartus* (1834)]

Work is the grand cure of all the
maladies and miseries that ever beset
mankind.

[Speech, 1886]

CLARKE, John (fl. 1639)
He that would thrive
Must rise at five;
He that hath thriven
May lie till seven.

[*Paraemiologia Anglo-Latina* (1639)]

CLUFF, Algy
[On the controversy over whether the
inhabitants of Hong Kong should be
allowed to enter Britain]
Energy, brains and hard work made
Hong Kong. If only a few of its people
would come here.

[*Daily Mail*, 1996]

**COLERIDGE, Samuel Taylor
(1772–1834)**
Work without hope draws nectar in a
sieve,
And hope without an object cannot
live.

['Work Without Hope' (1828)]

**COLLINGWOOD, Robin George
(1889–1943)**
Perfect freedom is reserved for the
man who lives by his own work and in
that work does what he wants to do.

[*Speculum Mentis* (1924)]

COWARD, Sir Noël (1899–1973)
Work is much more fun than fun.

[*The Observer*, 1963]

CUMBERLAND, Bishop Richard
(1631–1718)
It is better to wear out than to rust out.
[In Horne, *The Duty of Contending for the
Faith* (1786)]

CURIE, Marie (1867–1934)
One never notices what has been
done; one can only see what remains
to be done.
[Letter to her brother, 1894]

FRANCE, Anatole (1844–1924)
Man is so made that he can only find
relaxation from one kind of labour by
taking up another.
[*The Crime of Sylvestre Bonnard* (1881)]

GEORGE, Henry (1839–1897)
The man who gives me employment,
which I must have or suffer, that man
is my master, let me call him what I
will.
[*Social Problems* (1884)]

JEROME, Jerome K. (1859–1927)
I like work; it fascinates me. I can sit
and look at it for hours. I love to keep
it by me: the idea of getting rid of it
nearly breaks my heart.
[*Three Men in a Boat* (1889)]

KEROUAC, Jack (1922–1969)
We're really all of us bottomly broke. I
haven't had time to work in weeks.
[*On the Road* (1957)]

KOLLWITZ, Käthe (1867–1945)
For the last third of life there remains
only work. It alone is always stimu-
lating, rejuvenating, exciting and
satisfying.
[*Diaries and Letters* (1955)]

LANG, Ian (1940–)
Job insecurity is a state of mind.
[*The Observer Review*, 1995]

LARKIN, Philip (1922–1985)
Why should I let the toad work
Squat on my life?
Can't I use my wit as a pitchfork
And drive the brute off?
['Toads' (1955)]

LONDON, Jack (1876–1916)
In an English ship, they say, it is poor
grub, poor pay, and easy work; in an
American ship, good grub, good pay,
and hard work. And this is applicable
to the working populations of both
countries.
[*The People of the Abyss* (1903)]

LOWELL, James Russell (1819–1891)
No man is born into the world, whose
work
Is not born with him; there is always
work,
And tools to work withal, for those
who will:
And blessèd are the horny hands of
toil!
['A Glance Behind the Curtain' (1844)]

PARKINSON, C. Northcote (1909–1993)
Work expands so as to fill the time
available for its completion.
[*Parkinson's Law* (1958)]

PETER, Laurence J. (1919–1990)
In a hierarchy every employee tends to
rise to his level of incompetence.
[*The Peter Principle – Why Things Always Go
Wrong* (1969)]

PHILIP, Prince, Duke of Edinburgh
(1921–)
[Replying to a query as to what nature
of work he did]
I am self-employed.
[Attr.]

REAGAN, Ronald (1911–)
They say hard work never hurt
anybody, but I figure why take the
chance.
[Attr.]

ROOSEVELT, Theodore (1858–1919)
No man needs sympathy because he
has to work ... Far and away the best
prize that life offers is the chance to
work hard at work worth doing.
[Address, 1903]

ROWLAND, Helen (1875–1950)
When you see what some girls marry,

you realize how they must hate to work for a living.

[*Reflections of a Bachelor Girl* (1909)]

RUSSELL, Bertrand (1872–1970)
One of the symptoms of approaching nervous breakdowns is the belief that one's work is terribly important. If I were a medical man, I should prescribe a holiday to any patient who considered his work important.

[Attr.]

SHAKESPEARE, William (1564–1616)
The labour we delight in physics pain.

[*Macbeth*, II.iii]

SHAW, George Bernard (1856–1950)
A day's work is a day's work, neither more nor less, and the man who does it needs a day's sustenance, a night's repose, and due leisure, whether he be painter or ploughman.

[*An Unsocial Socialist* (1887)]

SPOONER, William (1844–1930)
[Many of the sayings attributed to Spooner are believed to have been made up by his friends]
You will find as you grow older that the weight of rages will press harder and harder upon the employer.

[In W. Hayter, *Spooner* (1977)]

STANTON, Elizabeth Cady (1815–1902)
Woman has been the great unpaid laborer of the world.

[In Anthony and Gage, *History of Woman Suffrage* (1881)]

TEBBITT, Norman (1931–)
[Of his father during the 1930s]
He didn't riot. He got on his bike and looked for work and he kept looking till he found it.

[Speech, 1981]

THOREAU, Henry (1817–1862)
For more than five years I maintained myself thus solely by the labor of my hands, and I found, that by working about six weeks in a year, I could meet all the expenses of living.

[*Walden* (1854)]

WATTS, Isaac (1674–1748)
In works of labour, or of skill,
I would be busy too;
For Satan finds some mischief still
For idle hands to do.

['Against Idleness and Mischief' (1715)]

WHITEHORN, Katherine (1926–)
The best careers advice to give to the young is 'Find out what you like doing best and get someone to pay you for doing it.'

[*The Observer*, 1975]

WILDE, Oscar (1854–1900)
Work is the curse of the drinking classes.

[In Pearson, *Life of Oscar Wilde* (1946)]

YEATS, W.B. (1865–1939)
The intellect of man is forced to choose
Perfection of the life, or of the work.

['The Choice' (1933)]

See CAREERS

THE WORLD

BALFOUR, A.J. (1848–1930)
This is a singularly ill-contrived world, but not so ill-contrived as all that.

[Attr.]

BROWNE, Sir Thomas (1605–1682)
The created world is but a small parenthesis in eternity.

[*Christian Morals* (1716)]

BUCKINGHAM, Duke of (1628–1687)
The world is made up for the most part of fools and knaves.

['To Mr. Clifford, on his Humane Reason']

BUTLER, Samuel (1835–1902)
The world will, in the end, follow only those who have despised as well as served it.

[*The Note-Books of Samuel Butler* (1912)]

CHAUCER, Geoffrey (c. 1340–1400)
This world nys but a thurghfare ful of wo,

And we been pilgrymes, passynge to
and fro.

[*The Canterbury Tales* (1387)]

CLOUGH, Arthur Hugh (1819–1861)
This world is bad enough, may-be,
We do not comprehend it;
But in one fact can all agree,
God won't, and we can't mend it.

[*Dipsychus* (1865)]

DIDEROT, Denis (1713–1784)
*Oh! que ce monde-ci serait une bonne
comédie si l'on n'y faisait pas un rôle.*
What a fine comedy this world would
be if one did not play a part in it!

[*Letters to Sophie Volland*]

FERLINGHETTI, Lawrence (1920–)
The world is a beautiful place
to be born into
if you don't mind some people dying
all the time
or maybe only starving
some of the time
which isn't half so bad
if it isn't you.

[*Pictures of the Gone World* (1955)]

FIRBANK, Ronald (1886–1926)
The world is disgracefully managed,
one hardly knows to whom to
complain.

[*Vainglory* (1915)]

HEMINGWAY, Ernest (1898–1961)
The world is a fine place and worth
the fighting for.

[*For Whom the Bell Tolls* (1940)]

KAFKA, Franz (1883–1924)
*Im Kampf zwischen dir und der Welt
sekundiere der Welt.*
In the struggle between you and the
world, support the world.

[*Reflections on Sin, Sorrow, Hope and the True
Way* (1953)]

LLOYD GEORGE, David (1863–1945)
The world is becoming like a lunatic
asylum run by lunatics.

[*The Observer*, 1953]

MCLUHAN, Marshall (1911–1980)
The new electronic interdependence
recreates the world in the image of a
global village.

[*The Gutenberg Galaxy* (1962)]

MACNEICE, Louis (1907–1963)
World is crazier and more of it than
we think,
Incorrigibly plural. I peel and portion
A tangerine and spit the pips and feel
The drunkenness of things being
various.

['Snow' (1935)]

O'CASEY, Sean (1880–1964)
Th' whole worl's in a terrible state o'
chassis!

[*Juno and the Paycock* (1924)]

SARTRE, Jean-Paul (1905–1980)
*Le monde peut fort bien se passer de la
littérature. Mais il peut se passer de
l'homme encore mieux.*
The world can survive very well
without literature. But it can survive
even more easily without man.

[*Situations*]

SHAKESPEARE, William (1564–1616)
I hold the world but as the world,
Gratiano –
A stage, where every man must play a
part,
And mine a sad one.

[*The Merchant of Venice*, I.i]

Why, then the world's mine oyster,
Which I with sword will open.

[*The Merry Wives of Windsor*, II.ii]

How many goodly creatures are there
here!
How beauteous mankind is! O brave
new world
That has such people in't!

[*The Tempest*, V.i]

SMITH, Sydney (1771–1845)
Bishop Berkeley destroyed this world
in one volume octavo; and nothing
remained, after his time, but mind;
which experienced a similar fate from

the hand of Mr Hume in 1739.

[*Sketches of Moral Philosophy* (1849)]

SMOLLETT, Tobias (1721–1771)
I consider the world as made for me, not me for the world: it is my maxim therefore to enjoy it while I can, and let futurity shift for itself.

[*The Adventures of Roderick Random* (1748)]

TRAHERNE, Thomas (c. 1637–1674)
You never enjoy the world aright, till the sea itself floweth in your veins, till you are clothed with the heavens, and crowned with the stars: and perceive yourself to be the sole heir of the whole world, and more than so, because men are in it who are every one sole heirs as well as you. Till you can sing and rejoice and delight in God, as misers do in gold, and kings in sceptres, you can never enjoy the world.

[*Centuries of Meditations*]

WORDSWORTH, William (1770–1850)
The world is too much with us; late
    and soon,
Getting and spending, we lay waste
    our powers:
Little we see in Nature that is ours;
We have given our hearts away, a
    sordid boon!

['The world is too much with us' (1807)]

WRITERS

ANONYMOUS
[A member of the Soviet Writers' Union, after the decision to urge publication of *The Gulag Archipelago*, in reply to Vladimir Karpov's comment 'I have never seen such unanimity among us']
At least, not since we voted to expel Solzhenitsyn.

[*The Independent*, 1989]

AUBREY, John (1626–1697)
How these curiosities would be quite forgot, did not such idle fellows as I am put them down.

[*Brief Lives* (c. 1693)]

AUDEN, W.H. (1907–1973)
No poet or novelist wishes he were the only one who ever lived, but most of them wish they were the only one alive, and quite a number fondly believe their wish has been granted.

[*The Dyer's Hand* (1963)]

AUSTEN, Jane (1775–1817)
I think I may boast myself to be, with all possible vanity, the most unlearned and uninformed female who ever dared to be an authoress.

[Letter to James Stanier Clarke, 1815]

BAGEHOT, Walter (1826–1877)
Writers, like teeth, are divided into incisors and grinders.

['The First Edinburgh Reviewers' (1858)]

BEAUVOIR, Simone de (1908–1986)
L'écrivain original, tant qu'il n'est pas mort, est toujours scandaleux.
Writers who stand out, as long as they are not dead, are always scandalous.

[*The Second Sex* (1950)]

BENNETT, Alan (1934–)
We were put to Dickens as children but it never quite took. That un-remitting humanity soon had me cheesed off.

[*The Old Country* (1978)]

BERNARD, Jeffrey (1932–)
Writers as a rule don't make fighters, although I would hate to have to square up to Taki or Andrea Dworkin.

[*Spectator*, 1992]

CANETTI, Elias (1905–1994)
Er legt Sätze wie Eier, aber er vergisst, sie zu bebrüten.
He lays sentences like eggs, but he forgets to incubate them.

[*The Human Province. Notes from 1942 to 1972*]

CHATEAUBRIAND, François-René (1768–1848)
L'écrivain original n'est pas celui qui n'imite personne, mais celui que personne ne peut imiter.
The original writer is not the one who

refrains from imitating others, but the one who can be imitated by none.

[*The Beauties of Christianity* (1802)]

CONNOLLY, Cyril (1903–1974)
An author arrives at a good style when his language performs what is required of it without shyness.

[*Enemies of Promise* (1938)]

Better to write for yourself and have no public, than write for the public and have no self.

[In Pritchett (ed.), *Turnstile One*]

EMERSON, Ralph Waldo (1803–1882)
Talent alone cannot make a writer. There must be a man behind the book.

['Goethe; or, the Writer' (1850)]

FAULKNER, William (1897–1962)
The writer's only responsibility is to his art ... If a writer has to rob his mother, he will not hesitate; the 'Ode on a Grecian Urn' is worth any number of old ladies.

[*Paris Review*, 1956]

FROST, Robert (1874–1963)
No tears in the writer, no tears in the reader.

[*Collected Poems* (1939)]

GORDIMER, Nadine (1923–)
The tension between standing apart and being fully involved; that is what makes a writer.

[*Selected Stories* (1975)]

HOBBES, Thomas (1588–1679)
The praise of ancient authors, proceeds not from the reverence of the dead, but from the competition, and mutual envy of the living.

[*Leviathan* (1651)]

JOHNSON, Samuel (1709–1784)
The greatest part of a writer's time is spent in reading, in order to write: a man will turn over half a library to make one book.

[In Boswell, *The Life of Samuel Johnson* (1791)]

The chief glory of every people arises from its authors.

[*A Dictionary of the English Language* (1755)]

JOSEPH, Michael (1897–1958)
Authors are easy to get on with – if you're fond of children.

[*The Observer*, 1949]

KOESTLER, Arthur (1905–1983)
A writer's ambition should be ... to trade a hundred contemporary readers for ten readers in ten years' time and for one reader in a hundred years' time.

[*New York Times Book Review*, 1951]

LAMB, Lady Caroline (1785–1828)
[Of Byron]
Mad, bad, and dangerous to know.

[*Journal*, 1812]

LANDOR, Walter Savage (1775–1864)
Clear writers, like clear fountains, do not seem so deep as they are; the turbid look the most profound.

[*Imaginary Conversations* (1824)]

LINCOLN, Abraham (1809–1865)
[On meeting Harriet Beecher Stowe]
So you're the little woman who wrote the book that made this great war!

[Attr.]

MACDIARMID, Hugh (1892–1978)
Our principal writers have nearly all been fortunate in escaping regular education.

[*The Observer*, 1953]

MACMANUS, Michael (1888–1951)
But my work is undistinguished
And my royalties are lean
Because I never am obscure
And not at all obscene.

['An Author's Lament']

PASCAL, Blaise (1623–1662)
Quand on voit le style naturel, on est tout étonné et ravi, car on s'attendait de voir un auteur, et on trouve un homme.
When we see a natural style, we are quite surprised and delighted, for we

expected to see an author and we find
a man.

[*Pensées* (1670)]

SINGER, Isaac Bashevis (1904–1991)
When I was a little boy they called me
a liar but now that I am a grown up
they call me a writer.

[*The Observer*, 1983]

VIDAL, Gore (1925–)
American writers want to be not good
but great; and so are neither.

[*Two Sisters* (1970)]

WAUGH, Evelyn (1903–1966)
No writer before the middle of the 19th
century wrote about the working
classes other than as grotesque or as
pastoral decoration. Then when they
were given the vote certain writers
started to suck up to them.

[*Paris Review*, 1963]

WHITLAM, Gough (1916–)
The challenge for the writer is to adapt
his ancient and difficult craft to a
generation that is largely insensitive to
its virtues and to a popular audience
increasingly distracted by the pace,
immediacy and materialism of
contemporary life.

[Speech, 1975]

YEATS, W.B. (1865–1939)
It's not a writer's business to hold
opinions.

[Attr.]

WRITING

ADDISON, Joseph (1672–1719)
[Of the difference between his
conversational and writing abilities]
I have but ninepence in ready money,
but I can draw for a thousand pounds.

[In Boswell, *The Life of Samuel Johnson*
(1791)]

ANONYMOUS
Inspiration is the act of drawing up a
chair to the writing desk.

ASCHAM, Roger (1515–1568)
He that will write well in any tongue,
must follow this counsel of Aristotle,
to speak as the common people do, to
think as wise men do; and so should
every man understand him, and the
judgment of wise men allow him.

[*Toxophilus* (1545)]

ATWOOD, Margaret (1939–)
Writing ... is an act of faith: I believe
it's also an act of hope, the hope that
things can be better than they are.

[Attr.]

AUSTEN, Jane (1775–1817)
Let other pens dwell on guilt and
misery.

[*Mansfield Park* (1814)]

BENTHAM, Jeremy (1748–1832)
Prose is when all the lines except the
last go on to the end. Poetry is when
some of them fall short of it.

[In Packe, *Life of John Stuart Mill* (1954)]

**BOILEAU-DESPREAUX, Nicolas
(1636–1711)**
*Qui ne sait se borner ne sut jamais
écrire.*
He who does not know how to limit
himself does not know how to write.

[*L'Art Poétique* (1674)]

BULWER-LYTTON, Edward (1803–1873)
Beneath the rule of men entirely great
The pen is mightier than the sword.

[*Richelieu* (1839)]

DE VRIES, Peter (1910–)
I write when I'm inspired, and I see to
it that I'm inspired at nine o'clock
every morning.

[*The Observer*, 1980]

DICKENS, Charles (1812–1870)
I hold my inventive faculty on the
stern condition that it must master my
whole life, often have complete
possession of me ... and sometimes for
months together put everything else
away from me.

[*The Letters of Charles Dickens*]

ELIOT, T.S. (1888–1965)
[On his ideal of writing]
The common word exact without
vulgarity, the formal word precise but
not pedantic, the complete consort
dancing together.

[*The Sunday Telegraph*, 1993]

FROST, Robert (1874–1963)
Writing free verse is like playing tennis
with the net down.

[Address, 1935]

GORKY, Maxim (1868–1936)
You must write for children just as you
do for adults, only better.

[Attr.]

JOHNSON, Samuel (1709–1784)
The only end of writing is to enable
the readers better to enjoy life, or
better to endure it.

[*Works* (1787)]

No man but a blockhead ever wrote,
except for money.

[In Boswell, *The Life of Samuel Johnson*
(1791)]

KEATS, John (1795–1821)
I am convinced more and more day by
day that fine writing is next to fine
doing, the top thing in the world.

[Letter to J.H. Reynolds, 1819]

LAWRENCE, D.H. (1885–1930)
I like to write when I feel spiteful: it's
like having a good sneeze.

[Letter to Lady Cynthia Asquith, 1913]

MURDOCH, Iris (1919–)
Writing is like getting married. One
should never commit oneself until one
is amazed at one's luck.

[*The Black Prince* (1989)]

ORWELL, George (1903–1950)
Good prose is like a window pane.

['Why I Write' (1946)]

PASCAL, Blaise (1623–1662)
*La dernière chose qu'on trouve en
faisant un ouvrage, est de savoir celle
qu'il faut mettre la première.*
The last thing one finds out when
constructing a work is what to put
first.

[*Pensées* (1670)]

RENARD, Jules (1864–1910)
The profession of letters is, after all,
the only one in which one can make
no money without being ridiculous.

[*Journal*]

SCOTT, Sir Walter (1771–1832)
But no one shall find me rowing
against the stream. I care not who
knows it – I write for the general
amusement.

[*The Fortunes of Nigel* (1822)]

SIDNEY, Sir Philip (1554–1586)
Byting my tongue and penne, beating
my selfe for spite:
'Foole,' saide My muse to mee, 'looke
in thy heart and write'.

[*Astrophel and Stella* (1591)]

SIMENON, Georges (1903–1989)
Writing is not a profession but a
vocation of unhappiness.

[*Writers at Work* (1958)]

STEPHEN, James Kenneth (1859–1892)
Will there never come a season
Which shall rid us from the curse
Of a prose which knows no reason
And an unmelodious verse ...
When there stands a muzzled stripling,
Mute, beside a muzzled bore:
When the Rudyards cease from kipling
And the Haggards ride no more.

[*Lapsus Calami* (1891)]

See CRITICISM; FICTION; LITERATURE; POETRY

YOUTH

ASQUITH, Herbert (1852–1928)
Youth would be an ideal state if it came a little later in life.

[*The Observer*, 1923]

BULWER-LYTTON, Edward (1803–1873)
In the lexicon of youth, which Fate reserves
For a bright manhood, there is no such word
As – *fail*!

[*Richelieu* (1839)]

CHANEL, Coco (1883–1971)
Youth is something very new: twenty years ago no one mentioned it.

[In Haedrich, *Coco Chanel, Her Life, Her Secrets* (1971)]

CONRAD, Joseph (1857–1924)
I remember my youth and the feeling that will never come back any more – the feeling that I could last for ever, outlast the sea, the earth, and all men; the deceitful feeling that lures us on to perils, to love, to vain effort – to death; the triumphant conviction of strength, the heat of life in the handful of dust, that glow in the heart that with every year grows dim, grows cold, grows small, and expires – and expires, too soon, too soon – before life itself.

[*Youth* (1902)]

CRISP, Quentin (1908–)
The young always have the same problem – how to rebel and conform at the same time. They have now solved this by defying their parents and copying one another.

[*The Naked Civil Servant* (1968)]

DISRAELI, Benjamin (1804–1881)
Youth is a blunder; Manhood a struggle; Old Age a regret.

[*Coningsby* (1844)]

GAY, John (1685–1732)
Youth's the season made for joys,
Love is then our duty.

[*The Beggar's Opera* (1728)]

IBSEN, Henrik (1828–1906)
Youth will come here and beat on my door, and force its way in.

[*The Master Builder* (1892)]

JOHNSON, Samuel (1709–1784)
Young men have more virtue than old men; they have more generous sentiments in every respect.

[In Boswell, *The Life of Samuel Johnson* (1791)]

JOWETT, Benjamin (1817–1893)
Young men make great mistakes in life; for one thing, they idealize love too much.

[*Life and Letters of Benjamin Jowett* (1897)]

OSBORNE, John (1929–1994)
I keep looking back, as far as I can remember, and I can't think what it was like to feel young, really young.

[*Look Back in Anger* (1956)]

PITT, William (1708–1778)
The atrocious crime of being a young man ... I shall neither attempt to palliate nor deny.

[Speech, House of Commons, 1741]

PORTER, Hal (1911–1984)
How ruthless and hard and vile and right the young are.

[*The Watcher on the Cast-iron Balcony* (1963)]

SHAKESPEARE, William (1564–1616)
He capers, he dances, he has eyes of youth, he writes verses, he speaks holiday, he smells April and May.

[*The Merry Wives of Windsor*, III.ii]

I would there were no age between ten and three and twenty, or that youth would sleep out the rest; for there is nothing in the between but getting wenches with child, wronging the ancientry, stealing, fighting.

[*The Winter's Tale*, III.iii]

SHAW, George Bernard (1856–1950)
Youth, which is forgiven everything, forgives itself nothing: age, which

forgives itself everything, is forgiven
nothing.

[*Man and Superman* (1903)]

It's all that the young can do for the
old, to shock them and keep them up
to date.

[*Fanny's First Play* (1911)]

[On youth]
Far too good to waste on children.

[Attr. in Copeland, *10,000 Jokes, Toasts, &
Stories* (1939)]

SMITH, Logan Pearsall (1865–1946)
The old know what they want; the
young are sad and bewildered.

['Last Words' (1933)]

THATCHER, Margaret (1925–)
Young people ought not to be idle. It is
very bad for them.

[*The Times*, 1984]

WHITMAN, Walt (1819–1892)
Youth, large, lusty, loving – youth full
    of grace, force, fascination,
Do you know that Old Age may come
    after you with equal grace, force,
    fascination?

['Youth, Day, Old Age and Night' (1855)]

WILDE, Oscar (1854–1900)
The old-fashioned respect for the
young is fast dying out.

[*The Importance of Being Earnest* (1895)]

WILSON, Woodrow (1856–1924)
Generally young men are regarded as
radicals. This is a popular misconcep-
tion. The most conservative
persons I ever met are college
undergraduates.

[Speech, 1905]

See AGE

LAST WORDS

ADDISON, Joseph (1672–1719)
See in what peace a Christian can die.
[Dying words]

**ALEXANDER THE GREAT
(356–323 BC)**
I am dying with the help of too many physicians.
[Attr.]

BAILLY, Jean Sylvain (1736–1793)
[Reflection on the evening before execution]
It's time for me to enjoy another pinch of snuff. Tomorrow my hands will be bound, so as to make it impossible.
[Attr.]

BARNUM, Phineas T. (1810–1891)
How were the receipts today in Madison Square Garden?
[Attr.]

BEHAN, Brendan (1923–1964)
Thank you, sister. May you be the mother of a bishop!
[Remark from his deathbed to a nun who was nursing him]

**BELL, Alexander Graham
(1847–1922)**
So little done. So much to do.
[Last words, 1922]

BRUCE, Robert (1554–1631)
Now, God be with you, my dear children: I have breakfasted with you and shall sup with my Lord Jesus Christ.
[Oral tradition]

BUTLER, Samuel (1835–1902)
[Last words to his servant and friend, Alfred Cathie]
Have you brought the cheque book, Alfred?
[In Henderson, *Samuel Butler: The Incarnate Bachelor* (1953)]

CAESAR, Gaius Julius (c. 102–44 BC)
Et tu Brute?

You too, Brutus?
[Attributed last words, on being stabbed by his friend]

CHANEL, Coco (1883–1971)
You see, this is how you die.
[In Madsen, *Coco Chanel* (1990)]

CHARLES I (1600–1649)
I dye a Christian, according to the profession of the Church of England, as I found it left me by my Father ... I go from a corruptible to an incorruptible Crown; where no disturbance can be, no disturbance in the world.
[In *King Charles His Speech Made Upon the Scaffold* (1649)]

CHESTERFIELD, Lord (1694–1773)
Give Dayrolles a chair.
[Attr.]

CHILDERS, Erskine (1870–1922)
[Last words before his execution by firing squad, 24 November 1922]
Take a step forward, lads. It will be easier that way.
[In Boyle, *The Riddle of Erskine Childers* (1977)]

**CHURCHILL, Sir Winston
(1874–1965)**
I'm so bored with it all.
[In M. Soames, *Clementine*]

CRANMER, Thomas (1489–1556)
[Said at the stake, 1556]
This is the hand that wrote it and therefore it shall suffer first punishment.
[In Green, *A Short History of the English People* (1874)]

CROMWELL, Oliver (1599–1658)
My design is to make what haste I can to be gone.
[Attr.]

CUVIER, Baron (1769–1832)
[On his deathbed when the nurse came to apply leeches]
Nurse, it was I who discovered that leeches have red blood.
[Attr.]

DAMIEN, Father (1840–1889)
[When asked on his deathbed
whether he would leave another
priest his mantle, like Elijah]
What would you do with it? It is full of
leprosy.
[In Acton, *Memoirs of an Aesthete*]

DANTON, Georges (1759–1794)
[Remark to his executioner]
Thou wilt show my head to the
people: it is worth showing.
[Attr.]

DE LA MARE, Walter (1873–1956)
[On being asked, as he lay seriously
ill, whether he would like fruit or
flowers]
Too late for fruit, too soon for flowers.
[Attr.]

DICKENS, Charles (1812–1870)
[Sydney Carton, before his execution]
It is a far, far better thing that I do,
than I have ever done; it is a far, far
better rest that I go to than I have
ever known.
[*A Tale of Two Cities* (1859)]

DISRAELI, Benjamin (1804–1881)
[Asked if Queen Victoria should visit
him during his last illness]
No, it is better not. She would only
ask me to take a message to Albert.
[Attr.]

DREISER, Theodore (1871–1945)
[Proposed last words]
Shakespeare, I come!
[In Mayfield, *The Constant Circle*]

DUNCAN, Isadora (1878–1927)
[Last words; she was about to test-
drive a Bugatti and was strangled
when her scarf caught in the spokes
of a wheel]
Adieu, mes amis, je vais à la gloire.
Goodbye, my friends, I go on to glory.
[Attr.]

ELIZABETH I (1533–1603)
All my possessions for a moment of
time.
[Attr., 1603]

EMMET, Robert (1778–1803)
[Before his execution]
When my country takes her place
among the nations of the earth, then
and not till then, let my epitaph be
written. I have done.
[Attr.]

EVANS, Dame Edith (1888–1976)
[Remark made a week before she
died]
Death is my neighbour now.
[Attr.]

FERRIER, Kathleen (1912–1953)
[Said shortly before her death]
Now I'll have *eine kleine Pause.*
[In Moore, *Am I Too Loud?*]

FONTENELLE, Bernard (1657–1757)
[Remark during his last illness]
It is high time for me to depart, for at
my age I now begin to see things as
they really are.
[Attr.]

[Remark made on his deathbed at the
age of 99]
I feel nothing, apart from a certain
difficulty in continuing to exist.
[In Conrad, *Famous Last Words*]

FOX, Charles James (1749–1806)
I die happy.
[Attr.]

GANDHI, Indira (1917–1984)
[Said 24 hours before she was
assassinated]
Even if I die in the service of this
nation, I would be proud of it. Every
drop of my blood, I am sure, will
contribute to the growth of this nation
and make it strong and dynamic.
[Speech, Orissa, 31 October 1984]

GEORGE V (1865–1936)
[To Lord Wigram, his secretary;
sometimes quoted as his last words]
How is the Empire?
[Attr.]

GOETHE (1749–1832)
Mehr Licht!
More light!

[Attr.]

**GRAHAM, James, Marquis of
Montrose (1612–1650)**
May God have mercy upon this
afflicted Kingdom.

[Attr.]

HAZLITT, William (1778–1830)
Well, I've had a happy life.
[In W.C. Hazlitt, *Memoirs of William
Hazlitt* (1867)]

HEGEL, Georg Wilhelm (1770–1831)
[Said on his deathbed]
Only one man ever understood me...
And he didn't understand me.
[In Conrad, *Famous Last Words* (1962)]

HEINE, Heinrich (1797–1856)
Dieu me pardonnera, c'est son métier.
God will forgive me. It is his
profession.
[In Meissner, *H H Erinnerungen* (1856)]

HENRY, O. (1862–1910)
[Attr. last words, quoting the song 'I'm
Afraid to Go Home in the Dark']
Don't turn down the light, I'm afraid to
go home in the dark.
[In Leacock, 'The Amazing Genius of
O. Henry' (1916)]

HOBBES, Thomas (1588–1679)
I am about to take my last voyage, a
great leap in the dark.
[In Watkins, *Anecdotes of Men of
Learning* (1808)]

HOKUSAI (1760–1849)
[Said on his deathbed]
If heaven had granted me five more
years, I could have become a real
painter.
[In Conrad, *Famous Last Words* (1962)]

HOLLAND, Lord (1705–1774)
[Said during his last illness]
If Mr Selwyn calls, let him in: if I am

alive I shall be very glad to see him,
and if I am dead he will be very glad to
see me.

[Attr.]

HOLT, Harold Edward (1908–1967)
I know this beach like the back of my
hand.
[Last words before disappearing,
presumed drowned; *Sydney Morning
Herald*, 1967]

HUME, David (1711–1776)
I am dying as fast as my enemies, if I
have any, could wish, and as cheer-
fully as my best friends could desire.
[Last words, 1776]

HUNTER, John (1728–1793)
If I had strength enough to hold a pen
I would write how easy and pleasant a
thing it is to die.
[Said on his deathbed]

HUSS, Jan (c. 1370–1415)
[At the stake, on seeing a peasant
bringing wood]
O sancta simplicitas!
O holy simplicity!
[In Zincgreff and Weidner,
Apothegmata (1653)]

IBSEN, Henrik (1828–1906)
[Ibsen's last words; his nurse had just
remarked that he was feeling a little
better]
On the contrary!

[Attr.]

JOHN XXIII (1881–1963)
[Remark made two days before he
died]
I am able to follow my own death step
by step. Now I move softly towards the
end.

[*The Guardian*, 1963]

JOHNSON, Samuel (1709–1784)
[On his deathbed]
I will be conquered; I will not ca-
pitulate.
[In Boswell, *The Life of Samuel Johnson*
(1791)]

KEATS, John (1795–1821)
I shall soon be laid in the quiet grave –
thank God for the quiet grave – O! I
can feel the cold earth upon me – the
daisies growing over me – O for this
quiet – it will be my first.

[Attr.]

KELLY, Ned (1855–1880)
[On the scaffold, 11 November 1880]
Ah well, I suppose it has come to this!
... Such is life!

[Attr.]

**LATIMER, Bishop Hugh
(c. 1485–1555)**
[Said shortly before being put to death
for heresy]
Be of good comfort, Master Ridley, and
play the man. We shall this day light
such a candle by God's grace in
England, as (I trust) shall never be put
out.

[In Foxe, *Actes and Monuments*
(1562–1563)]

LE MESURIER, John (1912–1983)
It's all been rather lovely.

[Last words, quoted in *The Times*,
1983]

LOUIS XIV (1638–1715)
[Noticing as he lay on his deathbed
that his attendants were crying]
Why are you weeping? Did you imagine that I was immortal?

[Attr.]

MCALPINE, Sir Alfred (1881–1944)
Keep Paddy behind the big mixer.

[Attr.]

MONMOUTH, Duke of (1649–1685)
[Words to his executioner]
Do not hack me as you did my Lord
Russell.

[In Macaulay, *History of England*
(1849)]

MORE, Sir Thomas (1478–1535)
After his head was upon the block,
[he] lift it up again, and gently drew
his beard aside, and said, This hath

not offended the king.

[In Bacon, *Apophthegms New and Old*
(1625)]

MORRIS, William (1834–1896)
I want to get Mumbo-Jumbo out of the
world.

[Attr.]

NELSON, Lord (1758–1805)
[Last words at the Battle of Trafalgar,
1805]
Thank God, I have done my duty.

[In Robert Southey, *The Life of Nelson*
(1860 edition)]

NERO (37–68)
Qualis artifex pereo!
What a great artist dies with me!

[In Suetonius, *Lives of the Caesars*,
'Nero']

**OATES, Captain Lawrence
(1880–1912)**
I am just going outside, and may be
some time.

[Last words, quoted in Captain Scott's
diary]

PALMERSTON, Lord (1784–1865)
Die, my dear Doctor, that's the last
thing I shall do!

[Attr.]

PHEIDIPPIDES (d. 490 BC)
[His last words, after he had run to
Athens with news of the Battle of
Marathon]
Greetings, we have won.

[In Lucian, 'Pro Lapsu inter
salutandum']

PITT, William (1759–1806)
I think I could eat one of Bellamy's
veal pies.

[Attr.]

MARCO POLO (c. 1254–1324)
I have not told half of what I saw.

[In Durant, *The Story of Civilization*]

POPE, Alexander (1688–1744)
Here am I, dying of a hundred good

symptoms.

[In Spence, *Anecdotes*]

RABELAIS, François
(c. 1494–c. 1553)
Je vais quérir un grand peut-être ... Tirez le rideau, la farce est jouée.
I am going to seek a great perhaps ...Bring down the curtain, the farce is played out.

[Attr.]

RALEIGH, Sir Walter (c. 1552–1618)
[On feeling the edge of the axe before his execution]
'Tis a sharp remedy, but a sure one for all ills.

[Attr.]

SAKI (1870–1916)
[Last words, said by Corporal Munro to one of his men who had lit up; he was killed by a German sniper]
Put that bloody cigarette out!

[In Langguth, *Life of Saki*]

SARO-WIWA, Ken (1941–1995)
Lord take my soul, but the struggle continues.

[*The Observer*, 1995]

SCARRON, Paul (1610–1660)
[As he lay dying]
At last I am going to be well!

[Attr.]

SCOTT, Captain Robert (1868–1912)
For God's sake look after our people.

[*Journal*, 25 March 1912]

Had we lived, I should have had a tale to tell of the hardihood, endurance, and courage of my companions which would have stirred the heart of every Englishman. These rough notes and our dead bodies must tell the tale.

[Message to the Public, 1912]

SIDNEY, Sir Philip (1554–1586)
[Offering his water-bottle, despite his own injuries, to a dying soldier on the battlefield near Zutphen, 1586]

Thy necessity is yet greater than mine.

[In Fulke Greville, *Life of Sir Philip Sidney* (1652)]

SMITH, Adam (1723–1790)
I believe we must adjourn this meeting to some other place.

[Attr.]

SOCRATES (469–399 BC)
Crito, we owe a cock to Asclepius. Pay it and do not neglect it.

[Attr. in Plato, *Phaedo*]

SPENCER, Sir Stanley (1891–1959)
[Thanking the nurse who had given him his nightly injection, just before he died]
Beautifully done.

[In Collis, *Stanley Spencer* (1962)]

STEIN, Gertrude (1874–1946)
Just before she [Stein] died she asked, 'What is the answer?' No answer came. She laughed and said, 'In that case, what is the question?' Then she died.

[In Sutherland, *Gertrude Stein* (1951)]

STEIN, Jock (1922–1985)
Let's not lose our dignity.

[Attr.]

STRACHEY, Lytton (1880–1932)
If this is dying, then I don't think much of it.

[In Holroyd, *Lytton Strachey: A Critical Biography* (1968)]

SWIFT, Jonathan (1667–1745)
[Learning of the arrival of Handel: Swift's last words]
Ah, a German and a genius! a prodigy, admit him!

[Attr.]

THURBER, James (1894–1961)
God bless ... God damn.

[Attr.]

TICHBORNE, Chidiock
(c. 1558–1586)
My prime of youth is but a frost of

cares;
My feast of joy is but a dish of pain;
My crop of corn is but a field of tares;
And all my good is but vain hope of
gain.
The day is past, and yet I saw no sun;
And now I live, and now my life is
done.
[*Elegy*, written in the Tower before
his execution]

TOLSTOY, Leo (1828–1910)
[Refusing to reconcile himself with the
Russian Orthodox Church as he lay
dying]
Even in the valley of the shadow of
death, two and two do not make six.
[Attr.]

**VEGA CARPIO, Félix Lope de
(1562–1635)**
[On learning that he was about to die]
All right, then, I'll say it: Dante makes
me sick.
[Attr.]

VESPASIAN (AD 9–79)
Vae, puto deus fio.
Woe is me, I think I am becoming a
god.
[In Suetonius, *Lives of the Caesars*,
'Vespasian']

WILDE, Oscar (1854–1900)
[Last words, as he lay dying in a drab
Paris bedroom]
Either that wallpaper goes, or I do.
[*Time*, 16 January 1984]

WILHELM I, Kaiser (1797–1888)
[Said during his last illness]
I haven't got time to be tired.
[Attr.]

WOLFE, James (1727–1759)
[Dying words]
Now God be praised, I will die in
peace.
[In Knox, *Historical Journal of
Campaigns* (1914 edition)]

EPITAPHS

ANONYMOUS
All who come my grave to see
Avoid damp beds and think of me.
[Epitaph of Lydia Eason, St Michael's,
Stoke]

[On a child dead of snake-bite]
From a subtle serpents Bite he cride
our RoseBud cut he drup'd his head
and died,
He was his Fathers glorey
And Mothers pride.
[Memorial to John Howorth, died aged
11 in 1804, St John's Churchyard,
Wilberforce, New South Wales]

God took our flour,
Our little Nell;
He thought He too
Would like a smell.
[In Thomas Wood, *Cobbers*]

Here lie I and my four daughters,
Killed by drinking Cheltenham waters.
Had we but stuck to Epsom salts,
We wouldn't have been in these here
vaults.
['Cheltenham Waters']

Here lie I by the chancel door;
They put me here because I was poor.
The further in, the more you pay,
But here lie I as snug as they.
[Epitaph, Devon churchyard]

Here lies a child that took one peep of
Life
And viewed its endless troubles with
dismay,
Gazed with an anguish'd glance upon
the strife
And sickening at the sight flew fast
away.
What though for many the gate of
Heaven is shut,
It stands wide open for this little Butt.
[Epitaph on Allena Butt, who died
when only 6 weeks old]

Here lies a man who was killed by
lightning;

He died when his prospects seemed to
be brightening.
He might have cut a flash in this world
of trouble,
But the flash cut him, and he lies in
the stubble.
[Epitaph, Torrington, Devon]

Here lies a poor woman who always
was tired,
For she lived in a place where help
wasn't hired.
Her last words on earth were, Dear
friends I am going
Where washing ain't done nor
sweeping nor sewing,
And everything there is exact to my
wishes,
For there they don't eat and there's no
washing of dishes ...
Don't mourn for me now, don't mourn
for me never,
For I'm going to do nothing for ever
and ever.
[Epitaph in Bushey churchyard]

Here lies Fred,
Who was alive and is dead;
Had it been his father,
I had much rather;
Had it been his brother,
Still better than another;
Had it been his sister,
No one would have missed her;
Had it been the whole generation,
Still better for the nation:
But since 'tis only Fred,
Who was alive and is dead, –
There's no more to be said.
[In Walpole, *Memoirs of George II*
(1847)]

Here lies my wife,
Here lies she;
Hallelujah!
Hallelujee!
[Epitaph, Leeds churchyard]

Here lies the body of Mary Ann
Lowder,
She burst while drinking a seidlitz
powder.
Called from the world to her heavenly
rest,

She should have waited till it
effervesced.
[Epitaph]

Here lies the body of Richard Hind,
Who was neither ingenious, sober, nor
kind.
[Epitaph]

Here lies Will Smith – and, what's
something rarish,
He was born, bred, and hanged, all in
the same parish.
[Epitaph]

Lo, Huddled up, together Lye
Gray Age, Grene youth, White Infancy.
If Death doth Nature's Laws dispence,
And reconciles All Difference
Tis Fit, One Flesh, One House Should
have
One Tombe, One Epitaph, One Grave:
And they that Liv'd and Lov'd Either,
Should Dye and Lye and Sleep
together.

Good reader, whether go or stay
Thou must not hence be Long Away.
[Epitaph, of William Bartholomew
(died 1662), his wife and some of their
children, St John the Baptist, Burford]

Mary Ann has gone to rest,
Safe at last on Abraham's breast,
Which may be nuts for Mary Ann,
But is certainly rough on Abraham.
[Epitaph]

My sledge and anvil lie declined
My bellows too have lost their wind
My fire's extinct, my forge decayed,
And in the Dust my Vice is laid
My coals are spent, my iron's gone
My Nails are Drove, My Work is done.
[Epitaph in Nettlebed churchyard]

Reader, one moment stop and think,
That I am in eternity, and you are on
the brink.
[Tombstone inscription in Perth,
Scotland]

Remember man, as thou goes by,
As thou art now so once was I,
As I am now so must thou be,

Remember man that thou must die.
[Headstone in Straiton, Ayrshire]

Rest in peace – until we meet again.
[Widow's epitaph for her husband; in Mitford, *The American Way of Death*]

Sacred to the memory of
Captain Anthony Wedgwood
Accidentally shot by his gamekeeper
Whilst out shooting
'Well done thou good and faithful servant'.
[Epitaph]

Stranger! Approach this spot with gravity!
John Brown is filling his last cavity.
[Epitaph of a dentist]

That we spent, we had:
That we gave, we have:
That we left, we lost.
[Epitaph of the Earl of Devonshire]

[On a cairn dedicated to the memory of the United Empire Loyalists]
They Sacrificed Everything Save Honour
[Inscription, 1964]

This is the grave of Mike O'Day
Who died maintaining his right of way.
His right was clear, his will was strong.
But he's just as dead as if he'd been wrong.
[Epitaph]

Warm summer sun shine kindly here:
Warm summer wind blow softly here:
Green sod above lie light, lie light:
Good-night, Dear Heart: good-night, good-night.
[Memorial to Clorinda Haywood, St Bartholomew's, Edgbaston]

ARBUTHNOT, John (1667–1735)
Here continueth to rot the body of Francis Chartres.
[First line of epitaph]

ATKINSON, Surgeon-Captain E.L. (1882–1929)
Hereabouts died a very gallant gentleman, Captain L.E.G. Oates of the Inniskilling Dragoons. In March 1912, returning from the Pole, he walked willingly to his death in a blizzard, to try and save his comrades, beset by hardships.
[Epitaph on a cairn and cross erected in the Antarctic, 1912]

AUDEN, W.H. (1907–1973)
Perfection, of a kind, was what he was after,
And the poetry he invented was easy to understand;
He knew human folly like the back of his hand,
And was greatly interested in armies and fleets;
When he laughed, respectable senators burst with laughter,
And when he cried the little children died in the streets.
['Epitaph on a Tyrant']

To save your world you asked this man to die:
Would this man, could he see you now, ask why?
['Epitaph for the Unknown Soldier' (1955)]

BARNFIELD, Richard (1574–1627)
[In memory of Sir John Hawkins]
The waters were his winding sheet, the sea was made his tomb;
Yet for his fame the ocean sea, was not sufficient room.
[*The Encomion of Lady Pecunia* (1598)]

BRAY, John Jefferson (1912–)
A hundred canvasses and seven sons
He left, and never got a likeness once.
['Epitaph on a Portrait Painter']

BROWNE, William (c. 1591–1643)
Underneath this sable hearse
Lies the subject of all verse,
Sidney's sister, Pembroke's mother;
Death! ere thou hast slain another,
Fair and learn'd, and good as she,
Time shall throw a dart at thee.
['Epitaph on the Countess of Pembroke' (1623)]

BURKE, Edmund (1729–1797)
His virtues were his arts.
> [Inscription on the statue of the
> Marquis of Rockingham in
> Wentworth Park]

BURNS, Robert (1759–1796)
Here lie Willie Michie's banes:
O Satan, when ye tak him,
Gie him the schulin' o' your weans,
For clever Deils he'll mak them!
> ['Epitaph for William Michie,
> Schoolmaster of Cleish Parish,
> Fifeshire' (1787)]

BYRON, Lord (1788–1824)
With death doomed to grapple,
Beneath this cold slab, he
Who lied in the chapel
Now lies in the Abbey.
> ['Epitaph for William Pitt' (1820)]

CAMDEN, William (1551–1623)
My friend, judge not me,
Thou seest I judge not thee.
Betwixt the stirrup and the ground
Mercy I asked, mercy I found.
> ['Epitaph for a Man Killed by Falling
> from His Horse' (1605)]

CARLYLE, Thomas (1795–1881)
[Epitaph for Jane Welsh Carlyle in
Haddington Church]
For forty years she was the true and
ever-loving helpmate of her husband,
and, by act and word, unweariedly
forwarded him as none else could, in
all of worthy that he did or attempted.
She died at London, 21st April 1866,
suddenly snatched away from him,
and the light of his life as if gone out.
> [In Macpherson, *Thomas Carlyle*
> (1896)]

CLEVELAND, John (1613–1658)
Here lies wise and valiant dust,
Huddled up, 'twixt fit and just:
Strafford, who was hurried hence
'Twixt treason and convenience.
He spent his time here in a mist,
A Papist, yet a Calvinist.
His Prince's nearest joy and grief;

He had, yet wanted, all relief:
The Prop and Ruin of the State,
The people's violent love and hate:
One in extremes lov'd and abhor'd.
Riddles lie here, or in a word,
Here lies blood; and let it lie
Speechless still, and never cry.
> ['Epitaph on the Earl of Strafford'
> (1647)]

**COLERIDGE, Samuel Taylor
(1772–1834)**
Ere sin could blight or sorrow fade,
Death came with friendly care:
The opening bud to Heaven convey'd
And bade it blossom there.
> ['Epitaph on an Infant' (1794)]

**CORNFORD, Frances Crofts
(1886–1960)**
Whoso maintains that I am humbled
   now
(Who wait the Awful Day) is still a liar;
I hope to meet my Maker brow to
   brow
And find my own the higher.
> ['Epitaph for a Reviewer' (1954)]

CRASHAW, Richard (c. 1612–1649)
To these, Whom Death again did wed,
This Grave's the second Marriage-Bed
...Peace, good Reader, doe not weepe;
Peace, the Lovers are asleepe:
They (sweet Turtles) folded lye,
In the last knot that love could tye.
> ['An Epitaph upon Husband and Wife,
> which died, and were buried together'
> (1646)]

DAY LEWIS, C. (1904–1972)
Now we lament one
Who danced on a plume of words,
Sang with a fountain's panache,
Dazzled like slate roofs in sun
After rain, was flighty as birds
And alone as a mountain ash.
The ribald, inspired urchin
Leaning over the lip
Of his world, as over a rock pool
Or a lucky dip,
Found everything brilliant and virgin.
> ['In Memory of Dylan Thomas']

DOUGLAS, James, Earl of Morton (c. 1516–1581)
[Said during the burial of John Knox, 1572]
Here lies he who neither feared nor flattered any flesh.
[Attr.]

DRYDEN, John (1631–1700)
Here lies my wife: here let her lie!
Now she's at rest, and so am I.
['Epitaph intended for his wife']

EVANS, Abel (1679–1737)
Under this stone, Reader, survey
Dead Sir John Vanbrugh's house of clay.
Lie heavy on him, Earth! for he
Laid many heavy loads on thee!
['Epitaph on Sir John Vanbrugh, Architect of Blenheim Palace' (died 1726)]

FIELDS, W.C. (1880–1946)
On the whole, I'd rather be in Philadelphia.
[His own epitaph]

FRANKLIN, Benjamin (1706–1790)
The body of
Benjamin Franklin, printer,
(Like the cover of an old book,
Its contents worn out,
And stript of its lettering and gilding)
Lies here, food for worms!
Yet the work itself shall not be lost,
For it will, as he believed, appear once
more
In a new
And more beautiful edition,
Corrected and amended
By its Author!
[Epitaph for himself, 1728]

FROST, Robert (1874–1963)
I would have written of me on my stone:
I had a lover's quarrel with the world.
['The Lesson for Today' (1942)]

GARRICK, David (1717–1779)
Here lies Nolly Goldsmith, for shortness call'd Noll,

Who wrote like an angel, but talk'd like poor Poll.
['Impromptu Epitaph on Goldsmith', 1774]

HALLECK, Fitz-Greene (1790–1867)
Green be the turf above thee,
Friend of my better days!
None knew thee but to love thee,
Nor named thee but to praise.
['On the Death of J.R. Drake' (1820)]

HOPE, Anthony (1863–1933)
His foe was folly and his weapon wit.
[Inscription to W.S. Gilbert, Victoria Embankment, London, 1915]

HOUSMAN, A.E. (1859–1936)
These, in the day when heaven was falling,
The hour when earth's foundations fled,
Followed their mercenary calling
And took their wages and are dead.

Their shoulders held the sky suspended;
They stood, and earth's foundations stay;
What God abandoned, these defended,
And saved the sum of things for pay.
['Epitaph on an Army of Mercenaries' (1922)]

HUME, David (1711–1776)
Within this circular idea
Call'd vulgarly a tomb,
The ideas and impressions lie
That constituted Hume.
[Epitaph on his monument on Calton Hill, Edinburgh]

JOHNSON, Samuel (1709–1784)
In lapidary inscriptions a man is not upon oath.
[In Boswell, *The Life of Samuel Johnson* (1791)]

Olivarii Goldsmith, Poetae, Physici, Historici, Qui nullum fere scribendi genus non tetigit, Nullum quod tetigit non ornavit.
To Oliver Goldsmith, A Poet,

Naturalist, and Historian, who left scarcely any style of writing un-touched, and touched none that he did not adorn.

[Epitaph on Goldsmith, 1776]

[On the death of Mr Levett]
Officious, innocent, sincere,
Of every friendless name the friend.
Yet still he fills affection's eye,
Obscurely wise, and coarsely kind.
[In Boswell, *The Life of Samuel Johnson* (1791)]

JONSON, Ben (1572–1637)
Weep with me, all you that read
This little story:
And know for whom a tear you shed
Death's self is sorry.
'Twas a child that so did thrive
In grace and feature,
As Heaven and Nature seem'd to strive
Which own'd the creature.
Years he number'd scarce thirteen
When Fates turn'd cruel,
Yet three fill'd Zodiacs had he been
The stage's jewel;
And did act, what now we moan,
Old men so duly,
As sooth the Parcae thought him one,
He play'd so truly.
So, by error, to his fate
They all consented;
But viewing him since, alas, too late!
They have repented;
And have sought (to give new birth)
In baths to steep him;
But being so much too good for earth,
Heaven vows to keep him.
['An Epitaph on Salomon Pavy, a Child of Queen Elizabeth's Chapel' (1616)]

O rare Ben Jonson.
[Epitaph in Westminster Abbey]

JOWETT, Benjamin (1817–1893)
Nowhere probably is there more true feeling, and nowhere worse taste, than in a churchyard – both as regards the monuments and the inscriptions.

Scarcely a word of the true poetry anywhere.
[In Abbott and Campbell (eds), *Life and Letters of Benjamin Jowett* (1897)]

KAUFMAN, George S. (1889–1961)
[Suggestion for his own epitaph]
Over my dead body!
[Attr.]

KEATS, John (1795–1821)
Here lies one whose name was writ in water.
[Epitaph for himself]

KIPLING, Rudyard (1865–1936)
I could not look on Death, which being known,
Men led me to him, blindfold and alone.
['Epitaphs – The Coward' (1919)]

LOCKHART, John Gibson (1794–1854)
Here lies that peerless peer Lord Peter,
Who broke the laws of God and man and metre.
[Epitaph for Patrick ('Peter'), Lord Robertson, 1890]

MACAULAY, Lord (1800–1859)
By those white cliffs I never more must see,
By that dear language which I spake like thee,
Forget all feuds, and shed one English tear
O'er English dust. A broken heart lies here.
['A Jacobite's Epitaph' (1845)]

MACDONALD, George (1824–1905)
Here lie I, Martin Elginbrodde:
Hae mercy o' my soul, Lord God;
As I wad do, were I Lord God,
And you were Martin Elginbrodde.
[*David Elginbrod* (1863)]

MARVELL, Andrew (1621–1678)
Who can foretell for what high cause
This Darling of the Gods was born! ...

Gather the flowers, but spare the buds.
['The Picture of Little T.C. in a Prospect of Flowers' (1681)]

MENCKEN, H.L. (1880–1956)
If, after I depart this vale, you ever remember me and have thought to please my ghost, forgive some sinner and wink your eye at some homely girl.

[*Smart Set*, 1921, Epitaph]

MILL, John Stuart (1806–1873)
Were there but a few hearts and intellects like hers this earth would already become the hoped-for heaven.

[Epitaph for his wife, Harriet, 1859]

MOORE, George (1852–1933)
[What he would like on his tombstone]
Here lies George Moore, who looked upon corrections as the one morality.

[Conversation with Geraint Goodwin]

NEWCASTLE, Margaret, Duchess of (c. 1624–1674)
Her name was Margaret Lucas youngest daughter of Lord Lucas, earl of Colchester, a noble family, for all the brothers were valiant, and all the sisters virtuous.

[Epitaph in Westminster Abbey; quoted by Joseph Addison]

PARKER, Dorothy (1893–1967)
He lies below, correct in cypress wood,
And entertains the most exclusive worms.

['Epitaph for a Very Rich Man' (1937)]

[Her own epitaph]
Excuse my dust.

[In Woollcott, *While Rome Burns* (1934)]

[Suggesting words for tombstone]
This is on me.

[In J. Keats, *You Might As Well Live* (1970)]

PEACOCK, Thomas Love (1785–1866)
Long night succeeds thy little day
Oh blighted blossom! can it be,
That this gray stone and grassy clay
Have closed our anxious care of thee?

[In Henry Cole (ed.), *Works of Peacock (1875)*, 'Epitaph on his Daughter']

PLOMER, William (1903–1973)
[In memory of the South African writers Ingrid Jonker and Nathaniel Nakasa, who committed suicide in 1965]
Her blood and his
Fed the slow, tormented
Tree that is destined
To bear what will be
Bough-bending plenty.

Let those who savour
Ripeness and sweetness,
Let them taste and remember
Him, her, and all others
Secreted in the juices.

['The Taste of the Fruit' (1966)]

POPE, Alexander (1688–1744)
Nature, and Nature's laws lay hid in night:
God said, *Let Newton be!* and all was light.

['Epitaph for Sir Isaac Newton' (1730)]

Of manners gentle, of affections mild;
In wit, a man; simplicity, a child:
With native humour temp'ring virtuous rage,
Formed to delight at once and lash the age.

['Epitaph: On Mr. Gay in Westminster Abbey', 1733]

RHYS, Ernest (b. 1859)
He had the plowman's strength
in the grasp of his hand:
He could see a crow
three miles away,
and the trout beneath the stone.
He could hear the green oats growing,
and the south-west wind making rain.
He could hear the wheel upon the hill
when it left the level road.
He could make a gate, and dig a pit,
And plow as straight as stone can fall.
And he is dead.

['Lost in France: Jo's Requiem']

ROCHESTER, Earl of (1647–1680)
Here lies our sovereign lord the King
Whose word no man relies on,
Who never said a foolish thing,
Nor ever did a wise one.

[Epitaph written for Charles II (1706)]

ROSSETTI, Christina (1830–1894)
O Earth, lie heavily upon her eyes;
Seal her sweet eyes weary of
watching.
['Rest' (1862)]

SASSOON, Siegfried (1886–1967)
Here sleeps the Silurist; the loved
physician;
The face that left no portraiture
behind;
The skull that housed white angels
and had vision
Of daybreak through the gateways of
the mind.
['At the Grave of Henry Vaughan'
(1928)]

SCOTT, Sir Walter (1771–1832)
Here lies one who might be trusted
with untold gold, but not with un-
measured whisky.
[Epitaph for his favourite servant, Tom
Purdie]

**SHAKESPEARE, William
(1564–1616)**
[Epitaph on his tomb]
Good friend, for Jesu's sake forbear,
To dig the dust enclosed here.
Blest be the man that spares these
stones,
And curst be he that moves my bones.
[Attr.]

SIMONIDES (c. 556–468 BC)
[Epitaph for the three hundred
Spartans under Leonidas who died at
Thermopylae in 480]
Go, tell the Spartans, thou who passest
by,
That here, obedient to their laws, we
lie.
[In Herodotus, *Histories*]

SMITH, Joseph (1805–1844)
No man knows my history.
[Funeral sermon, written by himself]

**STEVENSON, Robert Louis
(1850–1894)**
Under the wide and starry sky
Dig the grave and let me lie.
Glad did I live and gladly die,
And I laid me down with a will.

This be the verse you grave for me:
'Here he lies where he longed to be;
Home is the sailor, home from sea,
And the hunter home from the hill.'
['Requiem' (1887)]

SWIFT, Jonathan (1667–1745)
*Ubi saeva indignatio
Ulterius cor lacerare nequit.*
Where fierce indignation can no
longer tear his heart.
[Epitaph]

TURGOT, A.-R.-J. (1727–1781)
[Inscription for a bust of Benjamin
Franklin, who invented the lightning
conductor]
*Eripuit coelo fulmen, sceptrumque
tyrannis.*
He snatched the lightning shaft from
heaven, and the sceptre from tyrants.
[In A.N. de Condorcet, *Vie de Turgot*]

WILDE, Oscar (1854–1900)
All her bright golden hair
Tarnished with rust,
She that was young and fair
Fallen to dust.
['Requiescat' (1881)]

**WORDSWORTH, William
(1770–1850)**
Three years she grew in sun and
shower,
Then Nature said, 'A lovelier flower
On earth was never sown;
This child I to myself will take;
She shall be mine, and I will make
A Lady of my own'.
['Three years she grew' (1800)]

WOTTON, Sir Henry (1568–1639)
He first deceased; she for a little tried
To live without him: liked it not, and
died.
['Death of Sir Albertus Moreton's Wife'
(c. 1610)]

WREN, Sir Christopher (1632–1723)
Si monumentum requiris, circumspice.
If you are looking for his memorial,
look around you.
[Inscription written by his son, in St
Paul's Cathedral, London]

EPITAPHS

YEATS, W.B. (1865–1939)
Swift has sailed into his rest;
Savage indignation there
Cannot lacerate his breast.
Imitate him if you dare,
World-besotted traveller; he
Served human liberty.

['Swift's Epitaph' (1931)]

Under bare Ben Bulben's head
In Drumcliff churchyard Yeats is laid ...
On limestone quarried near the spot
By his command these words are cut:
Cast a cold eye
On life, on death.
Horseman, pass by!

['Under Ben Bulben' (Yeats' epitaph)
(1939)]

A

Abbott, Diane (1953–) British Labour politician

Accius, Lucius (170–86 BC) Roman poet

Ace, Jane (1905–1974) American comedian and radio personality

Achebe, Chinua (1930–) Nigerian writer, poet and critic

Acheson, Dean (1893–1971) American Democratic politician

Acton, Lord (1834–1902) English historian and moralist

Adamov, Arthur (1908–1970) Russian-born French surrealist and political dramatist

Adams, Douglas (1952–) English writer

Adams, Franklin P. (1881–1960) American writer, poet, translator and editor

Adams, Henry (1838–1918) American historian and memoirist

Adams, John Quincy (1767–1848) American lawyer, diplomat and President

Adams, Richard (1846–1908) Irish journalist, barrister and judge

Adams, Richard (1920–) English writer

Addams, Jane (1860–1935) American sociologist and writer

Addison, Joseph (1672–1719) English essayist, poet, playwright and statesman

Ade, George (1866–1944) American fabulist and playwright

Adenauer, Konrad (1876–1967) German Chancellor

Adler, Alfred (1870–1937) Austrian psychiatrist and psychologist

Adler, Freda (1934–) American educator and writer

Aeschylus (525–456 BC) Greek dramatist and poet

Aesop (6th century BC) Greek fabulist

Aga Khan III (1877–1957) Muslim leader

Agate, James (1877–1947) English drama critic and writer

Agathon (c.445–400 BC) Athenian poet

Ailesbury, Maria, Marchioness of (d.1902) English aristocrat

Alain (Emile-Auguste Chartier) (1868–1951) French philosopher, teacher and essayist

Albee, Edward (1928–) American dramatist

Albert, Prince Consort (1819–1861) German-born husband of Queen Victoria

Albertano of Brescia (c.1190–c.1270) Jurist, philosopher, magistrate and politician

Alcott, Bronson (1799–1888) American educator, reformer and trans-cendentalist

Alcott, Louisa May (1832–1888) American writer

Alcuin (735–804) English theologian, scholar and educationist

Aldiss, Brian (1925–) English writer

Aldrich, Henry (1647–1710) English scholar, divine and composer of songs

Alexander the Great (356–323 BC) Macedonian king and conquering army commander

Alfonso X (1221–1284) King of Castile and Leon; legal reformer

Ali, Muhammad (Cassius Clay) (1942–) American heavyweight boxer

Allen, Dave (1936–) Irish comedian and television personality

Allen, Fred (1894–1956) American vaudeville performer and comedian

Allen, Woody (1935–) American film director, writer, actor and comedian

Alley, Rewi (1897–1987) New Zealand reformer and educationist

Allingham, William (1824–1889) Irish poet and diarist

Allison, Malcolm (1927–) English footballer, coach and manager

Altman, Robert (1922–) American film director

Ambrose, Saint (c. 340–397) French-born churchman; writer of music and hymns

Ames, Fisher (1758–1808) American statesman and essayist

Amiel, Henri-Frédéric (1821–1881) Swiss philosopher and writer

Amis, Kingsley (1922–1995) English writer, poet and critic

Amis, Martin (1949–) English writer

Andersen, Hans Christian (1805–1875) Danish writer and dramatist

Anderson, Bruce British journalist

Andreotti, Giulio (1919–) Italian statesman and Prime Minister

Andrewes, Bishop Lancelot (1555–1626) English churchman

Angelou, Maya (1928–) American writer, poet and dramatist

Anka, Paul (1941–) American pop singer and songwriter

Anouilh, Jean (1910–1987) French dramatist and screenwriter

Anthony, Susan B. (1820–1906) American reformer, feminist and abolitionist

Antrim, Minna (1861–1950) American writer

Apollinaire, Guillaume (1880–1918) French poet and writer

Appius Claudius Caecus (4th–3rd century BC) Roman censor and writer

Appleton, Sir Edward (1892–1965) English physicist

Appleton, Thomas Gold (1812–1884) American epigrammatist

Arbuthnot, John (1667–1735) Scottish physician, pamphleteer and wit

Archer, Lord Jeffrey (1940–) British Conservative MP and popular novelist

Arendt, Hannah (1906–1975) German-born American theorist

Aristophanes (c.445–385 BC) Greek dramatist and satirist

Aristotle (384–322 BC) Greek philosopher

Armstrong, Dr John (1709–1779) Scottish physician, poet and writer

Armstrong, Louis (1900–1971) American jazz trumpeter, singer and bandleader

Armstrong, Neil (1930–) American astronaut and first man on the moon

Arnold, Harry British journalist

Arnold, Matthew (1822–1888) English poet, critic, essayist and educationist

Arnold, Thomas (1795–1842) English historian and educator

Artley, Alexandra British writer

Ascham, Roger (1515–1568) English scholar, educationist and archer

Ashdown, Paddy (1941–) British politician and leader of the Social and Liberal Democrat Party

Ashford, Daisy (1881–1972) English child author

Asimov, Isaac (1920–1992) Russian-born American scientist, academic and writer

Asquith, Herbert (1852–1928) English Liberal statesman and Prime Minister

Asquith, Margot (1864–1945) Scottish political hostess and writer

Astor, John (1763–1848) German-born American fur–trader and financier

Astor, Nancy (1879–1964) American-born British Conservative politician and hostess

Atkinson, Surgeon-Captain E.L. (1882–1929) British polar explorer, doctor and naval officer

Atkinson, Ti-Grace (c.1938–) American feminist

Attlee, Clement (1883–1967) English statesman and Prime Minister

Atwood, Margaret (1939–) Canadian writer, poet and critic

Auber, Daniel (1782–1871) French opera composer

Aubrey, John (1626–1697) English antiquary, folklorist and biographer

Auden, W.H. (1907–1973) English poet, essayist, critic, teacher and dramatist

Augier, Emile (1820–1889) French dramatist and poet

Augustine, Saint (354–430) Numidian-born Christian theologian, philosopher and scholar

Aung San Suu Kyi, Burmese politician

Aurelius, Marcus (121–180) Roman emperor and Stoic philosopher

Austen, Jane (1775–1817) English writer

Austin, Alfred (1835–1913) English poet and journalist

Austin, Warren Robinson (1877–1962) American politician and first US ambassador to the United Nations

Ayckbourn, Alan (1939–) English dramatist and theatre director

Ayer, A.J. (1910–1989) English philosopher

Aykroyd, Dan (1952–) American film actor

Aytoun, W.E. (1813–1865) Scottish poet, ballad writer and satirist

B

Bacon, Francis (1561–1626) English philospher, essayist, politician and courtier

Bacon, Francis (1909–1993) Irish painter

Baez, Joan (1941–) American folksinger and songwriter

Bagehot, Walter (1826–1877) English economist and political philosopher

Baillie, Joanna (1762–1851) Scottish dramatist and poet

Bailly, Jean Sylvain (1736–1793) French astronomer and politician

Bainbridge, Kenneth (1904–) American nuclear physicist

Bakewell, Joan (1933–) British journalist and television presenter

Bakunin, Mikhail (1814–1876) Russian anarchist and writer

Baldwin, James (1924–1987) American writer, dramatist, poet and civil rights activist

Baldwin, Stanley (1867–1947) English Conservative statesman and Prime Minister

Balfour, A.J. (1848–1930) Scottish Conservative statesman and Prime Minister

Ball, Alan (1943–) English international footballer and manager

Ballantyne, Sheila (1936–) American writer

Balzac, Honoré de (1799–1850) French writer

Bancroft, Richard (1544–1610) English churchman

Banda, Dr Hastings (1905–) Malawian politician and President

Bankhead, Tallulah (1903–1968) American actress

Banville, Théodore de (1823–1891) French poet, lyricist and dramatist

Barbarito, Luigi (1922–) Papal emissary

Barbour, John (c.1316–1395) Scottish poet, churchman and scholar

Bareham, Lindsey (1948–) Food critic and writer

Barker, George (1913–1991) English poet and writer

Barker, Ronnie (1929–) English comedian

Barnard, Robert (1936–) English writer

Barnes, Peter (1931–) English dramatist

Barnes, Simon (1951–) English writer

Barnfield, Richard (1574–1627) English poet

Barnum, Phineas T. (1810–1891) American showman and writer

Barrie, Sir J.M. (1860–1937) Scottish dramatist and writer

Barrington, George (1755–c.1835) Irish pickpocket and writer; transported to Australia

Barth, John (1930–) American writer

Barth, Karl (1886–1968) Swiss Protestant theologian

Barton, Bruce (1886–1967) American advertising agent and writer

Baruch, Bernard M. (1870–1965) American financier, government advisor and writer

Bashó, Matsuo (1644–1694) Japanese haiku poet

Bates, Daisy May (1863–1951) Irish-born journalist, anthropologist and reformer

Bateson, Mary (1939–) American anthropologist and writer

Baudelaire, Charles (1821–1867) French poet, translator and critic

Bax, Sir Arnold (1883–1953) English composer

Baxter, James K. (1926–1972) New Zealand poet and playwright

Baylis, Lilian (1874–1937) English theatrical manager

Bayly, Thomas Haynes (1797–1839) English songwriter, writer and dramatist

Beaumarchais (1732–1799) French dramatist, essayist, watchmaker and spy

Beaumont, Francis (1584–1616) English dramatist and poet

Beauvoir, Simone de (1908–1986) French writer, feminist critic and teacher of philosophy

Beaverbrook, Lord (1879–1964) Canadian-born British newspaper owner, politician and writer

Beckett, Samuel (1906–1989) Irish dramatist, writer and poet

Beckford, William (1760–1844) English writer, collector and politician

Becon, Thomas (1512–1567) English Protestant divine

Bede, The Venerable (673–735) English monk, historian and scholar

Beecham, Sir Thomas (1879–1961) English conductor and impresario

Beecher, Henry Ward (1813–1887) American clergyman, lecturer, editor and writer

Beeching, Rev. H.C. (1859–1919) English theologian, poet and essayist

Beer, Thomas (1889–1940) American writer

Beerbohm, Sir Max (1872–1956) English satirist, cartoonist, critic, essayist and parodist

Beethoven, Ludwig van (1770–1827) German composer

Behan, Brendan (1923–1964) Irish dramatist, writer and Republican

Behn, Aphra (1640–1689) English dramatist, writer, poet, translator and spy

Belasco, David (1853–1931) American theatre producer and playwright

Bell, Alexander Graham (1847–1922) Scottish-born American inventor and educator of the deaf

Bell, Clive (1881–1964) English art critic

Belloc, Hilaire (1870–1953) French-born English writer of verse, essayist and critic; Liberal MP

Bellow, Saul (1915–) Canadian–born American Jewish writer

Belloy, P.-L.B. du (1727–1775) French dramatist

Benchley, Robert (1889–1945) American essayist, humorist and actor

Bennett, Alan (1934–) English dramatist, actor and diarist

Bennett, Arnold (1867–1931) English writer, dramatist and journalist

Bentham, Jeremy (1748–1832) English writer and philosopher

Bentley, Edmund Clerihew (1875–1956) English writer

Bentley, Nicolas (1907–1978) English publisher and artist

Berkeley, Bishop (1685–1753) Irish philosopher and scholar

Berlin, Sir Isaiah (1909–) Latvian-born British philosopher

Berlioz, Hector (1803–1869) French composer and founder of modern orchestration

Bernard, Jeffrey (1932–) British columnist

Bernard, Tristan (1866–1947) French writer and dramatist

Bernhardt, Sarah (1844–1923) French actress

Betjeman, Sir John (1906–1984) English poet laureate

Betterton, Thomas (1635–1710) English actor and dramatist

Bevan, Aneurin (1897–1960) Welsh Labour politician, miner and orator

Beveridge, William (1879–1963) Indian-born British social reformer, economist and Liberal

Biagi, Enzo (1920–) Italian writer

Bickerstaffe, Isaac (c.1773–c.1808) Irish dramatist and author of ballad operas

Bierce, Ambrose (1842–c.1914) American writer, verse writer and soldier

Biko, Steve (1946–1977) Black South African civil rights leader

Billings, Josh (1818–1885) American writer, philosopher and lecturer

Bingham, Sir Thomas (1933–) English Master of the Rolls

Binyon, Laurence (1869–1943) English poet, art historian and critic

Bion (fl. 280 BC) Greek poet

Birley, Mark London nightclub owner

Birt, John (1944–) British television producer and Director-General of the BBC

Birtwistle, Harrison, Sir (1934–) English composer

Bismarck, Prince Otto von (1815–1898) German statesman; first Chancellor of the German Reich

Bissell, Claude T. (1916–) Canadian writer

Bjelke-Petersen, Sir Johannes (1911–) New Zealand-born Australian politician

Blackstone, Sir William (1723–1780) English judge, historian and politician

Blackwell, Antoinette Brown (1825–1921) American writer

Blainey, Geoffrey Norman (1930–) Australian writer

Blair, Tony (1953–) British Labour politician

Blake, Eubie (1883–1983) American jazz performer and songwriter

Blake, William (1757–1827) English poet, engraver, painter and mystic

Blücher, Prince (1742–1819) Prussian field marshal

Blue, Rabbi Lionel (1930–) English lecturer, writer and broadcaster

Blythe, Ronald (1922–) English writer

Bocca, Giorgio (1920–) Italian writer

Boethius (c. 475–524) Roman statesman, scholar and philosopher

Bogarde, Dirk (1921–) British actor and writer

Bohr, Niels (1885–1962) Danish nuclear physicist

Boileau-Despréaux, Nicolas (1636–1711) French poet, satirist and critic

Boleyn, Anne (1507–1536) Wife of Henry VIII and mother of Elizabeth I

Bolingbroke, Henry (1678–1751) English statesman, philosopher, historian and actor

Bolitho, William (1890–1930) South African-born British writer

Bombeck, Erma (1827–1996) American humorist and writer

Bone, James (1872–1962) Scottish journalist

Bongay, Amy President of the Models Guild

Bonhoeffer, Dietrich (1906–1945) German theologian, executed by the Nazis

Bono, Edward de (1933–) British physician and writer

Boorde, Andrew (c.1490–1549) English traveller, physician and writer

Boorstin, Daniel (1914–) American librarian, historian, lawyer and writer

Booth, General William (1829–1912) English founder of the Salvation Army

Borges, Jorge Luis (1899–1986) Argentinian writer, poet and librarian

Borovoy, A. Alan Canadian writer and civil liberties advocate

Borrow, George (1803–1881) English writer and linguist

Bosman, Herman (1905–1951) South African writer

Bosquet, Pierre (1810–1861) French general

Bossidy, John Collins (1860–1928) American oculist

Bottomley, Gordon (1874–1948) English poet and verse dramatist

Bottomley, Horatio William (1860–1933) English journalist, financier, politician and bankrupt

Boucicault, Dion (1822–1890) Irish dramatist, actor and theatrical manager

Boulay de la Meurthe, Antoine (1761–1840) French statesman and revolutionary

Boutros-Ghali, Boutros (1922–) Egyptian politician and minister; Secretary-General of the United Nations

Bowen, Elizabeth (1899–1973) Irish writer

Bowen, Lord (1835–1894) English judge and scholar

Bowra, Sir Maurice (1898–1971) English scholar

Boyd, Robin (1919–1971) Australian architect

BIOGRAPHIES

Boyd, William (1952–) Scottish writer and scriptwriter

'Boy George' (1961–) English singer-songwriter

Brack, (Cecil) John (1920–) Australian artist

Bradbury, Malcolm (1932–) English writer, critic and academic

Bradford, John (c.1510–1555) English Protestant martyr and writer

Bradley, F.H. (1846–1924) English philosopher

Bradley, Omar Nelson (1893–1981) American general

Bradshaw, Henry (d.1513) Monk and theologian

Bradshaw, John (1602–1659) English judge and republican

Bradstreet, Anne (c. 1612–1672) English-born American poet

Brahms, Johannes (1833–1897) German composer, pianist and conductor

Brando, Marlon (1924–) American actor

Braque, Georges (1882–1963) French painter

Brasch, Charles Orwell (1909–1973) New Zealand poet and editor

Braxfield, Lord (1722–1799) Scottish judge

Bray, John Jefferson (1912–) Australian lawyer and poet

Brecht, Berthold (1898–1956) German dramatist and poet

Brenan, Gerald (1894–1987) English writer

Brennan, Christopher (1870–1932) Australian poet

Breton, Nicholas (c.1545–c.1626) English writer and poet

Bridges, Robert (1844–1930) English poet, dramatist, essayist and doctor

Bridie, James (1888–1951) Scottish dramatist, writer and physician

Brien, Alan (1925–) British writer

Bright, John (1811–1889) English Liberal politician and social reformer

Brittain, Vera (1893–1970) English writer and pacifist

Broderick, John (1927–) Irish writer

Brodsky, Joseph (1940–1996) Russian poet, essayist, critic and exile

Brome, Richard (c.1590–1652) English dramatist

Bronowski, Jacob (1908–1974) Polish-born British mathematician, writer and television presenter

Brontë, Anne (1820–1849) English writer and poet

Brontë, Charlotte (1816–1855) English writer

Brontë, Emily (1818–1848) English poet and writer

Brooke, Rupert (1887–1915) English poet

Brookner, Anita (1928–) English writer

Brooks, Mel (1926–) American film actor and director

Brough, Robert (1828–1860) English journalist and writer

Brougham, Lord Henry (1778–1868) Scottish lawyer, politician, abolitionist and journalist

Brown, Ford Madox (1821–1893) French-born English painter and designer

Brown, Geoff (1949–) Film critic and writer

Brown, Helen Gurley (1922–) American writer and editor

Brown, Rita Mae (1944–) American writer and poet

Brown, Thomas Edward (1830–1897) Manx poet, teacher and curate

Brown, Tina (1953–) English journalist and editor

Browne, Sir Thomas (1605–1682) English physician, author and antiquary

Browne, William (c.1591–1643) English poet

Browning, Elizabeth Barrett (1806–1861) English poet; wife of Robert Browning

Browning, Robert (1812–1889) English poet

Bruce, Robert (1554–1631) Scottish churchman

Brummel, Beau (1778–1840) English dandy and wit

Bryan, William Jennings (1860–1925) American Democratic politician and editor

Buchan, John (1875–1940) Scottish writer, lawyer and Conservative politician

Buchanan, Robert Williams (1841–1901) British poet, writer and dramatist

Büchner, Georg (1813–1837) German playwright

Buchwald, Art (1925–) American humorist

Buck, Pearl S. (1892–1973) American writer and dramatist

Buckingham, Duke of (1628–1687) English courtier and dramatist

Buddha (c. 563–483 BC) Indian religious teacher; founder of Buddhism

Budgell, Eustace (1686–1737) English writer

Buffon, Comte de (1707–1788) French naturalist

Bulgakov, Mikhail (1891–1940) Russian writer and dramatist

Bullet, Gerald (1893–1958) English writer, poet and critic

Bullock, Alan (1914–) English historian and academic

Bulmer-Thomas, Ivor (1905–) Welsh politician and writer

Bulwer-Lytton, Edward (1803–1873) English writer, dramatist, poet and politician

Bunn, Alfred (1796–1860) English theatrical manager, librettist and poet

Buñuel, Luis (1900–1983) Spanish film director

Bunyan, John (1628–1688) English preacher, pastor and writer

Burchill, Julie (1960–) English writer

Burgess, Anthony (1917–1993) English writer, critic, teacher, linguist and composer

Burgon, John William (1813–1888) English churchman

Burke, Edmund (1729–1797) Irish-born British statesman and philosopher

Burnet, Sir Frank Macfarlane (1899–1985) Australian medical researcher

Burney, Fanny (1752–1840) English writer and diarist

Burns, Robert (1759–1796) Scottish poet and song writer; Scotland's national bard

Burton, Robert (1577–1640) English clergyman and writer

Bussy-Rabutin, Comte de (1618–1693) French soldier, writer and memoirist

Butler, Bishop Joseph (1692–1752) English philosopher and divine

Butler, Nicholas Murray (1862–1947) American teacher, lecturer, politican and writer

Butler, R.A. (1902–1982) Indian-born British Conservative politician

Butler, Samuel (1612–1680) English poet

Butler, Samuel (1835–1902) English writer, painter, philosopher and scholar

Bygraves, Max (1922–) English singer and entertainer

Byron, H.J. (1834–1884) English dramatist and actor

Byron, Lord (1788–1824) English poet, satirist and traveller

C

Cabell, James Branch (1879–1958) American writer, poet, genealogist and historian

Caesar, Gaius Julius (c.102–44 BC) Roman statesman, historian and army commander

Cage, John (1912–1992) American composer and writer

Caillavet, Arman de (1869–1915) French playwright

Calderón de la Barca, Pedro (1600–1681) Spanish dramatist and poet

Caligula (12–41) Roman emperor

Callaghan, James (1912–) English Labour statesman and Prime Minister

Calment, Jeanne (1875–) Frenchwoman, renowned for her longevity

Calverley, C.S. (1831–1884) English poet, parodist, scholar and lawyer

Calwell, Arthur Augustus (1894–1973) Australian Labour politician

Cambridge, Duke of (1819–1904) Field marshal and commander-in-chief of the British army

Camden, William (1551–1623) English scholar, antiquary and historian

Cameron, Simon (1799–1889) American statesman and newspaper editor

Campbell, David (1915–1979) Australian poet, rugby player and wartime pilot

Campbell, Joseph (1879–1944) Irish poet and republican

Campbell, Menzies (1941–) Scottish politician, lawyer and athlete

Campbell, Mrs Patrick (1865–1940) English actress

Campbell, Roy (1901–1957) South African poet and journalist

Campbell, Thomas (1777–1844) Scottish poet, ballad writer and journalist

Campbell-Bannerman, Sir Henry (1836–1908) British Liberal statesman and Prime Minister

Camus, Albert (1913–1960) Algerian-born French writer

Canetti, Elias (1905–1994) Bulgarian-born English writer, dramatist and critic

Canning, George (1770–1827) English statesman, Prime Minister, orator and poet

Canterbury, Tom American basketball player

Cantona, Eric (1966–) French footballer

Capone, Al (1899–1947) American gangster

Carew, Thomas (c.1595–1640) English poet, musician and dramatist

Carlyle, Jane Welsh (1801–1866) Scottish letter writer, literary hostess and poet

Carlyle, Thomas (1795–1881) Scottish historian, biographer, critic, essayist, teacher and translator

Carnegie, Andrew (1835–1919) Scottish-born American millionaire and philanthropist

Carr, J.L. (1912–1994) English writer and publisher

Carroll, Lewis (1832–1898) English mathematician, deacon, writer and photographer

Carson, Rachel (1907–1964) American marine biologist and writer

Carswell, Catherine (1879–1946) Scottish writer

Carter, Angela (1940–1992) English writer

Carter, Jimmy (1924–) American Democrat statesman and President

Cartland, Barbara (1902–) English writer

Casson, Sir Hugh (1910–) English architect and writer

Castellani, Maria (fl. 1930s) Italian educator and writer

Cather, Willa (1873–1947) American writer

Catherine the Great (1729–1796) German-born Empress of Russia and patron of the arts

Cato the Elder (234–149 BC) Roman statesman, writer and orator

Catullus (84–c.54 BC) Roman poet

Cavell, Edith (1865–1915) English nurse, executed by the Germans

Cecil, Lord David (1902–1986) English critic and writer

Cernuda, Luis (1902–1963) Spanish poet

Cervantes, Miguel de (1547–1616) Spanish writer and dramatist

Chamberlain, Neville (1869–1940) English statesman and Conservative Prime Minister

Chamfort, Nicolas (1741–1794) French writer

Chandler, Raymond (1888–1959) American crime writer

Chanel, Coco (1883–1971) French couturier and perfumer

Chaplin, Charlie (1889–1977) English comedian, film actor, director and satirist

Chapman, George (c.1559–c.1634) English poet, dramatist and translator

Charles I (1600–1649) Scottish-born British king

Charles II (1630–1685) English King of Great Britain and Ireland

Charles X (1757–1836) King of France; attempted to restore absolutism

Charles, Prince of Wales (1948–) Son and heir of Elizabeth II and Prince Philip

Chase, Ilka (1905–1978) American writer, actress and broadcaster

Chasen, Dave Hollywood restaurateur

Chateaubriand, François-René (1768–1848) French writer and statesman

Chaucer, Geoffrey (c.1340–1400) English poet, public servant and courtier

Chekhov, Anton (1860–1904) Russian writer, dramatist and doctor

Cher (1946–) American singer and actress

Cherry-Garrard, Apsley (1886–1959) English polar explorer, zoologist and writer

Chesterfield, Lord (1694–1773) English politician, statesman, letter writer and orator

Chesterton, G.K. (1874–1936) English writer, poet and critic

Chevalier, Maurice (1888–1972) French singer and actor

Chifley, Joseph (1885–1951) Australian politician

Child, Lydia M. (1802–1880) American writer, abolitionist and suffragist

Childers, Erskine (1870–1922) English writer and historian; Irish revolutionary politician

Chillingworth, William (1602–1644) English theologian and scholar

Chisholm, Caroline (1808–1977) English-born Australian humanitarian

Chomsky, Noam (1928–) American linguist and political critic

Chopin, Kate (1851–1904) American writer

Christie, Dame Agatha (1890–1976) English crime writer and playwright

Chuang Tse (c.369–286 BC) Chinese Taoist philosopher

Churchill, Charles (1731–1764) English poet, political writer and clergyman

Churchill, Sir Winston (1874–1965) English statesman and Conservative Prime Minister; writer and historian

Ciano, Count Galeazzo (1903–1944) Italian politician

Cicero (106–43 BC) Roman orator, statesman, essayist and letter writer

Clare, Dr Anthony (1942–) Irish professor, psychiatrist and broadcaster

Clare, John (1793–1864) English rural poet; died in an asylum

Clark, Alan (1928–) British Conservative politician and historian

Clark, Lord Kenneth (1903–1983) English art historian

Clarke, Arthur C. (1917–) English writer

Clarke, John (fl. 1639) English scholar

Clarke, Marcus (1846–1881) English-born Australian writer

Claudel, Paul (1868–1955) French dramatist, poet and diplomat

Clausewitz, Karl von (1780–1831) German general and military philosopher

Clayton, Keith (1928–) Professor of Environmental Sciences

Cleese, John (1939–) British comedian, actor and writer

Clemenceau, Georges (1841–1929) French statesman, Prime Minister and journalist

Cleveland, John (1613–1658) English poet

Clifford, William Kingdon (1845–1879) English mathematician

Clinton, Bill (1946–) American politician and President

Clive, Lord (1725–1774) English general, statesman and Indian administrator

Clough, Arthur Hugh (1819–1861) English poet and letter writer

Cluff, Algy Millionaire British businessman

Cobbett, William (1762–1835) English politician, reformer, writer, farmer and army officer

Cochran, Charles B. (1872–1951) English showman and theatrical producer

Cocteau, Jean (1889–1963) French dramatist, poet, film writer and director

Cody, Henry (1868–1951) Anglican churchman

Coetzee, John Michael (1940–) South African writer

Cohen, Sir Jack (1898–1979) Supermarket magnate

Coke, Sir Edward (1552–1634) English judge, writer and politician

Colby, Frank Moore (1865–1925) American editor, historian and economist

Coleman, David (1926–) English sports commentator and broadcaster

Coleridge, Hartley (1796–1849) English poet and writer

Coleridge, Samuel Taylor (1772–1834) English poet, philosopher and critic

Colette (1873–1954) French writer

Collingwood, Robin (1889–1943) English philosopher, archaeologist and historian

Collins, Michael (1890–1922) Irish revolutionary leader

Collins, Mortimer (1827–1876) English poet and writer

Colman the Elder, George (1732–1794) English dramatist and theatrical manager

Colman the Younger, George (1762–1836) English dramatist, theatrical manager and Examiner of Plays

Colton, Charles Caleb (c.1780–1832) English clergyman, poet, satirist, essayist and gambler

Coltrane, Robbie (1950–) Scottish comedian and actor

Comfort, Alex (1920–) British medical biologist and writer on sex

Compton-Burnett, Dame Ivy (1884–1969) English writer

Comte, Auguste (1798–1857) French philosopher, sociologist and mathematician

Condorcet, Antoine-Nicolas de (1743–1794) French mathematician and academician

Confucius, (c. 550–c. 478 BC) Chinese philosopher and teacher of ethics

Congreve, William (1670–1729) English dramatist

Connolly, Cyril (1903–1974) English literary editor, writer and critic

Connolly, James (1868–1916) Irish labour leader

Connors, Jimmy (1952–) American champion tennis player

Conrad, Joseph (1857–1924) Polish-born British writer, sailor and explorer

Conran, Shirley (1932–) English writer

Constable, John (1776–1837) English painter

Constant, Benjamin (1767–1834) Swiss-born French writer and politician

Coogan, Tim Pat (1935–) Irish writer

Cook, A.J. (1885–1931) English miners' leader

Cook, Peter (1937–1995) English comedian and writer

Coolidge, Calvin (1872–1933) American statesman and lawyer

Cooper, Roger British businessman, taken hostage in Iran

Cope, Wendy (1945–) English writer and poet

Coren, Alan (1938–) British humorist, writer and broadcaster

Corneille, Pierre (1606–1684) French dramatist, poet and lawyer

Cornford, F.M. (1874–1943) English Platonic scholar

Cornford, Frances Crofts (1886–1960) English poet and translator

Cornuel, Madame de (1605–1694) French society hostess

Cory, William (1823–1892) English poet, teacher and writer

Coubertin, Pierre de (1863–1937) French educationist and sportsman

Counihan, Noel (1913–1986) Australian cartoonist and artist

Coventry, Thomas (1578–1640) English Attorney-General and politician

Coward, Sir Noël (1899–1973) English dramatist, actor, producer and composer

Cowley, Abraham (1618–1667) English poet and dramatist

Cowley, Hannah (1743–1809) English dramatist and poet

Cowper, William (1731–1800) English poet, hymn and letter writer

Cozzens, James Gould (1903–1978) American writer

Crabbe, George (1754–1832) English poet, clergyman, surgeon and botanist

Craig, Sir Gordon (1872–1966) English actor, artist and stage designer

Craig, Maurice James (1919–) Poet and historian

Cranmer, Thomas (1489–1556) English Protestant martyr

Crashaw, Richard (c.1612–1649) English religious poet

Creighton, Mandell (1843–1901) English churchman, historian and biographer

Crick, Francis (1916–) British biologist

Crisp, Quentin (1908–) English writer, publicist and model

Critchley, Julian (1930–) English writer, broadcaster, journalist and politician

Crompton, Richmal (1890–1969) English writer and teacher

Cromwell, Oliver (1599–1658) English general, statesman and Puritan leader

Cronenberg, David (1943–) Canadian film director

Crooks, Garth (1958–) English footballer

Crowfoot (1821–1890) Blackfoot warrior and orator

Cumberland, Bishop Richard (1631–1718) English philosopher, divine and translator

cummings, e.e. (1894–1962) American poet, noted for his typography, and painter

Cunningham, Allan (1784–1842) Scottish poet, parliamentary reporter and biographer

Cunningham, Peter Miller (1789–1864) Scottish-born surgeon–superintendent on convict transports

Curie, Marie (1867–1934) Polish-born French physicist

Curnow, Allen (1911–) New Zealand poet and editor

Curran, John Philpot (1750–1817) Irish judge, orator, politician and reformer

Curry, George English churchman

Curtiz, Michael (1888–1962) Hungarian film director

Curzon, Lord (1859–1925) English statesman and scholar

Cuvier, Baron (1769–1832) French anatomist and politician

Cyprian, Saint (c. 200–258) Carthaginian churchman, theological writer and martyr

Cyrano de Bergerac, Savinien de (1619–1655) French writer, soldier and duellist

D

Dagg, Fred (1948–) Australian writer, actor and broadcaster

Dahl, Roald (1916–1990) British writer

Dali, Salvador (1904–1989) Spanish painter and writer

D'Alpuget, Blanche (1944–) Australian writer

Daly, Mary (1928–) American feminist and theologian

Damien, Father (1840–1889) Belgian Roman Catholic missionary

Dana, Charles Anderson (1819–1897) American newspaper editor and reformer

Daniel, Samuel (1562–1619) English poet, historian and dramatist

Danton, Georges (1759–1794) French revolutionary leader

Darling, Charles (1849–1936) English judge and Conservative politician

Darrow, Clarence (1857–1938) American lawyer, reformer and writer

Darwin, Charles (1809–1882) English naturalist

Darwin, Charles Galton (1887–1962) English physicist; grandson of Charles Darwin

David, Elizabeth (1913–1992) British cookery writer

Davies, David (1742–1819) Welsh churchman

Davies, Sir John (1569–1626) English poet and politician

Davies, Robertson (1913–) Canadian playwright, writer and critic

Davies, Scrope Berdmore (c.1783–1852) English conversationalist

Davies, William Henry (1871–1940) Welsh poet, writer and tramp

Davis, Bette (1908–1989) American film actress

Davis, Sammy, Junior (1925–1990) African-American entertainer and singer

Davis, Steve (1957–) English snooker player

Davison, Frank Dalby (1893–1970) Australian writer

Davy, Sir Humphry (1778–1829) English chemist and inventor

Dawe, (Donald) Bruce (1930–) Australian poet and lecturer

Day, Clarence Shepard (1874–1935) American essayist and humorist

Day Lewis, C. (1904–1972) Irish-born British poet, critic and writer

De Blank, Joost (1908–1968) Dutch-born British churchman

Debray, Régis (1942–) French writer

Debussy, Claude (1862–1918) French composer and critic

Decatur, Stephen (1779–1820) American naval commander

Defoe, Daniel (c.1661–1731) English writer and critic

Degas, Edgar (1834–1917) French painter and sculptor

De Gaulle, Charles (1890–1970) French statesman and general

De Klerk, F.W. (1936–) South African politician

De La Mare, Walter (1873–1956) English poet and writer

Delaney, Shelagh (1939–) English dramatist, screenwriter and writer

Delbanco, Andrew Writer and academic

Delille, Abbé Jacques (1738–1813) French poet and translator

Delors, Jacques (1925–) French politician

Demosthenes (c.384–322 BC) Athenian statesman and orator

Dempsey, Jack (1895–1983) American boxer

Denham, Sir John (1615–1669) Irish-born English poet, royalist and Surveyor–General

Denning, Lord (1899–) English judge and Master of the Rolls

Dennis, C.J. (1876–1938) Australian writer and poet

Dennis, John (1657–1734) English critic and dramatist

Dennis, Nigel (1912–1989) English writer, dramatist and critic

Dent, Alan (1905–1978) Scottish writer and critic

De Quincey, Thomas (1785–1859) English essayist and opium addict

Descartes, René (1596–1650) French philosopher and mathematician

Desmoulins, Camille (1760–1794) French pamphleteer, orator and revolutionary

Destouches, Philippe Néricault (1680–1754) French dramatist

De Valera, Eamon (1882–1975) American-born Irish statesman

Devlin, Bernadette (1947–) Irish politician

Devonshire, Duke of (1833–1908) English statesman

De Vries, Peter (1910–) American writer and humorist

Dewar, Lord (1864–1930) Scottish director of distilleries, Conservative politician and writer

Dewey, John (1859–1952) American educationist, philosopher and reformer

De Wolfe, Elsie (1865–1950) English actress, society leader and writer

Díaz, Porfirio (1830–1915) Mexican general and statesman

Dibdin, Charles (1745–1814) English songwriter, dramatist and actor

Dickens, Charles (1812–1870) English writer

Dickinson, Angie (1932–) American actress

Dickinson, Emily (1830–1886) American poet

Diderot, Denis (1713–1784) French philosopher, encyclopaedist, writer and dramatist

Didion, Joan (1934–) American writer and scriptwriter

Dietrich, Marlene (1901–1992) German-born American actress and singer

Diller, Phyllis (1917–1974) American comedian

Dillingham, Charles Bancroft (1868–1934) American theatrical producer

Diodorus Siculus (c.1st century BC) Sicilian-born Greek historian

Diogenes (the Cynic) (c. 400–325 BC) Greek philosopher

Dionysius of Halicarnassus (fl. 30–7 BC) Greek historian, critic and rhetorician

Disney, Walt (1901–1966) American film-maker and pioneer of animated films

Disraeli, Benjamin (1804–1881) English statesman and writer

Dix, Dorothy (1870–1951) American writer

Dix, George (1901–1952) English Anglican monk, historian and scholar

Dobbs, Kildare (1923–) Canadian writer

Dobrée, Bonamy (1891–1974) English academic, critic and editor

Dobson, Henry Austin (1840–1921) English poet, essayist and biographer

Dodd, Ken (1931–) English comedian, singer, entertainer and actor

Donatus, Aelius (fl. 4th century BC) Roman Latin grammarian and teacher

Donleavy, J.P. (1926–) American-born Irish writer and dramatist

Donne, John (1572–1631) English poet and divine

Dostoevsky, Fyodor (1821–1881) Russian writer

Douglas, Lord Alfred (1870–1945) English poet; intimate of Oscar Wilde

Douglas, James, Earl of Morton (c.1516–1581) Regent of Scotland

Douglas, Norman (1868–1952) Austrian-born Scottish writer

Douglas-Home, Sir Alec (1903–1995) Scottish statesman

Douglass, Frederick (c.1818–1895) American anti-slavery activist

Dowling, Basil Cairns New Zealand poet and pacifist

Dowson, Ernest (1867–1900) English poet

Doyle, Sir Arthur Conan (1859–1930) Scottish writer, doctor and war correspondent

Doyle, Roddy (1958–) Irish prizewinning writer

Drake, Sir Francis (c.1540–1596) English navigator

Drayton, Michael (1563–1631) English poet

Dreiser, Theodore (1871–1945) American writer

Drew, Elizabeth (1887–1965) English-born American writer and critic

Dring, Philip American preacher

Drummond, Thomas (1797–1840) Scottish statesman and engineer

Dryden, John (1631–1700) English poet, satirist, dramatist and critic

Du Bellay, Joachim (1522–1560) French poet

Du Bois, William (1868–1963) African-American sociologist, writer and political activist

Duffy, Jim Scottish football manager

Duhamel, Georges (1884–1966) French writer, poet, dramatist and physician

Dulles, John Foster (1888–1959) American statesman and lawyer

Dunbar, William (c.1460–c.1525) Scottish poet, satirist and courtier

Duncan, Isadora (1878–1927) American modern dance pioneer

Dundy, Elaine (1927–) American writer

Dunne, Finley Peter (1867–1936) American writer

Duppa, Richard (1770–1831) English artist and writer

Durant, Will (1885–1982) American philosopher and writer

Durrell, Lawrence (1912–1990) Indian-born British poet and writer

Dürrenmatt, Friedrich (1921–1990) Swiss dramatist and writer

Dworkin, Andrea (1946–) American writer and feminist

Dyer, Sir Edward (c.1540–1607) English poet and courtier

E

Eames, Emma (1865–1952) Chinese-born American opera singer

Earhart, Amelia (1898–1937) American aviator

Eastman, Max (1883–1969) American writer, editor and critic

Eastwood, Clint (1930–) American actor and film director

Eban, Abba (1915–) South African-born Israeli statesman and writer

Ebner-Eschenbach, Marie von (1830–1916) Austrian writer

Eco, Umberto (1932–) Italian critic and writer

Eddington, Sir Arthur (1882–1944) English astronomer, physicist and mathematician

Eddy, Mary Baker (1821–1910) American founder of Christian Science

Eden, Anthony (1897–1977) English Conservative statesman and Prime Minister

Edgeworth, Maria (1767–1849) English-born Irish writer

Edison, Thomas Alva (1847–1931) American inventor and industrialist

Edmond, James (1859–1933) Scottish-born Australian writer and editor

Edward VII (1841–1910) King of Great Britain and Ireland

Edward VIII (later Duke of Windsor) (1894–1972) Uncrowned British king; abdicated

Edward, Prince (1964–) Son of Queen Elizabeth II

Edwards, Oliver (1711–1791) English lawyer

Einstein, Albert (1879–1955) German-born American mathematical physicist

Eisenhower, Dwight D. (1890–1969) American statesman, Republican President and general

Ekland, Britt (1942–) Swedish actress

Eldershaw, M. Barnard (1897–1987) Australian writer, critic and librarian

Eliot, Charles W. (1834–1926) President of Harvard University

Eliot, George (1819–1880) English writer and poet

Eliot, T.S. (1888–1965) American-born British poet, verse dramatist and critic

Elizabeth I (1533–1603) Queen of England, scholar and letter writer

Elizabeth, the Queen Mother (1900–) Queen of the United Kingdom and mother of Elizabeth II

Elliot, Jean (1727–1805) Scottish lyricist

Elliott, Ebenezer (1781–1849) English poet and merchant

Ellis, Alice Thomas (1932–) British writer

Ellis, Bob (1942–) Australian dramatist

Ellis, George (1753–1815) West Indian-born British satirist and poet

Ellis, Havelock (1859–1939) English sexologist and essayist

Emerson, Ralph Waldo (1803–1882) American poet, essayist, transcendentalist and teacher

Emmet, Robert (1778–1803) Irish patriot

Engels, Friedrich (1820–1895) German socialist and political philosopher

Epicurus (341–270 BC) Greek philosopher and teacher

Erasmus (c.1466–1536) Dutch scholar and humanist

Ertz, Susan (1894–1985) English writer

Estienne, Henri (1531–1598) French scholar, lexicographer, printer and publisher

Etherege, Sir George (c. 1635–1691) English Restoration dramatist

Eubank, Chris (1966–) British champion boxer

Euclid (fl. c. 300 bc) Greek mathematician

Euripides (c.485–406 BC) Greek dramatist and poet

Evans, Abel (1679–1737) English churchman, poet and satirist

Evans, Dame Edith (1888–1976) English actress

Evans, Harold (1928–) English journalist and newspaper editor

Evarts, William Maxwell (1818–1901) American lawyer and statesman

Evelyn, John (1620–1706) English writer and diarist

Ewart, Gavin (1916–1995) English poet

Ewer, William (1885–1976) English journalist

F

Fadiman, Clifton (1904–) American writer, editor and broadcaster

Fairbairn, Sir Nicholas (1933–1995) Scottish Conservative MP and barrister

Fairbairn, Lady Sam Wife of Conservative MP, Sir Nicholas Fairbairn

Fairburn, A.R.D. (1904–1957) New Zealand poet

Falkland, Viscount (c.1610–1643) English politician and writer

Fanon, Frantz (1925–1961) West Indian psychoanalyst and philosopher

Faraday, Michael (1791–1867) English chemist and physicist

Farmer, Edward (c.1809–1876) English poet and writer

Farquhar, George (1678–1707) Irish dramatist

Faulkner, William (1897–1962) American writer

Faust, Beatrice (1939–) Australian writer and feminist

Feather, Vic, Baron (1906–1976) English trade unionist

Ferdinand I, Emperor (1503–1564) Spanish-born King of Hungary and Bohemia

Fergusson, Sir James (1832–1907) Scottish Conservative statesman

Ferlinghetti, Lawrence (1920–) American publisher, painter, poet and writer

Fern, Fanny (1811–1872) American writer

Ferrier, Kathleen (1912–1953) English singer

Feuerbach, Ludwig (1804–1872) German philosopher

Field, Eugene (1850–1895) American columnist, children's poet, translator and humorist

Fielding, Henry (1707–1754) English writer, dramatist and journalist

Fields, W.C. (1880–1946) American film actor

Figes, Eva (1932–) German-born British writer and critic

Firbank, Ronald (1886–1926) English writer

Fisher, Dorothy Canfield (1879–1958) American writer

Fisher, H.A.L. (1856–1940) English historian

FitzGerald, Edward (1809–1883) English poet, translator and letter writer

Fitzgerald, F. Scott (1896–1940) American writer

Fitzsimmons, Robert (1862–1917) English-born New Zealand world champion boxer

Flanders, Michael (1922–1975) English actor and lyricist

Flaubert, Gustave (1821–1880) French writer

Flecker, James Elroy (1884–1915) English poet, orientalist and translator

Flecknoe, Richard (d. c.1678) Irish priest, poet and dramatist

Fleming, Marjory (1803–1811) Scottish child diarist

Flers, Marquis de (1871–1927) French playwright

Fletcher, John (1579–1625) English dramatist

Fletcher, Phineas (1582–1650) English poet and clergyman

Florian, Jean-Pierre Claris de (1755–1794) French writer

Fo, Dario (1926–) Italian playwright and actor

Foch, Ferdinand (1851–1929) French marshal

Foley, Rae (1900–1978) American writer

Fonda, Jane (1937–) American actress, political activist and aerobics pioneer

Fontaine, Jean de la (1621–1695) French poet and fabulist

Fontenelle, Bernard (1657–1757) French librettist, philosopher and man of letters

Foot, Michael (1913–) English Labour politician

Foote, Samuel (1720–1777) English actor, dramatist and wit

Forbes, Miss C.F. (1817–1911) English writer

Ford, Anna (1943–) English television newscaster and reporter

Ford, Gerald R. (1913–) American politician and President

Ford, Henry (1863–1947) American car manufacturer

Ford, John (c.1586–1639) English dramatist and poet

Ford, John (1895–1973) Irish–American film director

Forgy, Howell (1908–1983) American naval chaplain

Forster, E.M. (1879–1970) English writer, essayist and literary critic

Foucault, Michel (1926–1984) French philosopher

Fourier, François (1772–1837) French social theorist

Fowles, John (1926–) English writer

Fox, Charles James (1749–1806) English statesman and abolitionist

Fox, Henry Stephen (1791–1846) English diplomat

Foyle, Christina (1911–) Member of famous British bookselling family

Frame, Janet (1924–) New Zealand writer

France, Anatole (1844–1924) French writer and critic

Francis, Clare (1946–) English yachtswoman and writer

Frank, Anne (1929–1945) Jewish diarist; died in Bergen-Belsen concentration camp

Frank, Otto (b.1889) Dutch concentration camp survivor and father of Anne Frank

Franklin, Benjamin (1706–1790) American statesman, scientist, political critic and printer

Franklin, Miles (1879–1954) Australian writer

Franks, Oliver, Baron (1905–1992) English diplomat, lecturer and banker

Frayn, Michael (1933–) English dramatist and writer

Frazer, Sir James (1854–1941) Scottish anthropologist and writer

Frederick the Great (1712–1786) King of Prussia and patron of the arts

French, Marilyn (1929–) American writer and critic

Freud, Clement (1924–) British Liberal politician, broadcaster and writer

Freud, Sigmund (1856–1939) Austrian physicist; founder of psychoanalysis

Friday, Nancy (1937–) American writer

Friedan, Betty (1921–) American feminist leader and writer

Friedman, Milton (1912–) American economist

Friel, Brian (1929–) Irish dramatist and writer

Frisch, Max (1911–1991) Swiss dramatist, writer and architect

Frost, Sir David (1939–) English television personality and writer

Frost, Robert (1874–1963) American poet

Froude, James Anthony (1818–1894) English historian and scholar

Fry, Christopher (1907–) English verse dramatist, theatre director and translator

Fry, Elizabeth (1780–1845) English social and prison reformer

Fry, Roger (1866–1934) English art critic, philosopher and painter

Fry, Stephen (1957–) British comedian and writer

Frye, Marilyn American feminist and writer

Frye, Northrop (1912–1991) Canadian critic and academic

Fuller, Richard Buckminster (1895–1983) American architect and engineer

Fuller, Thomas (1608–1661) English churchman and antiquary

Furphy, Joseph (1843–1912) Australian writer and poet

G

Gabor, Zsa-Zsa (1919–)
Hungarian–born American actress

Gaisford, Rev, Thomas (1779–1855)
English scholar and Dean of Christ
Church, Oxford

Gaitskell, Hugh (1906–1963) English
socialist and Labour politician

Galbraith, J.K. (1908–) Canadian-born
American economist, diplomat and
writer

Galileo Galilei (1564–1642) Italian
mathematician, astronomer, physicist,
inventor and teacher

Gallacher, William (1881–1965)
Scottish Communist politician

Galsworthy, John (1867–1933) English
writer and dramatist

Galt, John (1779–1839) Scottish writer
and Canadian pioneer

Gambetta, Léon (1838–1882) French
statesman and Prime Minister

Gandhi (1869–1948) Indian political
leader

Gandhi, Indira (1917–1984) Indian
statesman and Prime Minister

Garbo, Greta (1905–1990) Swedish-
born American film actress

García Márquez, Gabriel (1928–)
Colombian writer

Gardiner, Richard (b. c.1533) English
writer

Garel-Jones, Tristan (1941–) English
politician

Garibaldi, Giuseppe (1807–1882) Italian
soldier and patriot

Garland, Judy (1922–1969) American
film actress and singer

Garrick, David (1717–1779) English
actor, theatre manager, dramatist and
letter writer

Garrod, Heathcote William (1878–1960)
English scholar, academic and essayist

Gascoigne, Paul (1967–) English
football player

Gaskell, Elizabeth (1810–1865) English
writer

Gautier, Théophile (1811–1872) French
poet, writer and critic

Gay, John (1685–1732) English poet,
dramatist and librettist

Geldof, Bob (1954–) Irish rock
musician and charity fund raiser

George II (1683–1760) King of Great
Britain and Ireland

George V (1865–1936) King of Great
Britain and Northern Ireland

George VI (1895–1952) King of Great
Britain and Northern Ireland

George, Eddie (1938–) Governor of
the Bank of England

George, Henry (1839–1897) American
economist, editor and lecturer

Gerrish, Theodore American soldier

Getty, J. Paul (1892–1976) American oil
billionaire and art collector

Gibbon, Edward (1737–1794) English
historian, politician and memoirist

Gibbons, Orlando (1583–1625) English
organist and composer of church music

Gibbs, Sir Philip (1877–1962) British
journalist

Gibran, Kahlil (1883–1931) Lebanese
poet, mystic and painter

Gide, André (1869–1951) French writer,
critic, dramatist and poet

Gilbert, W.S. (1836–1911) English
dramatist, humorist and librettist

Gill, Eric (1882–1940) English stone-
carver, engraver, topographer and
writer

Gilman, Charlotte Perkins (1860–1935)
American writer, social reformer and
feminist

Gilmour, Sir Ian (1926–) Scottish
Conservative politician

Ginsberg, Allen (1926–) American
poet

Giraudoux, Jean (1882–1944) French
dramatist, poet, writer and satirist

Gladstone, William (1809–1898)
English statesman and reformer

Glover, Denis (1912–1980) New
Zealand poet and printer

Godard, Jean-Luc (1930–) French film
director and writer

Goebbels, Joseph (1897–1945) German
Nazi politician

Goering, Hermann (1893–1946) German Nazi leader and military commander

Goethe (1749–1832) German poet, writer, dramatist and scientist

Gogarty, Oliver St John (1878–1957) Irish poet, dramatist, writer, politician and surgeon

Gogol, Nicolai (1809–1852) Russian writer and soldier

Golding, William (1911–1993) English writer and poet

Goldman, Emma American anarchist

Goldsmith, Sir James (1933–) British business magnate and French MEP

Goldsmith, Oliver (c.1728–1774) Irish dramatist, poet and writer

Goldwater, Barry (1909–) American politician, presidential candidate and writer

Goldwyn, Samuel (1882–1974) Polish-born American film producer

Gonne, Maud (1865–1953) Irish patriot and philanthropist

Gordimer, Nadine (1923–) South African writer

Gordon, Adam Lindsay (1833–1870) Australian poet and ballad writer

Gorky, Maxim (1868–1936) Russian writer, dramatist and revolutionary

Gorton, John (1911–) Australian Parliamentarian

Goulburn, Edward (1818–1897) English divine and teacher

Gowers, Sir Ernest (1880–1966) English civil servant and champion of plain language

Grable, Betty (1916–1973) American film actress and wartime 'pin-up'

Grace, W.G. (1848–1915) English cricketer, physician and surgeon

Gracián, Baltasar (1601–1658) Spanish writer, philosopher and Jesuit preacher

Grade, Lew (1906–1994) Russian-born British film, television and theatrical producer

Graham, Clementina (1782–1877) Scottish writer, lyricist and translator

Graham, James, Marquis of Montrose (1612–1650) Scottish Covenanter, soldier, poet and Royalist

Grainger, James (c.1721–1766) Scottish poet, army surgeon and editor

Grant, Bruce Alexander (1925–) Australian writer, critic and civil servant

Grant, Cary (1904–1986) English-born American film actor

Grant, Ulysses S. (1822–1885) American Republican President, general and memoirist

Granville, George (1666–1735) English poet, dramatist and politician

Granville-Barker, Harley (1877–1946) English actor, dramatist, producer and critic

Graves, Robert (1895–1985) English poet, writer, critic, translator and mythologist

Gray, Patrick, Lord (d. 1612) Scottish courtier and ambassador at the court of Elizabeth I

Gray, Thomas (1716–1771) English poet and scholar

Greaves, Jimmy (1940–) English footballer and television commentator

Green, Michael (1927–) English writer and playwright

Greene, Graham (1904–1991) English writer and dramatist

Greer, Germaine (1939–) Australian feminist, critic, English scholar and writer

Gregory VII (c.1020–1085) Italian pope, saint and church reformer

Gregory, Lady Isabella (1852–1932) Irish dramatist, writer and translator

Grellet, Stephen (1773–1855) French missionary

Greville, Fulke (1554–1628) English poet, dramatist, biographer, courtier and politician

Grey, Edward (1862–1933) English statesman and writer

Grey Owl,(1888–1938) Canadian writer and naturalist

Griffith, D.W. (1874–1948) American film director

Griffith-Jones, Mervyn (1909–1979) British lawyer

Griffiths, Trevor (1935–) British dramatist and screenwriter

Grossmith, George (1847–1912) English singer, songwriter and writer

Grossmith, Weedon (1854–1919) English writer, painter and actor

Guedalla, Philip (1889–1944) English historian, writer and lawyer

Guinan, Texas (1884–1933) Canadian actress

Guinness, Sir Alec (1914–) British actor

Guitry, Sacha (1885–1957) Russian-born French actor, dramatist and film director

Gulbenkian, Nubar (1896–1972) British industrialist, diplomat and philanthropist

Gurney, Dorothy (1858–1932) English poet

Gwenn, Edmund (1875–1959) English actor

Gwyn, Nell (1650–1687) English actress and mistress of Charles II

H

Hadrian (76–138) Roman emperor and patron of the arts

Hahnemann, C.F.S. (1755–1843) German physician and founder of homeopathy

Haig, Douglas, Earl (1861–1928) Scottish military commander

Hailsham, Quintin Hogg, Baron (1907–) English Conservative politician

Hakim, Catherine British academic

Haldane, J.B.S. (1892–1964) British biochemist, geneticist and popularizer of science

Hale, Sir Matthew (1609–1676) English judge and writer

Hale, Nathan (1755–1776) American soldier and revolutionary

Halifax, Lord (1633–1695) English politician, courtier, pamphleteer and epigrammatist

Hall, Jerry (1956–) American fashion model

Hall, Rodney (1935–) Australian poet and writer

Halleck, Fitz-Greene (1790–1867) American poet, satirist and banker

Halsey, Margaret (1910–) American writer

Hamerton, P.G. (1834–1894) British artist and writer

Hamilton, Ian (1925–) Lawyer and Scottish Nationalist

Hamilton, Sir William (1788–1856) Scottish metaphysical philosopher

Hamilton, William (Willie) (1917–) British politician, teacher and anti-royalist

Hammarskjöld, Dag (1905–1961) Swedish statesman and Secretary-General of the United Nations

Hampton, Christopher (1946–) English dramatist

Hancock, Sir William (1898–1988) Australian historian

Handke, Peter (1942–) Austrian playwright

Hanrahan, Brian (1949–) Television news correspondent and reporter

Hanson, Lord James (1922–) English millionaire businessman

Hardwicke, Earl of (1690–1764) English judge and Lord Chancellor

Hardy, Rev. E.J. (1849–1920) Irish army chaplain and writer

Hardy, Thomas (1840–1928) English writer and poet

Hare, Augustus (1792–1834) English clergyman and writer

Hare, Maurice Evan (1886–1967) English limerick writer

Harlech, Lord (1918–1985) English politician, diplomat and television company chairman

Harman, Sir Jeremiah (1930–) British High Court judge

Harney, Bill (1895–1962) Australian writer

Harris, George (1844–1922) American churchman and educator

Harris, Max (1921–1995) Australian critic, poet and publisher

Harris, Sydney J. (1917–) American journalist

Hartley, L.P. (1895–1972) English writer and critic

Harwood, Gwen (1920–) Australian poet and music teacher

Haskins, Minnie Louise (1875–1957) English teacher and writer

Hattersley, Roy (1932–) British Labour politician and writer

Havel, Václav (1936–) Czech dramatist and statesman

Hawke, Bob (1929–) Australian statesman

Hawthorne, Nathaniel (1804–1864) American allegorical writer

Hazlitt, William (1778–1830) English writer and critic

Hazzard, Shirley (1931–) Australian writer

Healey, Denis (1917–) English Labour politician

Hearst, William Randolph (1863–1951) American newspaper proprietor

Heath, Sir Edward (1916–) English Conservative statesman, Prime Minister, writer and yachtsman

Hegel, Georg Wilhelm (1770–1831) German philosopher

Heine, Heinrich (1797–1856) German lyric poet, essayist and journalist

Heisenberg, Werner (1901–1976) German theoretical physicist

Heller, Joseph (1923–) American writer

Hellman, Lillian (1905–1984) American dramatist and screenwriter

Helpman, Sir Robert Murray (1909–1986) Australian dancer, actor, choreographer, producer and director

Helps, Sir Arthur (1813–1875) English historian and writer

Hemingway, Ernest (1898–1961) American writer and war correspondent

Henderson, Hamish (1919–) Scottish folklorist, composer, translator and poet

Hendrix, Jimi (1942–1970) American rock singer, songwriter and guitarist

Henley, W.E. (1849–1903) English poet, dramatist and critic

Henri IV (1553–1610) Huguenot leader turned Catholic king from 1589

Henry, O. (1862–1910) American short-story writer

Henry, Patrick (1736–1799) American lawyer, orator and statesman

Henshaw, Bishop Joseph (1603–1679) English churchman and writer

Hepworth, Dame Barbara (1903–1975) English sculptor

Hepworth, John (1921–) Australian writer

Heraclitus (c. 540–c.480 BC) Greek philosopher

Herbert, Sir A.P. (1890–1971) English humorist, writer, dramatist and politician

Herbert, George (1593–1633) English poet and priest

Herrick, Robert (1591–1674) English poet, royalist and clergyman

Hervey, Lord (1696–1743) English politician and memoirist

Hewart, Gordon (1870–1943) English Liberal politician and Lord Chief Justice

Hewett, Dorothy (1923–) Australian dramatist and poet

Hewitt, John (1907–1987) Irish poet and museum and art gallery director

Hightower, Jim (1933–) Texan agriculture commissioner

Higley, Brewster (19th century) American songwriter

Hill, Joe (1879–1914) Swedish-born American songwriter and workers' organizer

Hill, Reginald (1936–) British writer and playwright

Hill, Rowland (1744–1833) English preacher and hymn writer

Hillary, Sir Edmund (1919–) New Zealand mountaineer, explorer and apiarist

Hillel, 'The Elder', (c.60 BC–c.AD 10) Babylonian rabbi and doctor of Jewish law

Hillingdon, Lady Alice (1857–1940) English aristocrat

Hilton, James (1900–1954) English writer and screenwriter

Hippocrates (c.460–357 BC) Greek physician

Hirohito, Emperor (1901–1989) Emperor of Japan

Hirst, Damien (1965–) British artist

Hitchcock, Alfred (1899–1980) English film director

Hitler, Adolf (1889–1945) Austrian-born German Nazi dictator

Hobbes, Thomas (1588–1679) Political philosopher

Hobson, Sir Harold (1904–1992) British critic and writer

Hodgson, Ralph (1871–1962) English poet, illustrator and journalist

Hodson, Peregrine British author

Hoffer, Eric (1902–1983) American writer, philosopher and longshoreman

Hoffmann, Max (1869–1927) German general

Hoffnung, Gerard (1925–1959) British artist, illustrator and musician

Hogg, James (1770–1835) Scottish poet, ballad writer and writer

Hogg, Quintin (1907–) see Hailsham, Baron

Hoggart, Simon (1946–) British journalist

Hokusai (1760–1849) Japanese artist

Holland, Lord (1705–1774) English politician

Holland, Canon Henry Scott (1847–1918) English cleric, Professor of Divinity and Christian social reformer

Holmes, Hugh (Lord Justice Holmes) (1840–1916) Irish judge

Holmes, Rev. John H. (1879–1964) American Unitarian minister

Holmes, Oliver Wendell (1809–1894) American physician, anatomist, poet, writer and scientist

Holmes, Oliver Wendell Jr. (1841–1935) American jurist and judge

Holst, Gustav (1874–1934) English composer

Holt, Harold Edward (1908–1967) Australian statesman and Prime Minister

Hood, Thomas (1799–1845) English poet, editor and humorist

Hooker, Richard (c.1554–1600) English theologian and churchman

Hooper, Ellen Sturgis (1816–1841) American poet and hymn writer

Hooton, Harry (1908–1961) Australian philosopher and poet

Hoover, Herbert (1874–1964) American Republican President, engineer, public administrator and writer

Hope, Alec (1907–) Australian poet and critic

Hope, Anthony (1863–1933) English writer, dramatist and lawyer

Hopkins, Gerard Manley (1844–1889) English poet, classicist and Jesuit priest

Hopkins, Jane Ellice (1836–1904) English social reformer and writer

Hopper, Hedda (1890–1966) American actress and writer

Horace (65–8 BC) Roman lyric poet and satirist

Horne, Donald Richmond (1921–) Australian writer and lecturer

Horváth, Ödön von (1901–1938) German-Hungarian writer

Household, Geoffrey (1900–1988) English writer

Housman, A.E. (1859–1936) English poet and scholar

Howar, Barbara (1934–) American television correspondent and writer

Howard, Michael (1922–) English historian and writer

Howard, Philip (1933–) English journalist

Howells, W.D. (1837–1920) American writer, critic, editor and poet

Howkins, Alun (1947–) British historian and writer

Hubbard, Elbert (1856–1915) American printer, editor, writer and businessman

Hubbard, 'Kin' (1868–1930) American humorist and writer

Hudson, Louise (1958–) English poet and editor

Hughes, Howard (1905–1976) American millionaire industrialist, aviator and film producer

Hughes, Sean (1966–) Irish comedian

Hugo, Victor (1802–1885) French poet, writer, dramatist and politician

Huistra, Peter (1967–) Dutch international footballer

Hull, Josephine (1886–1957) American actress

Hume, Basil (1923–) British Roman Catholic Archbishop of Westminster

Hume, David (1711–1776) Scottish philosopher, political economist and historian

Humphries, Barry (1934–) Australian entertainer

Hunt, G.W. (1829–1904) British songwriter and painter

Hunt, Leigh (1784–1859) English writer, poet and literary editor

Hunter, John (1728–1793) British surgeon

Hurst, Fannie (1889–1968) American writer and playwright

Huss, Jan (c.1370–1415) Bohemian religious reformer, preacher and martyr

Hutcheson, Francis (1694–1746) Scottish philosopher

Huxley, Aldous (1894–1963) English writer, poet and critic

Huxley, Henrietta (1825–1915) English writer and poet; wife of T.H. Huxley

Huxley, Sir Julian (1887–1975) English biologist and Director-General of UNESCO

Huxley, T.H. (1825–1895) English biologist, Darwinist and agnostic

I

Ibárruri, Dolores ('La Pasionara') Spanish Basque Communist leader; exiled in USSR 1939–77

Ibsen, Henrik (1828–1906) Norwegian writer, dramatist and poet

Ignatieff, Michael (1947–) Canadian writer and media personality

Illich, Ivan (1926–) Austrian-born American educator, sociologist, writer and priest

Inge, William Ralph (1860–1954) English divine, writer and teacher

Ingersoll, Robert Greene (1833–1899) American lawyer, Republican orator, soldier and writer

Ingham, Sir Bernard (1932–) Chief Press Secretary to Margaret Thatcher; journalist

Ingrams, Richard (1937–) British journalist and editor of *Private Eye*

Ingres, J.A.D. (1780–1867) French painter

Iphicrates (419–353 bc) Athenian general

Irving, Washington (1783–1859) American writer and diplomat

Izetbegovic, Alija (1925–) Bosnian and Herzogovinian politician; President of Bosnia

J

Jackson, F.J. Foakes (1855–1941) English divine and church historian

Jackson, Robert (1946–) English Conservative politician and writer

Jacobs, Joe (1896–1940) American boxing manager

Jago, Rev. Richard (1715–1781) English poet

James I of Scotland (1394–1437) King of Scots and father of Mary, Queen of Scots

James VI of Scotland and I of England, (1566–1625) Son of Mary, Queen of Scots; essayist and patron of poetry

James, Brian (1892–1972) Australian writer

James, Henry (1843–1916) American-born British writer, critic and letter writer

James, William (1842–1910) American psychologist and philosopher

Jarrell, Randall (1914–1965) American poet, critic and translator

Jay, Douglas (1907–) British economist and writer

Jeans, Sir James Hopwood (1877–1946) English mathematician, physicist, astronomer and popularizer of science

Jefferson, Thomas (1743–1826) American Democratic President

Jenkins, David (1925–) English prelate and Bishop of Durham

Jenkins, Roy (1920–) Welsh politician and writer

Jerome, Jerome K. (1859–1927) English writer and dramatist

Jerrold, Douglas William (1803–1857) English dramatist, writer and wit

Jespersen, Otto (1860–1943) Danish philologist

Joad, C.E.M. (1891–1953) English popularizer of philosophy, scholar and teacher

John XXIII (1881–1963) Italian pope and promoter of ecumenicalism

Saint John of the Cross (1542–1591) Spanish mystic

John Paul II (1920–) First Polish pope

Johnson, Amy (1903–1941) English aviator

Johnson, Hiram (1866–1945) American Republican politician

Johnson, Paul (1928–) British editor and writer

Johnson, Samuel (1709–1784) English lexicographer, poet, critic, conversationalist and essayist

Johnston, Brian (1912–1994) British broadcaster

Johnston, Jill (1929–) English-born American dancer, critic and feminist

Jones, Sir William (1746–1794) English orientalist, translator and jurist

Jonson, Ben (1572–1637) English dramatist and poet

Joseph, Michael (1897–1958) English publisher and writer

Jowett, Benjamin (1817–1893) English scholar, translator, essayist and priest

Joyce, James (1882–1941) Irish writer and poet

Julia (39 BC–AD 14) Daughter of the Emperor Augustus

Junell, Thomas Host of Finland's seaborne drinking championships

Jung, Carl Gustav (1875–1961) Swiss psychiatrist and pupil of Freud

Jung Chang (1952–) Chinese author, now based in London

Junius (fl. 1769–1772) Pen-name of anonymous author

Justinian, Emperor (c. 482–565) Byzantine emperor

Juvenal (c. 60–130) Roman verse satirist and Stoic

K

Kael, Pauline (1919–) American writer and film critic

Kafka, Franz (1883–1924) Czech-born German-speaking writer

Kant, Immanuel (1724–1804) German idealist philosopher

Karr, Alphonse (1808–1890) French writer and editor

Kaufman, George S. (1889–1961) American scriptwriter, librettist and journalist

Kaufman, Sue (1926–) American writer and editor

Keats, John (1795–1821) English poet

Keenan, Brian (1950–) Irish journalist and hostage in Lebanon

Keillor, Garrison (1942–) American writer and broadcaster

Keith, Penelope (1940–) English actress

Keller, Helen (1880–1968) American writer and educator of the blind and deaf; deaf and blind herself

Kelly, Bert (1912–) Australian politician

Kelly, Ned (1855–1880) Australian outlaw and folk hero

Kemble, John Philip (1757–1823) English Shakespearian actor

Kempis, Thomas à (c. 1380–1471) German mystic, monk and writer

Keneally, Thomas (1935–) Australian writer and screenwriter

Kennedy, Florynce R. (1916–) American lawyer, feminist and civil rights activist

Kennedy, John F. (1917–1963) American Democrat President

Kennedy, Robert F. (1925–1968) American Democrat lawyer and politician

Kenny, Mary (1944–) Irish writer and broadcaster

Kerouac, Jack (1922–1969) American writer and poet

Kerr, Jean (1923–) American writer and dramatist

Kettle, Thomas (1880–1916) Irish writer and academic

Key, Ellen (1849–1926) Swedish feminist, writer and lecturer

Keynes, John Maynard (1883–1946) English economist

Khrushchev, Nikita (1894–1971) Russian statesman and Premier of the Soviet Union

Kierkegaard, Sören (1813–1855) Danish philosopher and theologian

Kilvert, Francis (1840–1879) English curate and diarist

King, Billie-Jean (1943–) American champion tennis player

King, Bishop Henry (1592–1669) English royal chaplain and bishop; poet and sermonist

King, Martin Luther (1929–1968) American civil rights leader and Baptist minister

Kingsley, Charles (1819–1875) English writer, poet, lecturer and clergyman

Kingsmill, Hugh (1889–1949) English critic and writer

Kinnock, Neil (1942–) Welsh politician

Kipling, Rudyard (1865–1936) Indian-born British poet and writer

Kissinger, Henry (1923–) German-born American diplomat and Secretary of State

Klee, Paul (1879–1940) Swiss painter, engraver and teacher

Klopstock, Friedrich (1724–1803) German poet

Knox, Philander Chase (1853–1921) American lawyer and Republican politician

Knox, Ronald (1888–1957) English priest, biblical translator and essayist

Knox, Vicesimus (1752–1821) English churchman and writer

Koestler, Arthur (1905–1983) Hungarian-born British writer, essayist and political refugee

Kollwitz, Käthe (1867–1945) German painter, sculptor and graphic artist

Kraus, Karl (1874–1936) Austrian scientist, critic and poet

Kubrick, Stanley (1928–) American screenwriter, producer and director

Kundera, Milan (1929–) Czech writer and critic

Kurtz, Irma (1935–) British writer and 'agony aunt'

Kyd, Thomas (1558–1594) English dramatist and poet

L

La Bruyère, Jean de (1645–1696) French moralist and satirist

Laing, R.D. (1927–1989) Scottish psychiatrist, psychoanalyst and poet

Lamartine, Alphonse de (1790–1869) French poet, historian, royalist and statesman

Lamb, Lady Caroline (1785–1828) English writer and poet

Lamb, Charles (1775–1834) English essayist, critic and letter writer

Lancaster, Sir Osbert (1908–1986) English writer, cartoonist and stage designer

Landers, Ann (1918–) Famous 'Agony Aunt' and columnist

Landor, Walter Savage (1775–1864) English poet and writer

Landseer, Sir Edwin Henry (1802–1873) English painter, engraver and sculptor

Lang, Andrew (1844–1912) Scottish poet, writer, mythologist, anthropologist and scholar

Lang, Ian (1940–) British Conservative politician

Langland, William (c.1330–c.1400) English poet

Lardner, Ring (1885–1933) American humorist and writer

Larkin, Philip (1922–1985) English poet, writer and librarian

La Rochefoucauld, Duc de (1613–1680) French moralist and epigrammatist

Latimer, Bishop Hugh (c.1485–1555) English Protestant churchman

Laver, James (1899–1975) English art, costume and design historian

Law, Bonar (1858–1923) Canadian–born British statesman and Conservative MP

Lawrence, D.H. (1885–1930) English writer, poet and critic

Lawrence, T.E. (1888–1935) British soldier, archaeologist, translator and writer; 'Lawrence of Arabia'

BIOGRAPHIES

Lawson, Henry (Hertzberg) (1867–1922) Australian writer and poet

Lazarre, Jane (1943–) American journalist

Lazarus, Emma (1849–1887) American poet and translator

Leach, Sir Edmund (1910–1989) English social anthropologist

Leacock, Stephen (1869–1944) English-born Canadian humorist, writer and economist

Leavis, F.R. (1895–1978) English critic, lecturer and writer

Le Corbusier (1887–1965) Swiss-born French architect and town planner

Ledru-Rollin, Alexandre Auguste (1807–1874) French lawyer and politician

Lee, Nathaniel (c.1653–1692) English dramatist

Lee, Robert E. (1807–1870) American Confederate general

Lefèvre, Théo (1914–1973) Belgian Prime Minister

Le Gallienne, Richard (1866–1947) English poet, writer and critic

Le Guin, Ursula (1929–) American writer and critic

Leith, Prue (1940–) English cookery writer and businesswoman

Le Mesurier, John (1912–1983) English actor

Lenin, V.I. (1870–1924) Russian revolutionary and Marxist theoretician

Lennon, John (1940–1980) English pop singer–songwriter; member of The Beatles

Léon, Fray Luis de (c.1527–1591) Spanish Augustinian monk, poet and translator

Leonard, Hugh (1926–) Irish dramatist and screenwriter

Leopold II (1835–1909) King of Belgium

Lermontov, Mikhail (1814–1841) Russian poet and writer

Lerner, Alan Jay (1918–1986) American lyricist and screenwriter

Lesage, Alain-René (1668–1747) French writer and dramatist

Lessing, Doris (1919–) British writer, brought up in Zimbabwe

Lessing, Gotthold Ephraim (1729–1781) German dramatist, critic and theologian

L'Estrange, Sir Roger (1616–1704) English writer, royalist, translator and politician

Levant, Oscar (1906–1972) American pianist and autobiographer

Levi, Primo (1919–1987) Italian writer, poet and chemist; survivor of Auschwitz

Lévi-Strauss, Claude (1908–) French structuralist and anthropologist

Levin, Bernard (1928–) British writer

Lévis, Duc de (1764–1830) French writer and soldier

Lewes, G.H. (1817–1878) English writer, philosopher, critic and scientist

Lewis, C.S. (1898–1963) Irish-born English academic, writer and critic

Lewis, D.B. Wyndham (1891–1969) British writer and biographer

Lewis, Sir George Cornewall (1806–1863) English statesman, Liberal politician and writer

Lewis, Sinclair (1885–1951) American writer

Lewis, Wyndham (1882–1957 American-born British painter, critic and writer

Liberace (1919–1987) American pianist and showman

Lichtenberg, Georg (1742–1799) German physicist, satirist and writer

Lie, Trygve (1896–1968) Norwegian Labour politician and Secretary-General of the United Nations

Lightner, Candy (1946–) American estate agent and founder of MADD (Mothers Against Drunk Driving)

Lincoln, Abraham (1809–1865) American statesman, lawyer, abolitionist and Republican President

Lindbergh, Anne Morrow (1906–) American aviator, poet and writer

Lindsay, Norman (1879–1969) Australian artist and writer

Linklater, Eric (1899–1974) Welsh-born Scottish writer and satirist

Linnaeus, Carl (1707–1778) Swedish botanist

BIOGRAPHIES

Linton, W.J. (1812–1897) English wood engraver, editor and printer

Lloyd George, David (1863–1945) English-born Welsh statesman and Prime Minister

Locke, John (1632–1704) English philosopher

Lockhart, John Gibson (1794–1854) Scottish writer, critic, editor and translator

Lockier, Francis (1667–1740) English churchman

Lodge, David (1935–) English writer, satirist and literary critic

Logau, Friedrich von (1605–1655) German epigrammatist

London, Jack (1876–1916) American writer, sailor, socialist and goldminer

Longfellow, Henry Wadsworth (1807–1882) American poet and writer

Longford, Lord (1905–) British politician, social reformer and biographer

Longworth, Alice Roosevelt (1884–1980) American writer

Loos, Anita (1893–1981) American writer and screenwriter

Louis XIV (1638–1715) French monarch, the 'Sun King', and patron of the arts

Louis XVIII (1755–1824) King of France

Louis, Joe (1914–1981) American champion boxer

Lovelace, Richard (1618–1658) English poet

Lover, Samuel (1797–1868) Irish songwriter, painter, writer and dramatist

Low, Sir David (1891–1963) New Zealand-born British political cartoonist

Lowe, Robert (1811–1892) English Liberal politician and lawyer

Lowell, James Russell (1819–1891) American poet, editor, abolitionist and diplomat

Lowell, Robert (1917–1977) American poet and writer

Lowry, Malcolm (1909–1957) English writer and poet

Luce, Clare Boothe (1903–1987) American diplomat, politician and writer

Lucretius (c. 95–55 BC) Roman poet and philosopher

Lunt, Alfred (1892–1977) American actor

Luther, Martin (1483–1546) German Protestant theologian and reformer

Lutyens, Sir Edwin Landseer (1869–1944) English architect

Lydgate, John (c.1370–c.1451) English poet, translator and monk

Lyly, John (c.1554–1606) English dramatist and politician

Lynne, Liz (1948–) English politician

M

McAlpine, Sir Alfred (1881–1944) Scottish building contractor

Macaulay, Lord (1800–1859) English historian, Liberal statesman, essayist and poet

Macaulay, Dame Rose (1881–1958) English writer

McAuley, James (1917–1976) Australian poet and critic

MacCarthy, Cormac American writer

MacCarthy, Sir Desmond (1878–1952) English critic

McCarthy, Abigail (c.1914–) American writer

McCarthy, Senator Eugene (1916–) American Independent politician, lecturer and writer

McCarthy, Senator Joseph (1908–1957) American Republican politician

McCarthy, Mary (1912–1989) American writer and critic

McCartney, Paul (1942–) English pop singer-songwriter, guitarist and member of The Beatles

McDermott, John W. Hawaiian travel writer

McDiarmid, Hugh (1892–1978) Scottish poet and writer

MacDonald, George (1824–1905) Scottish writer, poet and preacher

MacDonald, Ramsay (1866–1937) Scottish Labour politician and Prime Minister

McGonagall, William (c.1830–1902) Scottish poet, tragedian and actor

McGough, Roger (1937–) English poet and teacher

McGregor, Craig (1933–) Australian writer

McGuigan, Barry (1961–) British boxer

Machiavelli (1469–1527) Florentine statesman, political theorist and historian

MacInnes, Colin (1914–1976) English writer

McIver, Charles D. (1860–1906) American educationist

McKenney, Ruth (1911–1972) American writer

Mackenzie, Sir Compton (1883–1972) English-born Scottish writer and broadcaster

Mackintosh, Sir James (1765–1832) Scottish philosopher, historian, lawyer and politician

Maclaine, Shirley (1934–) American actress

McLean, Joyce Canadian writer

Macleod, Iain (1913–1970) English Conservative politician and writer

McLuhan, Marshall (1911–1980) Canadian communications theorist

Macmillan, Harold (1894–1986) British Conservative statesman and Prime Minister

McMillan, Joyce (1952–) Scottish writer and critic

MacNally, Leonard (1752–1820) Irish lawyer, dramatist and political informer

MacNeice, Louis (1907–1963) Belfast-born British poet, writer, radio producer, translator and critic

Madan, Geoffrey (1895–1947) English bibliophile

Madariaga, Salvador de (1886–1978) Spanish writer, diplomat and teacher

Maeterlinck, Maurice (1862–1949) Belgian poet, playwright and essayist

Mailer, Norman (1923–) American writer

Maistre, Joseph de (1753–1821) French diplomat and political philosopher

Major, John (1943–) English Conservative politician and Prime Minister

Mallarmé, Stéphane (1842–1898) French poet

Mallet, Robert (1915–) French university rector, poet and writer

Malouf, David (1934–) Australian writer and poet

Malthus, Thomas Robert (1766–1834) English political economist

Mandela, Nelson (1918–) South African President, lawyer and political prisoner

Mandelstam, Nadezhda (1899–1980) Russian writer, translator and teacher

Mankiewicz, Herman (1897–1953) American journalist and screenwriter

Mann, Horace (1796–1859) American educationist, politician, teacher and writer

Mann, Thomas (1875–1955) German writer and critic

Mann, W. Edward (1918–) Canadian sociologist

Manners, Lord John (1818–1906) English Conservative politician and writer

Manning, Frederic (1882–1935) Australian writer

Mansfield, Earl of (1705–1793) Scottish judge

Mansfield, Katherine (1888–1923) New Zealand writer

Mantel, Hilary (1952–) English writer

Mao Tse-Tung, (1893–1976) Chinese Marxist statesman

Marlowe, Christopher (1564–1593) English poet and dramatist

Marmion, Shackerley (1603–1639) English dramatist and poet

Maron, Monika (1941–) German writer

Marquis, Don (1878–1937) American columnist, satirist and poet

Marryat, Frederick (1792–1848) English naval officer and writer

Marshall, Alan (Jock) (1911–1968) Australian zoologist and explorer

Martial (c.40–c.104) Spanish–born Latin epigrammatist and poet

Martineau, Harriet (1802–1876) English writer

Marvell, Andrew (1621–1678) English poet and satirist

Marx, Groucho (1895–1977) American film comedian

Marx, Karl (1818–1883) German political philosopher and economist; founder of Communism

Mary, Queen of Scots (1542–1587) Daughter of James V; imprisoned and executed

Masefield, John (1878–1967) English poet, writer and critic

Massinger, Philip (1583 1640) English dramatist and poet

Matthews, Brander (1852–1929) American critic, lecturer, dramatist and writer

Maugham, William Somerset (1874–1965) English writer, dramatist and physician

Maxwell, Gavin (1914–1969) British writer and naturalist

Mayakovsky, Vladimir (1893–1930) Russian poet, dramatist and artist

Mayer, Louis B. (1885–1957) Russian–born American film executive

Mayhew, Christopher (1915–) British parliamentarian and writer

Maynard, Sir John (1602–1690) English judge, politician and royalist

Mead, Margaret (1901–1978) American anthropologist, psychologist, lecturer and writer

Medawar, Sir Peter (1915–1987) Brazilian-born British zoologist and immunologist

Medici, Cosimo de' (1389–1464) Member of prominent Medici family of bankers, merchants and rulers of Tuscany and Florence

Meir, Golda (1898–1978) Russian-born Israeli stateswoman and Prime Minister

Melba, Dame Nellie (1861–1931) Australian opera singer

Melbourne, Lord (1779–1848) English statesman

Mellon, Andrew (1855–1937) American, banker, public official and art collector

Melville, Herman (1819–1891) American writer and poet

Mencken, H.L. (1880–1956) American writer, critic, philologist and satirist

Menzies, Sir Robert (1894–1978) Australian statesman

Meredith, George (1828–1909) English writer, poet and critic

Meredith, Owen (1831–1891) English statesman and poet

Merritt, Dixon Lanier (1879–1972) American editor

Meudell, George Dick (1860–1936) Australian writer, traveller and social commentator

Meyer, Agnes (1887–c. 1970) American writer and social worker

Meynell, Hugo (1727–1780) Frequenter of London society and acquaintance of Dr Johnson

Michaelis, John H. (1912–1985) American army officer

Mikes, George (1912–1987) Hungarian-born British writer

Mill, John Stuart (1806–1873) English philosopher, economist, reformer and politician

Millay, Edna St Vincent (1892–1950) American poet and dramatist

Miller, Alice Swiss-born American psychotherapist and writer

Miller, Arthur (1915–) American dramatist and screenwriter

Miller, Henry (1891–1980) American writer

Miller, Jonathan (1934–) English writer, director, producer and physician

Milligan, Spike (1918–) Irish comedian and writer

Milne, A.A. (1882–1956) English writer, dramatist and poet

Milner, Alfred (1854–1925) British statesman and colonial administrator

Milton, John (1608–1674) English poet, parliamentarian, libertarian and pamphleteer

Minifie, James M. (1900–1974) Canadian broadcaster

Mitchell, Margaret (1900–1949) American writer

Mitford, Nancy (1904–1973) English writer

Mizner, Wilson (1876–1933) American writer, wit and dramatist

Moliére (1622–1673) French dramatist, actor and director

Moltke, Helmuth von (1800–1891) German field marshal

Monash, Sir John (1865–1931) Australian military commander

Monmouth, Duke of (1649–1685) Illegitimate son of Charles II

Monroe, Marilyn (1926–1962) American film actress and model

Montagu, Lady Mary Wortley (1689–1762) English letter writer, poet, traveller and introducer of smallpox inoculation

Montague, C.E. (1867–1928) English writer and critic

Montaigne, Michel de (1533–1592) French essayist and moralist

Montesquieu (1689–1755) French philosopher and jurist

Montessori, Maria (1870–1952) Italian doctor and educationist

Montgomery, Viscount (1887–1976) English field marshal

Mooney, Bel British journalist

Moore, Brian (1921–) Irish-born Canadian writer

Moore, George (1852–1933) Irish writer, dramatist and critic

Moran, Lord (1924–) British diplomat and politician

Moravia, Alberto (1907–1990) Italian writer

Mordaunt, Thomas (1730–1809) British officer

More, Hannah (1745–1833) English poet, dramatist and religious writer

More, Sir Thomas (1478–1535) English statesman and humorist

Morell, Thomas (1703–1784) English scholar, librettist, editor and clergyman

Morito, Akio Japanese Chairman of Sony Corporation

Morley, John British writer

Morley, Robert (1908–1992) British actor

Morris, Charles (1745–1838) English songwriter and soldier

Morris, Desmond (1928–) English biologist, anthropologist, broadcaster and writer

Morris, William (1834–1896) English poet, designer, craftsman, artist and socialist

Morrison, Danny (1950–) Irish political activist

Mortimer, John (1923–) English lawyer, dramatist and writer

Morton, Rogers (1914–1979) American government official

Moses, Grandma (1860–1961) American painter

Mosley, Sir Oswald (1896–1980) English politician; founder of the British Union of Fascists

Mountbatten of Burma, Earl (1900–1979) British naval commander; killed by IRA

Mourie, Graham (1952–) New Zealand rugby player

Mtshali, Oswald (1940–) South African poet

Muggeridge, Malcolm (1903–1990) English writer

Muir, Edwin (1887–1959) Scottish poet, critic, translator and writer

Muir, Frank (1920–) English writer, humorist and broadcaster

Mumford, Ethel (1878–1940) American writer, dramatist and humorist

Murdoch, Iris (1919–) Irish-born British writer, philosopher and dramatist

Murdoch, Rupert (1931–) Australian newspaperman, publisher and international businessman

Murdoch, Sir Walter (1874–1970) Scottish-born Australian writer and broadcaster

Murray, David (1888–1962) British writer

Murray, Les A. (1938–) Australian poet and writer

Murrow, Edward R. (1908–1965) American reporter, war correspondent and news analyst

Mussolini, Benito (1883–1945) Italian fascist dictator

N

Nabokov, Vladimir (1899–1977) Russian-born American writer, poet, translator and critic

Naipaul, Sir V.S. (1932–) Trinidadian writer

Nairn, Ian (1930–1983) English writer on architecture and journalist

Napier, Sir William (1785–1860) British general and historian

Napoleon I (1769–1821) French emperor, general and reforming administrator

Napoleon III (1808–1873) French emperor

Narayan, R.K. (1907–) Indian writer and translator

Narváez, Ramón María (1800–1868) Spanish general and statesman

Nash, Ogden (1902–1971) American humorous poet

Naylor, James Ball (1860–1945) American physician and writer

Neaves, Lord (1800–1876) English jurist

Nelson, Lord (1758–1805) English admiral

Nero (37–68) Roman emperor

Nerval, Gérard de (1808–1855) French poet and writer

Newby, P.H. (1918–) English writer and Director of the BBC

Newcastle, Margaret, Duchess of (c.1624–1674) English poet, dramatist and woman of letters

Newman, Ernest (1868–1959) English music critic and writer

Newman, John Henry, Cardinal (1801–1890) English theologian and poet

Newman, Paul (1925–) American actor

Newton, Sir Isaac (1642–1727) English scientist and philosopher

Nicholson, Sir Bryan (1932–) British businessman

Nicholson, Emma (1941–) British politician and computer consultant

Niebuhr, Reinhold (1892–1971) American Protestant theologian and writer

Niemöller, Martin (1892–1984) German Lutheran theologian

Nietzsche, Friedrich (1844–1900) German philosopher, critic and poet; noted for his concept of the Superman

Nin, Anais (1903–1977) American writer

Nixon, Richard (1913–1994) American Republican President, politician and lawyer

Nolan, Sir Sidney (1917–) Australian artist

Norris, Kathleen (1880–1966) American writer, pacifist and activist

North, Christopher (1785–1854) Scottish poet, writer, editor and critic

Northcliffe, Lord (1865–1922) Irish-born British newspaper proprietor

Novello, Ivor (1893–1951) Welsh actor, composer, songwriter and dramatist

O

Oates, Captain Lawrence (1880–1912) English Antarctic explorer

O'Brian, Patrick Irish writer

O'Brien, Edna (1936–) Irish writer and dramatist

O'Casey, Sean (1880–1964) Irish dramatist

Ochs, Adolph S. (1858–1935) American newspaper publisher and editor

O'Connell, Daniel (1775–1847) Irish politician and nationalist

O'Connor, Flannery (1925–1964) American writer

Ogden, C.K. (1889–1957) English linguist

Ogilvy, James (1663–1730) Scottish politician and lawyer

O'Keeffe, Georgia (1887–1986) American artist

Olivier, Laurence, Baron (1907–1989) English actor and director

Olsen, Tillie (1913–) American writer

Onassis, Aristotle (1906–1975) Turkish-born Greek shipping magnate

Ondaatje, Michael (1943–) Canadian writer

O'Neill, Eugene (1888–1953) American dramatist

Oppenheimer, J. Robert (1904–1967) American nuclear physicist

O'Reilly, Tony (1936–) Irish industrialist and international rugby player

O'Rourke, P.J. (1947–) American writer and humorist

Ortega y Gasset, José (1883–1955) Spanish philosopher and critic

Ortega Spottorno, José Spanish writer

Orton, Joe (1933–1967) English dramatist and writer

Orwell, George (1903–1950) English writer and critic

Osborne, John (1929–1994) English dramatist and actor

Osler, Sir William Canadian physician

O'Sullivan, John L. (1813–1895) American editor and diplomat

Otis, James (1725–1783) American lawyer, politician and pamphleteer

Otway, Thomas (1652–1685) English dramatist and poet

Ouida (1839–1908) English writer and critic

Ovett, Steve (1955–) English athlete

Ovid (43BC–AD18) Roman poet

Owen, John (c. 1560–1622) Welsh epigrammatist and teacher

Owen, Wilfred (1893–1918) English poet

Ozick, Cynthia (1928–) American writer

P

Paglia, Camille (1947–) American academic

Paine, Thomas (1737–1809) English-born American journalist, political theorist and pamphleteer

Palacio Valdés, Armando (1853–1938) Spanish writer

Paley, Rev. William (1743–1805) English theologian and philosopher

Palmer, Arnold (1929–) American golfer

Palmerston, Lord (1784–1865) English statesman and Prime Minister

Pankhurst, Dame Christabel (1880–1958) English suffragette

Pankhurst, Emmeline (1858–1928) English militant suffragette

Pankhurst, Sylvia (1882–1960) English suffragette, pacifist and internationalist

Park, Mungo (1771–1806) Scottish explorer, writer and physician

Parker, Charlie (1920–1955) American jazz musician and composer

Parker, Dorothy (1893–1967) American writer, poet, critic and wit

Parkes, Sir Henry (1815–1896) Australian politician, writer and poet

Parkinson, C. Northcote (1909–1993) English political scientist and historian

Parnell, Anna (1852–1911) Irish political activist

Parnell, Charles Stewart (1846–1891) Irish nationalist politician

Parris, Matthew (1949–) British politician and journalist

Parsons, Tony (1922–1996) British diplomat

Pascal, Blaise (1623–1662) French philosopher and scientist

Pasteur, Louis (1822–1895) French chemist, bacteriologist and immunologist

Pater, Walter (1839–1894) English critic, writer and lecturer

Paton, Alan (1903–1988) South African writer

Patten, Brian (1946–) British poet

Patton, General George S. (1885–1945) American general

Pavese, Cesare (1908–1950) Italian writer and translator

Pavlova, Anna (1881–1931) Russian ballet dancer

Payne, J.H. (1791–1852) American dramatist, poet and actor

Paz, Octavio (1914–) Mexican poet and critic

Peacock, Thomas Love (1785–1866) English writer and poet

Pearson, Hesketh (1887–1964) English biographer

Pearson, Lester B (1897–1972) Canadian diplomat and politician

Peary, Robert Edwin (1856–1920) American Arctic explorer, admiral and writer

Peck, Gregory (1916–) American actor

Péguy, Charles (1873–1914) French Catholic socialist, poet, writer, publisher and nationlist

Penn, William (1644–1718) English Quaker, religious and political writer; founder of Pennsylvania

Pepys, Samuel (1633–1703) English diarist, naval administrator and politician

Perelman, S.J. (1904–1979) American humorist, writer and dramatist

Pericles (c.495–429) Athenian statesman, democrat, general, orator and cultural patron

Pessoa, Fernando (1888–1935) Portuguese poet

Peter, Laurence J. (1919–1990) Canadian educationist and writer

Peters, Ellis (1913–1995) English writer

Pheidippides (d. 490 BC) Athenian athlete

Philip, Prince, Duke of Edinburgh (1921–) Greek-born British consort of Queen Elizabeth II

Philips, Ambrose (c.1675–1749) English poet and politician

Picasso, Pablo (1881–1973) Spanish painter, sculptor and graphic artist

Piggy, Miss Puppet character from The Muppets

Pindar, (518–438 bc) Greek lyric poet

Pinter, Harold (1930–) English dramatist, poet and screenwriter

Pirsig, Robert (1928–) American author

Pitt, William (1708–1778) English politician and Prime Minister

Pitt, William (1759–1806) English politician and Prime Minister

Plath, Sylvia (1932–1963) American poet, writer and diarist

Plato, (c. 429–347 BC) Greek philosopher

Pliny the Elder (23–79) Roman scientist, historian and soldier

Plomer, William (1903–1973) South African-born British writer, poet, librettist and editor

Plutarch (c. 46–c.120) Greek biographer and philosopher

Poe, Edgar Allan (1809–1849) American poet, writer and editor

Polo, Marco (c.1254–1324) Venetian merchant, traveller and writer

Pompidou, Georges (1911–1974) French statesman, Premier and President

Pope, Alexander (1688–1744) English poet, translator and editor

Popper, Sir Karl (1902–1994) Austrian-born British philosopher

Porson, Richard (1759 1808) English scholar

Porter, Sir George (1920–) English chemist

Porter, Hal (1911–1984) Australian writer, dramatist and poet

Portland, Duke of (1857–1943) British aristocrat and writer

Post, Emily (1873–1960) American writer

Potter, Stephen (1900–1969) English writer, critic and lecturer

Pound, Ezra (1885–1972) American poet, translator and critic

Powell, Anthony (1905–) English writer and critic

Powell, Enoch (1912–) English politician and scholar

Power, Marguerite, Countess of Blessington (1789–1849) English writer

Powys, John Cowper (1872–1963) English writer and poet

Prescott, John (1938–) British Labour politician

Preston, Keith (1884–1927) American poet, writer and teacher

Previn, André (1929–) German–born American conductor and composer

Priestley, J.B. (1894–1984) English writer, dramatist and critic

Pringle, John (1912–) Scottish–born Australian writer

Pringle, Thomas (1789–1834) Scottish poet

Propertius, Sextus Aurelius (c. 50–c.15 BC) Roman poet

Proudhon, Pierre–Joseph (1809–1865) French social reformer, anarchist and writer

Proust, Marcel (1871–1922) French writer and critic

Puzo, Mario (1920–) American writer

Pyrrhus, (319–272 BC) King of Epirus and army commander

Q

Quarles, Francis (1592–1644) English poet, writer and royalist

Quevedo y Villegas, Francisco Gómez de (1580–1645) Spanish poet and writer

Quiller-Couch, Sir Arthur ('Q') (1863–1944) English writer, poet, critic and academic

R

Rabelais, François (c.1494–c.1553) French satirist, humanist, physician and monk

Racine, Jean (1639–1699) French tragedian and poet

Rae, John (1931–) English educationist and writer

Rainborowe, Thomas (d. 1648) English parliamentarian and soldier

Rains, Claude (1889–1967) British actor

Raleigh, Sir Walter (c.1552–1618) English courter, explorer, military commander, poet, historian and essayist

Ramey, Estelle (1917–) American physiologist, educator and feminist

Rattigan, Terence (1911–1977) English dramatist and screenwriter

Reagan, Ronald (1911–) American Republican President and former film actor

Reed, Henry (1914–1986) English poet, radio dramatist and translator

Reed, Rex (1948–) American film and music critic and columnist

Reger, Max (1873–1916) German composer, conductor, teacher and pianist

Reinhardt, Gottfried (1911–) Austrian film producer

Reith, Lord (1889–1971) Scottish wartime minister, administrator, diarist and Director-General of the BBC

Renan, J. Ernest (1823–1892) French philologist, writer and historian

Renard, Jules (1864–1910) French writer and dramatist

Renoir, Jean (1894–1979) French film director

Renoir, Pierre-Auguste (1841–1919) French painter

Revson, Charles (1906–1975) American cosmetic company executive

Reynolds, Sir Joshua (1723–1792) English portrait painter

Reynolds, Malvina (1900–1978) American singer-songwriter

Rhodes, Cecil (1853–1902) English imperialist financier and South African statesman

Rhondda, Viscountess (1883–1958) English magazine editor and suffragette

Rhys, Ernest (b.1859) British poet

Rhys, Jean (1894–1979) West Indian-born British writer

Ribblesdale, Lord (1854–1925) British army officer and courtier

Rice, Grantland (1880–1954) American writer and poet

Richard, Sir Cliff (1940–) English singer and performer

Richards, I.A. (1893–1979) English critic, linguist, poet and teacher

Richardson, Sir Ralph (1902–1983) English actor

Richelieu, Cardinal (1585–1642) French statesman

Richelieu, Duc de (1766–1822) French courtier, soldier and Prime Minister

Rifkin, Jeremy American bioethicist

Riley, Janet (1915–) American lawyer, educator and civil rights activist

Rilke, Rainer Maria (1875–1926) Austrian poet, born in Prague

Rimbaud, Arthur (1854–1891) French poet

Rippon, Geoffrey (1924–) English Conservative politician

Robespierre, Maximilien (1758–1794) French revolutionary

Robinson, Mary (1944–) Irish barrister and politician

Robinson, Roland (1912–1992) Irish-born Australian poet

Rochester, Earl of (1647–1680) English poet, satirist, courtier and libertine

Rogers, Will (1879–1935) American humorist, actor, rancher, writer and wit

Roland, Madame (1754–1793) French revolutionary and writer

Roosevelt, Franklin Delano (1882–1945) American lawyer, statesman and President

Roosevelt, Theodore (1858–1919) American Republican President, statesman, soldier and writer

Ross, Harold (1892–1951) American editor

Ross, Nick (1947–) British broadcaster

Rossetti, Christina (1830–1894) English poet

Rossetti, Dante Gabriel (1828–1882) English poet, painter, translator and letter-writer

Rossini, Gioacchino (1792–1868) Italian composer

Rostand, Jean (1894–1977) French biologist

Rosten, Leo (1908–) Polish-born American social scientist, writer and humorist

Roth, Philip (1933–) American writer

Rousseau, Jean-Jacques (1712–1778) Swiss-born French philosopher, educationist and essayist

Rousselot, Fabrice French journalist

Roux, Joseph (1834–1886) French priest and epigrammatist

Rowbotham, David (1924–) Australian journalist, critic and poet

Rowland, Helen (1875–1950) American writer

Rowland, Richard (1881–1947) American film executive

Rubin, Jerry (1936–) American political activist

Rubinstein, Helena (c, 1872–1965) Polish-born American cosmetician and businesswoman

Rückriem, Ulrich (1938–) German sculptor

Runciman, Sir Steven (1903–) British scholar, historian and archaeologist

Runyon, Damon (1884–1946) American writer

Rushdie, Salman (1946–) Indian-born writer, resident in Britain; subject of a fatwa issued by the Ayatollah Khomeini

Rusk, Dean (1909–) American politician and diplomat

Ruskin, John (1819–1900) English art critic, philosopher and reformer

Russell, Bertrand (1872–1970) English philosopher, mathematician, essayist and social reformer

Russell, Lord John (1792–1878) English Liberal statesman, Prime Minister and writer

Rutskoi, Alexander (1947–) Russian politician

Ryle, Gilbert (1900–1976) English philosopher

S

Sabia, Laura Canadian writer and feminist

Sackville-West, Vita (1892–1962) English writer, poet and gardener

Sade, Marquis de (1740–1814) French soldier and writer

Sagan, Françoise (1935–) French writer

Sahl, Mort (1927–) Canadian-born American comedian

Saikaku, Ihara (1642–1693) Japanese writer and poet

Sainte-Beuve (1804–1869) French critic, essayist and poet

Saint-Exupéry, Antoine de (1900–1944) French writer and aviator

Saint-Pierre, Bernardin de (1737–1814) French writer

Saintsbury, George (1845–1933) English critic and historian

Saki (1870–1916) Burmese-born British writer

Salinger, J.D. (1919–) American writer

Salisbury, Lord (1830–1903) English statesman and Conservative Prime Minister

Salk, Jonas E. (1914–) American virologist

Sallust (86–c.34 BC) Roman historian and statesman

Salmon, George (1819–1904) Provost of Trinity College, Dublin

Sampson, Anthony (1926–) British writer

Samuel, Lord (1870–1963) English Liberal statesman, philosopher and administrator

Sand, George (1804–1876) French writer and dramatist

Sandburg, Carl (1878–1967) American poet, writer and song collector

Sanders, George (1906–1972) Russian-born British film actor

Santayana, George (1863–1952) Spanish-born American philosopher, poet, critic and writer

Sappho (fl. 7th–6th centuries BC) Greek poet

Sarasate (y Navascués) Pablo (1844–1908) Spanish violinist and composer

Sargent, John Singer (1856–1925) American painter

Sargent, Sir Malcolm (1895–1967) English conductor

Saro-Wiwa, Ken (1941–1995) Nigerian writer, environmentalist and human rights activist

Saroyan, William (1908–1981) American writer and dramatist

Sarton, May (1912–) American poet and writer

Sartre, Jean-Paul (1905–1980) French philosopher, writer, dramatist and critic

Sassoon, Siegfried (1886–1967) English poet and writer

Satie, Erik (1866–1925) French composer

Saunders, Ernest (1935–) British businessman and company director

Sayers, Dorothy L. (1893–1957) English writer, dramatist and translator

Scanlon, Hugh, Baron (1913–) British trade union leader

Scargill, Arthur (1941–) English trade union official

Scarron, Paul (1610–1660) French dramatist, writer and poet

Schelling, Friedrich von (1775–1854) German philosopher

Schiller, Johann (1759–1805) German writer, dramatist, critic, poet and historian

Schlegel, Friedrich von (1772–1829) German critic and philosopher

Schnabel, Artur (1882–1951) Austrian pianist and composer

Schopenhauer, Arthur (1788–1860) German philosopher

Schreiner, Olive (1855–1920) South African writer

Schubert, Franz (1797–1828) Austrian composer

Schulz, Charles (1922–) American cartoonist

Schumacher, E.F. (1911–1977) German-born British economist, essayist and lecturer

Schurz, Carl (1829–1906) German–born American lawyer, soldier, Republican politician and writer

Scott, C.P. (1846–1932) English newspaper editor and Liberal politician

Scott, Capt. Robert (1868–1912) English naval officer, Antarctic explorer and writer

Scott, Valerie Canadian prostitute and feminist

Scott, Sir Walter (1771–1832) Scottish writer, historian, folklorist, dramatist, editor and critic

Scott-Maxwell, Florida (1884–1979) American writer, suffragist, psychologist, playwright and actress

Seal, Christopher British churchman

Sedgwick, Catharine Maria (1789–1867) American writer and feminist

Seeley, Sir John (1834–1895) English historian, essayist and scholar

Segal, Erich (1937–) American scholar, lecturer and writer

Selden, John (1584–1654) English historian, jusrist and politician

Sellar, Walter (1898–1951) British writer and teacher

Seneca (c.4 BC–AD 65) Roman philosopher, poet, dramatist, essayist, rhetorician and statesman

Sévigné, Madame de (1626–1696) French letter-writer

Sexton, Anne (1928–1974) American poet and critic

Shahn, Ben (1898–1969) Lithuanian-born American painter and muralist

Shakespeare, William (1564–1616) English dramatist, poet and actor

Shankly, Bill (1914–1981) Scottish footballer and manager

Sharif, Omar (1932–) Egyptian film actor

Sharpe, Tom (1928–) English writer

Shaw, George Bernard (1856–1950) Irish socialist, writer, dramatist and critic

Sheen, J. Fulton (1895–1979) American Roman Catholic churchman and writer

Shelley, Percy Bysshe (1792–1822) English poet, dramatist, essayist and letter-writer

Sheridan, Philip Henry (1831–1888) American general

Sheridan, Richard Brinsley (1751–1816) Irish dramatist, politician and orator

Sherman, Alfred (1919–) British journalist

Sherman, William Tecumseh (1820–1891) American Civil War general

Shinwell, Emanuel (1884–1986) British Labour politician

Shirley, James (1596–1666) English poet and dramatist

Shorten, Caroline British spokesperson for Social and Liberal Democrat party

Shorter, Clement King (1857–1926) English writer and critic

Shuter, Edward (1728–1776) English actor and wit

Sibelius, Jean (1865–1957) Finnish composer

Sickert, Walter (1860–1942) German-born British painter and writer

Sidney, Sir Philip (1554–1586) English poet, critic, soldier, courtier and diplomat

Sigismund (1368–1437) King of Hungary, Bohemia and Holy Roman Emperor

Simenon, Georges (1903–1989) Belgian writer

Simon, Neil (1927–) American playwright and scriptwriter

Simonides (c. 556–468 BC) Greek poet and epigrammatist

Simpson, N.F. (1919–) English dramatist

Singer, Isaac Bashevis (1904–1991) Polish-born American Yiddish writer

Sinyavsky, Andrei: see Tertz, Abram

Sitwell, Dame Edith (1887–1964) English poet, anthologist, critic and biographer

Sitwell, Sir Osbert (1892–1969) English poet and writer

Skelton, Red (1913–) American comedian

Slater, Nigel Food writer

Smart, Christopher (1722–1771) English poet and translator

Smith, Adam (1723–1790) Scottish economist, philosopher and essayist

Smith, Alexander (1830–1867) Scottish poet and writer

Smith, Sir Cyril (1928–) British politician

Smith, Delia Cookery writer

Smith, F.E. (1872–1930) English politician and Lord Chancellor

Smith, Ian (1919–) Prime Minister of Rhodesia (now Zimbabwe)

Smith, Joseph (1805–1844) Founder of the Mormon Church

Smith, Logan Pearsall (1865–1946) American-born British epigrammatist, critic and writer

Smith, Stevie (1902–1971) English poet and writer

BIOGRAPHIES

Smith, Sydney (1771–1845) English clergyman, essayist, journalist, wit and lecturer

Smith, Sir Sydney (1883–1969) New Zealand-born British forensic scientist and writer

Smollett, Tobias (1721–1771) Scottish writer, satirist, historian, traveller and physician

Snagge, John (1904–) British television broadcaster and commentator

Snow, C.P. (1905–1980) English writer, critic, physicist and public administrator

Soames, Nicholas (1948–) English Conservative politician

Socrates (469–399 BC) Athenian philosopher

Solanas, Valerie (1940–) American artist and writer

Solon (C. 638–C. 559 BC) Athenian statesman, reformer and poet

Solzhenitsyn, Alexander (1918–) Russian writer, dramatist and historian

Somoza, Anastasio (1925–1980) President of Nicaragua

Sontag, Susan (1933–) American critic and writer

Soper, Donald (1903–) Methodist churchman and writer

Southern, Terry (1924–) American writer and screenwriter

Southey, Robert (1774–1843) English poet, essayist, historian and letter-writer

Spalding, Julian (1948–) English art administrator

Spark, Muriel (1918–) Scottish writer, poet and dramatist

Sparrow, John (1906–1992) English lawyer and writer

Spencer, Herbert (1820–1903) English philosopher and journalist

Spencer, Sir Stanley (1891–1959) English painter

Spender, Sir Stephen (1909–) English poet, critic, editor, translator, diarist and autobiographer

Spenser, Edmund (c.1522–1599) English poet

Spinoza, Baruch (1632–1677) Dutch philosopher and theologian

Spooner, William (1844–1930) English churchman and university warden

Squire, Sir J.C. (1884–1958) English poet, critic, writer and editor

Stacpoole, H. de Vere (1863–1951) Irish writer and physician

Staël, Mme de (1766–1817) French writer, critic, memoirist and hostess

Stalin, Joseph (1879–1953) Soviet Communist leader

Stanton, Elizabeth Cady (1815–1902) American suffragist, abolitionist, feminist, editor and writer

Stapledon, Olaf (1886–1950) British philosopher and writer

Stark, Dame Freya (1893–) French-born traveller and writer

Stassinopoulos, Ariana (1950–) Greek writer

Stead, Christina (1902–1983) Australian writer

Steele, Sir Richard (1672–1729) Irish-born English writer, dramatist and politician

Stefano, Joseph (1922–) American screenwriter

Steffens, Lincoln (1866–1936) American political analyst and writer

Stein, Gertrude (1874–1946) American writer, dramatist, poet and critic

Stein, Jock (1922–1985) Scottish football player and manager

Steinbeck, John (1902–1968) American writer

Steinem, Gloria (1934–) American writer and feminist activist

Stendhal (1783–1842) French writer, critic and soldier

Stenhouse, David (1932–) English-born New Zealand zoologist, educationist and writer

Stephen, Sir James Fitzjames (1829–1894) English judge and essayist

Stephen, James Kenneth (1859–1892) English writer and poet

Stephens, James (1882–1950) Irish poet and writer

Sterne, Laurence (1713–1768) Irish-born English writer and clergyman

Stevens, Wallace (1879–1955) American poet, essayist, dramatist and lawyer

Stevenson, Adlai (1900–1965) American lawyer, statesman and United Nations ambassador

Stevenson, Robert Louis (1850–1894) Scottish writer, poet and essayist

Stewart, Rod (1945–) English rock singer

Stocks, Mary, Baroness (1891–1975) English educationist, broadcaster and biographer

Stockwood, Mervyn (1913–) English Anglican churchman

Stone, I.F. (1907–1989) American writer and editor

Stone, Judith American science writer and humorist

Stoppard, Tom (1937–) British dramatist, born in Czechoslovakia

Storr, Dr Anthony (1920–) British writer and psychiatrist

Stowe, Harriet Beecher (1811–1896) American writer and reformer

Strachey, Lytton (1880–1932) English biographer and critic

Stravinsky, Igor (1882–1971) Russian composer and conductor

Streatfield, Sir Geoffrey (1897–1978) British judge

Stretton, Hugh (1924–) Australian political scientist and historian

Stromme, Sigmund Norwegian publisher

Stubbes, Philip (c.1555–1610) English Puritan pamphleteer and writer

Su Tung-P'o (Su Shih) (1036–1101) Chinese poet, writer, painter and public official

Sullivan, Annie (1866–1936) American lecturer, writer and teacher

Sullivan, Sir Arthur (1842–1900) English composer, particularly of operettas

Sully, Duc de (1559–1641) French statesman and financier

Surtees, R.S. (1805–1864) English writer

Suzuki, D.T. (1870–1966) Japanese Buddhist scholar and main interpreter of Zen to the West

Swaffer, Hannen (1879–1962) English writer

Swann, Donald (1923–1994) English composer and pianist

Swift, Jonathan (Dean Swift) (1667–1745) Irish satirist, poet, essayist and Anglican cleric

Swinburne, Algernon Charles (1837–1909) English poet, critic, dramatist and letter-writer

Synge, J.M. (1871–1909) Irish dramatist, poet and letter-writer

Szasz, Thomas (1920–) Hungarian-born American psychiatrist and writer

Szent-Györgyi, Albert von (1893–1986) Hungarian-born American biochemist

T

Taber, Robert (20th century) American writer

Tacitus (c. 56–c.120) Roman historian

Talleyrand, Charles-Maurice de (1754–1838) French statesman, memoirist and prelate

Tannen, Deborah (1945–) American linguist and academic

Tarkington, Booth (1869–1946) American writer and dramatist

Tawney, R.H. (1880–1962) Indian-born British economic historian and Christian socialist

Taylor, A.J.P. (1906–1990) English historian, writer, broadcaster and lecturer

Taylor, Bert Leston (1866–1921) American journalist

Taylor, Elizabeth (1912–1975) English writer

Taylor, Bishop Jeremy (1613–1667) English divine and writer

Tebbitt, Norman (1931–) English Conservative politician

Tecumseh (d. 1812) Leader of the Shawnee Indians

Teilhard de Chardin, Pierre (1881–1955) French priest, palaeontologist and philosopher

Temple, William (1881–1944) English prelate, social reformer, teacher and writer

Tennyson, Alfred, Lord (1809–1892) English lyric poet

Terence (c. 190–159 BC) Carthaginian-born Roman dramatist

Teresa, Mother (1910–) Roman Catholic missionary in India

Terry, Dame Ellen (1847–1928) English actress, theatrical manager and memoirist

Tertullian, (c. 160–225) Carthaginian theologian

Tertz, Abram (Andrei Sinyavsky) (1925–) Russian writer and dissident

Tessimond, A.S.J. (1902–1962) English poet

Thackeray, William Makepeace (1811–1863) Indian-born English writer and lecturer

Thales (c. 624–547BC) Ionian philosopher, mathematician and astronomer

Thatcher, Carol (1953–) English writer and broadcaster; daughter of Margaret Thatcher

Thatcher, Sir Denis (1915–) British businessman and husband of Margaret Thatcher

Thatcher, Margaret, Baroness (1925–) English stateswoman and Conservative Prime Minister

Theroux, Paul (1941–) American writer

Thiers, Louis Adolphe (1797–1877) French statesman and historian

Thomas, Dylan (1914–1953) Welsh poet, writer and radio dramatist

Thomas, Gwyn (1913–1981) Welsh writer, dramatist and teacher

Thomas, Irene (1920–) English writer and broadcaster

Thomas, Lewis (1913–) American pathologist and university administrator

Thomson, James (1700–1748) Scottish poet and dramatist

Thomson, Joseph (1858–1895) Scottish explorer, geologist and writer

Thoreau, Henry (1817–1862) American essayist, social critic and writer

Thorpe, Jeremy (1929–) English Liberal Pary politician

Thurber, James (1894–1961) American humorist, writer and dramatist

Thurlow, Edward (1731–1806) English lawyer, politician and Lord Chancellor

Tibullus (c. 54–19 BC) Roman poet

Tichborne, Chidiock (c.1558–1586) English Roman Catholic conspirator against Elizabeth I

Tindal, Matthew (1657–1733) English deist and writer

Titus Vespasianus (39–81) Roman emperor and public benefactor

Tocqueville, Alexis de (1805–1859) French political historian, politician, lawyer and memoirist

Todd, Ron (1927–) British trade union official

Tolstoy, Leo (1828–1910) Russian writer, essayist, philosopher and moralist

Tomalin, Nicholas (1931–1973) English journalist

Tomaschek, Rudolphe (b. c.1895) German scientist

Tomlin, Lily (1939–) American actress

Toner, Pauline (1935–1989) Australian politician

Toynbee, Arnold (1889–1975) English historian and scholar

Tracy, Spencer (1900–1967) American film actor

Traherne, Thomas (c.1637–1674) English religious writer and clergyman

Trapp, Joseph (1679–1747) English poet, pamphleteer, translator and clergyman

Tree, Sir Herbert Beerbohm (1853–1917) English actor and theatre manager

Trevelyan, G.M. (1876–1962) English historian and writer

Trollope, Anthony (1815–1882) English writer, traveller and post office official

Trotsky, Leon (1879–1940) Ukrainian-born Russian revolutionary and Communist theorist

Truman, Harry S. (1884–1972) American statesman and President

Tuchman, Barbara W. (1912–1989) American journalist and historian

Tucholsky, Kurt (1890–1935) German satirist and writer

Tucker, Sophie (1884–1966) Russian-born American vaudeville singer

Tupper, Martin (1810–1889) English writer, lawyer and inventor

Turenne, Henri, Vicomte (1611–1675) French marshal

Turgenev, Ivan (1818–1883) Russian writer and dramatist

Turgot, A-R-J. (1727–1781) French economist and statesman

Turnbull, Margaret (fl. 1920s–1942) Scottish-born American writer and dramatist

Tusser, Thomas (c.1524–1580) English writer, poet and musician

Tutu, Archbishop Desmond (1931–) South African churchman and anti-apartheid campaigner

Twain, Mark (1835–1910) American humorist, writer, journalist and lecturer

Tynan, Kenneth (1927–1980) English drama critic, producer and essayist

U

Unamuno, Miguel de (1864–1936) Spanish philosopher, poet and writer

Updike, John (1932–) American writer, poet and critic

Urey, Harold (1893–1981) American chemist

Ustinov, Sir Peter (1921–) English actor, director, dramatist, writer and raconteur

Uvavnuk Inuit singer and shaman

V

Vail, Amanda (1921–1966) American writer

Valéry, Paul (1871–1945) French poet, mathematician and philosopher

Vanbrugh, Sir John (1664–1726) English dramatist and baroque architect

Vanderbilt, William H. (1821–1885) American financier and railway magnate

Van der Post, Sir Laurens (1906–) South African writer, soldier and explorer

Vaughan, Henry (1622–1695) Welsh poet and physician

Vauvenargues, Marquis de (1715–1747) French soldier and moralist

Veblen, Thorstein (1857–1929) American economist and sociologist

Vega Carpio, Félix Lope de (1562–1635) Spanish dramatist, poet and writer

Vegetius Renatus, Flavius (fl. c. 375) Military writer

Vergniaud, Pierre (1753–1793) French politician and revolutionary

Verlaine, Paul (1844–1896) French poet and autobiographer

Vespasian (9–79) Roman emperor

Victoria, Queen (1819–1901) British Queen and Empress of India; diarist and writer

Vidal, Gore (1925–) American writer, critic and poet

Viera, Ondina Uruguayan football manager

Vigneaud, Vincent de (1901–1978) Canadian biochemist

Villiers de l'Isle-Adam, Philippe-Auguste (1838–1889) French poet, writer and dramatist

Virgil (70–19 BC) Roman poet

Vizinczey, Stephen (1933–) Hungarian-born writer, editor and broadcaster

Voltaire (1694–1778) French philosopher, dramatist, poet, historian writer and critic

Vorster, John (1915–1983) South African Nationalist politician, Prime Minister and President

Vulliamy, Ed British writer

W

Waddell, Helen (1889–1965) Irish scholar and writer

Wain, John (1925–) English poet, writer and critic

Walden, George (1939–) British Conservative politician and diplomat

Wales, Princess of (1961–) Diana Spencer, wife of Charles, Prince of Wales; divorced

Walker, Alice (1944–) American writer and poet

Wallace, Edgar (1875–1932) English writer and dramatist

Wallace, William Ross (c.1819–1881) American lawyer and poet

Wallach, Eli (1915–) American actor

Waller, Edmund (1606–1687) English poet and politician

Walpole, Horace (1717–1797) English writer and politician

Walpole, Sir Hugh (1884–1941) New Zealand-born English writer

Walpole, Robert (1676–1745) English statesman and first British Prime Minister

Walsh, William (1663–1708) English critic, poet and politician

Walton, Izaak (1593–1683) English writer

Ward, Artemus (1834–1867) American humorist, journalist, editor and lecturer

Warhol, Andy (c.1926–1987) American painter, graphic designer and film-maker

Warren, Earl (1891–1974) American lawyer and politician

Washington, George (1732–1799) American general, statesman and President

Watts, Isaac (1674–1748) English hymn-writer, poet and minister

Waugh, Auberon (1939–) English writer and critic

Waugh, Evelyn (1903–1966) English writer and diarist

Wax, Ruby (1953–) American actor and comedienne

Webb, Beatrice (1858–1943) English writer and reformer

Webb, Sidney (1859–1947) English reformer, historian and socialist

Webster, Daniel (1782–1852) American statesman, orator and lawyer

Webster, John (c.1580–c.1625) English dramatist

Wedgewood, Cicely (1910–) English historian

Wedgwood, Josiah (1730–1795) English potter, manufacturer and pamphleteer

Weil, Simone (1909–1943) French philosopher, essayist and mystic

Weiss, Peter (1916–1982) German dramatist, painter, film producer and writer

Welch, Raquel (1940–) American actress

Weldon, Fay (1931–) British writer and critic

Welles, Orson (1915–1985) American actor, director and producer

Wellington, Duke of (1769–1852) Irish-born British military commander and statesman

Wells, H.G. (1866–1946) English writer

Wesley, John (1703–1791) English theologian and preacher

Wesley, Samuel (1662–1735) English churchman and poet

West, Mae (1892–1980) American actress and scriptwriter

West, Dame Rebecca (1892–1983) English writer, critic and feminist

Wharton, Edith (1862–1937) American writer

Whately, Richard (1787–1863) English philosopher, theologian, educationist and writer

Whistler, James McNeill (1834–1903) American painter, etcher and pamphleteer

White, E.B. (1899–1985) American humorist and writer

White, Patrick (1912–1990) English-born Australian writer and dramatist

Whitehead, A.N. (1861–1947) English mathematician and philosopher

Whitehorn, Katharine (1926–) English writer

Whitelaw, William, Viscount (1918–) English Conservative politician and landowner

Whiting, William (1825–1878) English teacher, poet and hymn writer

Whitlam, Gough (1916–) Australian Labor statesman and Prime Minister

Whitman, Walt (1819–1892) American poet and writer

Whittier, John Greenleaf (1807–1892) American poet, abolitionist and journalist

Whorf, Benjamin (1897–1941) American anthropological linguist and engineer

Wilberforce, Bishop Samuel (1805–1873) English divine and writer

Wilcox, Ella Wheeler (1850–1919) American poet and writer

Wilde, Lady Jane (1826–1896) Irish poet and society hostess; mother of Oscar Wilde

Wilde, Oscar (1854–1900) Irish poet, dramatist, writer, critic and wit

Wilder, Billy (1906–) Austrian-born American film director, producer and screenwriter

Wilder, Thornton (1897–1975) American dramatist, writer and teacher

Wilhelm I, Kaiser (1797–1888) King of Prussia and first Emperor of Germany

William of Wykeham (1324–1404) English churchman and Chancellor of England

Williams, Kenneth (1926–1988) English actor and comedian

Williams, Tennessee (1911–1983) American dramatist and writer

Williams, William Carlos (1883–1963) American poet, writer and paediatrician

Williamson, Malcolm (1931–) Master of the Queen's Music

Williamson, Nicol Scottish actor

Willkie, Wendell (1892–1944) American lawyer, industrialist and Republican politician

Wilson, Charles E. (1890–1961) American industrialist, car manufacturer and politician

Wilson, Harold, Baron (1916–1995) English statesman and Labour Prime Minister

Wilson, Woodrow (1856–1924) American statesman and Democrat President

Winchell, Walter (1897–1972) American drama critic, columnist and broadcaster

Wittgenstein, Ludwig (1889–1951) Austrian-born British philosopher

Woddis, Roger British poet and scriptwriter

Wodehouse, P.G. (1881–1975) English humorist and writer

Wolfe, Humbert (1886–1940) Italian-born British poet, critic and civil servant

Wolfe, James (1727–1759) English major-general

Wolff, Charlotte (1904–1986) German-born British psychiatrist and writer

Wollstonecraft, Mary (1759–1797) English feminist, writer and teacher

Wolsey, Thomas (c.1475–1530) English cardinal and statesman

Wood, Mrs Henry (1814–1887) English writer and editor

Woolf, Virginia (1882–1941) English writer and critic

Woollcott, Alexander (1887–1943) American writer, drama critic and anthologist

Wordsworth, Dame Elizabeth (1840–1932) English educationist and writer

Wordsworth, William (1770–1850) English poet

Worsthorne, Sir Peregrine (1923–) English journalist

Wotton, Sir Henry (1568–1639) English diplomat, traveller and poet

Wren, Sir Christopher (1632–1723) English architect, mathematician and astronomer

Wright, Frank Lloyd (1869–1959) American architect and writer

Wright, Judith (1915–) Australian poet, critic and writer

Wycherley, William (c.1640–1716) English dramatist and poet

Wyllie, George (1921–) Scottish artist

Wynne-Tyson, Esme (1898–1972) British actress, dramatist and writer

X

X, Malcolm (1925–1965) Afro-American activist leader

Xerxes (c. 519–465BC) King of Persia

Y

Yankwich, Léon R. (1888–1975) Romanian-born American judge and writer

Ybarra, Thomas Russell (1880–) American writer and poet

Yeatman, Robert (1897–1968) British writer

Yeats, W.B. (1865–1939) Irish poet, dramatist, editor, writer and senator

Yeltsin, Boris (1931–) Russian politician and President

Yevtushenko, Yevgeny (1933–) Russian poet

Young, Andrew (1885–1971) Scottish poet, churchman and botanist

Young, Edward (1683–1765) English poet, dramatist, satirist and clergyman

Young, George W. (1846–1919) British writer

Z

Zamoyski, Jan (1541–1605) Polish Chancellor and army leader

Zangwill, Israel (1864–1926) English writer and Jewish spokesman

Zappa, Frank (1940–1993) American rock musician, songwriter and record producer

Ze Ami (1363–1443) Japanese playwright, theorist and director of Noh theatre